Problem Solving and Structured Programming in **Modula-2**

Problem Solving and Structured Programming in Modula-2

Elliot B. Koffman

ADDISON-WESLEY PUBLISHING COMPANY
Reading, Massachusetts Menlo Park, California New York
Don Mills, Ontario Wokingham, England Amsterdam
Bonn Sydney Singapore Tokyo Madrid San Juan

To my wife Caryn: With profound gratitude for the last twenty-five years and great expectations for the next twenty-five.

Keith Wollman, Sponsoring Editor
Bette J. Aaronson, Production Supervior
Nancy Benjamin, Production Editor
Joyce Cameron Weston, Text Design
Hugh Crawford, Manufacturing Supervisor
Dick Hannus, Cover Design

Library of Congress Cataloging-in-Publication Data

Koffman, Elliot B.
Problem solving and structured programming in Modula-2.

Includes index.
1. Modula-2 (Computer program language) 2. Structured programming. I. Title.
QA76.73.M63K65 1988 005.13'3 87-31902
ISBN 0-201-07828-7

Reprinted with corrections June, 1988

8 9 10 DO 95949392

Preface

The major goals of this text are to teach procedural and data abstraction and to introduce the use of abstract data types in a first course in programming methods. Because of the module feature, it is easier to accomplish these goals using Modula-2 as the instructional language than it would be using Pascal.

A Modula-2 module is a separately compilable program unit consisting of a definition part and an implementation part. The definition part serves as the interface between a module and other users of that module; the implementation part contains the details of data types and procedures which are hidden from users of the module.

The module feature of Modula-2 facilitates large-scale software development because it enables programmers to easily implement abstract data types and to create their own libraries of reusable procedures. Once Modula-2 has been mastered, it can be used effectively in later courses on algorithms, data structures, software engineering, compiler design, and operating systems.

Organization of the Book

This textbook on problem solving and programming methods covers all the topics in the ACM (Association for Computing Machinery) recommended first course in computer science, CS1,[1] and most of the topics in CS2.[2] The first nine chapters deal with material that is generally covered in CS1; the balance of the book deals with concepts generally covered in CS2. For students going on to CS2, the later chapters of this book may be used with additional material as the primary text for CS2. If another text is used for CS2, these chapters will serve as a useful reference and as a supplement to the primary textbook.

There is an emphasis on procedural abstraction right from the start. In Chapter 2, students are introduced to the advantages of implementing a program as a set of procedures. In Chapter 4, they learn how to use procedure parameters to provide communication paths between procedures. In Chapter 6, students learn how to define and implement separately compilable mod-

1. Koffman, E., Miller, P., and Wardle, C. Recommended Curriculum for CS1, 1984. Communications of the ACM 27, 10 (Oct. 1984), 998–1001.
2. Koffman, E., Stemple, D., and Wardle, C. Recommended Curriculum for CS2, 1984. Communications of the ACM 28, 8 (Aug. 1985), 815–818.

ules and how to use these modules in large program systems. A library module for simplifying input/output operations is implemented in this chapter. Chapter 6 also introduces data abstraction. As an example, an abstract data type consisting of an enumeration type and its operators is implemented.

Case studies in later chapters develop program systems that include one or more new modules and that import procedures and data types from previously designed modules. Chapter 13 describes the use of opaque types to enforce information hiding. The early and continued emphasis on the use of procedures and abstract data types enables students to adopt the important design techniques of procedural and data abstraction as their own from the beginning.

Another important feature of this text is the use of loop invariants in loop design. Loop invariants are introduced in Chapter 3 as a design technique rather than simply as a verification tool. Program examples illustrate this technique.

Other Features

- **Numerous program examples:** Each concept introduced in the text is illustrated with a complete sample program or procedure (see pp. 55, 77, 80, 214).
- **Case studies:** Each chapter contains one or more expanded problems, which are solved in their entirety. The solutions to the case studies are all carefully developed. Algorithms and structure charts are included in many of the solutions (see pp. 88, 176, 274).
- **Spiral approach:** The spiral approach is used to a limited degree to preview topics such as the `IF` statement, `FOR` statement, procedures, and data types. Features are introduced as needed rather than overwhelming the student by providing all the details at once.
- **Pedagogical aids:**
  Self-check exercises: Self-check exercises are found at the end of most sections (see pp. 35, 88). These exercises, for example, test a student's knowledge of the concepts covered or ask the student to provide a missing procedure for a large program system. Answers to odd-numbered exercises are provided at the end of the text; answers to even-numbered exercises are provided in the Instructor's Manual.
  Chapter review material: Each chapter ends with a summary, a table of new Modula-2 statements, and a set of review questions (see pp. 43, 93). Answers to all review questions are provided in the Instructor's Manual.
  Error warnings: Each chapter contains a section that discusses common programming errors (see pp. 40, 185). These sections help a student avoid program errors and assist students in debugging and correcting errors when they occur.

Boxed material: Syntax display boxes describe the syntax of each new Modula-2 statement as it is introduced. Program style displays discuss issues of good programming style (see pp. 22, 104).
Program comments: All programs are carefully commented. Loop invariants and assertions are shown for most loops. All procedures begin with a preamble that specifies a precondition and postcondition for that procedure (see pp. 128, 219, 253).

- **Reference appendixes:** Several appendixes cover Modula-2 operators, reserved words, standard identifiers, standard procedures, standard utility modules, syntax diagrams, and the ASCII table. There is also an appendix that discusses sequential and random-access file processing in Modula-2.

Overview of Content

Chapter 1 introduces the student to the computer, and provides a brief introduction to computer hardware and software. It describes the process of creating, compiling, linking, and loading a program. The last half of the chapter introduces Modula-2 and provides several sample program modules. Assignment statements and input/output procedures found in modules `InOut` and `RealInOut` are covered. The standard data types are also introduced.

Chapter 2 covers problem solving and algorithm design. We introduce problem decomposition and show how to use procedures without parameters to implement subproblems. We discuss the need for decisions and loops in algorithms and show how to implement them in programs using the `IF` statement and a simplified form of the `FOR` statement.

Chapter 3 discusses the `IF` statement in more detail and introduces the `WHILE` statement. We also describe how to use loop invariants as a design tool. We implement several program examples utilizing sequences and nests of control structures.

Chapter 4 covers the important topic of procedure parameters. It also illustrates how to perform stepwise (top-down) design and testing with procedures and procedure stubs. The Modula-2 scope rules for identifiers are also discussed.

Chapter 5 provides a thorough discussion of the standard data types and their Modula-2 operators. We describe the differences between the numeric types `CARDINAL`, `INTEGER`, and `REAL` and how to use the standard Modula-2 functions and functions imported from module `MathLib0`. The data type `CHAR` and operators for ordinal types are described. We also show how to declare subranges of the ordinal data types.

Chapter 6 discusses software development and the roles of procedural and data abstraction. We show how to create library modules and how to make use of them in the design of large-scale program systems. We also cover enumeration types and implement an abstract data type consisting of an enumeration type and its operators. The use of text files is introduced so that previously prepared data files can be used for program input and so that program output can be saved on disk.

Chapter 7 completes the discussion of control structures in Modula-2. We show how to use the `FOR` statement with loop control variables that are enumeration types and other ordinal types. The `REPEAT` statement and general `LOOP` statement are introduced and compared with `WHILE` and `FOR` statements. Function procedures are also discussed.

Chapter 8 introduces Modula-2 data structures, starting with the array type. There are application programs involving array types with a variety of subscript and element types. We also show how to declare and store strings as arrays of characters.

Chapter 9 describes the various forms of the record data structure, including hierarchical records and variant records. Also, an abstract data type for complex arithmetic is implemented in this chapter.

Chapter 10 describes arrays with structured elements, including arrays of arrays (multidimensional arrays) and arrays of records. Also, searching and sorting an array of records is discussed.

Chapter 11 describes the module `Strings` and illustrates text processing. The set data type and type `BITSET` are also covered.

Chapter 12 discusses recursion and provides many examples of recursive procedures and functions, including binary search and quicksort. Some faculty will prefer to introduce the rudiments of recursion earlier. The first two sections of this chapter can be covered anytime after Chapter 4 (Procedure Parameters); the remainder of this chapter can be covered after Chapter 8 (Arrays and String Variables).

Chapter 13 introduces the pointer data type and shows how to use opaque types in modules to enforce information hiding. We introduce the stack and queue abstract data types and provide array implementations of these important data structures.

Chapter 14 covers dynamic data structures including linked lists and trees. Linked-list implementations of stacks and queues are also discussed. Abstract data types for an ordered list and a binary search tree are implemented. Procedure types are also introduced.

Instructional Aids

A complete Instructor's Manual is available on request from your local representative of Addison-Wesley. A disk containing all modules and procedures is also available from the publisher.

Acknowledgments

Many people participated in the development of this text. The principal reviewers were most helpful in pointing out errors and suggesting improvements. They provided their time generously and their assistance and advice was invaluable in helping to shape this manuscript. I am especially indebted to Giorgio Ingargiola, a colleague at Temple University, with whom I spent several hours discussing how to properly use the module concept in a CS1 textbook. I am also grateful to the faculty listed below who carefully reviewed one or more drafts of this text and provided many constructive criticisms and comments:

Kevin Bowyer, University of South Florida
Albert L. Crawford, Southern Illinois University
Ron Curtis, Canisius College
Giorgio Ingargiola, Temple University
Deepak Kumar, State University of New York at Buffalo
Richard Pattis, University of Washington

I would also like to thank Ethan Waldman of Temple University for his help in editing and debugging all of the Modula-2 programs that appear in the textbook. Without Ethan's assistance, it would have been impossible to meet my deadline for this book. Thanks are also due to Carol Risher who provided solutions to several chapters of review questions and self-check exercises.

Finally, there were also many people involved with the actual production of the textbook. The sponsoring editor, Keith Wollman of Addison-Wesley, provided much encouragement and valuable help in seeing this manuscript through to completion. Bette Aaronson of Addison-Wesley supervised the design and production of the text. Nancy Benjamin did an excellent job of coordinating the conversion of the manuscript to a finished text. I am grateful to all of them for their considerable efforts in behalf of this project.

Philadelphia, PA E.B.K.

Contents

List of Case Studies

1 ▸ Introduction to Computers and Programming

FROM THE 1940s until today—a period of less than 50 years—the computer's development has spurred the growth of technology into realms only dreamed of at the turn of the century. It has changed the way we live and how we do business. Today we depend on computers to process our paychecks, send rockets into space, build cars and machines of all types, and help us do our shopping and banking. The role of the computer program in this technology is key; without a list of instructions to follow, the computer becomes virtually useless. Programming languages allow us to write those programs, and thus to communicate with computers.

You are about to begin the study of one of the most versatile, useful programming languages available today: the Modula-2 language. This chapter introduces you to the computer, its components, and the major categories of programming languages. It focuses on Modula-2 and shows you how to write some simple programs in the Modula-2 language.

1.1 Electronic Computers Then and Now

Just a short time ago, computers were fairly mysterious devices that only a few people knew much about. Computer "know-how" turned around when advances in solid-state electronics led to cuts in the size and the cost of electronic computers. Today a personal computer (see Fig. 1.1) costs less than $2000, sits on a desk, and has as much computational power as a computer that ten years ago cost more than $100,000 and filled a 9-by-12 room. This price reduction is even more remarkable when we consider the effects of inflation over the last decade.

If we take the literal definition for "computer" as "a device for counting or computing," then the abacus might be considered the first computer. The first electronic digital computer was designed in the late 1930s by Dr. John Atanasoff at Iowa State University. Atanasoff designed his computer to perform mathematical computations for graduate students.

The first large-scale, general-purpose electronic digital computer, called the ENIAC, was built in 1946 at the University of Pennsylvania and was funded by the U.S. Army. The ENIAC was used to compute ballistics tables, predict weather, and perform atomic energy calculations. It weighed 30 tons and occupied 1500 square feet (see Fig. 1.2).

Although we are often led to believe otherwise, computers cannot reason as we do. Computers are basically devices for performing computations at incredible speeds (more than one million operations per second) and with

Figure 1.1 ▸ *IBM Personal Computer*

great accuracy. However, to accomplish anything useful, a computer must be *programmed*, that is, given a sequence of explicit instructions (the *program*) to carry out.

Programming the ENIAC entailed connecting hundreds of wires and arranging thousands of switches in a certain way. In 1946, Dr. John von Neumann of Princeton University proposed the concept of a *stored-program computer*: the instructions of a program would be stored in computer memory rather than set by wires and switches. Since the contents of computer memory can be changed easily, it would not be nearly as difficult to reprogram such a computer to perform different tasks as it was to reprogram the ENIAC. Von Neumann's design is the basis of the digital computer as we know it today.

Figure 1.2 ▸ *The ENIAC Computer (Photo courtesy of Sperry Corporation)*

1.2 Components of a Computer

Despite large variations in cost, size, and capabilities, modern computers are remarkably similar in a number of ways. Basically, a computer consists of the five components shown in Fig. 1.3. The arrows connecting the components show the direction of information flow.

All information that is to be processed by a computer must first be entered into the computer *memory* via an *input device*. The information in memory is manipulated by the *central processor unit* (CPU), and the results of that manipulation are stored in memory. Information in memory can be displayed through an *output device*. A *secondary storage device* is often used for storing large quantities of information in a semipermanent form.

Many of you have seen or even used a personal computer. The memory, CPU, and secondary storage devices are usually housed in a single cabinet. The input device is a keyboard and the output device a television-like monitor or screen. These components and their interactions are described in more detail in the following sections.

Computer Memory

Computer memory is used to store information. All types of information—numbers, names, lists, and even pictures—can be represented and stored in computer memory.

Figure 1.3 ▸
Components of a Computer

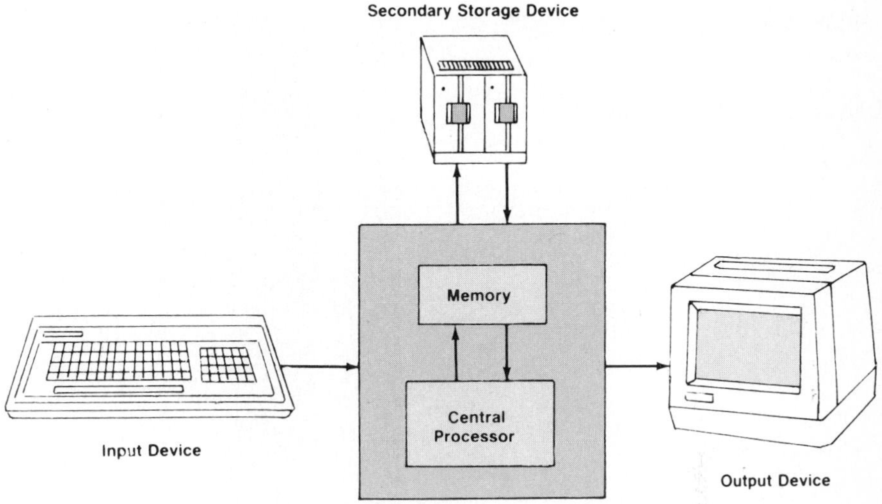

Picture the memory of a computer as an ordered sequence of storage locations called *memory cells*. For a computer to be able to store and *retrieve* (access) information, it must have some way to identify the individual memory cells. To accomplish this, each memory cell has a unique *address*, which indicates its relative position in memory. Figure 1.4 shows a computer memory consisting of 1000 memory cells, with addresses 0 through 999. Some large-scale computers have memories consisting of millions of individual cells.

The information stored in a memory cell is called the *contents* of a memory cell. In Fig. 1.4, the contents of memory cell 3 is the number −26, and the contents of memory cell 4 is the letter H. Every memory cell always contains some information, although we may have no idea what that information is. Whenever new information is placed in a memory cell, any information already there is destroyed and cannot be retrieved.

The memory cells shown in Fig. 1.4 are actually aggregates of smaller units called bytes. A *byte* is the amount of storage required to store a single character. The number of bytes in a memory cell depends on the kind of information stored in that cell and varies from computer to computer. A byte is an aggregate of even smaller units of storage called bits. A *bit* is a single binary digit (0 or 1). There are always eight bits to a byte.

To store a value, the computer sets each bit of a selected memory cell to 0 or 1, thereby destroying what was previously in that bit. Each value is represented by a particular pattern of 0s and 1s. To retrieve a value from a memory cell, the computer copies the pattern of the 0s and 1s stored in that

Figure 1.4 ▸ *A Computer Memory with 1000 Cells*

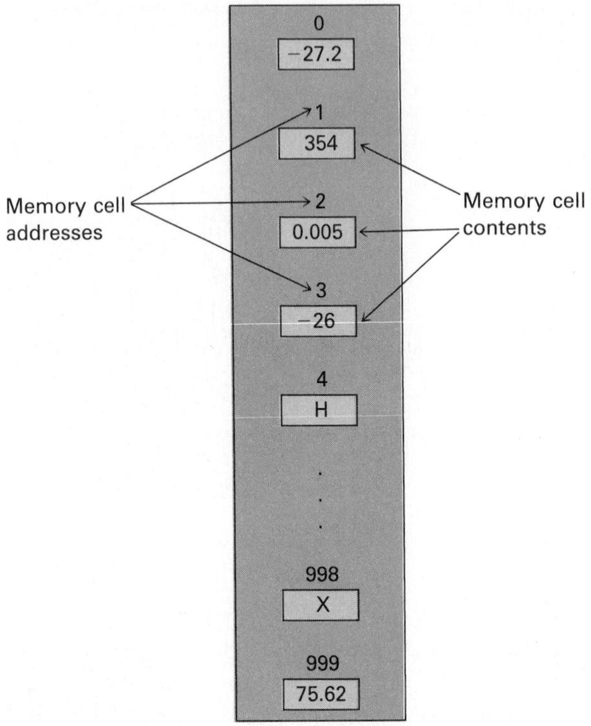

cell to another storage area called the *memory buffer register*, where the bit pattern can be processed. The copy operation does not destroy the bit pattern currently in the memory cell. This process is the same regardless of the kind of information stored in a memory cell (e.g., character, number, program instruction).

Central Processor Unit

The *central processor unit* (CPU) performs the actual processing or manipulation of information stored in memory. The CPU can retrieve information from memory. The information can be either data or instructions for manipulating data. The CPU can also store the results of manipulations back in memory for later use.

The *control unit* within the CPU coordinates all activities of the computer. It determines which operations should be carried out and in what order and then transmits coordinating control signals to the other computer components.

The CPU also contains the *arithmetic-logic unit* (ALU). The ALU consists of electronic circuitry to perform a variety of arithmetic operations, including addition, subtraction, multiplication, and division. These arithmetic operations are performed on data stored in memory; the computational results are then saved in memory. The ALU can perform each arithmetic operation in

Figure 1.5 ▸
A Computer Terminal

about one-millionth of a second. The ALU can also compare information and carry out operations based on the results of the comparison.

Input and Output Devices

The manipulative capability of the computer would be of little use if we were unable to communicate with the computer. Specifically, we must be able to enter data for a computation into memory. Later the computational results that are stored in memory can be displayed.

Many of you will be using a *computer terminal* (see Fig. 1.5) as both an input and an output device. A terminal consists of a *keyboard* (used for entering information) and a *monitor* (used for displaying information). A terminal keyboard is similar to a typewriter keyboard except that it has some extra keys for performing special functions. A monitor is similar to a television or video screen. If you are using a personal computer, the keyboard and the monitor will be separate devices.

Figure 1.6 ▸ *Macintosh Computer with Mouse*

Some terminals are equipped with *graphics capability* (see Fig. 1.6), which enables the output to be displayed as a two-dimensional graph or picture, not just as rows of letters and numbers. With some graphics devices, the user can communicate with the computer by using a *mouse* to move an electronic pointer.

The only problem with using a monitor as an output device is that there is no written record of the computation. Once the image disappears from the monitor screen, it is lost. If you want *hard-copy output*, you have to send your computational results to an output device called a *printer* (see Fig. 1.7) or use a *hard-copy terminal*.

Secondary Storage Device

Most computer systems have a secondary storage device, which provides additional data-storage capability. An example of a secondary storage device is a disk drive with its associated disk (see Fig. 1.8). Large quantities of information can be saved on a disk.

There are two kinds of disks: *hard disks* and *floppy disks*. A computer may have one or more disk drives of each kind. A hard disk normally cannot be removed from its drive, so the storage area on a hard disk is often shared by all users of a computer. However, each computer user may have his or her own floppy disks that can be inserted into a disk drive as needed. Hard disks

Figure 1.7 ▸
Printer

Figure 1.8 ▸
Inserting a Floppy Disk into a Disk Drive

can store much more data than floppy disks and operate much more quickly, but they are much more expensive than floppy disks.

The memory described in the section "Computer Memory" is often called *main memory* or *core memory* to distinguish it from *secondary memory* (disks). Main memory is much faster and more expensive than secondary memory. Also, most computers can have only limited quantities of main memory. The limit on main memory size depends on the number of digits in a memory cell's address. It is often necessary to expand a computer system's data-storage capacity by adding one or more secondary storage devices.

Information stored in secondary memory is organized into aggregates called *files*. Results generated by the computer can be saved as *data files* in secondary memory. Most of the programs that you write will be saved as *program files* in secondary memory. Any file can be transferred easily from secondary memory to main memory for further processing.

SELF-CHECK EXERCISES FOR SECTION 1.2

1. What are the contents of memory cells 0 and 999 in Fig. 1.4? What memory cell contains the letter X? The fraction 0.005?
2. Explain the purpose of each: the arithmetic-logic unit, memory, the central processor unit, the disk drive and disk. What input and output devices will be used with your computer?

1.3 Problem Solving and Programming

We mentioned earlier that a computer cannot think; therefore, for it to do any useful work, a computer must be provided with a *program*. Programming a computer is a lot more involved than simply writing a list of instructions. An important component of programming is problem solving. Before we can write a program to solve a particular problem, we must consider carefully all aspects of the problem and then organize its solution.

Like most programming students, you will probably spend a great deal of time in the computer laboratory entering your programs. Later you will spend more time removing the errors that inevitably will be present in your programs.

It is tempting to rush to the computer laboratory and start entering your program as soon as you have some idea of how to write it. Resist that temptation. Instead think carefully about the problem and its solution before you write any program statements. When you have a solution in mind, first plan it out on paper and modify it if necessary before writing the program.

Once you have written the program on paper, *desk check* your solution by "executing" it much as a computer would. Carefully determine the result of each program statement by using sample data that are easy to manipulate (e.g., small whole numbers). Compare those results with what would be expected; when the results are incorrect, make any necessary corrections to the program. Only then should you go to the computer laboratory and start to enter the program. Experience has shown that a few extra minutes spent evaluating the proposed solution in this way often saves hours of frustration later. The process you should follow is shown in Fig. 1.9.

This text stresses a methodology for problem solving that we have found useful in helping students learn to program. We will practice a technique called *structured programming* that should enable you to write programs that are relatively easy to read and understand and that contain fewer initial errors.

Most students have a very strong positive or negative feeling about programming; very few are ambivalent. Programming can be challenging for the following reasons:

- You are learning a new language with its own *syntax*, or rules of grammar.
- You must carefully plan out what actions you performed and their sequence.
- You must be explicit and accurate in describing what you want done.
- You must implement your solution in an existing programming language. What seems simple to write in English may require considerable effort to specify in a programming language.
- You must enter all program instructions and all data carefully. Each instruction must correspond exactly with the syntax of the programming language. Omitting a comma can cause your program to fail.
- You will be dealing with equipment that occasionally malfunctions and sometimes is not accessible when you want to use it.
- When you make a mistake (and you will make lots of mistakes), it is often difficult to determine what is wrong so that you can fix it.

Figure 1.9 ▸ *Programming Strategy*

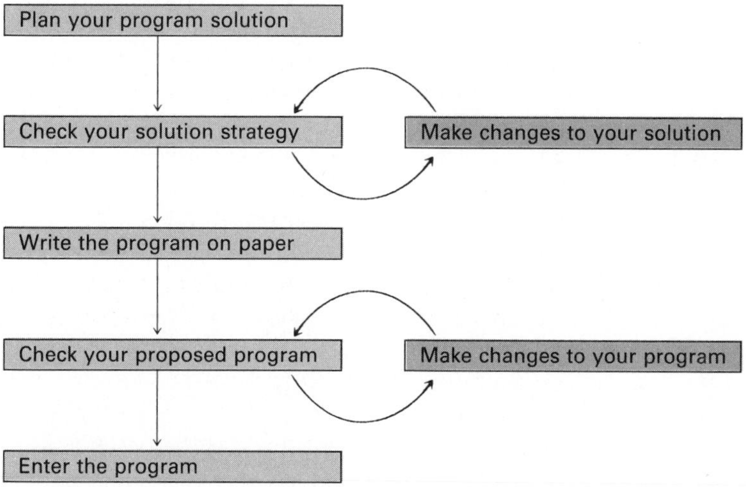

This list is not intended to scare you, but to alert you to some of the problems that you may encounter. If you are careful and patient and plan ahead, you can avoid some of these problems. Planning ahead includes scheduling your time so that you can use the computer laboratory during hours when it is less busy.

1.4 Programming Languages

Languages used for writing computer programs are called *programming languages*. Programming languages fall into three broad categories: machine, assembly, and high-level.

High-level languages are the ones most often used by *programmers* (program writers). One reason for the popularity of high-level languages is that they are much easier to use than machine and assembly languages. Another reason is that a high-level language program is *portable*, which means that it can be executed without modification on many different types of computers. An assembly-language or machine-language program, on the other hand, can execute on only one type of computer.

Some common high-level languages are BASIC, FORTRAN, COBOL, Pascal, and Modula-2. Each of these high-level languages has a *language standard* that describes the form and meaning of all its statements. Generally there are additional features available on a particular computer that are not part of the standard. A program will be portable if the programmer is careful to use only those features that are part of the standard.

One of the most important features of high-level languages is that they allow us to write program statements that resemble English. We can reference data that are stored in memory using descriptive names (e.g., `Name`, `Rate`) rather than numeric memory-cell addresses. We can also describe operations using familiar symbols. For example, in several high-level languages the statement

```
Z := X + Y
```

means add `X` to `Y` and store the result in `Z`.

We can also use descriptive names to reference data in assembly language; however, we must specify the operations to be performed on the data more explicitly. The high-level language statement above might be written in an assembly language as

```
LOAD X
ADD Y
STORE Z
```

Machine language is the "native tongue" of a computer. Each instruction in machine language is a *binary string* (string of 0s and 1s) that specifies an operation and the memory cells involved in the operation. The assembly-language statements above might be written in a machine language as

```
0010 0000 0000 0100
0100 0000 0000 0101
0011 0000 0000 0110
```

Obviously what is easiest for a computer to understand is most difficult for a person and vice versa.

A computer can execute only programs that are in machine language. Consequently, a program in high-level language must be translated into machine language before it can be executed. The next section describes the process of translating and executing a program written in a high-level language.

SELF-CHECK EXERCISE FOR SECTION 1.4

1. What do you think the high-level language statements below mean?

```
X := A + B + C;    X := Y / Z;    D := C - B + A
```

1.5 Processing a High-Level-Language Program

Before it can be processed, a high-level-language program must be entered at the terminal. The program will be stored on disk as a file called the *source file*. An *editor* program is used to enter and save the program.

Once the source file is saved, it must be translated into machine language. A *compiler* program processes the source file and attempts to translate each statement.

One or more statements in the source file may contain a *syntax error*, which means that the statement does not correspond exactly to the syntax of the high-level language. In that case, the compiler will cause error messages to be displayed.

At this point, you can make changes to your source file and have the compiler process it again. If there are no more errors, the compiler will create an *object file*, which is your program translated into machine language. The object file and any additional object files (e.g., programs for input and output operations) that may be needed by your program are combined into a *load file* by the *linker* program. Finally, the load file is placed into memory by the *loader* program and executed. The editor, compiler, linker, and loader programs are part of your computer system. This process is shown in Fig. 1.10.

Figure 1.10 ▸ *Preparing a Program for Execution*

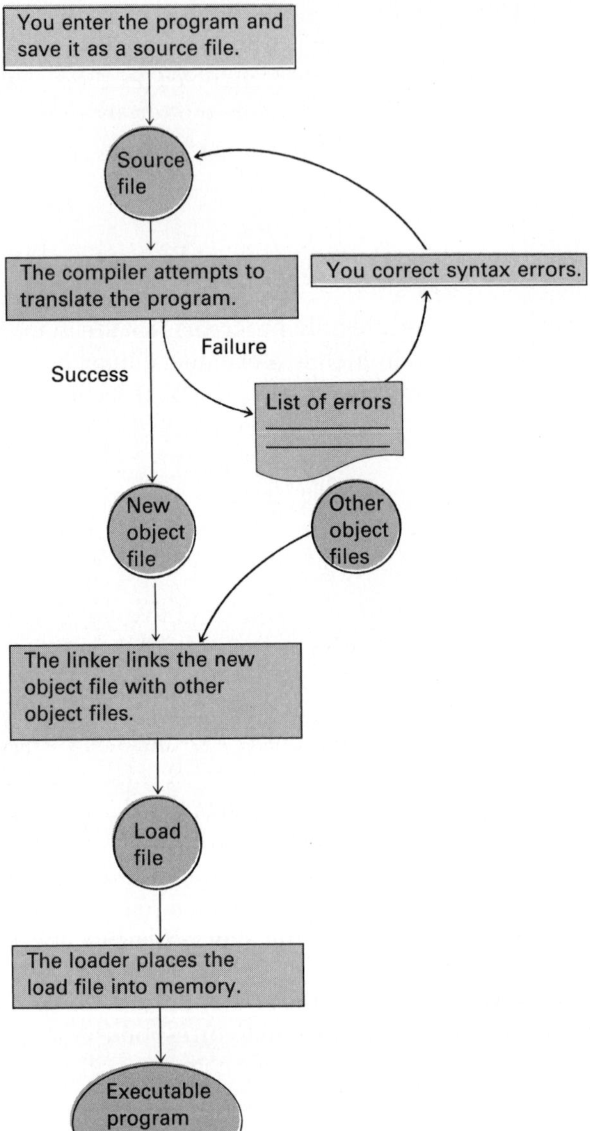

Executing a Program

To execute a program, the computer control unit must examine each program instruction in memory and send out the command signals required to carry out the instruction. Normally the instructions are executed in sequence; however, as we will see later, it is possible to have the control unit skip over some instructions or execute some instructions more than once. During execution,

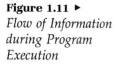

Figure 1.11 ▸ *Flow of Information during Program Execution*

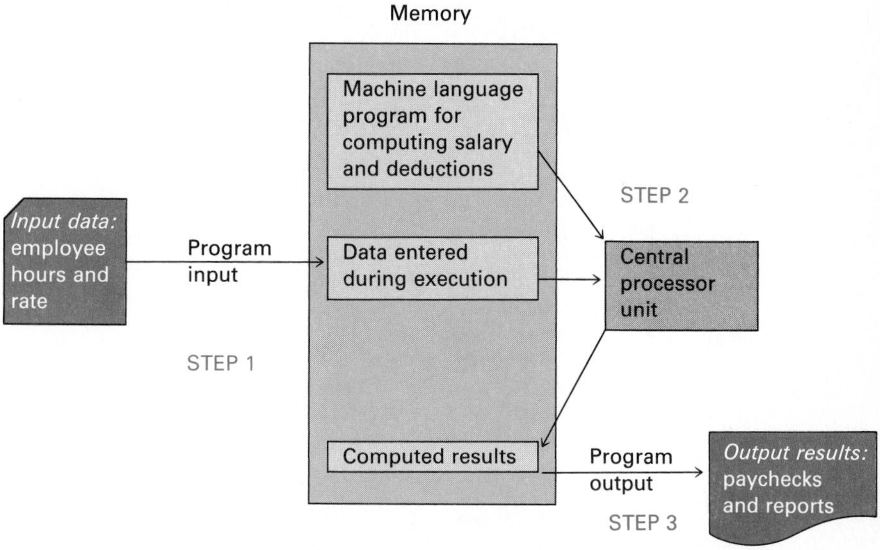

data are entered into memory and manipulated in some specified way. The result of that data manipulation will then be displayed.

Figure 1.11 shows the execution of a payroll program stored in memory. The first step of the program requires entering data into memory that describe the employee. In step 2, the employee data are manipulated by the central processor, and the results of computations are stored in memory. In the final step, the computational results are displayed as payroll reports or employee payroll checks. An example of a program that does this is provided later in the chapter.

SELF-CHECK EXERCISES FOR SECTION 1.5

1. What is the role of a compiler? What is a syntax error? In which file would you find a syntax error?
2. What is the difference between the source file and an object file? Which do you create and which does the compiler create? Which one is processed by the linker? What does the loader do?

1.6 Introduction to Modula-2

Modula-2 was developed in 1978 by Professor Nicklaus Wirth of Zurich, Switzerland, as a successor to Pascal, which he developed in 1971. Although it is widely used for teaching programming, Pascal has some limitations that

Figure 1.12 ▶
Printing a Welcoming Message

```
MODULE Hello;

  FROM InOut IMPORT
    WriteString, WriteLn, Read, Write;

  VAR
    Letter1, Letter2 : CHAR;

BEGIN
  WriteString ('Enter your two initials: ');
  Read (Letter1);  Read (Letter2);
  WriteLn;
  WriteString ('Hello ');
  Write (Letter1);  Write (Letter2);
  WriteString ('.  We hope you enjoy studying Modula-2!');
  WriteLn
END Hello.

Enter your two initials: EK
Hello EK. We hope you enjoy studying Modula-2!
```

restrict its use as a language for implementing large-scale program systems. Modula-2, however, can be used equally well for teaching introductory programming concepts and for developing practical computer systems. Both Pascal and Modula-2 have features that facilitate writing structured programs, that is, programs that are relatively easy to read, understand, and maintain (keep in good working order).

Two Sample Programs

Before beginning our study of Modula-2, let's examine two short *program modules*, or programs. Don't worry about understanding the details of these programs; it will all be explained later.

EXAMPLE 1.1 ▶ Figure 1.12 contains a Modula-2 program followed by a sample execution of that program. For easy identification, the first and last lines of the program are in color; the information entered by the program user in the sample execution also is in color.

The first three lines of the program will be explained in the next section. The program statement starting with `VAR` identifies the names of the two memory cells (`Letter1`, `Letter2`) that will be used to store each initial.

The part of the program that is translated into machine language for execution follows `BEGIN`. Each program statement starting with the word

WriteString or Write causes some information to be displayed during program execution. The statement

```
WriteString ('Enter your two initials: ');
```

displays the *string* enclosed in quotes on the first output line of the program. This string asks the program user to enter two letters. The statements

```
Read (Letter1);  Read(Letter2);
```

read the two letters EK (entered by the program user) into the two memory cells listed, one letter per cell. The last output line of the program is displayed by the statements

```
WriteString ('Hello ');
Write (Letter1);  Write (Letter2);
WriteString ('.  We hope you enjoy studying Modula-2!');
```

These statements display the string 'Hello ', the two letters just read, and finally the longer string.

The statement

```
WriteLn
```

terminates the line displayed on the video screen by advancing the *cursor* (a place marker) to the first column of the next line. ◂

EXAMPLE 1.2 ▸ The program in Fig. 1.13 converts inches to centimeters. The number of inches to be converted is read into the memory cell Inches by the statement

```
ReadReal (Inches);
```

The statement

```
Cent := CentPerInch * Inches;
```

computes the equivalent length in centimeters by multiplying the length in inches by the real constant 2.54 (the number of centimeters per inch); the product is stored in memory cell Cent.

The statement

```
WriteReal (Cent);
```

displays the value of Cent as a real number (7.6200E+001) in Modula-2 scientific notation. The value printed is equivalent to 7.62 × 10, or 76.2, as will be explained later. ◂

One of the nicest things about Modula-2 is that it lets us write program statements that resemble English. At this point, you probably can read and

Figure 1.13 ▸ *Converting Inches to Centimeters*

```
MODULE InchToCent;

  FROM InOut IMPORT
    WriteString, WriteLn;

  FROM RealInOut IMPORT
    ReadReal, WriteReal;

  CONST
    CentPerInch = 2.54;

  VAR
    Inches, Cent : REAL;

BEGIN
  WriteString ('Enter a length in inches: ');
  ReadReal (Inches);  WriteLn;
  Cent := CentPerInch * Inches;
  WriteString ('That equals ');
  WriteReal (Cent, 12);
  WriteString (' centimeters');
  WriteLn
END InchToCent.

Enter a length in inches: 30.0
That equals 7.6200E+001 centimeters
```

understand the sample programs, even though you may not know how to write your own programs. The following sections explain in detail the Modula-2 programs and statements seen so far.

Reserved Words and Identifiers

Each statement in the programs in Figs. 1.12 and 1.13 satisfies the syntax for Modula-2. Modula-2 statements contain a number of different elements: reserved words, standard identifiers, special symbols, and names for data, program modules, and procedures. *Reserved words* have special meaning and cannot be used for other purposes.

Reserved words in Figs. 1.12 and 1.13

```
MODULE, CONST, VAR, BEGIN,
END, FROM, IMPORT
```

Standard identifiers also have special meaning, but they can be used by the programmer for other purposes (such use, however, is not recommended).

Standard identifiers in Figs. 1.12 and 1.13

```
REAL, CHAR
```

Modula-2 is *case sensitive*, which means that you must be consistent in your use of case (e.g., `char` cannot be substituted for `CHAR`). All reserved words and standard identifiers must be written in uppercase.

There are also some symbols (e.g., =, *, :=) that have special meaning. Appendix A contains a complete list of reserved words, standard identifiers, and special symbols.

What is the difference between reserved words and standard identifiers? Although it is illegal to use a reserved word for the name of a data item, it is legal to use a standard identifier. If you do so, however, Modula-2 no longer associates any special meaning with that identifier. For example, say you decide to use `REAL` as the name of a data item. You then could not use `REAL` for its normal purpose (to identify a data item that is a real number). Obviously, this would be a silly thing to do, and we don't recommend it.

Besides standard identifiers, the programs in Figs. 1.12 and 1.13 contain other identifiers that are used as the names of program modules, utility modules, utility procedures, and data. These identifiers, written in a combination of uppercase and lowercase, are described in the next two sections.

Program Modules and Utility Modules

We must inform Modula-2 of the name and purpose of each identifier used in a program module (or program). The name of the program module itself is given in the first line following the reserved word `MODULE`, as in

```
MODULE Hello;
```

Next we must identify any utility procedures that will be needed by the program module. A *utility procedure* is a program unit that performs a specific operation, such as reading a real number (procedure `ReadReal`) or writing a string (procedure `WriteString`). The utility procedures perform useful operations that are frequently required for programming in Modula-2.

A *utility module* is a collection of utility procedures that perform related operations. For example, utility module `InOut` consists of procedures for performing input and output of individual characters, strings, and integers. The name of each utility procedure needed by a Modula-2 program and its associated module must be declared in an *import statement* at the beginning of the module.

The import statement

```
FROM InOut IMPORT
  Read, Write, WriteString, WriteLn;
```

specifies the name of a utility module (`InOut`) and lists four utility procedures (`Read, Write, WriteString, WriteLn`) found in that module. If a program module begins with this statement, then any of the four utility procedures after `IMPORT` may be used in that program module.

The utility modules provided by each Modula-2 system may vary. We will assume, however, that the modules described in Appendix B are available. We will have more to say about utility modules `InOut` and `RealInOut` in Section 1.7 and modules in general in Chapter 6.

The import statement is summarized in the syntax display below. Each syntax display describes the syntactic form of a statement followed by an example. Each syntactic element is described in the interpretation section.

Import Statement ▶

> FORM: `FROM` *utility module* `IMPORT` *procedure list*
>
> EXAMPLE: `FROM InOut IMPORT WriteString, WriteLn;`
>
> INTERPRETATION: The *procedure list* identifies the utility procedures that are being imported from a *utility module*. Commas separate the procedure names in the *procedure list*. In later chapters, we will see that procedures are not the only things that can be imported.

Constant and Variable Declarations

Each program begins with a *declaration part*, which consists of declarations for all identifiers (except reserved words and standard identifiers) used in the program. The programs seen so far contain declarations for constants and variables. The *constant declaration*

```
CONST
  CentPerInch = 2.54;
```

specifies the identifier `CentPerInch` as the name of the constant 2.54.

Identifiers declared in a constant declaration are called *constants*. Only data values that never change (e.g., the number of centimeters per inch is always 2.54) should be associated with an identifier that is a constant. It is incorrect to attempt to change the value of a constant in a Modula-2 program.

The *variable declaration*

```
VAR
  Letter1, Letter2 : CHAR;
```

in Fig. 1.12 gives the names of two identifiers used to reference data items that are individual characters as denoted by the standard identifier `CHAR`. The variable declaration

```
VAR
  Inches, Cent : REAL;
```

in Fig. 1.13 gives the names of two identifiers used to reference data items that are real numbers (e.g., 30.0 and 562.57) as denoted by the standard identifier `REAL`.

Identifiers declared in a variable declaration statement are called *variables*. The value stored in a variable may change as a program executes. Variables are used in a program for storing input data items and computational results. The standard identifiers (REAL, CHAR) used in the variable declaration statement describe the *type*, or kind, of data that will be stored in the variable. The *data types* REAL and CHAR will be discussed in more detail in Section 1.9.

You have quite a bit of freedom in selecting *identifiers*, but you must follow these syntactic rules:

1. An identifier must always begin with a letter.
2. An identifier must consist of letters and/or digits only.

Remember, you cannot use a reserved word as an identifier. Some valid and invalid identifiers are listed below.

Valid identifiers

```
LETTER1, letter1, Inches,
Cent, CentPerInch, hello
```

Invalid identifiers

```
1LETTER, CONST, VAR,
Two*Four, Joe's, Cent_Per_Inch
```

Although both uppercase and lowercase may be used, the case of each letter is significant. Every reference to an identifier in a program must be written in exactly the same way; otherwise a syntax error will result.

The category of each identifier used in Examples 1.1 and 1.2 is shown in Table 1.1.

The statements introduced in this section are summarized in the displays below. Each display describes the syntactical form of the statement and then provides an example and an interpretation of the statement. Elements in italics are described in the interpretation.

Table 1.1 ▸ *Category of Identifiers in Examples 1.1 and 1.2*

PROGRAM MODULES	UTILITY MODULES	UTILITY PROCEDURES	VARIABLES	CONSTANTS
Hello	InOut	Read	Letter1	CentPerInch
InchToCent		Write	Letter2	
		WriteString	Inches	
		WriteLn	Cent	
	RealInOut	ReadReal		
		WriteReal		

Constant Declaration ▶

FORM: `CONST` *constant* = *value*

EXAMPLE:
```
CONST
  MaxInt = 32767;
  Pi = 3.1459;
```

INTERPRETATION: The specified *value* is associated with the identifier *constant*. The value of *constant* cannot be changed by any subsequent program statements. More than one constant declaration may follow each occurrence of the word `CONST`.

Variable Declaration ▶

FORM: `VAR` *variable list* : *type*

EXAMPLE:
```
VAR
  X, Y : REAL;
  Me, You : INTEGER;
```

INTERPRETATION: A memory cell is allocated for each variable (an identifier) in the *variable list*. The *type* of data (`REAL`, `CHAR`, etc.) to be stored in each variable is specified following the ":". Commas separate the identifiers in the *variable list*. More than one list of variables may be declared after each occurrence of the word `VAR` in a program.

Program Style

Choosing Identifier Names

Throughout the text, issues of good programming style will be discussed in displays such as this one. Program-style displays will provide guidelines for improving the appearance and readability of programs. Because most programs will be examined or studied by someone else, a program that follows consistent style conventions will be easier to read and understand than one that is sloppy or inconsistent. Such conventions make it easier for humans to understand programs, but they have no effect whatsoever on the computer's interpretation.

It is important to pick meaningful names for identifiers so it will be easier to understand their use in a program. For example, the identifier `Salary` would be a good name for a variable used to store a person's salary; the identifiers `S` and `Bagel` would be bad choices.

There is no restriction on the length of an identifier. However, it is difficult to form meaningful names using fewer than three letters. On the other hand, typing errors are more likely when identifiers are too long. A reasonable rule of thumb is to use names between three and ten characters in length.

If you mistype an identifier, the compiler will usually detect this as a syntax error. Because mistyped identifiers sometimes look like other identifiers, avoid picking names that are very similar to each other. Names that are almost the same also can cause confusion. Do not choose two names that are identical except for their case.

Finally, we will use the convention of starting each identifier with an uppercase letter and using lowercase thereafter. If an identifier consists of multiple words, then each word will begin with an uppercase letter (e.g., StartSalary). This convention makes it easy to read multiple word identifiers and helps us to distinguish declared identifiers from reserved words and standard identifiers, which are all uppercase.

General Form of a Program Module

To summarize what we have learned so far, the program modules shown earlier have the general form described in Fig. 1.14. The first line of each module begins with the reserved word `MODULE`. The last line of each module begins with the reserved word `END`.

Figure 1.14 ▸ *General Form of a Program Module*

```
MODULE identifier1;
  FROM identifier IMPORT      )
    identifier list;          |
  CONST                       |
    identifier = constant;    }    Declaration part
    . . .                     |
  VAR                         |
    identifier list : type;   )
    . . .
BEGIN
  program statement;  )
    . . .             }            Statement sequence
  program statement   )
END identifer1.
```

The import statements (beginning with `FROM`) identify utility modules and procedures that are needed by the program module. The import statements must appear first, followed by any constant declarations (indicated by `CONST`) and variable declarations (indicated by `VAR`). There may be more than one occurrence of the reserved words `FROM`, `CONST`, and `VAR`. The words `CONST` and `VAR` may appear in any order. Commas separate identifiers in an identifier list (e.g., a list of variables).

The reserved word `BEGIN` signals the start of the statement sequence part of the module. The *statement sequence* consists of the program statements that are translated into machine language and executed. The program statements seen so far consist of statements that perform computations and input/output operations (these executable statements are described in Section 1.7). The last line in a program module has the form

END *identifier*$_1$.

where *identifier*$_1$ is the name of the module.

Semicolons separate Modula-2 statements and must be inserted between statements in a program. A semicolon is not needed before the first statement in a sequence or after the last statement. Consequently, a semicolon should not appear after the reserved word BEGIN. It is permissible, though not recommended, to use a semicolon after the last statement in a sequence. If present, this semicolon has the effect of inserting an "empty statement" between the last statement and the reserved word END.

As shown in Fig. 1.14, a Modula-2 statement can extend over more than one line. The import statements and the variable and constant declarations start on one line and finish on the next. Statements cannot be split in the middle of an identifier, a reserved word, a number, or a string.

We can also write more than one statement on a line. The line

```
Read (Letter1);  Read (Letter2);
```

contains two statements, each followed by a semicolon. Generally we do this only for statements that perform related input/output operations.

Program Style

Use of Blank Spaces

The consistent and careful use of blank spaces can significantly enhance the style of a program. A blank space is required between words in a program line (e.g., between MODULE and Hello).

Because extra blanks between words and symbols are ignored by the compiler you may insert them as desired to improve the style and appearance of a program. Always leave a blank space after a comma and before and after operators such as *, –, :=. The reserved words CONST, VAR, and BEGIN should be on separate lines so that they stand out. Indent all lines except the first and last lines of the program and the line BEGIN two or more spaces. Finally, use blank lines between sections of the program.

All of these measures are for the sole purpose of improving the style and the clarity of a program. They have no effect on the meaning of a program as far as the computer is concerned; however, they make it easier for people to read and understand the program.

Be careful not to insert blank spaces where they do not belong. For example, there cannot be a space between the characters : and = in the assignment operator :=. Also, do not write the identifier StartSalary as Start Salary.

SELF-CHECK EXERCISE FOR SECTION 1.6

1. Indicate which of the identifiers below are Modula-2 reserved words, standard identifiers, identifiers, and invalid identifiers.

```
END    Readln   BILL   MODULE   SUE'S   Rate   OPERATE   START
BEGIN   CONST   XYZ123   123XYZ   ThisIsALongOne   Y=Z
```

1.7 Performing Computations and Displaying Results

One of the main functions of a computer is to perform arithmetic computations and to display the results of those computations. First we will see how to specify computations.

Assignment Statements

The *assignment statement*

```
Cent := CentPerInch * Inches;
```

in Fig. 1.13 assigns a value to the variable `Cent`. In this case, `Cent` is assigned the result of the multiplication (* means multiply) of the constant `CentPerInch` by the variable `Inches`. Valid information must be stored in both `CentPerInch` and `Inches` before the assignment statement is executed. As shown in Fig. 1.15, only the value of `Cent` is affected by the assignment statement; `CentPerInch` and `Inches` retain their original values.

Figure 1.15 ▸ *Effect of Cent := CentPerInch * Inches;*

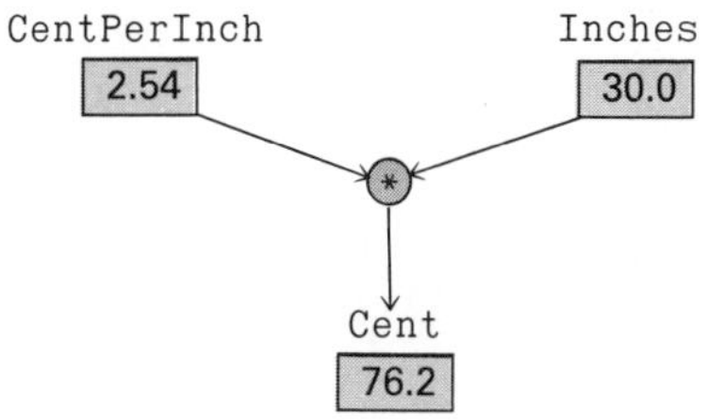

The symbol := is the *assignment operator* in Modula-2 and should be pronounced "becomes" or "takes the value of" rather than "equals." The : and = must be adjacent characters (no intervening space). The general form of the assignment statement is shown in the next display.

Assignment Statement (arithmetic) ▶

FORM: *result* := *expression*

EXAMPLE: `X := Y + Z + 2.0`

INTERPRETATION: The variable specified by *result* is assigned the value of *expression*. The previous value of *result* is destroyed. The *expression* can be a single variable or a single constant or involve variables, constants, and the arithmetic operators listed in Table 1.2. All variables and constants must be the same data type. The real division operator / can be used with type REAL operands only (a division operator for integers will be introduced in Chapter 5).

Table 1.2 ▸ *Some Arithmetic Operators*

ARITHMETIC OPERATOR	MEANING
+	addition
–	subtraction
*	multiplication
/	real division

EXAMPLE 1.3 ▸ In Modula-2, it is permissible to write assignment statements of the form

```
Sum := Sum + Item
```

where the variable `Sum` is on both sides of the assignment operator. This is obviously not an algebraic equation, but it illustrates something often done in programming. This statement instructs the computer to add the current value of the variable `Sum` to the value of `Item`; the result is saved temporarily and then stored back into `Sum`. The previous value of `Sum` is destroyed in the process, as illustrated in Fig. 1.16; the value of `Item`, however, is unchanged. ◂

Figure 1.16 ▸ *Effect of Sum := Sum + Item*

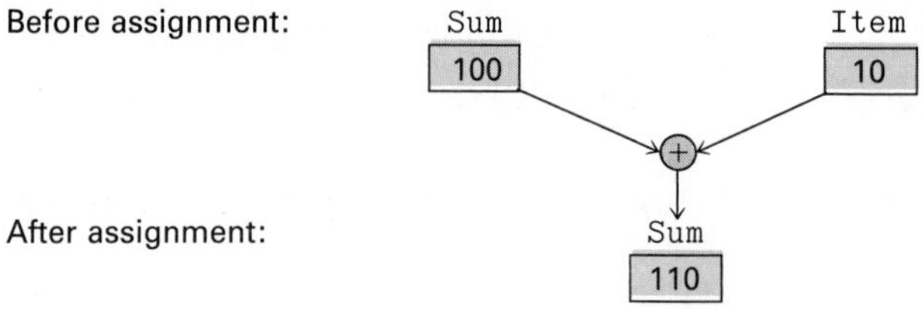

EXAMPLE 1.4 ▸ Assignment statements can also be written with an expression part that consists of a single variable or value. The statement

```
NewX := X
```

instructs the computer to *copy* the value of `X` into `NewX`. The statement

```
NewX := -X
```

instructs the computer to get the value of `X`, *negate* that value, and store the result in `NewX` (e.g., if `X` is 3.5, `NewX` is −3.5). Neither assignment statement changes the value of `X`. ◂

Modules InOut and RealInOut

Information cannot be manipulated by a computer unless it is first stored in main memory. There are three ways to place a data value in memory: associate it with a constant, assign it to a variable, or read it into memory. The first two approaches can be followed only when the value to be stored will be the same every time the program is run. If we wish to store different information each time, then the information must be read in as the program is executing (an *input* operation). As it executes, a program performs computations and assigns new values to variables. The results of a program's execution are displayed to the program user by an *output* operation.

All input/output operations in Modula-2 are performed by utility procedures that are included in a *library* of utility modules supplied with each Modula-2 compiler. Since these modules are not part of the basic Modula-2 language, these procedures can operate in slightly different ways. Most of the time, we will use utility procedures from the utility modules `InOut` and `RealInOut`.

The specific procedure used to read or display a data item is determined by the type of that data item. For the time being, we will manipulate four different types of data: characters, real numbers, integers, and cardinals. We will also need to display strings.

As you write each program module, be aware of the input/output operations that need to be performed and import the required procedures. For most programs, you will need to import procedure `WriteString` (to print prompts) and `WriteLn` (to terminate a line) from utility module `InOut`. You need to import procedures from utility module `RealInOut` only when real numbers are being manipulated. If you forget to import a particular input/output procedure referenced in your program, the compiler will detect this as an *undeclared identifier* syntax error.

Performing Input Operations

A *procedure call* statement is used to call or activate a procedure. The procedure call statement

```
ReadReal (Inches);
```

in Fig. 1.15 reads a *real number* (a number with a decimal point) into the variable `Inches`. This statement causes the number entered at the keyboard to be stored in the variable `Inches`. (After typing a number, the program user should press the RETURN or ENTER key or the space bar.) The effect of this statement is shown in Fig. 1.17.

Figure 1.17 ▸ *Effect of ReadReal (Inches);*

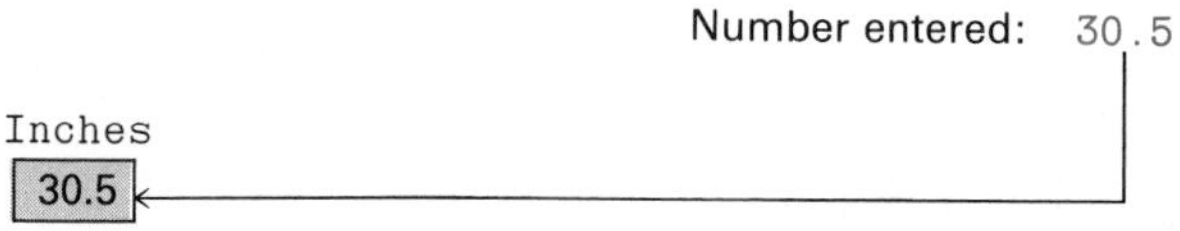

In Example 1.1, a user's initials were read. Because each person using the program probably will have different initials, the statements

```
Read (Letter1);  Read (Letter2);
```

are used to read in two initials. These statements cause the next two characters entered at the terminal to be stored in the variables `Letter1` and `Letter2` (type CHAR), one character per variable. Figure 1.18 shows the effect of these statements when the letters EK are entered.

Figure 1.18 ▸ *Effect of Read (Letter1); Read (Letter2);*

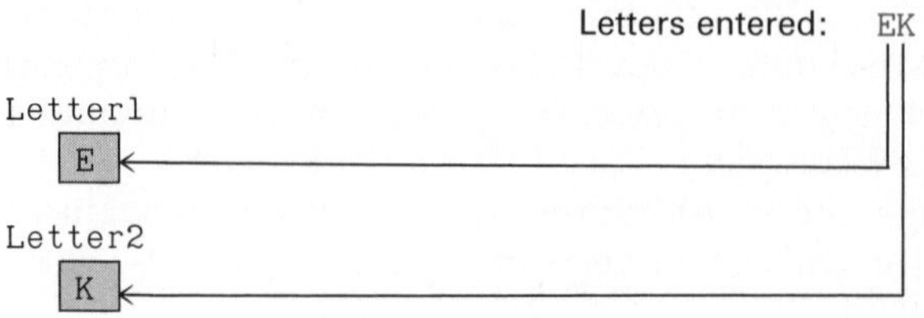

It may be necessary to press the RETURN key after typing in the data characters. Some systems read in characters as they are typed; others do not begin to read them until the RETURN key is pressed.

Some systems echo individual characters as they are entered, and others do not. If your system does not automatically echo these characters, you must follow each Read with a Write, as in

```
Read (Letter1);  Write (Letter1);
Read (Letter2);  Write (Letter2);
```

For the remainder of this text, we assume that Write statements are needed to echo individual character values.

It is interesting to note that the four input characters in Fig. 1.17 make up a single data value, the number 30.5, which is stored in the variable Inches (type REAL). In Fig. 1.18, each input character represents a separate data value and is stored in a different variable.

The procedure ReadInt is used to read an *integer* (a number without a decimal point), which may or may not be preceded by a sign. The variable into which this number is stored must be declared type INTEGER. The procedure ReadCard is used to read an unsigned integer (a *cardinal*) into a variable that is declared as type CARDINAL.

The number of characters read by an input operation depends on the procedure that is executed. Only one character is read by Read. When ReadReal, ReadInt, or ReadCard is executed, the computer skips over any leading blanks and continues to read characters until it reaches a character that cannot be part of a number (e.g., a blank or a letter) or until the RETURN key is pressed. All Modula-2 systems echo the numeric characters that are pressed; some also echo the data terminator (blank or RETURN), while others do not.

How does a program user know when to enter data and what data to enter? Your program should print a prompting message (as explained in the next section) to inform the user what data to enter and when. The cursor indicates the current position on the video screen. As each character is entered, the cursor advances to the next screen position.

After the data are entered and the RETURN key is pressed, the cursor may or may not advance to the beginning of the next display line. If the RETURN key does not advance the cursor on your system, include a `WriteLn` statement after each input operation to advance the cursor. The programs in this book will use the `WriteLn` statement for this purpose. If your system advances the cursor when RETURN is pressed, the extra `WriteLn` statement will cause a blank line to be displayed. Table 1.3 summarizes the four input procedures, which are described in detail in the displays that follow the table.

Table 1.3 ▸ *Utility Procedures for Data Entry*

UTILITY PROCEDURE	PURPOSE	UTILITY MODULE
`Read`	Reads a character	`InOut`
`ReadReal`	Reads a real number	`RealInOut`
`ReadInt`	Reads an integer	`InOut`
`ReadCard`	Reads a cardinal	`InOut`

Read Procedure ▶

FORM: `Read (`*variable*`)`

EXAMPLE: `Read (Letter1)`

INTERPRETATION: The next character pressed on the keyboard is read into *variable* (type `CHAR`). `Read` is part of utility module `InOut`. On some systems, the character read is not echoed.

ReadReal Procedure ▶

FORM: `ReadReal (`*variable*`)`

EXAMPLE: `ReadReal (Inches)`

INTERPRETATION: The next string of numeric characters entered at the keyboard is read into *variable* (type `REAL`). Any leading blank characters are ignored. The first nonblank character may be a sign (+ or –) or a digit. The data string is terminated when a character that cannot be part of a real number is entered or the space bar or RETURN key is pressed. `ReadReal` is part of utility module `RealInOut`.

ReadInt Procedure ▶

FORM: `ReadInt (`*variable*`)`

EXAMPLE: `ReadInt (N)`

INTERPRETATION: The next string of numeric characters entered at the keyboard is read into *variable* (type `INTEGER`). Any leading blank characters are ignored. The first nonblank character may be a sign (+ or –) or a digit. The data string is terminated when a nonnumeric character is entered or the space bar or RETURN key is pressed. `ReadInt` is part of utility module `InOut`.

ReadCard Procedure ▶

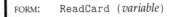

> FORM: `ReadCard (`*variable*`)`
>
> EXAMPLE: `ReadCard (N)`
>
> INTERPRETATION: The next string of characters entered at the keyboard is read into *variable* (type `CARDINAL`). Any leading blank characters are ignored. The first nonblank character must be a digit. The data string is terminated when a nonnumeric character is entered or the space bar or RETURN key is pressed. `ReadCard` is part of utility module `InOut`.

Output Operations

To see the results of a program execution, we must have some way of displaying the values of selected variables. In Fig. 1.13, the statements

```
WriteString  ('That equals ');
WriteReal  (Cent, 12);
WriteString  (' centimeters');
WriteLn
```

display the output line

```
That equals 7.6200E+001 centimeters
```

Procedure `WriteString` is called twice: first to display the string `'That equals '` and next to display the string `' centimeters'`. A string must be enclosed in single or double quotes. If single quotes are used to enclose the string, then double quotes may appear inside the string. Alternatively, if double quotes are used to enclose the string, then single quotes may appear inside the string. Most of the time, it makes no difference whether you use single or double quotes; however, double quotes are required if the string contains an apostrophe (e.g., `"Joe's hat"`). When the `WriteString` statement is executed the characters enclosed by the quotes are printed, but not the quotes.

In Fig. 1.13, procedure `WriteReal` displays the value of variable `Cent` (type `REAL`) between two strings. The output line is

```
That equals 7.6200E+001 centimeters
```

The number `7.6200E+001` is 76.2 expressed in *Modula-2 scientific notation*. In normal scientific notation, 7.62×10^1 means multiply 7.62 by 10 or move the decimal point right one digit. Since superscripts cannot be entered or displayed at the terminal, the capital letter `E` is used in Modula-2 to indicate scientific notation.

In Fig. 1.12, the statements

```
Write (Letter1);  Write (Letter2);
```

display the characters stored in two type `CHAR` variables (`Letter1`, `Letter2`). Each `Write` statement causes a single character to be displayed at the current cursor position.

Procedures WriteInt and WriteCard are used to display integer values and cardinal values, respectively. Both procedures are part of utility module InOut.

Whenever an output operation is performed, the characters to be displayed appear at the current cursor position. The WriteLn procedure is used to segment program output into lines. Each time WriteLn is executed, the cursor advances to the first column of the next line on the screen.

Prompting Messages

The WriteString statements

```
WriteString ('Enter your two initials: ');
WriteString ('Enter a length in inches: ');
```

are used to display *prompts*, or *prompting messages*, in Figs. 1.12 and 1.13, respectively. A prompting message is a string that is displayed just before an input operation is performed. Its purpose is to prompt the program user to enter data; it may also describe the format of the data expected. It is important to precede each input operation with a WriteString statement that prints a prompt; otherwise, the program user may have no idea that the program is waiting for data entry or what data to enter.

Specifying the Field Width of a Number

When displaying numbers, you must specify exactly how many columns of the screen should be used to display the number. The *field width* specification (a CARDINAL value or variable) appears after the output variable or value. For example,

```
WriteCard (1234, 5)
```

uses five columns (the first column is blank) to display the cardinal 1234. The statement

```
WriteInt (N, 6)
```

uses six columns to display the value of variable N (type INTEGER). In the statement

```
WriteCard (1234, NumDigits)
```

the number of columns used is determined by the value of NumDigits (type CARDINAL).

If the field width specified is longer than the number, the number is printed right-justified in the field preceded by blanks. If the field width specified is too short, it is extended so the number can be printed. A field width of ten or greater should be used to display type REAL values. Table 1.4 summarizes the procedures used for output operations. They are described in the syntax displays that follow.

Table 1.4 ▸ *Utility Procedures for Output Operations*

UTILITY PROCEDURE	PURPOSE	UTILITY MODULE
`Write`	Displays a character	`InOut`
`WriteReal`	Displays a real number	`RealInOut`
`WriteInt`	Displays an integer	`InOut`
`WriteCard`	Displays a cardinal	`InOut`
`WriteString`	Displays a string	`InOut`
`WriteLn`	Terminates a line	`InOut`

Write Procedure ▸

FORM: `Write (`*item*`)`

EXAMPLE: `Write ('A');   Write (Letter1)`

INTERPRETATION: The value of *item* (type `CHAR`) is displayed at the current cursor position, and the cursor is advanced to the next screen position. Procedure `Write` is part of utility module `InOut`.

WriteString Procedure ▸

FORM: `WriteString (`*string*`)`

EXAMPLE: `WriteString ('Hello ');   WriteString ("John")`

INTERPRETATION: The *string* is displayed at the current cursor position. The quotes are not displayed. Procedure `WriteString` is part of utility module `InOut`.

WriteLn Procedure ▸

FORM: `WriteLn`

INTERPRETATION: The current output line is terminated and the cursor is advanced to the first column of the next output line. Procedure `WriteLn` is part of utility module `InOut`.

WriteCard Procedure ▸

FORM: `WriteCard (`*item*`, `*width*`)`

EXAMPLE: `WriteCard (Count, 3)`

INTERPRETATION: The value of *item* (type `CARDINAL`) is displayed at the current cursor position. The value of *width* (type `CARDINAL`) determines the number of print positions used to display *item*. Procedure `WriteCard` is part of utility module `InOut`.

WriteInt Procedure ▶

FORM: `WriteInt (`*item*`,` *width*`)`

EXAMPLE: `WriteInt (Item, 5)`

INTERPRETATION: The value of *item* (type `INTEGER`) is displayed at the current cursor position. The value of *width* (type `CARDINAL`) determines the number of print positions used to display *item*. Procedure `WriteInt` is part of utility module `InOut`.

WriteReal Procedure ▶

FORM: `WriteReal (`*item*`,` *width*`)`

EXAMPLE: `WriteReal (Inches, 10)`

INTERPRETATION: The value of *item* (type `REAL`) is displayed at the current cursor position. The value of *width* (type `CARDINAL`) determines the number of print positions used to display *item*. Procedure `WriteReal` is part of utility module `RealInOut`.

Programs in Memory

In this section, we will look at a new sample program and see what happens to memory when the program is loaded and then executed.

EXAMPLE 1.5 ▶ The payroll program shown in Fig. 1.19 computes an employee's gross pay and net pay using the algebraic formulas

gross pay = hours worked × hourly rate
net pay = gross pay − tax amount

In Modula-2, these formulas are written as the assignment statements

```
Gross := Hours * Rate;
Net := Gross - Tax;
```

New values of `Hours` and `Rate` are read each time the program is executed; a constant `Tax` of $25.00 is always deducted.

The program first reads the data representing the hours worked and the hourly rate, then computes the gross pay as their product. Next it computes the net pay by deducting a constant tax amount of 25.00. Finally it displays the computed values of the gross pay and the net pay. ◀

Memory Area for the Payroll Program

Figure 1.20A shows the payroll program loaded into memory and the program memory area before execution of the program body. The question marks in memory cells `Hours`, `Rate`, `Gross`, and `Net` indicate that these variables are *undefined* (value unknown) before program execution begins. During program execution, the data values `40.0` and `4.50` are read into the variables

Figure 1.19 ▸
A Payroll Program

```
MODULE Payroll;

  FROM InOut IMPORT
    WriteString, WriteLn;

  FROM RealInOut IMPORT
    ReadReal, WriteReal;

  CONST
    Tax = 25.00;

  VAR
    Hours, Rate, Gross, Net : REAL;

BEGIN
  WriteString ('Enter hours worked: ');  ReadReal (Hours);  WriteLn;
  WriteString ('Enter hourly rate : ');  ReadReal (Rate);   WriteLn;
  Gross := Hours * Rate;
  Net := Gross - Tax;
  WriteString ('Gross pay is $ ');  WriteReal (Gross, 12);  WriteLn;
  WriteString ('Net pay is   $ ');  WriteReal (Net, 12);    WriteLn
END Payroll.


Enter hours worked: 40.0
Enter hourly rate : 4.50
Gross pay is $ 1.8000E+002
Net pay is   $ 1.5500E+002
```

Figure 1.20 ▸
Memory Before and After Execution of a Program

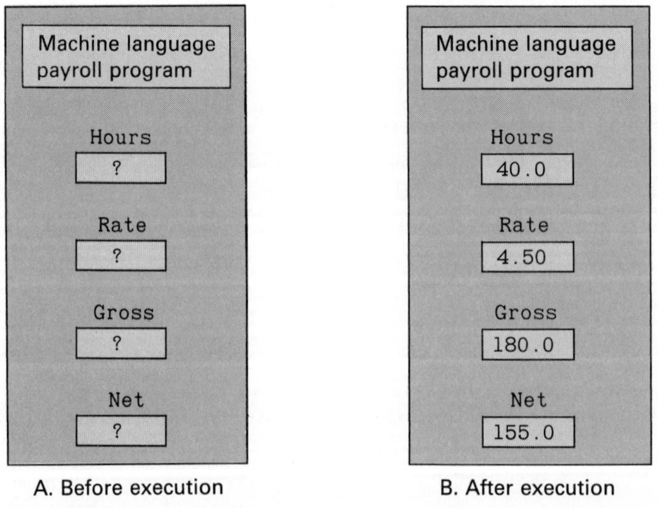

Hours and Rate, respectively. After the assignment statements are used to compute the values for Gross and Net, all variables are defined, as shown in Fig. 1.20B.

SELF-CHECK EXERCISES FOR SECTION 1.7

1. Correct the syntax errors in the program below and rewrite it so that it follows our style conventions. What does each statement of your corrected program do? What is printed?

```
module SMALL; VAR X, Y, X , real:
BEGIN 15.0 = Y; Z:= -Y + 3.5; Y + z =: x;
writeln (x; Y; z) end small;
```

2. Provide the statements needed to display the line below and display the value of X using 10 characters in the space provided.

```
The value of X is ---------- pounds.
```

1.8 Using the Computer

After a program is written, it must be entered at the terminal. Section 1.5 discussed the process of translating and executing a program. The mechanics of this process differ on each computer system; we will describe the general process next. Some of you will be using *time-shared* computers. In time-sharing, many users are connected by terminals to one large, central computer, and all users share the central facilities. Others of you will be using personal computers. A personal computer is a smaller, desktop computer used by one individual at a time.

Operating Systems

Regardless of what computer you are using, it will be necessary to interact with a supervisory program within the computer called the *operating system*. In large, time-shared computers, the operating system allocates the central resources among many users. Some tasks of the operating system are

1. validating user identification and account number
2. making the editor, compiler, or loader available to users
3. allocating memory and processor time
4. providing input and output facilities
5. retrieving files
6. saving new files

The operating system for a personal computer performs tasks 2 through 6.

Each computer has its own special *control language* for communicating with its operating system. We cannot really provide the details here, but we will discuss the general process. Your instructor will provide the specific commands for your system.

Creating a Program or Data File

To use an interactive system, you must first "boot up" a personal computer or "log on" to a time-shared computer. Once you have accomplished one of these tasks, you can begin to create a program.

In most cases, you will use a special program called an *editor* to enter your Modula-2 program. An editor is a program that creates and modifies program and data files. After accessing the editor, you can start to enter a new Modula-2 program. Once your program is entered, you must save the program as a permanent file on disk. To create and save a program file, follow these steps:

1. Log on to a time-shared computer or boot up a personal computer.
2. Access the editor program.
3. Indicate that you are creating a new file and specify its name.
4. Enter each line of your program.
5. Save your program as a permanent file in secondary memory.

Once your program is created and you are satisfied that you have entered each line correctly, you can attempt to compile, link, load, and execute it.

If your program will not compile because it contains syntax errors, you must edit it to eliminate the syntax errors before going further. To accomplish this, you will have to access the editor again, retrieve your program file, make the necessary changes to the Modula-2 program, save the modified program file, and attempt to recompile. The steps used to correct and reexecute a program file are

1. Reaccess the editor program.
2. Get your program file.
3. Correct the statements that have syntax errors.
4. Save your edited program file.
5. Compile, link, load, and execute the new program file.

1.9 Introduction to Data Types

First let's clarify exactly what is meant by a data type in a programming language. A *data type* is a set of values and a set of operations on those values. The data type of the object stored in a particular memory cell determines how the bit pattern in that cell is interpreted. For example, the same bit pattern will mean something different if it represents a type INTEGER object, or a type CHAR object, or a program instruction.

A *standard data type* is a data type that is predefined in the programming language (e.g., REAL, CHAR). Besides the standard data types, programmers can define their own data types in Modula-2.

The standard data types in Modula-2 represent familiar objects. For example, the data type REAL is the set of real numbers (in the mathematical sense) that can be represented on the computer. Every type REAL object in Modula-2 is a real number; however, not all real numbers can be represented in Modula-2. Some real numbers are too large or too small or cannot be represented precisely due to the finite size of a memory cell (more on this in Chapter 5).

The normal arithmetic operations (+, –, *, /) for real numbers and the assignment operation (:=) can be performed on type REAL objects in Modula-2. Input/output operations are performed using utility procedures ReadReal and WriteReal.

The other standard data types that represent numbers are CARDINAL and INTEGER. Except for real division, the arithmetic and assignment operations listed in the previous paragraph can be performed on these data types. The integer division operators DIV and MOD can be used with type INTEGER or CARDINAL operands. These operators will be described later; the Modula-2 operators are listed in Appendix A.

Type INTEGER objects in Modula-2 correspond to the integers in mathematics (e.g., −77, 0, 999, +999). However, because of the finite size of a memory cell, not all integers can be represented in Modula-2. Type CARDINAL objects correspond to the nonnegative integers, including zero.

The basic distinction between the three numeric data types is that a number with a decimal point and fractional part can be stored in a type REAL object, but only whole numbers can be stored in type INTEGER and CARDINAL objects. For this reason, type INTEGER and CARDINAL objects are more restricted in their use. Type CARDINAL objects are most often used to represent a count of items, because a count must always be nonnegative.

Objects of a data type may be variables, constants, or literals. A *literal* is a value that appears directly in a program. A type REAL literal is a number that begins with a digit and contains a decimal point (e.g., 0.112, 456.0, 123.456). A type REAL literal may have a scale factor, which is the capital letter E followed by an optional sign and an integer (e.g., 0.112E3, 456.0E−2). The scale factor means multiply the preceding real number by 10 raised to the power indicated by the integer (e.g., 0.112E3 is 112.0, 456.0E−2 is 4.56). A type REAL literal may be preceded by a sign when it appears in a program. Examples of valid and invalid REAL literals are shown in Table 1.5.

The last valid literal in Table 1.5, 1.15E−3, has the same value as 1.15×10^{-3} in normal scientific notation, where the *exponent* −3 causes the decimal point to be moved to the left three digits. A positive exponent causes the

Table 1.5 ▸
Valid and Invalid REAL *Literals*

VALID REAL LITERALS		INVALID REAL LITERALS	
3.14159		150	(no decimal point)
0.005		.12345	(no digit before .)
12345.		.16	(no digit before .)
15.0E-04	(value is 0.0015)	15E-03	(15 invalid real)
2.345E2	(value is 234.5)	12.5E.3	(.3 invalid exponent)
1.2E+6	(value is 1200000)	.123E3	(.123 invalid real)
1.15E-3	(value is 0.00115)		

decimal point to be moved to the right. When the exponent is positive, the + sign may be omitted.

EXAMPLE 1.6 ▸ The program in Fig. 1.21 determines the value of the coins (nickels and pennies only) you got for change. The variables are declared to be type CARDINAL, since it is impossible to have fractions of coins or fewer than zero coins. The assignment statement

```
Cents := 5 * Nickels + Pennies;
```

computes the value in cents of the collection of coins in the obvious way. ◂

Figure 1.21 ▸
Evaluating Coins

```
MODULE CountCoins;

  FROM InOut IMPORT
    WriteString, WriteLn, WriteCard, ReadCard;

  VAR
    Nickels, Pennies, Coins, Cents : CARDINAL;

BEGIN
  WriteString ('How many nickels do you have? ');
  ReadCard (Nickels);  WriteLn;
  WriteString ('How many pennies do you have? ');
  ReadCard (Pennies);  WriteLn;
  Coins := Nickels + Pennies;
  Cents := 5 * Nickels + Pennies;
  WriteString ('You have ');         WriteCard (Coins, 2);
  WriteString (' coins.');           WriteLn;
  WriteString ('Their value is ');   WriteCard (Cents, 3);
  WriteString (' cents.');           WriteLn
END CountCoins.


How many nickels do you have? 3
How many pennies do you have? 2
You have  5 coins.
Their value is  17 cents.
```

In Fig. 1.21, the statements

```
WriteString ('You have ');        WriteCard (Coins, 2);
WriteString (' coins.');          WriteLn;
```

display a string, a number, and another string before advancing the cursor to the next line. In the output shown, there are two spaces before the digit 5 and one space after. Why?

The fourth standard data type is type `CHAR`. We have already seen that type `CHAR` variables can be used to store any single character value. A type `CHAR` literal must be enclosed in quotes (e.g., `'A'` or `"A"`); however, quotes are not used when character data are entered at a terminal. When the `Read` procedure is used to read character data into a type `CHAR` variable, the next character entered at the terminal is stored in that variable. The blank character is entered by pressing the space bar; it is written in a program as the literal `' '` or `" "`.

EXAMPLE 1.7 ▶ The program in Fig. 1.22 first reads and echos three characters entered at the keyboard. Next it prints them in reverse order enclosed in asterisks. Each character is stored in a variable of type `CHAR`; the character value `'*'` is associated with the constant `Border`.

Figure 1.22 ▶ *Program for Example 1.7*

```
MODULE Reverse;

  FROM InOut IMPORT
    WriteString, WriteLn, Write, Read;

  CONST
    Border = '*';

  VAR
    First, Second, Third : CHAR;

BEGIN
  WriteString ('Enter 3 characters: ');
  Read (First);   Write (First);
  Read (Second);  Write (Second);
  Read (Third);   Write (Third);
  WriteLn;
  Write (Border);
  Write (Third);  Write (Second);  Write (First);
  Write (Border); WriteLn
END Reverse.


Enter 3 characters: E K
*K E*
```

The line

```
Write (Third);   Write (Second);   Write (First);
```

displays the three characters in reverse order. As shown in the program output, each character value is printed in a single print position. The second character read in the sample run of Fig. 1.22 is a blank. ◂

The fifth standard data type is type BOOLEAN (named after the mathematician George Boole). There are only two values associated with this data type, TRUE and FALSE. Examples of *Boolean expressions* (expressions that evaluate to TRUE or FALSE) are in the next chapter.

SELF-CHECK EXERCISE FOR SECTION 1.9

1. Identify the data type of each value below. Which are invalid?

```
15  'XYZ'  '*'  $  25.123  15.  -999  .123  'x'  "x"  '9'  '-5'
```

1.10 Common Programming Errors

One of the first things you will discover in writing programs is that a program very rarely runs correctly the first time it is submitted. Murphy's Law ("If something can go wrong, it will") seems to have been written with the computer programmer and the programming student in mind. In fact, errors are so common they have their own special name (*bugs*); and the process of correcting them is called *debugging a program.* To alert you to potential problems, a section on common errors appears at the end of each chapter.

When an error is detected, an error message will be printed indicating that you have made a mistake and what the cause of the error might be. Unfortunately, error messages are often difficult to interpret and are sometimes misleading. However, as you gain experience you will become more proficient at understanding them.

There are two basic categories of error messages: syntax error messages and run-time error messages. Syntax errors are detected and displayed by the compiler as it attempts to translate your program. If a statement has a syntax error, then it cannot be translated and your program will not be executed.

Run-time errors are detected by the computer and displayed during execution of a program. A run-time error occurs when the computer is directed to perform an illegal operation, such as dividing a number by zero or manipulating undefined or invalid data. When a run-time error occurs, your program will stop execution and a diagnostic message will be printed.

Figure 1.23 ▸
Compiler Listing of a Program with Syntax Errors

```
  1  MODULE Payroll
  2
  3    FROM InOut IMPORT
*****      ^ 23
* 23:  ';' expected
  4      WriteString, WriteLn;
  5
  6    FROM RealInOut IMPORT
  7      ReadReal, WriteReal;
  8
  9    CONST
 10      Tax : 25.00;
*****         ^ 43, 42
* 43: '=' expected
* 42: error in constant
 11
 12    VAR
 13      Hours, Rate, Gross, Net : REAL;
 14
 15    BEGIN
 16     WriteString('Enter hours worked:'); ReadReal(Hours); WriteLn;
 17     WriteString('Enter hourly rate:')   ReadReal(Rate);  WriteLn;
*****                                      ^ 23, 52
* 23: ';' expected
* 52: error in statement sequence
 18      Hours * Rate := Gross;
*****           ^ 23, 52
* 23: ';' expected
* 52:  error in statement sequence
 19      Net := Gross - Tax;
 20      WriteString ('Gross pay is $ '); WriteReal (GROSS, 12);
*****                                                ^ 73
* 73: identifier not declared
 21      WriteString ('Net pay is $ '); WriteReal (Net);
*****                                              ^ 137
* 137: expected parameters
 22      WriteLn
 23    END Payroll.
```

Syntax Errors

Figure 1.23 shows a *compiler listing* of an early payroll program with each line numbered. The program contains the following syntax errors:

- missing semicolon after the module header (line 1)
- use of : instead of = in the constant declaration (line 10)
- missing semicolon after the `WriteString` statement (line 17)
- assignment statement with transposed variable and expression part (line 18)
- wrong case for identifier `Gross` (line 20)
- missing width specification for procedure `WriteReal` (line 21)

The actual format of the listing and error messages produced by your compiler may differ from Fig. 1.23. In this listing, whenever an error is detected, the compiler prints a line starting with five asterisks, a caret symbol (^), and a list of numbers. The caret points to the position in the preceding line where the error was detected. Each number is a preassigned code for the error; the codes and their meaning are listed just below the error line.

The first error is detected after the symbol `FROM` is processed by the compiler. At this point the compiler recognizes that a semicolon is missing (after the word `Payroll`) and indicates this by printing error code 23 (`';' expected`). In this case, the position of the caret is misleading because the compiler could not detect the error until it started to process the import statement.

Two error codes are printed after line 10 to indicate an incorrect symbol (: instead of =). The transposed assignment statement in line 18 also causes two error codes to be printed.

One syntax error often generates multiple error messages. For example, failing to declare the variable `Net` results in an error message each time `Net` is used in the program. For this reason, it is a good idea initially to concentrate on correcting the errors in the declaration part of a program and then recompile rather than to attempt to fix all the errors at once. Many later errors will disappear once the declarations are correct.

As also indicated in Fig. 1.23 (line 20), an `identifier not declared` syntax error occurs if the compiler cannot find the declaration for an identifier referenced in the program body. This can happen because the programmer forgot the declaration, mistyped the name of the identifier, or forgot to import a utility procedure that is referenced in the program body.

Be consistent in your use of uppercase and lowercase. The reserved word `VAR` will not be recognized if it is typed in as `var` or `Var`. Similarly you must be consistent in the way you type in an identifier. The identifiers `Item`, `item`, and `ITEM` cannot be used interchangeably.

Syntax errors are often caused by the improper use of quotation marks as *string delimiters*. If the start of a string is marked by a single quote, then a single quote must be used to mark the end of the string. A single quote cannot appear inside a string that is delimited by single quotes (e.g., `'Joe's hat'` is invalid, but `"Joe's hat"` is okay). A string also must begin and end on the same line.

Run-Time Errors

A common run-time error is `division by zero`. This happens if the program attempts to divide one variable by another that has a value of zero. Another common error is `cardinal overflow`, which is detected when a program attempts to store a negative value in a type `CARDINAL` variable.

If you use a variable that is not yet defined as an operand of an arithmetic operator, the error will often go undetected. In this case, the computer will use whatever value happens to be stored in that memory cell as an operand. A careful inspection of your program output may reveal some unusually small or large values. To avoid this error, make sure that you initialize all variables with assignments or input operations before you use them.

As indicated earlier, debugging a program can be time-consuming. The best approach is to plan your programs carefully and desk check them beforehand to eliminate bugs before they occur. If you are not sure of the syntax for a particular statement, look it up. If you follow this approach, you will be much better off in the long run.

1.11 Chapter Review

The basic components of a computer are main and secondary memory, the central processor, and the input and output devices. A summary of important facts about computers that you should remember follows.

1. A memory cell is never empty, but its initial contents may be meaningless to your program.
2. The current contents of a memory cell are destroyed whenever new information is placed in that cell (via an assignment or read operation).
3. Programs must first be placed in the memory of the computer before they can be executed.
4. Data may not be manipulated by the computer without first being stored in memory.
5. A computer cannot think for itself; it must be instructed to perform a task in a precise and unambiguous manner, using a programming language.
6. Programming a computer can be fun—if you are patient, organized, and careful.

In this chapter, you saw how to use the Modula-2 programming language to perform some fundamental operations. You learned how to instruct the computer to read information into memory, perform some simple computations, and display the results of those computations. All of this was done using symbols (punctuation marks, variable names, and special operators such as *, −, and +) that are familiar, easy to remember, and easy to use. You do not have to know very much about your computer to understand and use Modula-2.

The remainder of the text will introduce more features of the Modula-2 language and provide rules for using them. Remember that the rules of Modula-2, unlike the rules of English, are precise and allow no exceptions.

The compiler will be unable to translate Modula-2 instructions that violate any rules. Remember to import every utility procedure needed, to declare every identifier used as a variable or constant, and to separate program statements with semicolons.

New Modula-2 Statements

The new Modula-2 statements introduced in this chapter are described in Table 1.6.

Table 1.6 ▸ *Summary of New Modula-2 Statements*

STATEMENT	EFFECT
Program Statement	

`FROM InOut IMPORT`
`WriteLn, WriteString,`
`WriteInt, ReadInt;`
	Identifies `InOut` as the name of the utility module that contains utility modules `WriteLn`, `WriteString`, etc.

Constant Declaration	

`CONST`
`Tax = 25.00;`
`STAR = '*';`
	Associates the constant `Tax` with the real value `25.00` and the constant `STAR` with the type `CHAR` value `'*'`.

Variable Declaration	

`VAR`
`X, Y, Z : REAL;`
`Me, It : INTEGER;`
	Allocates memory cells `X`, `Y`, and `Z` for storage of real numbers and `Me` and `It` for storage of integers.

Assignment Statement	
`Distance := Speed * Time`	Assigns the product of `Speed` and `Time` as the value of `Distance`.
Input Statement	
`ReadInt (Me)`	Enters data into the type `INTEGER` variable `Me`.
Output Statement	

`WriteString ('Value of Me: ');`
`WriteInt (Me, 4);`
`WriteLn`
	Displays the string `'Value of Me:` followed by the value of `Me` in a field of four columns, after which the display line is terminated.

CHAPTER 1 ▸ Review Questions

1. List at least three types of information stored in a computer.
2. List two functions of the CPU.

3. List two input/output devices and two secondary storage devices.
4. A computer can think. True or false?
5. List the three categories of programmming languages.
6. Give three advantages of programming in a high-level language such as Modula-2.
7. What processes are needed to transform a Modula-2 program to a machine-language program ready for execution?
8. What are three characteristics of a structured program?
9. Check the variables below that are syntactically correct.

```
Income  ________     TWO FOLD  ________
1time   ________     c3po      ________
CONST   ________     INCOME    ________
TOM'S   ________
```

10. What is illegal about the statements below?

```
CONST Pi = 3.14159;
VAR C, R : REAL;

BEGIN
  Pi := C / (2 * R * R)
```

11. What computer action is required by the statement below?

```
VAR Cell : REAL;
```

12. Write a program to read a five-character name and then print the name out backwards.
13. If the average size of a family is 2.8 and this value is stored in the variable `FamilySize`, provide the Modula-2 statement to display this fact in a readable way (leave the cursor on the same line).
14. List the four standard data types of Modula-2.

CHAPTER 1 ▸

Programming Projects

1. Write a program to convert a temperature in degrees Fahrenheit to degrees Celsius.

2. Write a program to read three data items into variables `X`, `Y`, and `Z`, and find and print their product and sum.

3. Write a program to read in the weight (in pounds) of an object and compute and print its weight in kilograms and grams. (Hint: One pound is equal to 0.453592 kilograms, or 453.59237 grams.)

4. Write a program that prints your initials in large block letters. (Hint: Use a 6×6 grid for each letter and print six strings. Each string should consist of a row of asterisks interspersed with blanks.)

5. Eight track stars entered the mile race at the Penn Relays. Write a program that will read in the race time in minutes (`Minutes`) and seconds (`Seconds`) for each runner

and compute and print the speed in feet per second (`FPS`) and in meters per second (`MPS`). (Hints: One mile equals 5,280 feet, and one kilometer equals 3,282 feet.) Test your program on each of the times below.

Minutes	*Seconds*
3	52.83
3	59.83
4	00.03
4	16.22

6. A cyclist coasting on a level road slows from a speed of 10 miles per hour to 2.5 miles per hour in one minute. Write a computer program that calculates the cyclist's constant rate of acceleration and determines how long it will take the cyclist to come to rest, given an initial speed of 10 miles per hour. (Hint: Use the equation

$$a = (v_f - v_i) / t$$

where a is acceleration, t is the time interval, v_i is the initial velocity, and v_f is the final velocity.)

7. If a human heart beats on the average of once a second for 78 years, how many times does the heart beat in a lifetime? (Use 365.25 for days in a year.) Rerun your program for a heart rate of 75 beats per minute.

8. In shopping for a new house, you must consider several factors. In this problem, you know the initial cost of the house, the estimated annual fuel costs, and the annual tax rate. Write a program that will determine the total cost after a five-year period for each set of house data below. You should be able to inspect your program output to determine the best buy.

Initial House Cost	*Annual Fuel Cost*	*Tax Rate*
$67,000	$2,300	0.025
$62,000	$2,500	0.025
$75,000	$1,850	0.020

To calculate the house cost, add the initial cost to the fuel cost for five years, then add the taxes for five years. Taxes for one year are computed by multiplying the tax rate by the initial cost.

2 ▸ Problem Solving, Procedures, Decisions, and Repetition

ALL YOUR LIFE, you have been solving problems using your own intuitive strategies. Problem solving on a computer, however, requires a more formal approach. In this chapter, you will learn how to analyze a problem and devise an algorithm, or list of steps, to describe a possible solution. You will also learn how to verify that a proposed algorithm does indeed solve the problem it is intended to solve.

We will discuss several different strategies for problem solving, such as generalization, divide and conquer, and solution by analogy. We will use the divide and conquer strategy to break a problem up into smaller, more manageable subproblems. We will introduce the use of procedures to write each subproblem's solution as a separate group of Modula-2 statements.

This chapter will also discuss how to represent decisions in algorithms by writing steps with two or more alternative courses of action and how to specify the repetition of one or more algorithm steps. We will also explain how to write decisions and repetition in a Modula-2 program.

2.1 Representing and Refining Algorithms

Divide and Conquer

One of the most fundamental methods of problem solving is to decompose a large problem into several smaller *subproblems*. This technique, often called *divide and conquer*, enables us to solve a large problem one step at a time.

As an example, let us assume it is the year 2000 and we have a household robot, named Robbie, to help with some simple chores. We would like Robbie to serve us breakfast. Because Robbie is an early-production model, we must provide the robot with a detailed list of instructions to get it to perform even the simplest task.

ROBBIE SERVING BREAKFAST

Problem: Robbie is at point R (for Robbie). We want Robbie to retrieve our favorite box of cereal (point C) and bring it to the table (point T) in the next room. These points and an additional point, D (a doorway), are shown in Fig. 2.1.

Discussion: We can accomplish our goal by having Robbie perform the four steps listed below.

1. Move from point R to point C.
2. Retrieve the cereal box at point C.
3. Move from point C to point T.
4. Place the cereal box on the table at point T.

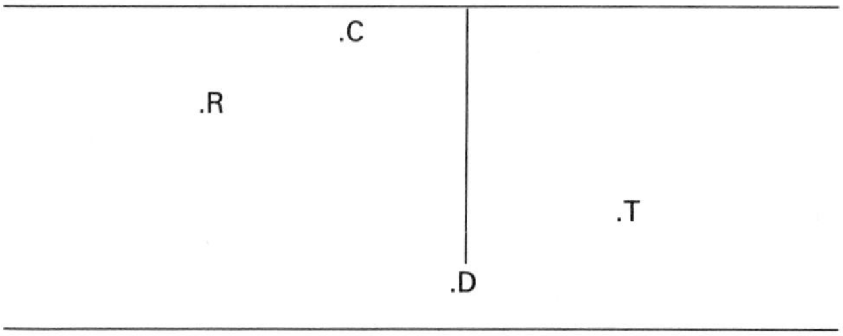

Figure 2.1 ▸ *Robbie Serving Breakfast*

Solving these four subproblems will give us the solution to the original problem stated earlier.

We can attack each subproblem independently. To solve any of these problems, we must have an idea of the basic operations that Robbie can perform. Assume that Robbie can rotate to face any direction, move straight ahead, and grasp and release specified objects. Given this information, subproblems 2 and 4 are basic operations, provided Robbie is in the correct position. First we will concentrate on moving Robbie (subproblems 1 and 3).

In solving the first subproblem

1. Move from point R to point C

we must allow for the fact that Robbie can move in only one direction at a time, and that direction is straight ahead. Consequently, the steps required to solve subproblem 1 are:

1.1 Turn to face point C.
1.2 Move from point R to point C.

Step 3 can be solved in a similar way. However, since Robbie cannot walk through walls, the steps for solving subproblem 3 might be:

3.1 Turn to face the doorway (point D) between the rooms.
3.2 Move from point C to point D.
3.3 Turn to face point T.
3.4 Move from point D to point T.

To summarize the events so far, we divided the original problem of getting Robbie to bring our breakfast cereal to the table into four subproblems, all of which can be solved independently. Two of these subproblems were broken up into even smaller subproblems.

The complete list of steps required to solve our problem is shown below. Such a list of steps is called an *algorithm*. The process of adding detail to a solution algorithm (e.g., rewriting step 1 as steps 1.1 and 1.2) is called *stepwise refinement*.

Algorithm

1. Move from point R to point C.
   1.1 Turn to face point C.
   1.2 Move from point R to point C.
2. Retrieve the cereal box at point C.
3. Move from point C to point T.
   3.1 Turn to face the doorway (point D) between the rooms.
   3.2 Move from point C to point D.
   3.3 Turn to face point T.
   3.4 Move from point D to point T.
4. Place the cereal box on the table at point T.

Algorithms in Everyday Life

Algorithms are not unique to the study of robots or computer programming. You have probably been using algorithms to solve problems without being aware of it.

CHANGING A FLAT TIRE

Problem: You are driving a car with two friends and suddenly get a flat tire. Fortunately a spare tire and jack are in the trunk.

Discussion: After pulling over to the side of the road, you might decide to subdivide the problem of changing a tire into the subproblems below.

Algorithm

1. Get the jack and jack up the car.
2. Loosen the lug nuts from the flat tire and remove it.
3. Get the spare tire, place it on the wheel, and tighten the lug nuts.
4. Lower the car.
5. Secure the jack and flat tire in the trunk.

Since these steps are relatively independent, you might decide to assign subproblem 1 to friend A, subproblem 2 to friend B, subproblem 3 to yourself, and so on. If friend A has used a jack before, then the whole process should proceed very smoothly; however, if friend A does not know how to use a jack, it might be necessary to refine step 1 further.

STEP 1 REFINEMENT

1.1 Get the jack from the trunk.
1.2 Place the jack under the car near the tire that is flat.
1.3 Insert the jack handle in the jack.

1.4 Place a block of wood under the car to keep it from rolling.
1.5 Jack up the car until there is enough room for the spare tire.

Step 1.4 requires a bit of decision making on your friend's part. The actual placement of the block of wood depends on whether the car is facing uphill or downhill, as described next.

STEP 1.4 REFINEMENT

1.4.1 If the car is facing uphill, place the block of wood in back of a tire that is not flat; if the car is facing downhill, place the block of wood in front of a tire that is not flat.

Finally step 1.5 involves a repetitive action: moving the jack handle until there is sufficient room to put on the spare tire. People often stop when the car is high enough to remove the flat tire, forgetting that an inflated tire requires more room. It may take a few attempts to complete step 1.5.

STEP 1.5 REFINEMENT

1.5.1 Move the jack handle repeatedly until the car is high enough off the ground that the spare tire can be put on the wheel.

Throughout the rest of this chapter (and book), we will discuss computer problem solving. Pertinent concepts from this section include

- dividing a problem into subproblems
- solving each subproblem separately
- assigning separate subproblems to independent program modules
- refining an algorithm step to provide solution detail
- decision making in an algorithm step
- repetition of an algorithm step

Understanding the Problem

An important skill in human communication is the ability to listen carefully. Often we are too busy thinking of what our response will be to really hear what the other person is saying. This can lead to a lack of understanding between the speaker and the listener.

Many of us suffer from a similar difficulty when we attempt to solve problems that are presented either verbally or in writing. We do not pay close enough attention to the problem statement to determine what really is being asked; consequently, either we are unable to solve the stated problem or our problem solution is incorrect because it solves the wrong problem.

This text is concerned with improving your problem-solving skills and will present hints and techniques for problem solving. It is important that you analyze a problem statement carefully before attempting to solve it. Read each problem statement two or three times if necessary. The first time you read a problem, you should get a general idea of what is being asked. The second time you read it, try to answer the questions

- What information should the solution provide?
- What data do I have to work with?

The answer to the first question will tell you the desired results, or the *problem outputs*. The answer to the second question will tell you what data are provided, or the *problem inputs*. It may be helpful to underline the phrases in the problem statement that identify the inputs and the outputs. In the problem statement that follows, the inputs and outputs are in italics.

FINDING THE AREA AND CIRCUMFERENCE OF A CIRCLE

Problem: Read in the *radius* of a circle and compute and print its *area* and *circumference*.

Discussion: After identifying the problem inputs and outputs, we must determine the amount and type of memory required to store these data. Clearly one memory cell is required for the input data and two memory cells are required for the output information. All memory cells should be type `REAL` since the inputs and outputs can contain fractional parts. We must also choose meaningful variable names for these cells. We will summarize these decisions below.

PROBLEM INPUTS

the radius of a circle (`Radius : REAL`)

PROBLEM OUTPUTS

the area of the circle (`Area : REAL`)
the circumference of the circle (`Circum : REAL`)

Once the problem inputs and outputs are known, list the steps necessary to solve the problem. Be sure to pay close attention to the order of the steps. The algorithm follows.

Algorithm

1. Read the value of `Radius`.
2. Find the area.
3. Find the circumference.
4. Print the values of the area and the circumference.

Next, refine any steps whose solution is not immediately obvious; for example, step 2 and step 3.

STEP 2 REFINEMENT

2.1 Multiply the radius squared by the value of pi (3.14159).

STEP 3 REFINEMENT

3.1 Compute the product of `2 * pi * Radius`.

Next, we must implement the algorithm as a program. This is done by first writing the declarations for the program using the problem input and the output descriptions. Additional variables or constants introduced in the algorithm also should be declared (e.g., the constant `pi`). Then the algorithm steps should be written in Modula-2. If an algorithm step is refined, the refinement is implemented instead.

Following this procedure, we obtain the program shown in Fig. 2.2. Algorithm steps 1, 2.1, 3.1, and 4 are implemented in the program body following the variable declarations.

Figure 2.2 ▸ *Finding the Area and Circumference of a Circle*

```
MODULE AreaAndCircum;

(* Finds and prints the area and circumference of a circle *)

   FROM InOut IMPORT
     WriteString, WriteLn;

   FROM RealInOut IMPORT
     ReadReal, WriteReal;

   CONST
     pi = 3.14159;

   VAR
     Radius,          (* input  - radius of a circle *)
     Area,            (* output - area of a circle *)
     Circum : REAL;   (* output - circumference of a circle *)

   BEGIN (* AreaAndCircum *)
     (* Read the value of the radius *)
     WriteString ('Enter radius? ');
     ReadReal (Radius);  WriteLn;

     (* Find the area *)
     Area := pi * Radius * Radius;
```

```
  (* Find the circumference *)
  Circum := 2.0 * pi * Radius;

  (* Print the values of Area and Circum *)
  WriteString ('The area is ');
  WriteReal (Area, 12);
  WriteLn;
  WriteString ('The circumference is ');
  WriteReal (Circum, 12);
  WriteLn
END AreaAndCircum.


Enter radius? 5.0
The area is 7.8540E+001
The circumference is 3.1416E+001
```

The program in Fig. 2.2 contains some English phrases enclosed in parentheses and asterisks. These phrases, called *comments*, make the program easier to understand by describing the purpose of the program (see the first comment line), the use of identifiers (see the comments in the variable declarations), and the purpose of each program step (see the comments in the program body). Comments are an important part of the *documentation* of a program, since they help others read and follow the program. They are ignored by the compiler, however, and are not translated into machine language.

As shown in Fig. 2.2, a comment can appear by itself on a program line, appear at the end of a line after a statement, or be embedded in a statement or even another comment. The comment at the end of the second line below

```
VAR
  Radius,          (* input - radius of a circle *)
```

is embedded within the variable declaration that is continued following the comment. We will document the use of most variables in this way.

Comments

FORM: (* *comment* *)

EXAMPLE: `(* This is a comment *)`

INTERPRETATION: The symbols `(*` indicate the start of a *comment*; the symbols `*)` indicate the end of a *comment*. Comments are listed with the program but are ignored by the Modula-2 compiler.

Program Style

Using Comments

Comments make a program more readable by describing the purpose of the program and the use of each identifier. Comments are used within the program body to describe the purpose of each section of the program. There will generally be one comment in the program body for each major algorithm step.

A comment within the program body should describe what the step does rather than simply restate the step in English. For example, the comment

```
(* Find the area *)
Area := pi * Radius * Radius
```

is more descriptive than and, hence, preferable to

```
(* Multiply the Radius by itself and pi *)
Area := pi * Radius * Radius
```

Begin each program with a header section that consists of a series of comments specifying

- the programmer's name
- the date of the current version
- a brief description of what the program does
- a description of the program inputs and outputs
- a list of any program variables and what they represent

Although space considerations prevent us from doing this in the text, we strongly recommend that you follow this practice. The header section for the program in Fig. 2.2 follows.

```
(*
   PROGRAMMER:  Ethan Waldman
   DATE:  July 15, 1990

   Finds and prints the area and circumference of a circle.

   INPUTS:
     Radius - The radius of the circle
   OUTPUTS:
     Area   - The area of the circle
     Circum - The circumference of the circle
*)
```

As shown above, the symbols (* and *) will be placed on separate lines at the beginning and end of a multiple-line comment.

SELF-CHECK EXERCISES FOR SECTION 2.1

1. Describe the problem inputs and outputs and the algorithm for computing the sum and the average of three numbers.
2. Describe the problem inputs and outputs and the algorithm for the following problem: Compute the discounted price for an item, given the list price and the percentage of the discount.

2.2 Using Procedures for Subproblems

The Structure Chart

As mentioned earlier, one of the most fundamental ideas in problem solving is to divide a problem into subproblems and solve each subproblem independently of the others. In the simple area/circumference problem just analyzed, this was not a difficult task. Only two subproblems required refinement, and those were not extensive. In many situations, one or more subproblems may require significant refinement, as shown next.

PRINTING A MOTHER'S DAY MESSAGE

Problem: Mother's Day is coming and you would like to do something special for your mother. Write a Modula-2 program to print the message ''HI MOM'' in large capital letters.

Discussion: There is more than one way to interpret this problem. We could simply print ''HI MOM'' as it appears on this line, but that would not be too impressive. It would be nicer to use large block letters, as shown in Fig. 2.3. Since program output tends to run from the top of the screen downward, it is easier and more interesting to print the letters in a vertical column rather than across the screen.

Algorithm

1. Print the word HI in block letters.
2. Print three blank lines.
3. Print the word MOM in block letters.

The obvious refinements for each step are shown next.

STEP 1 REFINEMENT

1.1 Print the letter H
1.2 Print the letter I

STEP 3 REFINEMENT

3.1 Print the letter M
3.2 Print the letter O
3.3 Print the letter M

We can illustrate what we have done so far by using a diagram to show the algorithm subproblems and their interdependencies. This diagram, called a *structure chart*, is shown in Fig. 2.4.

As we trace down this diagram, we go from an abstract problem to a more detailed subproblem. The original problem is shown at the top, or level 0, of

Figure 2.3 ▸ *Mother's Day Message*

```
*      *
*      *
*      *
********
*      *
*      *
*      *
   **
   **
   **
   **
   **
   **
   **

*      *
**    **
* *  * *
*  **  *
*      *
*      *
*      *
  ****
 **  **
**    **
*      *
**    **
 **  **
  ****
*      *
**    **
* *  * *
*  **  *
*      *
*      *
```

the structure chart. The major subproblems are shown at level 1. The different subproblems resulting from the refinement of each level-1 step are shown at level 2 and are connected to their respective level-1 subproblem. The right side of the diagram shows that the subproblem *Print MOM* depends on the solutions to the two subproblems: *Print M* and *Print O*. Since the subproblem *Print 3 blank lines* is not refined further, there are no level-2 subproblems connected to it.

Figure 2.4 ▸
Structure Chart for Mother's Day Message

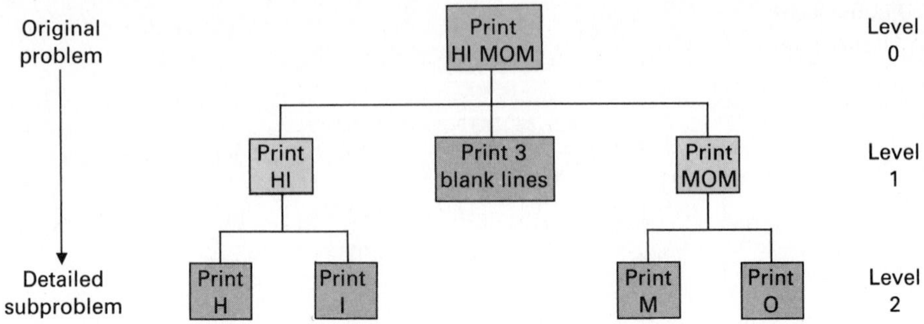

The purpose of a structure chart is to show the structural relationships among the subproblems. The algorithm (not the structure chart) shows the order in which each step must be carried out to solve the problem.

Procedure Declaration

It is desirable to implement each subproblem shown at level 2 in Fig. 2.4 as a separate program unit. In this way, we can concentrate on the design of each individual unit. This can be done in Modula-2 by using a *procedure*.

The procedure `PrintM` is shown in Fig. 2.5. A *procedure declaration* begins with a *procedure heading*, which consists of the word `PROCEDURE` followed by the procedure name (an identifier).

```
PROCEDURE  PrintM;
```

A comment describing the purpose of the procedure comes next, followed by the *procedure body*. The procedure body always starts with `BEGIN` and ends with `END` followed by the procedure name. In Fig. 2.5, the procedure body contains the seven `WriteString` statements needed to print the block letter M, followed by an additional `WriteLn` statement that displays a blank line.

Figure 2.5 ▸
Procedure PrintM

```
PROCEDURE PrintM;

(* Prints the block letter 'M'. *)

BEGIN (* PrintM *)
  WriteString ('*      *');  WriteLn;
  WriteString ('**    **');  WriteLn;
  WriteString ('* *  * *');  WriteLn;
  WriteString ('*  **  *');  WriteLn;
  WriteString ('*      *');  WriteLn;
  WriteString ('*      *');  WriteLn;
  WriteString ('*      *');  WriteLn;
  WriteLn
END PrintM;
```

In this text, the BEGIN that starts a procedure body will always be followed by a comment that identifies the procedure name. The comment is added for clarity and is not required by Modula-2.

The declaration of procedure PrintM must appear in the declaration part of any program that uses it. The procedure declaration indicates that the identifier PrintM is the name of a procedure and provides the list of statements that make up PrintM. The procedure declarations will generally follow the variable declarations in a program.

Procedure Call Statement

When procedure PrintM is referenced in a program, the procedure body is executed and the block letter M is printed. The *procedure call statement*

```
PrintM
```

may be used to reference, or *call*, this procedure, that is, to make it execute.

Figure 2.6 shows the body of the Mother's Day program, assuming that each subproblem at level 2 in Fig. 2.4 is implemented as a separate procedure. The program body (called the *main program*) implements the algorithm described earlier. Algorithm steps 1.1, 1.2, 3.1, 3.2, and 3.3 are implemented as procedure call statements; algorithm step 2 is a sequence of WriteLn statements.

Figure 2.6 ▸ *Main Program Body for the Mother's Day Problem*

```
BEGIN (* Mother *)
  (* Print the word HI *)
  PrintH;
  PrintI;

  (* Print three blank lines *)
  WriteLn;
  WriteLn;
  WriteLn;

  (* Print the word MOM *)
  PrintM;
  PrintO;
  PrintM
END Mother.
```

Besides the WriteLn statements, there are five procedure call statements in the main program shown in Fig. 2.6. Procedure call statement PrintM appears twice because the letter M must be printed twice.

The procedure call statement is used to call a procedure into execution. Modula-2 requires that each procedure called by the main program be declared in the declaration part of the program (before the program body). The

Figure 2.7 ▸ *Partially Completed Mother's Day Program*

```
MODULE Mother;

(* Prints a mother's day welcoming message. *)

  FROM InOut IMPORT
    WriteString, WriteLn;

  PROCEDURE PrintM;

  (* Prints the block letter M. *)

  BEGIN (* PrintM *)
    WriteString ('*       *');  WriteLn;
    WriteString ('**     **');  WriteLn;
    WriteString ('* *   * *');  WriteLn;
    WriteString ('*   **  *');  WriteLn;
    WriteString ('*       *');  WriteLn;
    WriteString ('*       *');  WriteLn;
    WriteString ('*       *');  WriteLn;
    WriteLn
  END PrintM;

  PROCEDURE PrintH;

  (* Prints the block letter H. *)

  BEGIN (* PrintH *)
    (* body of procedure PrintH goes here *)
  END PrintH;

  PROCEDURE PrintI;

  (* Prints the block letter I. *)

  BEGIN (* PrintI *)
    (* body of procedure PrintI goes here *)
  END PrintI;

  PROCEDURE PrintO;

  (* Prints the block letter O. *)

  BEGIN (* PrintO *)
    (* body of procedure PrintO goes here *)
  END PrintO;

BEGIN  (* Mother *)
  (* Print the word HI *)
  PrintH;
  PrintI;
```

```
  (* Print three blank lines *)
  WriteLn;
  WriteLn;
  WriteLn;

  (* Print the word MOM *)
  PrintM;
  PrintO;
  PrintM
END Mother.
```

only exceptions are procedures that are listed in import statements. The relative order of the individual procedures is irrelevant in this problem. The program so far is shown in Fig. 2.7; the remaining procedure declarations are left as an exercise.

A convenient aspect of using procedures in Modula-2 is that they allow us to delay the detailed implementation of a complicated subproblem until later (procedures `PrintH`, `PrintI`, `PrintO` are not yet written). That is, in fact, what we are trying to do when we divide a problem into subproblems and add details of the solution through stepwise refinement. Procedures also enable us to implement our program in logically independent sections in the same way that we develop the solution algorithm.

Another advantage is that procedures can be executed more than once. For example, procedure `PrintM` is called twice in Fig. 2.7. Each time `PrintM` is called, the list of output statements shown in Fig. 2.5 would be executed and the letter M would be printed. If we were not using procedures, these output statements would have to be listed twice in the program body, thereby increasing the program's length and the chances for error.

Finally, once a procedure is written and tested, it can be used in other programs. For example, the procedures discussed here could be used to write programs that display the messages "OH HIM" and "HI HO." It would be very easy to write these programs.

Each procedure declaration can contain declarations for its own constants, variables, and even for other procedures. These identifiers are considered *local* to the procedure and can be referenced only within the procedure (more on this later).

Procedure Declaration ▶

FORM: PROCEDURE *pname*;

local-declarations

BEGIN
procedure-body
END *pname*;

EXAMPLES:
```
PROCEDURE  Skip3;
(* Skips 3 lines *)
BEGIN (* Skip3 *)
  WriteLn;
  WriteLn;
  WriteLn
END Skip3;
```

INTERPRETATION: The procedure *pname* is declared. Any identifiers that are declared in the *local declarations* are defined only during the execution of the procedure and can be referenced only within the procedure. The *procedure body* describes the data manipulation to be performed by the procedure.

Procedure Call Statement ▶

FORM: *pname*

EXAMPLE: `PrintM`

INTERPRETATION: The procedure call statement initiates the execution of procedure *pname*.

Program Style

Use of Comments in a Program with Procedures

Several comments are included in Fig. 2.7. Each procedure begins with a comment that describes its purpose. The `BEGIN` that starts each procedure body and the main program body are followed by comments identifying that procedure or program. The first and last line of each procedure declaration is in color. This is to help you locate each procedure in the program listing.

Relative Order of Procedures and the Main Program

In the Mother's Day problem, the main program body was written as a sequence of procedure call statements before the details of all procedures were specified. The next step would be to provide the missing procedure declarations. We will use this technique to write Modula-2 programs for most problems in the text.

When we actually pull the separate procedures and main program together into a cohesive unit (the final program), the procedures must be listed in the declaration section of the program (before the main program body). This order will seem strange at first, since the main program body begins execution before the procedure bodies.

When the program is run, the first statement in the main program body is the first statement executed. When a procedure call statement is reached, control transfers to the procedure that is referenced. Any memory needed for the procedure's local data is allocated, and the first statement in the procedure body is executed. After the last statement in the procedure body is executed, control returns to the main program and the next statement after the procedure call statement will be executed. Any memory that was allocated to the procedure will be released to be reallocated for other purposes.

The sequence of execution of the Mother's Day program is illustrated in Fig. 2.8. The first statement in the main program body

```
PrintH;
```

is executed first and calls procedure `PrintH` into execution. After the body of procedure `PrintH` executes, control returns to the next statement in the main program body

```
PrintI;
```

The above procedure call statement would, of course, call procedure `PrintI` into execution.

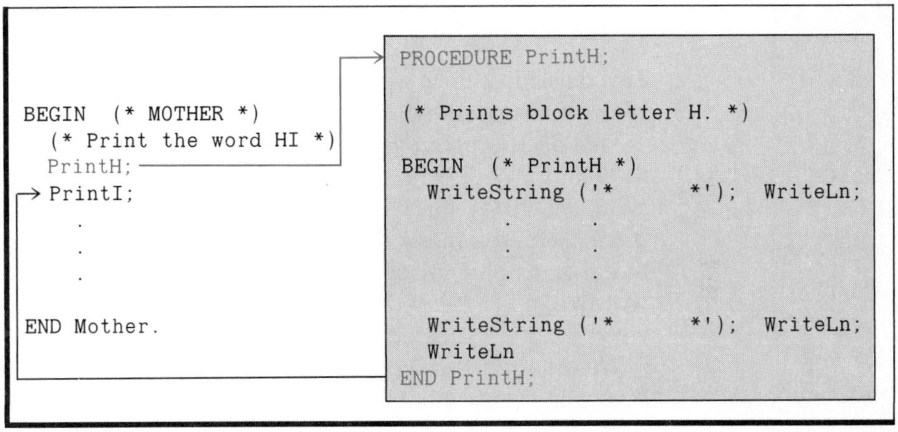
BEGIN (* MOTHER *)
(* Print the word HI *)
PrintH;
PrintI;
END Mother.
PROCEDURE PrintH;
(* Prints block letter H. *)
BEGIN (* PrintH *)
WriteString ('* *'); WriteLn;
WriteString ('* *'); WriteLn;
WriteLn
END PrintH;

Figure 2.8 ▶ *Flow of Control Between Main Program and Procedure*

SELF-CHECK EXERCISES FOR SECTION 2.2

1. Provide procedures `PrintH`, `PrintI`, and `PrintO` for the Mother's Day problem.
2. Write a program to print HI HO in block letters. Provide a structure chart for this problem.

2.3 Decision Steps in Algorithms

In all the algorithms illustrated, each algorithm step is executed exactly once in the order in which it appears. Often there are situations in which we must provide alternative steps that may or may not be executed, depending on the input data. For example, in the simple payroll problem discussed in Chapter 1, a tax of $25 was deducted regardless of the employee's salary. It would be more accurate to base the amount deducted on the employee's gross salary as described next.

If gross salary exceeds $100 deduct a tax of $25; otherwise, deduct no tax.

The refinement of this step should show that there are two courses of action: deduct a tax or do not deduct a tax. To determine what to do, a payroll clerk might ask, "Is gross salary greater than $100?" The clerk would perform one action (deduct tax) if the answer is "Yes" and the other action (deduct no tax) if the answer is "No."

We can describe the payroll clerk's decision process using the *decision step* below.

```
IF gross salary is greater than $100 THEN
  Deduct a tax of $25
ELSE
  Deduct no tax
END
```

This decision step is written in *pseudocode*, a mixture of English and Modula-2. We will use pseudocode to represent algorithms.

This decision step specifies that either the action "Deduct a tax of $25" or the action "Deduct no tax" will take place, but not both. The evaluation of the *condition* "gross salary is greater than $100" determines which action will take place. A condition is a *Boolean expression*, which is an expression that evaluates to either true or false. If the condition value is true, the task following the word `THEN` is executed; if the condition value is false, the task following the word `ELSE` is executed instead.

We can rewrite the condition "gross salary is greater than $100" in Modula-2 as `Gross > 100.00`, where the symbol > means greater than. Most conditions that we use will have one of the forms

variable relational operator variable
variable relational operator constant

where the *relational operators* are the familiar symbols < (less than), <= (less than or equal), > (greater than), >= (greater than or equal), = (equal), and # or <> (not equal).

EXAMPLE 2.1 ▶ The relational operators and some sample conditions are shown in Table 2.1. Each condition is evaluated assuming the variable values below. ◀

X	Power	MaxPow	Y	Item	MinItem	MomOrDad	Num	Sentinel
-5	1024	1024	7	1.5	-999.0	M	999	999

Table 2.1 ▸ *Modula-2 Relational Operators and Sample Conditions*

OPERATOR	CONDITION	MEANING	VALUE
<=	X <= 0	X less than or equal to 0	true
<	Power < MaxPow	Power less than MaxPow	false
>=	X >= Y	X greater than or equal to Y	false
>	Item > MinItem	Item greater than MinItem	true
=	MomOrDad = 'M'	MomOrDad equal to 'M'	true
#	MinItem # Item	MinItem not equal to Item	true
<>	Num <> Sentinel	Num not equal to Sentinel	false

Using a Decision Step in a Problem Solution

The problem that follows requires the use of a decision step in its solution.

MODIFIED-PAYROLL PROBLEM

Problem: Modify the simple payroll program to deduct a $25 tax only if an employee earns more than $100 and to deduct no tax otherwise.

Discussion: Analyze this problem using the tools developed so far in this chapter. First list the data requirements and the algorithm.

PROBLEM CONSTANTS

maximum salary without a tax deduction (TaxBracket = 100.00)
amount of tax deducted (Tax = 25.00)

PROBLEM INPUTS

hours worked (Hours : REAL)
hourly rate (Rate : REAL)

PROBLEM OUTPUTS

gross pay (Gross : REAL)
net pay (Net : REAL)

Algorithm

1. Enter hours worked and hourly rate.
2. Compute gross salary.
3. Compute net salary.
4. Print gross salary and net salary.

As shown previously, problem constants have the same values for each run of the program, whereas the values of the problem inputs may vary. Each constant value is associated with an identifier (`Tax` and `TaxBracket`). The reason for this will be discussed after the program is completed.

The structure chart for this algorithm is shown in Fig. 2.9; the complete program is shown in Fig. 2.10. The refinement of algorithm step 3 follows.

STEP 3 REFINEMENT

```
3.1 IF Gross > TaxBracket THEN
      Deduct a tax of $25
    ELSE
      Deduct no tax
    END
```

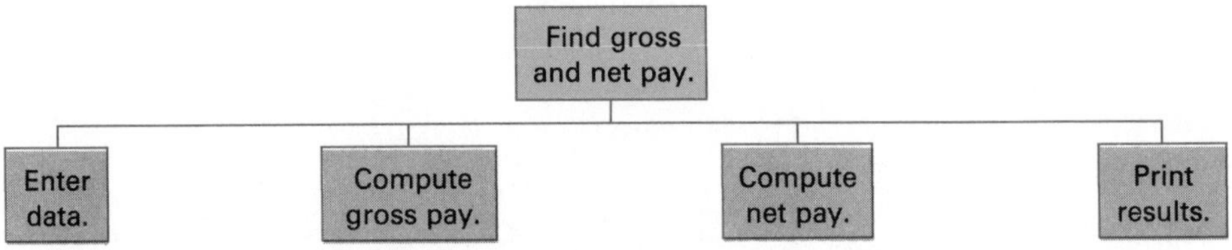

Figure 2.9 ▸ *Structure Chart for Modified Payroll Problem*

In Fig. 2.10, the `IF` statement

```
IF Gross > TaxBracket THEN
  Net := Gross - Tax        (* Deduct a tax amount *)
ELSE
  Net := Gross              (* Deduct no tax *)
END; (* IF *)
```

is used to implement the decision step (step 3) shown earlier. The comments on the right are embedded in the `IF` statement. The reserved word `END` terminates the `IF` statement. The semicolon after `END` separates the `IF` statement from the output statements that follow. The optional comment `(* IF *)` is added for clarity. Note that there is no semicolon after `THEN` or `ELSE`. The next section will provide more examples of the `IF` statement.

Figure 2.10 ▸ *Program for Modified Payroll Problem*

```
MODULE ModPay;
(*
   Computes and prints gross pay and net pay given an hourly
   rate and number of hours worked. Deducts a tax of $25 if
   gross salary exceeds $100; otherwise, deducts no tax.
*)
   FROM InOut IMPORT
     WriteString, WriteLn;

   FROM RealInOut IMPORT
     ReadReal, WriteReal;
```

```
  CONST
    TaxBracket = 100.00;  (* maximum salary for no deduction *)
    Tax = 25.00;          (* tax amount *)
  VAR

    Hours, Rate,        (* inputs - hours worked, hourly rate *)
    Gross, Net  : REAL; (* outputs - gross pay, net pay *)

BEGIN (* ModPay *)
  (* Enter Hours and Rate *)
  WriteString ('Hours worked? ');
  ReadReal (Hours);  WriteLn;
  WriteString ('Hourly rate? ');
  ReadReal (Rate);  WriteLn;
  (* Compute gross salary *)
  Gross := Hours * Rate;

  (* Compute net salary *)
  IF Gross > TaxBracket THEN
    Net := Gross - Tax      (* Deduct a tax amount *)
  ELSE
    Net := Gross            (* Deduct no tax *)
  END; (* IF *)

  (* Print Gross and Net *)
  WriteString ('Gross salary is $');
  WriteReal (Gross, 12);
  WriteLn;
  WriteString ('Net salary is $');
  WriteReal (Net, 12);
  WriteLn
END ModPay.

Hours worked? 40.0
Hourly rate? 5.0
Gross salary is $ 2.0000E+002
Net salary is $ 1.7500E+002
```

Program Style

Use of Constants

The constants `Tax` and `TaxBracket` appear in the `IF` statement in Fig. 2.10. We could just as easily have inserted the constant values directly into the `IF` statement and written

```
IF Gross > 100.00 THEN
  Net := Gross - 25.00
ELSE
  Net := Gross
END; (* IF *)
```

> There are two advantages to using constants. First, the original IF statement is easier to understand because it uses names (Tax and TaxBracket) that are descriptive, rather than numbers, which have no intrinsic meaning. Second, a program written with constants is much easier to modify than one that is not. If we wish to use different constant values in Fig. 2.10, we need to change only the constant declaration. If the constant values were inserted directly into the IF statement, we would have to change the IF statement and any other statements that manipulate the constant values.

More IF Statement Examples

The IF statement in Fig. 2.10 has two alternatives, but only one will be executed for a given value of Gross. An IF statement can also have a single alternative that is executed only when the condition is true, as shown next.

EXAMPLE 2.2 ▶ The IF statement below has one alternative, which is executed only when X is not equal to zero. It causes Product to be multiplied by X; the new value is then saved in Product and printed. If X is equal to zero, these steps are not performed.

```
(* Multiply Product by a nonzero X only *)
IF X # 0.0 THEN
  Product := Product * X;
  WriteString ('New product is ');
  WriteString (Product);  WriteLn
END (* IF *)
```

The semicolons in the program fragment above separate the statements within the IF statement. A semicolon is needed after END when more statements follow the IF statement. ◀

EXAMPLE 2.3 ▶ The IF statement below has two alternatives. It displays either Hi Mom or Hi Dad, depending on the character stored in variable MomOrDad (type CHAR).

```
IF MomOrDad = 'M' THEN
  WriteString ('Hi Mom')
ELSE
  WriteString ('Hi Dad')
END (* IF *)
```

The IF statement below has one alternative; it displays the message 'Hi Mom' only when MomOrDad has the value 'M'. Regardless of whether 'Hi Mom' is displayed, the message 'Hi Dad' is always displayed.

```
IF MomOrDad = 'M' THEN
  WriteString ('Hi Mom')
END; (* IF *)
WriteLn;
WriteString ('Hi Dad')
```

The `IF` statement below is incorrect because the line `END;` appears before the line `ELSE`. A syntax error would be detected when the compiler reaches the line `ELSE`, because the first `END;` terminates the `IF` statement and the next line cannot begin with `ELSE`. This error is called a *dangling else*. ◂

```
IF MomOrDad = 'M' THEN
  WriteString ('Hi Mom')
END;
ELSE
  WriteString ('Hi Dad')
END (* IF *)
```

The next problem illustrates the use of `IF` statements with one and two alternatives.

FINDING THE FIRST LETTER

Problem: Read three letters and find and print the one that comes first in the alphabet.

Discussion: From our prior experience with conditions and decision steps, we know how to compare two items at a time to see which is smaller, using the relational operator `¢`. In Modula-2, we can also use this operator to determine whether one letter precedes another in the alphabet. For example, the condition `'A' ¢ 'F'` is true because `A` precedes `F` in the alphabet. The problem inputs and outputs are listed next followed by the algorithm.

PROBLEM INPUTS

three letters (`Ch1, Ch2, Ch3 : CHAR`)

PROBLEM OUTPUTS

the alphabetically first letter (`AlphaFirst : CHAR`)

Algorithm

1. Read three letters into `Ch1`, `Ch2`, and `Ch3`.
2. Save the alphabetically first of `Ch1`, `Ch2`, and `Ch3` in `AlphaFirst`.
3. Print the alphabetically first letter.

Step 2 can be performed by first comparing `Ch1` and `Ch2` and saving the alphabetically first letter in `AlphaFirst`; this result can then be compared to `Ch3`. The refinement of step 2 follows.

STEP 2 REFINEMENT

2.1 Save the alphabetically first of `Ch1` and `Ch2` in `AlphaFirst`.
2.2 Save the alphabetically first of `Ch3` and `AlphaFirst` in `AlphaFirst`.

The structure chart corresponding to the algorithm is shown in Fig. 2.11; the program is shown in Fig. 2.12.

Figure 2.11 ▸ *Structure Chart for Finding Alphabetically First Letter*

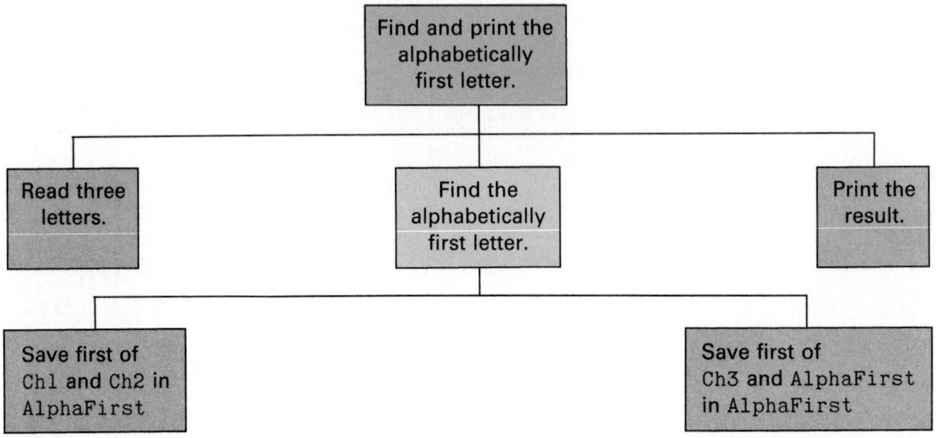
Find and print the alphabetically first letter.
Read three letters.
Find the alphabetically first letter.
Print the result.
Save first of Ch1 and Ch2 in AlphaFirst
Save first of Ch3 and AlphaFirst in AlphaFirst

Figure 2.12 ▸ *Finding the Alphabetically First Letter*

```
MODULE FirstLetter;

(* Finds and prints the  alphabetically first letter. *)

   FROM InOut IMPORT
     Read, Write, WriteString, WriteLn;

   VAR
     Ch1, Ch2, Ch3,              (* input  - three letters *)
     AlphaFirst     :  CHAR;     (* output - alphabetically
                                             first letter *)

BEGIN  (* FirstLetter *)
  (* Read three letters *)
  WriteString ('Enter any three letters: ');
  Read (Ch1);  Write (Ch1);
  Read (Ch2);  Write (Ch2);
  Read (Ch3);  Write (Ch3);
  WriteLn;

  (* Save the smaller of Ch1 and Ch2 in AlphaFirst *)
  IF Ch1 < Ch2 THEN
    AlphaFirst := Ch1       (* Ch1 comes before Ch2 *)
  ELSE
    AlphaFirst := Ch2       (* Ch2 comes before Ch1 *)
  END; (* IF *)

  (* Save the smaller of Ch3 and AlphaFirst in AlphaFirst *)
  IF Ch3 < AlphaFirst THEN
    AlphaFirst := Ch3 (* Ch3 comes before AlphaFirst *)
  END; (* IF *)
```

```
    (* Print result *)
    Write (AlphaFirst);
    WriteString (' is the first letter alphabetically');
    WriteLn
END FirstLetter.

Enter any three letters: EBK
B is the first letter alphabetically
```

In Fig. 2.12, the `IF` statement with two alternatives saves either `Ch1` or `Ch2` in `AlphaFirst`. The `IF` statement with one alternative stores `Ch3` in `AlphaFirst` if `Ch3` precedes the value already in `AlphaFirst`.

In the next chapter, we will see that `IF` statements with several (more than two) alternatives are also possible in Modula-2. The forms of the `IF` statement used so far are summarized in the displays that follow.

IF Statement (two alternatives)

FORM:
```
IF condition THEN
  statement sequence_T
ELSE
  statement sequence_F
END
```

EXAMPLE:
```
IF X >= 0.0 THEN
  WriteString ('Positive')
ELSE
  WriteString ('Negative')
END
```

INTERPRETATION: If *condition* evaluates to true, then *statement sequence*$_T$ is executed and *statement sequence*$_F$ is skipped; otherwise, *statement sequence*$_T$ is skipped and *statement sequence*$_F$ is executed.

IF Statement (one alternative)

FORM:
```
IF condition THEN
  statement sequence_T
END
```

EXAMPLE:
```
IF X > 0.0 THEN
  PosProd := PosProd * X;
  CountPos := CountPos + 1
END
```

INTERPRETATION: If *condition* evaluates to true, then *statement sequence*$_T$ is executed; otherwise, it is skipped.

Program Style

Formatting the IF Statement

In all the `IF` statement examples, *statement sequence*$_T$ and *statement sequence*$_F$ are indented. If the word `ELSE` appears, it is entered on a separate line and aligned with the words `IF` and `END`. The format of the `IF` statement makes its meaning apparent. Again, this is done solely to improve program readability; the format makes no difference to the compiler.

SELF-CHECK EXERCISES FOR SECTION 2.3

1. Modify the structure chart and program in the first-letter problem to find the alphabetically last of three letters.
2. Modify the structure chart and program in the first-letter problem to find the first of four letters.
3. Write Modula-2 statements to carry out the steps below.
   a. If `Item` is nonzero, then multiply `Product` by `Item` and save the result in `Product`; otherwise, skip the multiplication. In either case, print the value of `Product`.
   b. Store the absolute difference of `X` and `Y` in `Z`, where the absolute difference is `X - Y` or `Y - X`, whichever is positive.
   c. If `X` is zero, add 1 to `ZeroCount`; if `X` is negative, add `X` to `MinusSum`; if `X` is positive, add `X` to `PlusSum`.

2.4 Tracing a Program or Algorithm

A critical step in the design of an algorithm or program is to verify that it is correct before extensive time is spent entering or debugging it. Often a few extra minutes spent in verifying the correctness of an algorithm will save hours of testing time later.

One important technique is a hand trace or desk check of an algorithm or program. This consists of a careful, step-by-step simulation on paper of how the algorithm or program would be executed by the computer. The results of the simulation should show the effect of each step on data that are relatively easy to process by hand.

Table 2.2 shows a trace of the program in Fig. 2.12 for the data string `THE` Each program step is listed at the left in the order of its execution. The values of variables referenced by a program step are shown after the step. If a program step changes the value of a variable, then the new value is shown; the effect of each step is described at the far right. For example, the table shows that the statements

```
Read (Ch1);
Read (Ch2);
Read (Ch3);
```

store the letters T, H, and E in the variables CH1, CH2, and CH3.

Table 2.2 ▸ *Trace of Program in Figure 2.12*

STATEMENT	CH1	CH2	CH3	ALPHAFIRST	EFFECT
	?	?	?	?	
WriteString ('Enter ...')					Prints a prompt
Read (Ch1);	T				Reads Ch1
Read (Ch2);		H			Reads Ch2
Read (Ch3);			E		Reads Ch3
IF Ch1 < Ch2 THEN	T	H			Is 'T' < 'H' ? value is false
AlphaFirst := Ch2				H	'H' is first
IF Ch3 < AlphaFirst ...			E	H	Is 'E' < 'H' ? value is true
AlphaFirst := Ch3				E	'E' is first
Write (AlphaFirst); WriteString ('is first...')				E	Prints E is first letter...

The trace in Table 2.2 clearly shows that the alphabetically first letter, E, of the input string is stored in AlphaFirst and printed. To verify that the program is correct, it would be necessary to select other data that cause the two conditions to evaluate to different values. Since there are two conditions and each has two possible values (true or false), there are two × two, or four, different combinations that should be tried. (What are they?) An exhaustive desk check of the program would show that it works for all of these combinations.

Besides the four cases discussed above, verify that the program works correctly for unusual data. For example, what would happen if two or all three of the letters were the same? Would the program still provide the correct result? To complete the desk check, you would have to show that the program handles these special situations properly.

In tracing each case, be very careful to execute the program exactly as the computer would execute it. It is easy to carry out the operations that you expect will be performed without explicitly testing each condition and tracing each program step. A trace that is performed in this way is of little value.

SELF-CHECK EXERCISES FOR SECTION 2.4

1. Provide sample data and traces for the remaining three cases of the first-letter problem. Also test the case where all three letters are the same. What is the value of the conditions in this case?
2. Trace the program in Fig. 2.10 when `Hours` is 30.0 and `Rate` is 5.00. Perform the trace when `Hours` is 20.0 and `Rate` is 3.00.

2.5 Problem-Solving Strategies

Often what appears to be a new problem turns out to be a variation of one that you have already solved. Consequently an important skill in problem solving is the ability to recognize that a problem is similar to one solved earlier. As you progress through this course, you will start to build up a *library* of programs and procedures. Whenever possible, try to adapt or reuse parts of programs that have been shown to work correctly. Chapter 6 will show you how to create your own libraries of utility procedures.

Extending a Problem Solution

An experienced programmer usually writes programs that can be easily modified to fit other situations. One reason for this is that programmers (and program users) often want to make slight improvements to a program after having used it. If the original program is designed carefully from the beginning, the programmer may be able to modify one or two small procedures rather than rewrite the entire program.

COMPUTING OVERTIME PAY

Problem: We want to modify the payroll program so that employees who work more than 40 hours a week are paid double for all overtime hours.

Discussion: This problem is an extension of the modified-payroll problem (see Fig. 2.10). Overtime pay must be added for eligible employees. We can solve this problem by adding a new step (step 2A) after step 2 in the original algorithm. The data requirements are listed below, followed by the new algorithm and the refinement for step 2A.

PROBLEM CONSTANTS

maximum salary for no tax deduction (`TaxBracket = 100.00`)
amount of tax deducted (`Tax = 25.00`)
maximum hours without overtime pay (`MaxHours = 40.0`)

PROBLEM INPUTS

hours worked (`Hours : REAL`)
hourly rate (`Rate : REAL`)

PROBLEM OUTPUTS

gross pay (`Gross : REAL`)
net pay (`Net : REAL`)

Algorithm

1. Enter hours worked and hourly rate.
2. Compute gross salary.
2A. Add overtime pay to gross salary.
3. Compute net salary.
4. Print gross salary and net salary.

STEP 2A REFINEMENT

2A.1 `IF Hours > MaxHours THEN`
    2A.2 Add overtime pay to `Gross`
  `END`

As shown below, the `IF` statement that implements step 2A should follow the statement in Fig. 2.10 used to compute gross salary.

```
(* Compute gross salary *)
Gross := Hours * Rate;
(* Add overtime pay to Gross *)
IF Hours > MaxHours THEN
  Gross := Gross + ((Hours - MaxHours) * Rate)
END; (* IF *)
```

The assignment statement for step 2A.2 involves three arithmetic operators: +, –, *. We will talk more about how Modula-2 evaluates arithmetic expressions with multiple operators in Chapter 5. For the time being, it is sufficient to know that the parentheses cause the operators to be evaluated in this order: – first, * next, and + last. Consequently the overtime hours (`Hours - MaxHours`) will be multiplied by `Rate` and added to the value of `Gross` computed earlier; the result will be the new value of `Gross`.

Solution by Analogy

Sometimes a new problem is simply an old one presented in a different way. Try to determine whether you have solved a similar problem before and, if so, adapt the earlier solution. This requires a careful reading of the problem statement to detect similar requirements that may be worded differently.

COMPUTING INSURANCE DIVIDENDS

Problem: Each year an insurance company sends out dividend checks to its policyholders. The dividend amount is a fixed percentage (4.5%) of the insurance premium paid in. If there were no claims made by the policyholder, the dividend rate for that policy is increased by 0.5%. Write a program to compute dividends.

Discussion: This problem is quite similar to the payroll problem just completed. The dividend amount can be determined by first computing the basic dividend and then adding the bonus dividend when applicable. This is analogous to first computing gross pay and then adding in overtime pay when earned. The data requirements and algorithm are shown next; the structure chart is in Fig. 2.13.

PROBLEM CONSTANTS

the fixed dividend rate of 4.5% (`FixedRate = 0.045`)
the bonus dividend rate of 0.5% (`BonusRate = 0.005`)

PROBLEM INPUTS

premium amount (`Premium : REAL`)
number of claims (`Claims : REAL`)

PROBLEM OUTPUTS

dividend amount (`Dividend : REAL`)

Algorithm

1. Enter premium amount and number of claims.
2. Compute basic dividend.
3. Add bonus dividend to basic dividend.
4. Print total dividend.

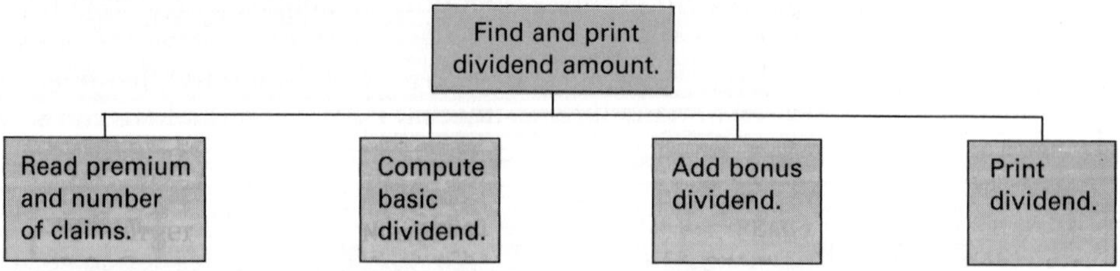

Figure 2.13 ▸ *Structure Chart for Insurance Dividend Problem*

The refinement of step 3 is similar to the refinement of step 2A in the payroll problem. This refinement is shown next. The complete program is in Fig. 2.14.

STEP 3 REFINEMENT

3.1 `IF Claims = 0 THEN`
    Add bonus dividend to `dividend`
  `END`

Figure 2.14 ▸ *Insurance Company Dividend Program*

```
MODULE CompDividend;

(* Finds and prints the insurance dividend. *)

  FROM InOut IMPORT
     WriteString, WriteLn;

   FROM RealInOut IMPORT
     ReadReal, WriteReal;

   CONST
     FixedRate = 0.045;       (* basic dividend rate *)
     BonusRate = 0.005;       (* bonus dividend rate *)

   VAR
     Premium,                  (* input  - premium amount *)
     Claims,                   (* input  - number of claims *)
     Dividend : REAL;          (* output - dividend amount *)

BEGIN (* CompDividend *)
  (* Enter Premium and Claims *)
  WriteString ('Premium amount: $');
  ReadReal (Premium);  WriteLn;
  WriteString ('Number of claims: ');
  ReadReal (Claims);  WriteLn;

  (* Compute basic dividend *)
  Dividend := Premium * FixedRate;

  (* Add any bonus dividend *)
  IF Claims = 0.0 THEN
    (* Add bonus *)
    Dividend := Dividend + (Premium * BonusRate)
  END; (* IF *)

  (* Print total dividend *)
  WriteString ('Total dividend is $');
  WriteReal (Dividend, 12);
  WriteLn
END CompDividend.

Premium amount: $1200
Number of claims: 0
Total dividend is $ 6.0000E+001
```

In Fig. 2.14, 4.5% and 0.5% are written as the decimal fractions 0.045 and 0.005, respectively. Since there is no % operator in Modula-2, decimal fractions are required. All real numbers must begin with a digit; therefore, the zero in front of the decimal point is always rquired for real values less than 1.0.

SELF-CHECK EXERCISES FOR SECTION 2.5

1. Provide the complete program for the overtime pay problem.
2. Rewrite the algorithm for the modified-payroll problem so that the computation of gross salary is performed in one step rather than two (i.e., combine steps 2 and 2A). Use an `IF` statement with two alternatives.
3. In Fig. 2.14, use an `IF` statement with two alternatives to combine the two steps that compute `Dividend` into one step.

2.6 Repetition in Programs—Counting Loops

Just as the ability to make decisions is an important programming tool, so is the ability to specify that a group of operations is to be repeated. For example, if there are six employees in a company, we would probably like to carry out the gross pay and net pay computations shown in Fig. 2.10 six times. We could express this in pseudocode as follows:

```
FOR each employee DO
  Read hours worked and hourly rate
  Compute gross salary
  Compute net salary
  Print gross pay and net pay
END
```

Modula-2 provides four control statements for specifying repetition. We will examine one of these in the next section.

The FOR Statement

The `FOR` statement can be used to specify some forms of repetition, as shown in the next examples.

EXAMPLE 2.4 ▶ The two sets of statements below have the same effect.

```
(* Print three blank lines *)   | (* Print three blank lines *)
WriteLn;                        | FOR Line := 1 TO 3 DO
WriteLn;                        |   WriteLn
WriteLn                         | END
```

If Line is declared as a cardinal variable, the FOR statement causes the WriteLn operation to be performed three times. ◄

EXAMPLE 2.5 ► Procedure PrintI for the Mother's Day problem (see Fig. 2.7) can be written using the FOR statement, as shown in Fig. 2.15. This procedure prints seven lines that contain asterisks in columns 4 and 5. ◄

Figure 2.15 ►
Procedure PrintI

```
PROCEDURE PrintI;

(* Prints the block letter 'I'. *)

   VAR
     NextLine : CARDINAL; (* Loop control variable -
                             from 1 to 7           *)

BEGIN (* PrintI *)
  FOR NextLine := 1 TO 7 DO
    WriteString ('   **');
    WriteLn
  END; (* FOR *)
  WriteLn
END PrintI;
```

The FOR statement is used to implement *counting loops*, which are loops where the exact number of loop repetitions can be specified as a variable or constant value. In Examples 2.4 and 2.5, the number of repetitions required were 3 and 7, respectively. The reserved word END terminates the FOR statement.

The FOR statement in Fig. 2.15 specifies that the variable NextLine should take on each of the values in the range 1 to 7 during successive loop repetitions. This means that the value of NextLine is 1 during the first loop repetition, 2 during the second loop repetition, and 7 during the last loop repetition.

NextLine is called the *loop control variable*, because its value controls the loop repetition. The loop control variable is initialized to 1 when the FOR statement is first reached; after each execution of the loop body, the loop control variable is incremented by one and tested to see whether loop repetition should continue.

The loop control variable may also be referenced in the loop body, but its value cannot be changed. The next example shows a FOR statement whose loop control variable is referenced in the loop body.

EXAMPLE 2.6 ▶ The program in Fig. 2.16 uses a `FOR` loop to print a list of integer values and their squares. During each repetition of the loop body, the statement

```
Square := I * I;
```

computes the square of the loop control variable `I`; then, the values of `I` and `Square` are displayed. A trace of this program is shown in Table 2.3.

Figure 2.16 ▶ *Program to Print a List of Integers and Their Squares*

```
MODULE Squares;

  FROM InOut IMPORT
    WriteString, WriteCard, WriteLn;

  CONST
    MaxI = 4;

  VAR
    I,                         (* loop control variable *)
    Square : CARDINAL;         (* output - square of I *)

BEGIN (* Squares *)
  (*Prints a list of integer values and their squares. *)
  WriteString ('         I         I * I');
  WriteLn;
  FOR I := 1 TO MaxI DO
    Square := I * I;
    WriteCard (I, 10);
    WriteCard (Square, 10);
    WriteLn
  END (* FOR *)
END Squares.

         I         I * I
         1           1
         2           4
         3           9
         4          16
```

The trace in Table 2.3 shows that the loop control variable `I` is initialized to `1` when the `FOR` loop is reached. After each loop repetition, `I` is incremented by one and tested to see whether its value is still less than or equal to `MaxI` (4). If the test result is true, the loop body is executed again, and the next values of `I` and `Square` are printed. If the test result is false, the loop is exited.

During the last loop repetition, `I` is equal to `MaxI`. After this repetition, the value of `I` becomes undefined (indicated by `?` in the last table line), and the loop is exited. The variable `I` should not be referenced again until it is given a new value. ◀

Table 2.3 ▸ *Trace of Program in Figure 2.16*

STATEMENT	i	SQUARE	EFFECT
	?	?	
`FOR I := 1 TO MaxI DO`	1		Initialize `I` to `1`
`Square := I * I`		1	Assign `1 * 1` to `Square`
`WriteCard (I, 10);`			Print `1`
`WriteCard (Square, 10);`			Print `1`
Increment and test `I`	2		`2 <= 4` is true
`SQUARE := I * I`		4	Assign `2 * 2` to `Square`
`WriteCard (I, 10);`			Print `2`
`WriteCard (Square, 10);`			Print `4`
Increment and test `I`	3		`3 <= 4` is true
`SQUARE := I * I`		9	Assign `3 * 3` to `Square`
`WriteCard (I, 10);`			Print `3`
`WriteCard (Square, 10);`			Print `9`
Increment and test `I`	4		`4 <= 4` is true
`SQUARE := I * I`		16	Assign `4 * 4` to `Square`
`WriteCard (I, 10);`			Print `4`
`WriteCard (Square, 10);`			Print `16`
Increment and test `I`	?		Exit loop

Counting Loops

FORM:

```
FOR counter := 1 TO repetitions DO
  statement sequence
END
```

EXAMPLE:

```
FOR I := 1 to 5 DO
  WriteCard (I, 4);
  WriteLn
END
```

INTERPRETATION: The number of times *statement sequence* is executed is determined by the value of *repetitions*. The value of the loop control variable *counter* is set to `1` before the first execution of *statement sequence; counter* is incremented by one after each execution of *statement sequence*. The variable *counter* must be type `CARDINAL` or `INTEGER`; *repetitions* may be an expression, a constant, or a variable with a type `CARDINAL` or `INTEGER` value.

Note: If the value of *repetitions* is less than `1`, *statement sequence* will not be executed. The value of *counter* must not be changed within *statement sequence*. The value of *counter* is considered undefined after loop exit.

Program Style

> *Loop Control Variables as Local Variables*
>
> In Fig. 2.15, the loop control variable `NextLine` is declared in procedure `PrintI`. Identifiers declared within a procedure are called *local identifiers*. All loop control variables used in a procedure must be declared as local variables.

Accumulating a Sum

We can use a counting loop to accumulate the sum of a collection of data values, as shown in the next problem.

SUM OF INTEGERS

Problem: Write a program that finds the sum of all integers from 1 to `N`.
Discussion: To solve this problem, we must find some way to form the sum of the first `N` integers. The data requirements and algorithm follow.

PROBLEM INPUTS

the last integer in the sum (`N : CARDINAL`)

PROBLEM OUTPUTS

the sum of integers from `1` to `N` (`Sum : CARDINAL`)

Algorithm

1. Read the last integer (`N`).
2. Find the sum (`Sum`) of all the integers from `1` to `N`, inclusive.
3. Print the sum.

Step 2 is the only step that needs refinement. One possible refinement follows.

STEP 2 REFINEMENT

2.0 Set `Sum` to zero
2.1 Add `1` to `Sum`
2.2 Add `2` to `Sum`
2.3 Add `3` to `Sum`
.
.
.
2.N Add `N` to `Sum`

For a large value of `N`, it would be time-consuming to write this list of steps. We would also have to know the value of `N` before writing the list; consequently, the program would not be general, since it would work only for one value of `N`.

Since steps 2.1 through 2.N are quite similar, we can represent each of them with the general step 2.i.

2.i Add `i` to `Sum`

This general step must be executed for all values of `i` from `1` to `N`, inclusive. This suggests the use of a counting loop, with `i` as the loop control variable.

ADDITIONAL VARIABLES

loop control variable—represents each integer from `1` to `N`
(`i : CARDINAL`)

The variable `i` will take on the successive values `1, 2, 3, ..., N`. Each time the loop is repeated, the current value of `i` must be added to `Sum`. The new refinement of step 2 follows.

STEP 2 REFINEMENT

```
2.1 FOR each integer i from 1 TO N DO
       Add i to Sum
    END
```

The statements

```
Sum := 0;              (* Initialize Sum to zero *)
FOR i := 1 TO N DO
  Sum := Sum + i     (* Add the next integer to Sum *)
END; (* FOR *)
```

are used to perform step 2. To ensure that the final sum is correct, the value of `Sum` must be *initialized* to zero (algorithm step 2.0) before the first addition operation. The `FOR` statement causes the assignment statement

```
Sum := Sum + i
```

to be repeated `N` times. Each time, the current value of `i` is added to the sum being accumulated and the result is saved back in `Sum`. Figure 2.17 illustrates the first two loop repetitions; the complete program is in Fig. 2.18.

A trace of the program for a data value of `3` is shown in Table 2.4. The trace verifies that, since the final value stored in `Sum` is 6 (1+2+3), the program performs as desired. The value of the loop control variable `i` becomes undefined after it reaches the value of `N` (3 in this case). As shown in the table, the statement

```
Sum := Sum + i
```

is executed exactly three times.

Figure 2.17 ▸ *First Two Loop Repetitions for Sum of Integers Problem*

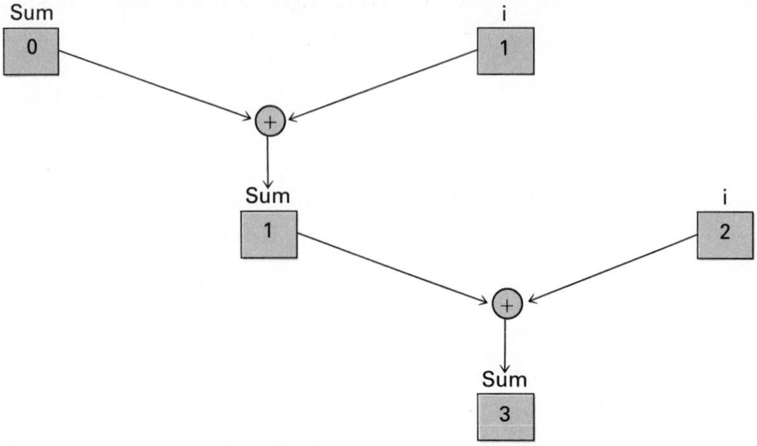

Figure 2.18 ▸ *Program for Sum of Integers from 1 to N*

```
MODULE SumIntegers;

(* Finds and prints the sum of all integers from 1 to N. *)

   FROM InOut IMPORT
     ReadCard, WriteCard, WriteString, WriteLn;

   VAR
     N,                 (* input  - the last integer added *)
     Sum,               (* output - the sum being accumulated *)
     i    : CARDINAL;   (* loop control - the next integer added *)

BEGIN (* SumIntegers *)
  (* Read the last integer, N *)
  WriteString ('Enter the last integer in the sum: ');
  ReadCard (N);  WriteLn;

  (* Find the sum (Sum) of all integers from 1 to N *)
  Sum := 0;             (* Initialize Sum to zero *)
  FOR i := 1 TO N DO
    Sum := Sum + i      (* Add the next integer to Sum *)
  END; (* FOR *)

  (* Print the sum *)
  WriteString ('The sum is ');
  WriteCard (Sum, 5);  WriteLn
END SumIntegers.

Enter the last integer in the sum: 6
The sum is 21
```

Table 2.4 ▸ *Trace of Program in Figure 2.18*

STATEMENT	i	N	SUM	EFFECT
	?	?	?	
`WriteString ('Enter ...')`				Print a prompt
`ReadCard (N)`		3		Read `3` into `N`
`Sum := 0`			0	Initialize `Sum`
`FOR i := 1 TO N DO`	1	3	0	Initialize `i` to `1`
`  Sum := Sum + i`			1	Add `1` to `Sum`
Increment and test `i`	2	3	1	`2 <= 3` is true
`  Sum := Sum + i`			3	Add `2` to `Sum`
Increment and test `i`	3	3	3	`3 <= 3` is true
`  Sum := Sum + i`			6	Add `3` to `Sum`
Increment and test `i`	?	3	6	Exit loop
`WriteString ('The sum is ')`				Print message
`WriteCard (Sum, 3)`			6	Print `6`

SELF-CHECK EXERCISES FOR SECTION 2.6

1. Generally there is more than one way to solve a problem. The algebraic formula

$$\frac{N(N + 1)}{2.0}$$

can be used to compute the sum of the integers from 1 to N, inclusive. Write a program that compares the results of both methods and prints an appropriate message indicating whether the results are the same.
2. Write a program that finds the product of the integers from 1 to N, inclusive. Test this program with values of N that are less than 8.

2.7 Generalizing a Solution

After you finish a program, someone may ask a "What if?" question. The person asking the question usually wants to know whether the program would still work if some of the restrictions implied by the problem statement were removed. If the answer is "No," you may have to modify the program to make it work. Try to anticipate such questions in advance and make your programs as general as possible right from the start. Sometimes this can be as easy as changing a program constant to a problem input.

One question that comes to mind for the last problem is: What if we wanted to find the sum of a list of any numbers, not just the sum of the first `N` integers; would the program still work? Clearly, the answer to this question is "No." However, it would not be too difficult to modify the program to solve this more general problem.

GENERAL SUM PROBLEM

Problem: Write a program that finds and prints the sum of a list of numbers.

Discussion: To add any list of numbers, a new variable (`Item`) would be needed to store each item to be summed. The numbers must be provided as input data. Since the numbers are not necessarily integers, we will make `Item` and `Sum` type `REAL`. The new data requirements and algorithm follow.

PROBLEM INPUTS

number of items to be summed (`NumItems : CARDINAL`)
each data value to be summed (`Item : REAL`)

PROBLEM OUTPUTS

sum of the data items (`Sum : REAL`)

Algorithm

1. Read in the number (`NumItems`) of items to be summed.
2. Read each data item and add it to the sum.
3. Print the sum.

This algorithm is very similar to the earlier one. Step 2 is modified slightly and refined below.

STEP 2 REFINEMENT

2.1 Initialize `Sum` to `0.0`.
2.2 `FOR` each data item `DO`
    Read the data item into `Item` and add `Item` to `Sum`.
  `END`

In this refinement, the variable `Item` is used to store each number to be summed. After each number is read into `Item`, it will be added to `Sum`. If there are more data items, the loop will be repeated and the next data item will replace the last one in `Item`.

The number of data items to be summed is read into `NumItems` before the loop is reached. This value determines the number of loop repetitions that are required. A loop control variable is needed to count the data items as they are processed and ensure that all data are summed.

ADDITIONAL VARIABLES

loop control variable—the number of data items added so far
(Count : CARDINAL)

The general program to find the sum of a list of data items is shown in Fig. 2.19.

Figure 2.19 ▶ *Program to Sum a List of Data Items*

```
MODULE SumItems;

(* Finds and prints the sum of a list of data items. *)

   FROM InOut IMPORT
     ReadCard, WriteString, WriteLn;

   FROM RealInOut IMPORT
     ReadReal, WriteReal;

   VAR
     NumItems : CARDINAL; (* input  - the number of data items *)
     Item,                (* input  - the next data item *)
     Sum    : REAL;       (* output - the sum being accumulated *)
     Count  : CARDINAL;   (* loop control -
                                   count of items added so far *)

BEGIN (* SumItems *)
  (* Read the number of data items to be summed *)
  WriteString ('Number of items to be summed? ');
  ReadCard (NumItems);  WriteLn;

  (* Find the sum (Sum) of NumItems data items *)
  Sum := 0.0;                   (* Initialize Sum to zero *)
  FOR Count := 1 TO NumItems DO
    WriteString ('Next item to be summed? ');
    ReadReal (Item);            (* Read next data item *)
    WriteLn;
    Sum := Sum + Item           (* Add it to Sum *)
  END; (* FOR *)

  (* Print the final value of Sum *)
  WriteString ('The sum is ');
  WriteReal (Sum, 12); WriteLn
END SumItems.

Number of items in the sum? 3
Next item to be summed? 4.5
Next item to be summed? 6.5
Next item to be summed? 7.0
The sum is 1.8000E+001
```

Program Style

Comments after END

The comment `(* FOR *)` follows the first `END` in Fig. 2.19. Comments are often used after the reserved word `END` to identify the type of statement (`IF` or `FOR`) that is being terminated by the `END`. The semicolon may come before or after the comment, since the comment is ignored by the compiler.

SELF-CHECK EXERCISE FOR SECTION 2.7

1. Write a general program to find the product of a list of data items. Ignore any data values of zero.

2.8 Repeating a Program Body

In the discussion of repetition in programs, we mentioned that we would like to be able to execute the payroll program for several employees in a single run. We will see how to do this next.

MULTIPLE-EMPLOYEE PAYROLL PROBLEM

Problem: Modify the payroll program to compute gross pay and net pay for a group of employees.

Discussion: The number of employees must be provided as input data along with each employee's hourly rate and hours worked. The same set of variables will be used to hold the data and computational results for each employee. The computations will be performed in the same way as before. The new data requirements and algorithm follow.

PROBLEM CONSTANTS

maximum salary for no tax deduction (`TaxBracket = 100.0`)
amount of tax deducted (`Tax = 25.00`)
maximum hours without overtime pay (`MaxHours = 40.0`)

PROBLEM INPUTS

number of employees (`NumEmp : CARDINAL`)
hours worked by each employee (`Hours : REAL`)
hourly rate for each employee (`Rate : REAL`)

PROBLEM OUTPUTS

gross pay (`Gross : REAL`)
net pay (`Net : REAL`)

Algorithm

1. Enter the number of employees (`NumEmp`).
2. `FOR` each employee `DO`
   Enter payroll data and compute and print gross and net pay.
   `END`

An additional variable is needed to count the number of employees processed and to control the `FOR` loop in step 2.

ADDITIONAL VARIABLE

loop control variable—counts the number of employees that are processed (`CountEmp : CARDINAL`)

The structure chart is shown in Fig. 2.20. (The structure chart for the subproblem "find gross and net pay" was drawn in Fig. 2.9.)

Figure 2.20 ▸ *Structure Chart for Multiple-Employee Payroll Problem*

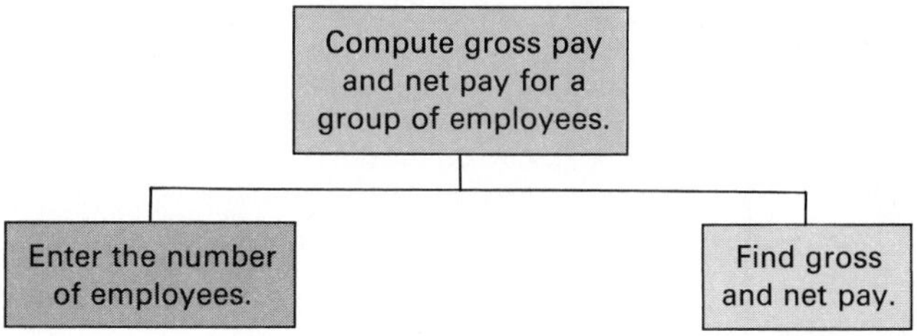

The declaration section of the program in Fig. 2.21 contains a large procedure (`ModPay`) that is based on the payroll program in Fig. 2.10. The main program body consists of statements to read in `NumEmp` (number of employees) and a `FOR` statement that repeatedly calls procedure `ModPay`. Each execution of `ModPay` causes the payroll computations to be performed for a different employee.

The only identifiers declared in the main program are `NumEmp`, `CountEmp`, and `ModPay`. All other identifiers are declared as local identifiers in procedure `ModPay` because they are manipulated only within the procedure.

Procedure `ModPay` contains exactly the same declaration section and body as program `ModPay` in Fig. 2.10. The only difference is that `ModPay` is now written as a procedure instead of a program; consequently its first line begins with the word `PROCEDURE` instead of `MODULE`, and its last line is terminated with a semicolon instead of a period.

The ability to convert an entire program into a procedure is a powerful programming tool. This capability enables us to reuse old programs as procedures in the solution of new problems. Thus, we can create new solutions from old ones.

Figure 2.21 ▸
Multiple-Employee Payroll Program

```
MODULE MultiPay;
(* Finds and prints gross pay and net pay for several employees. *)

   FROM InOut IMPORT
     ReadCard, WriteString, WriteLn;

   FROM RealInOut IMPORT
     ReadReal, WriteReal;

   VAR
     NumEmp,                   (* input - total number of employees *)
     CountEmp : CARDINAL;      (* loop control -
                                       count of employees processed *)

   PROCEDURE ModPay;
   (*
      Computes and prints gross pay and net pay given an hourly
      rate and number of hours worked. Deducts a tax of $25 if
      gross salary exceeds $100; otherwise, deducts no tax.
   *)
      CONST
        TaxBracket = 100.00; (* maximum salary for no deduction *)
        Tax = 25.00;         (* tax amount *)

      VAR
        Hours, Rate,         (* input - hours worked, hourly rate *)
        Gross, Net : REAL;   (* output - gross pay, net pay *)

  BEGIN (* ModPay *)
    (* Enter Hours and Rate *)
    WriteString ('Hours worked? ');
    ReadReal (Hours);  WriteLn;
    WriteString ('Hourly rate? ');
    ReadReal (Rate);  WriteLn;

    (* Compute gross salary *)
    Gross := Hours * Rate;

    (* Compute net salary *)
    IF Gross > TaxBracket THEN
      Net := Gross - Tax (* Deduct a tax amount *)
    ELSE
      Net := Gross       (* Deduct no tax *)
    END; (* IF *)

    (* Print Gross and Net *)
    WriteString ('Gross salary is $');
    WriteReal (Gross, 12);  WriteLn;
    WriteString ('Net salary is $');
    WriteReal (Net, 12);  WriteLn
  END ModPay;
```

```
BEGIN (* MultiPay *)
  (* Enter total number of employees *)
  WriteString ('How many employees? ');
  ReadCard (NumEmp);  WriteLn;

  (* Compute gross pay and net pay for NumEmp employees *)
  FOR CountEmp := 1 TO NumEmp DO
    ModPay;          (* Process next employee *)
    WriteLn
  END (* FOR *)
END MultiPay.

How many employees? 2
Hours worked? 25
Hourly rate? 3.50
Gross salary is $ 8.7500E+001
Net salary is $ 8.7500E+001

Hours worked? 40
Hourly rate? 4.80
Gross salary is $ 1.9200E+002
Net salary is $ 1.6700E+002
```

Program Style

Cohesion in Procedures

Procedure `ModPay` suffers from one important fault: it does too much. This procedure enters data, performs computations, and displays results. Ideally each procedure in a program system performs a single function. A procedure that performs a single function is said to be *highly cohesive*.

All three operations were combined in `ModPay` because currently we have no way of communicating between procedures. Consequently, if we had separate procedures for performing the computations and for displaying the computational results, there would be no way to pass the results computed in the first procedure to the second procedure. Chapter 4 will show how to use procedure parameters for communication between procedures.

Similarity Between Procedures and Programs

The problem just completed points out the similarity between a program and a procedure. Both have a declaration part followed by a body (`BEGIN` ... `END` *ModuleName*. or `BEGIN` ... `END` *ProcedureName*;). The declaration part describes the identifiers that can be referenced in the body; the body performs the data manipulation.

Although many procedures may be declared in a program, there can be only one program body. The program body always follows the last procedure declaration (if any).

Procedure bodies and program bodies are translated into machine language and saved in different sections of memory. When program execution begins, control transfers to the memory address of the first statement of the main program body. When a procedure call statement is executed, control transfers to the memory address of the first statement of that procedure body. After the procedure is done, control returns to the statement in the main program body that follows the procedure call statement.

In the next chapter, we will see that a procedure, like a program, can call other procedures. Later, we will see how to pass information between procedures and between procedures and the main program. All of these capabilities increase the utility of procedures.

2.9 Debugging and Testing Programs

Chapter 1 described the general categories of error messages that you are likely to see: syntax errors and run-time errors. It is also possible for a program to execute without generating any error messages but still produce incorrect results. Sometimes the cause of a run-time error or the origin of incorrect results is apparent and the error can easily be fixed. Often, however, the error is not obvious and requires considerable effort to locate.

The first step in attempting to find a hidden error is to try to determine what part of the program is generating incorrect results. Then insert extra output statements in your program to provide a trace of its execution. For example, if the summation loop in Fig. 2.19 is not computing the correct sum, you might want to insert extra diagnostic output statements such as the last two lines in the loop below.

```
FOR Count := 1 TO NumItems DO
  WriteString ('Next item to be summed? ');
  ReadReal (Item);  WriteLn;
  Sum := Sum + Item;
  WriteString ('Sum = ');     WriteReal (Sum, 12);
  WriteString ('Count = ');   WriteCard (Count, 2);   WriteLn
END; (* FOR *)
```

The extra output statements will display each partial sum that is accumulated and the current value of `Count`. Be careful when inserting extra diagnostic output statements, though, since they can be a source of syntax errors or additional run-time errors. Their inclusion may require changes to existing program statements. In this case, a semicolon must be inserted after the assignment statement in the loop body.

Once it appears that you have located the error, take out the extra diagnostic statements or, as a temporary measure, make these diagnostic statements comments by enclosing them with `(*` and `*)`. If errors crop up again in later testing, it is easier to remove these symbols than to retype the diagnostic statements.

Many computer systems have special *debugger programs,* which provide assistance in debugging. Such programs enable you to execute program statements one at a time and observe the results of each statement's execution. Using this feature, you can trace the values of specified program variables and see how those values change as the program executes.

Testing a Program

After all errors have been corrected and the program appears to execute as expected, the program should be tested thoroughly to make sure it works. Section 2.4 discussed tracing an algorithm and suggested that you provide enough sets of test data to ensure that all possible paths are traced. The same is true for testing the completed program. Make enough test runs to verify that the program works properly for representative samples of all possible data combinations.

2.10 Common Programming Errors

When using comments, be very careful to insert `(*` and `*)` where required. If the opening characters, `(*`, are missing, the compiler will not recognize the beginning of the comment and will attempt to process it as a Modula-2 statement. This should cause a syntax error. If the closing characters, `*)`, are missing, the comment will simply be extended to include the program statements that follow it. Modula-2 allows comments to be nested so the comment will not be terminated until an unmatched set of closing symbols is reached. If the comment is not terminated, the rest of the program will be included in the comment and a syntax error such as `incomplete program` will be printed.

Use semicolons to separate the individual statements inside a `FOR` loop or an `IF` statement. An `END` must be used to terminate a `FOR` loop or an `IF` statement. A semicolon is needed after the `END` if more statements follow. Semicolons should not be used after the reserved words `THEN` and `ELSE` in an `IF` statement, or after `DO` in a `FOR` statement.

2.11 Chapter Review

In the first part of this chapter, we outlined a method for solving problems on the computer. This method stressed six points:

1. Understand the problem.
2. Identify the input and output data for the problem, as well as other relevant data.
3. Formulate a precise statement of the problem.
4. Develop a list of steps for solving the problem (an algorithm).
5. Refine the algorithm.
6. Implement the algorithm in Modula-2.

We showed how to divide a problem into subproblems and how to use a structure chart to show the relationships among the subproblems. The procedure was introduced as a means of implementing subproblems as separate program modules.

Several guidelines for using program comments were discussed. Well-placed and carefully worded comments and a structure chart can provide all the documentation necessary for a program.

In the remainder of the chapter, we discussed the representation of the various steps in an algorithm and illustrated the stepwise refinement of algorithms. We used pseudocode to represent the loops and decision steps of an algorithm. We showed how to implement decisions in Modula-2 using the `IF` statement and repetition using the `FOR` statement.

Algorithm and program traces are used to verify that an algorithm or program is correct. Errors in logic can be discovered by carefully tracing an algorithm or program. Tracing an algorithm or program before entering the program into the computer will save you time in the long run.

New Modula-2 Statements in Chapter 2

The new Modula-2 statements introduced in this chapter are described in Table 2.5.

Table 2.5 ▸ *Summary of New Modula-2 Statements*

STATEMENT	EFFECT
Comment	
`(* This is a comment *)` `(* So is his! *)`	Comments document the use of variables and statements in a program. They are ignored by the compiler.
Procedure Declaration	

`PROCEDURE Display;`
 	
`(* Prints 3 lines *)`
	Procedure `Display` is declared and can be called to print three lines of asterisks. The local constant `Star` is defined only when `Display` is executing.

```
    CONST
      Star = '*';

  BEGIN (* Display *)
    Write (Star);  WriteLn;
    Write (Star);  WriteLn;
    Write (Star);  WriteLn
  END Display;
```

Procedure Call Statement

```
Display
```

Calls procedure `Display` and causes it to begin execution.

IF Statement (one alternative)

```
IF X# 0.0 THEN
     Product := Product * X
END
```

Multiplies `Product` by `X` only if `X` is nonzero.

IF Statement (two alternatives)

```
IF X >= 0.0 THEN
  WriteReal (X, 12);
  WriteString (' is positive');
  WriteLn
ELSE
  WriteReal (X, 12);
  WriteString (' is negative');
  WriteLn
END
```

If `X` is greater than or equal to `0.0`, `X` and the message `' is positive'` is printed; otherwise, the message `' is negative'` is printed.

FOR Statement

```
FOR NumStars := 1 TO 25 DO
  Write ('*')
END
```

Prints a row of 25 asterisks.

CHAPTER 2 ▸

Review Questions

1. Briefly describe the steps to derive an algorithm for a given problem.
2. The diagram that shows the algorithm steps and their interdependencies is called a ____________ .
3. What are three advantages of using procedures?
4. Where in the final program is the main program body found? Why?
5. When is a procedure executed? Where must it appear in the main program?
6. A decision in Modula-2 is actually an evaluation of a(n) ____________ expression.
7. List the seven relational operators discussed in this chapter.
8. What should be done by the programmer after the algorithm is written but before the program is entered (typed) into the computer?

9. Trace the following program fragment and indicate which procedure will be called if a data value of `27.34` is entered.

```
WriteString ('Enter a temperature: ');
ReadReal (Temp);  WriteLn;
IF Temp > 32.0 THEN
  NotFreezing
ELSE
  IceForming
END
```

10. Write the appropriate `IF` statement to compute `GrossPay` given that the hourly rate is stored in the variable `Rate` and the total hours worked is stored in the variable `Hours`. Pay time and a half for hours worked over 40.

CHAPTER 2 ▸

Programming Projects

1. a. Write a program to print the "message" `XXOXOX` in block letters.
   b. Modify your program so that any six-letter message consisting of `X`s and `O`s will be printed in block-letter form. The message to be printed should be entered and displayed one character at a time.

2. a. Write a program to simulate a state police radar gun. The program should read an automobile speed and print the message `Speeding` if the speed exceeds 55 mph.
   b. Modify your program so that ten speeds are handled in a single run. Also print a count of the number of speeding automobiles.

3. Write a program that computes the product of a collection of fifteen data values. Your program should ignore zero values.

4. Compute and print a table showing the first fifteen powers of 2.

5. A program is needed that will read a character value and a number. Depending on what is read, certain information will be printed. The character should be either an `S` or a `T`. If an `S` is read and the number is `100.50`, the program will print

```
Send money!  I need $100.50
```

If a `T` is read and the number is `100.50`, the program will print

```
The temperature last night was 100.50 degrees
```

6. Write a program that reads in twenty values and prints the number of values that are positive (greater than or equal to zero) and the number that are negative. Also print `'more positive'` or `'more negative'` based on the result.

7. Write an algorithm to compute the factorial ($n!$) of a single arbitrary integer n ($n! = n * (n - 1) * \ldots 2 * 1$). Your program should read and print the value of n and print $n!$ when done.

8. a. If n contains an integer, then we can compute x^n for any x simply by initializing a variable to 1 and multiplying it by x a total of n times. Write a program to read in a value of x and a value of n and to compute x^n via repeated multiplications. Check your program for

   $x = 6.0 \quad n = 4$

   $x = 2.5 \quad n = 6$

   $x = -8.0 \quad n = 5$

   b. Modify your program to handle positive or negative values of n. Hint: x^{-3} is equal to $1/x^3$.

9. Write a program that prints a table showing classroom number, maximum size, number of seats available, and a message indicating whether the class is filled. Before reading any data, call a procedure to print some table headings indicating what the output represents. In an interactive program, the headings should be printed to the right of the screen so that they are not confused with the input data. Call another procedure repeatedly to read and process the data for each classroom. Use the following classroom input data:

Room	Capacity	Enrollment
426	25	25
327	18	14
420	20	15
317	100	90

Sample output might begin:

Room number	Maximum size	Number enrolled	Remaining seats	Filled?
426	25	25	0	YES
327	18	14	4	NO

10. Write a program that will determine the additional state tax owed by an employee. The state charges a 4% tax on net income. Net income is determined by subtracting a $500 allowance for each dependent from gross income. Your program will read gross income, number of dependents, and tax amount already deducted. It will then compute the actual tax owed and print the difference between tax owed and tax deducted, followed by the message `'SEND CHECK'` or `'REFUND'` depending on whether the difference is positive or negative.

3 ▸ IF and WHILE Statements

THE CONTROL STATEMENTS of a programming language enable the programmer to control the sequence and the frequency of execution of segments of a program. Control statements call procedures into execution and implement decisions and repetition in programs. The control statements introduced so far are the procedure call statement, the `IF` statement, and the `FOR` statement.

In this chapter, we will see how syntax diagrams are used to specify the syntax of a Modula-2 statement, including control statements. An examination of the syntax diagram for the `IF` statement will show how to write `IF` statements with several (more than two) alternatives.

A new looping statement, the `WHILE` statement, will be introduced. The repetition of a `WHILE` loop is controlled by a condition; the loop is repeated as long as ("while") the condition is true. We will study how to design `WHILE` loops and use them in Modula-2 programs. We will also introduce the idea of verifying that a loop is correct and discuss special comments called assertions and loop invariants, which are helpful in loop design and verification.

3.1 Syntax Diagrams

Before discussing control statements, we will show how to use a *syntax diagram* to describe the syntax of any Modula-2 language feature. The syntax diagram in Fig. 3.1 describes a Modula-2 *identifier*. This syntax diagram references two other syntactical elements of Modula-2: *letter* (A-Z, a-z) and *digit* (0-9). You will recall that an *identifier* is a sequence of letters and digits starting with a letter.

Figure 3.1 ▸ *Syntax Diagram of a Modula-2 Identifier*

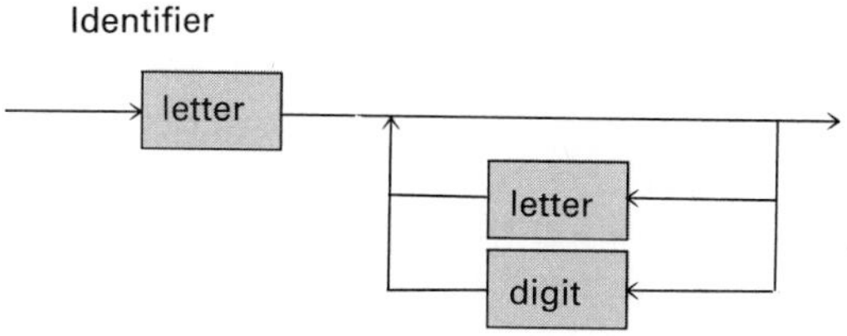

To use a syntax diagram, trace through the diagram following the arrows. Start at the arrow tail on the left and finish at the arrowhead on the right. The shortest path through the diagram in Fig. 3.1 is from left to right, passing through the top box labeled *letter*. This means that a Modula-2 identifier may be any single letter (e.g., `A`, `B`, `c`, `z`).

There are many other paths through the diagram. Instead of exiting at the right after passing through the top box labeled *letter*, you could follow either path leading down and to the left. These paths go through a box labeled *digit* and another box labeled *letter*. If you then exit the diagram, the identifier formed will consist of two characters (e.g., `it`, `ME`, `R2`, `D2`).

Since there is a closed cycle, or loop, in the diagram, you can pass through the lower box labeled *letter* and the box labeled *digit* several times before exiting the diagram. Each time, add a symbol from the box passed through to the identifier being formed. Examples of identifiers formed this way are `A`, `ABC`, and `A23b4cd5`. It is impossible to trace a path that establishes `123` or `12ABC` as a valid identifier.

EXAMPLE 3.1 ▸ Chapter 1 described a *real literal* as a number starting with one or more digits, then a decimal point, and zero or more digits, and possibly ending with a *scale factor*. The syntax diagrams for a real literal and a scale factor are shown in Fig. 3.2. ◂

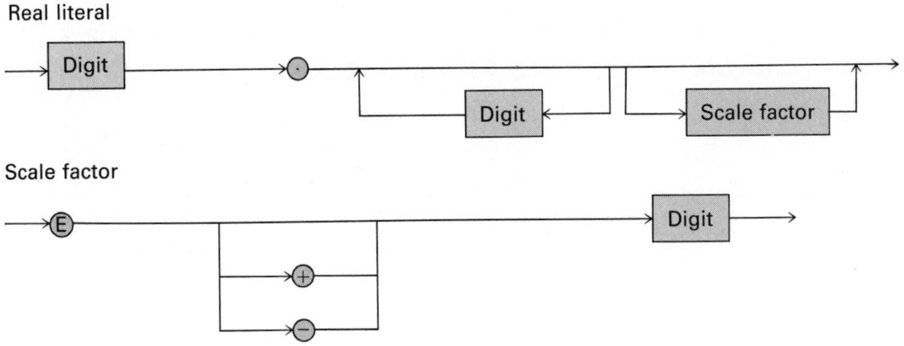

Figure 3.2 ▸ *Syntax Diagrams for a Real Literal and a Scale Factor*

You can use syntax diagrams to verify that a program statement is syntactically correct before you enter it. If the compiler detects a syntax error, you can refer to the appropriate syntax diagram to determine the correct form of the incorrect element. Appendix C contains all Modula-2 syntax diagrams.

SELF-CHECK EXERCISE FOR SECTION 3.1

1. Which syntax diagrams in Appendix C would you use to verify that the statement below is syntactically correct? The identifier `N` would be classified as what kind of syntactic element? Answer the same question for the identifiers `I` and `Sum`.

```
FOR I := 1 TO N DO
  Sum := Sum + I
END
```

3.2 The IF Statement Revisited

The syntax diagram for an `IF` statement is shown in Fig. 3.3. This diagram shows that the syntactic elements *expression* and *statement sequence* are components of an `IF` statement. Consult the appropriate syntax diagram in Appendix C for the form of these elements.

Figure 3.3 ▸ *Syntax Diagram for an IF Statement*

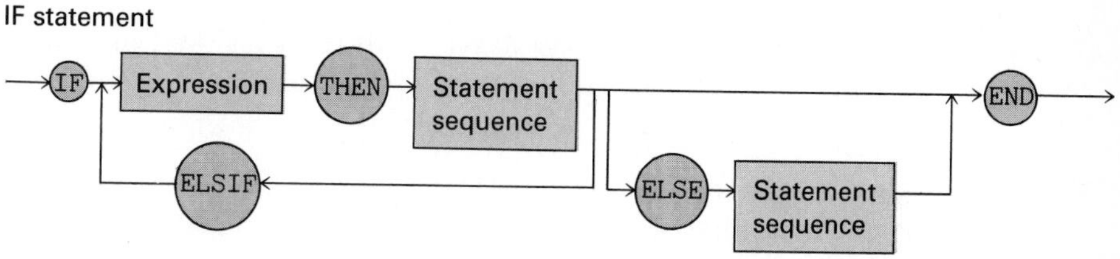

The reserved words `IF`, `THEN`, `ELSE`, `ELSIF`, and `END` are enclosed in ovals rather than boxes. When you pass through one of these ovals, insert the word inside into the `IF` statement being formed. The syntax diagram in Fig. 3.3 shows that `IF` statements can implement decisions with one alternative as in

```
IF expression THEN
  statement sequence
END
```

or decisions with two alternatives as in

```
IF expression THEN
  statement sequence1
ELSE
  statement sequence2
END
```

or decisions with several alternatives as in

```
IF expression1 THEN
  statement sequence1
ELSIF expression2 THEN
  statement sequence2
. . . . . . . . . . . . . . . .

ELSIF expressionk THEN
  statement sequencek
ELSE
  statement sequencen
END
```

```
IF expression1 THEN
  statement sequence1
ELSIF expression2 THEN
  statement sequence2
. . . . . . . . . . . . . . . . .

ELSIF expressionk THEN
  statement sequencek
END
```

More Examples of IF Statements

EXAMPLE 3.2 ▶ The following IF statement can be used to compute the discounted price of an item. It first determines the discount by multiplying the item price and the discount rate (a fraction); next it deducts the discount. The statement sequence is not executed when the discount rate is zero. ◀

```
IF DiscRate # 0.0 THEN
  Discount := Price * DiscRate;      (* Compute discount amount *)
  Price := Price - Discount          (* Deduct discount from price *)
END   (* IF *)
```

EXAMPLE 3.3 ▶ The following IF statement orders the values in X and Y so that the smaller number will be in X and the larger number in Y. If the two numbers are already in the proper order, the statement sequence will not be executed. ◀

```
IF X >  Y THEN
  (* switch X and Y *)
  Temp := X;                         (* Store old X in Temp *)
  X := Y;                            (* Store old Y in X *)
  Y := Temp                          (* Store old X in Y *)
END  (* IF *)
```

The variables X, Y, and Temp should all be the same type. Although the values of X and Y are being switched, an additional variable, Temp, is needed to store a copy of one of these values. The need for Temp is illustrated in the trace in Table 3.1, assuming X and Y have original values of 12.5 and 5.0, respectively.

Table 3.1 ▶ *Trace of IF Statement to Order X and Y*

STATEMENT PART	X	Y	Temp	EFFECT
	12.5	5.0	?	
IF X > Y THEN				12.5 > 5.0 is true
Temp := X;			12.5	Store old X in Temp
X := Y;	5.0			Store old Y in X
Y := Temp		12.5		Store old X in Y

EXAMPLE 3.4 ▶ The following IF statement can be used to process a positive transaction amount (TransAmount) that represents a check (TransType is 'C') or a deposit. In either case, an appropriate message is printed and the account balance (Balance) is updated. ◀

```
IF TransType = 'C' THEN
  (* check *)
  WriteString ('Check for $');
  WriteReal (TransAmount, 12);  WriteLn;
  Balance := Balance - TransAmount       (* Deduct check amount *)
ELSE
  (* deposit *)
  WriteString ('Deposit of $');
  WriteReal (TransAmount, 12);  WriteLn;
  Balance := Balance + TransAmount       (* Add deposit amount *)
END  (* IF *)
```

The semicolons in the IF statement separate the individual statements in each alternative. Note that a semicolon is not used after the last statement in each alternative or after THEN or ELSE.

EXAMPLE 3.5 ▶ The nested IF statement below has three alternatives. It causes one of three variables (NumPos, NumNeg, or NumZero) to be increased by one depending on if X is greater than zero, less than zero, or equal to zero, respectively.

```
(* Increment NumPos, NumNeg, or NumZero depending on X *)
IF X > 0 THEN
  INC (NumPos)
ELSIF X < 0 THEN
  INC (NumNeg)
ELSE  (* X = 0 *)
  INC (NumZero)
END  (* IF *)
```

The execution of this IF statement proceeds as follows: the first condition (X > 0) is tested; if it is true, the procedure call statement

```
INC (NumPos)
```

increments NumPos by one and the rest of the IF statement is skipped. If the first condition is false, the second condition (X < 0) is tested; if it is true, NumNeg is incremented; otherwise, NumZero is incremented. It is important to realize that the second condition is tested only when the first condition is false.

Fig. 3.4 diagrams the execution of this statement. Each condition is shown in a diamond-shaped box. If a condition is true, its arrow labeled T is followed. If a condition is false, its arrow labeled F is followed. This diagram shows that one and only one of the statement sequences in a rectangular box will be executed. (Don't confuse this diagram with the syntax diagram for an IF statement shown earlier.)

Figure 3.4 ▸
Diagram of the IF Statement in Example 3.5

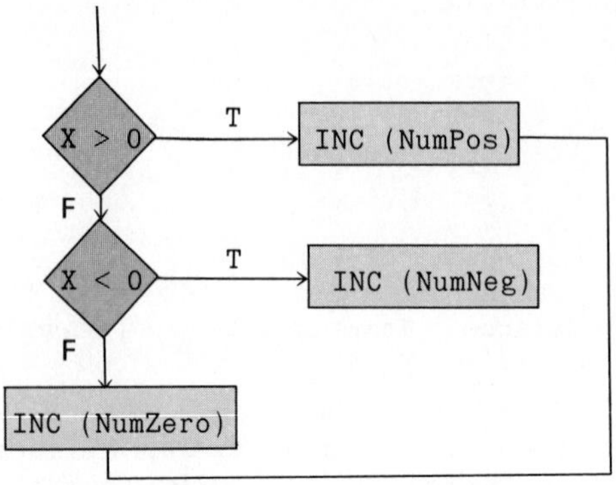

A trace of the IF statement for X = –7 is shown in Table 3.2. The statement

```
INC (NumNeg)
```

shown in this table is equivalent to

```
NumNeg := NumNeg + 1
```

Because the increment operation is performed frequently in programming, Modula-2 provides a standard procedure for this purpose. Procedure INC will be discussed further in Chapter 5. The multiple-alternative IF statement is described in the syntax display following Table 3.2. ◂

Table 3.2 ▸
Trace of IF Statement in Example 3.5 for X = –7

STATEMENT PART	X	EFFECT
	–7	
IF X > 0 THEN		–7 > 0 is false
ELSIF X < 0 THEN		–7 < 0 is true
INC (NumNeg)		Add 1 to NumNeg

Multiple-Alternative IF Statement ▶

FORM:

```
IF expression₁ THEN
  statement sequence₁
ELSIF expression₂ THEN
  statement sequence₂
.....................
ELSIF expressionₖ THEN
  statement sequenceₖ
ELSE
  statement sequenceₙ
END
```

EXAMPLES:
```
IF N >= 0 THEN
  WriteString ('Positive')
ELSIF N = 0 THEN
  WriteString ('Zero')
ELSE
  WriteString ('Negative')
END
```

INTERPRETATION: The *expressions* (conditions) in a multiple-alternative `IF` statement are evaluated from top to bottom until a true value is obtained. The *statement sequence* following the first true *expression* is executed and the rest of the `IF` statement is skipped. If every *expression* is false, then *statement sequence*$_n$ (between `ELSE` and `END`) is executed.

Notes: At most, one *statement sequence* is executed. If `ELSE` and *statement sequence*$_n$ are present, exactly one *statement sequence* is always executed. If `ELSE` and *statement sequence*$_n$ are omitted, then no *statement sequence* is executed when every *expression* is false.

Program Style

Writing a Multiple-Alternative IF Statement

When writing a multiple-alternative `IF` statement, align the reserved words `IF`, `ELSE`, `ELSIF`, and `END` and indent each statement sequence consistently. This is done to make the `IF` statement more readable; indentation is ignored by the compiler.

Order of Conditions

Often the conditions in a multiple-alternative decision are not *mutually exclusive*. This means that it may be possible for more than one condition to be true for a given data value. If this is the case, the order of the conditions is important because only the statement sequence following the first true condition is executed.

EXAMPLE 3.6 ▶ The table below describes the assignment of grades based on an exam score.

Exam Score	*Grade Assigned*
90 and above	A
80–89	B
70–79	C
60–69	D
below 60	F

The following multiple-alternative `IF` statement prints the letter grade assigned according to this table. The last three conditions are true for an exam score of 85; a grade of B is assigned, however, because the first true condition is Score >= 80.

```
(* correct grade assignment *)
IF Score >= 90 THEN
  Write ('A')
ELSIF Score >= 80 THEN
  Write ('B')
ELSIF Score >= 70 THEN
  Write ('C')
ELSIF Score >= 60 THEN
  Write ('D')
ELSE
  Write ('F')
END  (* IF *)
```

The order of conditions can also have an effect on program efficiency. If we know that low exam scores are much more likely than high scores, it would be more efficient to test first for scores below 60, then for scores between 60 and 69, and so on (see Exercise 4 at the end of this section).

It would be wrong to write the decision as shown next. All passing exam scores (60 or above) would be incorrectly categorized as a grade of D, because the first condition would be true and the rest would be skipped. ◄

```
(* incorrect grade assignment *)
IF Score >= 60 THEN
  Write ('D')
ELSIF Score >= 70 THEN
  Write ('C')
ELSIF Score >= 80 THEN
  Write ('B')
ELSIF Score >= 90 THEN
  Write ('A')
ELSE
  Write ('F')
END  (* IF *)
```

EXAMPLE 3.7 ► A multiple-alternative IF statement can be used to implement a *decision table* that describes several alternatives. Each line of Table 3.3 indicates a salary range and a base tax amount and tax percentage for that range. Given a salary amount, the tax is calculated by adding the base tax for that salary range to the product of the percentage of excess and the amount of salary over the minimum salary for that range. For example, the second line of the table specifies that the tax due on a salary of $2000.00 is $225.00 plus 16% of the excess salary over $1500.00 (i.e., 16% of $500.00). Therefore, the total tax due is $225.00 plus $80.00, or $305.00.

The IF statement in Fig. 3.5 implements the tax table. If the value of Salary is within the table range (0.00 to 14999.99), exactly one of the statements

Table 3.3 ▶ *Tax Table for Example 3.7*

RANGE	SALARY	BASE TAX	PERCENTAGE OF EXCESS
1	0.00–1499.99	0.00	15%
2	1500.00–2999.99	225.00	16%
3	3000.00–4999.99	465.00	18%
4	5000.00–7999.99	825.00	20%
5	8000.00–14999.99	1425.00	25%

assigning a value to `Tax` will be executed. A trace of the `IF` statement for `Salary = $2000.00` is shown in Table 3.4. The value assigned to `Tax` is $305.00. ◂

Figure 3.5 ▶ *IF Statement for Table 3.3*

```
IF Salary < 0.0 THEN
  WriteString ('Error!  Negative salary $');
  WriteReal (Salary, 12);  WriteLn
ELSIF Salary < 1500.00 THEN                    (* first range *)
  Tax := 0.15 * Salary
ELSIF Salary < 3000.00 THEN                    (* second range *)
  Tax := (Salary - 1500.00) * 0.16 + 225.00
ELSIF Salary < 5000.00 THEN                    (* third range *)
  Tax := (Salary - 3000.00) * 0.18 + 465.00
ELSIF Salary < 8000.00 THEN                    (* fourth range *)
  Tax := (Salary - 5000.00) * 0.20 + 825.00
ELSIF Salary < 15000.00 THEN                   (* fifth range *)
  Tax := (Salary - 8000.00) * 0.25 + 1425.00
ELSE
  WriteString ('Error!  Too large salary $');
  WriteReal (Salary, 12);  WriteLn
END  (* IF *)
```

Table 3.4 ▶ *Trace of IF Statement in Figure 3.3 for SALARY = $2000.00*

STATEMENT PART	SALARY	TAX	EFFECT
	2000.00	?	
IF Salary < 0.0			2000.0 < 0.0 is false
ELSIF Salary < 1500.00			2000.0 < 1500.0 is false
ELSIF Salary < 3000.00			2000.0 < 3000.0 is true;
Tax := (Salary - 1500.00)			difference is 500.00,
* 0.16			product is 80.00,
+ 225.00		305.00	sum is 305.00

Program Style

Validating the Value of Variables

It is important to validate the value of a variable before performing computations, to avoid using invalid or meaningless data. Instead of computing an incorrect tax amount, the `IF` statement in Fig. 3.3 prints an error message if the value of `Salary` is outside the range covered by the table (0.0 to 14999.99). The first condition detects negative salaries, and an error message is printed if `Salary` is less than zero. All conditions evaluate to false if `Salary` is greater than 14999.99, and the alternative following `ELSE` displays an error message.

SELF-CHECK EXERCISES FOR SECTION 3.2

1. Write an `IF` statement that assigns the larger of `X` and `Y` to `Larger` and the smaller to `Smaller`. Your statement should print `X Larger` or `Y Larger`, depending on the situation.
2. Trace the execution of the nested `IF` statement in Fig. 3.5 when `Salary` is `13500.00`.
3. What would be the effect of reversing the order of the first two conditions in the `IF` statement of Fig. 3.5?
4. Rewrite the `IF` statement for Example 3.6 to test for failure first, then a grade of D, then a grade of C, and so on.
5. Implement the following decision table using a nested `IF` statement. Assume that the grade point average is within the range 0.0 through 4.0.

Grade Point Average	*Transcript Message*
0.0–0.99	Failed semester—registration suspended
1.0–1.99	On probation for next semester
3.0–3.49	Dean's list for semester
3.5–4.0	Highest honors for semester

3.3 The WHILE Statement

In all the loops used so far, the exact number of loop repetitions required could be determined before the start of loop execution. We used the `FOR` statement to implement those counting loops.

In many programming situations, the exact number of loop repetitions cannot be determined before loop execution begins. It may depend on some aspect of the data not known beforehand, but that usually can be stated by a condition. For example, we may want to continue writing checks as long as our bank balance is positive, as indicated by the following pseudocode description.

```
WHILE the balance is still positive DO
   Read in the next transaction
   Update and print the balance
END
```

The actual number of loop repetitions performed depends on the type of each transaction (deposit or withdrawal) and its amount.

Modula-2 provides three additional looping statements (WHILE, REPEAT, and LOOP) to implement *conditional loops*. The WHILE statement is discussed next; the REPEAT and LOOP statements are discussed in Chapter 6.

EXAMPLE 3.8 ▶ The program in Fig. 3.6 traces the progress of a hungry worm approaching an apple. Each time it moves, the worm cuts the distance between itself and the apple in half until the worm is close enough to enter the apple. A WHILE loop is the correct looping structure to use because we have no idea beforehand how many moves will be required. ◀

Figure 3.6 ▶
Worm Bites Apple

```
MODULE WormAndApple;
(*
   Prints distances between a worm and an apple. The worm keeps
   cutting the distance in half until it is close enough to enter
   the apple.
*)

   FROM InOut IMPORT
     WriteString, WriteLn;

   FROM RealInOut IMPORT
     ReadReal, WriteReal;

   CONST
     Close = 0.5;        (* maximum distance for entry to apple *)

   VAR
     InitialDist, (* input - starting distance of worm from apple *)
     Distance : REAL; (* output - distance between worm and apple *)

BEGIN (* WormAndApple *)
  WriteString ('Enter initial distance between worm and apple: ');
  ReadReal (InitialDist);  WriteLn;

  (*
     Cut the distance between the worm and the apple in half
     until the worm is close enough to enter the apple
  *)
  Distance := InitialDist;
  WHILE Distance > Close DO
    WriteString ('The distance is ');
    WriteReal (Distance, 12);
    WriteLn;
    Distance := Distance / 2.0          (* cut Distance in half *)
  END; (* WHILE *)
```

```
  (* Print final distance before entering the apple. *)
  WriteLn;
  WriteString ('Final distance between the worm and the apple is ');
  WriteReal (Distance, 12);
  WriteLn;
  WriteString ('The worm enters the apple.');
  WriteLn
END WormAndApple.


Enter initial distance between worm and apple: 2.8
The distance is  2.8000E+000
The distance is  1.4000E+000
The distance is  7.0000E-001

Final distance between the worm and the apple is  3.5000E-001
The worm enters the apple.
```

Take a close look at the `WHILE` loop in Fig. 3.6. The assignment statement just before the loop initializes the variable `Distance` to the starting distance (`2.8`), which was previously read into `InitialDist`. Next the loop header is reached, and the *loop repetition condition* (or `WHILE` condition)

```
Distance > Close
```

is evaluated. Since this condition is true, the loop body (through `END`) is executed. The loop body displays the value of `Distance`, and the statement

```
Distance := Distance / 2.0          (* cut Distance in half *)
```

halves the value of `Distance`, thereby bringing the worm closer to the apple. The loop repetition condition is retested with the new value of `Distance` (`1.4`); and since `1.4 > 0.5` is true, the loop body displays `Distance` again, and `Distance` becomes `0.7`. The loop repetition condition is then tested a third time; since `0.7 > 0.5` is true, the loop body displays `Distance` again, which becomes `0.35`. The loop repetition condition is tested again and since `0.35 > 0.5` is false, loop exit occurs and the statements following the loop `END` are executed.

It is important to realize that the loop is not exited at the exact instant that `Distance` becomes `0.35`. If there were more statements in the loop body after the assignment to `Distance`, they would be executed. Loop exit does not occur until the loop repetition condition is retested at the top of the loop and found to be false.

There are three critical steps in Fig. 3.6 that involve the variable `Distance`.

1. `Distance` is initialized to `InitialDist` before the loop header is reached.

2. `Distance` is tested before the start of each loop repetition (called an *iteration* or a *pass*).
3. `Distance` is updated (divided by 2.0) during each iteration.

Similar steps (initialization, test, and update) must be performed for every `WHILE` loop. If the first step is missing, the initial test of `Distance` will be meaningless. The last step ensures that we make progress toward the final goal (`Distance <= Close`) during each repetition of the loop. If the last step is missing, the value of `Distance` cannot change, so the loop will execute "forever" (an *infinite loop*). The `WHILE` loop is described in the next display.

WHILE Statement ▶

FORM:

```
WHILE expression DO
  statement sequence
END
```

EXAMPLE:

```
(* Display powers of 2 *)
PowerOf2 := 1;
WHILE PowerOf2 < 10000 DO
  WriteCard (PowerOf2, 5);
  PowerOf2 := PowerOf2 * 2
END
```

INTERPRETATION: The *expression* (a condition) is tested and if it is true, the *statement sequence* is executed and the *expression* is retested. The *statement sequence* is repeated as long as (`WHILE`) the *expression* is true. When the *expression* is tested and found to be false, the `WHILE` loop is exited and the next program statement after `END` is executed.

Note: If the *expression* evaluates to false the first time it is tested, the *statement sequence* will not be executed.

EXAMPLE 3.9 ▶ It is instructive to compare the two loop forms that we already know how to write: the `FOR` loop and the `WHILE` loop. We can always implement a `FOR` loop using a `WHILE` loop, but not vice versa. The `WHILE` loop shown on the right of Fig. 3.7 behaves identically to the `FOR` loop shown on the left.

Figure 3.7 ▶ *Implementing a Counting Loop Using FOR and WHILE*

```
FOR i := 1 to 5 DO
  Square := i * i;
  WriteInt (i);
  WriteInt (Square);
  WriteLn
END (* FOR *)
```

```
i := 1;
WHILE i <= 5 DO
  Square := i * i;
  WriteInt (i);
  WriteInt (Square);
  WriteLn;
  INC (i)
END (* WHILE *)
```

We can make the following observations about the two loop forms shown in Fig 3.7.

1. The statement

```
i := 1;
```

   before the `WHILE` loop initializes `i` to `1`. The initialization of the `FOR` loop control variable `i` is specified in the `FOR` loop header statement.
2. The statement `INC (i)` in the `WHILE` loop body increments `i` by one. This step is implicit in the `FOR` loop.

Because both the initialization and the update of variable `i` are additional steps in the `WHILE` loop implementation, the `WHILE` loop is considerably longer than the `FOR` loop. Always use a `FOR` loop, rather than a `WHILE` loop, to implement counting loops. ◂

EXAMPLE 3.10 ▸ The distance traveled in t seconds by a body dropped from a tower is represented by the formula

$$distance = 1/2\ gt^2$$

where g is the gravitational constant. The program in Fig. 3.8 prints a table showing the height of a falling object at fixed time intervals after it is dropped from a tower and before it hits the ground.

The number of lines in the table depends on the time interval between lines (`DeltaT`) and the tower height (`Tower`), both of which are data values. During each iteration, the current elapsed time (`t`) and the current object height (`Height`) are displayed. Next the elapsed time is incremented by `DeltaT` and the new object height is computed. The message following the table is displayed when the object hits the ground. ◂

Figure 3.8 ▸ *Dropping an Object from a Tower*

```
MODULE FreeFall;
(*
   Displays the height of an object dropped
   from a tower until it hits the ground.
*)
   FROM InOut IMPORT
     WriteString, WriteLn;

   FROM RealInOut IMPORT
     WriteReal, ReadReal;

   CONST
     g = 9.80665;        (* gravitational constant *)
```

```
  VAR
    Height,            (* output-height of object *)
    Tower,             (* input-height of tower *)
    t,                 (* output-elapsed time *)
    DeltaT : REAL;     (* input-time interval *)

BEGIN
  (* Enter tower height and time interval. *)
  WriteString ('Tower height in meters: ');
  ReadReal (Tower);   WriteLn;
  WriteString ('Time in seconds between table lines: ');
  ReadReal (DeltaT);  WriteLn;  WriteLn;

  (* Display object height until it hits the ground. *)
  WriteString ('        Time      Height');  WriteLn;
  t := 0.0;
  Height := Tower;
  WHILE Height > 0.0 DO
    WriteReal (t, 12);  WriteReal (Height, 12);  WriteLn;
    t := t + DeltaT;
    Height := Tower - 0.5 * g * t * t
  END; (* WHILE *)

  (* Object hits the ground. *)
  WriteLn;  WriteString ('SPLATT!!!');
  WriteLn
END FreeFall.


Tower height in meters: 100.0
Time in seconds between table lines: 1.0

        Time      Height
 0.0000E+000 1.0000E+002
 1.0000E+000 9.5097E+001
 2.0000E+000 8.0387E+001
 3.0000E+000 5.5870E+001
 4.0000E+000 2.1547E+001

SPLATT!!!
```

Program Style

Displaying a Table

The program in Fig. 3.8 displays a table of output values. The table heading is displayed before the loop is reached by the statements

```
WriteString ('        Time      Height');  WriteLn;
```

The spaces in the string are used to align the column headings over their respective table values. We have left enough spaces to place the rightmost character of the first heading in column 12 and the second heading in column 24. Within the WHILE loop, the statements

```
WriteReal (t, 12);  WriteReal (Height, 12);  WriteLn;
```

display a pair of output values on each line of the table, using twelve columns per value.

SELF-CHECK EXERCISES FOR SECTION 3.3

1. What values would be printed if the assignment came first in the loop body of Fig. 3.6?
2. Write a program that prints a table showing n and 2^n while 2^n is less than 10000.

3.4 Loop Design

It is one thing to be able to analyze the operation of the loop in Fig. 3.6 and another to design our own loops. Let's consider the latter problem. The comment just before the loop

```
(* Cut the distance between the worm and the apple in half
   until the worm is close enough to enter the apple *)
```

summarizes the purpose of the loop. To accomplish this, we must concern ourselves with loop control and loop processing. Loop control involves making sure that loop exit occurs when it is supposed to; loop processing involves making sure the loop body performs the required operations.

To help us formulate the necessary loop control and loop processing steps, it is useful to list what we know about the loop. In this example, if `Distance` is the distance of the worm from the apple, we can make the following observations:

1. `Distance` is equal to `InitialDist` just before the loop begins.
2. `Distance` during pass i is half the value of `Distance` during pass i-1 (for $i > 1$).
3. `Distance` is between `Close/2.0` and `Close` just after loop exit.

Statement 1 simply indicates that `InitialDist` is the starting distance of the worm from the apple. Statement 2 derives from the fact that the distance of the worm from the apple must be cut in half during each iteration. Statement 3 derives from the fact that the worm enters the apple when `Distance <= Close`, so the loop must be exited if `Distance` is `Close`. Distance cannot be <= `Close/2.0` after loop exit, because then the loop should have been exited before the last pass.

Statement 1 by itself tells us what initialization must be performed. Statement 2 tells us how to process `Distance` within the loop body (i.e., divide it by 2.0). Finally statement 3 tells us when to exit the loop. Since `Distance` is decreasing, loop exit should occur when `Distance <= Close` is true. These considerations give us the following outline, which is the basis for the `WHILE` loop shown earlier in Fig. 3.6. The loop repetition condition, `Distance > Close`, is the opposite of the exit condition, `Distance <= Close`.

```
1. Initialize Distance to InitialDist
2. WHILE Distance > Close DO
     3. Display Distance
     4. Divide Distance by 2.0
   END
```

Working Backward to Determine Loop Initialization

It is not always so easy to come up with the initialization steps for a loop. In some cases, we must work backward from the results we know are required in the first pass to determine what initial values will produce these results.

EXAMPLE 3.10 ▶ We want to write a loop that displays all powers of a certain number (say, `N`) that are less than a certain value (say, 1000). Assuming that each power of `N` is stored in the variable `Power`, we can make the following observations about the loop.

1. `Power` during pass i is `N` times `Power` during pass i-1 (for $i > 1$)
2. `Power` is between `1000` and `N * 1000` just after loop exit.

Statement 1 derives from the fact that the powers of number `N` are all multiples of `N`. Statement 2 derives from the fact that only powers less than 1000 are displayed. From statement 1, we know that `Power` must be multiplied by `N` in the loop body. From statement 2, we know that the loop exit condition is `Power >= 1000`, so the loop repetition condition is `Power < 1000`. These considerations lead us to the following outline:

```
1. Initialize Power to ______
2. WHILE Power < 1000 DO
     3. Display Power
     4. Multiply Power by N
   END
```

One way to complete step 1 is to ask what value should be displayed during the first loop repetition. The value of `N` raised to the power zero is one for any number `N`. Therefore, if we initialize `Power` to `1`, the value displayed during the first loop repetition will be correct. ◀

1. Initialize Power to 1

WHILE Loops with Zero Iterations

The body of a WHILE loop is not executed if the loop repetition test fails (evaluates to false) when the loop is first reached. To verify that the initialization steps are correct, make sure that a program still generates the correct results for zero iterations of the loop body. If Close is greater than or equal to the value read into InitialDist (say, 0.4), the loop body in Fig. 3.6 would not execute, and the lines below would be correctly displayed.

```
Enter initial distance between worm and apple: 0.4

Final distance between the worm and the apple is  4.0000E-001
The worm enters the apple.
```

Processing an Unspecified Number of Data Items

Often we do not know exactly how many data items will be entered before a program begins execution. This may be because there are too many data items to count them beforehand (e.g., a stack of exam scores for a very large class), or because the number of data items provided may depend on how the computation proceeds.

There are two ways to handle this situation using a WHILE loop. One approach is to ask whether there are any more data before each data item is read. The user should enter Y (for yes) or N (for no) and the program would either read the next item (Y) or terminate data entry (N).

EXAMPLE 3.11 ▶ If this approach is used to design a loop that accumulates the sum (in Sum) of a collection of exam scores, the statements below are true, assuming that MoreData always contains the value 'Y' or 'N'.

1. Sum is the sum of all scores read so far.
2. MoreData is 'N' just after loop exit.

From statement 1, we know that we must add each score to Sum in the loop body and that Sum must be zero initially for its final value to be correct. From statement 2, we know that loop exit must occur when MoreData is 'N', so the loop repetition condition is MoreData = 'Y'. These considerations lead us to the following loop form:

1. Initialize Sum to zero
2. Initialize MoreData to ______
3. WHILE MoreData = 'Y' DO
    4. Read the next score into Score
    5. Add Score to Sum
    6. Read the next value of MoreData

   END

The loop repetition condition, MoreData = 'Y', derives from the facts that MoreData is either 'Y' or 'N', and that loop exit occurs, when MoreData is 'N'. To ensure that at least one pass is performed, step 2 should be

2. Initialize MoreData to 'Y'

In the Modula-2 loop in Fig. 3.9, the value of the type CHAR variable MoreData controls loop repetition. It must be initialized to the constant Affirmative (value is 'Y') before the loop is reached. A new character value ('Y' or 'N') is read into MoreData at the end of each loop repetition. The loop processing consists of reading each exam score (into Score) and adding it to Sum. Loop exit occurs when the value read into MoreData is not equal to Affirmative.

Figure 3.9 ▸ *Entering an Unspecified Number of Data Values*

```
Sum := 0;
MoreData := Affirmative;
WHILE MoreData = Affirmative DO
  WriteString ('Enter the next score: ');
  ReadCard (Score);  WriteLn;
  Sum := Sum + Score;
  WriteString ('Any more data?  Enter Y (Yes) or N (No): ');
  Read (MoreData);  Write (MoreData);  WriteLn;
  MoreData := CAP(MoreData)
END (* WHILE *)
```

Since it is possible that the program user may enter an uppercase or lowercase letter, the last statement in the loop

```
MoreData := CAP(MoreData);
```

uses the standard function CAP to set the character in MoreData to uppercase. This function will be explained in more detail in Chapter 5.

The following sample dialog would be used to enter the scores 33, 55, and 77. The problem with this approach is that the program user must enter an extra character value, Y, before entering each actual data item. ◂

```
Enter the next score: 33
Any more data?  Enter Y (Yes) or N (No): Y
Enter next data item: 55
Any more data?  Enter Y (Yes) or N (No): Y
Enter next data item: 77
Any more data?  Enter Y (Yes) or N (No): N
```

Sentinel-Controlled Loops

A second approach to solving the problem addressed in the last section would be to instruct the user to enter a unique data value, or *sentinel value*, when done. The program would test each data item and terminate when this sentinel value is read. The sentinel value should be carefully chosen and must be a value that could not normally occur as data. This approach is more convenient, because the program user then enters only the required data.

EXAMPLE 3.12 ▶ The statements below must be true for a sentinel-controlled loop that accumulates the sum of a collection of exam scores.

1. `Sum` is the sum of all scores read so far.
2. `Score` contains the sentinel value just after loop exit.

Statement 2 derives from the fact that loop exit occurs after the sentinel is read into `Score`. These statements lead to the following trial loop form:

Incorrect sentinel-controlled loop

```
1. Initialize Sum to zero
2. WHILE Score is not the sentinel DO
     3. Read the next score into Score
     4. Add Score to Sum
   END
```

Since `Score` has not been given an initial value, the `WHILE` condition in step 2 cannot be evaluated when the loop is first reached. One way around this would be to initialize `Score` to any value besides the sentinel and then read in the first score at step 3. A preferred solution is to read in the first score as the initial value of `Score` before the loop is reached and then switch the order of steps 3 and 4 in the loop body. The outline for this solution follows.

Correct sentinel-controlled loop

```
1. Initialize Sum to zero
2. Read the first score into Score
3. WHILE Score is not the sentinel DO
     4. Add Score to Sum
     5. Read the next score into Score
   END
```

Step 2 reads in the first score, which step 4 adds to zero (initial value of `Sum`). Step 5 reads all remaining scores, including the sentinel. Step 4 adds all scores, except the sentinel, to `Sum`.

The initial read (step 2) is often called the *priming read*, an analogy with the priming of a pump, in which a cup of water must first be poured into a pump before it can begin to draw water out of a well. The Modula-2 implementation shown in Fig. 3.10 uses `-1` (value of `Sentinel`) as the sentinel because all exam scores should be nonnegative.

Although it may look strange at first to see the statement

```
ReadInt (Score);
```

Figure 3.10 ▸
A Sentinel-Controlled Loop

```
Sum := 0;
WriteString ('When done, enter -1 to stop.');  WriteLn;
WriteString ('Enter the first score: ');
ReadInt (Score);  WriteLn;
WHILE Score # Sentinel DO
  Sum := Sum + Score;
  WriteString ('Enter the next score: ');
  ReadInt (Score);  WriteLn
END (* WHILE *)
```

at two different points in the program, this is perfectly good programming practice and causes no problems. Note that `ReadCard` cannot be used because the sentinel value is negative. The following sample dialog would be used to enter the scores 33, 55, and 77. Compare this with the previous dialog. ◂

```
When done, enter -1 to stop.
Enter the first score: 55
Enter the next  score: 77
Enter the next  score: -1
```

It is usually instructive (and often necessary) to question what happens when there are no data items to process. In that case, the sentinel value should be entered as the "first score." Loop exit would occur right after the first (and only) test of the loop repetition condition, so the loop body would not be executed (i.e., a loop with zero iterations). `Sum` would retain its initial value of zero, which would be correct.

In the first loop form shown, at least one exam score must always be entered because the prompt

```
Any more data?  Enter Y (Yes) or N (No):
```

does not appear until the end of the first pass through the loop. To be able to execute the program without any exam scores, you must modify the program to read the initial value of `MoreData` just before the loop is reached.

SELF-CHECK EXERCISE FOR SECTION 3.4

1. Write statements similar to the ones shown on page 114 that summarize the properties of the loop in Fig. 3.8.

3.5 Assertions and Loop Invariants

Once a loop is designed, you should verify that it works properly. One way to do this is to trace its execution for a variety of different sets of data, making sure that the loop always terminates and that it produces the correct results even when zero iterations are performed.

Exhaustive testing of a loop can be time-consuming. For this reason, computer scientists have devised techniques for proving that a loop is correct. Although this process is beyond the scope of the text, we will introduce some principles of loop verification that will be helpful in loop design.

A critical part of loop verification is documenting the loop with special comments called *assertions*, which are logical statements that are always true. One assertion should be placed just before the `WHILE` condition and another just after the loop `END`. The assertion that precedes the `WHILE` condition is called the *loop invariant*. Like the `WHILE` condition, the loop invariant is evaluated just before each repetition of the loop body. Even though the `WHILE` condition may be false (i.e., just before loop exit), the loop invariant must always be true. The loop from Fig. 3.6 is rewritten in Fig. 3.11 using assertions. Assertions, like all comments, are ignored by the compiler; consequently, it is all right to insert the invariant between the word `WHILE` and the loop repetition condition, as shown in Fig. 3.11.

Figure 3.11 ▸ *Worm-and-Apple Loop with Assertions*

```
(* Cut the distance between the worm and the apple in half
   until the worm is close enough to enter the apple       *)
Distance := InitialDist;
WHILE
  (* invariant:
       Distance > Close/2.0 and
       Distance in pass i is half Distance in pass i-1 (for i > 1)
  *)
     Distance > Close DO
  WriteString ('The distance is ');
  WriteReal (Distance, 12);
  WriteLn;
  Distance := Distance / 2.0            (* cut Distance in half *)
END; (* WHILE *)
(* assert: Distance <= Close *)
```

The invariant summarizes the loop properties and is similar to statements 2 and 3 listed on page 114 and repeated here:

- Distance during pass i is half the value of `Distance` during pass $i-1$ (for $i > 1$).
- Distance is between `Close/2.0` and `Close` just after loop exit.

The last line in Fig. 3.11

```
(* assert:  Distance <= Close *)
```

describes the relationship between `Distance` and `Close` just after loop exit.

EXAMPLE 3.13 ▸ The sentinel-controlled loop in Fig. 3.10 is rewritten in Fig. 3.12 using assertions. Compare the loop invariant with the following statements, which summarize the loop properties. ◂

- `Sum` is the sum of all scores read so far.
- `Score` is the sentinel just after loop exit.

Figure 3.12 ▸ *Sentinel-Controlled Loop with Assertions*

```
Sum := 0;
WriteString ('When done, enter -1 to stop.');  WriteLn;
WriteString ('Enter the first score: ');
ReadCard (Score);  WriteLn;
WHILE
  (* invariant:
       Sum is the sum of all scores read and
       no prior score was the sentinel
  *)
     Score # Sentinel DO
  Sum := Sum + Score;
  WriteString ('Enter the next  score: ');
  ReadInt (Score);  WriteLn
END (* WHILE *)
(* assert: Score is Sentinel and Sum is the sum of all scores *)
```

Although detailed discussion of the topic is beyond the scope of this text, some computer scientists use loop invariants for loop design as well as loop verification. By first writing the loop invariant as a comment inside the loop, they can discern from the invariant what initialization, testing, and processing steps are required. Our approach of describing the properties of a loop before refining the loop is similar but less formal.

SELF-CHECK EXERCISE FOR SECTION 3.5

1. Write the loop invariant for the loop in Fig. 3.8.

3.6 Nested Control Statements

The statement sequence inside a control statement can contain another control statement. The second control statement is said to be *nested* inside the first control statement.

EXAMPLE 3.14 ▶ Depending on a student's GPA (grade point average), the following fragment displays one of three messages. If the GPA is less than or equal to 1.5, the painful message following the second ELSE is displayed. If the GPA is greater than 1.5, the *inner* IF statement is executed, and a more pleasant message is displayed.

```
IF GPA > 1.5 THEN
  IF GPA < 3.0 THEN
    WriteString ('Progressing satisfactorily')
  ELSE
    WriteString ("Made the Dean's List - send money")
  END (* inner IF *)
ELSE
  WriteString ('Flunked out')
END (* outer IF *)
```

The following nested statements have the same effect as the previous ones. Again, the inner IF statement is executed when the GPA exceeds 1.5.

```
IF GPA <= 1.5 THEN
  WriteString ('Flunked out')
ELSE
  IF GPA < 3.0 THEN
    WriteString ('Progressing satisfactorily')
  ELSE
    WriteString ("Made the Dean's List - send money")
  END (* inner IF *)
END (* outer IF *)
```

A single multiple alternative IF statement can often replace nested IF statements, resulting in a more readable program. Verify for yourself that the following IF statement has the same effect as the previous nested IF statements. ◀

```
IF GPA <= 1.5 THEN
  WriteString ('Flunked out')
ELSIF GPA < 3.0 THEN
  WriteString ('Progressing satisfactorily')
ELSE
  WriteString ("Made the Dean's List - send money")
END (* IF *)
```

Remembering the Last Data Value in a Loop

In some situations it is necessary to remember the data value processed during the last iteration of a loop. For example, some keyboards are "bouncy," causing multiple occurrences of the same character to be sent when a single key is pressed. Some faculty are forgetful and may enter the same exam score twice in succession. An IF statement nested inside a loop can check whether the current data value is the same as the last data value.

EXAMPLE 3.15 ▶ The program in Fig. 3.13 finds the product of a collection of data values. If there are multiple consecutive occurrences of the same data value, only the first occurrence is included in the product. For example, the product of the numbers 10, 5, 5, 5, 10 is $10 \times 5 \times 10$, or 500. Assuming a new data value is read into `NextNum` during each loop iteration, we can make the following observations.

1. `Product` in pass i is the same as `Product` in pass $i-1$ if `NextNum` in pass i is `NextNum` in pass $i-1$; otherwise, `Product` during pass i is `NextNum` times `Product` in pass $i-1$ (for $i > 1$).
2. `NextNum` is the sentinel just after loop exit.

Statement 1 requires the loop to "remember" the value read into `NextNum` during the previous iteration. We will introduce a new program variable, `LastNum`, for this purpose. The current value of `NextNum` should be incorporated into the product only if it is different from the previous value of `NextNum` (saved in `LastNum`). A trial loop form follows.

Initial loop form

```
1. Initialize Product to _______
2. Initialize LastNum to _______
3. Read the first number into NextNum
4. WHILE NextNum is not the sentinel DO
     5. IF NextNum is not equal to LastNum THEN
          6. Multiply Product by NextNum
        END
     7. Set LastNum to NextNum
     8. Read the next number into NextNum
   END
```

For `Product` to be correct during the first pass, it must be initialized to 1 (step 1). We must also initialize `LastNum` so the condition in step 4 can be evaluated. To ensure that the first number read into `NextNum` is incorporated into the product, we must pick a value for `LastNum` that is different from the initial data value. The safest thing to do is to initialize `LastNum` to the sentinel. (Why?) These considerations lead to the following revised loop form.

Revised loop form

```
1. Initialize Product to 1
2. Initialize LastNum to the sentinel
3. Read the first number into NextNum
4. WHILE NextNum is not the sentinel DO
```

5. IF NextNum is not equal to LastNum THEN
    6. Multiply Product by NextNum
   END
7. Set LastNum to NextNum
8. Read the next number into NextNum
END

Within the loop, steps 7 and 8 prepare for the next iteration by saving the previous value of NextNum in LastNum before reading the next data value. (What happens if the order of these two steps is reversed?)

Figure 3.13 ▸ *Program to Multiply Nonzero Data*

```
MODULE Multiply;
(*
   Finds the product of a collection of nonzero integers. If there
   are multiple consecutive occurrences of the same value, only the
   the first value is included in the product.
*)
   FROM InOut IMPORT
     ReadInt, WriteInt, WriteString, WriteLn;

   CONST
     Sentinel = 0;                    (* sentinel value *)
   VAR
     NextNum,                         (* input - new data item *)
     LastNum,                         (* last data item *)
     Product : INTEGER;               (* output - product of data *)
BEGIN (* Multiply *)
  (* Compute product of nonzero, nonrepeating data items. *)
  Product := 1;
  LastNum := Sentinel;
  WriteString ('Enter 0 to stop.');  WriteLn;
  WriteString ('Enter first number: ');
  ReadInt (NextNum);  WriteLn;                        (* read first item *)
  WHILE
    (* invariant:
         No prior value of NextNum is the sentinel and
         Product in pass i is Product in pass i-1 if NextNum is
         LastNum; otherwise, Product in pass i is NextNum * Product
         in pass i-1 (for i > 1)
    *)
       NextNum # Sentinel DO
    IF NextNum # LastNum THEN
      Product := Product * NextNum          (* compute next product *)
    END; (* IF *)
    LastNum := NextNum
    WriteString ('Enter next  number: ');
    ReadInt (NextNum); WriteLn                        (* read next item *)
  END; (* WHILE *)
```

```
  (* assert:
       NextNum is the sentinel and Product is the product of
       every value of NextNum such that NextNum # LastNum
  *)

  WriteString ('The product is ');                (* print result *)
  WriteInt (Product, 6);
  WriteLn
END Multiply.


Enter 0 to stop.
Enter first number: 10
Enter next  number: 5
Enter next  number: 5
Enter next  number: 5
Enter next  number: 10
Enter next  number: 0
The product is    500
```

The program in Fig. 3.13 illustrates the proper form of a sentinel-controlled loop. The constant `Sentinel` has the value zero, since it is meaningless to include zero in a collection of numbers being multiplied. To determine whether or not to execute the loop, the program must compare each value read into `NextNum` to `Sentinel`. For this test to make sense in the beginning, the first data value must be read before the `WHILE` loop is reached. The next value must be read at the end of the loop so that it can be tested before starting another iteration. This general pattern is illustrated below.

> Read the first data item
> `WHILE` current data item is not the sentinel `DO`
>   Process current data item
>   Read the next data item
> `END`

Remember, in a sentinel-controlled loop, the read operation appears twice: before the `WHILE` header (the priming read) and at the end of the loop body.

SELF-CHECK EXERCISE FOR SECTION 3.6

1. What is the product computed by the program in Fig. 3.13 if only one data value besides the sentinel is supplied? What product would be computed if the assignment to `LastNum` followed `ReadInt` at the end of the loop body and several data items were provided?

3.7 Case Study

MONEY IN THE BANK

Problem: Now that you are finally graduating, your parents have some money to invest in a savings account and they want to know the best strategy for investment. They would like you to write a program that shows them how the value of a certificate of deposit increases annually. They want to use this program for fixed-rate or variable-rate (interest rate changes at the beginning of each year) certificates. Whenever it is run, your program should display a table showing the investment year, the annual interest, and the year-end certificate balance until the balance has passed a target amount.

Discussion: What is needed is a program that computes annual interest and new balance using the formulas

interest = *balance* * *rate*
new balance = *old balance* + *interest*

The program should display these values while the new balance is less than the target balance. We can use a single variable (`Balance`) to represent the old and the new balance where the initial value of `Balance` is the deposit amount (`Deposit`). The data requirements for the problem follow.

PROBLEM INPUTS

the deposit amount (`Deposit : REAL`)
the target balance (`TargetBal : REAL`)
the annual interest rate as a fraction (`Rate : REAL`)
an indicator of whether the interest rate is fixed or variable
(`FixedOrVar : CHAR`)

PROBLEM OUTPUTS

the current investment year (`Year : CARDINAL`)
the current balance (`Balance : REAL`)
the annual interest earned (`Interest : REAL`)

The type `CHAR` variable `FixedOrVar` indicates whether the annual interest rate is fixed (value is `'F'`) or varying (value is `'V'`). The algorithm is shown next.

Algorithm

1. Enter the deposit amount, the value of `FixedOrVar`, and the interest rate for a fixed-rate certificate.

2. Print a table showing the year, interest earned, and account balance as long as the balance has not passed the target balance. If the interest rate is variable, read in the new rate at the start of each year before computing the annual interest.

Step 2 requires a loop. Since we don't know how many iterations are needed, a `WHILE` loop should be used. The loop has the following properties:

1. `Year` is the number of loop iterations performed so far.
2. `Balance` is the sum of `Deposit` plus all prior values of `Interest`.
3. `Balance` is between `TargetBal` and `TargetBal + Interest` just after loop exit.

These statements suggest the following refinement for step 2 of the algorithm. The program and a sample run are shown in Fig. 3.14.

STEP 2 REFINEMENT

```
2.1 Initialize Year to zero
2.2 Initialize Balance to Deposit
2.3 Initialize Interest to zero
2.4 WHILE  Balance < TargetBal DO
      2.5 Increment Year by 1
      2.6 IF the interest rate is variable THEN
            2.7 Read this year's rate
          END
      2.8  Compute the interest for this year
      2.9  Compute the new value of Balance
      2.10 Display the table line for the current year
    END
```

Figure 3.14 ▸ *Increasing Your Money*

```
MODULE GrowMoney;
(*
   Prints a table of interest earned and account balance for each
   investment year for fixed- or varying-rate certificates.
*)
   FROM InOut IMPORT
     Read, Write,.WriteString, WriteCard, WriteLn;

  FROM RealInOut IMPORT
     ReadReal, WriteReal;

  CONST
    Fixed = 'F';
    Variable = 'V';
    Pad = '
```

```
  VAR
     FixedOrVar : CHAR;  (* input - fixed or varying rate *)
     Deposit,            (* input - initial amount of deposit *)
     Rate,               (* input - annual rate of interest *)
     TargetBal,          (* input - the target certificate amount *)
     Balance,            (* output - current certificate amount *)
     Interest : REAL;    (* output - amount of annual interest *)
     Year : CARDINAL;    (* output - year of investment *)

BEGIN (* GrowMoney *)
   WriteString ('Enter the deposit amount $');
   ReadReal (Deposit);  WriteLn;

   WriteString ('Enter the desired final balance $');
   ReadReal (TargetBal);  WriteLn;

   WriteString ('Is the interest rate fixed (F) or variable (V)? ');
   Read (FixedOrVar);  Write (FixedOrVar);  WriteLn;
   IF CAP(FixedOrVar) = Fixed THEN
     WriteString ('Enter the interest rate as a decimal fraction: ');
     ReadReal (Rate);  WriteLn
   END; (* IF *)

   (* Display table heading *)
   WriteLn;
   WriteString (Pad);
   WriteString ('Year        Interest        Balance');  WriteLn;

   (* Display the certificate balance for each year. *)
   Year := 0;
   Interest := 0.0;
   Balance := Deposit;
   WHILE
     (* invariant:
          Balance < TargetBal + Interest and
          Balance is the sum of Deposit and all values of Interest
     *)
       Balance < TargetBal DO
     INC (Year);
     IF CAP(FixedOrVar) = Variable THEN
       WriteString('Enter rate for year ');
       WriteCard (Year, 0);  Write (':');
       ReadReal(Rate);  WriteLn
     END; (* IF *)
     Interest := Balance * Rate;
     Balance := Balance + Interest;

     WriteString (Pad);                         (* print table line *)
     WriteCard (Year, 4);      WriteReal (Interest, 15);
     WriteReal (Balance, 15);  WriteLn
    END; (* WHILE *)
```

```
   (* assert:
        Balance >= TargetBal and Balance is the sum of Deposit and
        all values of Interest
   *)

   WriteLn;
   WriteString ('Certificate amount reaches target after ');
   WriteCard (Year, 2);
   WriteString (' years');  WriteLn;
   WriteString ('Final balance is $');
   WriteReal (Balance, 15);  WriteLn
END GrowMoney.


Enter the deposit amount $100.00
Enter the desired final balance $200.00
Is the interest rate fixed (F) or variable (V)? V

                                    Year         Interest          Balance
Enter rate for year 1: 0.075
                                       1 7.5000000E+000 1.0750000E+002
Enter rate for year 2: 0.080
                                       2 8.6000000E+000 1.1610000E+002
Enter rate for year 3: 0.085
                                       3 9.8685000E+000 1.2596850E+002
Enter rate for year 4: 0.090
                                       4 1.1337165E+001 1.3730567E+002
Enter rate for year 5: 0.095
                                       5 1.3044038E+001 1.5034970E+002
Enter rate for year 6: 0.100
                                       6 1.5034970E+001 1.6538467E+002
Enter rate for year 7: 0.150
                                       7 2.4807701E+001 1.9019237E+002
Enter rate for year 8: 0.200
                                       8 3.8038475E+001 2.2823085E+002

Certificate amount reaches target after  8 years
Final balance is $ 2.2823085E+002
```

The sample run uses a variable interest rate. Using a fixed rate would eliminate the lines needed to read each annual rate.

SELF-CHECK EXERCISES FOR SECTION 3.7

1. Write the `WHILE` loop for a program that prints all powers of an integer, *n*, less than a specified value, `MaxPower`. On each line of a table, show the power (0, 1, 2, ...) and the value of the integer *n* raised to that power.
2. Write the `WHILE` loop for a program that prints a table of equivalent Fahrenheit and Celsius temperature values. Use the formula

```
Fahrenheit = 1.8 * Celsius + 32.0
```

to convert from degrees Celsius to Fahrenheit. Assume that the initial and final Celsius values are available in `InitCel` and `FinalCel` (type `REAL`), respectively, and that the temperature change between table entries is given by `StepCel`.

3.8 Displaying a Table of Values

The program in Fig. 3.14 displays a table with three output columns. The string constant `Pad` is used to shift the table to the right portion of the screen so that the table will not be confused with any display lines used for data entry. After the cursor is shifted right, three column headings are displayed by the statement

```
WriteString ('Year        Interest        Balance');
```

which must appear before the `WHILE` loop.

Inside the `WHILE` loop, the statements

```
WriteCard (Year, 4);      WriteReal (Interest, 15);
WriteReal Balance, 15);   WriteLn
```

are used to display three values on each line of the table. The field widths were chosen so that each value would be right justified under its column heading, that is, the last digit of each number is aligned with the last letter of its column heading.

The table displayed on the right side of Fig. 3.14 is not very readable because all real values are in scientific notation. What is needed is a utility procedure that can display a real value in normal decimal form. Modula-2 does not provide such a procedure, but Chapter 6 will discuss how to write your own procedure called (`WriteRealFormat`) to do this.

If Procedure `WriteRealFormat` is available, the procedure call statements

```
WriteCard (Year, 4);
WriteRealFormat (Interest, 15, 2);
WriteRealFormat (Balance, 15, 2);    WriteLn;
```

could be used to display a table line. In the procedure call statement

```
WriteRealFormat (Interest, 15, 2);
```

`Interest`, `15`, and `2` are the *actual parameters* that are passed into the procedure; they specify what value will be printed (`Interest`), how many characters (15) will be used, and how many decimal places (2) will be displayed. (Procedure parameters are the subject of the next chapter.) Following are the first few lines of the table in Fig. 3.14 using `WriteRealFormat` instead of `WriteReal` to display `Interest` and `Balance`.

```
Year   Interest   Balance
 1       7.50     107.50
 2       8.60     116.10
 3       9.86     125.96
```

3.9 Common Programming Errors

Beginners sometimes confuse `IF` and `WHILE` statements because both statements contain a condition. Make sure you use an `IF` statement to implement a decision step and a `WHILE` statement to implement a conditional loop. Remember to terminate each control structure with an `END`, or the compiler will detect a syntax error.

Be careful when using tests for inequality to control the repetition of a `WHILE` loop. The following loop is intended to process all transactions for a bank account while the balance is positive.

```
WHILE Balance # 0.0 DO
  UpDate (Balance)
END
```

If the bank balance goes from a positive to a negative amount without being exactly 0.0, the loop will not terminate (an *infinite loop*). The loop below would be safer.

```
WHILE Balance > 0.0 DO
  UpDate (Balance)
END
```

Verify that the repetition condition for a `WHILE` loop will eventually become false. If you use a sentinel-controlled loop, remember to provide a prompt that tells the program user what value to enter as the sentinel. Make sure that the sentinel value cannot be entered as a normal data item.

3.10 Chapter Review

Syntax diagrams were introduced in this chapter, and we saw how to use them to check the syntax of a Modula-2 statement. A complete set of syntax diagrams for Modula-2 is in Appendix C.

The `IF` statement was examined more formally. We saw how to use multiple-alternative `IF` statements to implement decisions with several alternatives.

A conditional looping structure, the `WHILE` statement, was used to implement loops whose repetition is controlled by a condition. The `WHILE` statement is useful when the exact number of repetitions required is not known before the loop begins. In designing a `WHILE` loop, we must consider both the loop control and the loop processing operations that must be performed. Separate Modula-2 statements are needed to initialize and update variables appearing in the loop repetition condition.

A common technique for controlling the repetition of a `WHILE` loop is the use of a special sentinel value to indicate that all required data have been processed. In this case, an input variable must appear in the loop repetition condition. The variable is initialized when the first data value is read *(priming read)* and is updated at the end of the loop when the next data value is read. Loop repetition terminates when the sentinel value is read.

The use of assertions and loop invariants in loop verification and loop design was also introduced. Loop invariants can be used to document the processing performed by the loop body.

Table 3.5 ▸ *Summary of New Modula-2 Statements*

STATEMENT	EFFECT

Multiple-alternative Decision
`IF Score >= 90 THEN`
`  Write('A');`
`  INC. (CountA)`
`ELSIF Score >= 80 THEN`
`  Write('B');`
`  INC. (CountB)`
`ELSE`
`  Write('C');`
`  INC. (CountC)`
`END (* IF *)`
	`IF Score` is greater than or equal to `90`, `THEN` the first alternative is executed; otherwise, `IF Score` is greater than or equal to `80`, the second alternative is executed; otherwise, the third alternative is executed.

WHILE Statement
`Sum := 0;`
`WHILE Sum <= MaxSum DO`
`  Write ('Next integer: ');`
`  ReadInt (Next);`
`  WriteLn;`
`  Sum := Sum + Next`
`END (* WHILE *)`
	A collection of input data items is read and their sum is accumulated in `Sum`. This process stops when the accumulated sum exceeds `MaxSum`.

New Modula-2 Statements

The new Modula-2 statements introduced in Chapter 3 are described in Table 3.5.

CHAPTER 3 ▸

Review Questions

1. How can syntax diagrams aid a new user in becoming comfortable with an unfamiliar programming language?
2. Given the following syntax diagram, circle the words under the diagram that are valid.

Syntax Diagram for Words

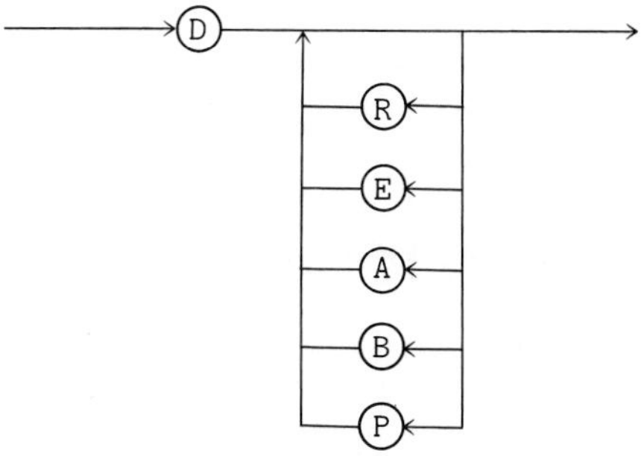

PEAR BREAD DREAR DEADEN DAD DRRAB

3. Define a sentinel value.
4. For a sentinel value to be used properly when data is being read, where should the input statements appear?
5. Write a program called `Sum` to sum and print a collection of payroll amounts entered at the keyboard until a sentinel value of `-1` is entered. Use a `WHILE` statement.
6. Hand trace the following program given the following data:

```
4,2,8,4,   1,4,2,1,   9,3,3,1,   -22,10,8,2

MODULE Slope;

  FROM InOut IMPORT
    WriteString, WriteLn;

  FROM RealInOut IMPORT
    ReadReal, WriteReal;

  CONST
    Sentinel = 0.0;

  VAR
    Slope, y2, y1, x2, x1 : REAL;
```

```
BEGIN (* Slope *)
  WriteString ('Enter four real numbers');  WriteLn;
  ReadReal (y2);  WriteLn;
  ReadReal (y1);  WriteLn;
  ReadReal (x2);  WriteLn;
  ReadReal (x1);  WriteLn;
  Slope := (y2 - y1) / (x2 - x1);
  WHILE Slope # Sentinel DO
    WriteString ('Slope is ');
    WriteReal (Slope, 5);  WriteLn;
    WriteLn;
    WriteString ('Enter four real numbers');  WriteLn;
    ReadReal (y2);  WriteLn;
    ReadReal (y1);  WriteLn;
    ReadReal (x2);  WriteLn;
    ReadReal (x1);  WriteLn;
    Slope := (y2 - y1) / (x2 - x1)
  END (* WHILE *)
END Slope.
```

7. Explain when it is appropriate to use semicolons within
   a. the variable declaration statement
   b. the constant declaration statement
   c. the program body
   d. an `IF` statement

8. Which of the statements below is incorrect?
   a. Loop invariants are used in loop verification.
   b. Loop invariants are used in loop design.
   a. A loop invariant is always an assertion.
   b. An assertion is always a loop invariant.

CHAPTER 3 ▸

Programming Projects

1. Write a program that will find the product of a collection of data values. Your program should terminate when a zero value is read.

2. Write a program to read in an integer `N` and compute `Slow` = `i` = `1 + 2 + 3 + ... + N` (the sum of all integers from 1 to *N*). Then compute `Fast` = `(N × (N + 1)) / 2` and compare `Fast` and `Slow`. Your program should print both `Fast` and `Slow` and indicate whether they are equal. (You will need a loop to compute `Slow`.) Which computation method is preferable?

3. Write a program to read a list of integer data items and find and print the index of the first and last occurrence of the number 12. Your program should print an index value of 0 if the number 12 is not found. The index is the sequence number of the data item 12. For example, if the `8th` data item is the only 12, then the index value 8 should be printed for the first and last occurrence.

4. Write a program to read in a collection of exam scores ranging in value from 1 to 100. Your program should count and print the number of outstanding scores (90–100), the number of satisfactory scores (60–89), and the number of unsatisfactory scores (1–59). Test your program on the following data:

63	75	72	72	78	67	80	63	75
90	89	43	59	99	82	12	100	

In addition, print each exam score and its category.

5. Write a program to process weekly employee time cards for all employees of an organization. Each employee will have three data items indicating an identification number, the hourly wage rate, and the number of hours worked during a given week. Each employee is to be paid time-and-a-half for all hours worked over 40. A tax amount of 3.625 percent of gross salary will be deducted. The program output should show the employee's number and net pay.

6. Suppose you own a beer distributorship that sells Piels (ID number 1), Coors (ID number 2), Bud (ID number 3), and Iron City (ID number 4) by the case. Write a program to (a) read in the case inventory for each brand for the start of the week; (b) process all weekly sales and purchase records for each brand; and (c) print out the final inventory. Each transaction will consist of two data items. The first item will be the brand identification number (an integer). The second will be the amount purchased (a positive integer value) or the amount sold (a negative integer value). The weekly inventory for each brand (for the start of the week) will also consist of two items: the identification and the initial inventory for that brand. For now, you may assume that you always have sufficient foresight to prevent depletion of your inventory for any brand. (*Hint:* Your data entry should begin with eight values representing the case inventory, which should be followed by the transaction values.)

7. Write a program to find the largest, smallest, and average value in a collection of N numbers where the value of N will be the first data item read.

4 ▸ Procedure Parameters

CHAPTER 2 INTRODUCED procedures to write separate program units corresponding to the individual steps in a problem solution. You have not used procedures extensively because we have not yet discussed how to pass information between individual procedures or between procedures and the main program. So far, our procedures can manipulate only data that are stored locally.

This chapter introduces an important concept in programming: the use of procedure parameters. You will see that parameters provide a convenient way to pass information between a main program and a procedure. Parameters also make procedures more versatile because they enable a procedure to manipulate different sets of data.

4.1 Actual Parameter Lists

We can make an analogy between a carefully designed program that uses procedures and a stereo system. Each stereo component is an independent device that performs a specific function. There may be similar electronic parts inside the tuner and amplifier, but each component uses its own internal circuitry to perform its required function.

Information in the form of electronic signals is passed back and forth between the components over wires. If you look at the rear of a stereo amplifier, you will find some plugs marked *inputs* and others marked *outputs*. The wires attached to the plugs marked *inputs* carry electronic signals into the amplifier, where they are processed. (The signals may come from a tape deck, a tuner, or a turntable.) New electronic signals are generated. These signals come out of the amplifier from the plugs marked *outputs* and go to the speakers or back to the tape deck for recording.

So far, we have discussed how to design the separate components (procedures) of a programming system, but not how to pass data between them. This chapter will explain how to use *parameter lists* to specify the inputs and outputs of a procedure.

Each procedure call statement has two parts: a procedure name and an *actual parameter list*. In the procedure call statement

```
WriteInt (Num, 3)
```

the actual parameter list is (`Num, 3`). The actual parameters, `Num` and `3`, pass information into utility procedure `WriteInt`. The first actual parameter, `Num`, specifies the variable whose value is displayed. The second actual parameter, `3`, specifies the number of columns used in displaying `Num`. We know that the first parameter for procedure WriteInt must be type INTEGER and the second parameter must be type CARDINAL (normally a constant).

Both Num and 3 are inputs to the procedure. There are no procedure outputs in that there is no information returned by WriteInt to the calling program. WriteInt does display a value, but it is considered an action of the procedure, not a procedure output. Next we will see how to declare a procedure with parameters.

4.2 Formal Parameter Lists

Let us assume that utility procedure Write and WriteCard are available but, for some reason, our Modula-2 system does not have procedure WriteInt. We can write our own procedure to display an integer value as shown in Fig. 4.1. We will call our procedure OurWriteInt to avoid confusing it with the missing procedure WriteInt.

Figure 4.1 ▸ *Procedure OurWriteInt*

```
PROCEDURE OurWriteInt (N : INTEGER;  Width : CARDINAL);

(*
   Displays an integer value, N, using Width characters.
*)
   CONST
     Minus = '-';

BEGIN (* OurWriteInt *)
  IF N < 0 THEN
    N := -N;             (* convert N to positive integer *)
    Write (Minus);                     (* display sign *)
    IF Width # 0 THEN
      DEC (Width)                   (* decrement Width *)
    END (* inner IF *)
  END; (* outer IF *)
  WriteCard (ORD(N), Width)  (* display N as a cardinal *)
END OurWriteInt;
```

The procedure header contains the *formal parameter list*

```
(N : INTEGER;  Width : CARDINAL)
```

This formal parameter list indicates that the first actual parameter will be represented in the procedure by N (type INTEGER) and the second actual parameter by Width (type CARDINAL). N and Width are called *formal parameters*.

If N is negative, the IF statement changes N to a positive value and displays a minus sign. Next, if Width is not zero, the standard procedure DEC decrements Width by one because a minus sign was displayed. Regardless of whether N was initially positive or negative, the statement

```
WriteCard (ORD(N), Width)  (* display N as a cardinal *)
```

displays the type CARDINAL number corresponding to the positive integer N using Width characters. (Function ORD, which converts the integer value in N to a cardinal number, will be described in the next chapter, along with procedure DEC.)

Table 4.1 traces the execution of OurWriteInt for the procedure call statement

```
OurWriteInt (-15, 3)
```

The procedure call sets the value of N to −15 and of Width to 3. Because N is negative, the IF statement causes a minus sign to be displayed and N and Width to be changed to 15 and 2, respectively. Procedure WriteCard displays 15 after the minus sign, using 2 characters as desired.

Table 4.1 ▸ *Trace of OurWriteInt (−15, 3)*

STATEMENT IN OurWriteInt	N	Width	CardN	EFFECT
	−15	3	?	
IF N < 0 THEN				−15 < 0 is true
N := −N;	15			
Write (Minus);				Displays a minus sign
IF Width # 0 ...				2 # 0 is true
DEC (Width);		2		decrement Width
WriteCard (ORD(N), ...)				Displays 15

We can use procedure OurWriteInt to display other integer values. For example, the procedure call statement

```
OurWriteInt (-5, 3)
```

sets the value of N to −5 and Width to 3. The procedure's execution displays the three characters −5. Unfortunately the space comes after the minus sign rather than before. (Why?)

If Num is a type INTEGER variable, the statement

```
OurWriteInt (Num, 0)
```

calls OurWriteInt to display the value of Num. Since the second actual parameter is 0, the procedure's execution displays this value using as many characters as necessary.

SIMPLE SORTING PROBLEM

In this section, we will write a procedure that orders a pair of real numbers and a main program that uses that procedure to order three numbers.

Problem: Write a program that reads any three numbers into the variables `Num1`, `Num2`, `Num3` and rearranges the data so that the smallest number is stored in `Num1`, the next smaller number in `Num2`, and the largest number in `Num3`.

Discussion: This is a special case of a *sorting problem*: rearranging a collection of data items so that the values are either in increasing or decreasing order. Because there are only three items to be sorted, we will solve this special case now; the general sorting problem is a bit more complicated and will be considered later. The problem inputs and outputs are described below.

PROBLEM INPUTS

three numbers (`Num1, Num2, Num3 : REAL`)

PROBLEM OUTPUTS

the three numbers stored in increasing order in `Num1`, `Num2`, `Num3`

Algorithm

1. Read the three numbers into `Num1`, `Num2`, and `Num3`.
2. Place the smallest number in `Num1`, the next smaller in `Num2`, and the largest number in `Num3`.
3. Print `Num1`, `Num2`, and `Num3`

Think of the three variables `Num1`, `Num2`, `Num3` as representing a list of consecutive storage cells. To perform step 2, we can compare pairs of numbers, always moving the smaller number of the pair closer to the front of the list (`Num1`) and the larger number closer to the end of the list (`Num3`). It should take three comparisons to sort the numbers in the list; one possible sequence of comparisons is shown next.

STEP 2 REFINEMENT

2.1 Compare `Num1` and `Num2`; store the smaller number in `Num1` and the larger number in `Num2`.
2.2 Compare `Num1` and `Num3`; store the smaller number in `Num1` and the larger number in `Num3`.
2.3 Compare `Num2` and `Num3` and store the smaller number in `Num2` and the larger number in `Num3`.

Table 4.2 traces this refinement for the input sequence: 8, 10, 6. The final order is correct.

Table 4.2 ▸ *Trace of Step 2 Refinement for Input Data 8, 10, 6*

ALGORITHM STEP	Num1	Num2	Num3	EFFECT
	8	10	6	
2.1	8	10		Num1, Num2 are in order
2.2	6		8	Switch Num1 and Num3
2.3		8	10	Switch Num2 and Num3

The structure chart for this algorithm is shown in Fig. 4.2. Since steps 2.1, 2.2, and 2.3 perform the same operation on different data, it would be a waste of time and effort to write a different procedure for each step. We would like to be able to write one general procedure to order any pair of numbers. This procedure is shown in Fig. 4.3.

Figure 4.2 ▸ *Structure Chart for Simple Sorting Problem*

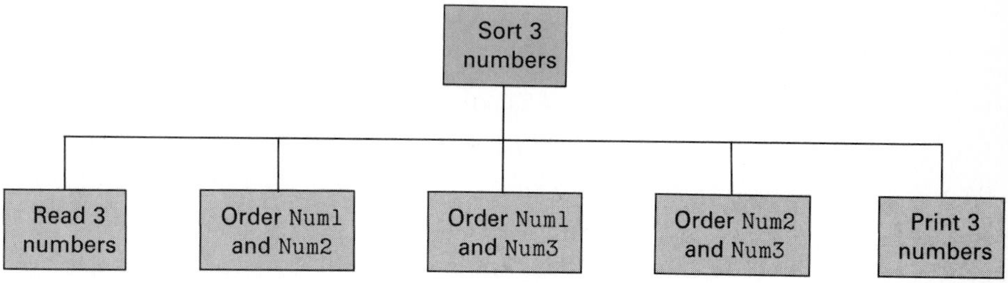

Figure 4.3 ▸ *Procedure Order*

```
PROCEDURE Order (VAR X, Y : REAL);
(*
  Orders a pair of numbers represented by X and Y so that the
  smaller number is in X and the larger number is in Y.
*)
   VAR
     Temp : REAL;            (* copy of number originally in X *)

BEGIN (* Order *)
  IF X > Y THEN
    (* Switch the values of X and Y *)
    Temp := X;                          (* Store old X in Temp *)
    X := Y;                             (* Store old Y in X *)
    Y := Temp                           (* Store old X in Y *)
  END (* IF *)
END Order;
```

The body of procedure `Order` consists of the `IF` statement from Example 3.3. The procedure heading contains the formal parameter list

```
(VAR X, Y : REAL)
```

This formal parameter list identifies the formal parameters (X and Y) that will be used within the procedure in place of the variable names; the actual variables to be manipulated are determined when the procedure is called. Think of X and Y as generic names for the procedure data; the specific names will be supplied later.

The use of formal parameters in a procedure is analogous to the use of the names *defendant* and *plaintiff* in a legal document. The name *defendant* in the body of the document refers to the individual who is accused; the name *plaintiff* refers to the individual doing the accusing. The actual names of the people involved are specified on a separate cover sheet preceding the document.

A formal parameter list describes a template or pattern that is partially filled in. The template described by the formal parameter list for procedure Order follows. The part that is filled in indicates that formal parameters X and Y represent type REAL variables. The missing entries in the template are the actual variables to be manipulated (actual parameters); these entries are filled in when the procedure call statement is executed.

Actual Parameters	*Formal Parameters*	*Description*
___________	X	REAL variable
___________	Y	REAL variable

The following procedure call statement contains an actual parameter list enclosed in parentheses.

```
Order (Num1, Num2)
```

This actual parameter list causes the template to be completed as follows:

Actual Parameters	*Formal Parameters*	*Description*
Num1	X	REAL variable
Num2	Y	REAL variable

The completed template shows that formal parameters X and Y represent the variables Num1 and Num2, respectively. This means that whenever X is referenced in the procedure, the variable Num1 will be manipulated. Thus, the procedure call statement

```
Order (Num1, Num2)
```

can be used to perform step 2.1 of the algorithm: store the smaller number in Num1 and the larger number in Num2.

The sequence of the actual parameters is important. The first actual parameter is paired with the first formal parameter, the second actual parameter is paired with the second formal parameter, and so on. The procedure call statement

```
Order (Num2, Num1)
```

would cause the smaller number to be stored in Num2 and the larger number in Num1 instead of the other way around. (Complete the partial template above to see why this is so.)

The final program is shown in Fig. 4.4. The main program body contains three statements that call procedure Order:

```
Order (Num1, Num2);        (* Order the data in Num1 and Num2 *)
Order (Num1, Num3);        (* Order the data in Num1 and Num3 *)
Order (Num2, Num3);        (* Order the data in Num2 and Num3 *)
```

Since each statement contains a different actual parameter list, a different pair of variables will be manipulated each time the procedure is called. We will see how this is done in the next section.

Figure 4.4 ▸ *Program to Order Three Numbers*

```
MODULE Sort3Numbers;
(*
   Reads three numbers and sorts them
   so that they are in increasing order.
*)
   FROM InOut IMPORT
     WriteString, WriteLn;

   FROM RealInOut IMPORT
     ReadReal, WriteReal;

   VAR
     Num1, Num2, Num3 : REAL;         (* a list of three cells *)


   PROCEDURE Order (VAR X, Y : REAL);
   (*
      Orders a pair of numbers represented by X and Y so that the
      smaller number is in X and the larger number is in Y.
      Pre : X and Y are assigned values.
      Post: X has the smaller value and Y has the larger value.
   *)
      VAR
        Temp : REAL;           (* copy of number originally in X *)

   BEGIN  (* Order *)
     IF X > Y THEN
       (* Switch the values of X and Y *)
       Temp := X;                          (* Store old X in Temp *)
       X := Y;                             (* Store old Y in X *)
       Y := Temp                           (* Store old X in Y *)
     END (* IF *)
   END Order;

BEGIN  (* Sort3Numbers *)
```

```
  WriteString ('Enter 3 numbers to be sorted, one per line.');
  WriteLn;
  ReadReal (Num1);  WriteLn;
  ReadReal (Num2);  WriteLn;
  ReadReal (Num3);  WriteLn;

  (* Sort the numbers *)
  Order (Num1, Num2);          (* Order the data in Num1 and Num2 *)
  Order (Num1, Num3);          (* Order the data in Num1 and Num3 *)
  Order (Num2, Num3);          (* Order the data in Num2 and Num3 *)

  (* Print the results. *)
  WriteString ('The three numbers in order are: ');
  WriteReal (Num1, 12);  WriteReal (Num2, 12);  WriteReal (Num3, 12);
  WriteLn
END Sort3Numbers.
```

```
Enter 3 numbers to be sorted, one per line.
8.0
10.0
6.0
The three numbers in order are:
 6.0000E+000 8.0000E+000 1.0000E+001
```

Program Style

Preconditions and Postconditions as Comments

The declaration for procedure `Order` begins with a lengthy comment that describes its operations. We use the commenting style

```
(*
   ... comments ...
*)
```

for comments that extend over multiple lines.

The comment line

```
Pre : X and Y are assigned values.
```

describes the condition that must be true before the procedure is called and is called the *precondition*. The comment line

```
Post: X has the smaller value and Y has the larger value.
```

describes the condition that must be true after the procedure execution is completed and is called the *postcondition*. The use of explicit preconditions and postconditions provides valuable documentation to other programmers who might want to use procedure `Order`. It also aids in verifying the correctness of a program that calls this procedure.

Executing a Procedure with Parameters

Figure 4.5 shows the data areas for the main program and procedure `Order` immediately after the execution of the procedure call statement

```
Order (Num1, Num2);       (* Order the data in Num1 and Num2 *)
```

This diagram shows the data values read into `Num1`, `Num2`, and `Num3`. It also shows that the local variable `Temp` is considered undefined immediately after the procedure is called.

Figure 4.5 also shows the parameter correspondence specified by the previous actual parameter list. The double-headed arrows symbolize the connection between formal parameters `X` and `Y` and main program variables `Num1` and `Num2`, respectively. Whenever `X` is referenced in the procedure, the data in variable `Num1` are manipulated.

Figure 4.5 ▸ *Parameter Correspondence for Order (Num1, Num2)*

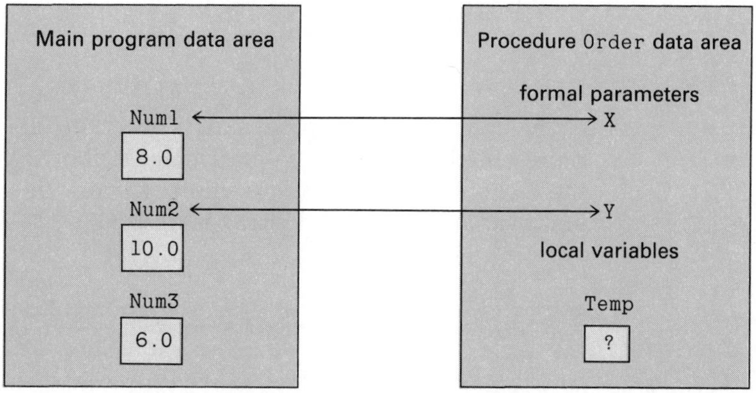

The execution of the procedure is traced in Table 4.3. The actual parameter represented by each formal parameter is shown in parentheses at the top of the table. Since the value of `Num1` is less than the value of `Num2`, the true alternative is skipped and the variable values are unchanged.

Table 4.3 ▸ *Trace of Procedure Execution for Order (Num1, Num2)*

STATEMENT IN ORDER	X(Num1)	Y(Num2)	Temp	EFFECT
	8.0	10.0	?	
IF X > Y THEN				8.0 > 10.0 is false; do nothing

The parameter correspondence specified by the procedure call statement

```
Order (Num1, Num3);
```

is pictured in Fig. 4.6. This time parameter `X` corresponds to variable `Num1`, and parameter `Y` corresponds to variable `Num3`. This means that whenever formal parameter `Y` is referenced in the procedure, the data in main program variable `Num3` are manipulated.

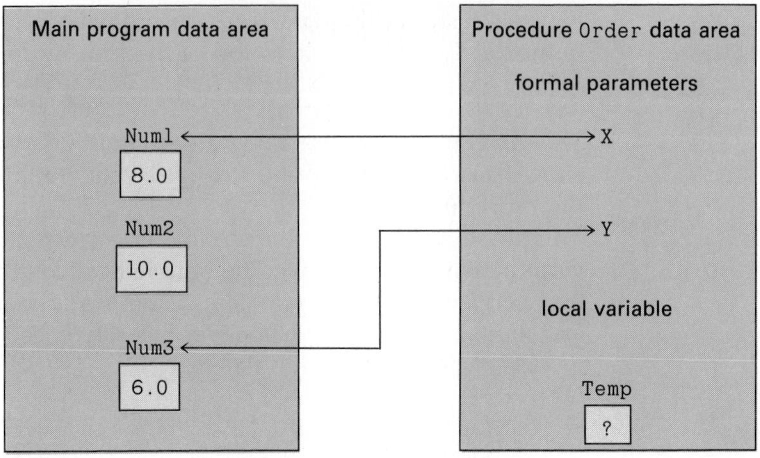

Figure 4.6 ▸ *Parameter Correspondence for Order (Num1, Num3)*

The execution of the procedure is traced in Table 4.4. The actual parameter represented by each formal parameter is shown in parentheses at the top of the table. The procedure execution switches the values stored in main program variables `Num1` and `Num3`, as desired.

Table 4.4 ▸ *Trace of Procedure Execution for Order (Num1, Num3)*

STATEMENT IN ORDER	X(Num1)	Y(Num3)	Temp	EFFECT
	8.0	6.0	?	
`IF X > Y THEN`				`8.0 > 6.0` is true;
`Temp := X;`			8.0	save old `Num1` in `Temp`;
`X := Y;`	6.0			save old `Num3` in `Num1`;
`Y := Temp`		8.0		save `Temp` in `Num3`

SELF-CHECK EXERCISES FOR SECTION 4.2

1. Draw the templates for parameter correspondence specified by the procedure calls

```
Order (Num1, Num3);
Order (Num2, Num3)
```

2. Trace the execution of the three procedure call statements

```
Order (Num3, Num2);
Order (Num3, Num1);
Order (Num2, Num1)
```

for the data sets: 8.0, 10.0, 6.0 and 10.0, 8.0, 6.0. What does this sequence do?

4.3 Variable and Value Parameters

In procedure `Order`, formal parameters `X` and `Y` are called *variable parameters*, because they correspond to actual parameters that are variables during each execution of the procedure. The reserved word `VAR` in the formal parameter list

```
(VAR X, Y : REAL)
```

indicates that `X` and `Y` are variable parameters. The parameters used with a Modula-2 input procedure (e.g., `Read`, `ReadCard`) are also variable parameters.

As we saw in Table 4.4, it is possible for a procedure execution to change the value of an actual parameter that corresponds to a variable formal parameter. Both `Num1` and `Num3` were changed by the procedure execution traced in Table 4.4. Only variables can be used as variable parameters (e.g., `Order(5.0, 3.7)` causes a syntax error).

In some situations, a parameter is used only to pass data into a procedure, and we know beforehand that the actual parameter value should not be changed by the procedure. Although a variable parameter could be used for this purpose, Modula-2 provides a second type of parameter, called a *value parameter*, which is usually preferred.

The Modula-2 utility procedures for displaying results use value parameters. `N` and `Width` in the formal parameter list shown in Fig. 4.1 and repeated in the following procedure header are also value parameters.

```
PROCEDURE OurWriteInt (N : INTEGER;  Width : CARDINAL);
```

The fact that neither parameter is preceded by the reserved word `VAR` indicates that they are value parameters.

An actual parameter that corresponds to a value parameter may be an expression of the same type as the value parameter where constants and variables are considered forms of expressions. The following procedure call statements show some typical actual parameter lists.

```
WriteString ('Value is ');
OurWriteInt (Num, 5);
WriteCard (ORD(N), Width-1)
```

The actual parameters are a string literal, a variable (`Num`), a cardinal literal (`5`), an expression (`ORD(N)`), and another expression (`Width-1`), in that order.

Modula-2 allocates a local memory cell in the procedure data area for each formal parameter that is a value parameter. Each local cell is initialized to the value of its corresponding actual parameter when the procedure is called, and there is no further connection between the actual and formal parameter. When a value parameter is referenced within the procedure, the local cell is manipulated. Consequently, even if the local data are modified, the actual parameter value cannot be changed.

The next two examples illustrate the use of value parameters.

EXAMPLE 4.1 ▶ Procedure PrintLine in Fig. 4.7 prints a row of asterisks. In the procedure heading

```
PROCEDURE PrintLine (NumStars : CARDINAL);
```

`NumStars` is declared to be a formal parameter of type `CARDINAL`; `NumStars` is a value parameter (indicated by the absence of the word `VAR`).

Figure 4.7 ▶
Procedure PrintLine

```
PROCEDURE PrintLine (NumStars : CARDINAL);
(*
   Prints a row of asterisks. The number of
   asterisks printed is determined by NumStars.
   Pre :  NumStars is assigned a value.
   Post:  A row of asterisks is displayed.
*)
   CONST
     Star = '*';                 (* symbol being printed *)

   VAR
     CountStar : CARDINAL;       (* loop control for PrintLine *)

BEGIN (* PrintLine *)
  (* Print a row of asterisks *)
  FOR CountStar := 1 TO NumStars DO
    Write (Star)
  END; (* FOR *)
  WriteLn
END PrintLine;
```

Parameter `NumStars` determines how many asterisks are printed, and its initial value is passed into procedure `PrintLine` when the procedure is called. Since there is no need for the procedure to change its parameter value, `NumStars` is declared to be a value parameter. The three procedure call statements

```
PrintLine (5);
PrintLine (3);
PrintLine (1)
```

would cause the three lines below to be printed.

```
*****
***
*
```

An integer value (5, 3, or 1) is assigned to NumStars when each procedure call statement is executed. ◂

EXAMPLE 4.2 ▸ Procedure Triangle in Fig. 4.8 uses procedure PrintLine to draw a triangle. This example shows that a procedure may be declared locally in another procedure and called by that procedure.

Figure 4.8 ▸ *Procedure Triangle*

```
PROCEDURE Triangle (NumRows : CARDINAL);
(*
   Prints a triangle by displaying lines of increasing length.
   The number of lines is determined by NumRows.
    Pre: NumRows is assigned a value.
   Post: A triangle is displayed.
   Uses: PrintLine
*)
   VAR
     Row : CARDINAL;            (* loop control for Triangle *)

   PROCEDURE PrintLine (NumStars : INTEGER);
   (*
      Prints a row of asterisks. The number of
      asterisks printed is determined by NumStars.
      Pre : NumStars is assigned a value.
      Post: A row of asterisks is displayed.
   *)
      CONST
        Star = '*';               (* symbol being printed *)

      VAR
        CountStar : CARDINAL;     (* loop control for PrintLine *)

   BEGIN (* PrintLine *)
     (* Print a row of asterisks *)
     FOR CountStar := 1 TO NumStars DO
        Write (Star)
     END; (* FOR *)
     WriteLn
   END PrintLine;
```

```
BEGIN (* Triangle *)
  (* Print lines of increasing length *)
  FOR Row := 1 TO NumRows DO
    PrintLine (Row)
  END (* FOR *)
END Triangle;
```

The `FOR` statement in the body of procedure `Triangle`

```
FOR ROW := 1 TO NumRows DO
  PrintLine (ROW)
END (* FOR *)
```

calls procedure `PrintLine` repeatedly; each time `PrintLine` is called, the current value of `Row` (`1` to `NumRows`) determines how many asterisks will be printed.

The parameter `NumRows` determines the number of lines in the triangle. The procedure call statement

```
Triangle (5)
```

assigns a value of `5` to `NumRows` and causes the triangle below to be drawn. ◂

```
*
**
***
****
*****
```

Because procedure `PrintLine` is declared within procedure `Triangle`, `PrintLine` is considered a local identifier in `Triangle`, and `PrintLine` can be called only by `Triangle` (or by `PrintLine` itself). The *scope of identifiers* will be discussed in detail in Section 4.6.

When to Use a Variable or a Value Parameter

You may be wondering how to tell when to use a variable parameter and when to use a value parameter. Some rules of thumb follow:

- If information is to be passed into a procedure and does not have to be returned, then the formal parameter representing that information can be a value parameter. Such a parameter is called an *input parameter* or a *procedure input* (e.g., `NumStars` and `NumRows` in Fig. 4.8).
- If information is to be passed out of a procedure, then the formal parameter representing that information must be a variable parameter. Such a parameter is called an *output parameter* or a *procedure output*.
- If information is to be passed into a procedure, perhaps modified, and a new value returned, then the formal parameter representing that informa-

tion must be a variable parameter. Such a parameter is called an *input/output parameter* or an *in/out parameter* (e.g., X and Y in Fig. 4.3).

Remember, it is all right to use an expression (or a variable or a constant) as an actual parameter corresponding to a value parameter; however, only a variable can be used as an actual parameter corresponding to a variable parameter. The reason for this restriction is that an actual parameter corresponding to a variable parameter may be modified when the procedure executes; it is illogical to allow a procedure to change the value of either a constant or an expression.

The next example shows a procedure with a value parameter (for input) and a variable parameter (for output).

EXAMPLE 4.3 ▶ Procedure `FindTax` in Fig. 4.9 implements the income tax table (see Table 3.3). The procedure body consists of the `IF` statement first shown in Fig. 3.5. A value is passed into parameter `Salary` (a value parameter) when the procedure is called. If `Salary` is within the range of the table, a value is assigned to parameter `Tax` (a variable parameter) during procedure execution. This value is *returned* or passed out of the procedure. The comments `(* input *)` and `(* output *)` document the use of formal parameters `Salary` and `Tax`, respectively.

Figure 4.9 ▶ *Driver Program with Procedure FindTax*

```
MODULE Driver;

(* Tests procedure FindTax *)

   FROM InOut IMPORT
     WriteString, WriteLn;

   FROM RealInOut IMPORT
     ReadReal, WriteReal;

   VAR
     MySalary, MyTax : REAL;              (* salary and tax *)

   PROCEDURE FindTax (Salary (* input *) : REAL;
                      VAR Tax (* output *) : REAL);
   (*
      Computes tax amount (Tax) owed for a
      salary (Salary) < $15000.
      Pre : Salary is assigned a value.
      Post: Tax is assigned a value or
            an error message is displayed.
   *)
   BEGIN  (* FindTax *)
```

```
      IF Salary < 0.0 THEN
        WriteString ('Error!  Negative Salary $');
        WriteReal (Salary, 12);
        WriteLn
      ELSIF Salary < 1500.00 THEN                  (* first range *)
        Tax := 0.15 * Salary
      ELSIF Salary < 3000.00 THEN                  (* second range *)
        Tax := (Salary - 1500.00) * 0.16 + 225.00
      ELSIF Salary < 5000.00 THEN                  (* third range *)
        Tax := (Salary - 3000.00) * 0.18 + 465.00
      ELSIF Salary < 8000.00 THEN                  (* fourth range *)
        Tax := (Salary - 5000.00) * 0.20 + 865.00
      ELSIF Salary < 15000.00 THEN                 (* fifth range *)
        Tax := (Salary - 8000.00) * 0.25 + 1425.00
      ELSE
        WriteString ('Error!  Too large Salary $');
        WriteReal (Salary, 12);
        WriteLn
      END (* IF *)
    END FindTax;

BEGIN  (* Driver *)
  WriteString ('Enter a Salary less than $15000.00:  $');
  ReadReal (MySalary);  WriteLn;
  FindTax (MySalary, MyTax);
  WriteString ('The tax on $');
  WriteReal (MySalary, 12);
  WriteString (' is $');
  WriteReal (MyTax, 12);  WriteLn
END Driver.


Enter a salary less than $15000.00:  $6000.00
The tax on $ 6.0000E+003 is $ 1.0650E+003
```

The parameter correspondence specified by the procedure call statement

```
FindTax (MySalary, MyTax)
```

is shown in Fig. 4.10. The dashed line leading to value parameter `Salary` indicates that the connection between the actual and the formal parameter is broken after the actual parameter value is stored locally. Assuming a data value of `6000.00` was read into `MySalary` before `FindTax` was called, the value `1065.00` would be assigned to `MyTax` during the execution of procedure `FindTax`. ◂

Figure 4.10 ▸ *Parameter Correspondence for FindTax (MySalary, MyTax)*

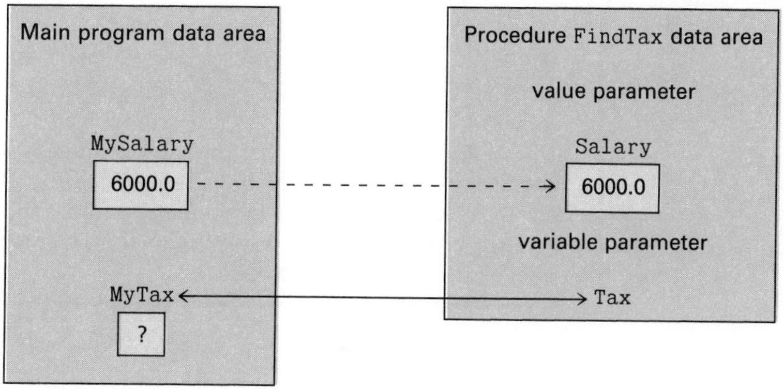

Program Style

Writing Formal Parameter Lists

In Fig. 4.9, the formal parameter list

```
(Salary (* input *) : REAL;
 VAR Tax (* output *) : REAL);
```

is written on two lines to improve program readability. The value parameter is written on the first line with the comment `(* input *)` inserted to document its use as a procedure input. The variable parameter is written on the second line with the comment `(* output *)`.

Generally we will follow the practice shown here in writing formal parameter lists. Input parameters will be listed first, then the input/output parameters, and any output parameters will be listed last. The order of the actual parameters in the procedure call must correspond to the order of the formal parameters.

Program Style

Cohesion Revisited

Procedure `FindTax` is concerned only with the tax computation. It does not read in a value for `Salary` or display the computed result. The result is returned to the calling program, which may display it or pass it on to another procedure that prints results. Only error messages are displayed by procedure `FindTax` in the event that the value passed to `Salary` is outside the range covered by the tax table. Now that you have seen how to use parameters to pass information between procedures and the main program, you can write cohesive procedures like `FindTax`, that is, procedures that perform a single operation (see Section 2.8).

Program Style

Writing Driver Programs to Test Procedures

The main program body in Fig. 4.9 consists of a statement for data entry, two statements for data display, and a procedure call statement. Its sole purpose is to test procedure `FindTax`. Such a program is called a *driver program*.

The use of driver programs to pretest procedures is highly recommended. Generally the small investment in time and effort required to write a short driver program will pay off by reducing the total time spent debugging a large program system containing several procedures.

The Procedure Data Area

Each time a procedure call statement is executed, an area of memory is allocated for storage of that procedure's data. Included in the procedure data area are storage cells for any local variables or constants that may be declared in the procedure. The procedure data area is always erased when the procedure terminates; it is re-created empty (all values undefined) when the procedure is called again.

Memory cells are allocated in the procedure data area for each formal parameter. These cells are used in different ways for value and variable parameters. For a value parameter, the local cell is used to hold a value; the value of the corresponding actual parameter is placed in this cell when the procedure is called. For a variable parameter, the local cell is used to hold a memory address; this is the address in the calling program data area of the corresponding actual parameter. This information enables the procedure to manipulate data stored in the calling program data area.

4.4 Syntax Rules for Parameter Lists

This section formally presents the syntax rules for procedure declarations and procedure call statements with parameters. The displays that follow summarize these rules.

Procedure Declaration (Procedure with Parameters) ▶

FORM:
```
PROCEDURE pname (formal parameters);
  declaration section
BEGIN
  procedure body
END pname;
```

EXAMPLE:
```
PROCEDURE Highlight (Ch : CHAR);
  CONST
    Border = '*';
```

```
BEGIN
  Write (Border);  Write (Ch);  Write (Border)
END Highlight;
```

INTERPRETATION: The procedure *pname* is declared. The *formal parameters* are enclosed in parentheses.

Any identifiers that are declared in the *declaration section* are defined only during the execution of the procedure.

The *procedure body* describes the data manipulation to be performed by the procedure. The formal parameter names are used in place of the actual parameter names in this description. For a variable parameter, the corresponding actual parameter is manipulated by the procedure; for a value parameter, a local memory cell is initialized to the actual parameter's value and is manipulated by the procedure without altering the actual parameter.

Procedure Call Statement (Procedure with Parameters)

FORM: *pname (actual parameters)*

EXAMPLE: `Highlight ('A')`

INTERPRETATION: The *actual parameters* are enclosed in parentheses. When procedure *pname* is called into execution, the first actual parameter is associated with the first formal parameter, the second actual parameter with the second formal parameter, and so on. For a value parameter, the actual parameter's value is saved in the procedure. For a variable parameter, the actual parameter's address is saved in the procedure.

Note: The actual parameters must satisfy the rules for parameter list correspondence (discussed later in this section).

Figure 4.11 *Syntax Diagram for a Formal Parameter List*

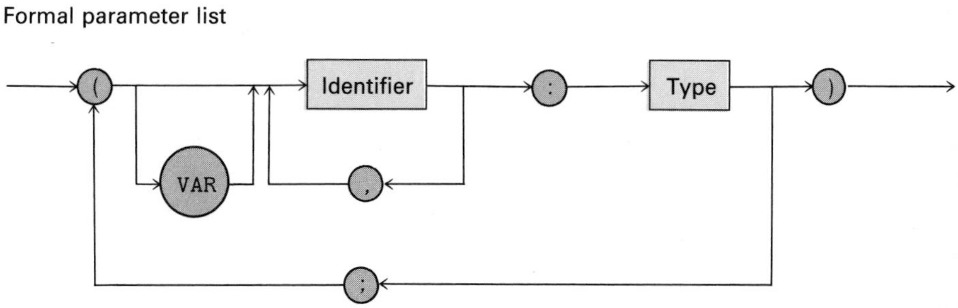

You must follow certain rules when writing parameter lists. The syntax diagram in Fig. 4.11 shows that a *formal parameter list* is always enclosed in parentheses. It consists of one or more lists of identifiers. Each list may be preceded by VAR. Identifiers are separated by commas, lists of identifiers are separated by semicolons, and each list must end with a colon followed by a data type name (e.g., REAL, CHAR).

EXAMPLE 4.4 ▶ Two formal parameter lists follow. Each list is printed on two or more lines to improve readability.

```
(Ch3 : CHAR;
 VAR X, Y, Z : REAL)

(M, N, O : INTEGER;
 A, B, C : REAL;
 VAR X, Y, Z : REAL)
```

In both lists above, X, Y, and Z are declared to be type REAL variable parameters; Ch3 is a type CHAR value parameter in the first list; A, B, C are type REAL value parameters in the second list; M, N, O are type INTEGER value parameters in the second list. ◀

The formal parameter list also determines the form of any actual parameter list that may be used to call the procedure. This form is determined during the translation of the program when the compiler processes the procedure declaration.

Later, when a procedure call statement is reached, the compiler checks the actual parameter list for consistency with the formal parameter list. An actual parameter list may be a list of expressions, variables, or constants separated by commas. The actual parameter list must satisfy the following rules.

Rules for Parameter List Correspondence

1. Correspondence between actual and formal parameters is determined by position in their respective parameter lists. These lists must be the same size. The names of corresponding actual and formal parameters may be different.
2. For variable parameters, the types of corresponding actual and formal parameters must be identical. For value parameters, the types of corresponding actual and formal parameters must be assignment compatible (discussed in Chapter 5).
3. For variable parameters, an actual parameter must be a variable. For value parameters, an actual parameter may be a variable, a constant, or an expression.

EXAMPLE 4.5 ▶ The main program contains the following declarations:

```
CONST
  MaxInt = 32767;
```

```
VAR
  X, Y : REAL;
  M : INTEGER;
  Next : CHAR;

PROCEDURE Test (A, B : INTEGER;
                VAR C, D : REAL;
                VAR E : CHAR);
```

where only the heading for procedure `Test` is shown. Any procedure call statement below would be syntactically correct in the main program.

```
Test (M + 3, 10, X, Y, Next)
Test (M, MaxInt, Y, X, Next)
Test (35, M * 10, Y, X, Next)
```

The correspondence specified by the first parameter list is shown in Table 4.5.

Table 4.5 ▸ *Parameter Correspondence for Test (M + 3, 10, X, Y, Next)*

ACTUAL PARAMETER	FORMAL PARAMETER	DESCRIPTION
`M + 3`	A	`INTEGER`, value
`10`	B	`INTEGER`, value
`X`	C	`REAL`, variable
`Y`	D	`REAL`, variable
`Next`	E	`CHAR`, variable

The last column in Table 4.5 describes each formal parameter. Table 4.5 shows that an expression (`M + 3`) or a constant (`10`) may be associated with a value parameter. All the procedure call statements in Table 4.6 contain syntax errors as indicated.

Table 4.6 ▸ *Invalid Procedure Call Statements*

PROCEDURE CALL STATEMENT	ERROR
`Test (30, 10, M, X, Next)`	Type of `M` is not `REAL`.
`Test (M, 19, X, Y)`	Not enough actual parameters.
`Test (M, 10, 35, Y, 'E')`	Constants `35` and `'E'` cannot correspond to variable parameters.
`Test (M, 3.5, X, Y, Next)`	Type of `3.5` is not `INTEGER`.
`Test (30, 10, X, X + Y, Next)`	Expression `X + Y` cannot correspond to a variable parameter.
`Test (30, 10, C, D, E)`	`C`, `D`, and `E` are not declared in the main program.

The last procedure call statement in Table 4.6 points out an error that is often made in using procedures. The actual parameter names `C`, `D`, `E` are the same as their corresponding formal parameter names. However, since these names are not declared in the main program, they cannot appear in an actual parameter list used in the main program. ◂

When writing relatively long parameter lists such as the ones in Table 4.6, you must be careful not to transpose two actual parameters. Doing so will result in a syntax error if it causes a violation of a parameter correspondence rule. Even if no syntax is violated, the procedure execution may generate incorrect results.

SELF-CHECK EXERCISES FOR SECTION 4.4

1. Provide a table similar to Table 4.5 for the other correct parameter lists shown in Example 4.5.
2. Correct the syntax errors in the formal parameter lists below.

```
(VAR A, B : INTEGER, C : REAL)
(VALUE M : INTEGER; VAR Next : CHAR)
(VAR Account, REAL; X + Y , REAL)
```

3. Assuming the declarations

```
CONST
  MaxInt = 32767;

VAR
  X, Y, Z : REAL;
  M, N : INTEGER;

PROCEDURE Massage (VAR A, B : REAL;
                           X : INTEGER);
```

what is wrong with each of the following incorrect procedure call statements?

a. `Massage (X, Y, Z)`
b. `Massage (X, Y, 8)`
c. `Massage (Y, X, N)`
d. `Massage (M, Y, N)`
e. `Massage (25.0, 15, X)`
f. `Massage (X, Y, M + N)`
g. `Massage (A, B, X)`
h. `Massage (Y, Z, M)`
i. `Massage (Y + Z, Y - Z, M)`
j. `Massage (Z, Y, X)`
k. `Massage (X, Y, M, 10)`
l. `Massage (Z, Y, MaxInt)`

4.5 Stepwise Design and Testing

Now that you know how to pass data into and out of procedures, you can make more use of procedures in programming. Many of the level-one subproblems shown in a structure chart will be implemented as separate procedures. Generally, if a subproblem requires more than a few lines of code, it will be written as a procedure.

This section will discuss how to add *data flow* information to a structure chart and how to practice *stepwise* design of programs. We will do this by example, reexamining the solution to the General Sum problem (see Section 2.7). The problem statement is repeated below, followed by its data description and algorithm.

GENERAL SUM PROBLEM REVISITED

Problem: Write a program to find and print the sum of a list of data items.

PROBLEM INPUTS

number of data items to be summed (`NumItems : CARDINAL`)
each data item (`Item : REAL`)

PROBLEM OUTPUTS

sum of data items (`Sum : REAL`)

Algorithm

1. Read the number of items (`NumItems`).
2. Read each item and add it to the sum (`Sum`).
3. Print the sum.

Step 2 is the only step that needs refinement. Rather than refine it now, we will implement it later as procedure `FindSum`.

The structure chart is drawn in Fig. 4.12, which documents the data flow between subproblems. Downward pointing arrows indicate inputs to a subproblem; upward pointing arrows indicate outputs from a subproblem. The variables involved in the data transfer are listed inside the arrow.

Since the step "Read the number of items" defines the value of the variable `NumItems`, `NumItems` is an output of this step. Procedure `FindSum` needs this value to know how many data items to read; consequently, `NumItems` is an input to procedure `FindSum`. The procedure result, `Sum`, is an output of `Find-Sum`. `Sum` must be provided as an input to the step that displays the program result.

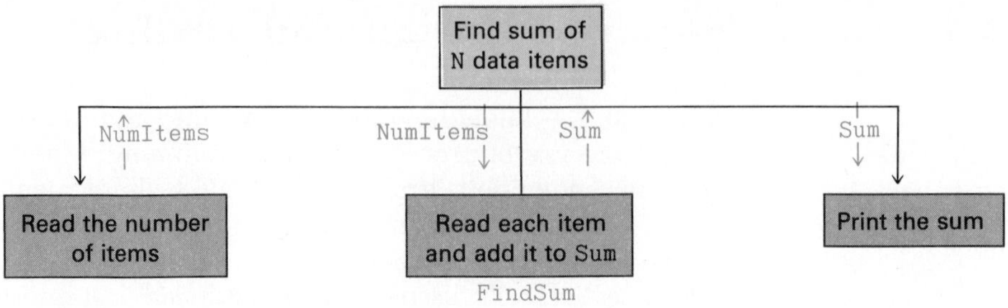

Figure 4.12 ▸ *Structure Chart with Data Flow Information*

Once the data flow information has been added to the structure chart, the main program can be written even if the details of the procedures are not yet known. For example, we know from the data flow information in Fig. 4.12 that the procedure call statement

```
FindSum (NumItems, Sum)
```

may be used to call `FindSum`. We also know that `NumItems` should correspond to a value parameter and `Sum` to a variable parameter.

The program is shown in Fig. 4.13 except for procedure `FindSum`. All the variables that appear in the structure chart should be declared in the main program.

Figure 4.13 ▸ *Main Program with a Stub for Procedure FindSum*

```
MODULE SumItems;

(* Finds and prints the sum of a list of data items. *)

  FROM InOut IMPORT
    ReadCard, WriteString, WriteLn;

  FROM RealInOut IMPORT
    ReadReal, WriteReal;

  VAR
    NumItems : CARDINAL;   (* input - number of items to be added *)
    Sum : REAL;            (* output - sum being accumulated *)

  PROCEDURE FindSum (n (* input *) : CARDINAL;
                     VAR Sum (* output *) : REAL);
  (*
     Finds the sum of a list of n data items.
      Pre: n is assigned a value.
     Post: n data items are read and their sum is stored in Sum.
  *)

  BEGIN  (* FindSum *)
    WriteString ('Procedure FindSum entered ');
```

```
    WriteLn;
    Sum := 0.0
  END FindSum;

BEGIN  (* SumItems *)
  (* Read the number of items to be summed *)
  WriteString ('How many items will be summed? ');
  ReadCard (NumItems);  WriteLn;

  (* Find the sum of a list of data items *)
  FindSum (NumItems, Sum);

  (* Print the sum *)
  WriteString ('The Sum is ');
  WriteReal (Sum, 8);  WriteLn
END SumItems.
```

The declaration for procedure `FindSum` shown in Fig. 4.13 is called a *stub*. Including this declaration enables the main program to be compiled, checked for syntax errors, and even run before `FindSum` is written. However, the program will not yet generate meaningful results, because the value returned by the stub for `FindSum` is always zero.

Since we already know how to perform the summation operation, it will be an easy matter to write procedure `FindSum`. The completed procedure, shown in Fig. 4.14, should replace the stub.

Figure 4.14 ▸ *Procedure FindSum*

```
PROCEDURE FindSum (n (* input *) : INTEGER;
                   VAR Sum (* output *) : REAL);
(*
   Finds the sum of a list of n data items.
   Pre : n is assigned a value.
   Post: n data items are read and their sum is stored in Sum.
*)
   VAR
     Count : CARDINAL;        (* count of items added so far *)
     Item  : REAL;            (* the next data item to be added *)

BEGIN  (* FindSum *)
  (* Read each data item and add it to Sum *)
  Sum := 0.0;
  FOR Count := 1 TO n DO
    WriteString ('Next number to be summed? ');
    ReadReal (Item);  WriteLn;
    Sum := Sum + Item
  END  (* FOR *)
END FindSum;
```

Because `Count` and `Item` are used only within procedure `FindSum`, they are declared as local variables in `FindSum`. The parameter correspondence specified by the procedure call statement

```
FindSum (NumItems, Sum);
```

is shown in Fig. 4.15, assuming the value `10` is read into `NumItems` just before the procedure call.

Figure 4.15 ▸ *Parameter Correspondence for FindSum (NumItems, Sum)*

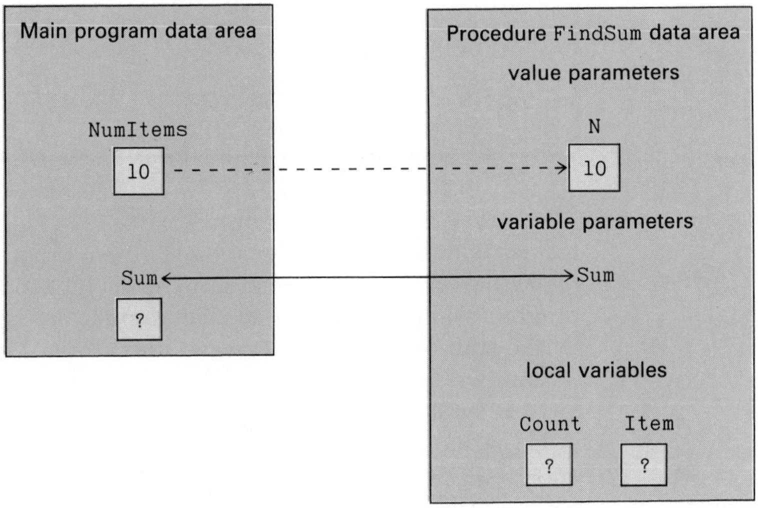

The body of the procedure begins by initializing to zero the main program variable `Sum`, which corresponds to variable parameter `Sum`. The `FOR` statement causes each data item to be read into the local variable `Item` and added to the main program variable `Sum`. The procedure exit will occur after ten items are added.

Program Style

Choosing Formal Parameter Names

The identifiers `n` and `Sum` are used as formal parameter names in procedure `FindSum`. In the procedure call statement shown, formal parameter `Sum` happens to correspond to an actual parameter also named `Sum`. This, of course, is not necessary, but it causes no difficulties either.

Choose meaningful generic names for formal parameters. When a procedure is developed for a particular program system, it is fairly common for a formal parameter to have the same name as its corresponding actual parameter. This may not be true if that procedure is used later with a different program system.

Top-Down and Bottom-Up Testing

In the program shown in Fig. 4.13, a stub is substituted for procedure `FindSum`, presumably because `FindSum` is not yet written. This is common practice when a team of programmers is working on a problem. Obviously not all procedures will be ready at the same time. Still, it would be useful to test and debug those that are available.

The stub for `FindSum` displays a message and assigns a value of zero to its output parameter `Sum`. The message provides a trace of procedure execution. Assigning a value of zero to the output parameter enables the rest of the program system to be tested. This process is called *top-down testing*.

When `FindSum` is completed, it can be tested separately by writing a short driver program to call it and print the actual value assigned to its output parameter. It is easier to locate and correct errors when dealing with a single procedure rather than a complete program system. Once we are confident that `FindSum` works properly, it can be substituted for its stub in the program system. The process of separately testing individual procedures before inserting them in the program system is called *bottom-up testing*.

By following a combination of top-down and bottom-up testing, the programming team can be fairly confident that the complete program system will be relatively free of errors when it is finally put together. Consequently the final debugging sessions should proceed quickly and smoothly.

SELF-CHECK EXERCISES FOR SECTION 4.5

1. Add data flow information to the structure chart shown in Fig. 2.13. Implement each subproblem as a procedure with parameters.
2. A procedure has four formal parameters: `W`, `X`, `Y`, and `Z` (all type `REAL`). The procedure execution stores the sum of `W` and `X` in `Y` and the product of `W` and `X` in `Z`. Which parameters are inputs and which are outputs? Write the procedure.

4.6 Nested Procedures and Scope of Identifiers

In Fig. 4.13, procedure `FindSum` is contained, or *nested*, in program `SumItems`. It is also possible for one procedure to be nested in another procedure. For example, procedure `PrintLine` is nested in procedure `Triangle` in Fig. 4.8. Nested procedures occur frequently in Modula-2 and are a natural consequence of the top-down design process.

Each procedure in a nest of procedures has its own declaration part and body; there are also a declaration part and body for the main program. A procedure's parameter list is included in its declaration part.

Figure 4.16 displays the organization of procedures in program `Nested`. Each box represents a procedure or program *block*. A block consists of the declaration part and body of a program or procedure. The name of the block is indicated just above it.

Figure 4.16 ▸
Procedure Nesting

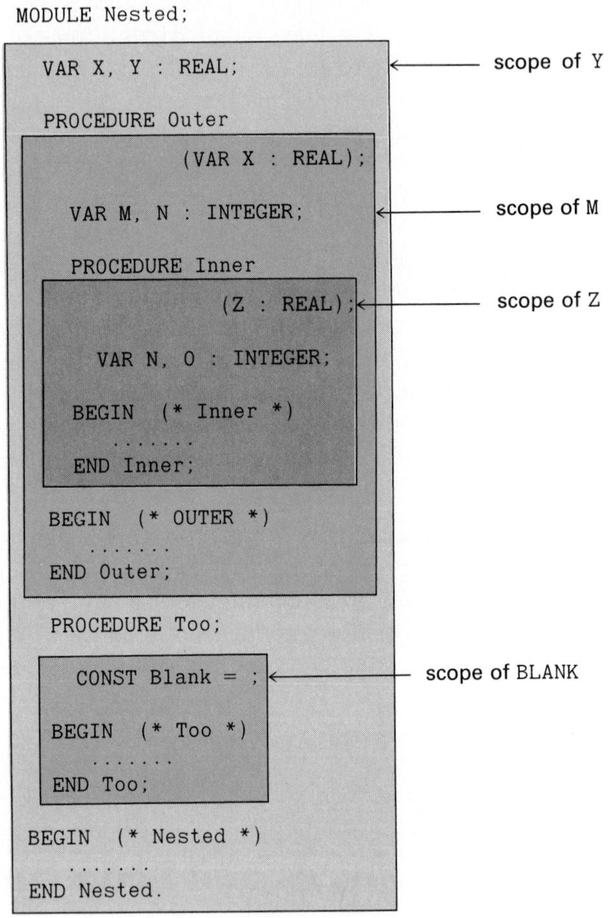
MODULE Nested;
VAR X, Y : REAL;
scope of Y
PROCEDURE Outer
(VAR X : REAL);
VAR M, N : INTEGER;
scope of M
PROCEDURE Inner
(Z : REAL);
scope of Z
VAR N, O : INTEGER;
BEGIN (* Inner *)
....
END Inner;
BEGIN (* OUTER *)
....
END Outer;
PROCEDURE Too;
CONST Blank = ;
scope of BLANK
BEGIN (* Too *)
....
END Too;
BEGIN (* Nested *)
....
END Nested.

Figure 4.16 shows procedures `Outer` and `Too` nested in the main program block. Procedure `Inner` is shown nested in the block for `Outer`.

Scope of Identifiers

The statements in each program or procedure body written so far manipulate only local identifiers. Although we have not done so yet, it is possible in Modula-2 to reference identifiers that are not declared locally.

The following Modula-2 scope rules tell us where an identifier may be referenced.

Modula-2 Scope Rules

1. The scope of an identifier is the block in which it is declared. Therefore, an identifier declared in procedure `P` may be referenced in procedure `P` and all procedures enclosed in procedure `P`.
2. If an identifier `I` declared in procedure `P` is redeclared in some inner procedure `Q` enclosed in `P`, then procedure `Q` and all its enclosed procedures are excluded from the scope of `I` declared in `P`.

According to rule 1, the *scope of an identifier* is the block in which it is declared. The scope of the constant `Blank` (see Fig. 4.16) is the block for procedure `Too`; therefore, `Blank` may be referenced only in procedure `Too`.

The scope of a procedure's formal parameters is the same as for all identifiers declared in that procedure. We illustrated this in Fig. 4.16 by placing the formal parameter list for each procedure in its block. Figure 4.16 shows the scope of formal parameter `Z` as the block for procedure `Inner`.

Since procedure `Inner` is nested in procedure `Outer`, the scope of an identifier declared in procedure `Outer` includes the block for procedure `Inner` (see Fig. 4.16). Therefore, an identifier declared in `Outer` (e.g., variable `M`) may be referenced in the body of either `Inner` or `Outer`, but not `Too`.

Rule 2 takes effect when there are multiple declarations of the same identifier. This rule will be discussed in the next section.

Since all procedures are nested within the main program block, an identifier declared in the main program may be referenced anywhere in the program system. For this reason, main program variables are called *global variables*.

Although global variables may be referenced in procedures, experience has shown this to be a dangerous practice. If a procedure references a global variable, it is possible for the value of that variable to change when the procedure is executed (called a *side effect*). Often there is no documentation to indicate that the procedure manipulates a global variable; consequently, it may be difficult to find a statement in a procedure that is responsible for assigning an incorrect or unexpected value to a global variable.

The formal parameter list and local declarations for a procedure explicitly document the data that will be manipulated. We will continue to manipulate only identifiers (including parameters) that are declared locally in a procedure. The only exceptions will be global constants and type identifiers (discussed in later chapters). It is all right to reference a global constant in a procedure, because Modula-2 does not allow the value of a constant to be changed. Hence, there cannot be a side effect when a global constant is referenced.

Multiple Declarations of Identifiers

Although an identifier may be declared only once in a given procedure, the same identifier may be declared in more than one procedure. In Fig. 4.16, for example, `X` is declared as a global variable in the main program and as a formal parameter in procedure `Outer`. Consequently when `X` is referenced in the program system, there may be some question in our minds as to which declaration takes precedence.

Scope rule 2 states that procedures `Outer` and `Inner` are excluded from the scope of global variable `X`, because `X` is declared as a formal parameter of `Outer`. Therefore, when `X` is referenced in the body of procedure `Outer` or `Inner`, formal parameter `X` is manipulated. When `X` is referenced anywhere else in the program system, global variable `X` is manipulated. In general, the declaration that takes precedence is the closest declaration with a scope that includes the point of reference. This will always be a local declaration if one exists.

If an identifier is not declared locally, then a declaration in an outer block containing the point of reference is used. For example, if identifier `N` is referenced in procedure `Inner` or procedure `Outer`, the corresponding local declaration for identifier `N` is used. If identifier `M` is referenced in procedure `Inner` where it is not declared locally, the declaration for variable `M` in procedure `Outer` is used. A reference to identifier `M` in either the main program body or procedure `Too` would cause an "identifier not declared" syntax error.

Table 4.7 shows the meaning of each valid reference to an identifier in the blocks of Fig. 4.16. Procedure names have been included with other identifiers in this table. They will be discussed in the next section.

Procedure Calls

Since procedure names are identifiers, the Modula-2 scope rules specify where a procedure may be referenced or called. Procedures `Outer` and `Too`

Table 4.7 ▸ *Valid Identifier References for Figure 4.16*

BLOCK	MEANING OF EACH IDENTIFIER
`Inner`	`Z` (parameter of `Inner`)
	`N, O` (local variables)
	`M` (variable declared in `Outer`)
	`X` (parameter of `Outer`)
	`Inner` (procedure declared in `Outer`)
	`Y` (variable declared in `Nested`)
	`Outer` (procedure declared in `Nested`)
`Outer`	`X` (parameter of `Outer`)
	`M, N` (local variables)
	`Inner` (local procedure)
	`Y` (variable declared in `Nested`)
	`Outer, Too` (procedure declared in `Nested`)

Too	Blank (local constant) X, Y (global variables) Outer, Too (procedures declared in Nested)
Nested	X, Y (global variables) Outer, Too (procedures declared in Nested)

are global identifiers (declared in the main program), so they may be called anywhere. Procedure Inner is declared in procedure Outer, so it may be called only by procedure Outer or by Inner itself (called a *recursive procedure call*).

As things stand now, a call to Inner in the body of procedure Too or the main program body would cause an "identifier is undeclared" syntax error. If we declare procedure Inner in the main program instead of in procedure Outer, then both the main program and procedure Too will be able to call Inner.

SELF-CHECK EXERCISES FOR SECTION 4.6

1. Explain why variable N declared in Outer cannot be referenced by the main program, procedure Inner, or procedure Too.
2. What would be the effect of executing the body of Inner, as follows?

```
BEGIN  (* Inner *)
  X := 5.5;
  Y := 6.6;
  M := 2;
  N := 3;
  O := 4
END Inner;
```

3. If the statement sequence above was the body of Outer, Too, or Nested, then some of the assignment statements would be syntactically incorrect. Identify the incorrect statements and indicate the effect of executing all the others in each block.

4.7 Case Studies

In this section, we will examine two programming problems that illustrate most of the concepts discussed in this chapter. Each problem makes extensive use of procedures with parameters.

The top-down design process will be demonstrated in solving these problems. The program solutions will be implemented in a stepwise manner, starting at the top of the structure chart, or with the main program.

BALANCING A CHECKBOOK

Problem: You have just received a new home computer and would like to write a program to help balance your checkbook. The program will read your initial checkbook balance and each transaction (check or deposit). It will print the new balance after each transaction and a warning message if the balance becomes negative. At the end of the session, the starting and final balances will be printed, along with a count of the number of checks and deposits processed.

Discussion: After the starting balance is read, each transaction will be read and processed separately. We can use a simple code (`'C'` or `'D'`) to distinguish between checks and deposits. The transaction amount will be a real number. Because the starting balance must be available at the end, we will save it in variable `StartBal` and use a different variable (`CurBal`) to keep track of the current balance.

PROBLEM INPUTS

starting checkbook balance (`StartBal : REAL`) transaction data
type of transaction (`TranType : CHAR`)
amount of transaction (`Amount : REAL`)

PROBLEM OUTPUTS

current balance after each transaction (`CurBal : REAL`)
number of checks (`NumCheck : CARDINAL`)
number of deposits (`NumDep : CARDINAL`)

Algorithm

1. Display the instructions and read the starting balance.
2. For each transaction, read the transaction, update and print the current balance, and increment the count of checks or deposits.
3. Print the starting and final balance and the number of checks and deposits processed.

The structure chart for this algorithm is shown in Fig. 4.17. The level-1 subproblems will be written as procedures `Instruct`, `Process`, and `Report`, respectively. The data flow information shows that `StartBal` is read by `Instruct` and passed to `Process`. Procedure `Process` defines the program results (`CurBal`, `NumCheck`, `NumDep`); these results are passed to `Report` and printed.

The variables shown in the structure chart should be declared in the main program, because each variable must be declared at the highest level in which it appears in the structure chart. Variables that are passed between the main program and a level-1 procedure must be declared in the main program.

Figure 4.17 ▸ *Structure Chart (Levels 0 and 1) for Checkbook Problem*

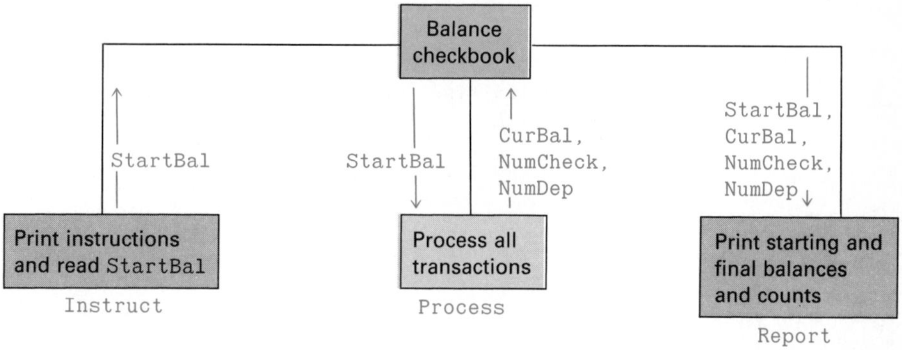

The data flow information is used to write the parameter lists in the program shown in Fig. 4.18. Because procedures `Instruct` and `Report` consist only of input/output statements, they are written now. Since procedure `Process` requires further refinement, it is written as a stub.

Figure 4.18 ▸ *Checkbook-Balancing Program with Stub for Process*

```
MODULE CheckBook;
(*
   Reads the starting balance for a checking account and processes
   all transactions. Prints the new balance after each transaction
   is processed. Also prints a count of the total number of checks
   and deposits processed.
*)
   FROM InOut IMPORT
     Read, Write, WriteString, WriteCard, WriteLn;

   FROM RealInOut IMPORT
     ReadReal, WriteReal;

   VAR
     StartBal,                    (* input - starting balance *)
     CurBal    : REAL;            (* output - current balance *)
     NumCheck,                    (* output - number of checks *)
     NumDep    : CARDINAL;        (* output - number of deposits *)

   PROCEDURE Instruct (VAR StartBal (* output *) : REAL);
   (*
      Displays the instructions and reads the starting balance.
      Pre : None
      Post: User instructions are displayed and StartBal is read in.
   *)
   BEGIN  (* Instruct *)
     WriteString ('Balance  our checking account!');  WriteLn;
     WriteLn;
     WriteString ('Enter C (Check), D (Deposit), or Q (Quit)');
```

```
    WriteLn;
    WriteString ('after prompt C, D, or Q: ');  WriteLn;
    WriteLn;
    WriteString ('Enter a positive number after prompt Amount $');
    WriteLn;  WriteLn;
    WriteString ('Begin by entering your starting balance $');
    ReadReal (StartBal);  WriteLn
  END Instruct;


  PROCEDURE Process (StartBal (* input *) : REAL;
                     VAR CurBal (* output *) : REAL;
                     VAR NumCheck, NumDep (* output *) : CARDINAL);

  BEGIN  (* Process stub *)
    WriteString ('Procedure Process entered.');  WriteLn;
    CurBal := 0.0;  NumCheck := 0;  NumDep := 0
  END Process;

  PROCEDURE Report (StartBal, CurBal (* input *) : REAL;
                    NumCheck, NumDep (* input *) : CARDINAL);
  (*
     Prints the starting and final balances and the count of checks
     and deposits.
     Pre : StartBal, CurBal, NumCheck, & NumDep are assigned values.
     Post: Program results are displayed.
  *)
  BEGIN  (* Report *)
    WriteLn;
    WriteString ('Starting balance was $');
    WriteReal (StartBal, 10);  WriteLn;
    WriteString ('Final    balance  is $');
    WriteReal (CurBal, 12);  WriteLn;
    WriteString ('Number of checks written: ');
    WriteCard (NumCheck, 3);  WriteLn;
    WriteString ('Number of deposits made : ');
    WriteCard (NumDep, 3);  WriteLn
  END Report;


BEGIN  (* CheckBook *)
  (* Display user instructions and read StartBal *)
  Instruct (StartBal);

  (* Process each transaction *)
  Process (StartBal, CurBal, NumCheck, NumDep);

  (* Print starting & final balances & count of checks/deposits *)
  Report (StartBal, CurBal, NumCheck, NumDep)
END CheckBook.
```

Procedure `Process` performs step 2 of the algorithm, which is repeated here.

Algorithm for PROCESS

2. For each transaction: read the transaction, update and print the current balance, and increment the count of checks or deposits.

It is obvious that a `WHILE` loop is needed. Assuming that we do not know how many transactions will occur, we can use a sentinel-controlled loop that compares the transaction code to a sentinel value. The loop properties follow.

- `Curbal` is `StartBal` plus all transactions that are deposits and minus all transactions that are checks.
- `NumCheck` is the count of checks so far.
- `NumDep` is the count of deposits so far.

The transaction code contains the sentinel value just after loop exit. These statements suggest the following refinement.

Algorithm for PROCESS

1. Initialize `NumCheck` and `NumDep` to zero.
2. Initialize `CurBal` to `StartBal`.
3. Read the first transaction.
4. `WHILE` the transaction code is not the sentinel `DO`
    5. Update `CurBal` and increment `NumCheck` or `NumDep`.
    6. Display `CurBal` and the transaction.
    7. Read the next transaction.

   END

The structure chart for `Process` is shown in Fig. 4.19. Procedure `ReadTran` performs steps 3 and 7 above, `UpDate` performs step 5, and `DisplayTran`

Figure 4.19 ▸ *Structure Chart for Procedure PROCESS*

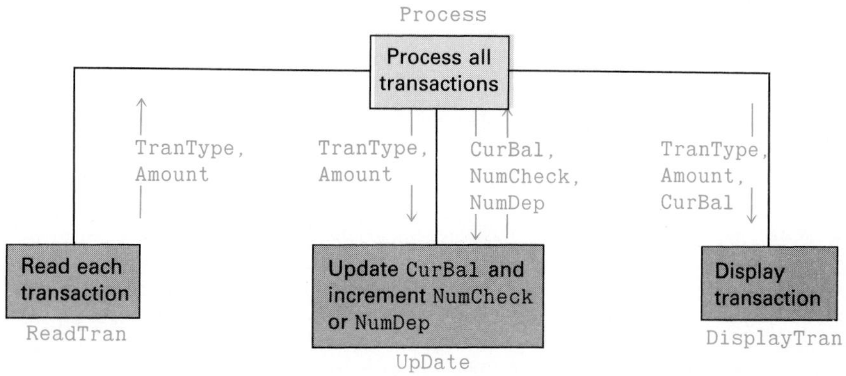

performs step 6. Two new variables, TranType and Amount, should be declared as local variables in procedure Process. Variables passed between a level-1 and a level-2 procedure should be declared in the level-1 procedure. The identifiers CurBal, NumCheck, and NumDep are declared already as formal parameters of Process.

LOCAL VARIABLES FOR PROCESS

the transaction type (TranType : CHAR)
the transaction amount (Amount : REAL)

The procedure nesting prescribed by this structure chart and the earlier one is summarized in Fig. 4.20. Each procedure that is subordinate to a higher-level procedure will be nested in that higher-level procedure. Figure 4.20 shows that ReadTran, Update, and DisplayTran are nested in Process, which is nested in CheckBook. Procedures Instruct and Report are also nested in CheckBook.

Figure 4.20 ▸ *Procedure Nesting for Checkbook Problem*

```
MODULE CheckBook
  PROCEDURE Instruct
  PROCEDURE Process
    PROCEDURE ReadTran
    PROCEDURE Update
    PROCEDURE DisplayTran
  PROCEDURE Report
```

Procedure UpDate will consist of an IF statement that implements the decision table shown in Table 4.8. Procedure Process is shown in Fig. 4.21; a sample run of program CheckBook is shown in Fig. 4.22.

Table 4.8 ▸ *Decision Table for UpDate*

CONDITION	DESIRED ACTION
TranType = 'D'	Increment NumDep, add Amount to CurBal.
TranType = 'C'	Increment NumCheck, subtract Amount from CurBal.

Figure 4.21 ▸ *Procedure Process for the Checkbook-Balancing Program*

```
PROCEDURE Process (StartBal (* input *) : REAL;
                   VAR CurBal (* output *) : REAL;
                   VAR NumCheck, NumDep (* output *) : CARDINAL);
(*
   Processes each transaction. Reads each transaction, updates and
   prints the current balance and increments the count of checks or
   deposits.
```

```
    Pre : StartBal is assigned a value.
    Post: CurBal is StartBal plus deposits and minus withdrawals.
          NumCheck is the count of checks.
          NumDep is the count of deposits.
    Uses: ReadTran, Update, and DisplayTran
*)
  CONST
    Sentinel = 'Q';         (* sentinel value *)
    Deposit = 'D';          (* deposit code *)
    Check = 'C';            (* check code *)

  VAR
    TranType : CHAR;        (* transaction type (check or deposit) *)
    Amount : REAL;          (* transaction amount *)


  PROCEDURE ReadTran (VAR TranType (* output *) : CHAR;
                      VAR Amount (* output *) : REAL);
  (* Reads each transaction. *)
     Pre : None
     Post: TranType and Amount are read in.
  *)
  BEGIN (* ReadTran *)
    WriteLn;
    WriteString ('C, D, or Q: ');
    Read (TranType);  Write (TranType);  WriteLn;
    TranType := CAP(TranType);
    IF TranType # Sentinel THEN
      (* Read amount *)
      WriteString ('Amount $');   ReadReal (Amount);   WriteLn
    END (* IF *)
  END ReadTran;


  PROCEDURE UpDate (TranType (* input *) : CHAR;
                    Amount (* input *) : REAL;
                    VAR CurBal (* in/out *) : REAL;
                    VAR NumCheck, NumDep (* in/out *) : CARDINAL);
  (*
     Updates CurBal and increments NumCheck for a check or
     NumDep for a deposit.
     Pre : TranType, Amount, CurBal, NumCheck, and NumDep are
           defined.
     Post: CurBal is increased (deposit) or decreased (check) by
           Amount. NumCheck or NumDep is increased by one.
  *)
  BEGIN (* UpDate *)
    IF TranType = Deposit THEN
      CurBal := CurBal + Amount;
      INC (NumDep)
    ELSIF TranType = Check THEN
```

```
        CurBal := CurBal - Amount;
        INC (NumCheck)
      END (* IF *)
    END UpDate;


    PROCEDURE DisplayTran  TranType (* input *) : CHAR;
                           Amount,
                           CurBal (* input *) : REAL);
    (*
       Displays current transaction and balance.
       Pre : TranType, Amount, and Curbal are assigned values.
       Post: Transaction data are displayed.
    *)
    BEGIN (* DisplayTran *)
      IF TranType = Deposit THEN
        WriteString ('Depositing $');
        WriteReal (Amount, 12);
        WriteString ('    Balance of $');
        WriteReal (CurBal, 12);  WriteLn
      ELSIF TranType = Check THEN
        WriteString ('Check for  $');
        WriteReal (Amount, 12);
        WriteString ('    Balance of $');
        WriteReal (CurBal, 12);  WriteLn;
        IF CurBal < 0.0 THEN
          WriteString ('Warning!  Your account is overdrawn.');
          WriteLn
        END (* inner IF *)
      ELSE  (* not check or deposit *)
        WriteString ('Invalid transaction type ');
        Write(TranType);
        WriteString (' -- transaction ignored');  WriteLn
      END (* outer IF *)
    END DisplayTran;


BEGIN  (* Process *)
  (* Initialize counters to zero and CurBal to StartBal *)
  NumCheck := 0;  NumDep := 0;  CurBal := StartBal;

  (* Read first transaction *)
  ReadTran (TranType, Amount);

  (* Process each transaction until done *)
  WHILE TranType # Sentinel DO
    UpDate (TranType, Amount, CurBal, NumCheck, NumDep);
    DisplayTran (TranType, Amount, CurBal);
    ReadTran (TranType, Amount)
  END (* WHILE *)
END Process;
```

Figure 4.22 ▸
Sample Run of Checkbook-Balancing Program

```
Balance your checking account!

Enter C (Check), D (Deposit), or Q (Quit)
after prompt C, D, or Q:

Enter a positive number after prompt Amount $

Begin by entering your starting balance $1000.00

C, D, or Q: D
Amount $100.00
Depositing $ 1.0000E+002    Balance of $ 1.1000E+003

C, D, or Q: C
Amount $1200.00
Check for  $ 1.2000E+003    Balance of $-1.0000E+002
Warning!  Your account is overdrawn.

C, D, or Q: X
Amount $500.00
Invalid transaction type X -- transaction ignored.

C, D, or Q: Q

Starting balance was $ 1.0000E+003
Final    balance  is $-1.0000E+002
Number of checks written:   1
Number of deposits made :   1
```

Procedure `Process` processes all transactions. `Process` calls `ReadTran` to read each transaction, `UpDate` to process the transaction just read, and `DisplayTran` to display the result. Since these three procedures are called only by `Process`, they are declared inside `Process`.

Procedure `DisplayTran` contains a nested `IF` statement that differentiates between checks and deposits. When `TranType` is `'C'`, the inner `IF` statement is executed and used to detect an overdrawn account (i.e., when `CurBal` is negative).

Program Style

Stepwise Design

The program system for the checkbook problem is a good illustration of the stepwise design process. It uses procedures to implement each subproblem shown in the structure chart. With the exception of procedure `Process`, each procedure is relatively short.

The main program at the bottom of Fig. 4.18 contains three procedure call statements. The second procedure call statement

```
Process (StartBal, CurBal, NumCheck, NumDep);
```

is used to process all transactions. Procedure `Process` calls procedures `ReadTran`, `UpDate`, and `DisplayTran` to perform the read, update, and display operations, respectively. These level-2 procedures are declared inside procedure `Process`.

The variables `TranType` and `Amount` are declared in `Process`, because they are used only by `Process` and the level-2 procedures. Similarly the constants `Sentinel`, `Check`, and `Deposit` are declared in `Process` and referenced as needed in the level-2 procedures.

The solution to the next problem also illustrates stepwise design with procedures. It also uses a `WHILE` statement and an `IF` statement.

GRADING AN EXAM

Problem: We want to write a grading program that will determine the number of exam scores that fall into each of three categories: outstanding, satisfactory, and unsatisfactory. The program will also print the highest score. The program user must specify the minimum satisfactory and outstanding scores and enter each student's name and exam score.

Discussion: The program must start by reading in the scale for the exam. The main processing step must read each student's data, categorize each score, and find the largest score. We will begin by describing the data requirements and the algorithm.

PROBLEM INPUTS

minimum satisfactory score (`MinSat : CARDINAL`)
minimum outstanding score (`MinOut : CARDINAL`)
each student's initials (`First, Last: CHAR`)
each student's score (`Score : CARDINAL`)

PROBLEM OUTPUTS

highest score (`High : CARDINAL`)
number of outstanding scores (`NumOut : CARDINAL`)
number of satisfactory scores (`NumSat : CARDINAL`)
number of unsatisfactory scores (`NumUns : CARDINAL`)

Algorithm

1. Read in the exam scale.
2. Read each student's initials and score, categorize each score, and find the highest score.
3. Print the number of scores in each category and the highest score.

Step 2 is the main processing step and requires further refinement. Rather than do this now, we will examine the structure chart for the problem, as shown in Fig. 4.23.

Figure 4.23 ▸ *Structure Chart (Levels 0 and 1) for Grading Problem*

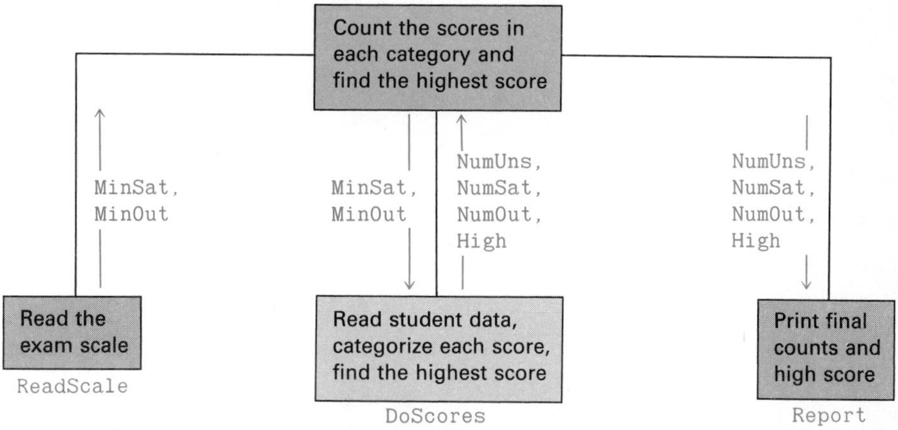

All level-1 subproblems will be implemented as procedures (ReadScale, DoScores, and Report, from left to right). The data flow information shows that the scale boundary values (MinSat, MinOut) are defined by procedure ReadScale and passed into procedure DoScores. Procedure DoScores determines all required output values (NumUns, NumSat, NumOut, and High); these values are then passed into Report to be printed.

The variables shown in the structure chart are all declared in the main program (see Fig. 4.24). The data flow information is used to write the parameter lists in the main program. Because procedure DoScores requires further refinement before it can be completed, it is written as a stub.

Figure 4.24 ▸ *Grading Program with Stub for DoScores*

```
MODULE Grader;
(*
   Reads an exam scale and uses it to find the number of students
   who received outstanding, satisfactory, and unsatisfactory grades
   on an exam. Also, finds the highest score.
*)
   FROM InOut IMPORT
     Read, ReadCard, Write, WriteCard, WriteString, WriteLn;

   VAR
     MinSat, MinOut,        (* input - boundaries for satisfactory
                               category *)
     NumUns, NumSat, NumOut,      (* output - counters for each
                                     category *)
```

```
    High                        : CARDINAL;    (* output - high score
                                                  so far *)

  PROCEDURE ReadScale (VAR MinSat, MinOut (* output *) : CARDINAL);
  (*
     Reads the exam scale.
     Pre : None
     Post: MinSat and MinOut are read in.
  *)
  BEGIN  (* ReadScale *)
    (* Enter the exam scale *)
    WriteString ('Enter the minimum satisfactory score: ');
    ReadCard (MinSat);  WriteLn;
    WriteString ('Enter the minimum outstanding  score: ');
    ReadCard (MinOut);  WriteLn
  END ReadScale;


  PROCEDURE DoScores (MinSat, MinOut (* input *) : CARDINAL;
            VAR NumUns, NumSat,
                NumOut, High (* output *) : CARDINAL);

  BEGIN  (* DoScores stub *)
    WriteString ('Procedure DoScores entered.');  WriteLn;
    NumUns := 0;  NumSat := 0;  NumOut := 0;  High := 0
  END DoScores;


  PROCEDURE Report (NumUns, NumSat,
                    NumOut, High (* input *) : CARDINAL);
  (*
     Prints the final counts and the highest score.
     Pre : NumUns, NumSat, NumOut, and High are assigned values.
     Post: The program results are displayed.
  *)
  BEGIN  (* Report *)
    WriteLn;
    WriteString ('Number of    outstanding scores: ');
    WriteCard (NumOut, 3);  WriteLn;
    WriteString ('Number of   satisfactory scores: ');
    WriteCard (NumSat, 3);  WriteLn;
    WriteString ('Number of unsatisfactory scores: ');
    WriteCard (NumUns, 3);  WriteLn;
    WriteLn;
    WriteString ('High score on exam: ');
    WriteCard (High, 3);  WriteLn
  END Report;


BEGIN  (* Grader *)
  (* Enter the exam scale *)
  ReadScale (MinSat, MinOut);
```

```
  (* Read and categorize all scores and find the high score *)
  DoScores (MinSat, MinOut, NumUns, NumSat, NumOut, High);

  (* Print count of scores in each category and the high score *)
  Report (NumUns, NumSat, NumOut, High)
END Grader.
```

Procedure `DoScores` performs step 2 of the original algorithm, which is repeated here.

Algorithm for DoScores

2. Read each student's initials and score, categorize each score, and find the highest score.

This time we will use a sentinel-controlled `WHILE` loop that compares a student's initials to a sentinel value. The loop properties follow.

- `NumUns` is the count of unsatisfactory scores.
- `NumSat` is the count of satisfactory scores.
- `NumOut` is the count of outstanding scores.
- `High` is the highest score so far.

The student's initials are the sentinel just after loop exit. These properties suggest the following refinement

Algorithm for DoScores

1. Initialize `NumUns`, `NumSat`, and `NumOut` to zero.
2. Initialize `High` to lowest possible score.
3. Read first student's initials and score.
4. `WHILE` the student's initials are not the sentinel `DO`
    5. Increment `NumUns`, `NumSat`, or `NumOut`.
    6. Set `High` to current score if it is the highest so far.
    7. Read the next student's initials and score.

   `END`

Step 5 can be implemented as a multiple-alternative decision, as outlined in Table 4.9. This step will be performed by procedure `Categorize`.

Table 4.9 ▸ *Decision Table for Step 5 of DoScores*

SCORE	ACTION
`< MinSat`	Score is unsatisfactory, increment `NumUns`.
`MinSat to MinOut-1`	Score is satisfactory, increment `NumSat`.
`>= MinOut`	Score is outstanding, increment `NumOut`.

To accomplish step 6 (check for highest score so far), the program must compare each score to the highest score so far (saved in `High`). If the current score is larger than the highest score so far, it becomes the new highest score. The "priming step" is to initialize `High` to the lowest possible score (zero), so that `High` is always set to the first score during pass 1. An example of this process is shown in Table 4.10.

Table 4.10 ▸ *Finding the Highest Score*

SCORE	HIGH	EFFECT
35	0	`35 > 0;` 35 is the new highest score.
60	35	`60 > 35;` 60 is the new highest score.
47	60	`47 < 60;` 60 is still the highest score.
80	60	`80 > 60;` 80 is the new highest score.
75	80	`75 < 80;` 80 is still the highest score.

Now that the algorithm for `DoScores` is refined, we can draw the system structure chart (see Fig. 4.25) that describes this step and its subproblems. Each subproblem is implemented as a procedure. The structure chart shows that `Score` is an output of procedure `ReadStu` and an input to procedures `Categorize` and `CheckHigh`. Because `Categorize` must increment a category counter, the counters are input/output parameters for this subproblem. Since `High` may be modified by `CheckHigh`, it is also an input/output parameter.

Figure 4.25 ▸ *Structure Chart for Procedure DoScores*

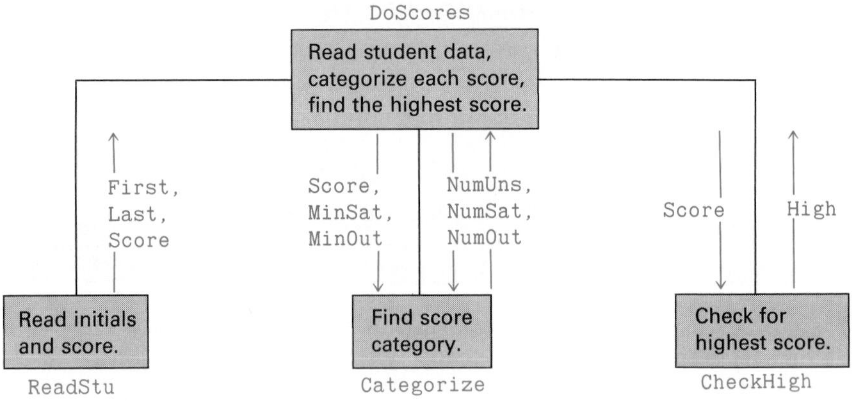

The nesting of procedures prescribed by this structure chart and the earlier one is summarized in Fig. 4.26. Procedure `DoScores` is shown in Fig. 4.27. `First`, `Last`, and `Score` are declared as local variables in `DoScores`; `Sentinel` and `MinScore` are local constants. A sample run of the complete program is shown in Fig. 4.28.

Figure 4.26 ▸ *Procedure Nesting for Grading Problem*

```
MODULE Grader
  PROCEDURE ReadScale
  PROCEDURE DoScores
    PROCEDURE ReadStu
    PROCEDURE Categorize
    PROCEDURE CheckHigh
  PROCEDURE Report
```

Figure 4.27 ▸ *Procedure DoScores (replaces the stub in Fig. 4.23)*

```
PROCEDURE DoScores (MinSat, MinOut (* input *) : CARDINAL;
                    VAR NumUns, NumSat,
                        NumOut, High (* output *) : CARDINAL);
(*
   Reads each student's initials and score, categorizes each score,
   and finds the highest score.
    Pre: MinSat and MinOut are assigned values.
   Post: NumUns, NumSat, and NumOut are the counts of scores in
         each category. High is the highest score.
   Uses: ReadStu, Categorize, and CheckHigh
*)
   CONST Sentinel = '*';                   (* sentinel value *)
   MinScore = 0;                           (* lowest possible score *)

   VAR
     Score : CARDINAL;                     (* each exam score *)
     First, Last : CHAR;                   (* student's initials *)

   PROCEDURE ReadStu (VAR First, Last (* output *) : CHAR;
                      VAR Score (* output *) : CARDINAL);
   (*
      Read a student's initials and score.
      Pre : None
      Post: First, Last, and Score are read in.
   *)
   BEGIN (* ReadStu *)
     WriteLn;
     WriteString ('Enter two initials, first and last, or **: ');
     Read (First);  Write (First);              (* Get initials *)
     Read (Last);   Write (Last);  WriteLn;
     IF First # Sentinel THEN
       WriteString ('Enter Score: ');
       ReadCard (Score);  WriteLn               (* Get Score *)
     END (* IF *)
   END ReadStu;

   PROCEDURE Categorize (Score, MinSat, MinOut (* input *) :
                                                  CARDINAL;
                         VAR NumUns, NumSat,
                             NumOut (* in/out *) : CARDINAL);
```

```
  (*
     Categorize score and increment the appropriate counter.
     Pre : Score, MinSat, MinOut, NumUns, NumSat, NumOut are
           defined.
     Post: Increments NumUns, NumSat, or NumOut by one based
           on Score.
  *)
     CONST
       Pad = '                 ';

  BEGIN  (* Categorize *)
    WriteString (Pad);
    IF Score < MinSat THEN
      (* unsatisfactory score *)
      WriteString ('Unsatisfactory');
      WriteLn;
      INC (NumUns)
    ELSIF Score < MinOut THEN
      (* satisfactory score *)
      WriteString ('Satisfactory');
      WriteLn;
      INC (NumSat)
    ELSE
      (* outstanding score *)
      WriteString ('Outstanding');
      WriteLn;
      INC (NumOut)
    END (* IF *)
  END Categorize;

  PROCEDURE CheckHigh (Score (* input *) : CARDINAL;
                       VAR High (* in/out *) : CARDINAL);
  (*
     Checks whether score is the highest score so far.
     Pre :  High is assigned a value.
     Post: High becomes Score if Score > old value of High.
  *)
  BEGIN (* CheckHigh *)
    IF Score > High THEN
      High := Score               (* Save New high score *)
    END  (* IF *)
  END CheckHigh;


BEGIN (* DoScores *)
  (* Intialize category counters and  High *)
  NumUns := 0;  NumSat := 0;  NumOut := 0;
  High := MinScore;

  (* Categorize each score and find High *)
  ReadStu (First, Last, Score);       (* Read first student's data *)
```

```
  WHILE First # Sentinel DO
    (* Categorize Score and increment appropriate counter *)
    Categorize (Score, MinSat, MinOut, NumUns, NumSat, NumOut);
    CheckHigh (Score, High);         (* Check for high score *)
    ReadStu (First, Last, Score)     (* Read next student's data *)
  END (* WHILE *)
END DoScores;
```

Figure 4.28 ▶ *Sample Run of Program Grader*

```
Enter the minimum satisfactory score: 75
Enter the minimum outstanding  score: 90

Enter two initials or **: EK
Enter score: 100
                Outstanding

Enter two initials or **: RK
Enter score: 75
                Satisfactory

Enter two initials or **: HH
Enter score: 89
                Satisfactory

Enter two initials or **: **

Number of    outstanding scores: 1
Number of   satisfactory scores: 2
Number of unsatisfactory scores: 0

Highest score on exam: 100
```

Procedure `DoScores` begins by initializing all category counters and `High` to zero. It calls `ReadStu` to read each student's initials and score and calls `Check-High` to check for the highest score so far.

Procedure `DoScores` calls procedure `Categorize` to find and print the category of each score. `Categorize` displays a blank string, `Pad`, at the beginning of each output line so it will be easy to distinguish the program output from the input data. The multiple-alternative decision in `Categorize` prints the score category and increments a counter.

SELF-CHECK EXERCISES FOR SECTION 4.7

1. Modify the checkbook program so that a penalty amount of $15.00 is deducted for each overdrawn check and a count of overdrawn checks is maintained and printed next to each overdrawn check. Reset the count of overdrafts to zero whenever the balance becomes positive.

2. What would be the effect of transposing the parameters `MinSat` and `MinOut` in the call to procedure `DoScores` or `ReadScale` in Fig. 4.24? Would the compiler detect this error?
3. What would happen if the person using this program became confused and switched the data values entered for `MinSat` and `MinOut`? Rewrite procedure `ReadScale` so that it checks for this error and takes corrective action if necessary.

4.8 Debugging a Program System

As the number of modules and statements in a program system grows, the possibility of error also increases. If each module is kept to a manageable size, the likelihood of error will increase much more slowly. Each module will also be easier to read and test. Finally the limited use of global variables will minimize the chance of harmful side effects that are always difficult to locate.

Whenever possible, test each procedure separately by writing a short driver program that contains all necessary declarations. The body of the driver program should assign values to the input and input/output parameters, call the procedure, and display the procedure results.

Even before all procedures are written, you can test the main program flow by substituting stubs for the missing procedures. If you do this, make sure that any output parameters are defined in the stub.

A list of suggestions for debugging a program system follows.

Debugging Tips for Program Systems

1. Carefully document each procedure parameter and local identifier using comments. Also describe the procedure operation using comments.
2. Leave a trace of execution by printing the procedure name as it is entered.
3. Print the values of all input and input/output parameters upon entry to a procedure. Check that these values make sense.
4. Print the values of all output parameters after returning from a procedure. Hand-compute these values to be sure they are correct. Make sure that all input/output and output parameters are declared as variable parameters.

It is a good idea to plan for debugging as you write each procedure, rather than after the fact. Include the output statements required for tips 2 through 4 in the original Modula-2 code for the procedure. When you are satisfied that the procedure works as desired, you can remove the debugging statements. An efficient way to remove the statements is to change them to comments by enclosing them with the symbols `(*` and `*)`. If you have a problem later, you can remove these symbols, thereby changing the comments back to executable statements.

4.9 Common Programming Errors

The Modula-2 scope rules determine where an identifier may be referenced. If an identifier is referenced outside its scope, an "identifier not declared" syntax error will result.

There are many opportunities for error when using procedures with parameter lists. The proper use of parameters is difficult for beginning programmers to master. An obvious pitfall is not making sure that the actual parameter list has the same number of parameters as the formal parameter list. The syntax error "number of parameters does not agree with declaration" will indicate this problem.

Each actual parameter must be the same data type as its corresponding formal parameter. An actual parameter that corresponds to a variable formal parameter must be a variable. A violation of either of these rules will result in an "illegal parameter substitution" syntax error.

A procedure result should be returned to the calling module by assigning a value to a variable parameter. Any value assigned to a value parameter will be stored locally in the procedure and will not be returned.

4.10 Chapter Review

This chapter discussed the use of procedure parameters for passing data to and from procedures. The parameter list provides a highly visible communication path between the procedure and the calling program. By using parameters, we can cause different data to be manipulated by a procedure each time we call it. This makes it easier to reuse the procedure in other program systems.

There are two types of parameters: value and variable. A value parameter is used only for passing data into a procedure. A variable parameter is used to return results from a procedure. The actual parameter corresponding to a value parameter may be an expression or a constant; the actual parameter corresponding to a variable parameter must be a variable.

We discussed the scope of identifiers. An identifier may be referenced anywhere within the block that declares it. If one block is nested inside another and an identifier is declared in the outer block, the identifier's meaning in the inner block is determined by its declaration in the outer block. If the identifer is declared in both blocks, its meaning in the inner block is determined by its declaration in the inner block.

A global variable is one that is declared in the main program; a local variable is one that is declared in a procedure. A local variable is defined only during the execution of the procedure; its value is lost when the procedure is finished.

New Modula-2 Statements

Table 4.11 describes the new Modula-2 statements introduced in this chapter.

Table 4.11 ▸ *Summary of New Modula-2 Statements*

STATEMENT	EFFECT
Procedure with Parameters	

`PROCEDURE A (X : REAL;`
`             Op : CHAR;`
`             VAR XTo3 : REAL);`
 	
`BEGIN (* A *)`
`  IF Op = '*' THEN`
`    XTo3 := X * X * X`
`  ELSIF Op = '+' THEN`
`    XTo3 := X + X + X`
`  ELSE`
`    WriteString ('Invalid ')`
`  END  (* IF *)`
`END A;`
	Procedure `A` has two value parameters (`X` and `Op`) and one variable parameter (`XTo3`). If `Op` is `'*'`, then the value returned is `X * X * X`; otherwise, If `Op` is `'+'`, then the value returned is `X + X + X`; otherwise, an error message is printed. A result is returned by assigning a new value to the actual parameter (a variable) that corresponds to parameter `XTo3`.

Procedure Call Statement	
`A (5.5, '+', Y)`	Calls procedure `A`. `5.5` is passed into `X`, `'+'` into `Op`, and the value `16.5` is stored in `Y`.

CHAPTER 4 ▸

Review Questions

1. Write the procedure heading statement for a procedure called `SCRIPT` that accepts three parameters passed to it. The first parameter will be the number of spaces to print at the beginning of a line; the second parameter will be the character to print after the spaces; and the third parameter will be the number of times to print the second parameter on the same line.
2. Write a procedure called `LetterGrade` that has one input parameter called `Grade`, and that will print out the corresponding letter grade using a straight scale (90–100 is an A, 80–89 is a B, etc.).
3. Explain the difference between a value parameter and a variable parameter with respect to the parameter's relationship to the variables in the calling program.
4. Explain the allocation of memory cells when a procedure is called.

5. Write the procedure header statement for a procedure named `Pass` that will be passed two integer parameters. The first parameter should be a value parameter and the second a variable parameter.
6. Explain the use of a stub in refining an algorithm.
7. In the following chart, write YES for each procedure on the right that can be referenced (called) by the procedure on the left, and NO for each procedure that is inaccessible.

```
MODULE ProcScope;

PROCEDURE A;

   PROCEDURE B;

      PROCEDURE C;

      .........

      END C;

      PROCEDURE D;

      .........

      END D;

   ..........

   END B;

.........

END A;

.........

END ProcScope.
```

Calling procedure \ *Callable procedure*	A	B	C	D
A				
B				
C				
D				

CHAPTER 4 ▸

Programming Projects

1. a. Write a program to process a collection of savings account transactions (deposits or withdrawals). Your program should begin by reading in the previous account balance and then read and process each transaction. Enter positive values for deposits and negative values for withdrawals. For each transaction, print the message `'WITHDRAWAL'` or `'DEPOSIT'` and the new balance. Print an error message if a withdrawal would result in a negative balance but do not change the balance.

b. Compute and print the number of deposits, the number of withdrawals, the number of invalid withdrawals, and the total dollar amount for each type of transaction.

2. a. Write a program that computes and prints the fractional powers of two (1/2, 1/4, 1/8, etc.). The program should also print the decimal value of each fraction, as follows.

Power	*Power*	*Decimal Value*
1	1/2	0.5
2	1/4	0.25
3	1/8	0.125

Print all values through power equal to ten.

b. Add an extra output column that shows the sum of all decimal values so far. The first three sums are 0.5, 0.75, and 0.875.

3. a. The trustees of a small college are considering voting a pay raise for the twelve faculty. They want to grant a 5.5 percent pay raise; before doing so, however, they want to know how much this will cost. Write a program that will print the pay raise for each faculty member and the total amount of the raises. Also, print the total faculty payroll before and after the raise. Test your program for the salaries:

$12500	$14029.50	$16000	$13250
$15500	$12800	$20000.50	$18900
$13780	$17300	$14120.25	$14100

b. Redo the program assuming that faculty earning less than $14,000 receive a 4-percent raise, faculty earning more than $16,500 receive a 7-percent raise, and all others receive a 5.5-percent raise. For each faculty member, print the raise percentage as well as the amount.

4. The assessor in your town has estimated the market value of all fourteen properties and would like a program that determines the tax owed on each property and the total tax to be collected. The tax rate is 125 mils per dollar of assessed value. (A mil is 0.1 of a penny.) The assessed value of each property is 28 percent of its estimated market value. The market values are as follows:

$50000	$48000	$45500	$67000	$37600	$47100	$65000
$53350	$28000	$58000	$52250	$48000	$56500	$43700

5. Patients required to take many kinds of medication often have difficulty remembering when to take their medicine. Given the following set of medications, write a program that prints an hourly table indicating what medication to take at any given hour. Use a counter variable `Clock` to go through a 24-hour day. Print the table based upon the following prescriptions:

Medication	*Frequency*
Iron pill	0800, 1200,1800
Antibiotic	Every 4 hours starting at 0400
Vitamin	0800, 2100
Calcium	1100, 2000

6. A monthly magazine wants a program that will print out renewal notices to its subscribers and cancellation notices when appropriate. Utilize procedures when advisable and write a program that first reads in the current month number (1 through 12) and year. For each subscription processed, read in four data items: the account number, the month and year the subscription started, and the number of years paid for the subscription.

   Read in each set of subscription information and print a renewal notice if the current month is either the month prior to expiration or the month of expiration. A cancellation notice should be printed if the current month comes after the expiration month.

   Sample input might be:

`10, 85`	for a current month of October 1985 for account 1364,
`1364, 4, 83, 3`	whose 3-year subscription began in April 1983

7. The square root of a number N can be approximated by repeated calculation using the formula

   $$NG = .5(LG + N / LG)$$

   where NG stands for next guess and LG stands for last guess. Write a procedure that implements this process where the first parameter will be a positive real number, the second will be an initial guess of the square root, and the third will be the computed result.

   The initial guess will be the starting value of LG. The procedure will compute a value for NG using the formula above. The difference between NG and LG is checked to see whether these two guesses are almost identical. If so, the procedure is exited and NG is the square root; otherwise, the new guess (NG) becomes the last guess (LG) and the process is repeated (i.e., another value is computed for NG, the difference is checked, etc.).

   The loop in this procedure should be repeated until the difference is less than 0.005 (`Delta`). Use an initial guess of 1.0 and test the procedure for the numbers 4, 120.5, 88, 36.01, and 10000.

5 ▸ Simple Data Types

SO FAR IN our programming, we have used five standard data types: CARDINAL, INTEGER, REAL, CHAR, and BOOLEAN (conditions in IF and WHILE statements). This chapter takes a closer look at these data types and introduces new operators and operations that can be performed on them. It describes the standard functions and procedures of Modula-2 and demonstrates how they are used to simplify computations.

You will also learn how to declare new data types called subrange types. All of the data types in this chapter are *simple* data types, that is, only one value can be stored in a single variable. Later chapters will examine *structured* data types, that is, data types that can be used to store multiple values in a single variable.

5.1 Constant Declarations

This chapter begins by reexamining constants in Modula-2. Each constant declaration has the form

constant identifier = *constant expression*

where *constant expression* is an expression consisting of operators and operands that are constants. The allowable operands include numbers, strings, sets (defined in Chapter 11), and previously defined constants. The operators include all the Modula-2 operators listed in Appendix A. Each *constant identifier* assumes the value of its *constant expression* as its initial value; this value cannot be changed.

EXAMPLE 5.1 ▶ Some valid constant declarations follow.

```
CONST
  Rows = 24;
  Columns = 80;
  ScreenSize = Rows * Columns;
  SpeedOfLight = 2.998E+5;
  Name = 'Alice';
```

The constant declaration for ScreenSize uses the previously defined constants Rows and Columns. Since Rows has the value 24 and Columns has the value 80, ScreenSize has the value 1920. The constant SpeedOfLight is associated with a real value (299800.0) expressed in scientific notation. The string 'Alice' is associated with the constant Name.

As mentioned earlier, there are two reasons for using constants. First, the name SpeedOfLight has more meaning to a reader of a program than the value 2.998E+5. Second, if we change the declaration of a constant, we also change the value of that constant wherever it is referenced in the program. ◀

5.2 Numeric Data Types

The data types CARDINAL, INTEGER, and REAL are used to represent numeric information. We used CARDINAL variables as loop counters and INTEGER variables to represent data such as exam scores that were whole numbers. In most other instances we used type REAL numeric data.

Differences Between Numeric Types

You may be wondering why it is necessary to have so many numeric types. Can the data type REAL be used for all numbers? The answer is yes. On many computers, however, operations involving integers are faster, and integers require less storage space. Also, whereas there may be some loss of accuracy when dealing with real numbers, operations with integers are always precise.

These differences result from how real numbers and integers are represented internally in memory. All data are represented in memory as *binary strings*, strings of 0's and 1's; however, the binary string stored for the integer 13 is not the same as the binary string stored for the real number 13.0. The actual internal representation used is computer dependent, but normally it will have the format shown in Fig. 5.1. In most computers, real format uses more bits than integer format.

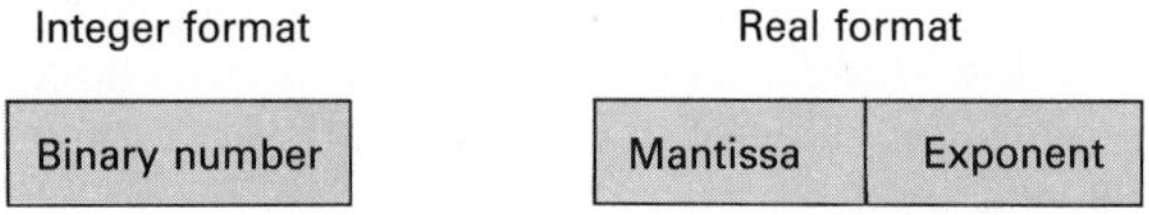

Figure 5.1 ▸ *Integer and Real Formats*

As Fig. 5.1 shows, integers are represented by standard binary numbers. If you are familiar with the binary number system, you know that the integer 13 is represented by the binary number 01101.

Real format is analogous to scientific notation. The storage area occupied by a real number is divided into two parts: the *mantissa* and the *exponent*. The mantissa is a binary fraction between 0.5 and 1.0 (−0.5 and −1.0 for a negative number). The exponent is a power of two. The mantissa and the exponent are chosen so that the formula below is correct.

$$real\ number = mantissa \times 2^{exponent}$$

Besides the capability of storing fractions, the range of numbers that may be represented in real format is considerably larger than for integer format. For example, in the LOGITECH Modula-2 compiler on the IBM personal computer, real numbers range in value from 10^{-308} (a very small fraction) to 10 + +308, whereas the range of integers extends from −32768 to 32767. In this compiler, a real number uses twice the storage space that an integer uses.

The CARDINAL data type may be used to represent positive whole numbers. Since there is no need to save the sign, the range of cardinal values extends from 0 to 65535. The main advantage of using type CARDINAL over type INTEGER is in documenting that a variable cannot be negative. Multiplication and division may be faster for operands of type CARDINAL.

Numeric Literals

A constant value appearing in an expression is called a literal. The data type of a numeric literal is determined in the following way. If the literal has a decimal point, it is considered type REAL. A type REAL literal may also have a decimal scale factor. For example, in the literal 2.998E+5, the scale factor is 10^5.

When an unsigned integer literal appears in an expression, Modula-2 uses its context to determine whether it is represented as type INTEGER or type CARDINAL. If the literal is manipulated with a type INTEGER operand, then the literal is type INTEGER. If the literal is manipulated with a type CARDINAL operand, then the literal is type CARDINAL.

Type of an Expression

The type of an expression is determined by the type of its operands and all operands of an expression must be the same type. For example, in the expression

```
X + 3.5
```

the variable X must be the same type (REAL) as the literal 3.5; the expression is type REAL. The expression

```
10 - I
```

is type INTEGER or CARDINAL depending on the type of variable I. If I is type CARDINAL and I is assigned a value greater than 10, a CARDINAL overflow run-time error will occur when the expression is evaluated because its value is negative.

Numeric Operators

The arithmetic operators +, −, *, and / can be used with real operands. However, since the *real division operator*, /, always yields a real result, it cannot be used with cardinals or integers. Instead, the *integer division operator*, DIV, must be used to divide two integer or cardinal values.

The expression M DIV N (M and N both integers or both cardinals) is equal to the truncated quotient of M divided by N. For example, if M is 7 and N is 2, the value of M DIV N is the truncated quotient of 7 divided by 2 or 3. The result of M DIV N has the same type (INTEGER or CARDINAL) as its operands.

EXAMPLE 5.2 ▶ Table 5.1 shows some examples of valid and invalid expressions involving the operators / and `DIV`. The result of integer division is always zero when the magnitude of the first operand is less than the magnitude of the second operand.

Table 5.1 ▶ *The DIV and / Operators*

3 DIV 15 = 0	3 DIV -15 = 0	15.0 / 3.0 = 5.0
15 DIV 3 = 5	15 DIV -3 = -5	15.0 DIV 3.0 is invalid
16 DIV 3 = 5	16 DIV -3 = -5	15 / 3 is invalid
17 DIV 3 = 5	-17 DIV 3 = -5	15 / 3.0 is invalid
18 DIV 3 = 6	-18 DIV -3 = 6	15.0 DIV 3 is invalid

The modulus operator, `MOD`, can also be used with integer or cardinal operands. The expression `M MOD N` (`M` and `N` are both type `INTEGER` or both type `CARDINAL`) is equal to the remainder of `M` divided by `N`. For example, `7 MOD 2` is equal to the remainder of 7 divided by 2 or 1. The second operand of `MOD` must always be greater than zero.

The formula

```
      M = (M DIV N) * N + (M MOD N)
e.g., 7 = (7 DIV 2) * 2 + (7 MOD 2) = 3 * 2 + 1 = 7
```

defines the relationship between the operators `DIV` and `MOD`. This relationship is illustrated by the following division example. The quotient is 3 (`7 DIV 2`), and the remainder is 1 (`7 MOD 2`). ◀

```
7 DIV 2
  |
  |
  ↓
  3 R1 <----7 MOD 2
 _______
2)7
  6
  -
  1
```

EXAMPLE 5.3 ▶ The `MOD` operator is illustrated in Table 5.2. The magnitude of the result is always less than the second operand (the divisor). The `MOD` operation is undefined when its second operand is negative. By comparing the second and third columns, we see that `M MOD N` is the negation of `-M MOD N`. ◀

Table 5.2 ▶ *The MOD Operator*

3 MOD 5 = 3	5 MOD 3 = 2	-5 MOD 3 = -2
4 MOD 5 = 4	5 MOD 4 = 1	-5 MOD 4 = -1
5 MOD 5 = 0	15 MOD 5 = 0	-15 MOD 5 = 0
6 MOD 5 = 1	15 MOD 6 = 3	-15 MOD 6 = -3
7 MOD 5 = 2	15 MOD 7 = 1	-15 MOD 7 = -1
8 MOD 5 = 3	15 MOD 8 = 7	-15 MOD 8 = -7

Operators DIV and MOD ▶

FORM: *operand*$_1$ `DIV` *operand*$_2$
operand$_1$ `MOD` *operand*$_2$

INTERPRETATION: The operator `DIV` yields the integral part of the result of *operand*$_1$ divided by *operand*$_2$; any remainder is truncated. The operator `MOD` yields the integer remainder of this division. Both operands must be the same data type (`INTEGER` or `CARDINAL`).

Note: If *operand*$_2$ is 0, the result of the `DIV` or `MOD` operation is undefined. If *operand*$_2$ is negative, the result of the `MOD` operation is undefined.

EXAMPLE 5.4 ▶ Procedure `PrintDigits` in Fig. 5.2 prints each digit of its parameter `Decimal` in reverse order (e.g., if `Decimal` is `738`, the digits printed are `8`, `3`, `7`). This is accomplished by printing each remainder (`0` through `9`) of `Decimal` divided by 10; the integer quotient of `Decimal` divided by 10 becomes the new value of `Decimal`.

The parameter `Decimal` is used as the loop-control variable. Within the `WHILE` loop, the `MOD` operator assigns to `Digit` the rightmost digit of `Decimal`, and the `DIV` operator assigns the rest of the number to `Decimal`. The loop is exited when `Decimal` becomes `0`. Since `Decimal` is a value parameter, the actual parameter value is not changed by the procedure execution. ◂

Figure 5.2 ▶ *Printing Decimal Digits*

```
PROCEDURE PrintDigits (Decimal (* input *) : CARDINAL);
(*
   Prints the digits of Decimal in reverse order.
   Pre : Decimal is assigned a value.
   Post: Each digit of Decimal is displayed, starting with the
         least significant one.
*)
   CONST
     Base = 10;                          (* number system base *)

   VAR
     Digit : CARDINAL;                   (* each digit *)

BEGIN  (* PrintDigits *)
  (* Find and print remainders of Decimal divided by 10 *)
  WHILE
    (* invariant:
         Decimal is the quotient of Decimal divided
         by Base and Digit is the remainder of
         Decimal divided by Base.
    *)
       Decimal # 0 DO
    Digit := Decimal MOD Base;       (* Get next remainder *)
    WriteCard (Digit, 1);
```

```
    Decimal := Decimal DIV Base      (* Get next quotient *)
  END; (* WHILE *)
  (* assert: Decimal is zero *)

  WriteLn
END PrintDigits;
```

Table 5.3 shows a trace of the procedure execution for an actual parameter of 43. The digits 3 and 4 are printed.

Table 5.3 ▸ *Trace of Execution of PrintDigits(43)*

STATEMENT	Decimal	Digit	EFFECT
	43		
WHILE Decimal # 0 DO	43		43 # 0 is true;
Digit := Decimal MOD Base	43	3	remainder is 3;
WriteCard (Digit, 1)		3	print 3;
Decimal := Decimal DIV Base	4		quotient is 4.
WHILE Decimal # 0 DO	4		4 # 0 is true;
Digit := Decimal MOD Base	4	4	remainder is 4;
WriteCard (Digit, 1)		4	print 4;
Decimal := Decimal DIV Base	0		quotient is 4.
WHILE Decimal # 0 DO	0		0 # 0 is false; exit.

Assignment Compatibility

An expression involving type REAL operands can be assigned only to a type REAL variable. An expression involving all INTEGER or all CARDINAL operands may be assigned to either a type INTEGER or a type CARDINAL variable. However, if a type INTEGER expression is assigned to a type CARDINAL variable, a CARDINAL overflow run-time error will result when the expression value is negative. We will discuss *assignment compatibility* in Section 5.6.

Expressions with Multiple Operators

To write expressions that compute the desired results, we must know the Modula-2 rules for evaluating expressions. For example, in the expression A + B * C, is * performed before +, or vice-versa? Is the expression X / Y * Z evaluated as (X / Y) * Z or X / (Y * Z)?

Some expressions with multiple operators are

```
1.8 * Celsius + 32.0
(Salary - 5000.00) * 0.20 + 1425.00
```

where Celsius and Salary are type REAL variables. In both cases, the algebraic rule that multiplication is performed before addition is applicable. The use of parentheses in the second expression ensures that the subtraction is done first. The Modula-2 rules for expression evaluation in the following syntax display are based on standard algebraic rules.

Rules for Expression Evaluation ▶

a. All parenthesized subexpressions must be evaluated first. Nested parenthesized subexpressions must be evaluated inside out, with the innermost subexpression evaluated first.
b. Operator precedence. Operators in the same subexpression are evaluated in the following order:

`*, /, DIV, MOD`	first
`+, -`	last

c. Left associative. Operators in the same subexpression and at the same precedence level (such as + and –) are evaluated left to right.

EXAMPLE 5.5 ▶ The formula for the area of a circle

$$a = \pi \times r^2$$

may be written in Modula-2 as

```
AREA := Pi * Radius * Radius
```

where `Pi` is the constant 3.14159. The *evaluation tree* for this formula is shown in Fig. 5.3. In this tree, the arrows connect each operand with its operator. The order of operator evaluation is shown by the number to the left of each operator; to the right is the letter that matches the applicable rule, as listed in the previous syntax display. ◀

Figure 5.3 ▶ *Evaluation Tree for Area := Pi * Radius * Radius*

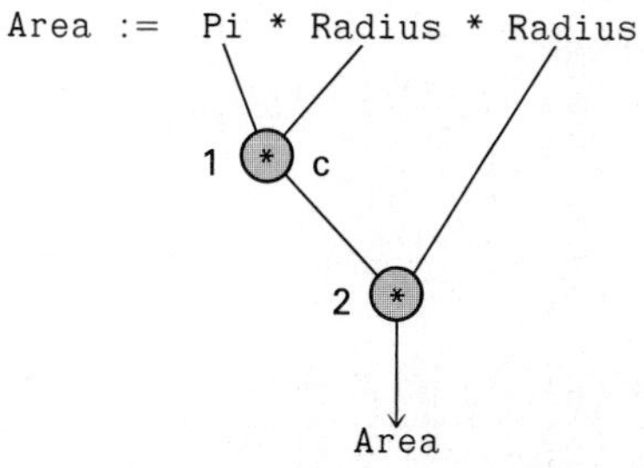

EXAMPLE 5.6 ▶ The formula for the average velocity, v, of a particle traveling on a line between points p_1 and p_2 in time t_1 to t_2 is

$$v = \frac{p_2 - p_1}{t_2 - t_1}$$

This formula can be written and evaluated in Modula-2 as shown in Fig. 5.4.

Figure 5.4 ▸
Evaluation Tree for V := (P2 − P1) / (T2 − T1)

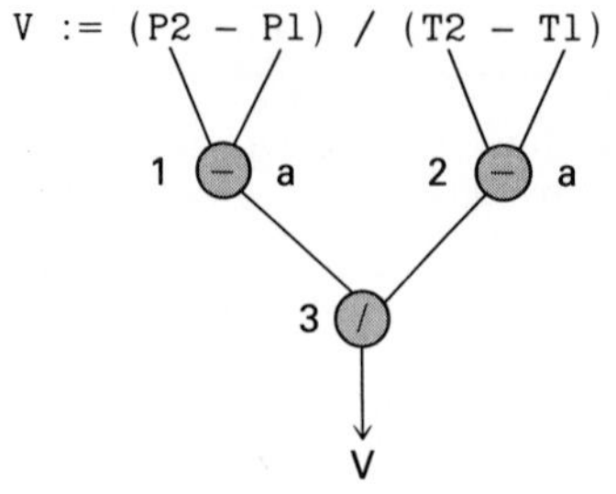

Inserting parentheses in an expression affects the order of operator evaluation. Parentheses should be used freely to clarify the order of evaluation. ◂

EXAMPLE 5.7 ▸ Consider the expression

```
Z - (A + B DIV 2) + W * Y
```

containing `INTEGER` variables only. The parenthesized subexpression `(A + B DIV 2)` is evaluated first (rule a), beginning with `B DIV 2` (rule b). Once the value of `B DIV 2` is determined, it can be added to `A` to obtain the value of `(A + B DIV 2)`. Next, the multiplication operation is performed (rule b) and the value for `W * Y` is determined. Then the value of `(A + B DIV 2)` is subtracted from `Z` (rule c), and finally this result is added to `W * Y`. The evaluation tree is shown in Fig. 5.5. ◂

Figure 5.5 ▸
*Evaluation Tree for Z − (A + B DIV 2) + W * Y*

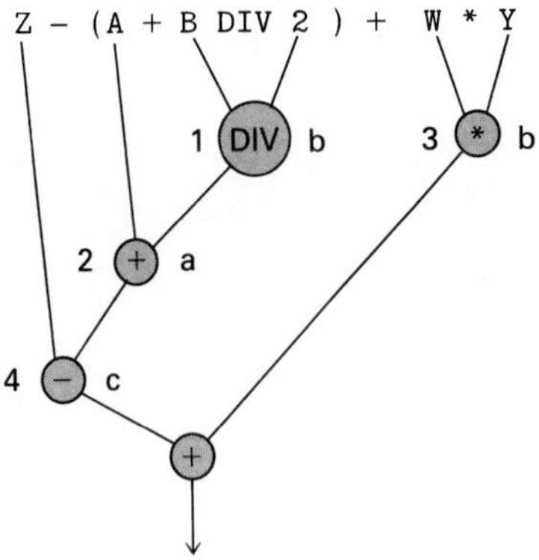

Writing Mathematical Formulas in Modula-2

There are two problem areas in writing a mathematical formula in Modula-2; one concerns multiplication and the other division. Multiplication can often be implied in a mathematical formula by writing the two items to be multiplied next to each other, for example, $a = bc$. In Modula-2, however, the * operator must *always* be used to indicate multiplication, as in

```
A := B * C
```

The other difficulty arises in formulas involving division. We normally write the numerator and denominator on separate lines:

$$m = \frac{y - b}{x - a}$$

In Modula-2, all assignment statements must be written in a linear form; consequently, parentheses are often needed to enclose the numerator and the denominator and to clearly indicate the order of evaluation of the operators in the expression. The preceding formula would be written as

```
M := (Y - B) / (X - A)
```

EXAMPLE 5.8 ▶ This example illustrates how several mathematical formulas can be written in Modula-2.

MATHEMATICAL FORMULA	MODULA-2 EXPRESSION
1. $b^2 - 4ac$	`B * B - 4.0 * A * C`
2. $a + b - c$	`A + B - C`
3. $\frac{a + b}{c + d}$	`(A + B) / (C + D)`
4. $\frac{1}{1 + x^2}$	`1.0 / (1.0 + X * X)`
5. $a \times -(b + c)$	`A * (-(B + C))`

The points illustrated are summarized as follows:

- Always specify multiplication explicitly by using the operator * (1).
- Use parentheses to control the order of operator evaluation (3, 4).
- Never write two arithmetic operators in succession; they must be separated by an operand or a parenthesis (5).
- Never mix operand types in an expression (1, 4).
- Never use integer literals with the real division operator (4). ◀

SELF-CHECK EXERCISES FOR SECTION 5.2

1. What happens if the constant `Base` is 2 instead of `10` in procedure `PrintDigits`? What result is generated for the procedure call statements `PrintDigits(23)` and `PrintDigits(64)` if `Base` is 2? If `Base` is 8?
2. Evaluate the following expressions with 7 and 22 as operands.
   `22 DIV 7`   `7 DIV 22`   `22 MOD 7`   `7 MOD 22`
   Repeat this exercise for these pairs of integers:
   15, 16   3, 23   4, 16
3. Given the declarations

```
CONST
  Pi = 3.14159;
  MaxI = 1000;

VAR
  X, Y : REAL;
  A, B, I : INTEGER;
```

find the value of each valid statement below. Also indicate which statements are invalid and why. Assume that `A` is 3, `B` is 4, and `Y` is `-1.0`.

a. `I := A MOD B`
b. `I := (990 - MaxI) DIV A`
c. `I := A MOD Y`
d. `X := Pi * Y`
e. `I := Y DIV 2.0`
f. `X := A DIV B`
g. `X := A MOD (A DIV B)`
h. `I := B DIV 0`
i. `I := A MOD (990 - MaxI)`
j. `I := (MaxI - 990) DIV A`
k. `X := A / Y`
l. `I := Pi * A`
m. `X := Pi DIV Y`
n. `X := A DIV B`
o. `I := (MaxI - 990) MOD A`
p. `I := A MOD 0`
q. `I := A MOD (MaxI - 990)`

4. What values are assigned by the legal statements in Exercise 3, assuming `A` is 5, `B` is 2, and `Y` is `2.0`?
5. Assume that you have the following variable declarations:

```
VAR
  Color, Lime, Straw, Yellow, Red, Orange : INTEGER;
  Black, White, Green, Blue, Purple, Crayon : REAL;
```

Evaluate each of the following statements given these values: `Color` is 2, `Black` is `2.5`, `Crayon` is `-1.3`, `Straw` is 1, `Red` is 3, `Purple` is `0.3E1`.

a. `White := Color * 2.5 / Purple;`
b. `Green := Color / Purple;`
c. `Orange := Color DIV Red;`
d. `Blue := (Color + Straw) / (Crayon + 0.3);`
e. `Lime := Red DIV Color + Red MOD Color;`
f. `Purple := Straw / Red * Color`

6. Let `A`, `B`, `C`, and `X` be the names of four type `REAL` variables and `I`, `J`, and `K` the names of three type `INTEGER` variables. Each of the following statements contains a violation of the rules for forming arithmetic expressions. Rewrite each statement so that it is consistent with the rules.

a. `X := 4.0 A * C`
b. `A := AC`
c. `I := 2 * -J`
d. `K := 3(I + J)`
e. `K := 5I DIV 3J`
f. `I := 5JK`

5.3 Standard Functions

This section describes the use of functions in expressions. A function is a procedure that performs a specific operation that is often mathematical (e.g., square root, cosine) and returns a single value. Functions are referenced directly in an expression; the value computed by the function is then substituted for the function reference.

EXAMPLE 5.9 ▶ `ABS` is the name of a function that computes the absolute value of a number. If the value of `X` is `-3.5`, the statement

```
Y := 5.7 + ABS(X + 0.5)
```

assigns a value of `8.7` to the type `REAL` variable `Y`. The execution of this statement is traced below. ◀

1. The expression argument (`X + 0.5`) is evaluated as `-3.0`.
2. The function returns 3.0, the absolute value of its argument.
3. The sum of `5.7` and the function result (`3.0`) is assigned to `Y` (`8.7`).

Standard Mathematical Functions

Modula-2 provides a number of standard mathematical functions. The names (in uppercase) and descriptions of some of these functions are given in Table 5.4. Others will be discussed as needed in the text. The function name is always followed by its *argument* (an actual parameter) enclosed in parentheses, as shown in Example 5.8 (argument is `X + 0.5`). Any legal expression of the proper type may be used as an argument for a function.

Table 5.4 ▶ *Standard Functions with Numeric Arguments and Results*

FUNCTION	PURPOSE
`ABS(X)`	Returns the absolute value of its argument (type `REAL`, `INTEGER`, or `CARDINAL`). The result type is the same as the argument type.
`FLOAT(N)`	Returns the type `REAL` representation of its type `CARDINAL` argument.
`MAX(T)`	Returns the maximum value of its argument (a type identifier). The type of the result is based on its argument. This function is not available in all Modula-2 systems.
`MIN(T)`	Returns the minimum value of its argument (a type identifier). The type of the result is based on its argument. This function is not available in all Modula-2 systems.

Table 5.4 ▶ *(continued)*

FUNCTION	PURPOSE
`ODD(N)`	Returns `TRUE` if its `INTEGER` or `CARDINAL` argument is an odd number; otherwise, returns `FALSE`.
`TRUNC(X)`	Returns the integral part of its `REAL` argument `X`. The result type is `CARDINAL`.

Function `ABS` may have a type `REAL`, `INTEGER`, or `CARDINAL` argument. The type of the result returned is the same as the type of the argument.

Functions `MIN` and `MAX` are included in the revised version of Modula-2 proposed in 1984 and are not supported on all Modula-2 compilers. The argument for `MIN` or `MAX` is a type identifier; the function `MIN` returns the minimum value for that data type, while function `MAX` returns the maximum value. On a computer that uses sixteen bits to represent an integer, the value of `MIN(INTEGER)` is `-32768` and the value of `MAX(INTEGER)` is `32767`. The value of `MIN(CARDINAL)` is always zero.

Function `ODD` may have a type `INTEGER` or `CARDINAL` argument. The function determines whether its argument is an odd number. The `BOOLEAN` value `TRUE` is returned if the function `ODD` has an odd number as its argument (e.g., `ODD(3)` is `TRUE`); otherwise, the `BOOLEAN` value `FALSE` is returned (e.g., `ODD(4)` is `FALSE`).

Type-Conversion Functions

The functions `FLOAT` and `TRUNC` convert between `CARDINAL` and `REAL` values. Function `FLOAT` accepts a type `CARDINAL` argument and returns the floating point representation of that argument (e.g., `FLOAT(3)` is `3.0`). The function `TRUNC` accepts a positive `REAL` argument and returns the integral part of that argument (e.g., `TRUNC(9.657)` is the cardinal `9`). Note that the value of the argument `9.657` is not rounded; its fractional part is simply *truncated*, or removed. If the argument of `TRUNC` is negative, a run-time error will result.

EXAMPLE 5.10 ▶ If `NumItems` is type `CARDINAL` and `SumOfItems` is type `REAL`, the expression

```
SumOfItems / FLOAT(NumItems)
```

divides the value of `SumOfItems` by the real equivalent of `NumItems`. This expression is used in the following assignment statement to store the "average value" in `Average`.

```
Average := SumOfItems / FLOAT(NumItems)
```

Note that the expression

```
SumOfItems / NumItems
```

is invalid, since the type `INTEGER` operand `NumItems` cannot be used with the real division operator. ◂

Utility Module MathLib0

Besides the standard functions, several functions are available in utility module `MathLib0` (pronounced "math-lib-zero"). They are described in Table 5.5 and must be imported into any module that references them. For the trigonometric functions, all angles must be in radians.

Table 5.5 ▸ *Functions in Utility Module MathLib0*

FUNCTION	PURPOSE
`arctan(X)`	Returns the angle y in radians satisfying `X` = tan(y) where $-\pi/2 \le y \le \pi/2$.
`cos(X)`	Returns the cosine of angle `X` (in radians).
`entier(X)`	Returns the largest integer less than or equal to `X`.
`exp(X)`	Returns e^X where $e = 2.71828\ldots$
`ln(X)`	Returns the natural logarithm of `X` for `X > 0.0`.
`real(X)`	Returns the `REAL` representation of its type `INTEGER` argument.
`sin(X)`	Returns the sine of angle `X` (in radians).
`sqrt(X)`	Returns the square root of `X` for `X` ≥ 0.0.

Functions `entier` and `real` are type-conversion functions. Function `entier` returns the largest integer that is less than or equal to its argument. This means that `entier(10.2)` is the integer `10`, and `entier(-10.2)` is the integer `-11`. Unlike `TRUNC`, `entier` can be passed a negative argument. Function `real` converts its integer argument to a real number in a manner similar to function `FLOAT` (e.g., `real(3)` is `3.0`).

The other utility functions in module `MathLib0` perform common mathematical computations. All of them accept type `REAL` arguments and return type `REAL` results. The arguments for `ln` and `sqrt` must be positive. The arguments for `sin` and `cos` must be expressed in radians, not degrees. The functions `exp` and `ln` are used in Example 5.11.

EXAMPLE 5.11 ▸ There is no exponentiation operator in Modula-2. This means that it is not possible to write x^y directly. However, from the study of logarithms we know that

$$\ln(x^y) = y \times \ln(x)$$

and

$$z = e^{\ln(z)}$$

where e is 2.71828.... So we can derive that

$$x^y = e^{(y \times \ln(x))}$$

This formula can be implemented in Modula-2 as ◂

```
XToPowerY := exp(y * ln(x))
```

EXAMPLE 5.12 ▸ The function `sqrt` (square root) can be used to compute the roots of a quadratic equation in X of the form

$$aX^2 + bX + c = 0$$

where a, b, and c are type `REAL`. The two roots are expressed in algebraic form as

$$Root1 = \frac{-b + \sqrt{b^2 - 4ac}}{2a}, \qquad Root2 = \frac{-b - \sqrt{b^2 - 4ac}}{2a}$$

The Modula-2 implementation is

```
Disc := b * b - 4 * a * c;
IF Disc > 0.0 THEN
  Root1 := (-b + sqrt(Disc)) / (2.0 * a);
  Root2 := (-b - sqrt(Disc)) / (2.0 * a)
END
```

where the variable `Disc` represents the *discriminant* ($b^2 - 4ac$) of the equation. ◂

EXAMPLE 5.13 ▸ The program in Fig. 5.6 illustrates the use of several arithmetic functions. The function references are used as actual parameters for procedures `WriteInt` and `WriteReal`. The `ABS` function is used to find the absolute value of `X` before the `sqrt` and `ln` functions are called.

Figure 5.6 ▸ *Using the Arithmetic Functions*

```
MODULE ArithFunc;

(* Illustrates the arithmetic functions. *)

  FROM InOut IMPORT
    WriteString, WriteCard, WriteInt, WriteLn;

  FROM RealInOut IMPORT
    ReadReal, WriteReal;

  FROM MathLib0 IMPORT
    entier, exp, ln, sqrt;
```

```
  CONST
    Sentinel =  0.0;          (* sentinel value *)

  VAR
    x : REAL;                 (* input each data value *)

BEGIN  (* ArithFunc *)
  (* Print the user instructions and table heading *)
  WriteString ('After each output line enter ');
  WriteString ('a real number or 0.0 to stop');
  WriteLn;  WriteLn;
  WriteString ('x     entier(x)       ABS(x)');
  WriteString ('       exp(x)   ln(ABS(x))  sqrt(ABS(x))');
  WriteLn;

  (* Read and process each value of x *)
  ReadReal (x);  WriteLn;                   (* Get first number *)
  WHILE x # Sentinel DO
    WriteInt (entier(x), 17);
    WriteReal (ABS(x), 13);
    WriteReal (exp(x), 13);
    WriteReal (ln(ABS(x)), 13);
    WriteReal (sqrt(ABS(x)), 14);
    WriteLn;
    ReadReal (x);  WriteLn                  (* Get next number *)
  END (* WHILE *)
END ArithFunc.


After each output line enter a real number or 0.0 to stop

x     entier(x)       ABS(x)        exp(x)   ln(ABS(x))  sqrt(ABS(x))
10.0
             10 1.00000E+001 2.20265E+004 2.30259E+000 3.162278E+000
2.71828
              2 2.71828E+000 1.51542E+001 9.99999E-001 1.648721E+000
25.0
             25 2.50000E+001 7.20049E+010 3.21888E+000 5.000000E+000
-15.15
            -16 1.51500E+001 2.63293E-007 2.71800E+000 3.892300E+000
0.0
```

CASE STUDY

Problem: A number of mathematical quantities can be represented using a series approximation, where a series is represented by a summation of an infinite number of terms. For example, the base of the natural logarithms, *e* (value is 2.71828...), can be determined by evaluating the expression

$1 + 1/1! + 1/2! + 1/3! + \ldots + 1/n! + \ldots$

where $n!$ is the factorial of n as defined here:

$0! = 1$
$n! = n \times (n-1)!$ (for $n > 1$)

Discussion: We can get an approximation to the value of e by summing the series for a finite value of n. Obviously, the larger the value of n, the more accurate the computed result. This expression can be represented using *summation notation* as

$$\sum_{i=0}^{n} 1/i!$$

where the first term is obtained by substituting 0 for i (1/0! is 1/1), the second term is obtained by substituting 1 for i (1/1!), and so on. A counting loop can be used to easily implement the preceding formula. The data requirements and algorithm follow.

PROBLEM INPUTS

the number of terms, n, in the sum (`n : CARDINAL`)

PROBLEM OUTPUTS

the approximate value of e (`e : REAL`)

PROGRAM VARIABLE

the ith term of the series (`ithTerm : REAL`)

Algorithm

1. Read in the value of `n`.
2. Initialize `e` to 1.0.
3. Initialize the ith term to 1.0.
4. `FOR` each `i` from `1` to `n DO`.
    5. Compute the ith term in the series.
    6. Add the ith term to `e`.

   END
7. Print the approximate value of `e`.

The program is shown in Fig. 5.7. Inside the `FOR` loop, the statement

```
ithTerm := ithTerm / FLOAT(i);
```

computes the value of the `ithTerm` in the series by dividing the previous term by the type `REAL` representation of the loop-control variable `i`. The formula below shows that this division does indeed produce the next term in the series.

$(1 / (i-1)!) / i = 1 / (i \times (i-1)!) = 1 / i!$

Since `0!` is `1`, `ithTerm` must be initialized to `1.0`. The statement

```
e = e + ithTerm
```

adds the new value of `ithTerm` to the sum being accumulated in `e`. Trace the execution of this loop to satisfy yourself that `ithTerm` takes on the values `1/1!`, `1/2!`, `1/3!`, and so on, during successive loop iterations.

Figure 5.7 ▸ *Series Approximation to e*

```
MODULE eSeries;

 (* Computes the value of e by a series approximation. *)

   FROM InOut IMPORT
     WriteString, WriteLn, ReadCard;

   FROM RealInOut IMPORT
     WriteReal;

   VAR
     e,                      (* output the value being approximated *)
     ithTerm : REAL;         (* ith term in series *)
     n,                      (* input number of terms in series *)
     i  : CARDINAL;          (* loop control variable *)

BEGIN
  WriteString('Enter the number of terms in the series: ');
  ReadCard(n);  WriteLn;

  (* Compute each term and add it to the accumulating sum. *)
  e := 1.0;                (* initial sum *)
  ithTerm := 1.0;          (* first term *)
  FOR i := 1 TO n DO
    ithTerm := ithTerm / FLOAT(i);
    e := e + ithTerm
  END;  (* FOR *)

  (* Print the result. *)
  WriteString('The approximate value of e is ');
  WriteReal(e, 20);  WriteLn
END eSeries.

Enter the number of terms in the series: 10
The approximate value of e is  2.718281801146E+000
```

Numerical Inaccuracies

One of the problems in processing real numbers is that there is sometimes an error in representing real data. Just as there are certain numbers that cannot be represented exactly in the decimal number system (e.g., the fraction 1/3 is 0.333333...), so there are numbers that cannot be represented exactly in real format. The *representational error* will depend on the number of binary digits (bits) used in the mantissa: the more bits the smaller the error.

The number 0.1 is an example of a real number that has a representational error. The effect of a small error is often magnified through repeated computations. Because the result of adding 0.1 ten times is not exactly 1.0, the following loop may fail to terminate on some computers.

```
Trial := 0.0;
WHILE Trial # 1.0 DO
  ................

  Trial := Trial + 0.1
END  (* WHILE *)
```

If the loop repetition test is changed to `Trial < 1.0`, the loop may execute ten times on one computer and eleven times on another. For this reason, it is best to use integers or cardinals whenever possible in loop repetition tests.

Other problems occur when manipulating very large and very small real numbers. In adding a large number and a small number, the larger number may "cancel out" the smaller number (a *cancellation error*). If `X` is much larger than `Y`, then `X + Y` and `X` may have the same value (e.g., 1000.0 + 0.0001234 is equal to 1000.0 on some computers).

For this reason, you can sometimes obtain more accurate results by carefully selecting the order in which computations are performed. For example, in computing the value of `e` in the preceding case study, the terms of the series

```
1 + 1/1! + 1/2! + ... + 1/n!
```

were generated in left-to-right order and added to a sum being accumulated in `e`. When `n` is large, the value of `1/n!` is very small, so the effect of adding a very small term to a sum that is larger than `2.0` may be lost. If the terms were generated and summed in right-to-left order instead, the computation result might be more accurate.

If two very small numbers are multiplied, the result may be too small to be represented accurately and thus will become zero. This is called *arithmetic underflow*. Similarly, if two very large numbers are multiplied, the result may be too large to be represented. This is called *arithmetic overflow* and is handled in different ways by Modula-2 compilers. Arithmetic underflow and overflow can also occur when processing very large and very small integer values. Arithmetic overflow can also occur when processing large cardinal values, or when a cardinal expression becomes negative.

SELF-CHECK EXERCISES FOR SECTION 5.3

1. Write a procedure that computes

$$e^{a \times \ln(b)}$$

Call this procedure with several different values of a and b and display the result. Verify for yourself that the result is correct.

2. Using the function `entier`, write a Modula-2 statement to round the value of real variable `X` to the nearest integer. Then write a statement sequence to round the value of `X` to two decimal places. Hint: You will have to multiply `X` by `100.0` before rounding.
3. The value of e^x is represented by the series

   $$1 + x + x^2/2! + x^3/3! + \ldots + x^n/n! + \ldots$$

   Write a procedure to compute and print the value of this series for any x and n. Compare the result to `exp(x)` and print a message `O.K.` or `Not O.K.`, depending on whether the difference between these results is less than 0.001.

5.4 Data Type BOOLEAN

Chapter 1 introduced the `BOOLEAN` data type. We have used `BOOLEAN` expressions (expressions that evaluate to `TRUE` or `FALSE`) to control loop repetition and to select one of the alternatives in an `IF` statement. Some examples of `BOOLEAN` expressions are:

```
Gross > TaxBracket
Item # Sentinel
TranType = 'C'
```

The simplest `BOOLEAN` expression is a `BOOLEAN` variable or constant. A `BOOLEAN` variable or constant can be set to either of the *Boolean values*, `TRUE` or `FALSE`. The statement

```
CONST
  Debug = TRUE;
```

specifies that the `BOOLEAN` constant `Debug` has the value `TRUE`; the statement

```
VAR
  Switch, Flag : BOOLEAN;
```

declares `Switch` and `Flag` to be `BOOLEAN` variables; that is, variables that may be assigned only the values `TRUE` and `FALSE`.

BOOLEAN Operators

A `BOOLEAN` variable or constant is the simplest form of a `BOOLEAN` expression (e.g., `Switch`). We have used the relational operators (=, < , > , etc.) with numeric data to form conditions, or `BOOLEAN` expressions (e.g., `Salary < MinSal`).

There are three `BOOLEAN` operators: `AND`, `OR`, `NOT`. These operators are used with operands that are `BOOLEAN` expressions.

```
(Salary < MinSal) OR (NumDepend > 5)
(Temp > 90.0) AND (Humidity > 0.90)
Athlete AND (NOT Failing)
```

The first BOOLEAN expression can determine whether an employee pays income tax. It evaluates to true if either condition in parentheses is true. The second BOOLEAN expression can describe an unbearable summer day: temperature and humidity both above 90. The expression evaluates to true only when both conditions are true. The third BOOLEAN expression has two BOOLEAN variables (Athlete and Failing) as its operands. Any individual for whom this expression is true is eligible for intercollegiate sports.

The symbol & may be used in place of AND. Therefore, the last expression can also be written as

```
Athlete & (NOT Failing)
```

(In the revised version of Modula-2, the symbol ~ may be used in place of NOT. However, we will not use ~ in the text.)

The BOOLEAN operators can be used with BOOLEAN expressions only. The BOOLEAN operators are summarized in Tables 5.6, 5.7, and 5.8.

Table 5.6 ▸ *AND (&) Operator*

OPERAND1	OPERAND2	OPERAND1 & OPERAND2
true	true	true
true	false	false
false	true	false
false	false	false

Table 5.7 ▸ *OR Operator*

OPERAND1	OPERAND2	OPERAND1 OR OPERAND2
true	true	true
true	false	true
false	true	true
false	false	false

Table 5.8 ▸ *NOT Operator*

OPERAND1	NOT OPERAND1
true	false
false	true

Table 5.6 shows that the AND operator yields a true result only when both its operands are true; Table 5.7 shows that the OR operator yields a false result

only when both its operands are false. The NOT operator has a single operand; Table 5.8 shows that the NOT operator yields the *logical complement*, or negation, of its operand.

The precedence of an operator determines its order of evaluation. Table 5.9 shows the precedence of all operators in Modula-2 that may occur in an expression.

Table 5.9 ▸ *Operator Precedence*

OPERATOR	PRECEDENCE
NOT	highest (evaluated first)
*, /, DIV, MOD, AND or &	↓
+, −, OR	↓
<, <=, =, # or <>, >=, >	lowest (evaluated last)

This table shows that the NOT operator has the highest precedence. Next are the multiplicative operators (including AND), the additive operators (including OR), and, last, the relational operators. Since the relational operators have the lowest precedence, they should generally be used with parentheses to prevent syntax errors.

EXAMPLE 5.14 ▸ The expression

```
X < Y + Z
```

involving the type REAL variables X, Y, and Z is interpreted as

```
X < (Y + Z)
```

since + has higher precedence than <.

The expression

```
X < Y OR Z < Y
```

causes the syntax error `invalid type of operands`. It is interpreted as

```
X < (Y OR Z) < Y
```

since OR has higher precedence than <. This is an error because the type REAL variables Y and Z cannot be operands of the BOOLEAN operator OR. The parentheses in the following expression prevent a syntax error. ◂

```
(X < Y) OR (Z < Y)
```

EXAMPLE 5.15 ▸ The following are all legal BOOLEAN expressions if X, Y, and Z are type REAL, and Flag is type BOOLEAN. Assuming that X is 3.0, Y is 4.0, Z is 2.0, and Flag is TRUE, the value of each expression is shown in brackets.

```
1. (X > Z) & (Y > Z)                      [TRUE]
2. (X + Y / Z) <= 3.5                     [FALSE]
3. (Z > X) OR (Z > Y)                     [FALSE]
4. NOT Flag                               [FALSE]
5. (X = 1.0) OR (X = 3.0)                 [TRUE]
6. (0.0 < X) & (X < 3.5)                  [TRUE]
7. (X <= Y) & (Y <= Z)                    [FALSE]
8. NOT Flag OR ((Y + Z) >= (X - Z))       [TRUE]
9. NOT (Flag OR ((Y + Z) >= (X - Z)))     [FALSE]
```

Expression 1 gives the Modula-2 form of the relationship "X and Y are greater than Z." It is often tempting to write this as

```
X & Y > Z
```

However, this is an illegal `BOOLEAN` expression because the real variable `X` cannot be an operand of the `BOOLEAN` operator `&`. Similarly, expression 5 shows the correct way to express the relationship "X is equal to 1.0 or to 3.0."

Expression 6 is the Modula-2 form of the relationship $0.0 < X < 3.5$, that is, "X is in the range 0.0 to 3.5." Similarly, expression 7 shows the Modula-2 form of the relationship $X \le Y \le Z$; that is, "Y is in the range X to Z, inclusive."

Finally, expression 8 is evaluated in Fig. 5.8; the values given at the beginning of Example 5.14 are shown above the expression. ◂

Figure 5.8 ▸ *Evaluation Tree for NOT Flag OR ((Y +Z) >= (X − Z))*

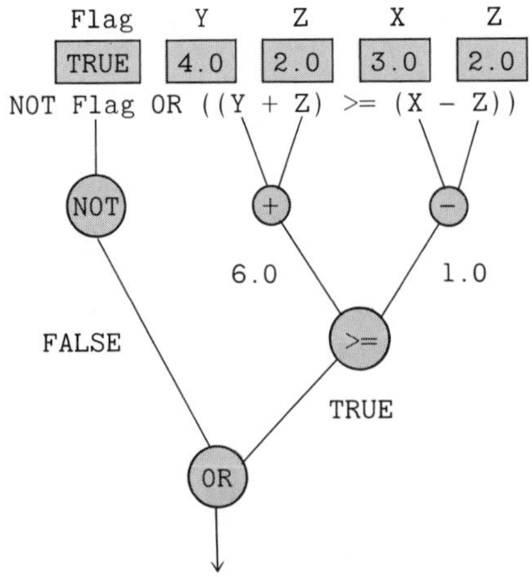

The expression in Fig. 5.8 is rewritten as follows, with parentheses enclosing the term `NOT Flag`. Although these parentheses are not required, they do clarify the meaning of the expression—we recommend their use.

```
(NOT Flag) OR ((Y + Z) >= (X - Z))
```

Short-Circuit Evaluation of BOOLEAN Expressions

When evaluating BOOLEAN expressions, Modula-2 employs a technique called short-circuit evaluation. This means that the evaluation of the expression is terminated as soon as the value of the expression can be determined.

EXAMPLE 5.16 ▶ If the value of Flag is FALSE, then NOT Flag is TRUE. Therefore, the expression in Fig. 5.8 must evaluate to TRUE regardless of the value of the parenthesized expression following OR (i.e., TRUE OR ... must always be TRUE). Consequently, the parenthesized expression following OR is not evaluated when Flag is FALSE. ◀

EXAMPLE 5.17 ▶ If X is zero, the expression

```
(X # 0.0) & (Y / X > 5.0)
```

is FALSE because (X # 0.0) is FALSE, and FALSE & ... must always be FALSE. Consequently, there is no need to evaluate the subexpression (Y / X > 5.0) when X is zero. We should point out that it is a good thing that this expression is not evaluated. If it were, a division by zero run-time error would occur because the divisor X is zero. The use of short-circuit evaluation by Modula-2 can prevent the occurrence of potential run-time errors. ◀

BOOLEAN Assignment Statements

We can write assignment statements that assign a BOOLEAN value to a BOOLEAN variable. The statement

```
Same := X = Y
```

assigns the value TRUE to the BOOLEAN variable Same when X and Y are equal; otherwise, the value FALSE is assigned. This assignment statement is more efficient than the IF statement

```
IF X = Y THEN
  Same := TRUE
ELSE
  Same := FALSE
END
```

which has the same effect.

EXAMPLE 5.18 ▶ Either of the following assignment statements assigns the value TRUE to Even if N is an even number.

```
Even := NOT ODD(N)        Even := (N MOD 2) = 0
```

The statement on the left assigns to Even the complement of the value returned by the BOOLEAN function ODD; the one on the right assigns a value of

TRUE to Even when the remainder of N divided by 2 is 0. (All even numbers are divisible by 2.) ◂

Using BOOLEAN Variables as Program Flags

BOOLEAN variables are often used as *program flags* to signal whether a special event occurs in a program. That such an event occurs is important to the future execution of the program. A BOOLEAN variable used as a program flag is initialized to one of its two possible values (TRUE or FALSE) and reset to the other as soon as the event being monitored occurs.

EXAMPLE 5.19 ▸ Procedure EnterInt in Fig. 5.9 continues to read integer values until a value between its two input parameters, MinN and MaxN, is entered. The first data value within range is returned as the procedure result.

The procedure begins with an IF statement that tests whether MinN is greater than MaxN. If it is, a warning message is displayed, and the values in MinN and MaxN are exchanged.

The BOOLEAN variable Between is used as a program flag to signal whether the event "data entry of an integer between MinN and MaxN" has occurred. The variable Between is initialized to FALSE before the WHILE loop. Inside the WHILE loop, the assignment statement

```
Between := (MinN <= N) & (N <= MaxN)
```

resets Between to TRUE when a value between MinN and MaxN is read into N. The loop is repeated as long as Between is still FALSE. ◂

Figure 5.9 ▸ *Procedure EnterInt*

```
PROCEDURE EnterInt (MinN, MaxN (* input *) : INTEGER;
                    VAR N (* output *) : INTEGER);
(*
   Reads an integer between MinN and MaxN into N.
   Pre :  MinN and MaxN are assigned values.
   Post: A value between MinN and MaxN is read into N.
*)
   VAR
     Between : BOOLEAN;      (* program flag -- loop control *)
     TempN : INTEGER;        (* temporary copy of MinN *)

BEGIN (* EnterInt *)
  IF MinN > MaxN THEN
    WriteString ('Error -- empty range for EnterInt');  WriteLn;
    WriteString ('MinN and MaxN were exchanged');       WriteLn;
    (* Exchange MinN and MaxN *)
    TempN := MinN;  MinN :=MaxN;  MaxN := TempN
  END; (* IF *)
```

```
  (* Keep reading until a valid number is read. *)
  Between := FALSE;    (* Assume a valid number is not read *)
  WHILE
    (* invariant:
         All prior values of N are outside the range MinN to MaxN
    *)
      NOT Between DO
    WriteString ('Enter an integer between ');
    WriteInt (MinN, 0);  WriteString (' and ');
    WriteInt (MaxN, 0);  WriteString (': ');
    ReadInt (N);         WriteLn;
    Between := (MinN <= N) & (N <= MaxN)
  END (* WHILE *)
  (* assert: N is in the range MinN to MaxN *)

END EnterInt;
```

Program Style

Defensive Programming

The IF statement in Fig. 5.9 exchanges the values of MinN and MaxN if MinN is larger than MaxN, which redefines the range of acceptable values for N. If the exchange was omitted, it would not be possible to enter a value of N that was in range, and the program user would have to terminate the program.

This tactic is called *defensive programming*. Whenever possible, you should anticipate common errors and take steps to counteract them. Make sure, however, that you display an error message so that the program user is aware of the mistake that was made and the corrective action that was taken.

Reading and Writing BOOLEAN Values

There are no utility procedures that can be used to read a BOOLEAN value or display the value of a BOOLEAN variable directly. However, the utility procedures Read and WriteString from module InOut can be used to perform input and output of BOOLEAN values, as shown in the next example.

EXAMPLE 5.20 ▶ Procedure ReadBool in Fig. 5.10 enters a character and uses the BOOLEAN assignment statement

```
BoolVar := CAP(InChar) = 'T'
```

to define the value of the output parameter BoolVar (type BOOLEAN). BoolVar is TRUE if InChar is 'T' or 't'; otherwise, BoolVar is FALSE. Function CAP returns the uppercase form of a lowercase letter and is described in the next section.

Figure 5.10 ▶
Procedure ReadBool

```
PROCEDURE ReadBool (VAR BoolVar (* output *) : BOOLEAN);
(*
   Enters a character to determine the value of BoolVar.
   Pre : None
   Post: BoolVar is TRUE if t or T is read;
         otherwise, BoolVar is FALSE.
*)
   VAR
     InChar : CHAR;          (* data character *)
BEGIN (* ReadBool *)
  Read (InChar);
  BoolVar := CAP(InChar) = 'T'
END ReadBool;
```

Procedure `WriteBool` in Fig. 5.11 displays the value of its `BOOLEAN` parameter. The input parameter `BoolVar` is the `BOOLEAN` expression in the `IF` statement.

Figure 5.11 ▶
Procedure WriteBool

```
PROCEDURE WriteBool (BoolVar (* input *) : BOOLEAN);
(*
   Displays the value of BoolVar.
   Pre : BoolVar is assigned a value.
   Post: 'TRUE' is displayed if BoolVar is TRUE;
         otherwise, 'FALSE' is displayed.
*)
BEGIN (* WriteBool *)
  IF BoolVar THEN
    WriteString ('TRUE')
  ELSE
    WriteString ('FALSE')
  END
END WriteBool;
```

If `Switch` is type `BOOLEAN`, the statements

```
WriteString ('Enter T or F': ');
ReadBool (Switch);
WriteBool (Switch)
```

read and echo the value of `Switch`. If the program user enters `T` or `t`, the string `'TRUE'` is displayed; otherwise, the string `'FALSE'` is displayed. ◂

Using a Global BOOLEAN Constant for Debugging

As mentioned earlier, a programmer should plan for debugging by including diagnostic print statements in the original code. One way to prevent the diagnostic print statements from executing during production runs is to declare a global BOOLEAN constant (say, Debug) whose value is TRUE during debugging and FALSE during production runs. The declaration part of the main module will contain the constant declaration

```
CONST
  Debug = TRUE;        (* turn debugging diagnostics on *)
```

during debugging runs and the constant declaration

```
CONST
  Debug = FALSE;        (* turn debugging diagnostics off *)
```

during production runs. The following diagnostic print statements will be executed only when Debug is TRUE (i.e., during debugging runs).

```
IF Debug THEN
  WriteString ('Procedure ProcessGoods entered'); WriteLn;
  WriteString ('Input parameter Salary is ');
  WriteReal (Salary, 12);  WriteLn
END; (* IF *)
```

SELF-CHECK EXERCISES FOR SECTION 5.4

1. Draw the evaluation tree for expression 9 of Example 5.15.
2. Write the following BOOLEAN assignment statements:
   a. Assign a value of TRUE to Positive if the value of N lies between 1 and Max inclusive; otherwise, assign a value of FALSE.
   b. Assign a value of TRUE to UpCase if CH is an uppercase letter; otherwise, assign a value of FALSE.
3. Assign a value of TRUE to Divisor if M is a divisor of N; otherwise, assign a value of FALSE.
4. Rewrite Procedure EnterInt to use a BOOLEAN variable OutOfRange that has the value TRUE if N is less than Min or greater than Max. OutOfRange, rather than Between, should be used to control loop repetition.

5.5 Data Type CHAR

Modula-2 provides a character data type that can be used to store individual characters. Character variables are declared using the data type CHAR. A character value consists of a single printable character (letter, digit, punctuation mark, etc.) enclosed in quotes. A character value may be assigned to a character variable or associated with a constant identifier, as shown in the following examples:

```
CONST
  Star = '*';
```

```
VAR
  NextLetter : CHAR;

BEGIN
  NextLetter := 'A'
```

The character variable `NextLetter` is assigned the character value `'A'` by the assignment statement. A single character variable or value may appear on the right side of a character assignment statement. Character values can also be compared, read, and printed.

EXAMPLE 5.21 ▶ The program in Fig. 5.12 reads a sentence ending in a period and counts the number of blanks in the sentence. Each character entered after the prompting message is read into the variable `Next` and tested to see if it is a blank.

The statement

```
Read (Next)
```

appears twice in the program and is used to read one character at a time from the data line, because `Next` is type `CHAR`. The `WHILE` loop is exited when the last character read is a period. ◀

Figure 5.12 ▶ *Counting Blanks in a Sentence*

```
MODULE BlankCount;

(* Counts the number of blanks in a sentence. *)

   FROM InOut IMPORT
     Read, Write, WriteString, WriteCard, WriteLn;

   CONST
     Blank =  ' ';                (* character being counted *)
     Sentinel =  '.';             (* sentinel character *)

   VAR
     Next  : CHAR;                (* input next character in sentence *)
     Count : CARDINAL;            (* output number of blank characters *)

BEGIN  (* BlankCount *)
  WriteString ('Enter a sentence ending with a period.');
  WriteLn;

  (* Process each input character up to the period *)
  Count :=  0;                    (* Initialize Count *)
  Read (Next);                    (* Get first character *)
  Write (Next);
```

```
  WHILE
    (*
       invariant: Count is the count of blanks so far and
         no prior value of Next is the sentinel
    *)
       Next # Sentinel DO
    IF Next = Blank THEN
      INC(Count)              (* Increment blank count *)
    END; (* IF *)
    Read (Next);                 (* Get next character *)
    Write (Next)
  END; (* WHILE *)
  (* assert: Count is the count of blanks and Next is the sentinel *)

  WriteLn;
  WriteString ('The number of blanks is ');
  WriteCard (Count, 2);
  WriteLn
END BlankCount.

Enter a sentence ending with a period.
There was an old woman who lived in a shoe.
The number of blanks is 9
```

Using Relational Operators with Characters

In Fig. 5.12, the BOOLEAN expressions

```
Next = Blank
Next # Sentinel
```

are used to determine whether two character variables have the same value or different values. Order comparisons can also be performed on character variables using the relational operators < , <=, >, >=.

To understand the result of an order comparison, we must know something about the way characters are represented internally. Each character has its own unique numeric code; the binary form of this code is stored in a memory cell that has a character value. These binary numbers are compared by the relational operators in the normal way. The character code we will use is called ASCII (American Standard Code for Information Interchange) and is shown in Appendix D.

The printable characters have codes from 32 (code for a blank or space) to 126 (code for the symbol ˜). The other codes represent nonprintable control characters. Sending a control character to an output device causes the device to perform a special operation, such as returning the cursor to column one, advancing the cursor to the next line, or ringing a bell.

Some features of ASCII are

- The digits are an increasing sequence of consecutive characters: `'0'<'1'<'2'<'3'<'4'<'5'<'6'<'7'<'8'<'9'`

- The uppercase letters are an increasing sequence of consecutive characters: `'A'<'B'<'C'< ...<'X'<'Y'<'Z'`
- The lowercase letters are an increasing sequence of consecutive characters: `'a'<'b'<'c'< ...<'x'<'y'<'z'`
- The digit characters precede the uppercase letters; the uppercase letters precede the lowercase letters: `'0'<'9'<'A'<'Z'<'a'< 'z'`

The Function CAP

We have used the function `CAP` to simplify testing for a particular letter of the alphabet. For example, in Fig. 5.10, the `BOOLEAN` assignment statement

```
BoolVar := CAP(InChar) = 'T'
```

assigns a value of `TRUE` to `BoolVar` if `InChar` is either `'t'` or `'T'`. This is because `CAP` returns the uppercase form of the lowercase letter used as a parameter. Without the `CAP` function, we would have had to write

```
BoolVar := (InChar = 'T') OR (InChar = 't')
```

If `InChar` is already an uppercase letter, then `CAP(InChar)` returns that uppercase letter. However, if `InChar` is not a letter, the result of `CAP(InChar)` is undefined.

Ordinal Types and the Function ORD

An *ordinal type* is a data type in which each value (except the first) has a unique predecessor and each value (except the last) has a unique successor (e.g., the predecessor of 5 is 4 and the successor of 5 is 6). The data types `BOOLEAN`, `CARDINAL`, `CHAR`, and `INTEGER` are all ordinal types. The data type `REAL` is not an ordinal type because a real number does not have a unique successor. For example, is the successor of 3.1415 the number 3.1416 or the number 3.14151?

The order or sequence of an ordinal data type is well defined. For example, if sixteen bits are used for integer and cardinal values, the cardinal numbers follow the sequence 0, 1, 2, 3, ..., 65535. The order of the `BOOLEAN` values is `FALSE`, `TRUE`.

The Modula-2 function `ORD` determines the *ordinal number*, or relative position of an ordinal value in its sequence of values, starting with 0 as the ordinal number of the first value in the sequence (e.g., `ORD(FALSE)` is `0`). Function `ORD(X)` returns a type `CARDINAL` result. If the argument `X` is a positive integer or cardinal, the value of `ORD(X)` is `X`. For all other ordinal types, the ordinal number of the first value in the sequence is zero, the ordinal number of the second value is one, and so on. Thus, `ORD(FALSE)` is zero and `ORD(TRUE)` is one. If `A` and `B` belong to the same ordinal type and `A < B` is true, then `ORD(A) < ORD(B)` must also be true.

EXAMPLE 5.22 ▶ Table 5.10 shows the result of using the `ORD` function with type `CARDINAL`, `BOOLEAN`, and `CHAR` arguments.

Table 5.10 ▶ *Result of ORD Function*

ARGUMENT	ORD(ARGUMENT)
0	0
30	30
65535	65535
FALSE	0
TRUE	1
'C'	67
'7'	55
'y'	121
blank	32

Because the digit characters are in increasing sequence, the expression

```
ORD('7') - ORD('0')
```

must have the value 7. From the table above, we see that the digit character '7' has the ordinal number 55, so the digit character '0' must have the ordinal number 48 (55 − 7). Also from this table and our knowledge of ASCII, we know that the letter 'D' is the successor of the letter 'C' (ordinal number 67) so the ordinal number of 'D' must be 68. ◀

EXAMPLE 5.23 ▶ Sometimes, instead of using `ReadCard` or `ReadInt`, we prefer to read a number as a string of individual characters. This enables the program to detect and ignore input errors. For example, if the program user enters a letter instead of a number, the error can be detected and the program can prompt again for a data value. Similarly, if the program user types in $15,400 instead of the number 15400, the extra characters can be ignored.

Procedure `ReadIntString` in Fig. 5.13 reads in a string of characters ending with the sentinel % and ignores any character that is not a digit. It also computes the value of the number (a cardinal) formed by the digits only. For example, if the characters `$15,43AB0%` are entered, the value returned through `NumData` will be `15430`.

Figure 5.13 ▸
Reading a Number as a String of Characters

```
PROCEDURE ReadIntString (VAR NumData (* output *) : CARDINAL);
(*
   Reads consecutive characters ending with the symbol %. Computes
   the integer value of the digit characters, ignoring nondigits.
   Pre : None
   Post: NumData is the value of the digit characters read.
*)
  CONST
    Base = 10;              (* the number system base *)
    Sentinel = '%';         (* the sentinel character *)

  VAR
    Next : CHAR;            (* input each character read *)
    Digit : CARDINAL;       (* the value of each numeric character *)

BEGIN (* ReadIntString *)
  (* Accumulate the numeric value of the digits in NumData *)
  NumData := 0;                  (* initial value is zero *)
  Read (Next);                   (* Read first character *)
  Write (Next);
  WHILE
    (* invariant:
         No prior value of Next is the sentinel and
         NumData is the number formed from all digit characters read
         into next.
    *)
      Next # Sentinel DO
    IF (Next >= '0') & (Next <= '9') THEN
      (* Process digit *)
      Digit := ORD(Next) - ORD('0');      (* Get digit value *)
      NumData := Base * NumData + Digit   (* Add digit value *)
    END;  (* IF *)
    Read (Next);                         (* Read next character *)
    Write (Next)
  END (* WHILE *)
  (* assert:
       Next is the sentinel and
       NumData is the number in base Base formed from the digit
       characters read as data
  *)

END ReadIntString;
```

In Fig. 5.13, the statements

```
Digit := ORD(Next) - ORD('0');       (* Get digit value *)
NumData := Base * NumData + Digit    (* Add digit value *)
```

assign to `Digit` an integer value between `0` (for character value `'0'`) and `9` (for character value `'9'`). The number being accumulated in `NumData` is multiplied by `10`, and the value of `Digit` is added to it. Table 5.11 traces the procedure execution for the input characters `3N5%`; the value returned is `35`. ◂

Table 5.11 ▸ *Trace of Execution of Procedure ReadIntString for Data Characters 3N5%*

STATEMENT	Next	Digit	NumData	EFFECT OF STATEMENT
	?	?	?	
`NumData := 0`			0	Initialize `NumData`.
`Read (Next)`	3			Get character.
`WHILE Next # Sentinel DO`	3			`'3' # '%'` is true
`IF (Next>='0') & (Next<='9')`	3			`'3'` is a digit
`Digit := ORD(Next) - ORD('0')`		3		Digit value is `3`.
`NumData := Base*NumData + Digit`			3	Add `3` to `0`.
`Read (Next)`	N			Get character.
`WHILE Next # Sentinel DO`	N			`'N' # '%'` is true.
`IF (Next>='0') & (Next<='9')`				`'N'` is not a digit.
`Read (Next)`	5			Get character.
`WHILE Next # Sentinel DO`	5			`'5' # '%'` is true.
`IF (Next>='0') & (Next<='9')`	5			`'5'` is a digit.
`Digit := ORD(Next) - ORD('0')`		5		Digit value is `5`.
`NumData := Base*NumData + Digit`			35	Add `5` to `30`.
`Read (Next)`	%			Get character.
`WHILE Next # Sentinel DO`	%			`'%' # '%'` is false

Character Constants

Because the control characters in Modula-2 cannot be printed, they cannot be represented in programs in the usual way (i.e., by enclosing them in quotes). A control character in Modula-2 is specified by its ordinal number (see Appendix D) represented as an octal (base 8) number followed by the letter `C`. For example, the character constant `12C` represents the line-feed character; the character constant `7C` is the bell character. The statements

```
Write(12C);
Write(7C);   Write(7C)
```

should cause the output device to perform a line feed and then ring its bell twice.

The Function CHR

The function CHR returns a character as its result. The character returned is the one whose ordinal number is the function argument. Therefore, the result of the function reference CHR(67) is the character with ordinal number 67 (the character 'C' in ASCII).

The characters returned by the references to function CHR that follows are control characters.

```
Write(CHR(12));
Write(CHR(7));    Write(CHR(7));
```

These statements should have the same effect as the Write statements in the preceding subsection (i.e., perform a line feed and ring the bell twice).

If NextChar is a type CHAR variable, the *nested function reference*

```
CHR(ORD(NextChar))
```

has the same value as NextChar. Therefore, the function CHR is the *inverse* of the ORD function for the characters.

EXAMPLE 5.24 ▶ The following IF statement sets LowCase to the lowercase form of a capital letter stored in NextChar, where NextChar, and LowCase, are both type CHAR. If NextChar does not contain a capital letter, LowCase is assigned the same value as NextChar.

```
IF (NextChar >= 'A') & (NextChar <= 'Z') THEN
  LowCase := CHR(ORD('a') + ORD(NextChar) - ORD('A'))
ELSE
  LowCase := NextChar
END
```

If NextChar has the value 'C', the BOOLEAN expression is TRUE and the assignment statement is evaluated as shown below. ◀

```
LowCase := CHR(ORD('a') + ORD('C') - ORD('A'))
           CHR(ORD('a') + 2)
           CHR(99) = 'c'
```

EXAMPLE 5.25 ▶ A *collating sequence* is a sequence of characters arranged by ordinal number. The program in Fig. 5.14 prints part of the Modula-2 collating sequence. It lists the characters with ordinal numbers 32 through 90, inclusive. The sequence shown is for ASCII; the first character printed is a blank (ordinal number 32). ◀

Figure 5.14 ▶ *Printing Part of a Collating Sequence*

```
MODULE Collate;

(* Prints part of the collating sequence. *)

FROM InOut IMPORT
  Write, WriteLn;
```

```
CONST
  MinOrd = 32;              (* smallest ordinal number *)
  MaxOrd = 90;              (* biggest ordinal number *)

VAR
  NextOrd : CARDINAL;       (* each ordinal number *)

BEGIN  (* Collate *)
  (* Print characters CHR(32) through CHR(90) *)
  FOR NextOrd := MinOrd TO MaxOrd DO
    Write (CHR(NextOrd))
  END; (* FOR *)
  WriteLn
END Collate.

 !"#$%&'()*+,-./0123456789:;<=>?@ABCDEFGHIJKLMNOPQRSTUVWXYZ
```

Table of Functions

The functions described in this section are summarized in Table 5.12.

Table 5.12 ▸ *Standard Functions for Data Type CHAR*

FUNCTION	PURPOSE
`CAP(Ch)`	If `Ch` is a lowercase letter, returns the corresponding uppercase letter. If `Ch` is an uppercase letter, returns that letter.
`CHR(N)`	Returns the character with ordinal number `N`.
`ORD(X)`	Returns the ordinal number (type `CARDINAL`) of its argument (an expression of any ordinal type).

SELF-CHECK EXERCISES FOR SECTION 5.5

1. Evaluate the following:
   a. `ORD(TRUE)`
   b. `CHR(ORD(' '))`
   c. `CHR(ORD('A') + 5)`
   d. `ORD(TRUE) - ORD(FALSE)`
   e. `ORD(CAP('a')) - ORD('A')`
   f. `CHR(ORD(CAP('z')))`
   g. `ORD(30 MOD 7)`
2. Evaluate the following using the ASCII character set.
   a. `ORD('D') - ORD('A')`
   b. `ORD('d') - ORD(CAP('a'))`
   c. `CHR(ORD('C'))`

d. `CHR(ORD('C') - ORD('A') + ORD('a'))`
e. `ORD('7') - ORD('6')`
f. `ORD('9') - ORD('0')`
g. `CHR(ORD('A') - 5)`

5.6 Functions and Procedures for Ordinal Types

We defined ordinal types in the last section and mentioned that all the standard types except REAL are ordinal types. This section describes functions and procedures that have ordinal type arguments.

Procedures INC and DEC

Ordinal types are characterized by the fact that each value has a unique predecessor and a unique successor. Often we want to assign to a variable the predecessor or successor of its current value. The assignment statements

```
I := I + 1
```

and

```
I := I - 1
```

accomplish this when I is type INTEGER or CARDINAL.

The standard procedures INC (for increment) and DEC (for decrement) perform these operations for a variable of any ordinal type. The preceding statements can be rewritten as

```
INC(I, 1) or INC(I)
```

and

```
DEC(I, 1) or DEC(I)
```

As shown, the second parameter can be omitted when it is 1.

EXAMPLE 5.26 ▶ Procedures DEC and INC are used in the following statements with several different argument types. The variable Ch is type CHAR, Switch is type BOOLEAN, and N is type CARDINAL. The comment at the right of each statement describes its effect. ◀

```
Switch := FALSE;
INC(Switch);            (* Switch is TRUE *)
DEC(Switch):            (* Switch is FALSE *)
```

```
Ch := 'A';
INC(Ch, 3);                (* Ch is 'D' *)
DEC(Ch, 2);                (* Ch is 'B' *)

N := 15;
INC(N, 10);                (* N is 25 *)
DEC(N, N);                 (* N is 0 *)
INC(N);                    (* N is 1 *)
DEC(N)                     (* N is 0 *)
```

The result of applying the procedure `INC` to the last value of an ordinal type is undefined. For example, if the `BOOLEAN` variable `Switch` has the value `TRUE`, then the result of `INC(Switch)` is undefined. Similarly, the result of applying the procedure `DEC` to the first value of an ordinal type is undefined. On some Modula-2 systems, these operations will result in an `overflow error` or a `range error` during execution.

Type Conversion and Function VAL

Section 5.5 discussed how to use the function `ORD` to convert from any ordinal type to an ordinal number and how to use the function `CHR` to convert an ordinal number to a type `CHAR` value. It is also possible to convert from an ordinal number to its corresponding value in any ordinal type using the type-conversion function `VAL`. `VAL` requires two arguments: the first is an ordinal type identifier, and the second is the ordinal number being converted to that type (e.g., `VAL(CHAR, 5)` returns the character with ordinal number 5).

EXAMPLE 5.27 ▶ Table 5.13 uses function `VAL` to return a value associated with each ordinal type encountered so far. Note that the function reference `VAL(CHAR, n)` returns the type `CHAR` value with ordinal number `n`. This is equivalent to the function reference `CHR(n)`.

Table 5.13 ▶ *The VAL Function*

FUNCTION REFERENCE	RESULT RETURNED	
`VAL(BOOLEAN, 0)`	`FALSE`	(type `BOOLEAN`)
`VAL(BOOLEAN, 1)`	`TRUE`	(type `BOOLEAN`)
`VAL(CHAR, 65)`	`'A'`	(type `CHAR`)
`VAL(CHAR, ORD('A'))`	`'A'`	(type `CHAR`)
`VAL(INTEGER, 37)`	`37`	(type `INTEGER`)
`VAL(CARDINAL, 37)`	`37`	(type `CARDINAL`)

The first two lines in Table 5.13 use function `VAL` to return the two `BOOLEAN` values, `FALSE` and `TRUE`. The function reference

```
VAL(BOOLEAN, 2)
```

causes the syntax error `index out of range or conversion error` because there is no BOOLEAN value with ordinal number 2. ◂

EXAMPLE 5.28 ▸ If I is type INTEGER and C is type CARDINAL, the mixed-type expression

```
I + C
```

is invalid; however, any of the following expressions is valid and may be used instead.

```
I + VAL(INTEGER, C)
VAL(CARDINAL, I) + C
ORD(I) + C
```

The first expression evaluates the sum of I and C in type INTEGER format; the last two expressions evaluate the sum of I and C in type CARDINAL format. In the latter expressions, a run-time error occurs if I is a negative number. ◂

Table of Functions and Procedures

The standard functions and procedures described in this section are summarized in Table 5.14.

Table 5.14 ▸ *Standard Functions and Procedures for Ordinal Types*

EXAMPLE	PURPOSE
DEC (X, n)	Procedure — assigns to X (a variable of ordinal type) the nth value that precedes the current value of X. If n is 1, it may be omitted.
INC (X, n)	Procedure — Assigns to X (a variable of ordinal type) the nth value that follows the current value of X. If n is 1, it may be omitted.
VAL(T, n)	Function — Returns the value in ordinal type T with ordinal number n.

SELF-CHECK EXERCISE FOR SECTION 5.6

1. Evaluate the following when NextChar is 'A'.
   a. VAL(CHAR, 32) = CHR(32)
   b. VAL(BOOLEAN, ORD(CHR(1)))
   c. VAL(BOOLEAN, ORD(0C))
   d. VAL(BOOLEAN, ORD(VAL(CHAR, 0)))
   e. INTEGER, ORD('c') - ORD('C'))
   f. CHAR, ORD(NextChar) + 2)
   g. (NextChar, 2)
   h. (INC (NextChar, 25), 25)

5.7 Subrange Types

One of the most important features of Modula-2 is that it permits the declaration of new data types. Many of these data types will be discussed in the next few chapters. This section discusses new data types that are subranges of the ordinal types where a *subrange* defines a subset of the values associated with an ordinal type (the *base type*). Subranges are used to make a program more readable and to enable Modula-2 to detect when a variable is given a value that is unreasonable in the problem environment.

EXAMPLE 5.29 ▶ Type declarations begin with the reserved word `TYPE` and are used to declare a new data type. The Modula-2 scope rules for identifiers apply to names of data types. The following statements declare three subrange types as well as a variable of each new type.

```
TYPE
  Letter = ['A'..'Z'];
  DaysInMonth = [1..31];
  SmallInt = [-50..50];

VAR
  NextChar : Letter;
  InDay : DaysInMonth;
  Volts : SmallInt;
```

The first subrange, `Letter`, has the base type `CHAR`. Any character from A through Z may be stored in a variable of type `Letter`. An error message will be printed and the program will stop execution if an attempt is made to store any other character in a variable of type `Letter`. For example, the assignment statement

```
NextChar := 'a'
```

causes the syntax error `index out of range or conversion error` because the character a is not included in data type `Letter`.

`DaysInMonth` is a subrange with base type `CARDINAL`. A variable of type `DaysInMonth` can be used to keep track of the current date, a value between 1 and 31, inclusive. The statement

```
ReadCard (InDay)
```

reads a data value into `InDay` (type `Date`). A `CARDINAL overflow` run-time error occurs if the data value is greater than 31.

`SmallInt` is a subrange with base type `INTEGER`. The compiler determines that `SmallInt` is a subrange of `INTEGER` and not `CARDINAL`, because its lower limit, −50, is a negative number. `DaysInMonth` is considered a subrange of base type `CARDINAL` because its lower limit, 1, is nonnegative. ◀

In the revised version of Modula-2, a programmer may specify the base type of a subrange, as follows:

```
TYPE
  Letter = CHAR ['A'..'Z'];
  DaysInMonth = CARDINAL  [1..31];
  SmallInt = INTEGER [-50..50];
```

Consequently, a programmer could declare `DaysInMonth` to be a subrange with base type `INTEGER`.

Subrange Type Declaration

FORM: `TYPE` *subrange type* = `[`*minvalue* `..` *maxvalue*`];`
or `TYPE` *subrange type* = *type id* `[`*minvalue* `..` *maxvalue* `];`

EXAMPLE: `TYPE Uppercase = ['A'..'Z'];`
or `TYPE Uppercase = CHAR ['A'..'Z'];`

INTERPRETATION: A new data type named *subrange type* is defined. A variable of type *subrange type* may be assigned a value from *minvalue* through *maxvalue*, inclusive. The values *minvalue* and *maxvalue* must belong to the same ordinal type (called the base type), and `ORD(`*minvalue*`)` must be less than `ORD(`*maxvalue*`)`.

Note: *minvalue* and *maxvalue* must be constant identifiers or literals of the same type. In the revised version of Modula-2, *type id* may be used to specify the base type.

All the operators that can be used with the base type of a subrange may also be used with the subrange. It is important to realize, however, that a subrange type is different from its base type and that the subrange type cannot be used interchangeably with its base type. Type compatibility is discussed in the next subsection.

Program Style

Motivation for Using Subranges

You may be wondering why we bother with subranges. While they don't seem to provide any new capabilities, they do provide additional opportunity for your program to "bomb"—any attempt to store an out-of-range value in a variable whose type is a subrange stops program execution. However, this should happen only as the result of an error by the programmer or the program user. If `Volts` is type `INTEGER` (instead of `SmallInt`), the program continues to execute regardless of what value is assigned to `Volts`. Assigning an overly large value (say, `1000`) to `Volts` may cause a later statement to fail or the program to generate incorrect results. In the former case, the program user may have difficulty finding the statement that was actually at fault (i.e., the statement that assigned the out-of-range value). In the latter case, if program execution is completed in a normal manner, the program user may not even be aware that an error occurred. The use of subranges ensures the immediate detection of an out-of-range value.

Type and Assignment Compatibility

We have already seen that it is not possible to mix the types of operands for an operator. This means, for example, that the expression `I + J` would lead to a syntax error such as `type incompatible operands` if `I` is one data type (say, `INTEGER`) and `J` is another (say, `CARDINAL`). But what if `I` is type `INTEGER` and `J` is type `SmallInt` (a subrange of `INTEGER`)? In this case, the expression is valid because `SmallInt` and `INTEGER` are considered *compatible types*. The following syntax display describes the compatibility relationships for simple data types.

Compatibility Relationships for Simple Types ▶

IDENTICAL

- The two types are exactly the same (i.e., they use the same identifier).

COMPATIBLE

- The two types are identical.
- One type is declared equal to the other (e.g., `TYPE T1 = INTEGER` declares `T1` to be the same as `INTEGER`, so `T1` and `INTEGER` are compatible).
- One type is a subrange of the other (e.g., `TYPE T2 = [-1..1000]` declares `T2` a subrange of `INTEGER`, so `T2` and `INTEGER` are compatible).
- Both types are subranges of the same base type (e.g., `TYPE T3 = [-100..100]` declares `T3` a subrange of `INTEGER`, so `T2` and `T3` are compatible).

ASSIGNMENT COMPATIBLE

- The two types are compatible.
- One is compatible with `INTEGER` and the other is compatible with `CARDINAL`.
- One type is `CHAR` and the other is a string of length one (defined in Chapter 11).

INCOMPATIBLE

- None of the above.

The strength of the compatibility relationship decreases as we move down this display. Identical types are also compatible and assignment compatible; compatible types are also assignment compatible.

The compatibility relationship between operands determines what operators may be used with the operands. Operands that have identical types may be used with any Modula-2 operator. Operands that have compatible types may also be used with any Modula-2 operator except that type compatibility is not sufficient for variable parameters. This means that the type of an actual parameter must be identical to the type of its corresponding formal parameter if the formal parameter is a variable parameter. Assignment compatibility is sufficient for the assignment operator and for value parameters. There are no operators that will accept incompatible operands. This information is summarized in Table 5.15.

Table 5.15 ▸ *Compatibility Requirements for Modula-2 Operators*

OPERATION	COMPATIBILITY REQUIREMENTS
assignment	assignment compatible, compatible, identical
numerical, logical, relational	compatible, identical
passing value parameters	assignment compatible, compatible, identical
passing variable parameters	identical

EXAMPLE 5.30 ▸ Given the declarations

```
TYPE
  Letter : ['A'..'Z'];

VAR
  NextCh : Letter;
  InChar : CHAR;
```

the data types `Letter` and `CHAR` are considered compatible (i.e., `Letter` is a subrange of `CHAR`). This means that the `BOOLEAN` expression

```
(NextCh # InChar) & (NextCh > K')
```

is valid in Modula-2. Also, the procedure call statement

```
Write (NextCh)
```

is valid, because the actual parameter `NextCh` corresponds to a value parameter. Similarly, the assignment statement

```
NextCh := InChar;
```

is also valid; however, a run-time range error will occur if the character stored in `InChar` is not an uppercase letter. ◂

SELF-CHECK EXERCISE FOR SECTION 5.7

1. Identify the illegal subranges:
   a. `['a'..'Z']`   d. `[0..'9']`
   b. `['A'..'Z']`   e. `[15..-15]`
   c. `[-15..15]`   f. `['ACE'..'HAT']`

5.8 Case Study

The case study that follows involves the manipulation of type `CARDINAL` data. It also illustrates the use of `BOOLEAN` variables as program flags.

TESTING FOR A PRIME NUMBER

Problem: Write a program that tests a positive integer to determine whether it is a prime number.

Discussion: A prime number is an integer that has no divisors other than 1 and itself. Examples of prime numbers are the integers 2, 3, 5, 7, and 11. Our program will either print a message indicating that its data value is a prime number, or it will print the smallest divisor of the number if it is not prime. The data requirements and the algorithm follow.

PROBLEM INPUTS

the number to be tested for a prime number (`N : CARDINAL`)

PROBLEM OUTPUTS

the smallest divisor if `N` is not prime (`FirstDiv : CARDINAL`)

Algorithm

1. Read in the number to be tested for a prime number.
2. Find the smallest divisor >1 or determine that the number is prime.
3. Print a message that the number is prime or print its smallest divisor.

We will use the `BOOLEAN` variable `Prime` as a program flag to indicate the result of step 2. The system structure chart is shown in Fig. 5.15.

Figure 5.15 ▸ *Structure Chart for Prime Number Problem*

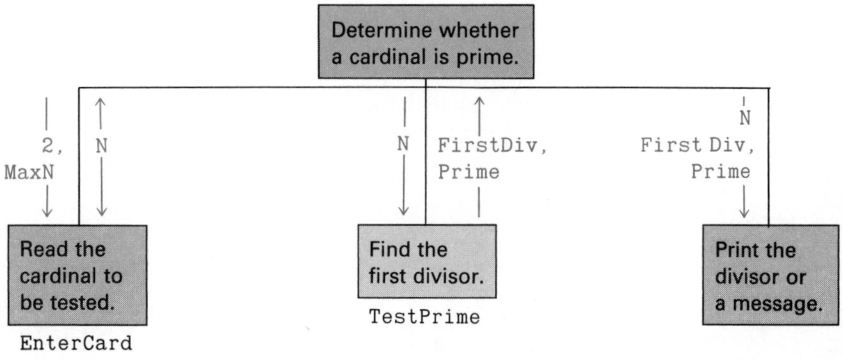

ADDITIONAL PROGRAM VARIABLES

program flag that will be set to TRUE if N is prime and
to FALSE if N is not prime (Prime : BOOLEAN)

Step 3 of the algorithm is relatively simple and will be included in the main program. The refinement for step 3 follows.

STEP 3 REFINEMENT

```
3.1 IF N is prime THEN
       Print a message that N is prime
     ELSE
       Print the first divisor of N
    END
```

Step 1 will be implemented by procedure `EnterCard` and is included with the main program shown in Fig. 5.16. Procedure `EnterCard` is based on procedure `EnterInt`, shown in Fig. 5.9, and reads a cardinal value between its two input parameter values. Step 2 is performed by procedure `TestPrime`, which is described next.

Figure 5.16 ▸ *Main Program to Test for a Prime Number*

```
MODULE PrimeNumber;
(*
   Prints the smallest divisor (other than 1) of the cardinal N if
   a divisor exists; otherwise, prints a message that N is prime.
*)
   FROM InOut IMPORT
     ReadCard, WriteCard, WriteString, WriteLn;
   FROM MathLib0 IMPORT
     sqrt;

   CONST
     MaxN = 1000;                (* largest n to be tested *)

   TYPE
     SmallCard = [2..MaxN];      (* range of values for n *)

   VAR
     N : CARDINAL;              (* input - number being tested *)
     FirstDiv : SmallCard;      (* output - first divisor if found *)
     Prime    : BOOLEAN;        (* flag - signals whether N is prime
                                     (TRUE) or not prime (FALSE)       *)

   PROCEDURE EnterCard (MinN, MaxN (* input *) : CARDINAL;
                        VAR N (* output *) : CARDINAL);
    (*
      Reads a cardinal number between MinN and MaxN into N.
      Pre:  MinN and MaxN are assigned values.
```

```
     Post: A value between MinN and MaxN is read into N if
           MinN <= MaxN is true; otherwise, N is set to MinN.
  *)
     VAR
       Between : BOOLEAN;       (* program flag - loop control *)
       TempN : CARDINAL;        (* temporary copy of MinN *)

  BEGIN (* EnterCard *)
    IF MinN > MaxN THEN
      WriteString ('Error - empty range for EnterCard');  WriteLn;
      WriteString ('MinN and MaxN were exchanged');       WriteLn;
      (* Exchange MinN and MaxN *)
      TempN := MinN;  MinN := MaxN;  MaxN := TempN
    END; (* IF *)

    (* Keep reading until a valid number is read. *)
    Between := FALSE;      (* Assume a valid number is not read *)
    WHILE
      (* invariant:
           All prior values of N are outside range MinN to MaxN
      *)
         NOT Between DO
      WriteString ('Enter an integer between ');
      WriteCard (MinN, 0);  WriteString (' and ');
      WriteCard (MaxN, 0);  WriteString (': ');
      ReadCard (N);         WriteLn;
      Between := (N >= MinN) & (N <= MaxN)
    END (* WHILE *)
    (* assert: N is in the range MinN to MaxN *)
  END EnterCard;

  PROCEDURE TestPrime (N (* input *) : CARDINAL;
                       VAR FirstDiv (* output *) : SmallCard;
                       VAR Prime (* output *) : BOOLEAN);
  (*
     Finds first divisor (FirstDiv) of N if it exists.
     Pre:  N is assigned a value.
     Post: FirstDiv is the first divisor of N besides 1 and N.
           Prime is TRUE if a divisor is not found; otherwise,
           Prime is FALSE.
  *)
  BEGIN  (* TestPrime stub *)
    WriteString ('Procedure TestPrime entered');  WriteLn;
    FirstDiv := 2;  Prime := FALSE
  END TestPrime;

BEGIN  (* PrimeNumber *)
  (* Enter an integer to test for a prime number *)
  WriteString ('Enter a number that you think is a prime.');
  WriteLn;
  EnterCard (2, MaxN, N);
```

```
  (*
     Find smallest divisor FirstDiv or determine that N is prime.
     Set Prime to indicate whether or not N is a prime number.
  *)
  TestPrime (N, FirstDiv, Prime);

  (* Print first divisor or a message that N is prime *)
  IF Prime THEN
    WriteCard (N, 5);
    WriteString (' is a prime number');
    WriteLn
  ELSE
    WriteCard (FirstDiv, 5);
    WriteString (' is the smallest divisor of ');
    WriteCard (N, 5);
    WriteLn
  END (* IF *)
END PrimeNumber.
```

The subrange type `SmallCard` declared in the main program includes the cardinal numbers from 2 to `MaxN (1000)`. Variable `FirstDiv` (the first divisor) is type `SmallCard`. The procedure call statement

```
TestPrime (N, FirstDiv, Prime);
```

calls procedure `TestPrime` to define the values of `FirstDiv` and `Prime`.

Procedure `TestPrime` determines whether `N` has any divisors other than 1 and itself. If `N` is an even integer, then it is divisible by 2. Therefore, 2 is the only even integer that can be prime, and 2 is the smallest divisor of all other even integers.

If `N` is an odd integer, its only possible divisors are the odd integers less than `N`. In fact, it can be proved that a number is prime if it is not divisible by any odd integer less than or equal to its square root. These considerations form the basis for the algorithm shown next.

Algorithm for TestPrime

1. `IF N = 2 THEN`
    2. `N` is a prime number

   `ELSIF N` is even `THEN`
    3. 2 is the smallest divisor and `N` is not prime

   `ELSE`
    4. Test each odd integer between 3 and the square root of `N` to see whether it is a divisor of `N`

   `END`

Step 4 must test each odd integer as a possible divisor of `N` until a divisor is found. We will write a separate procedure `(TestOdd)` to accomplish this. `TestOdd` should contain a `WHILE` loop with the loop invariant below.

```
(* invariant:
     FirstDiv during pass i is 1 + 2 * i (3, 5, 7, ... ) and
     no prior value of FirstDiv is a divisor of N and
     FirstDiv is less than or equal to the square root of N
*)
```

This invariant suggests the following algorithm; the structure chart for `TestPrime` is shown in Fig. 5.17.

Algorithm for TestOdd

1. Assume `N` is a prime number (i.e., set `Prime` to `TRUE`)
2. Initialize `FirstDiv` to `3`
3. `WHILE Prime` is still `TRUE` and `FirstDiv` is less than `sqrt(N) DO`
    4. `IF FirstDiv` is a divisor of `N THEN`
        5. Set `Prime` to `FALSE` (`N` is not a prime number)

       `ELSE`

        6. Set `FirstDiv` to the next odd number

       `END (* IF *)`

   `END (* WHILE *)`

Figure 5.17 ▸ *Structure Chart for TestPrime*

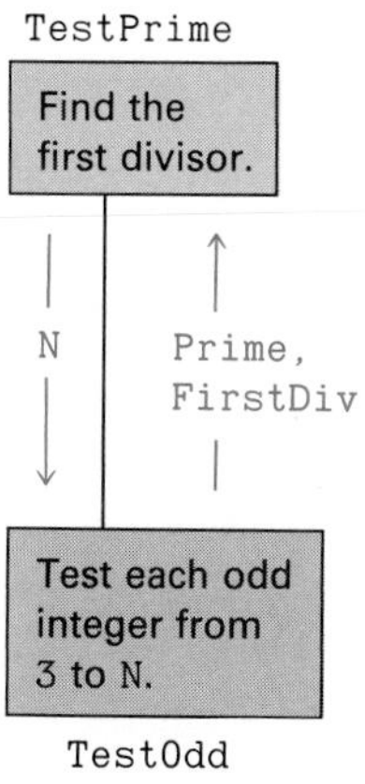

The nesting of procedures for the entire program system is shown in Fig. 5.18. Procedure `TestPrime` (with nested procedure `TestOdd`) is shown in Fig. 5.19, and four sample runs are shown in Fig. 5.20.

Figure 5.18 ▸ *Nesting of Procedures in Module PrimeNumber*

```
MODULE PrimeNumber
  PROCEDURE EnterCard
  PROCEDURE TestPrime
    PROCEDURE TestOdd
```

Figure 5.19 ▸ *Procedure TestPrime with TestOdd*

```
PROCEDURE TestPrime (N (* input *) : CARDINAL;
                     VAR FirstDiv (* output *) : SmallCard;
                     VAR Prime (* output *) : BOOLEAN);
(*
   Finds first divisor (FirstDiv) of N if it exists.
   Pre : N is assigned a value.
   Post: FirstDiv is the first divisor of N besides 1 and N.
         Prime is TRUE if a divisor is not found; otherwise,
         Prime is FALSE.
*)
   PROCEDURE TestOdd (N (* input *) : CARDINAL;
                      VAR FirstDiv (* output *) : SmallCard;
                      VAR Prime (* output *) : BOOLEAN);
   (*
      Tests each odd integer from 3 to the square root of N as a
      divisor of N.
      Pre : N is assigned a value.
      Post: FirstDiv is the smallest divisor if one is found.
            Prime is TRUE if a divisor is not found; otherwise,
            Prime is FALSE.
   *)
      VAR
        MaxPossibleDiv : SmallCard; (* largest possible divisor *)

   BEGIN  (* TestOdd *)
     Prime := TRUE;                      (* Assume that N is prime *)
     FirstDiv := 3;                              (* Try 3 first *)
     MaxPossibleDiv := TRUNC(sqrt(FLOAT(N)));
     WHILE
       (* invariant:
          FirstDiv during pass i is 1 + 2 * i (3, 5, 7, ... ) and
          no prior value of FirstDiv is a divisor of N and
          FirstDiv is less than or equal to the square root of N
       *)
          Prime AND (FirstDiv <= MaxPossibleDiv) DO
       IF N MOD FirstDiv = 0 THEN
         Prime := FALSE                       (* N is not prime *)
       ELSE
         INC (FirstDiv, 2)              (* Try next odd number *)
       END (* IF *)
     END (* WHILE *)
     (* assertion:
          Prime is TRUE and FirstDiv > sqrt(N) or
          Prime is FALSE and FirstDiv is the smallest divisor of N
     *)

   END TestOdd;

BEGIN  (* TestPrime *)
  IF N = 2 THEN
    Prime := TRUE                  (* 2 is a prime number *)
```

```
  ELSIF NOT ODD(N) THEN
    (* N is even *)
    Prime := FALSE;
    FirstDiv := 2                     (* 2 is first divisor *)
  ELSE (* N is odd *)
    TestOdd (N, FirstDiv, Prime)   (* Test for a divisor *)
  END (* IF *)
END TestPrime;
```

Figure 5.20 ▸
Four Sample Runs of the Prime Number Program

```
Enter a number that you think is a prime.
Enter an integer between 2 and 1000: 1000
    2 is the smallest divisor of  1000


Enter a number that you think is a prime.
Enter an integer between 2 and 1000:  997
  997 is a prime number


Enter a number that you think is a prime.
Enter an integer between 2 and 1000: 35
    5 is the smallest divisor of    35


Enter a number that you think is a prime.
Enter an integer between 2 and 1000: 0
Enter an integer between 2 and 1000: 1001
Enter an integer between 2 and 1000: 2
    2 is a prime number
```

The program flag `Prime` is set within `TestOdd` or `TestPrime` to indicate whether `N` is a prime number. In `TestOdd`, `Prime` is initialized to `TRUE` before any candidate divisors are tested. If a divisor is found, `Prime` is reset to `FALSE` and the `WHILE` loop is exited. If no divisors are found, `Prime` will remain `TRUE` and the loop is exited when `FirstDiv` becomes greater than `sqrt(N)`. The values of `Prime` and `FirstDiv` are returned to the main program.

Program Style

Removing Unnecessary Computation from Loops

In procedure `TestOdd`, the local variable `MaxPossibleDiv` is used to hold the maximum possible divisor ($\sqrt{N}$) and is assigned its value by the statement

```
MaxPossibleDiv := TRUNC(sqrt(FLOAT(N)));
```

just before the `WHILE` loop. The `FLOAT` function returns the real equivalent of `N` (required by `sqrt`); the `TRUNC` function returns the integral part of the result.

If `MaxPossibleDiv` is not declared as a local variable, the preceding expression would be included in the `WHILE` loop condition and would be reevaluated each time the loop is repeated. This is not necessary, since the expression value never changes. We recommend that you examine loops carefully and remove any computations that always generate the same results.

Program Style

Planning for Reuse

The identifier `N` is used as a main program variable and formal parameter in the prime number program. In Fig. 5.16, the procedure call statement

```
EnterCard (2, MaxN, N);
```

establishes a correspondence between main program variable `N` and formal parameter `N` (both type `CARDINAL`).

Since we know the value of main program variable `N` must be between 2 and `MaxN`, it is tempting to declare `N` as type `SmallCard` (`[2..MaxN]`) in the main program. This would require that we declare formal parameter `N` in procedure `EnterCard` as type `SmallCard`, since corresponding variable parameters must be the same type. This was not done because the operation of reading a cardinal value in a specified range is something we might like to do in later programs. If we use type `SmallCard` now instead of type `CARDINAL`, we would have to modify procedure `EnterCard` later to reuse it. It is always better to write procedures that can be reused without modification.

Selection of Test Cases

Several sample runs of the prime-number program were shown in Fig. 5.20. The test values used for `N` were selected to exercise all parts of the program and to verify that the program works for numbers that are prime as well as numbers that are not prime. The operation of the program at the boundaries (`2` and `1000`) was also checked, as well as the operation of the program for invalid data values (`0` and `1001`). A very large prime number (997) was used as a test case, as well as odd and even numbers that were not prime. Although many valid data values were not tested, the sample selected is representative and provides a fair indication that the program is correct.

Use a similar strategy when you select test data to exercise your programs. Avoid choosing sample test data that are similar. Also, select test data that are at or near any boundary values.

SELF-CHECK EXERCISE FOR SECTION 5.8

1. Write a procedure that prints all divisors of `N` where `N` may be any positive integer (odd or even). If `N` is prime, the divisors printed should be only `1` and `N`.

5.9 Common Programming Errors

A good deal of care is required when you are working with complicated expressions. It is easy to omit parentheses or operators inadvertently. If an operator or a single parenthesis is omitted, a syntax error will be detected. If a pair of parentheses is omitted, then the expression, although syntactically correct, will compute the wrong value.

Sometimes it is beneficial to break a complicated expression into subexpressions that are separately assigned to *temporary variables* and then to manipulate these temporary variables. For example, it is easier to write correctly the three assignment statements below

```
Templ := sqrt(X + Y);
Temp2 := 1 + Templ;
Z := Templ / Temp2
```

than the single assignment statement

```
Z := sqrt(X + Y) / (1 + sqrt(X + Y))
```

which has the same effect. Using three assignment statements is also more efficient because the square root operation is performed only once; it is performed twice in the single assignment statement.

Be careful to use the correct type of operands with each operator. The arithmetic operators can be used only with type CARDINAL, INTEGER, or REAL operands. The operator / can be used only with type REAL operands; the operators DIV and MOD can be used only with type CARDINAL and INTEGER operands. The relational operators can be used with any simple data type. The BOOLEAN operators can be used only with type BOOLEAN operands.

Make sure an operator does not have incompatible type operands. For example, the BOOLEAN expression

```
3 # '3'
```

is invalid because it compares an integer to a character value. All operators except the assignment operator require compatible operands; the assignment operator requires assignment-compatible operands. Identical operands must be used for variable parameter correspondence; assignment-compatible operands are sufficient for value-parameter correspondence.

Make sure that you use parentheses where required. In the expression

```
Flag & (X <= Y)
```

the variable Flag must be type BOOLEAN, and the parentheses shown are required (the statement would be invalid without them). Use parentheses freely to clarify the meaning of an expression.

Syntax or run-time errors may occur when you are using standard functions and procedures. The argument of the functions CHR and ODD must be type INTEGER or CARDINAL. The argument of the function ORD and the first argument of procedures DEC and INC must be an ordinal type (not type REAL). If the argument of utility procedure sqrt or ln is negative, an error will occur.

Subranges can be used to detect erroneous computations or data. If a value being assigned is outside the subrange, an out-of-range error occurs.

5.10 Chapter Review

This chapter described how to write arithmetic expressions involving several operators and the standard functions of Modula-2. It also discussed the manipulation of other simple data types, including the standard types, BOOLEAN and CHAR, and programmer-defined subrange types. Several new operators were introduced, including DIV and MOD, for manipulating integers and cardinals, and AND (&), OR, and NOT, for manipulating BOOLEAN data.

The concept of an ordinal number was discussed and several functions and procedures were introduced for the manipulation of ordinal data types. The function CHR, which is the inverse of ORD, was used to find the character corresponding to a given ordinal number. Appendix A lists the standard functions and procedures of Modula-2; Appendix B lists the utility functions in module MathLib0.

Subrange types were also introduced. Subranges are used to improve program readability and to enable the detection of out-of-range values. The operators that can be used with a subrange are the same as for its base type.

We also discussed type compatiblity. A subrange is compatible with its base type, which means that an operator can have one operand whose type is the subrange and one operand whose type is the base type. The only restriction is that a variable whose type is a subrange cannot correspond to a variable formal parameter whose type is the base type.

New Modula-2 Statements

The new Modula-2 statements introduced in this chapter are described in Table 5.16.

Table 5.16 ▸ *Summary of New Modula-2 Statements*

STATEMENT	EFFECT
Arithmetic Assignment	
`I := J DIV K + (L + 5) MOD N`	Adds the result (an integer) of J DIV K to the result (an integer) of (L + 5) MOD N. J, K, L, and N must all be type INTEGER or CARDINAL.
Character Assignment	
`NextCh := 'A'`	Assigns the character value 'A' to NextCh.

BOOLEAN Assignment	
`EVEN := NOT ODD(N)`	If `N` is an even number, assigns the value `TRUE` to `EVEN`; otherwise, assigns the value `FALSE` to `EVEN`.
Subrange Declaration	
`TYPE` `Digit = ['0'..'9'];`	A subrange of the characters is declared. This subrange (named `Digit`) consists of the digit characters `'0'` through `'9'`.

CHAPTER 5 ▸

Review Questions

1. What are the advantages of data type `INTEGER` over data type `REAL`?
2. Given the following declarations, indicate the data type of the result of each expression.

```
VAR
  X, Y : REAL;
  A, B : INTEGER;
```

	type
`X * Y`	______
`A * B`	______
`B / Y`	______
`B DIV A`	______
`X / Y`	______
`A MOD B`	______
`X MOD Y`	______

3. List the answers to the following operations.

`11 MOD 2`	______	`11 DIV 2`	______
`12 MOD -3`	______	`12 DIV -3`	______
`27 MOD 4`	______	`-25 DIV 4`	______
`18 MOD 6`	______	`-18 DIV -5`	______

4. What is the result of the expression `(3 + 4 DIV 2) + 8 - 15 MOD 4`?
5. Write an assignment statement that rounds a real variable `Num1` to two digits after the decimal point and leave the result in `Num1`.
6. Write a procedure called `Change` that has one real parameter `C` and four cardinal parameters `Q`, `D`, `N`, and `P`. `C` will be a value parameter; the others will be variable parameters. The procedure will return the number of quarters in `Q`, the number of dimes in `D`, the number of nickels in `N`, and the number of pennies in `P` to make change with the minimum number of coins. `C` (the change amount) is less than $1.00. Hint: Use the `MOD` and `DIV` operators.
7. List and explain three computational errors that may occur in type `REAL` expressions.

8. Write an `IF` statement that will write out `TRUE` or `FALSE` according to the following conditions: (1) `Flag` is `TRUE` or `Color` is `'RED'`, or (2) both `Money` is `'PLENTY'` and `Time` is `'UP'`.
9. Write the statement to assign a value of `TRUE` to the `BOOLEAN` variable `OverTime` only if a worker's `Hours` are greater than `40`.
10. Write a `BOOLEAN` expression using the `ORD` function that will determine whether the ordinal value for `'a'` is greater than the ordinal value for `'Z'`. What is the value of this expression in ASCII?
11. Write the Modula-2 statements necessary to enter a cardinal between `0` and `9` inclusive and convert it to an equivalent character value (e.g., `0` to `'0'`, `1` to `'1'`) to be stored in a character variable `Num`.

CHAPTER 5 ▸

Programming Projects

1. A company has `ten` employees, many of whom work overtime (more than 40 hours) each week. They want a payroll program that reads the weekly time records (containing employee name, hourly rate (`rate`), and hours worked (`hours`) for each employee) and computes the gross salary and net pay as follows:

$$\text{gross} = \begin{cases} \text{hours} \times \text{rate} & (\text{if hours} \leq 40) \\ 1.5 \times \text{rate} \times (\text{hours} - 40) + 40 \times \text{rate} & (\text{if hours} > 40) \end{cases}$$

$$\text{net} = \begin{cases} \text{gross} & (\text{if gross} <= \$65) \\ \text{gross} - (15 + 0.45 \times \text{gross}) & (\text{if gross} > \$65) \end{cases}$$

The program should print a five-column table listing each employee's name, hourly rate, hours worked, gross salary, and net pay. The total amount of the payroll should be printed at the end. It can be computed by summing the gross salaries for all employees. Test your program on the following data:

Name	*Rate*	*Hours*
IVORY HUNTER	3.50	35
TRACK STAR	4.50	40
SMOKEY BEAR	3.25	80
OSCAR GROUCH	6.80	10
THREE BEARS	1.50	16
POKEY PUPPY	2.65	25
FAT EDDIE	2.00	40
PUMPKIN PIE	2.65	35
SARA LEE	5.00	40
HUMAN ERASER	6.25	52

2. Write a program to read in a collection of integers and determine if each is a prime number. Test your program with the four integers 7, 17, 35, and 96. All numbers should be processed in one run.

3. Let n be a positive integer consisting of up to nine digits, $d_9 d_8 \ldots d_1$. Write a program to list in one column each digit in the number n. The rightmost digit d_1 should be listed at the top of the column. Hint: If $n = 3704$, what is the value of `Digit` as computed according to the following formula?

```
Digit = n MOD 10
```

Test your program for values of n equal to 6, 3704, and 170498.

4. An integer N is divisible by 9 if the sum of its digits is divisible by 9. Use the algorithm developed for project 3 to determine if the following numbers are divisible by 9.

$N = 154368$
$N = 621594$
$N = 123456$

5. Redo project 4 by reading each digit of the number to be tested into the type `CHAR` variable `Digit`. Form the sum of the numeric values of the digits. Hint: The numeric value of `Digit` (type `CHAR`) is `ORD(Digit) - ORD('0')`.

6. The interest paid on a savings account is compounded daily. This means that if you start with `StartBal` dollars in the bank, at the end of the first day you will have a balance of

`StartBal` $\times (1 + rate/365)$

dollars, where *rate* is the annual interest rate (0.10 if the annual rate is 10 percent). At the end of the second day, you will have

`StartBal` $\times (1 + rate/365) \times (1 + rate/365)$

dollars, and at the end of N days you will have

`StartBal` $\times (1 + rate/365)^N$

dollars. Write a program that processes a set of data records, each of which contains values for `StartBal`, `rate`, and `N`, and computes the final account balance.

7. Compute the monthly payment and the total payment for a bank loan, given:
   a. the amount of the loan
   b. the duration of the loan in months
   c. the interest rate for the loan

   Your program should read in one record at a time (each containing values for loan amount, months, and rate), perform the required computation, and print the values of the loan, months, rate, the monthly payment, and the total payment.

Test your program with at least the following data (and more if you want).

Loan	*Months*	*Rate*
16000	300	12.50
24000	360	13.50
30000	300	15.50
42000	360	14.50
22000	300	15.50
300000	240	15.25

Notes: The formula for computing monthly payment is

$$monthpay = \frac{ratem \times expm^{months} \times loan}{expm - 1.0}$$

where

$$ratem = rate \,/\, 1200.0$$
$$expm = (1.0 + ratem)$$

The formula for computing the total payment is

$$totalpay = monthly \times months$$

Hint: You will need a loop to multiply *expm* by itself *months* times.

6 ▸ Programming in the Large

UP UNTIL NOW, we have been primarily concerned with writing small, "throwaway" programs that solve particular programming problems but that otherwise have little general use. This chapter will begin to consider large-scale programming, called *programming in the large*. Your goal will be to write reusable components (i.e., procedures) and to build libraries of those components. You will use those components as building blocks to construct programs that solve new problems.

To accomplish that, you need to learn more about abstraction and its use in programming. You also must learn how to create and use your own library modules.

To make large programs more readable, you can declare new data types whose values you specify and whose values depend on the problem domain. You can then combine these data types with relevant operator procedures in library modules that can be compiled and reused.

Finally you will learn how to use files of data with your programs. You will be able to enter program data from data files and save program output on output files. Using data files frees you from having to continually reenter test data while debugging a program. Using output files enables you to save output on disk rather than simply view it on the screen.

6.1 The Software Life Cycle

Programming in college is somewhat different from programming in the real world. In college, you are generally given the problem specification by an instructor. In many cases, the problem specification is ambiguous or incomplete, and interaction between the instructor and the class is needed to pin down the details.

In the real world, the initial specification for a software product (a large program system) may also be incomplete initially. The details are determined through extensive interaction between the prospective users of the software and its designers. Through this interaction, the software designers determine precisely what the proposed software is supposed to do, and the users determine what to expect from the software product. Although it may seem like common sense to proceed in this manner, very often a "final" software product does not perform as expected. The reason for this is a communication gap between those responsible for the product's design and its eventual users, and both parties are generally at fault.

One cause of the communication gap is that software users often are not familiar enough with computers and their capabilities to know what is reasonable to request or how to specify what they want. Software designers, on the other hand, often assume that they are the best judges of what the user really wants and are quick to interpret an incomplete specification as a "blank check" to do what they think best. To avoid these problems, it is imperative that a complete, written description of the *requirements specification* for a new software product be generated in the beginning, and that both users and designers sign the document.

The design process begins as soon as the requirements specification is completed. A major part of software design is decomposing the complete software system into a set of subsystems. Each subsystem is further decomposed into a set of smaller program modules and procedures. It is important to determine whether any modules or procedures from existing systems can be reused in the new system.

Another critical part of the design process is determining what internal data representation will be used. In college, the instructor often recommends or requires the use of a particular data type or data structure. In the real world, the programmer must choose the internal representation that will lead to the most efficient and effective solution.

Once the design is complete, it is *coded*, that is, implemented as a program in a particular programming language. Some of the programmers may have been involved with the design; others, however, will be new to the project. For this reason, it is critical that the software design be carefully documented in a report that contains structure charts and high-level pseudocode. Part of the coding task involves removing all apparent program bugs (debugging) and performing preliminary tests on each procedure, module, subsystem, and system. Once the bugs are removed, the coding and debugging phase is complete, and it is time to exhaustively test the software product.

In college, the same person designs, codes, debugs, and tests a program. Testing a program often consists of making several sample runs in which you hope to avoid discovering any errors. Once you are satisfied that the program is correct, you hand it in to the instructor and go on to something else.

In the real world, testing is a more rigorous process that should be performed by a group other than the programmers. It is important to identify all bugs early, since the software used to control a rocket or to process payroll checks must be absolutely free of errors before its first use. Also, a software product usually must continue to perform effectively over a long period, sometimes in a changing environment. This may require periodic updating, or *maintenance*, of the program to correct new errors or to incorporate changes, for example, revised tax laws.

The *software life cycle* consists of at least the following phases:

1. Requirements specification
2. Design
3. Coding and debugging
4. Testing
5. Operation and maintenance

This cycle is iterative. During the design phase, problems may arise that make it necessary to modify the requirements specification. Any such changes will require approval of the users. Similarly, during coding it may become necessary to reconsider decisions made in the design phase. Again, any changes must be approved by the system designers and users.

There are varying estimates as to the percentage of time spent in each phase. For example, a typical system may require a year to proceed through the first three phases, three months of testing, and then four years of operation and maintenance. So you can see why it is so important to design and document software in such a way that it can be easily understood and maintained.

You may be wondering what relevance all of this has to your current course. Those of you majoring in computer science will begin to participate in the design of large program systems in the next course. Consequently, a major goal of this course is to prepare you to work on increasingly larger and more complex problems. Some of the techniques may seem out of place or unnecessary to solve the simpler problems assigned in this class, but it is important for you to learn and practice these techniques now so you will be able to apply them when needed.

6.2 Using Abstraction to Manage Complexity

One of the biggest problems faced by beginning programmers is getting started on a problem. They are often reluctant to start writing the code for a program until they have worked out the solution to every detail. While we enthusiastically support preplanning and concern for detail, this can be overdone to the extent that it blocks the problem-solving process. We have used the strategy of "divide and conquer" to decompose a problem into more manageable subproblems.

Procedural Abstraction

Abstraction is a powerful technique used by programmers to help them deal with complex issues in a piecemeal fashion. The dictionary defines *abstraction* as the act or process of separating the inherent qualities or properties of something from the actual physical object to which they belong. An example of the use of abstraction is our earlier description of a memory cell as a storage location in a computer for a data value. We are not concerned with the details of the physical structure of memory and memory cells, because we don't need to know them to use a memory cell in programming.

So far, you have practiced *procedural abstraction*, which is the philosophy that procedure development should separate the concern of *what* is to be achieved by a procedure from the details of *how* it is to be achieved. In other words, you can go ahead and specify what you expect a procedure to do and then use that procedure in the design of a problem solution before you know how to implement the procedure. You have even been able to perform a preliminary test of an overall design by using procedure stubs. Of course, each procedure stub must be replaced by an actual procedure before you can execute the final program.

Modula-2 enables you to fully realize the potential of procedural abstraction. Once you have designed and implemented a procedure that has some general use, you can encapsulate that procedure with others in your own *library module*. You can then import that procedure into another program that needs the same operation performed and call it to carry out the operation. In this way, you can truly separate the *what* from the *how*. You can use a procedure as long as you know what it does and how to call it even if you have no idea of how the procedure is implemented.

You can make use of your own library modules in much the same way you use predefined modules that are part of the Modula-2 system (e.g., `InOut` and `RealInOut`). You can compile each library module individually and later, link the object code for a procedure in a compiled module to a program that calls it. The next section discusses how to create and use your own modules.

Programming Teams

Nowadays, it is rare for a large software project to be implemented by a single programmer. Most often, a large project is assigned to a team of programmers. The use of library modules facilitates the allocation of separate pieces of a project to individual team members. As long as the requirements of each library module are clearly specified beforehand, team members can work independently to write, test, and debug their modules. As each module is completed and compiled, it can be linked into the main program. This approach allows team members to use modules from other programmers' libraries as well as their own and promotes the reuse of previously compiled modules in new programs.

6.3 Creating Library Modules

You have become rather proficient at decomposing a program solution into a collection of procedures. Although this has helped you practice procedural abstraction, the programs that result can be quite lengthy. You may find that you have to read through page after page of procedure definitions before reaching the main program body.

As you continue to write programs, you will have the opportunity to reuse procedures from library modules that you have already implemented, compiled, and tested. There are several advantages to this:

1. The object code for procedures in library modules is accessible, thereby saving compilation time.
2. The new program modules will be simpler, because declarations of previously compiled procedures are not needed.
3. It is easier to reuse old procedures in new programs.
4. It is easier to apportion a large project to individual team members.
5. You can change the details of a module's code without affecting its client modules.

As you develop and debug new program systems, you will find that you have to compile only the main program modules and any new procedures not present in a library module. This speeds up the program development process. The final programs will also be more concise and more readable because you can use import statements to bring in procedures contained in your own libraries (the procedure declarations should not appear in the module that imports them).

Case Study

This section will demonstrate how to create library modules by defining and implementing a module for simple input/output. So far, we have identified a number of important input/output features that are not part of Modula-2, including procedures for reading and writing `BOOLEAN` values, reading cardinal and integer values within a prespecified range, and writing real numbers using normal decimal notation. The availability of this module should simplify our programming chores and make program output more readable.

SIMPLE INPUT/OUTPUT MODULE

Problem: Develop a library module, `SimpleIO`, that can be used to simplify input/output tasks.

Interpretation: The first step is the module *specification*, which is like a contract between the module designer and its potential users. The specification tells the module user what procedures are available and how to call each procedure. It also tells the module designer what features he or she must provide, but not how to write the module.

In Modula-2, the specification is provided in the definition module. The definition module for `SimpleIO` is shown in Fig. 6.1. Save this module as file `SimpleIO.DEF`. The extension `DEF` will be used to identify all definition modules.

Figure 6.1 ▸
Definition Module for SimpleIO

```
DEFINITION MODULE SimpleIO;
(*
   Definition module for simple input/output module. Contains
   procedures for reading and writing BOOLEAN values, for reading
   an integer or cardinal within a specified range, and for writing
   a real number using normal decimal notation.
*)

   EXPORT QUALIFIED
     EnterInt, EnterCard, ReadBool, WriteBool, WriteRealFormat;


  PROCEDURE EnterInt (MinN, MaxN (* input *) : INTEGER;
                      VAR N (* output *) : INTEGER);
  (*
     Reads an integer between MinN and MaxN into N.
     Pre : MinN and MaxN are assigned values.
     Post: A value between MinN and MaxN is read into N.
  *)


  PROCEDURE EnterCard (MinN, MaxN (* input *) : CARDINAL;
                       VAR N (* output *) : CARDINAL);
  (*
     Reads a cardinal between MinN and MaxN into N.
     Pre : MinN and MaxN are assigned values.
     Post: A value between MinN and MaxN is read into N.
  *)


  PROCEDURE ReadBool (VAR BoolVar (* output *) : BOOLEAN);
  (*
     Enters a character to determine the value of BoolVar.
     Pre : None
     Post: BoolVar is TRUE if t or T is read;
           otherwise, BoolVar is FALSE.
  *)


  PROCEDURE WriteBool (BoolVar (* input *) : BOOLEAN);
  (*
     Displays the value of BoolVar.
     Pre : BoolVar is assigned a value.
     Post: 'TRUE' is displayed if BoolVar is TRUE;
           otherwise, 'FALSE' is displayed.
  *)


  PROCEDURE WriteRealFormat (X (* input *) : REAL;
                             Width,
                             DecimalPlaces (* input *) : CARDINAL);
```

```
  (*
     Displays the value of X in Width columns using DecimalPlaces
     digits after the decimal point. If Width is too small to
     accommodate the number, as many columns as are needed will be
     used.
     Pre : X, Width, and DecimalPlaces are assigned.
     Post: X is displayed using Width columns when possible.
  *)

END SimpleIO.
```

The definition module contains an export statement that identifies the names of procedures in `SimpleIO` that may be used by other client modules. The export statement is not needed in newer versions of Modula-2, because all objects declared in a definition module are automatically exported. The definition module also contains procedure headers for all procedures included in module `SimpleIO`. The complete procedure declarations are provided later.

Note that only standard identifiers are used as parameter types in the procedure headers. If the definition module references constants, data types, or variables declared elsewhere, these identifiers must be imported into the definition module.

The definition module serves as the *interface* between a module and its environment. It contains all the information that the Modula-2 system needs to verify that another module (called the *client module*) is correctly using the procedures provided in module `SimpleIO`. Any actual parameter lists can be checked against the formal parameter lists provided in the definition module.

The Implementation Module

The implementation module shown in Fig. 6.2 contains the procedure declarations. If a procedure body references procedures from other modules, these procedures must be imported into the implementation module for `SimpleIO`, not the definition module. Each procedure declared in `SimpleIO` lists the name of the procedures that it references in a comment line following the procedure header.

Figure 6.2 ▸ *Implementation Module for SimpleIO*

```
IMPLEMENTATION MODULE SimpleIO;
(*
   Definition module for simple input/output module. Contains
   procedures for reading and writing BOOLEAN values, for reading
   an integer or cardinal within a specified range, and for writing
   a real number using normal decimal notation.
*)

  FROM InOut IMPORT
```

```
  WriteString, WriteLn, WriteInt, WriteCard, Write,
  Read, ReadInt, ReadCard;

FROM RealInOut IMPORT
  WriteReal, ReadReal;

PROCEDURE EnterInt (MinN, MaxN (* input *) : INTEGER;
                    VAR N (* output *) : INTEGER);
(*
   Reads an integer between MinN and MaxN into N.
   Pre : MinN and MaxN are assigned values.
   Post: A value between MinN and MaxN is read into N.
   Uses: ReadInt, WriteInt, WriteString, WriteLn from InOut
*)
   VAR
     Between : BOOLEAN;     (* program flag -- loop control *)
     TempN : INTEGER;       (* temporary copy of MinN *)

BEGIN (* EnterInt *)
  IF MinN > MaxN THEN
    WriteString ('Error - empty range for EnterInt'); WriteLn;
    WriteString ('MinN and MaxN were exchanged');     WriteLn;
    (* Exchange MinN and MaxN *)
    TempN := MinN;  MinN := MaxN;  MaxN := TempN
  END; (* IF *)

  (* Keep reading until a valid number is read. *)
  Between := FALSE;   (* Assume a valid number is not read *)
  WHILE
    (* invariant:
         All prior values of N are outside the range MinN to MaxN
    *)
       NOT Between DO
    WriteString ('Enter an integer between ');
    WriteInt (MinN, 0);  WriteString (' and ');
    WriteInt (MaxN, 0);  WriteString (': ');
    ReadInt (N);         WriteLn;
    Between := (N >= MinN) & (N <= MaxN)
  END (* WHILE *)
  (* assert: N is in the range MinN to MaxN *)

END EnterInt;


PROCEDURE EnterCard (MinN, MaxN (* input *) : CARDINAL;
                     VAR N (* output *) : CARDINAL);
(*
   Reads a cardinal number between MinN and MaxN into N.
   Pre : MinN and MaxN are assigned values.
   Post: A value between MinN and MaxN is read into N.
   Uses: ReadCard, WriteCard, WriteString, WriteLn from InOut
*)
```

```
    VAR
      Between : BOOLEAN;      (* program flag -- loop control *)
      TempN : CARDINAL;       (* temporary copy of MinN *)

BEGIN (* EnterCard *)
  IF MinN > MaxN THEN
    WriteString ('Error - empty range for EnterCard');  WriteLn;
    WriteString ('MinN and MaxN were exchanged');       WriteLn;
    (* Exchange MinN and MaxN *)
    TempN := MinN;  MinN := MaxN;  MaxN := TempN
  END; (* IF *)

  (* Keep reading until a valid number is read. *)
  Between := FALSE;     (* Assume a valid number is not read *)
  WHILE
    (* invariant:
         All prior values of N are outside range MinN to MaxN
    *)
       NOT Between DO
    WriteString ('Enter an integer between ');
    WriteCard (MinN, 0);  WriteString (' and ');
    WriteCard (MaxN, 0);  WriteString (': ');
    ReadCard (N);         WriteLn;
    Between := (N >= MinN) & (N <= MaxN)
  END (* WHILE *)
  (* assert: N is in the range MinN to MaxN *)

END EnterCard;


PROCEDURE ReadBool (VAR BoolVar (* output *) : BOOLEAN);
(*
   Enters a character to determine the value of BoolVar.
   Pre : None
   Post: BoolVar is TRUE if t or T is read;
         otherwise, BoolVar is FALSE.
   Uses: Read from InOut
*)
   VAR
     InChar : CHAR;          (* data character *)

BEGIN (* ReadBool *)
  Read (InChar);
  BoolVar := CAP(InChar) = 'T'
END ReadBool;


PROCEDURE WriteBool (BoolVar (* input *) : BOOLEAN);
(*
   Displays the value of BoolVar.
   Pre : BoolVar is assigned a value.
   Post: 'TRUE' is displayed if BoolVar is TRUE;
```

```
        otherwise, 'FALSE' is displayed.
  Uses: WriteString from InOut
*)
BEGIN (* WriteBool *)
  IF BoolVar THEN
    WriteString ('TRUE')
  ELSE
    WriteString ('FALSE')
  END (* IF *)
END WriteBool;


PROCEDURE WriteRealFormat (X (* input *) : REAL;
                           Width,
                           DecimalPlaces (* input *) : CARDINAL);
(*
   Displays the value of X in Width columns using DecimalPlaces
   digits after the decimal point. If Width is too small to
   accommodate the number, as many columns as are needed will be
   used.
   Pre : X, Width, and DecimalPlaces are assigned.
   Post: X is displayed using Width columns with DecimalPlaces
         digits following the decimal point when physically
         possible.
         If X > MAX(CARDINAL), X is displayed in scientific
         notation.
   Uses: Write, WriteCard from InOut; WriteReal from RealInOut
*)
   CONST
     Minus = '-';               (* the minus sign *)
     DecimalPoint = '.';        (* the decimal point *)
     MaxCard = 65535;           (* value of MAX(CARDINAL) *)

   VAR
     i,                         (* loop control variable *)
     Whole : CARDINAL;          (* the whole part of X *)
     Digit : [0..9];            (* each decimal digit *)
     Fraction : REAL;           (* the fractional part of X *)

   BEGIN (* WriteRealFormat *)
     (* Display X unformatted if it is too large. *)
     IF ABS(X) > FLOAT(MaxCard) THEN
       WriteReal (X, Width);
       RETURN
     END; (* IF *)

     (* Print a minus sign if X negative & change X to positive *)
     IF X < 0.0 THEN
       X := -X:                  (* convert X to a positive number *)
       Write (Minus);                              (* display sign *)
       IF Width > 0 THEN
         DEC (Width)                           (* decrement Width *)
```

```
      END (* IF *)
    END; (* IF *)

    (* Print whole part of X *)
    Whole := TRUNC(X);
    IF Width > DecimalPlaces THEN
      WriteCard (Whole, Width-DecimalPlaces-1)
    ELSE
      WriteCard (Whole, 0)
    END; (* IF *)

    (* Print decimal point and fractional part *)
    Write (DecimalPoint);
    Fraction := X - FLOAT(Whole);          (* get fractional part *)
    FOR i := 1 TO DecimalPlaces DO
      Fraction := 10.0 * Fraction;      (* form new integral part *)
      Digit := TRUNC(Fraction);                (* get next digit *)
      WriteCard (Digit, 1);                 (* display next digit *)
      Fraction := Fraction - FLOAT(Digit)  (* get next fraction *)
    END (* FOR *)
  END WriteRealFormat;

END SimpleIO.
```

The implementation module for SimpleIO closely resembles a main program module. It begins with import statements and procedure declarations. However, the reserved word BEGIN and the statement sequence are missing; a main program module always contains a statement sequence. The implementation module should be saved as file SimpleIO.MOD. The definition and implementation parts of a module are described in the following syntax display. Procedure WriteRealFormat is discussed in the next subsection.

Definition Part of a Module ▶

FORM: DEFINITION MODULE *module name*;
  import statements
 EXPORT QUALIFIED *export list*;
  declarations
 END *module name*.

INTERPRETATION: The *import statements* should import only those items needed in the definition part itself. The standard identifiers are automatically imported into all modules. The *export list* contains all the identifiers that may be imported by a client of *module name*. Each identifier must be declared in the *declarations*. If procedures are exported, only their headers are provided in the *declarations*.

Note: In revised versions of Modula-2, the export statement is not needed, and any identifier declared in the *declarations* may be imported by a client of *module name*.

Implementation Part of a Module

FORM:
```
IMPLEMENTATION MODULE module-name ;
   import statements
   declarations
BEGIN
   statement sequence
END module name.
```

INTERPRETATION: The *import statements* import all identifiers needed in the module. Identifiers imported into the definition module and the standard identifiers are automatically available. The word BEGIN and the *statement sequence* are optional. If present, the *statement sequence* is executed only once, before the code in the client module.

Displaying a Formatted Real Number

Procedure `WriteRealFormat` in Fig. 6.2 is the only procedure declaration we have not seen before. `WriteRealFormat` can be used to display a real number (its first parameter) in a specified number of columns (its second parameter) using a specified number of decimal places (its third parameter).

The first `IF` statement tests whether the absolute value of `X` is too large to be displayed by the procedure. If it is, procedure `WriteReal` is called to display `X`. Next, the statement

```
RETURN
```

returns control to the calling program, skipping the rest of the procedure body. If your Modula-2 system supports function `MAX`, there is no need to declare constant `MaxCard`, and the first `IF` condition can be written as

```
ABS(X) > FLOAT(MAX(CARDINAL))
```

The second `IF` statement displays a minus sign if `X` is negative and changes `X` to a positive number. The statement

```
Whole := TRUNC(X);
```

stores the integral part of `X` in `Whole`, and the last `IF` statement then calls `WriteCard` to display `Whole`. Ideally, `Width−DecimalPlaces−1` columns will be used, but more columns will be used if needed.

Next the decimal point is displayed. Then the statement

```
Fraction := X - FLOAT(Whole);        (* get fractional part *)
```

stores the fractional part of X in Fraction, and the FOR loop displays the decimal digits. This is done by multiplying Fraction by 10.0, thereby moving the most significant decimal digit to the left of the decimal point. This digit is then stored in Digit, displayed, and removed from Fraction. These steps are repeated DecimalPlaces times.

As an example, the procedure call statement

```
WriteRealFormat (-100.2345, 8, 2)
```

passes the value -100.2345 into X. X is changed to 100.2345, a minus sign is displayed, and Width is changed to 7. Next, Whole is assigned the value 100 and is displayed using four columns (7–2–1 is 4). Then the decimal point is displayed, Fraction is assigned the value 0.2345, and the FOR loop is executed (the trace of the FOR loop is shown in Table 6.1). The procedure execution displays the eight characters – 100.23, as specified in the procedure call.

Table 6.1 ▸ *Trace of FOR Loop for WriteRealFormat (−100.2345, 8, 2)*

STATEMENT	i	Fraction	Digit	EFFECT
	?	0.2345	?	
FOR i := 1 TO ...	1			1 <= 2 is true; execute loop.
Fraction := 10.0 * ...		2.3450		
Digit := TRUNC(Fraction)			2	
WriteCard (Digit, 1)				Display 2;
Fraction := Fraction − FLOAT(Digit)		0.3450		compute 2.3450 - 2.0.
FOR i := 1 TO ...	2			2 <= 2 is true; execute loop.
Fraction := 10.0 * ...		3.4500		
Digit := TRUNC(Fraction)			3	
WriteCard (Digit, 1)				Display 3
Fraction := Fraction − FLOAT(Digit)		0.4500		compute 3.4500 - 3.0.
FOR i := 1 TO ...	3			3 <= 2 is false; exit loop.

RETURN Statement ▶

FORM: RETURN

INTERPRETATION: Returns control to the calling program or procecdure.

Program Style

Use of RETURN with Exception Tests

The `RETURN` statement in Fig. 6.2 causes an immediate exit from procedure `WriteRealFormat`. It is usually not considered good programming style to exit from the middle of a procedure. The only time we recommend doing so is when an *exception* is detected that preempts the normal processing performed by the procedure. Calling `WriteCard` to display the whole part of a real number larger than `MAX(CARDINAL)` would cause a cardinal overflow error, so the use of the `RETURN` statement to exit the procedure is perfectly appropriate.

Using Module SimpleIO

You can use module `SimpleIO` just as you use any predefined module provided in the Modula-2 system. Program `ArithFunc` in Fig. 5.6 displays a table of values computed by several standard functions of Modula-2. The revised version of this program, shown in Fig. 6.3, calls `WriteRealFormat` to display the table using formatted decimal numbers. The value of `exp(25.0)` is still displayed in scientific notation because it is larger than `MAX(CARDINAL)`. The table shown in Fig. 6.3 is considerably easier to read than the table shown earlier in Fig. 5.6.

Figure 6.3 ▸ *Displaying a Table of Formatted Real Numbers*

```
MODULE ArithFunc;

(* Illustrates the arithmetic functions. *)

   FROM InOut IMPORT
     WriteString, WriteCard, WriteInt, WriteLn;

   FROM RealInOut IMPORT
     ReadReal, WriteReal;

   FROM MathLib0 IMPORT
     entier, exp, ln, sqrt;

   FROM SimpleIO IMPORT
     WriteRealFormat;

   CONST
     Sentinel = 0.0;           (* sentinel value *)

   VAR
     x : REAL;                 (* input each data value *)

BEGIN  (* ArithFunc *)
  (* Print the user instructions and table heading *)
  WriteString ('After each output line enter ');
```

```
  WriteString ('a real number or 0.0 to stop');
  WriteLn;  WriteLn;
  WriteString ('x        entier(x)        ABS(x)');
  WriteString ('       exp(x)    ln(ABS(x))  sqrt(ABS(x))');
  WriteLn;

  (* Read and process each value of x *)
  ReadReal (x);  WriteLn;                  (* Get first number *)
  WHILE x # Sentinel DO
    WriteInt (entier(x), 17);
    WriteRealFormat (ABS(x), 13, 5);
    WriteRealFormat (exp(x), 13, 5);
    WriteRealFormat (ln(ABS(x)), 13, 5);
    WriteRealFormat (sqrt(ABS(x)), 14, 5);
    WriteLn;
    ReadReal (x);  WriteLn                 (* Get next number *)
  END (* WHILE *)
END ArithFunc.


After each output line enter a real number or 0.0 to stop

x        entier(x)      ABS(x)          exp(x)   ln(ABS(x))  sqrt(ABS(x))
10.0
                10    10.00000   22026.46579      2.30258       3.16227
2.71828
                 2     2.71827      15.15423      0.99999       1.64872
25.0
                25    25.00000  7.20049E+010      3.21887       5.00000
-15.15
               -16    15.15000       0.00000      2.71800       3.89230
0.0
```

In Fig. 6.3, the last import statement

```
FROM SimpleIO IMPORT
  WriteRealFormat;
```

imports procedure `WriteRealFormat` from our module `SimpleIO`. To run program `ArithFunc`, we must now carry out the following steps:

1. Compile the definition module for `SimpleIO`.
2. Compile the implementation module for `SimpleIO`.
3. Compile the main program module `ArithFunc`.
4. Link `ArithFunc` to its environment.
5. Load and execute `ArithFunc`.

Step 1 must be performed first because the definition module is the interface between module `SimpleIO` and any client module. It does not matter whether step 2 or step 3 is performed next. Once these two compilations are completed, steps 4 and 5 can be carried out.

If at a later time we decide to modify the implementation module for `SimpleIO` by rewriting the body of procedure `WriteRealFormat`, we will need to redo step 2. As long as we do not change the header for procedure `WriteRealFormat`, the definition module for `SimpleIO` will stay the same. If the definition module is unchanged, we do not have to recompile it or any of the client modules for `SimpleIO`. To rerun program `ArithFunc` using the new procedure `WriteRealFormat`, it will be necessary to redo steps 4 and 5.

If we modify the definition module for `SimpleIO`, we will need to repeat all the steps above in order to rerun program `ArithFunc`. If we neglect to perform any of the compilations in steps 1 through 3, Modula-2 will detect a `version conflict` error while attempting to link `ArithFunc`. For this reason, you should take exceptional care when writing a definition module. Remember that any changes will require you to recompile all of its client modules. If your program library is extensive, this could have a significant impact.

Module Initialization and Static Variables

It is possible for an implementation module to have a statement sequence. If present, the statement sequence normally initializes variables that are declared in the module declaration section. This code is executed before the statement sequence in the client program.

A variable declared in the module declaration section is called a *module variable*. A module variable has global scope within the module in which it is declared. A module variable is considered a *static variable*, which means that it retains its value as long as its client program is still running. A local variable declared in a procedure retains its value only while the procedure itself is executing.

A module variable may also be imported into a client module. In this case, the module variable's scope is global within the client module as well.

Qualified Identifiers

As you write more library modules, the odds increase that a particular identifier will appear in more than one module. If a client module references the same identifier from two different modules, that identifier must be qualified wherever it appears in the body of the client module. To *qualify* an identifier, prefix it with the name of the module that declares it. A period must separate the module name and the identifier name.

EXAMPLE 6.1 ▶ Assume that `WriteInt` is declared in both module `SimpleIO` and module `InOut`. The qualified identifier `InOut.WriteInt` references procedure `WriteInt` declared in module `InOut`; the qualified identifier `SimpleIO.WriteInt` references procedure `WriteInt` declared in module `SimpleIO`.

Unfortunately, the appearance of the identifier `WriteInt` in two import statements leads to an `identifier specified twice in import list` syntax error. To avoid this error, use *qualified import*. Simply specify the module name in the import statement:

```
IMPORT InOut;
IMPORT SimpleIO;
```

In this form, the keyword FROM is dropped and only the module name is listed. If this form is used, the client module may reference any of the identifiers in the export list of InOut or SimpleIO provided each identifier is qualified wherever it appears in the client module. ◄

SELF-CHECK EXERCISE FOR SECTION 6.3

1. Discuss the changes required to the main program in Fig. 5.16 to use module SimpleIO.

6.4 Predefined Modules and User-Defined Modules

The modules that are predefined in Modula-2 are implemented the same as user-defined modules. The only difference is that they are implemented earlier and are supplied as part of the Modula-2 system by the company that writes the Modula-2 system and compiler.

As an example, the definition module for RealInOut is shown in Fig. 6.4. Besides the two procedures used already (WriteReal and ReadReal), module RealInOut exports a BOOLEAN flag (Done) and a third procedure WriteRealOct. The flag Done is set as a side-effect of procedure ReadReal and will be discussed in Section 6.8. The implementation module (not shown) contains the procedure declarations.

Figure 6.4 ► *Module RealInOut*

```
DEFINITION MODULE RealInOut;

(* Supports input/output of type REAL values. *)

   EXPORT QUALIFIED
     ReadReal, WriteReal, WriteRealOct, Done;

   VAR Done : BOOLEAN;                    (* flag *)


  PROCEDURE ReadReal(VAR X : REAL);
  (*
     Reads a real number.
     Pre : None.
     Post: X is the number read.
           Done is set to TRUE if the read was successful; otherwise,
           Done is set to FALSE.
  *)
```

```
  PROCEDURE WriteReal(X : REAL; n : CARDINAL);
  (*
     Writes X using n characters. If fewer than n
     characters are needed, leading blanks are inserted.
     Pre : X and n are assigned values.
     Post: X is displayed using n characters. If fewer than n
           characters are needed to display X, leading blanks are
           displayed. If more than n characters are needed, X is
           displayed in a field width that is larger than n.
  *)


  PROCEDURE WriteRealOct(X : REAL);
  (*
     Writes X in octal form with an exponent and mantissa.
     Pre : X is assigned a value.
     Post: X is displayed in octal (base 8) form.
  *)

END RealInOut.
```

6.5 Enumeration Types

This section introduces a feature of Modula-2 that improves the readability of large programs. In many programming situations, the standard data types and their values are inadequate. For example, in a budget program you might want to distinguish among the following categories of expenditures: entertainment, rent, utilities, food, clothing, automobile, insurance, miscellaneous. You could always assign an arbitrary code that associates entertainment with a character value of `'e'`, rent with a character value of `'r'`, and so on. Modula-2 allows you to create *enumeration types*, each with its own set of values.

For example, the following enumeration type, `Expenses`, has eight possible values enclosed in parentheses.

```
TYPE
  Expenses = (entertainment, rent, utilities, food,
              clothing, automobile, insurance, miscellaneous);

VAR
  ExpenseKind : Expenses;
```

The variable `ExpenseKind` (type `Expenses`) can contain any of the eight values. The following `IF` statement can be used to test the value stored in `ExpenseKind`.

```
IF ExpenseKind = entertainment THEN
  WriteString ('Postpone until after your payday.')
ELSIF ExpenseKind = rent THEN
  WriteString ('Pay before the first of the month!')
.....

END (* IF *)
```

EXAMPLE 6.2 ▶ The enumeration type `Day` has the values `Sunday`, `Monday`, and so on.

```
TYPE
  Day = (Sunday, Monday, Tuesday, Wednesday,
         Thursday, Friday, Saturday);        (* days of the week *)
```

The values associated with an enumeration type must be identifiers; they cannot be numeric, character, or string literals (e.g., `'Sunday'` cannot be used as a value for an enumeration type). An enumeration-type value is also called a *scalar value*. ◀

The scope rules for identifiers apply to enumeration types and their values. Each enumeration-type value (also called a *scalar value*) is treated as a constant identifier in the block containing the type-declaration statement. The type declaration must precede any variable declaration that references it.

Enumeration Type Declaration ▶

FORM: `TYPE` *enumeration type* = (*identifier list*);

EXAMPLE: `TYPE Class = (Freshman, Sophomore, Junior, Senior);`

INTERPRETATION: A new data type named *enumeration type* is declared. The values associated with this type are specified in the *identifier list*. Each value is defined as a constant identifier in the block containing the type declaration statement.

Note: A particular identifier can appear in only one *identifier list* in a given block.

The note in the preceding syntax display states that an identifier cannot appear in more than one enumeration type declaration. If type `Day` is already declared, the type declaration

```
TYPE
  TDay = (Tuesday, Thursday);
```

is invalid.

Enumeration Type Operators

Each enumeration type is considered an ordinal type, so the order relationship between its values is fixed when the enumeration type is declared. For type `Day`, the first value in its list (`Sunday`) has ordinal number `0`, the next value (Monday) has ordinal number 1, and so on. The only operators that can be used with ordinal types are the relational operators and assignment. The following order relations are all true:

```
Sunday < Monday
Wednesday # Tuesday
Wednesday = Wednesday
Wednesday >= Tuesday
entertainment < rent
```

The order relation

```
entertainment < Wednesday
```

would cause a syntax error because the values shown are associated with two different enumeration types.

The assignment operator can be used to define the value of a variable whose type is an enumeration type. The variable declaration

```
VAR
  Today,                                (* current day of the week *)
  Tomorrow : Day;                       (* day after Today *)
```

specifies that Today and Tomorrow are type Day; therefore, they can be assigned any of the values listed in the declaration for type Day. Consequently, the assignment statements

```
Today := Friday;
Tomorrow := Saturday;
```

assign the value Friday to variable Today and Saturday to variable Tomorrow. After the assignments, the following order relations are all true.

```
Today = Friday
Tomorrow = Saturday
Today < Tomorrow
Today # Wednesday
Today >= Sunday
```

We can use all the procedures and functions listed in Table 5.14 with enumeration types. Some examples are given below, assuming that Today is Friday and Tomorrow is Saturday.

```
ORD(Today) is 6
ORD(Tomorrow) is 7
VAL(Day, 0) is Sunday
VAL(Day, 6) is Saturday
INC (Today) changes the value of Today to Saturday
DEC (Tomorrow, 2) changes the value of Tomorrow to Thursday
INC (Today) is undefined when Today is Saturday
```

The last example above is undefined because there is no value of type Day that follows Saturday. Similarly, if Today is Sunday, the value of DEC (Sunday) is undefined. INC or DEC operations leading to undefined results may cause a range error or overflow error during program execution.

EXAMPLE 6.3 ▶ The IF statement below reassigns the value of Today (type Day) to the next day of the week. Assume that the days of a week are cyclical, so that Sunday is the day after Saturday.

```
IF Today = Saturday THEN
  Today := Sunday
ELSE
  INC (Today)
END
```

The last value (Saturday) in the enumeration type Day is treated separately because INC (Today) is undefined when Today is Saturday. This IF statement is rewritten as follows using the standard functions MIN and MAX (available in revised versions of Modula-2). ◀

```
IF Today = MAX(Day) THEN
  Today := MIN(Day)
ELSE
  INC (Today)
END
```

Subranges of Enumeration Types

We can declare subranges of enumeration types. The following declarations specify that WeekDay (values Monday through Friday) is a subrange of type Day and variable SchoolDay is type WeekDay.

```
TYPE
  Day = (Sunday, Monday, Tuesday, Wednesday,
         Thursday, Friday, Saturday);        (* days of the week *)
  WeekDay = [Monday..Friday];                (* week days only *)

VAR
  SchoolDay : WeekDay;
```

The assignment statement

```
SchoolDay := Monday;
```

is valid; however, the assignment statement

```
SchoolDay := Sunday;
```

causes a constant out of range syntax error.

Reading and Writing Values for Enumeration Types

Enumeration types are defined by the programmer; thus, their values are not known in advance. There are no utility procedures available in Modula-2 for reading and writing enumeration type values. You can, however, write your own utility procedures.

EXAMPLE 6.4 ▶ Given the declarations

```
TYPE
  Color = (Red, Green, Blue, Yellow);

VAR
  Eyes : Color;
```

the statement

```
WriteCard (ORD(Eyes), 1)
```

can be used for diagnostic printing during debugging. It does not print the value of `Eyes`, but it does display the ordinal number of the value that is an integer from `0` (for `Red`) to `3` (for `Yellow`).

Procedure `WriteColor` in Fig. 6.5 prints a string that represents a value of type `Color`. If the value of `Eyes` is defined, the statement

```
WriteColor (Eyes)
```

displays the value of `Eyes` as a string. Make sure you understand the difference between the string `'Blue'` and the constant identifier `Blue`. ◀

Figure 6.5 ▶ *Procedure to Print a Value of Type Color*

```
PROCEDURE WriteColor (InColor (* input *) : Color);
(*
   Displays the value of InColor.
   Pre : InColor is assigned a value.
   Post: The value of InColor is displayed as a string.
   Uses: WriteString from InOut
*)
BEGIN (* WriteColor *)
  IF InColor = Red THEN
    WriteString ('Red')
  ELSIF InColor = Green THEN
    WriteString ('Green')
  ELSIF InColor = Blue THEN
    WriteString ('Blue')
  ELSIF InColor = Yellow THEN
    WriteString ('Yellow')
  END (* IF *)
END WriteColor;
```

It is slightly more difficult to read the value of an enumeration type variable. Two methods are shown in the following examples.

EXAMPLE 6.5 ▶ Procedure `ReadColor1` in Fig. 6.6 returns one value of type `Color` and one of type `BOOLEAN`. If `Eyes` is type `Color` and `ValidColor` is type `BOOLEAN`, the procedure call statement

```
ReadColor1 (Eyes, ValidColor)
```

attempts to read the value of `Eyes` and sets `ValidColor` to indicate the success (`ValidColor` is `TRUE`) or failure (`ValidColor` is `FALSE`) of this operation. (If `Black` and `Brown` are added to the list of values for `Color`, it becomes necessary to read additional characters when the first letter read is `B`. We will leave this as an exercise.) ◀

Figure 6.6 ▶ *Procedure ReadColor1*

```
PROCEDURE ReadColor1 (VAR ItemColor (* output *) : Color;
                      VAR ValidColor (* output *) : BOOLEAN);
(*
   Assigns a value to ItemColor based on an input character. Sets
   ValidColor to indicate whether the assignment was made.
   Pre : None
   Post: ItemColor is defined if the uppercase form of the
         character read is 'R', 'G', 'B', or 'Y'.
         ValidColor is set to TRUE if ItemColor is defined;
         otherwise, ValidColor is set to FALSE.
   Uses: Read, Write, WriteString from InOut
*)
   VAR
     ColorChar : CHAR;          (* first letter of color name *)

BEGIN  (* ReadColor1 *)
  ValidColor := TRUE;          (* Assume valid color will be read *)
  WriteString ('Enter first letter of color: ');
  Read (ColorChar);  Write (ColorChar);
  ColorChar := CAP(ColorChar);

  (* Assign the color value *)
  IF ColorChar = 'R' THEN
    ItemColor := Red
  ELSIF ColorChar = 'G' THEN
    ItemColor := Green
  ELSIF ColorChar = 'B' THEN
    ItemColor := Blue
  ELSIF ColorChar = 'Y' THEN
    ItemColor := Yellow
  ELSE
    ValidColor := FALSE        (* valid color was not read *)
  END (* IF *)
END ReadColor1;
```

EXAMPLE 6.6 ▶ Another procedure that reads a color value, `Color2` is shown in Fig. 6.7. `ReadColor2` uses function `VAL` to convert an integer code (read by `EnterCard` into a type `Color` value. `ReadColor2` requires only one output parameter, because it always returns a valid color value. ◀

Figure 6.7 ▶ *Procedure ReadColor2*

```
PROCEDURE ReadColor2 (VAR ItemColor (* output *) : Color);
(*
   Assigns a value to ItemColor based on an ordinal value.
   Pre : None
   Post: ItemColor is set to the color value whose ordinal
         number is read in.
   Uses: WriteString and WriteLn from InOut
         and EnterCard from SimpleIO
*)
   CONST
     MaxColorNum = 3;            (* value of MAX(Color) *)

    VAR
     ColorNum : [0..MaxColorNum];  (* ordinal number of color *)

BEGIN  (* ReadColor2 *)
  WriteString ('Enter 0 for Red');       WriteLn;
  WriteString ('Enter 1 for Green');     WriteLn;
  WriteString ('Enter 2 for Blue');      WriteLn;
  WriteString ('Enter 3 for Yellow');    WriteLn;

  EnterCard (0, MaxColorNum, ColorNum);  (* Get ordinal number *)

  (* Assign the color value *)
  ItemColor := VAL(Color, ColorNum)
END ReadColor2;
```

Program Style

Program Flags as Procedure Results

In Fig. 6.6, the variable parameter `ValidColor` is used to signal to the calling program (or procedure) whether or not a color value was assigned to `ItemColor`. This information will enable the caller to take appropriate action based on the `BOOLEAN` value returned. This use of the parameter `ValidColor` is consistent with our prior usage of `BOOLEAN` variables a program flags to signal the occurrence of an event.

Motivation for Using Enumeration Types

A legitimate concern at this point would be whether it is worth using enumeration types, considering that it is so much trouble to read and write their values. Also, if we need to use a numeric code to enter the value of an enumeration type variable, why not use that code throughout the program? The answer is that the use of enumeration types in a program makes that program considerably easier to read and understand. Also, the use of enumeration types automatically limits the range of values that can be assigned to a variable.

For example, the `IF` statement

```
IF DayNum = 1 THEN
  PayFactor = 2.0          (* double pay for Sunday *)
ELSIF DayNum = 7 THEN
  PayFactor := 1.5         (* time and a half for Saturday *)
ELSE
  PayFactor := 1.0         (* regular pay *)
END
```

might appear in a payroll program without enumeration types if `Sunday` and `Saturday` are "coded" as the integers 1 and 7, respectively. If we use the enumeration type `Day` and variable `Today` (type `Day`), we can write this statement as

```
IF Today = Sunday THEN
  PayFactor := 2.0
ELSIF Today = Saturday THEN
  PayFactor := 1.5
ELSE
  PayFactor := 1.0
END
```

The latter form is obviously more readable because, instead of an obscure code, it uses values (`Saturday` and `Sunday`) that are meaningful to the problem. Consequently, the comments on the right are not needed.

In a lengthy program, the extra overhead in the form of procedures required to read and write the values associated with an enumeration type will be insignificant. If these procedures are placed in library modules, it will be easy to reuse read and write procedures that have already been written.

SELF-CHECK EXERCISES FOR SECTION 6.5

1. Evaluate each of the following, assuming before each operation that `Today` (type `Day`) is `Thursday` before each operation.
   a. `ORD(Monday)`
   b. `ORD(Today)`
   c. `VAL (Today, 6)`
   d. `Today < Tuesday`
   e. `INC (Today, 2)`
   f. `DEC (Today, 2)`
   g. `VAL (Today, 0)`
   h. `Today >= Thursday`
2. Rewrite procedure `ReadColor1` (see Fig. 6.6), assuming that `Black` and `Brown` are also values for enumeration type `Color`.

6.6 Data Abstraction and Abstract Data Types

When we begin to analyze the solution to a case study, we list its data requirements and the algorithm. Procedural abstraction has helped us design and implement the algorithm. However, we have not yet paid much attention to a problem's data requirements.

Data abstraction is a powerful tool in programming. *Data abstraction* is the conceptual approach of combining a data type with a set of operations on that data type, and the philosophy that such data types can be used without knowing the details of the underlying computer system representation. Just as procedural abstraction enables us to focus on what a procedure does without worrying about how it does it, data abstraction enables us to consider what data objects are needed and what operations must be performed on those objects without our being concerned with unnecessary details.

You have already practiced data abstraction in that you have used the `REAL` data type to represent real numbers without knowing much about the internal representation of this data type on a computer. The specification for the Modula-2 data type `REAL` is shown in the following display.

Specification for Data Type REAL ▶

ELEMENTS: The elements are real numbers within the range `MIN(REAL)` to `MAX (REAL)`. Not all real numbers in this range are included, because of the imprecise nature of the representation. Type `REAL` literals are written as decimal numbers with an optional scale factor. There must be a decimal point and at least one digit before the decimal point in each `REAL` literal.

OPERATORS: The arithmetic operators are +, −, *, /. The relational operators are <=, <, =, <>, #, >, >=. The assignment operator is :=. The standard procedures are `ABS` and `TRUNC`. Revised versions of Modula-2 also support `MIN` and `MAX`. In addition, each Modula-2 system provides predefined modules containing utility procedures that accept type `REAL` parameters (e.g., module `RealInOut` for input/output and module `MathLib0` for mathematical computations).

Abstract Data Types

The combination of a data type and its operators is called an *abstract data type*. Through its type declaration facility and user-defined modules, Modula-2 enables us to create our own abstract data types. We can declare a new data type and write operators for that type in the form of procedures. We can encapsulate the data type and procedures (operators) together in a library module. Whenever we want to use the data type in a program, we can import it along with any operators that may be needed.

SELF-CHECK EXERCISE FOR SECTION 6.6

1. Write the specifications for the data types INTEGER, CARDINAL, CHAR, and BOOLEAN.

6.7 Case Study

The next case study will implement an abstract data type for an enumeration type. Two enumeration types will be declared in this abstract data type, along with operators for reading and displaying the values associated with each enumeration type.

ABSTRACT DATA TYPE DATESADT

Problem: In many programming problems, we need to process information relating to the day of the week or the month of the year. To facilitate this processing, we can implement an abstract data type containing the relevant data types and operators.

Discussion: Our abstract data type should contain declarations for data types Month and Day and procedures ReadDay, WriteDay, ReadMonth, and WriteMonth. In Modula-2, the definition module serves as the specification for an abstract data type. The definition module is the interface between the abstract data type and its client modules. As such, it contains all the information needed to compile a client module. The definition module for the abstract data type shown in Fig. 6.8 contains declarations for the enumeration types and header statements for the four procedures. Each header statement gives the name of a procedure and the form of its parameter list. The comment following the header statement provides additional documentation for each procedure.

Figure 6.8 ▸ *Definition Module for DatesADT*

```
DEFINITION MODULE DatesADT;
(*
   Contains declarations for two enumeration types, Day and Month,
   and procedures for reading and displaying value of these types.
*)

  EXPORT QUALIFIED
    Day, Month,                                      (* data types *)
    ReadDay, WriteDay, ReadMonth, WriteMonth;        (* procedures *)

(* Data types *)
```

```
  TYPE
    Day = (Sunday, Monday, Tuesday, Wednesday,
           Thursday, Friday, Saturday);

    Month = (January, February, March, April, May, June, July,
             August, September, October, November, December);

(* Operators *)

  PROCEDURE ReadDay (VAR InDay (* output *) : Day;
                     VAR ValidDay (* output *) : BOOLEAN);
  (*
     Reads a value into InDay.
     Pre : None
     Post: InDay is assigned a value if the uppercase form of the
           two characters read is SU, MO, TU, WE, TH, FR, or SA;
           otherwise, InDay is undefined.
           ValidDay is set to TRUE if InDay is defined; otherwise,
           ValidDay is set to FALSE.
  *)

  PROCEDURE WriteDay (OneDay (* input *) : Day);
  (*
     Displays the value of OneDay.
     Pre : OneDay is assigned a value.
     Post: The value of OneDay is displayed as a string.
  *)


  PROCEDURE ReadMonth (VAR InMonth (* output *) : Month);
  (*
     Reads a value into InMonth.
     Pre :  None
     Post: InMonth is set to the month value whose number is
           read in (1 for January, 2 for February, and so on.)
  *)

  PROCEDURE WriteMonth (OneMonth (* input *) : Month);
  (*
     Displays the value of OneMonth.
     Pre : OneMonth is assigned a value.
     Post: The value of OneMonth is displayed as a string.
  *)

END DatesADT.
```

The implementation module for DatesADT is shown in Fig. 6.9. The import statements identify input/output procedures for the standard data types that are needed in this module. Procedure EnterCard is also imported from user-defined module SimpleIO (see Fig. 6.2). The type declarations for Day and Month are not needed here because they are included in the definition module, which must be compiled before the implementation module. Due to space limitations, we have shown stubs for ReadDay and WriteMonth rather than complete procedures.

Figure 6.9 ▸ *Implementation Module for DatesADT*

```
IMPLEMENTATION MODULE DatesADT;
(*
   Contains declarations for two enumeration types, Day and Month,
   and procedures for reading and displaying value of these types.
*)

  FROM InOut IMPORT
    Read, Write, WriteString;

  FROM SimpleIO IMPORT
    EnterCard

(* Data types Day and Month are declared in the definition module. *)

(* Operators *)

  PROCEDURE ReadDay (VAR InDay (* output *) : Day;
                     VAR ValidDay (* output *) : BOOLEAN);
  (*
     Reads a value into InDay.
     Pre : None
     Post: InDay is assigned a value if the uppercase form of the two
           characters read is SU, MO, TU, WE, TH, FR, or SA;
           otherwise, InDay is undefined.
           ValidDay is set to TRUE if InDay is defined; otherwise,
           ValidDay is set to FALSE.
     Uses: Read, Write, WriteString from InOut
  *)
  BEGIN (* ReadDay stub *)
    WriteString ('Procedure ReadDay entered');
    InDay := Sunday;  ValidDay := TRUE
  END ReadDay;


  PROCEDURE WriteDay (OneDay (* input *) : Day);
  (*
     Displays the value of OneDay.
     Pre : OneDay is assigned a value.
     Post: The value of OneDay is displayed as a string.
```

```
    Uses: WriteString from InOut
  *)
  BEGIN (* WriteDay *)
    IF OneDay = Sunday THEN
      WriteString ('Sunday')
    ELSIF OneDay = Monday THEN
      WriteString ('Monday')
    ELSIF OneDay = Tuesday THEN
      WriteString ('Tuesday')
    ELSIF OneDay = Wednesday THEN
      WriteString ('Wednesday')
    ELSIF OneDay = Thursday THEN
      WriteString ('Thursday')
    ELSIF OneDay = Friday THEN
      WriteString ('Friday')
    ELSIF OneDay = Saturday THEN
      WriteString ('Saturday')
    END (* IF *)
  END WriteDay;


  PROCEDURE ReadMonth (VAR InMonth (* output *) : Month);
  (*
     Reads a value into InMonth.
     Pre : None
     Post: InMonth is set to the month value whose
           number is read in.
     Uses: WriteString from InOut and EnterCard from SimpleIO
  *)
     VAR
       MonthNumber : CARDINAL;    (* a number from 1 to 12 *)

  BEGIN (* ReadMonth *)
    WriteString ('Enter the month number.');
    EnterCard (1, 12, MonthNumber);
    InMonth := VAL (Month, MonthNumber-1)
  END ReadMonth;

  PROCEDURE WriteMonth (OneMonth (* input *) : Month);
  (*
     Displays the value of OneMonth.
     Pre : OneMonth is assigned a value.
     Post: The value of OneMonth is displayed as a string.
     Uses: WriteString from InOut
  *)
  BEGIN (* WriteMonth stub *)
    WriteString ('Procedure WriteMonth entered.')
  END WriteMonth;

END DatesADT.
```

Using Module DatesADT

Module `DatesADT` can be used by any client module that imports its data types and operators. To use this module, follow these steps:

1. Compile the definition module for `SimpleIO`.
2. Compile the definition module for `DatesADT`.
3. Compile the implementation module for `SimpleIO`.
4. Compile the implementation module for `DatesADT`.
5. Compile the client module.
6. Link the client module to its environment.
7. Load and execute the client module.

The relative order of steps 3, 4, and 5 is not critical.

Module `DatesADT` shown in Fig. 6.9 can be used to test the overall flow of a client module. However, it is not ready to provide accurate test results.Once each input/output procedure is written, it can be inserted in place of its stub. The only steps that need to be repeated are steps 4, 6, and 7. It will not be necessary to recompile the definition module for `DatesADT` or the client module. If the client module is changed later on, only steps 5 through 7 need to be repeated. Modules `DatesADT` and `SimpleIO` should not be touched.

SELF-CHECK EXERCISE FOR SECTION 6.7

1. Write procedures `ReadDay` and `WriteMonth`.

6.8 Using Text Files

In all the programs so far, the keyboard and the screen were used as input and output devices, respectively. This is fine as long as you are writing rather small programs. As you begin to write larger programs, however, it will be to your advantage to be able to read data from a previously prepared data file and to save the program output as a disk file. This will enable you to rerun a program with the same test data during debugging without having to reenter the test data each time the program is run. You can also list the program's output file on a printer and examine it more carefully after the program finishes execution.

This section will show you how to get a Modula-2 program to read from a data file and write to an output file. The files that you will process are called *text files*, or files of characters. Special characters called *end-of-line characters* can be used to separate a text file into lines.

This section will also introduce two utility procedures that are called to prepare files for input or output (*open the files*) and two utility procedures that can be used to disconnect those files after you are finished using them (*close the files*). These procedures are part of module `InOut`. See Appendix E for more discussion of file processing.

Opening and Closing Input and Output Files

A data file can be created using the same editor you use to write a Modula-2 program. Once the data file is created, you can instruct a Modula-2 program to read data from that file by using an `OpenInput` statement. The statements

```
WriteString ('Enter the data file name: ');
OpenInput ('TXT');
```

display the prompt message and read the name of a data file from the keyboard. The *default extension* `'TXT'` is appended to the file name if the user does not specify an extension. If the program user responds to the prompt by entering the data string `MyData` or `MyData.TXT`, all subsequent program input will be read from data file `MyData.TXT`.

In a similar way, the statement

```
OpenOutput ('TXT')
```

reads the name of the output file from the keyboard, and appends the default extension `'TXT'` if none is specified. (Note that the output file name is read from the keyboard even if all other input is coming from a data file.) All subsequent output is sent to the output file whose name is entered at the keyboard.

The statements

```
CloseInput;
CloseOutput
```

close the current input and output files, respectively, and cause input/output to be redirected to the keyboard/screen. These statements should always be executed before the program terminates.

The Module Variable Done

Instead of reporting input or output errors, module `InOut` assigns a value of `TRUE` (operation performed successfully) or `FALSE` (operation not performed) to the module variable `Done` (type `BOOLEAN`). This means that the value of `Done` can be tested after returning from certain procedures in `InOut` to determine whether the procedure performed its intended operation. Variable `Done` can be imported by a user program in the same way that a utility procedure is imported (i.e., by including it in an import list).

The variable `Done` is set whenever an `OpenInput` or `OpenOutput` statement is executed. If the specified file is opened, `Done` is set to `TRUE`; if the file cannot be opened for some reason (e.g., it is not on the disk), then `Done` is set to `FALSE`.

EXAMPLE 6.7 ▶ Procedure `GetInputFile` in Fig. 6.10 reads in an input file name. If the file cannot be opened, `Done` is set to `FALSE`, the `WHILE` loop is entered (`NOT Done` is `TRUE`), and the prompt

```
Error in file name - try again:
```

is printed. This prompt will continue to be printed until the user enters the name of a file that can be opened for input.

Figure 6.10 ▸ *Procedure GetInputFile*

```
PROCEDURE GetInputFile;
(*
   Opens the input file whose name is read from the keyboard.
   Pre : None
   Post: Done is TRUE and an input file is opened.
*)
BEGIN (* GetInputFile *)
  WriteString ('Enter input file name: ');
  OpenInput ('TXT');
  WHILE
    (* invariant:
         No prior input file was opened.
    *)
       NOT Done DO
    WriteString ('Error in file name - try again: ');
    OpenInput ('TXT')
  END (* WHILE *)
  (* assert: Done is TRUE - file opened successfully *)

 END GetInputFile;
```

The `WHILE` loop in `GetInputFile` gives the user more than one chance to enter a valid file name. This repeated prompting and reading of file names is automatically performed by many Modula-2 systems. If your system does this, then the `WHILE` loop shown in Fig. 6.10 is not needed.

The variable `Done` is also set after each call to an input procedure (e.g., `ReadInt`). If the input operation is performed successfully, `Done` is set to `TRUE`; otherwise, `Done` is set to `FALSE`. For example, if `ReadCard` or `ReadInt` is executed and a nonnumeric data value is entered, `Done` is set to `FALSE` instead of `TRUE`. This may be the only indication that the data value was invalid. ◂

EXAMPLE 6.8 ▸ The program in Fig. 6.11 reads a series of integer values from a data file and writes the numbers and their sum to an output file. Fig. 6.12 shows the output file (bottom) created by the program for a sample data file (top). Note that all seven numbers are summed and that it is not necessary for the numbers to appear on separate lines of the data file. The three output lines displayed on the screen appear in the usual position at the bottom of Fig. 6.11.

Figure 6.11 ▶
Reading and Writing Text Files

```
MODULE UseFiles;

(* Demonstrates use of data file and output file. *)

   FROM InOut IMPORT
     Done,                                              (* variable *)
     ReadInt, WriteInt, WriteString, WriteLn,         (* procedures *)
     OpenInput, OpenOutput, CloseInput, CloseOutput;

   VAR
     Sum : INTEGER;         (* output sum of data *)

   (* Insert GetInputFile here. *)


   PROCEDURE ReadAndSum (VAR Sum  (* output *) : INTEGER);
   (*
      Reads integers from a data file, copies them to an output
      file, and returns their sum.
      Pre : None
      Post: Sum is the sum of all data values read and
            each data value is copied to the output file.
   *)
      VAR
        NextInt : INTEGER;       (* each data value *)
        MoreData : BOOLEAN;      (* TRUE if more data remains *)

   BEGIN (* ReadAndSum *)
     WriteString ('Numbers being summed:');  WriteLn;
     Sum := 0;                             (* initialize Sum *)
     ReadInt (NextInt);
     MoreData := Done;                     (* more data remains? *)
     WHILE
       (* invariant:
            Sum is the sum of all data values read so far and
            each read attempt was successful
       *)
          MoreData DO
       WriteInt (NextInt, 5);             (* echo to output file *)
       WriteLn;                           (* terminate file line *)
       Sum := Sum + NextInt;
       ReadInt (NextInt);
       MoreData := Done                    (* more data remains? *)
     END (* WHILE *)
     (* assert:
          Sum is the sum of all data values and
          the last read attempt failed
     *)

   END ReadAndSum;
```

```
BEGIN (* UseFiles *)
  (* Get name of input file. *)
  GetInputFile;

  (* Get name of output file. *)
  WriteString ('Enter output file name: ');
  OpenOutput ('TXT');

  (* Read, echo, and print sum of input data. *)
  ReadAndSum (Sum);

  (* Copy result to output file. *)
  WriteString ('Sum is ');
  WriteInt (Sum, 5);  WriteLn;

  (* Close files. *)
  CloseInput;
  CloseOutput;
  WriteString ('Data file read and output file created.');
  WriteLn
END UseFiles.

Enter input file name: MyData.TXT
Enter output file name: MyOut.TXT
Data file read and output file created.
```

Figure 6.12 ▸ *Sample Data File (top) and Output File (bottom)*

```
DATA FILE

 30   20
-52  -18
 30

OUTPUT FILE

Numbers being summed:
   30
   20
  -52
  -18
   30
Sum is    10
```

From the sample output at the bottom of Fig. 6.11, you can see that the prompts for the file names are written to the screen instead of the output file. This is because the `WriteString` statements that display the prompts precede the `OpenOutput` operation. After the input and output files are opened, procedure `ReadAndSum` is called.

Procedure `ReadAndSum` begins by writing the string `'Numbers being summed:'` to the output file. The `ReadInt` statements in `ReadAndSum` read integer values from the data file. The `WHILE` loop is repeated as long as there are data items remaining on the data file. Within the loop, the `WriteInt` statement sends the next integer value to the output file, and the `WriteLn` statement terminates each line of the output file. When the `ReadInt` operation cannot be performed because there are no data remaining, `Done` and `MoreData` are set to `FALSE`, and the loop is exited.

In procedure `ReadAndSum`, local variable `MoreData` may seem redundant because it is set to the same value as module variable `Done` after each read operation. The reason `MoreData` is introduced is to make the `WHILE` loop header more readable. The `WHILE` loop header

```
WHILE MoreData DO
```

more clearly specifies the intent of the loop (iterate while there are more data items) than the logically equivalent header

```
WHILE Done DO
```

After returning from `ReadAndSum`, the `WriteString` and `WriteInt` statements in the main program write the last line of the output file. Finally, the last `WriteString` statement displays its message on the screen because it follows the `CloseOutput` operation. The four operators introduced in this section are summarized in the following display. ◂

Operators OpenInput and OpenOutput ▶

FORM: `OpenInput (`*defext*`);`
`OpenOutput (`*defext*`);`

EXAMPLE: `OpenInput ('TXT');`
`OpenOutput ('');`

INTERPRETATION: `OpenInput` is used to read (from the keyboard) the name of a data file; `OpenOutput` is used to read the name of an output file. RETURN is pressed after the name is entered. The string parameter *defext* is the default extension appended to the file name if the user does not specify an extension. No extension is appended if the string `''` is passed to *defext*. If the file specified can be opened, the `InOut` variable `Done` is set to `TRUE`; otherwise, `Done` is set to `FALSE`.

Note: On most systems, the backspace key can be used to edit the file name before RETURN is pressed. Some systems will continue to prompt for a file name if the specified file cannot be opened. If a file opened by `OpenOutput` already exists, some systems will ask if you want to overwrite (replace) the file with the new program output.

Operators CloseInput and CloseOutput ▶

FORM:
```
CloseInput;
CloseOutput;
```

INTERPRETATION: `CloseInput` closes the input file and redesignates the keyboard as the source of program input. `CloseOutput` closes the output file and redirects program output to the screen.

Effect of OpenOutput Statement on Prompts

It is difficult to interact with a program after an `OpenOutput` statement is executed, because all program output, including prompts, is sent to the output file. If the prompts do not appear on the screen, the user has no way of knowing what data are expected and when to enter the required data. For this reason, a program that sends its output to a file usually reads its data from a data file. Make sure the `OpenInput` statement is executed before the `OpenOutput` statement; otherwise, the prompt for the data file name may be sent to the output file instead of the screen.

The Module Constant EOL

We mentioned that a data file is separated into lines by an end-of-line character. This character is actually entered into an output file when the `WriteLn` statement is entered. Think of the screen as a file of characters. When the end-of-line character is displayed, a new output line is started on the screen.

The end-of-line character is different on each system and is defined as the constant `EOL` in module `InOut`. For example, the `InOut` module for the LOGITECH Modula-2 compiler contains the statement

```
CONST
  EOL = 36C;
```

This specifes the code for the constant `EOL` as 36 octal (30 decimal). The constant `EOL` can be imported from `InOut` and used in a program to detect the end of a data line.

EXAMPLE 6.9 ▶ Procedure `EchoLine` in Fig. 6.13 echos a line of data characters. The `WHILE` loop is exited when the character just read is `EOL`. After loop exit, the statement

```
Write (EOL)
```

writes the `EOL` character to the output file. This is equivalent to the `WriteLn` operation. ◀

Figure 6.13 ▶
Procedure EchoLine

```
PROCEDURE EchoLine;
(*
   Reads and echos a data line.
   Pre : None
```

```
   Post: A data line is read from the keyboard and echoed on the
         screen.
   Uses: EOL, Read, and Write from InOut
*)
   VAR
     NextCh : CHAR;

BEGIN (* EchoLine *)
  Read (NextCh);
  WHILE NextCh # EOL DO
    Write (NextCh);                        (* echo *)
    Read (NextCh)
  END; (* WHILE *)
  (* assert: The last character read is EOL. *)

  Write(EOL)                 (* terminate output line *)
END EchoLine;
```

The line of characters can be read from a data file or the screen. If data is being read from the screen, all characters pressed will be echoed until RETURN is pressed. To use `EchoLine`, `Read`, `Write`, and `EOL` must be imported from `InOut`.

Using Text Files for Debugging

During debugging, it may be necessary to reenter the same data during several runs of the program. Often a debugging run is terminated or aborted before very much of the program has executed. It becomes tiresome to reenter the data during each debugging run. To free yourself from this task, take the time to prepare a data file before beginning the debugging process and instruct your program to read its test data from this file. It is also helpful to have debugging output sent to an output file so that it can be reexamined carefully later. Output sent to the screen is lost as soon as it scrolls off the screen.

SELF-CHECK EXERCISES FOR SECTION 6.8

1. Write a driver program that calls `EchoLine` to read and echo on the screen three data lines entered at the keyboard. Display the prompt `'>'` before each data line.
2. Write a program that copies one text file to another. Your program should read characters from the data file and write them to the output file until there are no characters remaining.

6.9 Common Programming Errors

When writing user-defined modules, include only the procedure headers in the definition module; the complete procedure declarations must appear in the implementation module. A constant, type, or variable that is exported should be declared in the definition module. If your version of Modula-2 requires an export statement, remember to include each identifier to be exported in the export list of the definition module.

Be careful to import identifiers declared elsewhere into the correct module. For example, type identifiers appearing in parameter lists should be imported into the definition module; procedures called in a procedure body should be imported into the implementation module.

If the implementation part of a module is being changed but not the definition part, it is not necessary to recompile any clients of the module being modified. You must, however, repeat the link step before rerunning a client module. If the definition module is also changed, make sure you recompile it and all client modules as well. If you forget to recompile any of these modules, a `version conflict` error will be detected when you attempt to link a client module.

When declaring enumeration types, remember that only identifiers can appear in the list of values for an enumeration type. Strings, characters, or numbers are not allowed. Make sure that the same constant identifier does not appear in more than one enumeration type declaration in a given block. It is permissible for a given constant identifier to appear in more than one subrange type declaration. Remember that there are no standard procedures available to read or write the values of an enumeration type.

If you are sending program output to a file, make sure that any data not read from a data file are entered by the program user before the `OpenOutput` statement is executed. After the `OpenOutput` statement is executed, all prompt messages are sent to the output file and do not appear on the screen.

6.10 Chapter Review

This chapter described how to write user-defined modules. You saw that the definition module serves as an interface between each user-defined module and its client modules. Each constant, type, or variable that is exported from the module is declared in the definition module. The procedure headers are also shown, but their actual implementations are provided in the implementation module.

You also saw that there were many advantages to creating and using your own modules. Modules are the building blocks of larger programs. The use of modules makes it easier to assign pieces of a large project to different members of a programming team. Once a module is completed, it can be compiled and its procedures can be imported and reused by other modules. We can change the client program for a module without having to recompile the module being imported. If we rewrite the body of a procedure in an implementation module, then we have to recompile only the implementation module. As long as the procedure header does not change, the definition module and any client modules need not be recompiled.

We discussed how to declare enumeration types with a list of values tailored to a particular application. The use of enumeration types makes large programs more readable. You also saw how to encapsulate an enumeration type together with its operators as an abstract data type.

You learned how to instruct a program to read its data from a data file rather than the keyboard and how to save the output generated by a program as a file on disk. Both features make it easier to debug large programs.

New Modula-2 Statements

The new Modula-2 statements introduced in this chapter are described in Table 6.2.

Table 6.2 ▸ *Summary of New Modula-2 Statements*

STATEMENT	EFFECT
User-defined Modules	

`DEFINITION MODULE MyMod;`
 	
`  EXPORT QUALIFIED`
`    Message;`
 	
`  PROCEDURE Message;`
`  (* Prints a message *)`
 	
`END MyMod.`
 	
`IMPLEMENTATION MODULE MyMod;`
 	
`  FROM InOut IMPORT`
`    WriteString, WriteLn;`
 	
`  PROCEDURE Message;`
`  (* Prints a message *)`
`  BEGIN`
`    WriteString ('Much ado about nothing');`
`    WriteLn`
`  END Message;`
`END MyMod.`
	A very simple module is defined that can be used to print the message `'Much ado about nothing'`. The definition module specifies that procedure `Message` can be exported `Message` is described as a parameterless procedure. The implementation module imports lower-level modules `WriteString` and `WriteLn` and declares procedure `Message`.

RETURN Statement	
`RETURN`	Returns control from the executing procedure to the calling program or procedure.

Table 6.2 ▸ *(continued)*

STATEMENT	EFFECT
Enumeration Type Declaration	
`TYPE` `  BColor = (Blue, Black, Brown);`	An enumeration type `BColor` is declared with values `Blue`, `Black`, and `Brown`.
File Open and Close	
`OpenInput ('TXT');`	Reads the name of a data file and attempts to open it for input. Uses `TXT` as a default extension.
`OpenOutput ('');`	Reads the name of a data file and attempts to open it for output. There is no default extension.
`CloseInput`	Closes the data file previously opened and resumes reading from the keyboard.
`CloseOutput`	Closes the output file previously opened and resumes writing to the screen.

CHAPTER 6 ▸

Review Questions

1. Give four advantages to creating and using library modules.
2. A module variable may be referenced only in the module in which it is declared. True or false?
3. The scope of a module variable is global; it can be referenced anywhere in the program system. True or false?
4. What is the major difference between an implementation module and a main program module? Between a definition module and an implementation module?
5. Into which module should the following objects be imported?
   a. a type identifier used as the type of a formal parameter for a procedure that is exported
   b. a type identifier used as the type of a formal parameter for a procedure that is not exported
   c. a type identifier used as the type of a module variable that is exported
   d. a type identifier used as the type of a module variable that is not exported
   e. a type identifier used as the type of a local variable declared in a procedure that is exported
   f. a type identifier used as the type of a local variable declared in a procedure that is not exported
6. Specify where each object should be declared (definition module, implementation module, or both):
   a. the header of a procedure that is exported
   b. the header of a procedure that is not exported
   c. a data type that is exported

d. the body of a procedure that is exported
e. the body of a procedure that is not exported
f. a module variable that is exported
g. a module variable that is not exported
h. a local variable for a procedure

7. Write an enumeration type declaration for `Fiscal` as the months from `July` through `June`. Declare the subrange `Winter` as `December` through `February`.
8. Write an abstract data type for the positions on a baseball team (pitcher, catcher, infield, outfield) and operators to read and write these positions.
9. Explain the purpose of variable `Done` declared in module `InOut`.
10. Discuss how to terminate a line using procedure `Write` instead of `WriteLn`. Write the import statement that would be required to do this.
11. Write a loop that reads up to `10` integer values from a data file and displays them on the screen. If there are not `10` integers in the file, the message `That's all folks` should be displayed after the last number.

CHAPTER 6 ▶

Programming Projects

1. Write an abstract data type that consists of data type `PrimaryColor` and operators for reading and writing the colors (red, yellow, green, blue, black, and white).

2. Add a procedure for entering a character value within a specified range to module `SimpleIO`. Redo the prime number program in Fig. 5.16 to use procedure `EnterCard` declared in module `SimpleIO`.

3. Write a program to read in a collection of positive integers and print all divisors of each, except for 1 and the number itself. If the number has no divisors, print a message indicating that it is prime. Import procedure `TestPrime` (see Fig. 5.19) to perform the prime determination and list the divisors.

4. Each month, a bank customer deposits $50 into a savings account. The account earns 6.5 percent interest, calculated on a quarterly basis (one-fourth of 6.5 percent every three months). Write a program to compute the total investment, total amount in the account, and the interest accrued for each of the 120 months of a 10-year period. Assume that the rate is applied to all funds in the account at the end of a quarter regardless of when the deposits were made.

   Print all values accurate to two decimal places. The table printed by your program should begin as follows:

MONTH	INVESTMENT	NEW AMOUNT	INTEREST	TOTAL SAVINGS
1	50.00	50.00	0.00	50.00
2	100.00	100.00	0.00	100.00
3	150.00	150.00	2.44	152.44
4	200.00	202.44	0.00	202.44
5	250.00	252.44	0.00	252.44
6	300.00	302.44	4.91	307.35
7	350.00	357.35	0.00	357.35

5. Read a series of integers and determine the following information about each integer:
   a. Is it a multiple of 7, 11, or 13?
   b. Is the sum of the digits odd or even?
   c. What is the square root value (if positive)?
   d. Is it a prime number?

   You should have at least four procedures and label all output. Some sample input data might be `104 3773 13 121 77 30751`.

6. Whatsamata U. offers a service to its faculty in computing grades at the end of each semester. A program will process three weighted test scores and will calculate a student's average and letter grade (based on an A is 90–100, a B is 80–89, etc.).

   Write a program to provide this valuable service. The data will consist of the three test weights followed by three test scores and a student ID number (four digits) for each student. Calculate the weighted average for each student and the corresponding grade. This information should be printed along with the initial three test scores. The weighted average for each student is equal to:

   ```
   weight1 * grade1 + weight2 * grade2 + weight3 * grade3
   ```

   For summary statistics print the highest average, lowest average, average of the averages, and total number of students processed. Sample data might be:

   ```
   .35  .25  .40
   100   76   88  1014
    96   91   99  2222
    45   15   65  3051
    35   88   86  4067
   ```

7. Write a program that reads several lines from a data file and prints each word of the file on a separate line of an output file followed by the number of letters in that word. Also print a count of words in the file on the screen when done. Assume that words are separated by one or more blanks.

8. An employee time card is represented as one long string of characters. Write a program that processes a collection of these strings stored on a data file and writes the results to an output file.
   a. Compute gross pay using the formula

   $$gross = regular\ hours \times rate + overtime\ hours \times 1.5 \times rate$$

   b. Compute net pay by subtracting the following deductions

   $federal\ tax = .14 \times (gross - 13 \times dependents)$
   $social\ security = 0.052 \times gross$
   $city\ tax$ = 4% of *gross* if employee works in the city
   $union\ dues$ = 6.75% of *gross* for union member

The data string for each employee has the form

Positions	*Data*
`1-10`	Employee last name
`11-20`	Employee first name
`21`	Contains a `C` for City Office or `S` for suburban office
`22`	Contains a `U` (union) or `N` (nonunion)
`23-26`	Employee identification number
`27`	blank
`28-29`	Number of regular hours (a whole number)
`30`	blank
`31-36`	Hourly rate (dollars and cents)
`37`	blank
`38-39`	Number of dependents
`40`	blank
`41-42`	Number of overtime hours (a whole number)

7 ▶ More Control Statements

THIS CHAPTER INTRODUCES more control statements. You are already familiar with how to use the IF statement to implement decisions; the CASE statement is another way to select among several alternative tasks.

Chapter 7 also reexamines control structures for repetition. The FOR statement is reviewed and and its general form described. Another conditional loop (REPEAT statement) and a general loop (LOOP statement) are introduced, and the use of nested loops is described.

You have used standard functions and mathematical functions that are predefined in module MathLib0 to simplify expressions. In this chapter, you will see how to declare and use your own function procedures.

7.1 The CASE Statement

The CASE statement is used in Modula-2 to select one of several alternatives. It is especially useful when the selection is based on the value of a single variable or a simple expression. This variable or expression must be an ordinal type.

EXAMPLE 7.1 ▶ The CASE statement

```
CASE CAP(MomOrDad) OF
  'M' : WriteString ("Hello Mom - Happy Mother's Day")
| 'D' : WriteString ("Hello Dad - Happy Father's Day")
ELSE
  WriteString ('Invalid character ');
  Write (MomOrDad)
END (* CASE *)
```

behaves the same as the following IF statement.

```
IF CAP(MomOrDad) = 'M' THEN
  WriteString ("Hello Mom - Happy Mother's Day")
ELSIF CAP(MomOrDad) = 'D' THEN
  WriteString ("Hello Dad - Happy Father's Day")
ELSE
  WriteString ('Invalid character ');
  Write (MomOrDad)
END (* IF *)
```

The message displayed by the CASE statement depends on the value of the CASE *selector* CAP(MomOrDad). If the CASE selector matches the first CASE *label*, 'M', the first message is displayed. If the CASE selector matches the second CASE label, 'D', the second message is displayed. Otherwise, the ELSE clause is executed.

The vertical bar | preceding the second case label separates the first case from the second. A vertical bar is not needed to separate the last case from the ELSE clause. ◀

EXAMPLE 7.2 ▶ Procedure WriteDay in Fig. 7.1 uses a CASE statement to print a string that indicates the value of a variable whose type is the enumeration type Day. This procedure can replace the stub used in the implementation module for DatesADT shown in Fig. 6.9.

Figure 7.1 ▶ *Procedure WriteDay*

```
PROCEDURE WriteDay (OneDay (* input *) : Day);
(*
   Displays the value of OneDay.
   Pre : OneDay is assigned a value.
   Post: The value of OneDay is displayed as a string.
   Uses: WriteString from InOut
*)
BEGIN (* WriteDay *)
  CASE OneDay OF
     Sunday    : WriteString ('Sunday')
   | Monday    : WriteString ('Monday')
   | Tuesday   : WriteString ('Tuesday')
   | Wednesday : WriteString ('Wednesday')
   | Thursday  : WriteString ('Thursday')
   | Friday    : WriteString ('Friday')
   | Saturday  : WriteString ('Saturday')
  END (* CASE *)
END WriteDay;
```

Seven different alternatives are shown in Fig. 7.1; the value of OneDay (type Day) is used to select one of these for execution. The seven possible values of OneDay are listed as CASE labels to the left of each colon; the task for that CASE label follows the colon. After the WriteString statement selected is executed, the CASE statement and the procedure are exited. ◀

EXAMPLE 7.3 ▶ The CASE statement could be used to compute the numeric value of the hexadecimal digit stored in HexDigit (type CHAR). In the hexadecimal number systems, the valid "digits" are the characters '0' through '9' and 'A' through 'F'. The characters '0' through '9' have the numeric value 0 through 9; the characters 'A' through 'F' have the numeric values 11 (for 'A') through 15 (for 'F').

```
CASE HexDigit OF
  '0','1','2','3','4','5','6','7','8','9' :
                Decimal := ORD(HexDigit) - ORD('0')
| 'A','B','C','D','E','F' :
                Decimal := ORD(HexDigit) - ORD('A') + 10
```

```
ELSE
  WriteString ('Illegal hexadecimal digit ');
  Write (HexDigit);  WriteLn
END (* CASE *)
```

This CASE statement causes the first assignment statement to be executed when HexDigit is one of the digits '0' through '9'; the second assignment statement is executed when HexDigit is one of the letters 'A' through 'F'. If HexDigit is not one of the characters listed above, the ELSE task executes and prints an error message. The assignments to Decimal assume that the characters 'A' through 'F' and the characters '0' through '9' are consecutive.

We can use subrange notation to abbreviate CASE labels. The last CASE statement is rewritten as follows using subranges. Note that most Modula-2 systems do not allow large subranges in case labels. ◂

```
CASE HexDigit OF
  '0'..'9' : Decimal := ORD(HexDigit) - ORD('0')
| 'A'..'F' : Decimal := ORD(HexDigit) - ORD('A') + 10
ELSE
  WriteString ('Illegal hexadecimal digit ');
  Write (HexDigit);  WriteLn
END (* CASE *)
```

EXAMPLE 7.4 ▸ The CASE statement in Fig. 7.2 can be used in a student transcript program that computes grade point averages (GPAs). For each case shown, the total points (Points) earned toward the GPA increase by an amount based on the letter grade (Grade); the total credits earned toward graduation (GradCredits) increase by 1 if the course is passed. Assuming that the letters are in consecutive order, the expression

```
ORD('A') - ORD(Grade) + 4
```

evaluates to 4 when Grade is 'A', 3 when Grade is 'B', and so on.

Figure 7.2 ▸ *CASE Statement for GPA Computation*

```
CASE Grade OF
  'A'..'D'      : Points := Points + (ORD('A') - ORD(Grade) + 4);
                  GradCredits := GradCredits + 1
| 'P'           : GradCredits := GradCredits + 1
| 'F', 'I', 'W' : WriteString ('No points to GPA or graduation');
                  WriteLn
ELSE
  WriteString ('Illegal grade ');
  Write (Grade);  WriteLn
END (* CASE *)
```

In Fig. 7.2, a grade of A through D earns a variable number of points (4 for an A, 3 for a B, etc.) and 1 graduation credit; a grade of P earns 1 graduation credit; and a grade of F, I, or W earns no graduation credit and no points. The ELSE clause displays an error message if the program user enters a grade not listed in a CASE label. ◂

CASE Statement ▸

FORM:

CASE *selector* OF
  $label_1$: *statement sequence*$_1$
| $label_2$: *statement sequence*$_2$
  .
  .
  .
| $label_n$: *statement sequence*$_n$
ELSE
  statement sequence$_E$
END

EXAMPLE:

```
CASE N OF
  1, 2 : WriteString ('Buckle my shoe')
 | 3, 4 : WriteString ('Shut the door')
 | 5, 6 : WriteString ('Pick up sticks')
ELSE
  WriteString ('Whatever ... ')
END
```

INTERPRETATION: The *selector* expression is evaluated and compared to each of the CASE *labels*. Each *label* is a list of one or more possible values for the *selector*, separated by commas. Only one *statement sequence* will be executed; if the *selector* value is listed in $label_i$, then *statement sequence*$_i$ is executed. If the *selector* value is not listed in any $label_i$, *statement sequence*$_E$ is executed if present. Control is then passed to the first statement following the CASE END. The vertical bar is used as a separator between cases.

Notes: If the value of the *selector* is not listed in any $label_i$, a run-time error occurs unless an ELSE clause is provided.

A particular *selector* value may appear in, at most, one $label_i$.

The type of each value listed in $label_i$ must correspond to the type of the *selector* expression.

Any ordinal data type is permitted as the *selector* type.

Program Style

Use of ELSE Clause with CASE

We recommend that you use an `ELSE` clause with each `CASE` statement to display an error message in the event that the `CASE` selector takes on an unexpected value; otherwise, a run-time error such as `case-tag error` will occur and program execution will terminate. If you are using a variable whose type is an enumeration type or a `BOOLEAN` variable, there is no need to provide an `ELSE` clause, as long as every possible value appears in the case labels.

Comparison of Multiple-Alternative IF Statement and CASE Statement

The multiple-alternative `IF` statement is more general than the `CASE` statement and can always be used to implement a multiple-alternative decision. The `CASE` statement, however, is more readable and should be used whenever practical. The `CASE` statement cannot be used when the selection criteria involve a type `REAL` expression or strings. Its use should be avoided when the `CASE` selector is an ordinal type, but there are large gaps in the values occurring as `CASE` labels.

SELF-CHECK EXERCISES FOR SECTION 7.1

1. Rewrite the `CASE` statement in Fig. 7.1 as a nested `IF` statement.
2. If type `Color` is described as the list of identifiers (`Red, Green, Blue, Brown, Yellow`), write a `CASE` statement that assigns a value to `Eyes` (type `Color`) given that the first two letters of the color name are stored in `Letter1` and `Letter2`.
3. Write a `CASE` statement that prints a message indicating whether `NextCh` (type `CHAR`) is an operator symbol (+,–,*, =,#, <,>,&), a punctuation symbol in Modula-2 (comma, semicolon, parenthesis, bracket, vertical bar), a digit, a letter, or something else. Your statement should print the category selected. Write the equivalent `IF` statement.

7.2 The General FOR Statement

We have used the `FOR` statement to implement counting loops in which the loop-control variable (type `CARDINAL`) was always incremented by one. The `FOR` statement is more general than the examples we have seen so far and, in fact, the loop-control variable may be any ordinal type. It is also possible for the loop-control variable to decrease (rather than increase) in value after each loop repetition. The value may be increased or decreased by more than one.

EXAMPLE 7.5 ▶ The program in Fig. 7.3 prints a table of Celsius and equivalent Fahrenheit temperatures for the range of temperatures from 20 degrees Celsius to −20 degrees Celsius in steps of −5 degrees. The following `FOR` statement header contains three type `INTEGER` constants: `CStart`, `CLimit`, and `CStep`.

```
FOR Celsius := CStart TO CLimit BY CStep DO
```

`CStart` is the starting value of the `INTEGER` loop-control variable `Celsius`, `CLimit` is the limit value, and `CStep` is the step value. The loop is executed for values of `Celsius` in the sequence `20, 15, 10, ... , -15, -20`. The assignment statement

```
Fahrenheit := 1.8 * real(Celsius) + 32.0;
```

converts each Celsius value in this range to a real Fahrenheit value. Function `real` returns the type `REAL` equivalent of the value of `Celsius`. ◀

Figure 7.3 ▶ *Displaying a Temperature Table*

```
MODULE TempTable;
(*
   Displays a table of Fahrenheit and
   equivalent Celsius temperatures.
*)
   FROM InOut IMPORT
     WriteString, WriteLn, WriteInt;

   FROM MathLib0 IMPORT
     real;

   FROM SimpleIO IMPORT
     WriteRealFormat;

   CONST
     CStart = 20;        (* initial Celsius temp *)
     CStep = -5;         (* change in Celsius temp *)
     CLimit = -20;       (* final Celsius temp *)

   VAR
     Celsius : INTEGER;         (* Celsius temp *)
     Fahrenheit : REAL;         (* output Fahrenheit temp *)

BEGIN (* TempTable *)
  WriteString ('Celsius     Fahrenheit');  WriteLn;
  FOR Celsius := CStart TO CLimit BY CStep DO
    Fahrenheit := 1.8 * real(Celsius) + 32.0;
    WriteInt (Celsius, 7);  WriteString ('        ');
    WriteRealFormat (Fahrenheit, 7, 1);  WriteLn
  END (* FOR *)
END TempTable.
```

```
Celsius   Fahrenheit
     20         68.0
     15         59.0
     10         50.0
      5         41.0
      0         32.0
     -5         23.0
    -10         14.0
    -15          4.9
    -20       -  4.0
```

The FOR loop may be used with other ordinal types besides INTEGER and CARDINAL. The examples that follow use loop-control variables of type CHAR and the enumeration type Day.

EXAMPLE 7.6 ▶ The following FOR loop prints each uppercase letter and its ordinal number. The FOR loop control variable, Next, must be type CHAR. ◀

```
FOR Next := 'A' TO 'Z' DO
  Write(Next);  WriteCard(ORD(Next), 4);  WriteLn
END
```

EXAMPLE 7.7 ▶ The following FOR loop reads and accumulates hours worked for employees who work every other day of the week. The type of variable Today is the enumeration type Day (see Fig. 6.8). The loop is executed for Today equal to Monday, Wednesday, and Friday. During each iteration, procedure WriteDay displays the day name at the end of the prompting message. Each value read into DayHours is added to WeekHours. ◀

```
WeekHours := 0.0;
FOR Today := Monday TO Friday BY 2 DO
  WriteString ('Enter hours for day ');  WriteDay (Today);
  ReadReal (DayHours);  WriteLn;
  WeekHours := WeekHours + DayHours
END; (* FOR *)
WriteString ('Total weekly hours are ');
WriteReal (WeekHours, 12);  WriteLn;
```

The general form of the FOR statement is described in the next display.

FOR Statement ▶

FORM:

FOR *loop-control variable* := *start* TO *limit* BY *step*
  statement sequence
END

EXAMPLES:

```
FOR I := 1 TO N BY 2 DO
  Square := I * I;
  WriteInt(I, 4);  WriteInt(Square, 4);  WriteLn
END
```

INTERPRETATION: The *statement sequence* is executed once for each value of the *loop-control variable* (*lcv*) between *start* and *limit*, inclusive. *start* and *limit* may be constants, variables, or expressions of the same ordinal type as *lcv*. *step* must be a type `INTEGER` or `CARDINAL` constant expression. If the `BY` *step* clause is omitted, *step* is assumed to be 1.

Notes: The value of *lcv* should not be modified in the *statement sequence*.

The value of *limit* is computed once, just before loop entry. Any subsequent changes in the variables that make up the *limit* expression will not change the number of times the loop body is repeated.

Upon exit from the `FOR` loop, the value of *lcv* is considered undefined.

If *start* is greater than *limit* and *step* is positive, the *statement sequence* will not be executed. If *start* is less than *limit* and *step* is negative, the *statement sequence* will not be executed.

SELF-CHECK EXERCISES FOR SECTION 7.2

1. Write a `FOR` statement that prints each digit character and its ordinal number on the same line.
2. Given the constants `CStart`, `CLimit`, and `CStep` shown in Fig. 7.3, indicate what values of `Celsius` would be printed if the `FOR` loop header was rewritten as shown below.
   a. `FOR Celsius := CLimit TO CStart BY CStep DO`
   b. `FOR Celsius := CLimit TO CStart BY -CStep DO`
   c. `FOR Celsius := CLimit TO CStep BY CStart DO`
   d. `FOR Celsius := CStep TO CStart BY CLimit DO`

7.3 The REPEAT Statement

The `REPEAT` statement is used to specify a conditional loop that is repeated until its repetition condition becomes true. Such a loop is called a `REPEAT-UNTIL` loop.

EXAMPLE 7.8 ▶ Both program segments in Fig. 7.4 print all powers of 2 between 1 and 1000.

Figure 7.4 ▸ *WHILE and REPEAT Statements for Computing Powers of 2*

`Power := 1;`
`WHILE Power < 1000 DO`
`  WriteCard (Power, 5);`
`  Power := Power * 2`
`END (* WHILE *)`
	`Power := 1;`
	`REPEAT`
	`  WriteCard (Power, 5);`
	`  Power := Power * 2`
	`UNTIL Power >= 1000`

The test used in the REPEAT–UNTIL loop (Power >= 1000) is the *complement*, or opposite, of the test used in the WHILE loop. The loop body is repeated until the value of Power is greater than or equal to 1000. Since loop repetition stops when the condition is true, the test is called a *loop-termination test* rather than a loop-repetition test. ◂

REPEAT Statement (REPEAT-UNTIL Loop) ▶

FORM:

```
REPEAT
  statement sequence
UNTIL termination condition
```

EXAMPLE:

```
REPEAT
  WriteString ('Enter an uppercase letter: ');
  Read(Ch);  Write (Ch);  WriteLn
UNTIL Ch = CAP(Ch)
```

INTERPRETATION: After each execution of the *statement sequence*, the *termination condition* is evaluated. If the *termination condition* is true, loop exit occurs and the program statement following the loop is executed. If the *termination condition* is false, the *statement sequence* is repeated.

EXAMPLE 7.9 ▶ A REPEAT statement is often used to ensure that a data value is in range. For example, some interactive programs print a *menu* of choices from which the program user selects a program operation. The menu for a statistics program might look as follows.

```
Select one of the operations below.

1. Compute an average
2. Compute a standard deviation
3. Find the median
4. Find the smallest and largest value
5. Plot the data
6. Exit the program

Enter a number between 1 and 6:
```

The menu of choices can be displayed using a sequence of `WriteString` statements. Procedure `EnterCard` in Fig. 7.5 can be used to print repeatedly the line

```
Enter an integer between 1 and 6:
```

and read a cardinal value until a valid data item is entered. Compare procedure `EnterCard` with the version in Fig. 6.2 that uses a `WHILE` loop. ◄

Figure 7.5 ► *Procedure EnterCard*

```
PROCEDURE EnterCard (MinN, MaxN (* input *) : CARDINAL;
                     VAR N (* output *) : CARDINAL);
(*
   Reads an integer between MinN and MaxN into N.
   Pre : MinN and MaxN are assigned values.
   Post: A value between MinN and MaxN is read into N.
   Uses: ReadCard, WriteCard, WriteString, WriteLn from InOut
*)
   VAR
     TempN : CARDINAL;        (* temporary copy of MinN *)

BEGIN (* EnterCard *)
  IF MinN > MaxN THEN
    WriteString ('Error - empty range for EnterCard');  WriteLn;
    WriteString ('MinN and MaxN were exchanged');       WriteLn;
    (* Exchange MinN and MaxN *)
    TempN := MinN;  MinN := MaxN;  MaxN := TempN
  END; (* IF *)

  (* Keep reading until a valid number is read. *)
  REPEAT
    (* invariant:
         All prior values of N are outside range MinN to MaxN
    *)
    WriteString ('Enter an integer between ');
    WriteCard (MinN, 0);  WriteString (' and ');
    WriteCard (MaxN, 0);  WriteString (': ');
    ReadCard (N);         WriteLn;
  UNTIL (N >= MinN) & (N <= MaxN);
  (* assert: N is in the range MinN to MaxN *)

END EnterCard;
```

An important difference between the two conditional loops (`WHILE` and `REPEAT`) is that the `REPEAT–UNTIL` loop is always executed at least once since the *loop-termination condition* is evaluated after execution of the loop body. This limits the usefulness of the `REPEAT–UNTIL` loop, because many times we would like to have the option of not executing the loop body even one time. The REPEAT–UNTIL loop is ideal for the situation described in this example, because the program user must always enter at least one data value.

Complementing a Condition

Figure 7.4 shows a simple BOOLEAN expression (Power < 1000) and its complement (Power >= 1000). The complement of a condition can be formed by reversing the relational operator. For example, the operator < can be reversed to >=, <= reversed to >, # reversed to =, and so on.

DeMorgan's Theorem explains how to complement a compound Boolean expression involving the AND (&), OR operators: write the complement of each individual Boolean expression and change each AND (&) to OR and each OR to AND (&). Another way to complement a BOOLEAN expression is to precede the expression by NOT. Table 7.1 shows the complements of some BOOLEAN expressions.

DeMorgan's Theorem ▶

NOT ($expression_1$ & $expression_2$) = (NOT $expression_1$) OR (NOT $expression_2$)
NOT ($expression_1$ OR $expression_2$) = (NOT $expression_1$) & (NOT $expression_2$)

Table 7.1 ▶ *Complements of Boolean Expressions*

EXPRESSION	COMPLEMENT
(X >= 1) & (X <= 5)	(X < 1) OR (X > 5)
NOT Flag OR (X <= Y)	Flag & (X > Y)
(N MOD M = 0) & Flag	(N MOD M # 0) OR (NOT Flag)
(Next = 'A') OR (Next = 'a')	(Next # 'A') & (Next # 'a')
(Next = 'A') OR (Next = 'a')	NOT((Next = 'A') OR (Next = 'a'))

In Table 7.1, Flag is a Boolean variable, and X, Y, M, and N are type INTEGER. In the complement of the expression on the first line, the relational operators are reversed (e.g., >= changed to <) and the operator & is changed to OR. The last two lines show two complements of the same expression. In the last line, the expression is complemented by simply inserting the Boolean operator NOT before the entire expression. Any Boolean expression can be complemented in this way.

Review of FOR, WHILE, and REPEAT

So far, we have examined three kinds of loops: FOR, WHILE, and REPEAT. The FOR loop should be used as a counting loop, that is, a loop where the number of iterations required can be determined at the beginning of loop execution. The loop-control variable of a FOR loop must belong to an ordinal type.

The WHILE and REPEAT loops are both conditional loops, that is, the number of iterations depends on whether the value of a condition is true or false. The WHILE loop is repeated as long as its loop repetition condition is true; the REPEAT loop is repeated until its loop-termination condition becomes true. Remember, a REPEAT loop body will always be executed at least once, whereas a WHILE or FOR loop body may be skipped entirely. For this reason, a WHILE loop is preferred over a REPEAT loop unless you are certain that at least one loop iteration must always be performed.

As an illustration of the three loop forms, a simple counting loop is written in Fig. 7.6 (the dotted lines represent the loop body). The FOR loop is preferable in this situation. The REPEAT loop is nested in an IF statement to prevent it from being executed when StartValue is greater than StopValue.

Figure 7.6 ▸
Comparison of Three Loop Forms

```
FOR Count := StartValue TO StopValue DO
   .........

END  (* FOR *)
```

```
Count := StartValue;
WHILE Count <= StopValue DO
   .........

   INC (Count)
END  (* WHILE *)
```

```
Count := StartValue;
IF StartValue <= StopValue THEN
   REPEAT
      .........

      INC (Count)
   UNTIL Count > StopValue
END (* IF *)
```

In Fig. 7.6, Count, StartValue, and StopValue must all be the same ordinal type, but not necessarily CARDINAL or INTEGER. The procedure INC is used in both the WHILE and REPEAT–UNTIL loops to update the loop control variable Count to its next value. If the initial value of StartValue is greater than StopValue, the loop bodies will not be executed, and Count will be equal to StartValue. If the loop bodies are executed, the value of Count after loop exit is not defined for the FOR loop.

Of the three forms shown, the `FOR` loop is the most readable. The form using the `REPEAT` statement is the least readable because the loop is nested inside an `IF` statement.

SELF-CHECK EXERCISES FOR SECTION 7.3

1. Write procedure `PrintStatMenu` to display the menu in Example 7.9.
2. Write the complement of each expression below.
   a. `(X <= Y) & (X # 15)`
   b. `(X <= Y) & (X # 15) OR (Z = 7.5)`
   c. `(X # 15) OR (Z = 7.5) & (X <= Y)`
   d. `Flag OR (X # 15.7)`
   e. `NOT Flag & ((NextCh >= 'A') & (NextCh <= 'Z'))`
3. Rewrite the `WHILE` statement below using a `FOR` statement and a `REPEAT` statement.

```
Num := 10;
WHILE Num < 100 DO
  WriteCard (Num, 2);
  WriteLn;
  INC (Num, 10)
END (* WHILE *)
```

4. Write a procedure that reads the next character that is not a letter or a digit from an input line. Write two versions: one using `REPEAT` and the other using `WHILE`.
5. The approximate value of e^x is given by the series

   $$1 + x + x^2/2! + x^3/3! + \ldots + x^n/n! + \ldots$$

   Write a program to compute and print the value of this series for any x. Compare the result so far to `exp(x)` and continue to add terms until the error in the approximation is less than the error limit `Delta` (a constant). Use a `REPEAT` statement.

7.4 LOOP and EXIT Statements

There is another conditional loop statement in Modula-2 that is more general than either `REPEAT` or `WHILE`. It is called the `LOOP` statement. The main difference between the `LOOP` statement and the others is that the condition that controls loop repetition may be placed anywhere within the loop.

EXAMPLE 7.10 ▶ The `LOOP` statement shown in Fig. 7.7 displays all powers of two that are less than 1000. The `EXIT` statement is executed when the exit condition `Power >= 1000` becomes `TRUE`. The `EXIT` statement causes a transfer of control to the statement after the loop END. Compare the LOOP form in Fig. 7.7 with the WHILE and REPEAT forms shown in Fig. 7.4. You should reach the conclusion that the LOOP form is the least desirable of the three. ◄

Figure 7.7 ► *LOOP Statement for Computing Powers of 2*

```
Power := 1;
LOOP
  WriteCard (Power, 5);
  Power := Power * 2;
  IF Power >= 1000 THEN
    EXIT
  END (* IF *)
END (* LOOP *)
```

EXIT Statement ►

FORM: EXIT

INTERPRETATION: Causes the immediate termination of the LOOP statement in which it is enclosed. The statement following the loop END is executed next.

LOOP Statement ►

FORM:
```
LOOP
  statement sequence
END
```

EXAMPLE:
```
LOOP
  WriteString ('Enter an uppercase letter: ');
  Read (Ch);  Write (Ch);  WriteLn;
  IF Ch = CAP(Ch) THEN
    EXIT
  END; (* IF *)
  WriteString ('Wrong, try again!');
  WriteLn
END
```

INTERPRETATION: The *statement sequence* is repeated. When an EXIT statement inside the *statement sequence* is executed, loop exit occurs and the statement following the loop END is executed.

Note: If the *statement sequence* does not contain an EXIT statement, the loop is infinite and will execute until an error occurs or the program is terminated.

EXAMPLE 7.11 ► The program fragment in Fig. 7.8 calls procedure PrintStatMenu to display the statistics menu and EnterCard to read the user's choice into Option (see Example 7.9). If the choice is the constant ExitChoice, the loop is exited.

Otherwise, procedure `ProcessChoice` is called and the loop is repeated. A program whose repetition is controlled in this manner is called a *menu-driven* program. ◂

Figure 7.8 ▸ *Using the LOOP Statement for a Menu Driver*

```
LOOP
  PrintStatMenu;
  EnterCard (1, ExitChoice, Option);
  IF Option = ExitChoice THEN
    EXIT
  END; (* IF *)
  ProcessChoice (Option)
END (* LOOP *)
```

For comparison, the `WHILE` and `REPEAT` forms of this loop are shown side by side in Fig. 7.9. The `FOR` statement is not an option for implementing a conditional loop of this form. Of the three forms, the `LOOP` statement is preferable. Since the loop is always executed at least once, the `REPEAT` statement is a good second choice, but it requires an extra condition to ensure that `ProcessChoice` is not called just before loop exit. The `WHILE` statement is least desirable because it requires placing calls to `PrintStat` and `EnterCard` before loop entry and at the end of the loop body.

Figure 7.9 ▸ *REPEAT and WHILE Forms of a Menu Driver*

```
REPEAT
  PrintStatMenu;
  EnterCard (1, ExitChoice,
             Option);
  IF Option # ExitChoice THEN
    ProcessChoice (Option)
  END (* IF *)
UNTIL Option = ExitChoice
```

```
PrintStatMenu;
EnterCard (1, ExitChoice,
           Option);
WHILE Option # ExitChoice DO
  ProcessChoice (Option);
  PrintStatMenu;
  EnterCard (1, ExitChoice,
             Option)
END (* WHILE *)
```

The `LOOP` statement is convenient to use when there is some processing that occurs before the loop-control test and some that comes after. If all processing comes after the loop-control test, use the `WHILE` statement. If all processing is done before the loop-control test and the loop is always executed at least once, then use the `REPEAT` statement.

Program Style

Warning Regarding the LOOP Statement

Many computer scientists are wary about overusing the `LOOP` statement. They prefer to use a `WHILE` or `REPEAT` statement, because the loop-control condition for these loops is always in the same place (the beginning or the end of the loop). The consistent placement of the loop-control condition makes it easier to verify that a program using these loop forms is correct; it also allows the compiler to check that the loop-control condition has not been inadvertently omitted by the programmer.

For these reasons, we prefer to use the WHILE and REPEAT statements. We will restrict our use of the LOOP statement to situations similar to the one shown in Fig. 7.8, where it is most convenient to place the loop-control condition in the middle of the loop body. Both the WHILE and REPEAT implementations of this loop are less readable.

SELF-CHECK EXERCISE FOR SECTION 7.4

1. Implement the loop in Fig. 7.6 using a LOOP statement. How does this form compare with the others shown?

7.5 Nested Loops

This section examines nested loops. You have seen examples of nested loops in earlier programs, but the nesting was not apparent because the inner loop was contained in a procedure. Nested loops consist of an outer loop with one or more inner loops. Each time the outer loop is repeated, the inner loops are reentered, their loop-control parameters are reevaluated, and all required iterations are performed.

EXAMPLE 7.12 ▶ Figure 7.10 shows a sample run of a program with two nested FOR loops. The outer loop is repeated three times (for I equals 1, 2, 3). Each time the outer loop is repeated, the statements

```
WriteString('OUTER');  WriteCard(I, 7);  WriteLn;
```

display the string 'OUTER' and the value of I (the outer loop-control variable). Next, the inner loop is entered, and its loop-control variable J is reset to 1. The number of times the inner loop is repeated depends on the current value of I. Each time the inner loop is repeated, the statements

```
WriteString ('  INNER');  WriteCard (J, 10);  WriteLn;
```

display the string ' INNER' and the value of J. ◀

Figure 7.10 ▶ *Nested FOR Loop Program*

```
MODULE NestLoop;

(* Illustrates a pair of nested FOR loops. *)
```

```
    FROM InOut IMPORT
      WriteString, WriteCard, WriteLn;

    TYPE
      SmallCard = [1..3];

    VAR
      I, J : SmallCard;             (* loop control variables *)

BEGIN (* NestLoop *)
  WriteString ('            I    J');     (* Print heading *)
  WriteLn;
  FOR I := 1 TO 3 DO
    WriteString ('OUTER');  WriteCard (I, 7);  WriteLn;
    FOR J := 1 TO I DO
      WriteString ('  INNER');  WriteCard (J, 10);  WriteLn;
    END (* FOR J *)
  END (* FOR I *)
END NestLoop.


            I    J
OUTER       1
  INNER          1
OUTER       2
  INNER          1
  INNER          2
OUTER       3
  INNER          1
  INNER          2
  INNER          3
```

In Fig. 7.10, the outer loop-control variable `I` is used as the limit expression that determines the number of repetitions of the inner loop. Although this is perfectly valid, you cannot use the same variable as the loop-control variable of both an outer and inner `FOR` loop in the same nest.

EXAMPLE 7.13 ▶ The program in Fig. 7.11 prints the addition table for integer values between `0` and `9` (type `SmallInt`). For example, the table line beginning with the digit `9` shows the result of adding to `9` each of the digits `0` through `9`. The initial `FOR` loop prints the table heading, that is, the operator + and the list of digits from `0` through `9`.

The nested `FOR` loops are used to print the table body. The outer `FOR` loop (loop-control variable `Addend1`) first prints the current value of `Addend1`. In the inner `FOR` loop, each value of `Addend2` (`0` through `9`) is added to `Addend1` and the individual sums are printed. Each time the outer loop is repeated, 10 additions are performed; in all, 100 sums are printed. ◂

Figure 7.11 ▸ *Printing an Addition Table*

```
MODULE AddTable;

(* Prints an addition table. *)

   FROM InOut IMPORT
     Write, WriteCard, WriteLn;

   CONST
     MaxDigit = 9;                         (* largest digit *)

   TYPE
     SmallInt = [0..MaxDigit];             (* range of digits *)

   VAR
     Addendl,                              (* first addend *)
     Addend2  : SmallInt;                  (* second addend *)
     Sum      : INTEGER;                   (* sum of addends *)

BEGIN  (* AddTable *)
  (* Print the table heading. *)
  Write ('+');
  FOR Addend2 := 0 TO MaxDigit DO
    WriteCard (Addend2, 3)     (* Print each digit in heading *)
  END; (* FOR Addend2 *)
  WriteLn;                                   (* Terminate heading *)

  (* Print the table body. *)
  FOR Addendl := 0 TO MaxDigit DO
    (* Print each row of the table *)
    WriteCard (Addendl, 1);                (* Display first addend *)
    FOR Addend2 := 0 TO MaxDigit DO
      Sum := Addendl + Addend2;
      WriteCard (Sum, 3)                   (* Print sum of addends *)
    END; (* FOR Addend2 *)
    WriteLn                                 (* Terminate table row *)
  END (* FOR Addendl *)
END AddTable.


+  0  1  2  3  4  5  6  7  8  9
0  0  1  2  3  4  5  6  7  8  9
1  1  2  3  4  5  6  7  8  9 10
2  2  3  4  5  6  7  8  9 10 11
3  3  4  5  6  7  8  9 10 11 12
4  4  5  6  7  8  9 10 11 12 13
5  5  6  7  8  9 10 11 12 13 14
6  6  7  8  9 10 11 12 13 14 15
7  7  8  9 10 11 12 13 14 15 16
8  8  9 10 11 12 13 14 15 16 17
9  9 10 11 12 13 14 15 16 17 18
```

EXAMPLE 7.14 ▶ The program in Fig. 7.12 draws a sine curve. It uses the Modula-2 function `sin`, which returns the trigonometric sine of its parameter, an angle expressed in radians. The outer `FOR` loop is executed for values of `Theta` equal to `0`, `18`, `36`, ... , `360` degrees. For each `Theta`, the first assignment statement below

```
Radian := FLOAT(Theta) * RadPerDegree;
Pad := TRUNC(Scale * (1.0 + sin(Radian)) + 0.5);
```

computes the number of radians corresponding to `Theta`. Then the variable `Pad` is assigned a value based on `sin(Radian)`. This value increases from `0` when `sin(Radian)` is `-1.0` to twice the value of `Scale` when `sin(Radian)` is `1.0`. Since `Pad` is the limit variable in the inner `FOR` loop, its value determines how many blanks precede each character `'*'` displayed on the screen. In this way, the position of each `'*'` displayed represents the sine of the current angle. The sine value is also displayed as a real number after each `*`.

Figure 7.12 ▶ *Plotting a Sine Curve*

```
MODULE SineCurve;

(* Plots a sine curve. *)

   FROM InOut IMPORT
     Write, WriteString, WriteLn;

   FROM RealInOut IMPORT
     WriteReal;

   FROM MathLib0 IMPORT
     sin;

   CONST
     Pi = 3.14159;                   (* constant Pi *)
     RadPerDegree = Pi / 180.0;      (* radians per degree *)
     MinAngle = 0;                   (* smallest angle *)
     MaxAngle = 360;                 (* largest angle *)
     PlotWidth = 40;                 (* width of plot *)
     PlotHeight = 20;                (* height of plot *)
     StepAngle = (MaxAngle-MinAngle) DIV PlotHeight;
                                     (* change in angle *)
     Star = '*';                     (* symbol being plotted *)
     Blank = ' ';                    (* blank symbol *)

   TYPE
     AngleRange = [MinAngle..MaxAngle];
     ColumnRange = [0..PlotWidth];
```

```
  VAR
    Theta  : AngleRange;      (* angle in degrees *)
    Radian,                   (* angle in radians *)
    Scale : REAL;             (* scale factor *)
    Pad,                      (* size of blank padding *)
    I     : ColumnRange;      (* inner loop control variable *)

BEGIN  (* SineCurve *)
  WriteString ('                    Sine curve plot');
  WriteLn;  WriteLn;
  Scale := FLOAT(PlotWidth DIV 2);
  FOR Theta := MinAngle TO MaxAngle BY StepAngle DO
    Radian := FLOAT(Theta) * RadPerDegree;
    Pad := TRUNC(Scale * (1.0 + sin(Radian)) + 0.5);
    (* Display blank padding *)
    FOR I := 1 TO Pad DO
      Write (Blank)
    END; (* FOR I *)
    Write (Star);                  (* Plot * in next column *)
    WriteString ('        ');
    WriteReal (sin(Radian), 12);   (* Print sine value *)
    WriteLn
  END (* FOR Theta *)
END SineCurve.
```

```
                   Sine curve plot

                    *         0.0000E+000
                          *         3.0902E-001
                                *         5.8778E-001
                                    *         8.0902E-001
                                       *         9.5106E-001
                                        *         1.0000E+000
                                       *         9.5106E-001
                                    *         8.0902E-001
                                *         5.8779E-001
                          *         3.0902E-001
                    *         2.6536E-006
              *         -3.0901E-001
        *         -5.8778E-001
    *         -8.0901E-001
 *         -9.5106E-001
*         -1.0000E+000
 *         -9.5106E-001
    *         -8.0902E-001
        *         -5.8779E-001
              *         -3.0902E-001
                    *         -5.3072E-006
```

Program Style

Checking Boundary Values

The discussion for Example 7.14 states that the value of `Pad` ranges from `0` to twice `Scale` as the sine value goes from `-1.0` to `1.0`. It is a good idea to check the accuracy of these assumptions; you can usually do this by checking the boundaries of the range, as follows.

```
SIN(Radian) is -1.0, Pad is TRUNC(Scale * (1.0 + (-1.0)) + 0.5)
                     Pad is TRUNC(20.0 * 0.0 + 0.5)
                     Pad is TRUNC(0.5) = 0

SIN(Radian) is +1.0, Pad is TRUNC(Scale * (1.0 + 1.0) + 0.5)
                     Pad is TRUNC(20.0 * 2.0 + 0.5)
                     Pad is TRUNC(40.5) = 40
```

Since function `TRUNC` removes the fractional part of its argument, the fraction `0.5` is added before `TRUNC` is called so that the value assigned to `Pad` will be correct to the nearest whole number.

It is also a good idea to check the boundary values for all loop-control variables to see that they make sense. For example, the outer loop control variable, `Theta`, has an initial value of `MinAngle` (0) and a final value of `MaxAngle` (360). The inner-loop control variable, `I`, has an initial value of `1` and a final value of `Pad`.

SELF-CHECK EXERCISES FOR SECTION 7.5

1. Write a program that prints the multiplication table. Use separate procedures to print the table heading and the table body.
2. Show the output printed by the following nested loops.

```
FOR I := 1 TO 2 DO
  WriteString ('OUTER');
  WriteCard (I, 5);
  WriteLn;
  FOR J := 1 TO 3 DO
    WriteString ('  INNER');
    WriteCard (I, 3);
    WriteCard (J, 3);
    WriteLn
  END; (* FOR J *)
  FOR K := 2 TO 1 BY -1 DO
    WriteString ('  INNER');
    WriteCard (I, 3);
    WriteCard (K, 3);
    WriteLn
  END (* FOR K *)
END;  (* FOR I *)
```

3. Write a nest of loops that causes the following output to be printed.

```
1
1 2
1 2 3
1 2 3 4
1 2 3
1 2
1
```

4. Write a nest of loops that prints the following triangle.

```
    *
   ***
  *****
 *******
*********
```

7.6 User-Defined Function Procedures

Chapter 5 introduced some of the functions that are part of Modula-2, such as `ABS`, `ORD`, and `ODD`. It also described the functions in the library module `MathLib0`. In this section, you will learn how to declare your own *function procedures*, that is, procedures that return a single result. These function procedures can be referenced in expressions the same as the predefined functions. Generally the parameters of a function procedure are value parameters and cannot be modified by the function execution.

EXAMPLE 7.15 ▶ Function procedure `Square` in Fig. 7.13 returns the square of its argument. If `A` and `B` represent two sides of a right triangle, the assignment statement

```
Hypotenuse := sqrt(Square(A) + Square(B))
```

is the Modula-2 implementation of the formula

$$\text{Hypotenuse} = \sqrt{A^2 + B^2}$$

The expression in the preceding assignment statement calls function procedure `Square` twice, once with `A` as its argument and once with `B` as its argument.

Figure 7.13 ▶ *Function Procedure Square*

```
PROCEDURE Square (X : REAL) : REAL;
(*
   Returns the square of its argument.
   Pre : X is assigned a value.
   Post: X * X is returned.
```

```
*)

BEGIN (* Square *)
  RETURN X * X
END Square;
```

The procedure header

```
PROCEDURE Square (X : REAL) : REAL;
```

ends with a type identifier, which indicates that a function procedure is being declared and specifies the type (`REAL`) of the result returned. The procedure header also identifies the function procedure name (`Square`) and its parameter list. The formal parameters for a function procedure are always input parameters, so the comment `(* input *)` is omitted.

Unlike other procedures that return results by modifiying one or more variable parameters, a function procedure returns its single result by executing a statement of the form

RETURN *expression*

This statement causes an immediate return from the function procedure with its result equal to the value of *expression*. The type of *expression* must be assignment compatible with the declared type of the function procedure. In Fig. 7.13, executing the statement

```
RETURN X * X
```

causes an immediate return from the function procedure with the value of X^2 returned as the result.

The expression

```
sqrt(Square(A) + Square(B))
```

calls function `Square` twice and function `sqrt` (in module `MathLib0`) once. The *function designator* `Square(A)` is executed first and calls function `Square` with `A` as its argument. Next, the function designator `Square(B)` is executed. A function procedure must always be called by including a function designator in an expression; a procedure call statement cannot be used to call a function procedure. ◂

Function Procedure Declaration ▶

FORM: PROCEDURE *fname* (*formal parameters*) : *result type*;
local declaration section

BEGIN
function body
END *fname*;

EXAMPLES:

```
PROCEDURE SquareInt (N : INTEGER) : INTEGER;

BEGIN
  RETURN N * N
END SquareInt;
```

INTERPRETATION: The function procedure *fname* is declared. The list of formal parameters is enclosed in parentheses. The data type of the function result is indicated by the identifier *result type*. Any identifiers declared in the *local declaration section* are defined only during the execution of the function procedure.

The *function body* describes the data manipulation to be performed by the function. At least one statement of the form

`RETURN` *expression*

should appear in the function body. The value of *expression* is returned as the function result when the `RETURN` statement is executed. This value replaces the function reference in the expression that calls the function. The *expression* type must be assignment compatible with *result type*. If the `RETURN` statement is not executed, the function result is undefined and a `function return error` will result.

Notes: The identifier *result type* must be the name of a standard data type (`BOOLEAN`, `INTEGER`, `REAL`, or `CHAR`), a previously defined enumeration type, a subrange type, or a pointer type (described in Chapter 13).

If there are no formal parameters, omit the parentheses following *fname*.

Function Designator ▶

FORM: *fname* (*actual parameters*)

EXAMPLE: `Square(C + D)`

INTERPRETATION: The function *fname* is executed, and its result replaces the function designator. During the function execution, the first actual parameter is associated with the first formal parameter, the second actual parameter with the second formal parameter, and so on.

Notes: The actual parameters are separated by commas. There should be the same number of actual and formal parameters. Each actual parameter that is an expression is evaluated when *fname* is called; this value is assigned to the corresponding formal parameter. Each actual parameter must be assignment compatible with its corresponding formal parameter.

If there are no formal parameters, an empty pair of parentheses must follow the function name.

EXAMPLE 7.16 ▶ Function procedure `Powers` in Fig. 7.14 raises its first parameter, `X` (type `REAL`), to the power indicated by its second parameter, `N` (type `INTEGER`). If `X` is zero, the statement

```
RETURN 0.0                    (* 0.0 to any power is 0.0 *)
```

executes and the function is exited. Otherwise, `X` is multiplied by itself `N` times and the result is saved in `Product`. The `FOR` loop limit expression, `ABS(N)`, ensures that the required number of multiplications are performed, even when `N` is negative. If `N` is negative, the statement

```
Product := 1.0 / Product
```

executes and changes `Product` to a fraction. The statement

```
RETURN Product
```

returns the last value assigned to `Product`. ◂

Figure 7.14 ▸
The Function Powers

```
PROCEDURE Powers (X : REAL; N : INTEGER) : REAL;
(*
   Returns the value of X raised to the power N.
   Pre : X and N are assigned.
   Post: Returns X to the power N.
*)
   VAR
     Product : REAL;              (* the accumulated product *)
     Count   : CARDINAL;          (* loop control variable *)

BEGIN (* Powers *)
  (* Test for special case *)
  IF X = 0.0 THEN
    RETURN 0.0                    (* 0.0 to any power is 0.0 *)
  END; (* IF *)
  (* assert: X is non-zero *)

  (* Multiply X by itself N times accumulating result in Product *)
  Product := 1.0;                 (* Initialize Product *)
  FOR Count := 1 TO ABS(N) DO
    Product := Product * X
  END; (* FOR *)

  (* Define function result for negative N *)
  IF N < 0 THEN
    Product := 1.0 / Product
  END; (* IF *)

  RETURN Product
END Powers;
```

The following assignment statement computes the actual amount, `Amount`, in a savings account after `N` days have passed. `Deposit` is the initial amount deposited; `DailyRate` is the daily interest rate.

```
Amount := Deposit * Powers(1.0 + DailyRate, N)
```

This statement is derived from the formula

$$amount = deposit \times (1.0 + dailyrate)^n$$

The function designator

```
Powers(1.0 + DailyRate, N)
```

calls function `Powers` to raise the expression `1.0 + DailyRate` to the power `N`. After execution of the function body, the function result replaces the function designator in the calling expression; this result is then multiplied by the value of `Deposit` and the product is stored in `Amount`.

Program Style

Checking Special Cases

What happens in function `Powers` if the value of `X` or `N` happens to be zero? If `X` is zero, the statement

```
RETURN 0.0
```

executes and the function exit occurs. If `N` is zero, the assignment statement

```
Product := 1.0;
```

executes and the `FOR` loop is skipped. Since `1.0` is the last value assigned to `Product`, the correct result is returned (i.e., $X^0 = 1$, for $X \neq 0.0$).

Often a procedure or a function will fail for special cases such as these. It is important to identify special cases and verify that they are handled properly.

Program Style

Single Entry and Exit Points for Control Structures

Many computer scientists believe that a control structure should always have a single entry point and a single exit point. This applies to loops and decisions as well as procedures and functions. There will be times, however, when a function with multiple `RETURN` statements is easier to read and understand, for example, when the main processing step should be skipped because of a special parameter value. If this is the case, we suggest you write the function using multiple `RETURN`s. The body of function `Powers` is rewritten below with a single `RETURN`. Compare it with the version shown in Fig. 7.14. Which do you think is simpler?

```
BEGIN (* Powers *)
  (* Test for special case *)
  IF X = 0.0 THEN
    Product := 0.0                (* 0.0 to any power N is 0.0 *)
  ELSE (* X is non-zero *)
    (* Multiply X by itself N times - save result in Product *)
```

```
      Product := 1.0;                       (* Initialize Product *)
      FOR Count := 1 TO ABS(N) DO
        Product := Product * X
      END; (* FOR *)

      (* Define function result for negative N *)
      IF N < 0 THEN
        Product := 1.0 / Product
      END (* IF *)
    END; (* IF *)

    RETURN Product
  END Powers;
```

Functions with Nonnumeric Results

A function can return a value belonging to any of the standard types—an enumeration type, a subrange type, or a pointer type (discussed in Chapter 13). This section provides examples of functions with different result types.

EXAMPLE 7.17 ▶ Function `DayConvert` in Fig. 7.15 converts a number representing the day of the week (`1` through `7`) to a value of enumeration type `Day` (`Sunday` through `Saturday`). The statement

```
RETURN VAL(Day, DayNum - 1)
```

calls the standard function `VAL` to perform the conversion. In the event that `DayNum` is outside the range `1` through `7`, the function displays an error message. Since the `RETURN` statement is not executed, a `function return error` will occur. ◀

Figure 7.15 ▶ *Function DayConvert*

```
PROCEDURE DayConvert (DayNum : CARDINAL) : Day;
(*
   Converts a day number to a value of type Day.
   Pre : DayNum is assigned a value between 1 and 7.
   Post: Returns the corresponding value of type Day assuming
         1 for Sunday, 2 for Monday, etc.
*)
BEGIN (* DayConvert *)
  IF (DayNum < 1) OR (DayNum > 7) THEN
    WriteString ('Invalid parameter for DayConvert');
    WriteLn
  ELSE
    RETURN VAL(Day, DayNum - 1)
  END (* IF *)
END DayConvert;
```

EXAMPLE 7.18 ▶ Figure 7.16 shows a function that can be used to determine the number of days in any month of the twentieth century. The data types `YearRange` and `DayRange` are defined below; `Month` can be imported from module `DatesADT` (see Fig. 6.8).

Figure 7.16 ▶ *Function DaysInMonth*

```
TYPE
  YearRange = [1900..1999];
  DayRange = [1..31];


PROCEDURE DaysInMonth (CurMonth : Month;
                       ThisYear : YearRange) : DayRange;
(*
   Determines the number of days in a given month and year.
   Pre : CurMonth and ThisYear are assigned values.
   Post: Returns a cardinal between 28 and 31 representing
         the number of days in month CurMonth for year ThisYear.
*)
   VAR
     NumberOfDays : Days;

BEGIN  (* DaysInMonth *)
  CASE CurMonth OF
    April, June, September, November :          NumberOfDays := 30
  | January, March, May, July, August, October, December :
                                                NumberOfDays := 31
  | February : IF ThisYear MOD 4 = 0 THEN
                 NumberOfDays := 29             (* leap year *)
               ELSE
                 NumberOfDays := 28
               END (* IF *)
  END; (* CASE *)

  RETURN NumberOfDays
END DaysInMonth;
```

The `IF` statement following `CASE` label `February` has a condition that is true every leap year. An example of a function designator that calls the function `DaysInMonth` is

```
DaysInMonth(May, 1942)
```

EXAMPLE 7.19 ▶ `BOOLEAN` functions are often used to make `BOOLEAN` expressions more readable. The `BOOLEAN` function `IsUppercase` in Fig. 7.17 determines whether its argument is an uppercase letter (returns `TRUE`) or not (returns `FALSE`). This function can be used to simplify the writing of `IF` statements that require a test for an uppercase letter. This function assumes that the uppercase letters are consecutive characters in the collating sequence. (A similar function called `IsLowercase` is left as an exercise at the end of this section.) ◂

Figure 7.17 ▸ *Function IsUppercase*

```
PROCEDURE IsUppercase (Ch : CHAR) : BOOLEAN;
(*
   Determines whether Ch is an uppercase letter.
   Pre : Ch is assigned a value.
   Post: Returns TRUE if Ch is an uppercase letter;
         otherwise, returns FALSE.
*)
BEGIN (* IsUppercase *)
  RETURN (Ch >= 'A') & (Ch <= 'Z')
END IsUppercase;
```

Function `ChangeCase` (see Fig. 7.18) uses functions `IsLowercase` and `IsUppercase` and returns a result that is type `CHAR`. It changes an uppercase letter to lowercase and vice versa. If its argument `Ch` is an uppercase letter, the assignment statement

```
ChangeCase := CHR(ORD(Ch) - ORD('A') + ORD('a'))
```

is executed. If `Ch` is `'C'`, then the argument of function `CHR` is 2 + `ORD('a')` and the value `'c'` is assigned to `ChangeCase`. The analysis is similar when `Ch` is a lowercase letter.

Figure 7.18 ▸ *Function ChangeCase*

```
PROCEDURE ChangeCase (Ch : CHAR) : CHAR;
(*
   Changes the case of Ch when Ch is a letter.
   Pre : Ch is assigned a value.
   Post: If Ch is lowercase, returns its uppercase form.
         If Ch is uppercase, returns its lowercase form.
         If Ch is not a letter, returns Ch unchanged.
*)
   VAR
     NewCase : CHAR;

BEGIN  (* ChangeCase *)
  IF IsUppercase(Ch) THEN              (* Change to lowercase *)
    NewCase := CHR(ORD(Ch) - ORD('A') + ORD('a'))
  ELSIF IsLowercase(Ch) THEN           (* Change to uppercase *)
    NewCase := CHR(ORD(Ch) - ORD('a') + ORD('A'))
  ELSE
    NewCase := Ch                      (* Ch is not a letter *)
  END; (* IF *)

  RETURN NewCase
END ChangeCase;
```

All the function examples shown in this section have the property that they transform one or more input values into a single output value. A variety of result types were illustrated: `REAL`, `CHAR`, `BOOLEAN`, enumeration type `Day`, and subrange type `DayRange`. Because a function does not normally return a result by modifying its parameters, all the function parameters were value parameters.

Procedures versus Functions

Some of the procedures that we wrote earlier can also be implemented as function procedures. Any procedure that returns a single result can be rewritten as a function procedure.

As a general rule of thumb, always use a regular procedure when more than one result is returned. If a single result is returned, use a function procedure when a pure computation is performed that requires no data beyond what is provided through the parameter list. If input or output operations are also performed, use a regular procedure instead of a function procedure, even if only a single result is returned. The reason for this is that a function call may be inserted in an expression, and it is generally not useful to read or display information as part of an expression evaluation.

SELF-CHECK EXERCISES FOR SECTION 7.6

1. Write a function that computes the cube of any number.
2. Write a function that computes the tuition owed for a specified number of credit hours taken at a university. Assume that the charge per credit is $100 for up to 12 credit hours and that a flat fee of $1000 is charged when more than 12 credits are taken.
3. Function `Powers` in Fig. 7.14 works perfectly well for an integer exponent; however, the exponent cannot be type `REAL`. Write a new function that will handle type `REAL` exponents. Hint: Use the `ln` and `exp` functions of Modula-2.
4. Write a program that uses function `Powers` to compute and print a table showing the powers of two.
5. Write two versions of function `IsLowercase`. Use the standard function `CAP` in one version.

7.7 Case Study

This section presents a problem that illustrates many of the concepts discussed in the last two chapters. The problem involves printing a check amount in words.

CHECK WRITING PROBLEM

Problem: As part of a check writing program, it would be desirable to have a procedure that writes a check amount in words. Some examples of the desired procedure output are shown below.

Check	*Output*
43.55	`forty three dollars and fifty five cents`
62.05	`sixty two dollars and five cents`
15.20	`fifteen dollars and twenty cents`
0.95	`zero dollars and ninety five cents`
35.00	`thirty five dollars and zero cents`

Discussion: The procedure must separate the check amount into two integers, `Dollars` and `Cents`. Once this is done, `Dollars` can be printed, followed by the string `' dollars and '`, the value of `Cents`, and the string `' cents'`. For the sake of simplicity, we will restrict the check writing procedure to amounts less than $100. A description of the procedure data requirements and algorithm follows.

PROBLEM INPUTS

check amount as a real number (`Check : REAL`)

PROBLEM OUTPUTS

description of check amount in words

LOCAL VARIABLES FOR PRINTCHECK

dollar amount (`Dollars : [0..99]`)
number of cents (`Cents : [0..99]`)

Algorithm for PrintCheck

```
1. IF check amount is invalid THEN
       Print an error message
   ELSE
       Separate check amount into Dollars and Cents
       Print Dollars in words
       Print ' dollars and '
       Print Cents in words
       Print ' cents'
   END
```

The structure chart for procedure `PrintCheck` is shown in Fig. 7.19. Procedure `Print2Digits` is called twice: first to print the value of `Dollars` in words and then to print the value of `Cents` in words. Since the operation of printing a two-digit number in words is fairly general and may be needed by other programs that we develop, we will include procedure `Print2Digits` in a separate module called `PrintWords`. For this reason, there is no stub for procedure `Print2Digits` in procedure `PrintCheck` (see Fig. 7.20). Any program that calls `PrintCheck` will have to import procedure `Print2Digits` from `PrintWords`.

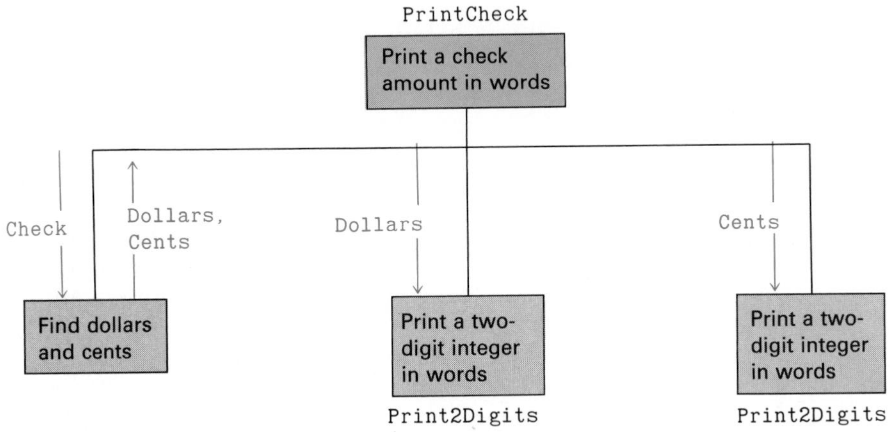

Figure 7.19 ▸ *Structure Chart for Procedure PrintCheck*

Figure 7.20 ▸ *Procedure PrintCheck*

```
PROCEDURE PrintCheck (Check (* input *) : REAL);
(* Prints a check amount in words.
   Pre : Check is assigned a value between 0.0 and 99.99.
   Post: Displays the value of Check in words.
   Uses: Print2Digits from PrintWords; WriteString from InOut;
         WriteReal from RealInOut
*)
   CONST
     MaxCard = 99;

   TYPE
     SmallCard = [0..MaxCard];      (* range of check amount *)

   VAR
     Dollars,                       (* the dollar amount *)
     Cents     : SmallCard;         (* the cents amount *)
     CheckPennies : CARDINAL;       (* total check in pennies *)

BEGIN (* PrintCheck *)
  IF (Check <= 0.0) OR (TRUNC(Check) > MaxCard) THEN
    WriteString ('Check amount ');
    WriteReal (Check, 12);
    WriteString (' is invalid.')
```

```
  ELSE
    (* valid amount *)
    CheckPennies := TRUNC(100.0 * Check + 0.5);    (* round to
                                                 nearest penny *)
    Dollars := CheckPennies DIV 100;
    Cents := CheckPennies MOD 100;
    Print2Digits (Dollars);        (* Print dollar amount *)
    WriteString (' dollars and ');
    Print2Digits (Cents);          (* Print cents amount *)
    WriteString (' cents')
  END (* IF *)
END PrintCheck;
```

In Fig. 7.20 the assignment statements

```
CheckPennies := TRUNC(100.0 * Check + 0.5);    (* round to
                                             nearest penny *)
Dollars := CheckPennies DIV 100;
Cents := CheckPennies MOD 100;
```

are used to determine the value of `Dollars` and `Cents`. For example, if `Check` is `95.63`, then `CheckPennies` is `9563`, `Dollars` is `95`, and Cents is `63`.

Procedure `Print2Digits` prints an integer value less than 100 in words. Its parameter value is separated into a tens digit (stored in `Tens`) and a units digit (stored in `Units`). Once this separation is performed, the two digits are printed in words. The data requirements and algorithm for `Print2Digits` follow.

PROCEDURE INPUTS

a number less than 100 (`In2Digits : CARDINAL`)

PROCEDURE OUTPUTS

a two-digit integer printed in words

LOCAL VARIABLES FOR PRINT2DIGITS

the tens digit (`Tens : [0..9]`)
the units digit (`Units : [0..9]`)

Algorithm for Print2Digits

1. Separate `In2Digits` into `Tens` and `Units`.
2. Print the `Tens` digit and `Units` digit in words.

Step 2 of `Print2Digits` must be able to print integers that are less than 10 (`Tens` is `0`), in the teens (`Tens` is `1`), and above the teens (`Tens` >= `2`). If `Tens` is `0`, only the `Units` digit is displayed. If `Tens` is `1`, then the string for a number between `10` (`'ten'`) and `19` (`'nineteen'`) is displayed. If `Tens` is between 2 and 9, then a string ('twenty' through 'ninety') representing the Tens digit is displayed, followed by a string for the Units digit, provided the latter is not 0.

REFINEMENT OF STEP 2

```
2.1 CASE Tens OF
        0 : Print the Units digit
        1 : Select and print a string based on the Units digit
        2 : Print 'twenty' and a non-zero Units digit
        3 : Print 'thirty' and a non-zero Units digit
        4 : Print 'forty' and a non-zero Units digit
        5 : Print 'fifty' and a non-zero Units digit
        8 : Print 'eighty' and a non-zero Units digit
        6, 7, 9 : Print the Tens digit followed by 'ty '
                  and a non-zero Units digit
    END
```

The definition module for PrintWords is shown in Fig. 7.21. It contains procedure headings for procedures Print2Digits and Print1Digit. The latter is used to display the string corresponding to the Units digit. The implementation module is shown in Fig. 7.22.

Figure 7.21 ▸ *Definition Module for PrintWords*

```
DEFINITION MODULE PrintWords;

(* Definition module for displaying one- and two-digit cardinals. *)

   EXPORT QUALIFIED
     Print1Digit, Print2Digits;

   PROCEDURE Print1Digit (InDigit (* input *) : CARDINAL);
   (*
      Prints its argument in words.
      Pre : InDigit is assigned a value between 0 and 9.
      Post: InDigit is displayed in words.
   *)

   PROCEDURE Print2Digits (In2Digits (* input *) : CARDINAL);
   (*
      Prints its argument in words.
      Pre : In2Digits is assigned a value between 0 and 99.
      Post: In2Digits is displayed in words.
      Uses: Print1Digit
   *)

END PrintWords.
```

Figure 7.22 ▸ *Implementation Module for PrintWords*

```
IMPLEMENTATION MODULE PrintWords;
(*
   Implementation module for displaying one- and two-digit
   cardinals.
*)
   FROM InOut IMPORT
     WriteString, Write, WriteLn;

   PROCEDURE Print1Digit (InDigit (* input *) : CARDINAL);
   (*
      Prints its argument in words.
      Pre : InDigit is assigned a value between 0 and 9.
      Post: InDigit is displayed in words.
   *)
   BEGIN (* Print1Digit *)
     CASE InDigit OF
       0 : WriteString('zero')
     | 1 : WriteString ('one')
     | 2 : WriteString ('two')
     | 3 : WriteString ('three')
     | 4 : WriteString ('four')
     | 5 : WriteString ('five')
     | 6 : WriteString ('six')
     | 7 : WriteString ('seven')
     | 8 : WriteString ('eight')
     | 9 : WriteString ('nine')
     ELSE
       WriteString ('Invalid parameter for Print1Digit');
       WriteLn
     END (* CASE *)
   END Print1Digit;


PROCEDURE Print2Digits (In2Digits (* input *) : CARDINAL);
(*
   Prints its argument in words.
   Pre : In2Digits is assigned a value between 0 and 99.
   Post: In2Digits is displayed in words.
   Uses: Print1Digit
*)
   TYPE
     Digit = [0..9];

   VAR
     Tens,                                 (* tens digit *)
     Units : Digit;                        (* units digit *)

   PROCEDURE CallDigit (Units (* input *) : Digit);
   (*
      Calls procedure Print1Digit with parameter Units if
```

```
      Units is not zero.
      Pre : Units is assigned a value between 0 and 9.
      Post: Calls Print1Digit if Units is not 0.
   *)
   BEGIN (* CallDigit *)
     IF Units # 0 THEN
       Write (' ');
       Print1Digit (Units)
     END (* IF *)
   END CallDigit;

BEGIN (* Print2Digits *)
  Tens := In2Digits DIV 10;                     (* Get tens digit *)
  Units := In2Digits MOD 10;                    (* Get units digit *)
  CASE Tens OF
    0 : Print1Digit (Units)                     (* less than ten *)
   | 1 : CASE Units OF                          (* in the teens *)
           0 : WriteString ('ten')
         | 1 : WriteString ('eleven')
         | 2 : WriteString ('twelve')
         | 3 : WriteString ('thirteen')
         | 5 : WriteString ('fifteen')
         | 8 : WriteString ('eighteen')
         | 4, 6, 7, 9 : Print1Digit (Units);  (* Print ...teen *)
                        WriteString ('teen')
         END (* CASE Units *)
   | 2 : WriteString ('twenty');              (* Print twenty ... *)
         CallDigit (Units)
   | 3 : WriteString ('thirty');              (* Print thirty ... *)
         CallDigit (Units)
   | 4 : WriteString ('forty');               (* Print forty ... *)
         CallDigit (Units)
   | 5 : WriteString ('fifty');               (* Print fifty ... *)
         CallDigit (Units)
   | 8 : WriteString ('eighty');              (* Print eighty ... *)
         CallDigit (Units)
   | 6, 7, 9 : Print1Digit (Tens);            (* Print ...ty ... *)
               WriteString ('ty');
               CallDigit (Units)
   ELSE
     WriteString ('Invalid parameter for Print2Digits');
     WriteLn
   END (* CASE Tens *)
  END Print2Digits;

END PrintWords.
```

Procedure `Print2Digits` uses a local procedure, `CallDigit`, to determine whether to call procedure `Print1Digit`. If `Units` is non-zero, `Print1Digit` is called to display `Units`; otherwise, it is not. `CallDigit` is not exported.

Program Style

Validating Parameter Values in Modules

Both procedures `Print1Digit` and `Print2Digits` end with an `ELSE` clause that validates the procedure parameter; an error message is printed if the parameter is not valid. This is generally a good idea. We used actual parameters whose types are subrange types (`SmallCard` and `Digit`) to prevent calling `Print2Digits` or `Print1Digit` with out-of-range parameter values; however, there is no guarantee that other users will do this. To protect against generating incorrect results, include parameter validation tests whenever you write a procedure that will become part of a library module.

7.8 Common Programming Errors

When using a `CASE` statement, make sure the `CASE` selector and labels are of the same ordinal type. Remember that only lists of ordinal values (not strings or reals) may be used as `CASE` labels and that no value may appear in more than one `CASE` label. It is generally a good idea to include an `ELSE` clause; otherwise, a run-time error will occur in the event that no `CASE` label matches the selector.

The main problem in using a `REPEAT` statement is the possibility of too many loop repetitions. A `REPEAT–UNTIL` loop will execute forever if its conditional test remains false. This is indicated by a program exceeding its time limit or running out of input data. Remember that a `REPEAT–UNTIL` loop is always executed at least once because the loop termination test follows the loop body.

Be careful when you use the `LOOP` statement. Make sure to include at least one `EXIT` statement. Check that an `EXIT` statement eventually will execute; otherwise, the loop will not terminate.

Be sure to trace each nest of loops carefully, checking all loop parameters at their boundary values. A loop-control variable for a `FOR` statement should not be changed inside the loop body. Don't try to use the same loop-control variable for two nested `FOR` statements.

When using functions, make sure that a `RETURN` statement followed by an expression is always executed. If the end of a function is reached without a `RETURN` being executed, the function result is undefined and an execution error may occur.

7.9 Chapter Review

The CASE statement was introduced in this chapter as a convenient way to implement decisions with several alternatives. You saw how to use the CASE statement to implement decisions that are based on the value of a variable or simple expression (the CASE selector). The CASE selector must have an ordinal data type.

The REPEAT statement was used to implement conditional loops. The REPEAT statement can be used to implement a loop that will always execute at least one time.

The general LOOP statement was also introduced. It is particularly useful for writing loops when some processing comes before the loop-control test and some after. We advise against overuse of this loop form.

Nested loops were analyzed. Every inner loop of a nest is reentered and executed to completion each time an outer loop is repeated.

Function procedures are procedures that return a single result. Function procedures generally have value parameters. A RETURN statement inside the function body is used to define the function result. A function is called by using it in an expression; the function name and actual parameters (function arguments) are inserted directly into the expression.

New Modula-2 Statements

The new Modula-2 statements introduced in this chapter are shown in Table 7.2.

Table 7.2 ▸ *Summary of New Modula-2 Statements*

STATEMENT	EFFECT
CASE Statement	

`CASE CAP(NextCh) OF`
`  'A' : WriteString ('Excellent')`
`| 'B' : WriteString ('Good')`
`| 'C' : WriteString ('O.K.')`
`| 'D', 'E', 'F' :`
`        WriteString ('Poor');`
`        Probation (ID)`
`ELSE`
`  WriteString ('Invalid grade')`
`END (* CASE *)`
	One of five messages is printed based on the value of NextCh (type CHAR). If NextCh is 'D', 'E', or 'F', procedure Probation is also called with ID as an actual parameter.

General FOR Statement	

`FOR CurMonth := Jan TO Dec DO`
`  ReadReal (MonthSales);`
`  YearSales := YearSales +`
`             MonthSales`
`END (* FOR *)`
	The loop body is repeated for each value of CurMonth from Jan through Dec, inclusive. For each month, the value of MonthSales is read and added to YearSales.

REPEAT Statement

```
REPEAT
  WriteString ('Next item: ');
  ReadInt (Item);  WriteLn;
  IF Item # Sentinel THEN
    Process (Item)
  END (* IF *)
UNTIL Item = Sentinel
```

The loop body is repeated until the value read into `Item` is `Sentinel`. Procedure `Process` is passed each data value except the last one.

LOOP Statement

```
LOOP
  WriteString ('Next item: ');
  ReadInt (Item);  WriteLn;
  IF Item = Sentinel THEN
    EXIT
  END; (* IF *)
  Process (Item)
END (* LOOP *)
```

The loop body is repeated until the value read into `Item` is `Sentinel`. Procedure `Process` is passed each data value except the last one.

Declaring a Function

```
PROCEDURE Sign (X : REAL) : CHAR;
(* Finds the sign ('+' or '-') of X *)
BEGIN (* Sign *)
  IF X >= 0.0 THEN
    RETURN '+'
  ELSE
    RETURN '-'
  END (* IF *)
END Sign;
```

Returns a character value that indicates the sign (`'+'` or `'-'`) of its type `REAL` argument.

CHAPTER 7 ▸

Review Questions

1. When should a multiple-alternative `IF` statement be used instead of a `CASE` statement?
2. Write a `CASE` statement to select an operation based on `Inventory`. Increment `TotalPaper` by `PaperOrder` if `Inventory` is `'B'` or `'C'`; increment `TotalRibbon` by `RibbonOrder` if `Inventory` is `'L'`, `'T'`, or `'D'`; increment `TotalLabel` by `Labe-lOrder` if `Inventory` is `'A'` or `'X'`. Take no action if `Inventory` is `'M'`. Al- low lowercase and uppercase.
3. (a) Write the `FOR` statement that displays the character values of the ordinal numbers 21 through 126, inclusive. Use `OrdNum` as the loop-control variable.
   (b) What is the value of `OrdNum` after completion of the loop?
4. Write a `REPEAT` statement that will accept only a valid response to a menu. A valid response would be any of the following: `'A'`, `'a'`, `'B'`, or `'b'`.
5. Write the complement of each Boolean expression below.

```
Flag AND (I < 20)
(ORD(NextCh) = 0) OR Flag
```

```
NOT (Vowel AND Consonant)
(TRUNC(N) = M) OR (N < sqrt(R))
```

6. (a) Write an `IF` statement that tests to see if `Today` is a working day. Print the message `'Workday'` or `'Weekend'`. Assume that `Today` is type `Day`, an enumeration type that has the days of the week as its values.
   (b) Write an equivalent `CASE` statement.
7. Write a `FOR` statement that runs from `'Z'` to `'A'` and prints only the consonants.
8. Write a nested loop that prints the first six letters of the alphabet on a line, the first five letters on the next line, and so on, down to and including the first two letters on the last line. Use uppercase or lowercase letters.
9. Write a function called `FindGross` that computes a worker's weekly gross pay given `Hours` (an `INTEGER`) and `Rate` (a `REAL`) as input parameters. Pay time and a half for any hours worked over 40 and subtract 30% for taxes. For 30 or more hours but less than 40, subtract 20% for taxes. For 20 or more hours but less than 30, subtract 10% for taxes. Do not deduct any taxes for under 20 hours. Be sure to check for a valid number of hours (0 < `Hours` <= 168).

CHAPTER 7 ▸

Programming Projects

1. Write a program that reads in a positive real number and finds and prints the number of digits to the left and the right of the decimal point. Hint: Separate both parts and repeatedly divide or multiply by 10 until it becomes less than 1. Test the program with the following data:

```
4703.62   0.01   0.47   5764   10.12   40000
```

2. Write a program that finds the largest value, the smallest value, and the sum of the input data. After all data are processed, call two functions to find the average value and the range of values in the data collection. Print the results.

3. Redo Programming Project 6 in Chapter 3 using the enumeration type

```
TYPE
  Brand = (Piels, Coors, Bud, IronCity);
```

Write an abstract data type that provides input/output operators for this data type.

4. Write a savings account transaction program that will process the following set of data

```
ADAM    1054.37  ⎫
W         25.00  ⎪
D        243.35  ⎬  group 1
W        254.55  ⎪
Z                ⎭
EVE     2008.24  ⎫
W         15.55  ⎬  group 2
Z                ⎭
```

```
MARY       128.24 ⎫
W           62.48 ⎪
D           13.42 ⎬ group 3
W           84.60 ⎪
Z                 ⎭
SAM          7.77 ⎫ group 4
Z                 ⎭
JOE         15.27 ⎫
W           16.12 ⎪
D           10.00 ⎬ group 5
Z                 ⎭
BETH    12900.00  ⎫
D        9270.00  ⎬ group 6
Z                 ⎭
```

The first record in each group (header) gives the name for an account and the starting balance in the account. All subsequent records show the amount of each withdrawal (`W`) or deposit (`D`) that was made for that account, followed by a sentinel value (`Z`). Print out the final balance for each account processed. If a balance becomes negative, print an appropriate message and take whatever corrective steps you deem proper. If there are no transactions for an account, print a message so indicating.

5. Write a program to print a table of the following form.

Rate (Percent)	*Duration (Years)*	*Monthly Payment*	*Total Payment*
10.00	20	________	________
10.00	25	________	________
10.00	30	________	________
10.25	20	________	________

Your program should print a table showing the monthly and total payments on a loan of $1,000 for interest rates from 10% to 14% with increments of 0.25%. The loan duration should be 20, 25, and 30 years. Your program should contain nested loops, some of which may be inside separate procedures, depending upon your solution. Be careful to remove all redundant computations from inside your loops.

6. Write a program to read in a string of up to ten characters representing a number in the form of a Roman numeral. Print the Roman numeral form and then convert to Arabic form (an integer). The character values for Roman numerals are

M	1000
D	500
C	100
L	50
X	10
V	5
I	1

Test your program on the following data: LXXXVII (87), CCXIX (219), MCCCLIV (1354), MMDCLXXIII (2673), MCDLXXVI (?).

7. A problem encountered in writing compilers or determining efficient means of storing data on disks is converting a name into a unique or a reasonably unique numeric value. This procedure is called hashing. Several algorithms are used to accomplish this task.

   One simple method is to use the numeric representation of each letter in some type of equation. In this problem, you are to convert a word into a reproducible integer value between 0 and 500. To get this value, add each ordinal value of a letter times that letter's position within the word. This should generate a rather large number that may not be within the required range. To calculate a number within the range, determine the modulus of this large number and 500. For example, the number for Ace would be: 1 * 65 + 2 * 67 + 3 * 69, or 406.

   Test your program with several words and print out the calculated value for each word.

8. Generate a table that indicates the rainfall for the city of Bedrock and that can be used to compare the average rainfall for the city with the previous year's rainfall. When you set up the limits for the table, assume a maximum monthly rainfall of 15 inches per month. In addition, provide some summary statistics that will indicate (1) annual rainfall for last year, (2) average annual rainfall, and (3) the difference between the two. The input data will consist of twelve pairs of numbers. The first number in each pair will be the average rainfall for a month, the second number will be what fell the previous year. The first data pair will represent January, second will be February, and so forth. The output should resemble the following:

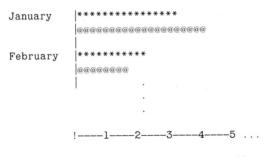

```
January    |****************
           |@@@@@@@@@@@@@@@@@@@@
           |
February   |***********
           |@@@@@@@@
           |
                     .
                     .
                     .

           !----1----2----3----4----5 ...

* - average rainfall for a given month

@ - previous year's rainfall for a given month
```

The data for the chart above begin with: 3.2 4 (for January)
2.2 1.6 (for February)

8 ▸ Arrays and String Variables

In the programs written so far, each variable was associated with a single memory cell. These variables are called simple variables, and their data types are simple or unstructured types. In this chapter, we will begin the study of data structures. A *data structure* is a collection of related data values. The items in a data structure can be processed individually, although some operations may be performed on the structure as a whole.

Modula-2 provides *type constructors*, which can be used to form new data types from simpler objects. The type constructor ARRAY is described in this chapter. The type constructors RECORD and SET will be discussed in subsequent chapters.

The *array* is a data structure used for storage of a collection of data items that are all the same type (e.g., all the exam scores for a class). By using an array, we can associate a single variable name (e.g., Scores) with the entire collection of data. This enables us to save the entire collection of data in main memory (one item per memory cell) and to reference individual items easily. To process an individual item, we need to specify the array name and indicate which array element is being manipulated (e.g., Scores[3] might reference the third item in the array Scores).

Since each score is saved in a separate cell in main memory, we can process the individual items more than once and in any order. In previous programs, we reused the same cell to store each exam score. Consequently, we could not, for example, access the third score after the fourth score was read.

The use of arrays of characters makes it easier to store character strings in memory. String variables or strings will be introduced for this purpose, and you will see how to read textual data into strings.

8.1 The Array Data Type

This section illustrates the basic operations that can be performed on an array. First, we will show how to allocate memory space for an array in Modula-2.

Array Type Declaration

Normally we first describe the structure of an array in an *array type declaration*. Then we allocate storage for one or more arrays of that type. The array type RealArray and array X of type RealArray are declared as follows.

```
TYPE
  RealArray = ARRAY [1..8] OF REAL;

VAR
  X : RealArray;
```

Modula-2 associates eight memory cells with the name `X`; these memory cells will be adjacent to each other in memory. Each element of array `X` can contain a single real value, so a total of eight real values can be stored and referenced using the array name `X`. (Note: The fact that an array's elements are in adjacent memory cells is not required by Modula-2, but it enables the compiler to access all elements of an array because it knows where the first element is stored.)

Referencing Elements of an Array

To process the data stored in an array, we must be able to reference each individual element. The *array subscript* is used to differentiate among elements of the same array. For example, if `X` is the array with eight elements declared previously, then we can refer to the elements of the array `X` as shown in Fig. 8.1.

Figure 8.1 ▸ *The Eight Elements of the Array X*

X[1]	X[2]	X[3]	X[4]	X[5]	X[6]	X[7]	X[8]
16.0	12.0	6.0	8.0	2.5	12.0	14.0	-54.5
First element	Second element	Third element					Eighth element

The *subscripted variable* `X[1]` (read as "`X` sub `1`") can be used to reference the first element of the array `X`, `X[2]` the second element, and `X[8]` the eighth element. The number enclosed in brackets is the array subscript. As you will see later, the subscript does not have to be a constant.

EXAMPLE 8.1 ▸ Let `X` be the array shown in Fig. 8.1. Some statements that manipulate this array are shown in Table 8.1.

Table 8.1 ▸ *Statements that Manipulate Array X*

STATEMENT	EXPLANATION
`WriteReal(X[1], 12)`	Displays the value of `X[1]`, or `16.0`.
`X[4] := 25.0`	Stores the value `25.0` in `X[4]`.
`Sum := X[1] + X[2]`	Stores the sum of `X[1]` and `X[2]`, or `28.0`, in the variable `Sum`.
`Sum := Sum + X[3]`	Adds `X[3]` to `Sum`. The new `Sum` is `34.0`.
`X[4] := X[4] + 1.0`	Adds `1.0` to `X[4]`. The new `X[4]` is `26.0`.
`X[3] := X[1] + X[2]`	Stores the sum of `X[1]` and `X[2]` in `X[3]`. The new `X[3]` is `28.0`.

The contents of array `X` after execution of these statements are as follows: Only `X[3]` and `X[4]` are changed. ◂

X[1]	X[2]	X[3]	X[4]	X[5]	X[6]	X[7]	X[8]
16.0	12.0	28.0	26.0	2.5	12.0	14.0	-54.5
First element	Second element	Third element					Eighth element

EXAMPLE 8.2 ▶ Two array types (BoolArray and ScoreArray) and two arrays (Answers and Scores) are declared as follows.

```
TYPE
  BoolArray = ARRAY [1..10] OF BOOLEAN;
  ScoreArray = ARRAY [1..50] OF CARDINAL;

VAR
  Answers : BoolArray;
  Scores : ScoreArray;
```

The array Answers has ten elements, and each element can store a BOOLEAN value. This array could be used to store the ten answers for a true-false quiz (e.g., Answers[1] is TRUE, Answers[2] is FALSE).

The array Scores has fifty elements, and each element can store a cardinal number. This array could be used to store exam scores for up to fifty students (e.g., Scores[1] is 90, Scores[2] is 65).

A slightly longer set of declarations for these two arrays follows.

```
CONST
  MaxQuestions = 10;
  MaxStudents = 50;

TYPE
  QuestionRange = [1..MaxQuestions];
  StudentRange = [1..MaxStudents];
  BoolArray = ARRAY QuestionRange BOOLEAN;
  ScoreArray = ARRAY StudentRange OF CARDINAL;

VAR
  Answers : BoolArray;
  Scores : ScoreArray;
```

There are three advantages to this set of declarations. First, it becomes very easy to change the declared size of the arrays. By simply redefining a constant value, we change the array size. Second, the subrange types QuestionRange and StudentRange can be used as type identifiers elsewhere in the program. You will see later that it is convenient to declare arrays and loop-control variables using the same subrange types. The third advantage is that the constants MaxQuestions and MaxStudents can be referenced in the program body. ◀

Array Type Declaration ▶

FORM: *array type* = `ARRAY` *subscript type* `OF` *element type*

EXAMPLE: `RealArray = ARRAY BOOLEAN OF REAL`

INTERPRETATION: The identifier *array type* describes a collection of array elements; each element can store an item of type *element type*. The *subscript type* can be either of the standard types `BOOLEAN` or `CHAR`, any enumerated type, or any subrange type. There is an array element corresponding to each value in the *subscript type*. All elements of an array are the same *element type*.

Notes: The standard types `REAL`, `INTEGER`, and `CARDINAL` may not be used as a *subscript type*; however, a subrange with base type `INTEGER` or `CARDINAL` may be a *subscript type*.

The *element type* may be any standard or user-defined simple or structured type.

It is important to realize that an array type declaration does not require allocation of storage space in memory. The array type describes the structure of an array only. Only variables actually store information and require storage. Storage space is not allocated until a variable of this type is declared.

Abstract Array

We can summarize the discussion so far about arrays in the following specification for an abstract array.

Specification for Abstract Array ▶

STRUCTURE: An array is an indexed collection of elements of the same data type. For each array, an ordinal subscript type is specified. There is an array element corresponding to each value in the ordinal type. The ordinal types `INTEGER` and `CARDINAL` cannot be subscript types; however, subranges of these types may be subscript types.

OPERATORS: There are two basic operations that act on elements of an array: *store* and *retrieve*. The store operation inserts a value into the array. If `A` is an array, `C` is an expression that is assignment compatible (defined in Section 5.7) with the base type of `A`, `i` is an expression that is assignment compatible with the subscript type, the statement

```
A[i] := C
```

stores the contents of `C` in element `i` of array `A`. If `C` is a variable that is assignment compatible with the base type of `A`, the statement

```
C := A[i]
```

retrieves element `i` of array `A` and copies its value into `C`. For both of these statements, the value of subscript `i` must be in the range of the array subscript type; otherwise, an execution error will occur.

The assignment operator can also be used to copy the contents of one array to another if they are *assignment compatible arrays* (defined in Section 8.4). If A and B are assignment compatible arrays, the statement

```
A := B
```

copies all values associated with array B to array A.

The preceding display summarizes all the information that you need to know to use an array. You do not need to know how Modula-2 stores the elements of an array in memory or how it implements the retrieve and store operators. If these operators were not included as part of the Modula-2 language, we would need to write procedures to perform the store and retrieve operations. For example, the procedure call statement

```
Store (C, A, i)
```

could be used to store the contents of C in A[i], and the statement

```
Retrieve (A, i, C)
```

could be used to copy A[i] into C.

8.2 Arrays with Numeric Subscripts

As indicated in Section 8.1, the subscript type of an array may be any ordinal type (except type CARDINAL or INTEGER) or a subrange. In the next few sections, most of the examples will deal with arrays whose subscript type is a subrange of type CARDINAL. We do this because it is expedient; keep in mind that the features described carry over to other subscript types as well. We will discuss arrays with nonnumeric subscripts in Section 8.7.

The subscript (sometimes called an *index*) used to reference an array element must be an expression that is assignment compatible with the declared subscript type. Often the subscript type is a subrange with a minimum value of 1 (e.g., [1..MaxSize]). Because the minimum subscript value is positive, the base type of such a subrange is CARDINAL, not INTEGER, and the subscript must be an expression whose value is in the range specified by the subscript type. For the array Scores declared in Example 8.2, the allowable subscript values are the cardinals from 1 through 50.

EXAMPLE 8.3 ▶ Table 8.2 shows some sample statements involving the array X shown in Fig. 8.1. I is assumed to be a type CARDINAL variable with value 6. Make sure you understand each statement.

Table 8.2 ▸ *Some Sample Statements for Array X in Fig. 8.1*

STATEMENT	EFFECT
`WriteReal (X[4], 12)`	Displays 8.0 (value of X[4]).
`WriteReal (X[I], 12)`	Displays 12.0 (value of X[6]).
`WriteReal (X[I]+1.0, 12)`	Displays 13.0 (value of 12.0 + 1.0).
`WriteReal (X[I+1], 12)`	Displays 14.0 (value of X[7]).
`WriteReal (X[I+I], 12)`	Illegal attempt to display X[12].
`WriteReal (X[2*I], 12)`	Illegal attempt to display X[12].
`WriteReal (X[2*I-4], 12)`	Displays -54.5 (value of X[8]).
`X[I] := X[I+1]`	Assigns 14.0 (value of X[7]) to X[6].
`X[I-1] := X[I]`	Assigns 14.0 (new value of X[6]) to X[5].
`X[I] - 1 := X[I]`	Illegal assignment statement
`X[TRUNC(X[4])] := 17.5`	Assigns 17.5 to X[8].

The last assignment statement uses `TRUNC(X[4])` as a subscript expression. Since this evaluates to 8, the value of `X[8]` (and not `X[4]`) is changed. If the value of `TRUNC(X[4])` is outside the range 1 through 8, this would be an illegal subscript expression.

In Table 8.2, there are two illegal attempts to display element `X[12]`, which is not in the array. These attempts will result in an `index out of range` run-time error. ◂

Array Reference ▶

FORM: *name*[*subscript*]

INTERPRETATION: The *subscript* must be an expression that is assignment compatible with the subscript type specified in the declaration for array *name*. If the expression is the wrong data type, a `type mismatch` syntax error will be detected. A value for *subscript* that is outside the declared bounds for the subscript type causes an `index out of range` run-time error.

Sequential Access to Arrays

Often we want to process the elements of an array in sequence, starting with the first. An example would be entering data into the array or printing its contents. This can be acccomplished using a `FOR` loop whose loop-control variable (e.g., `I`) is also used as the array subscript (e.g., `X[I]`). Increasing the value of the loop-control variable by `1` causes the next array element to be processed.

EXAMPLE 8.4 ▸ The array `Cubes` declared below will be used to store the cubes of the first ten integers (e.g., `Cubes[1]` is `1`, `Cubes[10]` is `1000`).

```
CONST
  Size = 10;
```

```
TYPE
  Index = [1..Size];                    (* subrange of cardinals *)
  IntArray = ARRAY Index OF INTEGER;

VAR
  Cubes : IntArray;                     (* array of cubes *)
  I : Index;                            (* loop-control variable *)
```

The FOR statement

```
FOR I := 1 TO Size DO
  Cubes[I] := I * I * I
END; (* FOR *)
```

initializes this array as follows: ◄

array Cubes

[1]	[2]	[3]	[4]	[5]	[6]	[7]	[8]	[9]	[10]
1	8	27	64	125	216	343	512	729	1000

EXAMPLE 8.5 ► In Fig. 8.2, the declarations

```
CONST
  MaxItems = 8;                          (* number of data items *)

TYPE
  Index = [1..MaxItems];                 (* subrange of cardinals *)
  RealArray = ARRAY Index OF REAL;

VAR
  X : RealArray;                   (* array of real numbers *)
  I : Index;                       (* loop control and subscript *)
```

allocate storage for an array X with subscripts in the range 1..8. The program uses three FOR loops to process the array X. The loop-control variable I (1 <= I <= 8) is also used as the array subscript in each loop.

The first FOR loop

```
FOR I := 1 TO MaxItems DO
  ReadReal(X[I]);  WriteLn
END; (* FOR *)
```

is used to read one data value into each array element (the first item is stored in X[1], the second item in X[2], etc.) The ReadReal procedure is called once for each value of I from 1 to 8; each call causes a new data value to be read and stored in X[I]. The subscript I determines which array element receives the next data value. The data lines shown in the sample run cause the array to be initialized as in Fig. 8.1.

The second FOR loop is used to accumulate (in Sum) the sum of all values stored in the array; this loop will be traced later. The last FOR loop

```
FOR I := 1 TO MaxItems DO
  WriteCard (I, 4);  WriteString ('    ');
  WriteRealFormat (X[I], 8, 2);  WriteString ('    ');
  WriteRealFormat (X[I]-Average, 8, 2);  WriteLn
END (* FOR *)
```

is used to display a table showing each array element, X[I], and the difference between that element and the average value, X[I] − Average. ◄

Figure 8.2 ▸
Table of Differences

```
MODULE ShowDiff;
(*
   Computes the average value of an array of data and
   prints the difference between each value and the average.
*)
   FROM InOut IMPORT
     WriteString, WriteCard, WriteLn;

   FROM RealInOut IMPORT
     ReadReal, WriteReal;

   FROM SimpleIO IMPORT
     WriteRealFormat;

   CONST
     MaxItems = 8;                        (* number of data items *)

   TYPE
     Index = [1..MaxItems];              (* subrange of cardinals *)
     RealArray = ARRAY Index OF REAL;

   VAR
     X : RealArray;                (* input - array of data *)
     Average,                      (* output - average value of data *)
     Sum      : REAL;              (* output - sum of the data *)
     I : Index;                    (* loop-control variable *)

BEGIN (* ShowDiff *)
  (* Enter the data. *)
  WriteString ('Enter ');
  WriteCard (MaxItems, 0);
  WriteString (' numbers: ');  WriteLn;
  FOR I := 1 TO MaxItems DO
    ReadReal (X[I]);
    WriteLn
  END; (* FOR *)
  WriteLn;
```

```
  (* Compute the average value. *)
  Sum := 0.0;                                      (* Initialize SUM *)
  FOR I := 1 TO MaxItems DO
    Sum := Sum + X[I]                    (* Add each element to Sum *)
  END; (* FOR *)
  Average := Sum / FLOAT(MaxItems);          (* Get average value *)
  WriteString ('Average value is ');
  WriteRealFormat (Average, 8, 2);  WriteLn;

  (* Display the difference between each item and the average. *)
  WriteString ('Table of differences between X[I] and average');
  WriteLn;
  WriteString ('   I        X[I]      Difference');  WriteLn;
  FOR I := 1 TO MaxItems DO
    WriteCard (I, 4);  WriteString ('     ');
    WriteRealFormat (X[I], 8, 2);  WriteString ('     ');
    WriteRealFormat (X[I]-Average, 8, 2);  WriteLn
  END (* FOR *)
END ShowDiff.

Enter  8 numbers:
16.0
12.0
6.0
8.0
2.5
12.0
14.0
-54.5

Average value is     2.00

Table of differences between X[I] and average
   I        X[I]      Difference
   1       16.00       14.00
   2       12.00       10.00
   3        6.00        4.00
   4        8.00        6.00
   5        2.50        0.50
   6       12.00       10.00
   7       14.00       12.00
   8    -  54.50    -  56.50
```

The program fragment

```
Sum := 0.0;                                      (* Initialize SUM *)
FOR I := 1 TO MaxItems DO
  Sum := Sum + X[I]                    (* Add each element to SUM *)
END; (* FOR *)
```

accumulates the sum of all eight elements of array X in the variable Sum. Each time the FOR loop is repeated, the next element of array X is added to Sum. The execution of this program fragment is traced in Table 8.3 for the first three repetitions of the loop.

Table 8.3 ▸ *Partial Trace of FOR Loop*

STATEMENT PART	I	X[I]	Sum	EFFECT
`Sum:= 0;`			0	Initialize Sum.
`FOR I := 1 TO MaxItems DO`	1	16.0		Initialize I to 1;
`Sum := Sum + X[I]`			16.0	add X[1] to Sum.
increment and test I	2	12.0		2 <= 8 is true;
`Sum := Sum + X[I]`			28.0	add X[2] to Sum.
increment and test I	3	6.0		3 <= 8 is true;
`Sum := Sum + X[I]`			34.0	add X[3] to Sum.

In Fig. 8.2, the subscripted variable X[I] is an actual parameter for procedure ReadReal and WriteRealFormat. It is always necessary to read data into an array one element at a time, as shown in this example. In most instances it is also necessary to display one array element at a time.

SELF-CHECK EXERCISE FOR SECTION 8.2

1. Describe the effect of each statement in Table 8.2, assuming I is 5.

8.3 Case Study: Budget Program

We have written programs that accumulate the sum of all input data items in a single variable. Often we have different categories of data items, and we might want to accumulate a separate total for each category rather than lump all items together. The problem that follows uses an array to accomplish this.

HOME BUDGET PROBLEM

Problem: We want to write a program that keeps track of our monthly expenses in each of ten categories. The program should read each expense amount, add it to the appropriate category total, and print the total expenditure by category. The input data consists of the category number and amount of each purchase made during the past month.

Discussion: There are ten separate totals to be accumulated; each total can be associated with a different element of a ten-element array. The program must read each expenditure, determine to which category it belongs, and then add that expenditure to the appropriate array element. When done with all expenditures, the program should print a table showing each category and its accumulated total. As in all programs that accumulate a sum, each total must be initialized to zero. The problem inputs and outputs and algorithm follow.

PROBLEM INPUTS

each expenditure and its category

PROBLEM OUTPUTS

the array of ten expenditure totals (`Budget`)

Algorithm

1. Initialize all category totals to zero.
2. Read each expenditure and add it to the appropriate total.
3. Print the accumulated total for each category.

The structure chart in Fig. 8.3 shows the relationships among the three steps. The array `Budget` is manipulated by all three procedures in the program solution. Procedures `Initialize` and `Post` store information in the array; this information is displayed by procedure `Report`. The main program is shown in Fig. 8.4, along with procedures `Initialize` and `Report`.

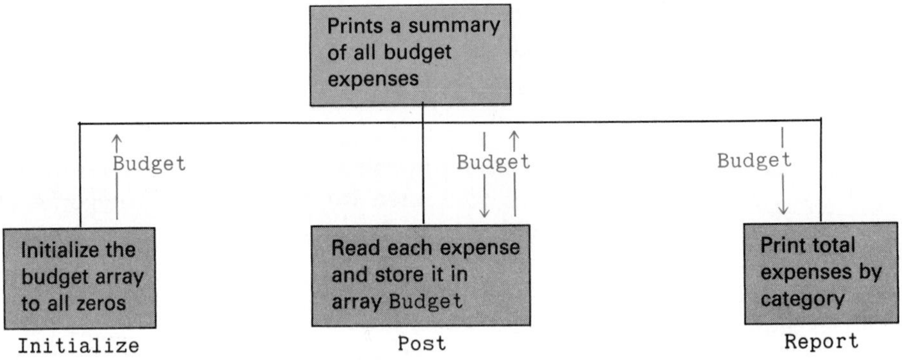

Figure 8.3 ▸ *Structure Chart for Home-Budget Problem*

Figure 8.4 ▸ *Home-Budget Main Program*

```
MODULE HomeBudget;

(* Prints a summary of all expenses by budget category. *)

   FROM InOut IMPORT
     WriteString, WriteCard, WriteLn;
```

```
FROM RealInOut IMPORT
  ReadReal;

FROM SimpleIO IMPORT
  EnterCard, WriteRealFormat;

CONST
  NumCategory = 10;                       (* number of categories *)

TYPE
  Index = [1..NumCategory];                     (* subscript type *)
  BudgetArray = ARRAY Index OF REAL;                (* array type *)

VAR
  Budget : BudgetArray;                  (* output - array of ten
                                            totals *)

PROCEDURE Initialize (VAR Budget (* output *) : BudgetArray);
(*
   Initializes array Budget to all zeros.
   Pre : None
   Post: Each array element Budget[i] is 0.0
*)
   VAR
     Category : Index;                   (* loop-control variable
                                           -- array subscript   *)
BEGIN  (* Initialize *)
  FOR Category := 1 TO NumCategory DO
    Budget[Category] := 0.0
  END (* FOR *)
END Initialize;

PROCEDURE Post (VAR Budget (* input/output *) : BudgetArray);
(*
   Reads each expenditure amount and adds it to the appropriate
   element of array Budget.
   Pre : Each array element Budget[i] is 0.0
   Post: Each array element Budget[i] is the sum of expense
         amounts for category i.
*)
BEGIN  (* Post stub *)
  WriteString ('Procedure Post entered');  WriteLn
END Post;


PROCEDURE Report (Budget (* input *) : BudgetArray);
(*
   Prints the expenditures in each budget category.
   Pre : Each array element Budget[i] is assigned a value.
   Post: Each array element Budget[i] is displayed.
*)
   VAR
```

```
      Category : Index;                    (* loop-control variable --
                                            array subscript         *)
  BEGIN  (* Report *)
    WriteLn;
    WriteString ('Category  Expenses');     (* Print heading *)
    WriteLn;

    (* Print each category number and the expenditure *)
    FOR Category := 1 TO NumCategory DO
      WriteCard (Category, 8);                          (* Print row *)
      WriteRealFormat (Budget[Category], 10, 2);  WriteLn
    END (* FOR *)
  END Report;

BEGIN  (* HomeBudget *)
  (* Initialize array Budget to all zeros. *)
  Initialize (Budget);

  (* Read and process each expenditure. *)
  Post (Budget);

  (* Print the expenditures in each category. *)
  Report (Budget)
END HomeBudget.
```

The main program contains declarations for a constant NumCategory and two types (Index and BudgetArray), as well as the array Budget. The array Budget (type BudgetArray) appears in each parameter list shown in Fig. 8.4 and is passed between each procedure and the main program. When passing an entire array, no subscript is used. We will discuss the use of arrays as parameters later.

The constant NumCategory (10) determines the limit value of the loop-control variable in each procedure. The loop-control variable Category (type Index) is declared as a local variable in Initialize and Report.

In procedure Initialize, the assignment statement

```
Budget[Category] := 0.0
```

is repeated once for each value of Category from 1 to 10 and is used to set each element of Budget to zero.

In procedure Report, the statements

```
WriteCard (Category, 8);                        (* Print row *)
WriteRealFormat (Budget[Category], 10, 2);  WriteLn
```

are used to print each category number (from 1 to 10) and its associated total.

Procedure Post must read each expenditure and add it to the appropriate array element. The total of all expenditures in category 1 is accumulated in Budget[1], the total of all expenditures in category 2 is accumulated in

Budget[2], and so on. Procedure Post is shown in Fig. 8.5; it uses procedure EnterCard from the utility module SimpleIO (see Fig. 6.1) to read a value into NextCategory. EnterCard and WriteRealFormat are imported into the main program.

Figure 8.5 ▸ *Procedure Post for Home-Budget Problem*

```
PROCEDURE Post (VAR Budget (* input/output *) : BudgetArray);
(*
   Reads each expenditure amount and adds it to the appropriate
   element of array Budget.
   Pre : Each array element Budget[i] is 0.0
   Post: Each array element Budget[i] is the sum of expense
         amounts for category i.
*)
   CONST
     Sentinel = 0;                    (* sentinel category *)

   VAR
     NextCategory : CARDINAL;         (* expenditure category *)
     Expense : REAL;                  (* expenditure amount *)

BEGIN  (* Post *)
  (* Read each  budget category and expense and add it to Budget. *)
  WriteString ('Enter each budget category after the prompt: ');
  WriteLn;
  WriteString ('"Enter a cardinal between 0 and ... "');  WriteLn;
  WriteString ('Enter a category of 0 to stop the program');
  WriteLn;  WriteLn;
  LOOP
    (* invariant:
         No prior value of NextCategory is Sentinel and
         Budget[i] is the sum of prior budget entries for
         category i.
    *)
    EnterCard (0, NumCategory, NextCategory);
    IF NextCategory = Sentinel THEN
      EXIT
    END; (* IF *)
    WriteString ('Enter the expenditure amount $');
    ReadReal (Expense);  WriteLn;  WriteLn;
    Budget[NextCategory] := Budget[NextCategory] + Expense
  END (* LOOP *)
END Post;
```

One advantage to using arrays in Fig. 8.5 is that there is no need to process each expense category as a separate case using an IF or a CASE statement. In procedure Post, the assignment statement

```
Budget[NextCategory] := Budget[NextCategory] + Expense
```

adds the expense amount to whatever element of array `Budget` is selected by the subscript `NextCategory`.

The loop control variable `Category` is declared as type `Index` (the subrange `[1..NumCategory]`) in procedures `Initialize` and `Report` (see Fig. 8.4). However, the type of `NextCategory` in `Post` is `CARDINAL`. The reason for this difference is that the type of `NextCategory` must be identical to the type of the third parameter of `EnterCard`. This also enables the sentinel value (`0`) to be returned in `NextCategory`.

A sample run of the home-budget program is shown in Fig. 8.6. As illustrated in this run, it is not necessary for the data to be in order by category.

Figure 8.6 ▶ *Sample Run of Home-Budget Program*

```
Enter each budget category after the prompt:
"Enter a cardinal between 0 and ... "
Enter a category of 0 to stop the program

Enter a cardinal between 0 and 10: 3
Enter the expenditure amount $25.00

Enter a cardinal between 0 and 10: 10
Enter the expenditure amount $25.00

Enter a cardinal between 0 and 10: 3
Enter the expenditure amount $15.00

Enter a cardinal between 0 and 10: 1
Enter the expenditure amount $675.00

Enter a cardinal between 0 and 10: 0

Category  Expenses
       1    675.00
       2      0.00
       3     40.00
       4      0.00
       5      0.00
       6      0.00
       7      0.00
       8      0.00
       9      0.00
      10     25.00
```

Program Style

Allowing for Array Expansion

The constant `NumCategory` is used throughout the home-budget program to represent the number (`10`) of budget categories. This enables us to easily extend the program to handle more budget categories by changing the value of a single constant. This is consistent with our prior use of program constants to write general programs.

Sequential versus Random Access to Arrays

The home-budget program illustrates two common ways of selecting array elements for processing. Often we need to manipulate all elements of an array in some uniform manner (e.g., initialize them all to zero). In situations like this, it makes sense to process the array elements in sequence (*sequential access*), starting with the first and ending with the last. In procedures `Initialize` and `Report`, this is accomplished by using a `FOR` loop whose loop-control variable is also the array subscript.

In procedure `Post`, the order in which the array elements are accessed depends completely on the order of the data. The value read into `NextCategory` determines which element is incremented. This is called *random access,* since the order cannot be predicted beforehand.

SELF-CHECK EXERCISES FOR SECTION 8.3

1. Write a procedure that copies each value stored in one array to the corresponding element of another array of the same type (e.g,. if the arrays are `InArray` and `OutArray`, copy `InArray[1]` to `OutArray[1]`, then copy `InArray[2]` to `OutArray[2]`).
2. Write a procedure that reverses the values stored in an array. If array `X` has `N` elements, then `X[1]` will become `X[N]`, `X[2]` will become `X[N-1]`, and so on.

8.4 Arrays as Operands and Parameters

Most Modula-2 operators (e.g., <, =, >, +, *) can manipulate only one array element at a time. Consequently an array name in an expression generally will be followed by its subscript.

Copying an Array

An exception to the above rule is the assignment operation. It is possible to assign the contents of one array to another array provided the arrays are assignment compatible. Section 5.7 defined assignment compatible for simple types. Two arrays are considered *assignment compatible* if their types are identical or they are renamings of the same type. Given the declarations

```
CONST
  MaxSize = 100;
```

```
TYPE
  Index = [1..MaxSize];
  TestArray = ARRAY Index OF REAL;
  MyTestArray = TestArray; (* identical types *)

VAR
  X, Y : TestArray;
  W : MyTestArray;
  Z : ARRAY Index OF REAL;
  I : Index;
```

the assignment statements

```
X := Y                    (* valid array copy *)
W := Y                    (* valid array copy *)
```

copy each value in array `Y` to the corresponding element of arrays `X` and `W` (i.e., `Y[1]` is copied to `X[1]` and `W[1]`, `Y[2]` is copied to `X[2]` and W[2], etc.).

It is important to realize that the assignments

```
Z := Y;                   (* invalid array copy *)
X := Z                    (* invalid array copy *)
```

are invalid. Even though array `Z` has the same structure as arrays `X` and `Y` (i.e., 100 type `REAL` elements), the type of array `Z` (an *anonymous* type) is not considered assignment compatible with type `TestArray`. Therefore, you must either declare array `Z` as type `TestArray` or `MyTestArray` or use a loop to copy each element individually. In general, the use of anonymous types (unnamed types) should be avoided.

Arrays as Parameters

If several elements of an array are being manipulated by a procedure, it is generally better to pass the entire array of data instead of individual array elements. In Fig. 8.4, the procedure call statements

```
Initialize (Budget);
Post (Budget);
Report (Budget)
```

pass the entire array `Budget` to each procedure. `Budget` is declared as a variable parameter in procedures `Initialize` and `Post` and as a value parameter in procedure `Report`.

In all three procedures, the formal parameter is declared as type `BudgetArray`. This is necessary since the formal and actual parameter must be the same array type. The procedure heading

```
PROCEDURE Initialize (VAR Budget : ARRAY [Index] OF REAL);
```

is invalid because an identifier must be used to specify the parameter type. An exception to this rule is discussed in Section 8.5.

When an array is used as a variable parameter, Modula-2 passes the address of the first actual array element into the procedure data area. Since the array elements are stored in adjacent memory cells, the entire array of data can be accessed. The procedure manipulates the actual array directly.

When an array is used as a value parameter, a local copy of the array is made when the procedure is called. The local array is initialized so that it contains the same values as the corresponding actual array at the time of the call. The procedure manipulates the local array, and any changes made to the local array are not reflected in the actual array.

The next two examples illustrate the use of arrays as parameters, assuming the following declarations.

```
CONST
  MaxSize = 5;

TYPE
  Index = [1..MaxSize];
  TestArray = ARRAY Index OF REAL;

VAR
  X, Y, Z : TestArray;
```

EXAMPLE 8.6 ▶ Although it is possible to use a single assignment statement to copy one array to another, the assignment statement

```
Z := X + Y            (* illegal addition of arrays *)
```

is invalid because the operator + cannot have an array as an operand. Procedure `AddArray` in Fig. 8.7 can be used to add two arrays of type `TestArray`. ◀

Figure 8.7 ▶ *Procedure AddArray*

```
PROCEDURE AddArray (A, B  (* input *)  : TestArray;
                    VAR C (* output *) : TestArray);
(*
   Stores the sum of A[i] and B[i] in C[i]. Array elements
   with subscripts 1..MaxSize are summed, element by element.
   Pre : A[i] and B[i] (1 <= i <= MaxSize) are assigned values
   Post: C[i] := A[i] + B[i] (1 <= i <= MaxSize).
*)
   VAR
     I : Index;                     (* loop-control variable and
                                       array subscript           *)
BEGIN  (* AddArray *)
  (* Add corresponding elements of each array *)
  FOR I := 1 TO MaxSize DO
    C[I] := A[I] + B[I]
  END (* FOR *)
END AddArray;
```

The parameter correspondence established by the procedure call statement

```
AddArray (X, Y, Z)
```

is shown in Fig. 8.8. Arrays A and B in the procedure data area are local copies of arrays X and Y. As indicated by the arrow, the address of the first element of array Z is stored in parameter C. The procedure results are stored directly in array Z. After execution of the procedure, Z[1] will contain the sum of X[1] and Y[1]; or 3.5, Z[2] will contain 6.7; and so on. Arrays X and Y will be unchanged.

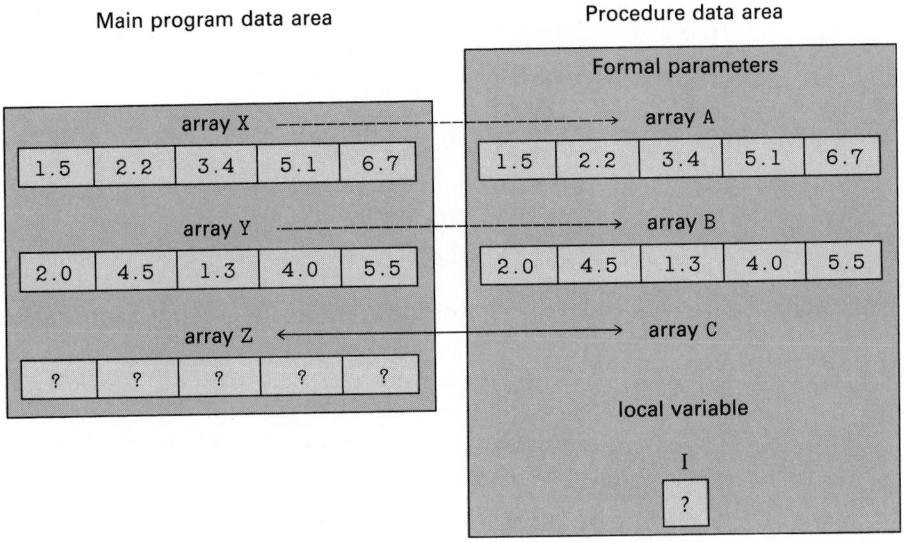

Figure 8.8 ▶ *Parameter Correspondence for AddArray (X, Y, Z)*

EXAMPLE 8.7 ▶ Function procedure SameArray in Fig. 8.9 is used to determine whether two arrays of type TestArray are identical. Two arrays are considered identical if the first element of one is the same as the first element of the other, the second element of one is the same as the second element of the other, and so on.

We can determine that the arrays are not identical by finding a single pair of unequal elements. Consequently, the REPEAT–UNTIL loop can be executed anywhere from one time (first elements unequal) to MaxSize times. The loop is exited when a pair of unequal elements is found or after all elements have been tested. The subscript I is initialized to 0; however, it becomes 1 before the first pair of array elements is tested.

Figure 8.9 ▶ *Function SameArray with REPEAT-UNTIL Loop*

```
PROCEDURE SameArray (A, B : TestArray) : BOOLEAN;
(*
   Returns a value of TRUE if the arrays A, B are identical;
   otherwise, returns a value of FALSE.
```

```
   Pre : A[i] and B[i] (1 <= i <= MaxSize) are assigned values.
   Post: Returns TRUE if A[i] = B[i] for all i in range
         1..MaxSize; otherwise, returns FALSE.
*)
   VAR
     I : Index;                    (* Array subscript *)

BEGIN (* SameArray *)
  I := 0;      (* I is incremented before first array reference *)

  (* Test corresponding elements of arrays A and B. *)
  REPEAT
    (* invariant:
         I <= MaxSize and
         A[i] = B[i] for 1 <= i <= I
    *)
    INC (I)                   (* Advance to next pair of elements *)
  UNTIL (I = MaxSize) OR (A[I] # B[I]);
  (* assert: all elements compared or an unequal pair was found *)

  RETURN A[I] = B[I]                      (* Define result *)
END SameArray;
```

The statement

```
RETURN A[I] = B[I]                      (* Define result *)
```

defines the function result. If the `REPEAT-UNTIL` loop is exited because the pair of elements with subscript `I` is unequal, then the function result is `FALSE`; otherwise, the function result is `TRUE`.

An alternative form of the body of function `SameArray` that uses a `FOR` loop is shown in Fig. 8.10. Convince yourself that the result returned would be the same for either version.

Figure 8.10 ▸ *Function SameArray with FOR Loop*

```
PROCEDURE SameArray (A, B : TestArray) : BOOLEAN;
(*
   Returns a value of TRUE if the arrays A, B are identical;
   otherwise, returns a value of FALSE.
   Pre : A[i] and B[i] (1 <= i <= MaxSize) are assigned values.
   Post: Returns TRUE if A[i] = B[i] for all i in range
         1..MaxSize; otherwise, returns FALSE.
*)
   VAR
     I : Index;                    (* Array subscript *)

BEGIN (* SameArray *)
  (* Test corresponding elements of arrays A and B. *)
  FOR I := 1 TO MaxSize DO
    (* invariant:
```

```
      I <= MaxSize and
      A[i] = B[i] for 1 <= i < I
    *)
    IF A[I] # B[I] THEN
      RETURN FALSE          (* pair at subscript I is unequal *)
    END (* IF *)
  END; (* FOR *)
  (* assert: all pairs are equal *)

  RETURN TRUE
END SameArray;
```

As an example of how function procedure `SameArray` might be used, the `IF` statement

```
IF SameArray(X, Y) THEN
  Z := X
ELSE
  AddArray (X, Y, Z)
END
```

either copies array `X` to array `Z` (`X` and `Y` are identical) or stores the sum of arrays `X` and `Y` in array `Z` (`X` and `Y` are not identical). ◂

Program Style

Efficiency of Variable Parameters versus Protection of Value Parameters

Parameters `A` and `B` in Fig. 8.7 are declared as value parameters because they are used only to store data passed into procedure `AddArray` and their values should not be changed by `AddArray`.

Modula-2 must create a local copy of these two arrays each time procedure `AddArray` is called. This uses valuable computer time and memory space. If the arrays being copied are very large, the program may terminate with an error because all of its memory space has been used up.

To conserve time and memory space, experienced programmers sometimes declare arrays that are used only for input as variable parameters instead of value parameters. However, this means that the corresponding actual parameter is no longer protected from accidental modification by the procedure. Any changes made by the procedure (either by accident or by design) will be saved in an actual array that corresponds to a variable parameter. If an array corresponds to a value parameter, the changes are made to a local copy, and the actual array is unaffected.

Individual Array Elements as Parameters

It is also all right to use a single array element as an actual parameter. For example, the expression

```
TRUNC(Budget[5])
```

truncates the value stored in the fifth element of array `Budget`, where the subscripted variable `Budget[5]` is the actual parameter passed to function `TRUNC`.

EXAMPLE 8.8 ▶ Procedure `Exchange` in Fig. 8.11 exchanges the values of its two type `REAL` parameters.

Figure 8.11 ▶ *Procedure Exchange*

```
PROCEDURE Exchange (VAR P, Q (* input/output *) : REAL);
(*
   Exchanges the values of P and Q.
   Pre : P and Q are assigned values.
   Post: P has the value passed into Q and vice-versa.
*)
   VAR
     Temp : REAL;        (* temporary variable for the exchange *)

BEGIN  (* Exchange *)
  Temp := P;  P := Q;  Q := Temp
END Exchange;
```

The procedure call statement

```
Exchange (X[1], X[2])
```

uses this procedure to exchange the contents of the first two elements (type `REAL`) of array `X`. The identifier `X` is the name of an array in the calling program. The actual parameter `X[1]` corresponds to formal parameter `P`; the actual parameter `X[2]` corresponds to formal parameter `Q`. This correspondence is shown in Fig. 8.12 for the array `X` shown earlier in Fig. 8.8. ◀

Figure 8.12 ▶ *Parameter Correspondence for Exchange (X[1], X[2])*

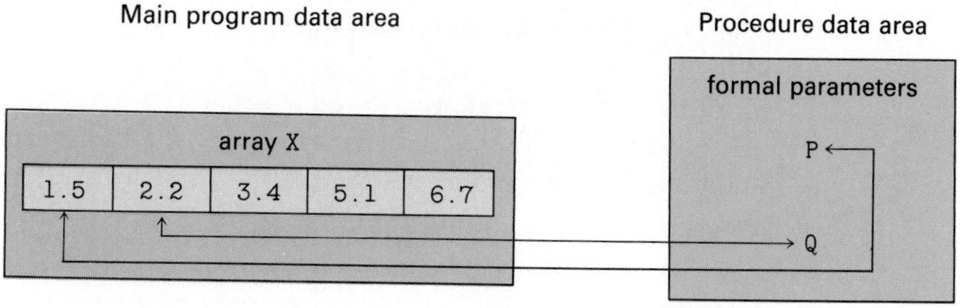

It is illegal to use a subscripted variable as a formal parameter. For example, the procedure declaration

```
PROCEDURE Exchange (VAR X[i], X[j] (* in/out *) : REAL);
```

would cause a syntax error.

8.5 Open-Array Parameters

Procedure AddArray and function procedure SameArray declared earlier in this section can be used with array parameters that are type TestArray only. We cannot use these procedures to process any other array types. This means that we would have to write different procedures to perform the same operation on arrays with ten type REAL elements or 1,000 type REAL elements.

To circumvent this problem, Modula-2 allows us to declare procedures with *open-array parameters*. Only the element type of an open array is specified, not the index range. Therefore, an open array may correspond to any array of the required element type. In the following revised procedure heading, the formal parameters A, B, and C are declared as open-array parameters.

```
PROCEDURE AddArray (A, B  (* input *)  : ARRAY OF REAL;
                    VAR C (* output *) : ARRAY OF REAL);
```

Within the procedure body, it may be necessary to reference individual elements of the actual array corresponding to open-array C. This is complicated by the fact that the actual index range is not known when the procedure is written and may be different each time the procedure is called. Consequently, within the procedure Modula-2 uses a lower bound of 0 for each open array. The upper bound for open-array C is HIGH(C) where HIGH is a standard function that returns the number of elements minus one declared in the actual array type. Therefore, the index range 0..HIGH(C) can be used in AddArray to reference all elements of any actual array corresponding to parameter C. Note that function HIGH may be used with any valid subscript type, and it always returns a type CARDINAL result regardless of the subscript type.

If open-array C corresponds to an actual array P with index range m..n, the value of HIGH(C) is n–m. Within the procedure, C[i] denotes P[m+i]. At the boundary points, C[0] denotes P[m] and C[HIGH(C)] denotes P[n]. For example, if array D with index range 1..100 is the actual array corresponding to open-array C, then HIGH(C) is 99 and array elements C[0]..C[99] in the procedure body correspond to elements D[1]..D[100] in the actual array.

Procedure AddArray is rewritten in Fig. 8.13 with open-array parameters. The procedure begins by testing that all three arrays have the same subscript range.

Figure 8.13 ▸ *Procedure AddArray with Open-Array Parameters*

```
PROCEDURE AddArray (A, B  (* input *)  : ARRAY OF REAL;
                    VAR C (* output *) : ARRAY OF REAL);
(*
   Stores the sum of A[I] and B[I] in C[I]. Array elements
   with subscripts 0..HIGH(C) are summed, element by element. *)
   Pre : Arrays A and B are assigned values.
```

```
    Post: C[i] := A[i] + B[i] for 0 <= i <= HIGH(C)
*)
    VAR
      I : CARDINAL;                  (* loop-control variable and
                                        array subscript          *)
BEGIN (* AddArray *)
  (* Verify that the subscript range is the same for all arrays *)
  IF (HIGH(A) # HIGH(B)) OR (HIGH(A) # HIGH(C)) OR
                          (HIGH(B) # HIGH(C)) THEN
    WriteString ('Invalid parameters for procedure AddArray');
    WriteLn;
    RETURN
  END; (* IF *)

  (* Add corresponding elements of each array *)
  FOR I := 0 TO HIGH(C) DO
    C[I] := A[I] + B[I]
  END (* FOR *)
END AddArray;
```

EXAMPLE 8.9 ▸ Procedures `Initialize` and `Report` (see Fig. 8.4) are rewritten in Fig. 8.14 with an open-array parameter. They are shown in the implementation module for `RealArrayManip` (the definition part is left as an exercise at the end of this section). The only change in the body of procedure `Initialize` is to the `FOR` loop header. In `Report`, the statements that display the table heading are removed because this heading may be different each time `Report` is used. ◂

Figure 8.14 ▸ *Implementation Module RealArrayManip*

```
IMPLEMENTATION MODULE RealArrayManip;
(*
   Implementation module for manipulating arrays with REAL
   elements.
*)
  FROM InOut IMPORT
    Write, WriteString, WriteCard, WriteLn;

  FROM SimpleIO IMPORT
    WriteRealFormat;

  PROCEDURE Initialize (VAR X (* output *) : ARRAY OF REAL);
  (*
     Initializes array X to zero.
     Pre : None
     Post: X[i] is 0.0 for 0 <= i <= HIGH(X)
  *)
     VAR
       Next : CARDINAL;               (* loop-control variable --
                                         array subscript        *)
```

```
BEGIN (* Initialize *)
  FOR Next := 0 TO HIGH(X) DO
    X[Next] := 0.0
  END (* FOR *)
END Initialize;


PROCEDURE Report (X (* input *) : ARRAY OF REAL;
                  Min, Max (* input *) : CARDINAL;
(*
   Prints each subscript and element value of its array parameter.
   Pre : 0 <= Min <= Max <= HIGH(X) and elements X[Min]
         through X[Max] are defined.
   Post: Displays i and X[i] for Min <= i <= Max. The last
         digit of i is in screen position 10; X[i] is displayed
         in positions 11 through 20 with two decimal digits.
*)
   VAR
     Next : CARDINAL;                 (* loop-control variable --
                                         array subscript        *)
 BEGIN (* Report *)
   (* Validate Min and Max *)
   IF (Min < 0) OR (Min > Max) OR
                   (Max > HIGH(X)) THEN
     WriteString ('Invalid subscript range');  WriteLn;
     RETURN
   END; (* IF *)

   (* Print each subscript and element value. *)
   FOR Next := Min TO Max DO
     WriteCard (Next, 10);                            (* Print row *)
     WriteRealFormat (X[Next], 10, 2);  WriteLn
   END (* FOR *)
 END Report;

END RealArrayManip.
```

Module `HomeBudget` is rewritten in Fig. 8.15, assuming these procedures are imported from module `RealArrayManip`. The statements that display the table heading are placed at the end of the main program body just before the call to procedure `Report`. The procedure call statement

```
Report (Budget, 0, HIGH(Budget))
```

displays the entire array Budget.

Figure 8.15 ▸ *Home-Budget Main Program Using RealArrayManip*

```
MODULE HomeBudget;

(* Prints a summary of all expenses by budget category. *)
```

```
FROM InOut IMPORT
  WriteString, WriteCard, WriteLn

FROM RealInOut IMPORT
  ReadReal;

FROM SimpleIO IMPORT
  EnterCard, WriteRealFormat;

FROM RealArrayManip IMPORT
  Initialize, Report;

CONST
  NumCategory = 10;                    (* number of categories *)

TYPE
  Index = [1..NumCategory];                  (* subscript type *)
  BudgetArray = ARRAY Index OF REAL;              (* array type *)

VAR
  Budget : BudgetArray;                 (* array of ten totals *)

PROCEDURE Post (VAR Budget (* inout *) : BudgetArray);
(*
   Reads each expenditure amount and adds it to the appropriate
   element of array Budget.
   Pre : Each array element Budget[i] is 0.0
   Post: Each array element Budget[i] is the sum of expense
         amounts for category i.
*)
   CONST
     Sentinel = 0;                      (* sentinel category *)

   VAR
     NextCategory : CARDINAL;           (* expenditure category *)
     Expense : REAL;                    (* expenditure amount *)

   BEGIN  (* Post *)
     (* Enter each budget category and expense *)
     WriteString ('Enter each budget category after prompt: ');
     WriteLn;
     WriteString ('"Enter a cardinal between 0 and ... "');
     WriteLn;
     WriteString ('Enter a category of 0 to stop the program');
     WriteLn;  WriteLn;
     LOOP
       (* invariant:
            no prior value of NextCategory is Sentinel
            and Budget[i] is the sum of prior budget entries for
            category i.
       *)
       EnterCard (0, NumCategory, NextCategory);
```

```
      IF NextCategory = Sentinel THEN
        EXIT
      END; (* IF *)
      WriteString ('Enter the expenditure amount $');
      ReadReal (Expense);  WriteLn;  WriteLn;
      Budget[NextCategory] := Budget[NextCategory] + Expense
    END (* LOOP *)
  END Post;

BEGIN  (* HomeBudget *)
  (* Initialize array Budget to all zeros. *)
  Initialize (Budget);

  (* Read and process each expenditure. *)
  Post (Budget);

  (* Print the expenditures in each category. *)
  WriteString ('The first table line represents category #1');
  WriteLn;  WriteLn;
  WriteString ('Category-1  Expenses');  WriteLn;
  Report (Budget, 0, HIGH(Budget))
END HomeBudget.
```

The revised program shown in Fig. 8.15 will generate a slightly different output table. The subscript values printed by procedure `Report` are in the range `0..NumCategory-1` (9). The first few lines of the sample output table follow (the first line represents category #1; compare with Fig. 8.6):

```
Category-1  Expenses
         0    675.00
         1      0.00
         2     40.00
```

EXAMPLE 8.10 ▶ Function `FindMax` (see Fig. 8.16) is a function that finds the largest value in an array of type `REAL` numbers in the subscript range `Min` to `Max`.

`FindMax` begins by testing whether the subscript range is invalid. If it is invalid, a value of 0.0 is returned. Otherwise, the statement

```
MaxSoFar := X[Min];    (* Assume first element is largest *)
```

saves the first element in the search range in `MaxSoFar`. The `FOR` loop examines the rest of the array, redefining `MaxSoFar` whenever a larger value is found. ◀

Figure 8.16 ▶ *Function Procedure FindMax*

```
PROCEDURE FindMax (X (* input *) : ARRAY OF REAL;
                   Min, Max (* input *) : CARDINAL) : REAL;
(*
   FindMax locates the largest value in array X in the
```

```
    subscript range Min..Max.
    Pre : 0 <= Min <= Max <= HIGH(X) and elements X[Min]
          through X[Max] are defined.
    Post: Returns the largest value in X[Min]..X[Max].
*)
    VAR
       MaxSoFar : REAL;                    (* largest value so far *)
       I : CARDINAL;                      (* loop-control variable *)

BEGIN (* FindMax *)
  IF (Min < 0) OR (Min > Max) OR
                 (Max > HIGH(X)) THEN
    WriteString ('Invalid subscript range');  WriteLn;
    RETURN 0.0
  END; (* IF *)

  (* Search for largest element *)
  MaxSoFar := X[Min];          (* Assume first element is largest *)
  (* Examine rest of array *)
  FOR I := Min+1 TO Max DO
    IF X[I] > MaxSoFar THEN                   (* Is X[I] larger? *)
      MaxSoFar := X[I]                       (* Redefine largest *)
    END (* IF *)
  END; (* FOR *)
  RETURN MaxSoFar                              (* Define result *)

END FindMax;
```

Be careful in specifying the parameters `Min` and `Max` that designate the subrange to be searched. To find the largest value in an array with subscript type `[1..N]`, pass `0` to `Min` and `N−1` to `Max`. For the array `Y` declared below

```
VAR
  Y : ARRAY [-30..30] OF REAL;
```

the function designator

```
FindMax(Y, 0, HIGH(Y))
```

returns the largest value stored in array `Y`; these parameter values always cause an entire array to be searched, regardless of the actual subscript type. The function designator

```
FindMax(Y, 0, 29)
```

returns the largest value stored in the subarray with negative subscripts (`Y[-30].. Y[-1]`); and the function designator

```
FindMax(Y, 31, 60)
```

returns the largest value stored in the subarray with positive subscripts (Y[1]..Y[30]).

We will insert FindMax in module RealArrayManip. If you are writing a procedure that is a candidate for general use or inclusion in a library, we recommend that you use open-array parameters for maximum flexibility.

EXAMPLE 8.11 ▶ Another candidate for inclusion in module RealArrayManip is procedure GraphIt shown in Fig. 8.17. This procedure displays the contents of a real array in the form of a *bar graph*. Each line of the bar graph corresponds to the value of an array element, and the first line corresponds to the first array element. The length of a line is proportional to the value it represents (i.e., the larger the value, the longer the line).

Figure 8.17 ▶ *Procedure GraphIt*

```
PROCEDURE GraphIt (VAR X (* input *) : ARRAY OF REAL;
                   Min, Max (* input *) : CARDINAL);
(*
   Displays the bar graph corresponding to its array parameter.
   One line is plotted for each value in the subscript range
   Min..Max. The graph is scaled so that the longest line is
   approximately 50 characters.
   Pre : Min, Max, and elements X[Min]..X[Max] are assigned values.
         0 <= Min <= Max <= HIGH(X)
   Post: Displays Max-Min+1 lines where the length of line i
         corresponds to the value of X[Min+i-1].
   Uses: WriteRealFormat from SimpleIO; Write, WriteCard, WriteLn,
         WriteString from InOut.
*)
   CONST
     Star = '*';                    (* symbol plotted *)
     MaxPoints = 50;                (* longest line length *)

   VAR
     MinVal,                        (* the smallest value plotted *)
     MaxVal,                        (* the largest value plotted *)
     Increment : REAL;              (* the amount represented by each
                                       point *)
     I,                             (* loop-control variable *)
     Next,                          (* subscript for array X *)
     NumStars : CARDINAL;           (* the number of stars in a line *)

BEGIN (* GraphIt *)
  (* Validate parameters *)
  IF (Min < 0) OR (Min > Max) OR
                (Max > HIGH(X)) THEN
    WriteString ('Invalid subscript range');  WriteLn;
    RETURN                          (* bar graph not plotted *)
```

```
    END; (* IF *)

    (* Determine the value represented by each point of the plot *)
    MaxVal := FindMax (X, Min, Max);
    MinVal := 0.0;
    Increment := (MaxVal - MinVal) / FLOAT(MaxPoints);

    (* Print a bar for each element of X. *)
    FOR Next := Min TO Max DO
      WriteCard (Next, 10);              (* Print the subscript *)
      Write (' |');
      NumStars := TRUNC((X[Next] - MinVal) / Increment + 0.5);
      (* Plot points until value plotted matches element value. *)
      FOR I := 1 TO NumStars DO
        Write (Star)
      END; (* FOR I *)
      (* assert: X[Next] is plotted *)

      WriteLn
    END; (* FOR Next *)
    (* assert: array X is plotted *)

    (* Identify scale *)
    WriteRealFormat (MinVal, 10, 2);
    WriteString ('^         ^         ');
    WriteString ('^         ^         ^         ^');
    WriteRealFormat (MaxVal, 10, 2);  WriteLn;
    WriteString ('              Each point represents a value of ');
    WriteRealFormat (Increment, 10, 2);  WriteLn
  END GraphIt;
```

First, procedure `GraphIt` verifies that parameters `Min` and `Max` are passed valid values. Next, `GraphIt` calls function `FindMax` to find the largest value (saved in `MaxVal`) in its array parameter. The difference between `MaxVal` and `MinVal` (0.0) is divided by `MaxPoints` to get the value, `Increment`, represented by each point plotted.

The outer `FOR` loop selects the next element of `X` to be plotted. The assignment statement

```
NumStars := TRUNC((X[Next] - MinVal) / Increment + 0.5);
```

determines the length of the line required to represent `X[Next]`. The value of `NumStars` is proportional to `X[Next]` and is equal to `0` when `X[Next]` is `MinVal` and is equal to `MaxPoints` when `X[Next]` is `MaxVal`. The inner `FOR` loop plots each point of the line. The `WriteString` and `WriteRealFormat` statements at the end of the procedure display a scale for the graph.

A sample execution of procedure `GraphIt` is shown in Fig. 8.18. The six element values plotted are `0.0`, `10.0`, `20.0`, `30.0`, `40.0`, and `50.0`. ◂

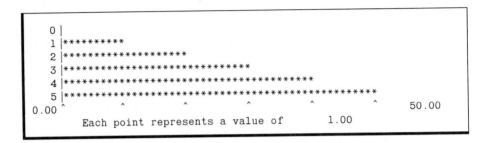

Figure 8.18 ▸ *Sample Graph Generated by GraphIt*

```
   0 |
   1 |**********
   2 |********************
   3 |******************************
   4 |****************************************
   5 |**************************************************
0.00 ^         ^         ^         ^         ^         ^    50.00
        Each point represents a value of        1.00
```

Open-Array Parameters ▸

FORM: `ARRAY OF` *element type*;

EXAMPLE: `ARRAY OF CHAR;`

INTERPRETATION: A formal array parameter can be declared as an open-array type. Only the *element type* of an open array is declared; the subscript type is not specified. The first array element has a subscript of `0` inside the procedure. The subscript of the last element is determined by calling the standard function `HIGH` with the open array as its argument.

SELF-CHECK EXERCISES FOR SECTION 8.5

1. Write the definition module for `RealArrayManip`.
2. Write function `FindMin`, a function that returns the smallest value in its array parameter.
3. Write a procedure that assigns a value of `TRUE` to element `i` of its output array if element `i` of one input array has the same value as element `i` of the other input array; otherwise, assign a value of `FALSE`. Assume that the input arrays are type `ARRAY OF CHAR`.
4. Rewrite function procedure `SameArray` with open-array parameters.

8.6 Reading Part of an Array

Usually we don't know exactly how many elements there will be in an array. For example, if we are processing exam scores, there might be 150 students in one class, 200 in the next, and so on. In this situation, we should declare an array that can accommodate the largest class. Only part of this array will actually be processed for a smaller class.

EXAMPLE 8.12 ▸ The following array `Scores` can accommodate a class of up to 250 students. Each array element can contain an integer value between 0 and 100.

```
CONST
  MaxSize = 250;
  MaxScore = 100;

TYPE
  ClassIndex = [1..MaxSize];
  ScoreRange = [0..100];
  ScoreArray = ARRAY ClassIndex OF ScoreRange;
  ClassRange = [0..MaxSize];

VAR
  Scores : ScoreArray;
  ClassSize : ClassRange;
```

Procedure `ReadScores` in Fig. 8.19 reads up to 250 exam scores. It prints a warning message when the array is filled. The actual number of scores read is returned as the value of `ClassSize`. ◄

Figure 8.19 ► *Reading Part of an Array*

```
PROCEDURE ReadScores (VAR Scores (* output *) : ScoreArray;
                      VAR ClassSize (* output *) : ClassRange);
(*
   Reads an array of exam scores (Scores)
   for a class of up to MaxSize students.
   Pre : None
   Post: The data values are stored in array Scores.
         The number of values read is stored in ClassSize.
   Uses: EnterInt from SimpleIO; WriteString, WriteLn from InOut
*)
CONST
  Sentinel = -1;                   (* Sentinel value *)

VAR
  TempScore : INTEGER;          (* Temporary storage for a score *)

BEGIN
  WriteString ('Enter next score after the prompt or -1 to stop.');
  WriteLn;

  ClassSize := 0;                        (* initial class size *)
  (* Read each array element until done. *)
  LOOP
    (* invariant:
         No prior value read is Sentinel and
         ClassSize <= MaxSize
    *)
    EnterInt (Sentinel, 100, TempScore);      (* Read next score *)
    IF (TempScore = Sentinel) OR (ClassSize = MaxSize) THEN
      EXIT
    END; (* IF *)
```

```
    INC (ClassSize);
    Scores[ClassSize] := TempScore      (* Save the score *)
  END; (* LOOP *)
  (* assert:
       Last value read is Sentinel or
       ClassSize is MaxSize
  *)

  IF ClassSize = MaxSize THEN
    WriteString ('Array is filled.');  WriteLn
  END (* IF *)
END ReadScores;
```

In any subsequent processing of array Scores, the variable ClassSize should be used to limit the number of array elements processed. Only the subarray with subscripts 1..ClassSize is defined. All array elements with subscripts larger than ClassSize are still undefined and should not be manipulated. Any attempt to process or display them may cause a run-time error. ClassSize should be passed as a parameter to any procedure that processes the partially filled array.

8.7 General Arrays

The subscript type of each array examined so far has been a subrange of the cardinals. This, of course, is not required in Modula-2, since the subscript type may be any ordinal type (except CARDINAL or INTEGER) or a subrange. A number of different array types are described in Table 8.4.

Table 8.4 ▸ *Some Array Types and Applications*

ARRAY DECLARATION	APPLICATION
`Name : ARRAY [1..10] OF CHAR;`	`Name[1] := 'A';` storing a person's name (up to 10 letters)
`Fahrenheit : ARRAY [-10..10] OF REAL;`	`Fahrenheit[-10] := 14.0;` storing Fahrenheit temperatures corresponding to −10 through 10 degrees Celsius
`LetterCount : ARRAY ['A'..'Z'] OF CARDINAL;`	`LetterCount['A'] := 0;` storing the number of times each capital letter occurs

`LetterFound : ARRAY ['A'..'Z'] OF BOOLEAN;`	`LetterFound['X'] := FALSE;` storing a set of flags indicating which letters occurred and which did not
`Answers : ARRAY BOOLEAN OF CARDINAL;`	`Answers[TRUE] := 15;` storing the number of `TRUE` answers and `FALSE` answers to a quiz.

The array `Name` has ten elements and can be used to store the letters of a person's name. The array `Fahrenheit` has twenty-one elements and can be used to store the Fahrenheit temperature corresponding to each Celsius temperature in the range −10 through +10 degrees Celsius. For example, `Fahrenheit[0]` would be the Fahrenheit temperature that corresponds to 0 degrees Celsius. Arrays `LetterCount` and `LetterFound` have the same subscript type (i.e., the uppercase letters) and will be discussed in Example 8.14. The array `Answers` has only two elements, with subscript values `FALSE` and `TRUE`.

EXAMPLE 8.13 ▶ The array `MonthSales` could be used to keep track of the amount of sales in each month. The subscript type is `Month` (imported from module `DatesADT` in Fig. 6.8) so the subscript values are the constants `January` to `December`.

```
TYPE
  SalesArray = ARRAY Month OF REAL;

VAR
  CurMonth   : Month;
  MonthSales : SalesArray;
  CurSales : REAL;
```

If procedure `Initialize` is imported from module `RealArrayManip` (see Fig. 8.14), the statement

```
Initialize (MonthSales)
```

initializes this array to all zeros. The statement

```
MonthSales[CurMonth] := MonthSales[CurMonth] + CurSales
```

adds the value of `CurSales` to the element of `MonthSales` selected by the subscript `CurMonth`. ◀

EXAMPLE 8.14 ▶ The arrays `LetterCount` and `LetterFound` described in Table 8.4 have the subscript type `['A'..'Z']`. Hence, there is an array element for each uppercase letter. `LetterCount['A']` could be used to count the number of occurrences of the letter A in a line; LetterFound['A'] could be used to indicate whether the letter A occurs. If the letter A occurs, LetterFound['A'] would be TRUE; otherwise, LetterFound['A'] would be FALSE.

The program in Fig. 8.20 uses the arrays LetterCount and LetterFound to print the number of occurrences of each letter in a line of text. The case of the letter is ignored (e.g., 't' or 'T' are considered the same letter). Only counts greater than zero are printed.

Figure 8.20 ▸ *Counting Letters in a Line*

```
MODULE Concordance;
(*
   Finds and prints the number of occurrences of each letter.
   The case of each letter is immaterial. Letters with counts
   of zero are not displayed.
*)
   FROM InOut IMPORT
     Read, Write, WriteCard, WriteString, WriteLn;

   CONST
     Sentinel = '.';

   TYPE
     Letter = ['A'..'Z'];

   VAR
     LetterCount : ARRAY Letter OF CARDINAL; (* array of counts *)
     LetterFound : ARRAY Letter OF BOOLEAN;    (* array of flags *)
     NextChar : CHAR;                    (* each input character *)

BEGIN (* Concordance *)
  (* Initialize LetterCount and LetterFound. *)
  FOR NextChar := 'A' TO 'Z' DO
    LetterCount[NextChar] := 0;               (* Initialize counts *)
    LetterFound[NextChar] := FALSE             (* Initialize flags *)
  END; (* FOR *)

  (* Read and process each data character. *)
  WriteString('Enter a line of text ending with a period.');
  WriteLn;
  REPEAT
    Read (NextChar);  Write (NextChar);
    NextChar := CAP(NextChar);

    (* Increment the count for each letter character. *)
    IF ('A' <= NextChar) & (NextChar <= 'Z') THEN
      INC (LetterCount[NextChar]);
      LetterFound[NextChar] := TRUE           (* Set letter flag *)
    END (* IF *)
  UNTIL NextChar = Sentinel;
```

```
  (* Print counts of letters that are in the line. *)
  WriteLn;  WriteLn;
  WriteString ('Letter     Occurrences');  WriteLn;
  FOR NextChar := 'A' TO 'Z' DO
    IF LetterFound[NextChar] THEN
      WriteString ('     ');
      Write (NextChar);
      WriteCard (LetterCount[NextChar], 16);
      WriteLn
    END (* IF *)
  END (* FOR *)
END Concordance.

Enter a line of text ending with a period.
This is it.

Letter      Occurrences
     H              1
     I              3
     S              2
     T              2
```

In Fig. 8.20, the array `LetterFound` is not really needed. The condition in the last `IF` statement

```
LetterFound[NextChar]
```

could be written just as easily as

```
LetterCount[NextChar] > 0
```

It would be more efficient to do this and eliminate the extra array.

CASE STUDY: GENERATING CRYPTOGRAMS

Problem: A cryptogram is a coded message formed by substituting a code character for each letter of an original message. The substitution is performed uniformly through the original message, for example, all A's are replaced by Z's, all B's by Y's, and so on. We will assume that all punctuation (including blanks between words) remains unchanged.

Discussion: The program must examine each character in the message and replace each character that is a letter with its code symbol. We will store the code symbols in an array `Code` with subscript type `['A'..'Z']` and element type `CHAR`. The character stored in `Code['A']` will be the code symbol for the letter `'A'`. This will allow us to simply "look up" the code symbol for a letter by using that letter as an index to the array `Code`. The problem data requirements and algorithm follow; the structure chart is shown in Fig. 8.21.

PROBLEM INPUTS

the array of code symbols (`Code : ARRAY ['A'..'Z'] OF CHAR`)
each message character

PROBLEM OUTPUTS

each character of the cryptogram

Algorithm

1. Read in the code symbol for each letter.
2. Read each message character and display the cryptogram.

Figure 8.21 ▸ *Structure Chart for Cryptogram-Generating Program*

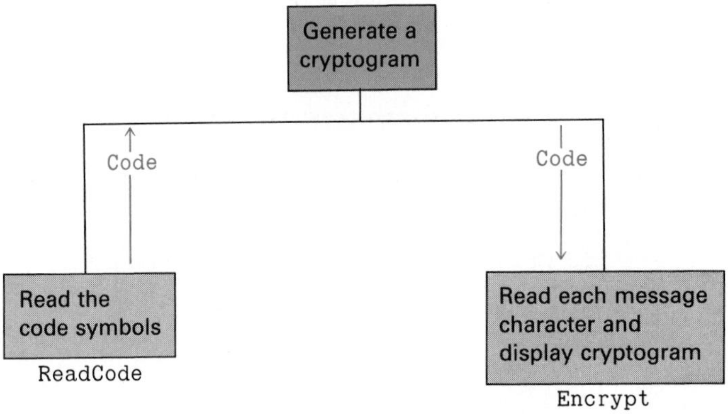

The data requirements and algorithms for procedures `ReadCode` and `Encrypt` follow. The complete program and a sample run are shown in Fig. 8.22.

LOCAL VARIABLE FOR READCODE

each code symbol (`CodeSymbol : CHAR`)
loop-control variable for accessing array `Code`
(`NextLetter : ['A'..'Z']`)

Algorithm for ReadCode

1. Display the alphabet.
2. `FOR` each letter `DO`
   Read in the code symbol and store it in array `Code`.
   `END`

LOCAL CONSTANT FOR ENCRYPT

the sentinel character for the message (`Sentinel = '.'`)

LOCAL VARIABLE FOR ENCRYPT

each message character (`NextChar : CHAR`)

Algorithm for Encrypt

1. REPEAT
    2. Read the next message character.
    3. IF it is a letter THEN
        4. Convert to the corresponding code symbol.

       END
    5. Display the cryptogram character.

   UNTIL the message is complete

Figure 8.22 ▸ *Cryptogram Generator*

```
MODULE Cryptogram;

  FROM InOut IMPORT
    Read, Write, WriteString, WriteLn;

  TYPE
    Letter = ['A'..'Z'];
    CodeArray = ARRAY Letter OF CHAR;

  VAR
    Code : CodeArray;                    (* input - array of code
                                            symbols *)

  PROCEDURE ReadCode (VAR Code (* output *) : CodeArray);
  (*
     Reads in the code symbol for each letter.
     Pre : None
     Post: 26 code symbols are read into array Code.
  *)
     VAR
       NextLetter : Letter;                 (* each letter *)
       CodeSymbol : CHAR;

  BEGIN (* ReadCode *)
    WriteString ('Enter a code symbol under each letter.');
    WriteLn;
    WriteString ('ABCDEFGHIJKLMNOPQRSTUVWXYZ');  WriteLn;

    (* Read each code symbol into array Code. *)
```

```
    FOR NextLetter := 'A' TO 'Z' DO
      Read (CodeSymbol);
      Write (CodeSymbol);
      Code[NextLetter] := CodeSymbol
    END; (* FOR *)

    WriteLn;  WriteLn
  END ReadCode;

  PROCEDURE Encrypt (Code (* input *) : CodeArray);
  (*
     Reads each character and prints it or its code symbol.
     Pre : The code for letter i is saved in Code[i].
     Post: Displays a message down column 1
           and its cryptogram down column 6.
  *)
     CONST
       Sentinel = '.';                  (* sentinel character *)

     VAR
       NextChar : CHAR;

   BEGIN (* Encrypt *)
     WriteString ('Enter each character of your message.');
     WriteLn;
     WriteString ('Enter the symbol "." after your  message.');
     WriteLn;
     REPEAT
       Read (NextChar);  Write (NextChar);  WriteString ('    ');
       NextChar := CAP(NextChar);
       IF ('A' <= NextChar) & (NextChar <= 'Z') THEN
         NextChar := Code[NextChar];  (* Convert to code symbol *)
       END; (* IF *)
       Write (NextChar);            (* Print cryptogram character *)
       WriteLn
     UNTIL NextChar = '.'
 END Encrypt;

BEGIN (* Cryptogram *)
  (* Read in the code symbol for each letter. *)
  ReadCode (Code);

  (* Read each character and print the cryptogram *)
  Encrypt (Code)
END Cryptogram.


Enter a code symbol under each letter.
ABCDEFGHIJKLMNOPQRSTUVWXYZ
BCDEFGHIJKLMNOPQRSTUVWXYZA
```

```
Enter each character of your message.
Enter the symbol "." after your message.
A    B

t    U
i    J
n    O
y    Z

O    P
N    O
E    F
!    !
.    .
```

In the sample run, the code symbol for each letter is entered directly beneath that letter and read by procedure `ReadCode`. Procedure `Encrypt` generates two columns of output. The original message can be seen by reading down the first column; the cryptogram appears in the second column.

SELF-CHECK EXERCISES FOR SECTION 8.7

1. Describe the following array types:
   a. `ARRAY [1..20] OF CHAR`
   b. `ARRAY ['0'..'9'] OF BOOLEAN`
   c. `ARRAY [-5..5] OF REAL`
   d. `ARRAY [BOOLEAN] OF CHAR`
2. If procedure `Read` in your Modula-2 system does not echo the character read, modify the cryptogram program so that only the cryptogram is displayed. The cryptogram should appear across one line of the screen.

8.8 String Variables

Until now, our use of character data has been quite limited. Variables of type `CHAR` were used to save individual characters. We used procedure `WriteString` to display strings. In this section, you will learn how to read and process string variables or strings.

Declaring a String

The declarations

```
CONST
  StringSize = 11;
```

```
TYPE
  Index = [0..StringSize-1];
  ShortString = ARRAY Index OF CHAR;

VAR
  FirstName, LastName : ShortString;
  i : Index;
```

allocate storage for two string variables: `FirstName` and `LastName`. String variables `FirstName` and `LastName` can store eleven characters each (subscript range `0..10`). In general, a string variable of type

```
ARRAY [0..n-1] OF CHAR
```

can be used to store a string of up to *n* characters.

Referencing Individual Characters in a String

We can manipulate individual characters in a string variable the same way we manipulate individual elements of an array. For example, the program fragment below reads eleven characters into string variable `FirstName` and displays all characters stored in the string.

```
WriteString ('Enter your first name and an initial ');
WriteString ('using 11 characters: ');  WriteLn;
FOR i := 0 TO StringSize-1 DO
  Read (FirstName[i]);  Write (FirstName[i])
END; (* FOR *)
WriteLn;

WriteString ('Hello ');
FOR i := 0 TO StringSize-1 DO
  Write (FirstName[i])
END; (* FOR *)
Write('!');  WriteLn;
```

A sample run of this program segment follows:

```
Enter your first name and an initial using 11 characters:
Jonathon B.
Hello Jonathon B.!
```

Eleven data characters are read into string variable `FirstName` after the prompt in the first line is displayed. The string variable `FirstName` (echoed on the last line) is shown next.

String `FirstName`

[0]	[1]	[2]	[3]	[4]	[5]	[6]	[7]	[8]	[9]	[10]
J	o	n	a	t	h	o	n		B	.

The statements

```
FirstName[8] := "'";
FirstName[9] := 's';
```

replace the contents of `FirstName[8]` (the blank character) and `FirstName[9]` (capital B) with the two characters shown above (an apostrophe and the letter s). Next, the `IF` statement

```
IF FirstName[i] = "'" THEN
  WriteString ('possessive form')
END
```

displays the message `'possessive form'` when the value of `i` is `8`.

Compatibility of Strings of Length One and Type CHAR

`OneString` declared below is a string variable of length one.

```
VAR
  OneString : ARRAY [0..0] OF CHAR;
  NextCh : CHAR;
```

On all Modula-2 systems, the assignment statements

```
OneString[0] := NextCh;
NextCh := OneString[0];
```

are valid and store a copy of `NextCh` in string `OneString`.

On some Modula-2 systems, the assignment statements

```
OneString := NextCh;
NextCh := OneString;
```

are invalid and cause a `type compatibility` syntax error. However, in revised versions of Modula-2 they are valid, because the data type `CHAR` is considered compatible with strings of length one. If this is the case on your system, it is possible to assign a type `CHAR` variable to a string of length one or to pass a type `CHAR` variable or value to a procedure expecting a string parameter.

Assigning and Displaying a String

Besides manipulating individual characters in a string variable, we can manipulate the string as a unit. The assignment statement

```
LastName := 'Appleseed';        (* assign a string to LastName *)
```

stores the string value `'Appleseed'` in the string variable `LastName` declared earlier (subscript range `0..10`). The string variable `LastName` is defined as shown below.

String `LastName`

[0]	[1]	[2]	[3]	[4]	[5]	[6]	[7]	[8]	[9]	[10]
A	p	p	l	e	s	e	e	d	@	?

Since `'Appleseed'` contains only nine characters, Modula-2 stores the null character (denoted by @ in the preceding diagram) after the last character (`'d'`). The ? in the diagram indicates that `LastName[10]` is undefined.

The statements

```
WriteString (LastName);
WriteString (', ');
WriteString (FirstName);
WriteLn
```

display the output line

```
Appleseed, Jonathon B.
```

As shown above, all characters through the null character stored in string variable `LastName` are displayed. Because the null character does not occupy a print position when it is displayed, the string `', '` follows the last character (d) in `LastName` that precedes the null character.

Any string of up to eleven characters may be assigned to `LastName`. A string shorter than eleven characters is always terminated with a null character before it is stored. Attempting to store a string longer than eleven characters will cause a `type incompatibility` syntax error.

As with other array types, we can copy the contents of one string variable to another of the same type. The statement

```
FirstName := LastName         (* copy LastName to FirstName *)
```

copies the string value stored in `LastName` to `FirstName`.

Reading Strings

Modula-2 provides a utility procedure `ReadString` (in module `InOut`) for entering a string value. The statement

```
ReadString (FirstName);
```

reads up to eleven characters into the string variable `FirstName`. The data-entry operation is terminated by pressing the RETURN key or the space bar after entering a nonblank character. It is not possible to read more than eleven characters into `FirstName`. If fewer than eleven characters are entered, the string is terminated with a null character before it is stored.

EXAMPLE 8.15 ▶ The statements

```
WriteString ('Enter your first name: ');
ReadString (FirstName);  WriteLn;
```

```
WriteString ('Enter your last name: ');
ReadString (LastName);  WriteLn;
```

can be used to enter string values into the string variables `FirstName` and `LastName`. Up to eleven characters can be stored in each `FirstName` and `LastName`. If the data characters `Jonathon` are entered after the first prompt and the data characters `Appleseed` are entered after the second prompt, the strings are defined as follows, with the symbol @ denoting the null character.

String `FirstName`

[0]	[1]	[2]	[3]	[4]	[5]	[6]	[7]	[8]	[9]	[10]
J	o	n	a	t	h	o	n	@	?	?

String `LastName`

[0]	[1]	[2]	[3]	[4]	[5]	[6]	[7]	[8]	[9]	[10]
A	p	p	l	e	s	e	e	d	@	?

The statements

```
WriteString(FirstName);  Write(' ');
WriteString(LastName);   Write ('.')
```

display the strings stored in `Firstname` and `LastName` with exactly one space between them. For the strings defined above, the line

```
Jonathon Appleseed.
```

will be displayed. Only the characters through the null character that are stored in `FirstName` and `LastName` are actually displayed.

Procedure ReadString ▶

FORM: `ReadString (`*string*`)`

EXAMPLE: `ReadString (FirstName)`

INTERPRETATION: If variable *string* has type `ARRAY [0..n-1] OF CHAR`, the `ReadString` procedure can be used to read up to `n` data characters into *string*. Any leading blanks are ignored. Once begun, data entry is terminated when the space bar or RETURN key is pressed. The BACKSPACE key can be used to edit the string being entered before data entry is terminated. Procedure `ReadString` is part of utility module `InOut`.

Note: Because data entry is terminated when the space bar is pressed, embedded blanks cannot appear in the data string. Since `ReadString` is part of a utility module, its operation may not be the same on all Modula-2 systems.

SELF-CHECK EXERCISES FOR SECTION 8.8

1. Write a function that returns the length of the string value stored in its string argument. The length of a string is always less than or equal to the declared length of the string variable in which it is stored. If the string length is less than the declared length, the string length is the number of characters that precede the null character in the string variable.
2. Write a procedure that stores the reverse of its input string in its output string (e.g., if the input string is `'happy'`, the output string should be `'yppah'`). Use the function from exercise 1 to determine the input string length.
3. Write a program that uses the procedure from exercise 2 to determine if a string is a palindrome. A palindrome is a string that reads the same left to right as it does right to left. (e.g., `'LEVEL'` is a palindrome.)

8.9 Case Study: Printing a Form Letter

Problem: We would like a program that can help in writing job application letters. Each letter will be sent to an output file for final editing and printing.

Discussion: Each letter consists of a heading, salutation, body, and closing. The heading, salutation, and first line of the body will be different for each letter, but the body and closing will be the same. We will need two procedures: `Preamble` and `WriteBody` to handle the two parts of the letter. `Preamble` enters the data for the first part of the letter, which is individualized, and writes it to an output file; `WriteBody` copies the rest of the letter from an input file to an output file. The structure chart is shown in Fig. 8.23; the main program body is shown in Fig. 8.24.

Figure 8.23 ▸ *Structure Chart for Form-Letter Program*

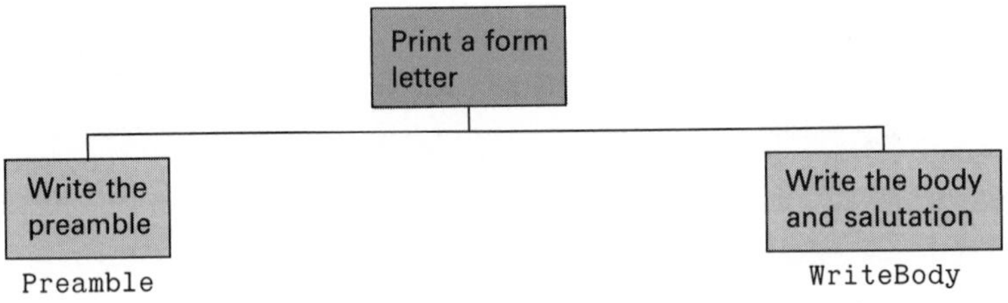

Figure 8.24 ▸ *Form-Letter Program*

```
MODULE FormLetter;
(*
   Writes a job application letter to an output file. The data
   for the letter preamble is read from the keyboard; the letter
   body is copied from a data file to the output file.
*)
```

```
  FROM InOut IMPORT
    Done,                                              (* variable *)
    WriteString, Write, WriteLn,                       (* procedures *)
    OpenInput, OpenOutput, CloseInput, CloseOutput;

  FROM SimpleIO IMPORT
    MyReadString;

  PROCEDURE Preamble;
  (*
     Writes a preamble for a job application letter to an output
     file.
     Pre : None
     Post: Writes the heading, salutation, and first sentence of a
           job application letter. Also opens the input file where
           the body of the letter is stored and opens the output
           file.
  *)
  BEGIN (* Preamble stub *)
    WriteString ('Procedure Preamble entered');  WriteLn
  END Preamble;

  PROCEDURE WriteBody;
  (*
     Copies the body of a job application letter from a data file
     to an output file.
     Pre : The input file and output file are opened.
     Post: Writes the letter body to the output file.
  *)
  BEGIN (* WriteBody stub *)
    WriteString ('    ... body of letter goes here ...');  WriteLn
  END WriteBody;

BEGIN (* FormLetter *)
  WriteString ('Writing job application letter.');  WriteLn;
  Preamble;
  WriteBody;
  CloseInput;
  CloseOutput;
  WriteString ('Letter copied to output file.');  WriteLn
END FormLetter.
```

Procedure `Preamble` (see Fig. 8.25) reads the strings needed for the letter heading and salutation. The data-entry process is shown in the sample run of program `FormLetter` found in Fig. 8.26. After data entry, the strings read into `DateString`, `Employer`, `Company`, `Address`, `CityStZip` are written to the output file in the form shown in Fig. 8.27.

Figure 8.25 ▶ *Procedure Preamble*

```
PROCEDURE Preamble;
(*
   Writes a preamble for a job application letter to an output file.
   Pre : None
   Post: Writes the heading, salutation, and first sentence of a
         job application letter. Also opens the input file where the
         body of the letter is stored and opens the output file.
   Uses: Done, Write, WriteString, WriteLn from InOut and
         MyReadString from SimpleIO
*)
   CONST
     StringSize = 40;
     Pad = '

   TYPE
     StringType = ARRAY [0..StringSize-1] OF CHAR;

   VAR
     DateString : StringType;
     Employer, Company  : ARRAY [0..StringSize-1] OF CHAR;
     Address, CityStZip : ARRAY [0..StringSize-1] OF CHAR;

BEGIN  (* Preamble *)
  (* Enter all data *)
  WriteString ("Today's date          -> ");
  MyReadString (DateString);                     WriteLn;
  WriteString ('Employer name         -> ');
  MyReadString (Employer);                       WriteLn;
  WriteString ('Company name          -> ');
  MyReadString (Company);                        WriteLn;
  WriteString ('Address               -> ');
  MyReadString (Address);                        WriteLn;
  WriteString ('City, state, and zip -> ');
  MyReadString (CityStZip);   WriteLn;           WriteLn;

  (* Open input file *)
  WriteString ('Letter body is in file: ');
  OpenInput ('TXT');
  IF NOT Done THEN
    WriteString ('Error in opening input file');  WriteLn;
    RETURN
  END; (* IF *)

  (* Open output file *)
  WriteString ('Enter output file name: ');
  OpenOutput ('TXT');
  IF NOT Done THEN
    WriteString ('Error in opening output file');  WriteLn;
    RETURN
  END; (* IF *)
```

```
    (* Start letter preamble. *)
    WriteString (Pad);  WriteString (DateString);  WriteLn;  WriteLn;
    WriteString (Employer);   WriteLn;
    WriteString (Company);    WriteLn;
    WriteString (CityStZip);  WriteLn;  WriteLn;
    WriteString ('Dear ');    WriteString (Employer);   Write (';');
    WriteLn;  WriteLn;
    WriteString('     I am interested in applying for a job at ');
    WriteString (Company);    Write ('.');  WriteLn;  WriteLn
  END Preamble;
```

Figure 8.26 ▸ *Interaction at Terminal during Sample Run of Form-Letter Program*

```
Writing job application letter.
Today's date          -> July 27, 1989
Employer name         -> Peter Liacouras
Company name          -> Temple University
Address               -> Broad and Montgomery Streets
City, state, and zip -> Philadelphia, PA  19122

Letter body is in file: MyLetter.TXT
Enter output file name: Temple.TXT
Letter copied to output file.
```

Figure 8.27 ▸ *Sample Output File for Form-Letter Program*

```
                                                July 27, 1989

Peter Liacouras
Temple University
Broad and Montgomery Streets
Philadelphia, PA  19122

Dear Peter Liacouras;

     I am interested in applying for a job at Temple University.

    ... body of letter goes here ...
```

Procedure `Preamble` uses `MyReadString` (imported from `SimpleIO`) to enter each data string instead of using `ReadString`. The reason for not using `ReadString` is that data strings read by it cannot contain embedded blanks. (Procedure `MyReadString` is discussed in the next subsection.)

Procedure `WriteBody` copies the rest of the letter (not shown) from the input file to the output file. Procedure `WriteBody` is shown in Fig. 8.28. The `REPEAT–UNTIL` loop copies each line of the data file to the output file. It is not necessary to call `WriteString` to copy each string read to the output file, because procedure `MyReadString` (like `ReadString`) automatically echo-prints its data string to the output file.

Figure 8.28 ▸ *Procedure WriteBody*

```
PROCEDURE WriteBody;
(*
   Copies the body of a job application letter from a data file
   to an output file.
   Pre : The input file and output file are opened.
   Post: Writes the letter body to the output file.
   Uses: Done, WriteLn from InOut and MyReadString from SimpleIO.
*)
   CONST
     LineSize = 80;

   VAR
     OneLine : ARRAY [0..LineSize-1] OF CHAR; (* next data line *)
     MoreLines : BOOLEAN;                     (* program flag *)

BEGIN (* WriteBody *)
  (* Copy each line until done *)
  REPEAT
    MyReadString (OneLine);
    WriteLn;
    MoreLines := Done
  UNTIL NOT MoreLines
END WriteBody;
```

String Input/Output Procedures in Module SimpleIO

As you saw in the last section, it would be convenient to include a procedure that can read strings with embedded blanks in module `SimpleIO`. Procedure `MyReadString` is shown in Fig. 8.29.

Figure 8.29 ▸ *Procedure MyReadString*

```
PROCEDURE MyReadString (VAR InString (* output *) : ARRAY OF CHAR);
(*
   Reads a string of characters that may contain an
   embedded blank into InString. Data entry is terminated
   when <Return> is pressed.
   Pre : None
   Post: The data string read from the input file is stored in
         InString and echo printed on the output file.
   Uses: EOL, Read, Write from InOut
*)
```

```
  CONST
    Null = 0C;              (* the null character *)

  VAR
    NextCh : CHAR;          (* each data character *)
    Next   : CARDINAL;      (* next array element *)

BEGIN (* MyReadString *)
  Next := 0;                  (* start with first element *)
  Read (NextCh);
  WHILE
    (* invariant:
         no prior character read was EOL and
         Next <= HIGH(InString) + 1
    *)
      (NextCh # EOL) AND (Next <= HIGH(InString)) DO
    Write (NextCh);
    InString[Next] := NextCh;     (* store data character *)
    INC (Next);                 (* advance to next element *)
    Read (NextCh)
  END; (* WHILE *)
  (* assert:
       the last character read was EOL or
       Next > HIGH(InString)
  *)

  (* Terminate a short string with the null character. *)
  IF Next <= HIGH(InString) THEN
    InString[Next] := Null
  END (* IF *)
END MyReadString;
```

Each data character is read into `NextCh` and echoed. Within the `WHILE` loop, the statement

```
InString[Next] := NextCh;    (* store data character *)
```

stores each data character into the string variable being formed, starting with position `0` in the string variable. The loop is exited after the RETURN key is pressed (`NextCh` contains `EOL`) or the string variable is filled. After loop exit, the `IF` statement stores the null character (`0C`) following the last character in a string variable that is not filled.

The character constant `EOL` represents the end-of-line character and should be imported into `SimpleIO` from module `InOut`. If the RETURN key is pressed when `Read(NextCh)` is executed, the contents of `NextCh` becomes `EOL`.

EXAMPLE 8.16 ▶ There is a problem with displaying strings. Procedure `WriteString` displays all characters stored in a string through the null character. Because the null character can appear anywhere in the string, not all strings of the same type will require the same number of print positions. Consequently, if an output table begins with a string value, the table columns may not be aligned because the strings at the beginning of each line may have different widths. Procedure `WriteStringFormat` (Fig. 8.30) pads each output string (its first parameter) with blanks so that the total number of characters displayed matches its second parameter. ◂

Figure 8.30 ▸ *Procedure WriteStringFormat*

```
PROCEDURE WriteStringFormat (OutString (* input *) : ARRAY OF CHAR;
                             Width (* input *) : CARDINAL);
(*
   Displays string OutString in Width columns.
   Pre : OutString and Width are assigned values.
   Post: OutString is displayed. If the number of characters in
         OutString is greater than Width, then the entire string
         will be displayed. If the number of characters in
         OutString (up to the null character) is less than Width,
         then blanks will be displayed after OutString until
         Width columns are filled.
   Uses: Write, WriteString from InOut; Length from Strings
*)

   CONST
     Blank = ' ';

   VAR
     I,                         (* loop-control variable *)
     StringLength : CARDINAL;   (* the actual length of OutString *)

BEGIN (* WriteStringFormat *)
  WriteString (OutString);
  StringLength := Length(OutString);

  (* Pad a short string with blanks at the right end *)
  FOR I := StringLength+1 TO Width DO
    Write (Blank)
  END (* FOR *)
END WriteStringFormat;
```

Module Strings

Most Modula-2 systems have a module called `Strings`, which consists of a variety of string-manipulation operators. Procedure `WriteStringFormat` uses function `Length` defined in module `Strings` to determine the actual length of a string (i.e., the number of characters preceding the null character). We will discuss function `Length` and module `Strings` in Chapter 11.

SELF-CHECK EXERCISES FOR SECTION 8.9

1. Rewrite the import statements in the implementation module for `SimpleIO` to enable inclusion of procedures `WriteStringFormat` and `MyReadString`. Discuss changes required in the definition module.
2. Write procedure `RightStringJustify` that displays a string with leading blanks instead of trailing blanks.

8.10 Common Programming Errors

The most common error in using arrays is a subscript-range error. This occurs when the subscript value is outside the subrange specified for that array type. Subscript-range errors are not syntax errors; they will not be detected until program execution begins. They are most often caused by an incorrect subscript expression, a loop-parameter error, or a nonterminating loop. Before you spend considerable time debugging, carefully check all suspicious subscript calculations for out-of-range errors. You can do this most easily by inserting diagnostic output statements in your program to print subscript values that might be out of range.

If an out-of-range subscript occurs inside a loop, make sure the loop is terminating properly. If the loop-control variable is not being updated as expected, the loop may be repeated more often than required. This could happen, for example, if the update step came after the loop `END` statement.

Double-check the subscript values at the loop boundaries as well. If these values are in range, it is likely that all other subscript references in the loop also will be in range.

As with all Modula-2 data types, make sure that there are no type inconsistencies. The subscript type and element type used in all array references must correspond to the types specified in the array declaration. Similarly, the types of two arrays used in an array copy statement or as corresponding parameters must be assignment compatible. Remember to use only identifiers without subscripts as formal array parameters and to specify the types of all formal array parameters using identifiers.

A string variable of length n can be assigned a string value consisting of n characters or less. An `incompatible type` syntax error is detected if a string value that is too long is assigned to a string variable. If one string variable is assigned to another, they must both be the same length.

8.11 Chapter Review

This chapter introduced a data structure called an array, which is a convenient facility for naming and referencing a collection of like items. We discussed how to declare an array type and how to reference an individual array element by placing a subscript in brackets, following the array name.

The `FOR` statement enables us to easily reference the elements of an array in sequence. We used `FOR` statements to initialize, read and print arrays, and control the manipulation of individual array elements.

We introduced the open array as a technique for relaxing the type-checking performed by Modula-2 on array parameters. An open-array parameter may correspond to any actual array that has the same element type; the index type of the actual array is immaterial. Within the procedure body, the elements of open-array `S` have subscripts `0..HIGH(S)`, where `HIGH` is a standard function.

Finally, we introduced string variables, or arrays of characters, and showed how to read, display, and assign strings. A string of up to *n* characters can be stored in a string variable of length `n` (type `ARRAY [0..n-1] OF CHAR`).

New Modula-2 Statements

The new Modula-2 statements introduced in this chapter are described in Table 8.5.

Table 8.5 ► *Summary of New Modula-2 Statements*

STATEMENT	EFFECT

Array Declaration
`TYPE`
`  IntArray = ARRAY [1..10] OF INTEGER;`
 	
`VAR`
`  Cube, Count : IntArray`
	The data type `IntArray` describes an array with ten type `INTEGER` elements. `Cube` and `Count` are arrays with this structure.

Array References
`FOR I := 1 TO 10 DO`
`  Cube[I] := I * I * I`
`END`
	Saves I^3 in the `I`th element of array `Cube`.

`IF Cube[5] > 100 THEN`	Compares `Cube[5]` to `100`.
`WriteInt (Cube[1], 5);` `WriteInt (Cube[2], 5)`	Displays the first two cubes.
Array Copy `Count := Cube`	Copies contents of array `Cube` to array `Count`.

String Declaration	
`VAR Name : ARRAY [0..10] OF CHAR;`	Declares a string variable (`Name`) of length `11`.
String Assignment	
`Name := 'Daffy Duck'`	Saves `'Daffy Duck'` in array `Name`. The null character is stored in `Name[10]`.
String Input/Output	
`ReadString (Name);` `WriteString (Name)`	A data string of up to eleven characters is read into `Name` and displayed.

CHAPTER 8 ▸

Review Questions

1. (a) Identify the error in the Modula-2 program below.

```
MODULE TestArray;

  TYPE
    ArrayType = ARRAY [1..8] OF INTEGER;

  VAR
    X : ArrayType;
    I : INTEGER;

BEGIN
  FOR I := 1 TO 9 DO
    X[I] := I
  END (* FOR *)
END TestArray.
```

   (b) When will the error be detected?
2. Declare an array of real numbers called `Week` that can be referenced by using any day of the week as a subscript, where `Sunday` is the first subscript.
3. Identify the error in the following Modula-2 program.

```
MODULE ArrayTest;

  TYPE
    ArrayType = ARRAY CHAR OF REAL;

  VAR
    X : ArrayType;
    I : INTEGER;

BEGIN
  I := 1;
  X[I] := 8.384
END ArrayTest.
```

4. The statement (*a*) in the following Modula-2 program is a valid Modula-2 statement. True or false?

```
MODULE ArrayTest;

  TYPE
    RealArray = ARRAY [1..8] OF REAL;

  VAR
    X : RealArray;
    I : INTEGER;

BEGIN
  I := 1;
  X[I] := 8.384    (*a*)
END ArrayTest.
```

5. What are the two common ways of selecting array elements for processing?
6. Write a Modula-2 program segment to print out the index of the smallest and largest numbers in an array `X` of 20 integers with values from 0 to 100. Assume array `X` already has values assigned to each element.
7. The parameters for a procedure are two arrays (type `RealArray`) and an integer representing the length of the arrays. The procedure copies the first array in the parameter list to the other array in reverse order using a loop structure. Write the procedure.
8. Declare an array that can be used to store each title of the Top 40 hits, given that the `TitleLength` will be twenty characters.
9. What would be a valid reason for not passing an array as a value parameter to a procedure?
10. Write the declaration of the array `Hours` to store the hours an employee works each day of the week.

CHAPTER 8 ▸

Programming Projects

1. Write a program to read `N` data items into two arrays `X` and `Y` of size `20`. Store the product of corresponding elements of `X` and `Y` in a third array, `Z`, also of size `20`. Print a three-column table displaying the arrays `X`, `Y`, and `Z`. Then compute and print the square root of the sum of the items in `Z`. Make up your own data, with `N` less than 20.

2. Assume for the moment that your computer has the very limited capability of being able to read and print only single decimal digits at a time and to add together two integers consisting of only one decimal digit each. Write a program to read in two integers of up to ten digits each, add these numbers together, and print the result. Test your program on the following numbers.

```
X =  1487625
Y =    12783
```

```
X = 60705202
Y = 30760832

X = 1234567890
Y = 9876543210
```

Hints: Store the numbers X and Y in two string arrays X, Y of size 10, one decimal digit per element. If the number is less than 10 digits in length, enter enough leading zeros (to the left of the number) to make the number 10 digits long.

array X

[1]	[2]	[3]	[4]	[5]	[6]	[7]	[8]	[9]	[10]
0	0	0	1	4	8	7	6	2	5

array Y

[1]	[2]	[3]	[4]	[5]	[6]	[7]	[8]	[9]	[10]
0	0	0	0	0	1	2	7	8	3

You will need a loop to add together the digits in corresponding array elements, starting with the element with subscript 10. Don't forget to handle the carry, if there is one. Use a BOOLEAN variable Carry to indicate whether the sum of the last pair of digits is greater than 9.

3. Write a program for the following problem. You are given a collection of scores for the last exam in your computer course. You are to compute the average of these scores and then assign grades to each student according to the following rule.

   If a student's score is within ten points (above or below) of the average, assign the student a grade of Satisfactory. If the score is more than ten points higher than the average, assign the student a grade of Outstanding. If the score is more than ten points below the average, assign the student a grade of Unsatisfactory.

   Hint: The output from your program should consist of a labeled three-column list containing the name, exam score, and grade of each student.

4. It can be shown that a number is prime if there is no smaller prime number that divides it. Consequently, to determine if N is prime, it is sufficient to check only the prime numbers less than N as possible divisors. Use this information to write a program that stores the first 100 prime numbers in an array. Have your program print the array after it is done.

5. The results of a true-false exam given to a Computer Science class have been coded for input to a program. The information available for each student consists of a student identification number and the student's answers to 10 true-false questions. The available data are as follows:

Student identification	*Answer string*
0080	FTTFTFTTFT
0340	FTFTFTTTFF
0341	FTTFTTTTTT
0401	TTFFTFFTTT
0462	TTFTTTFFTF
0463	TTTTTTTTTT
0464	FTFFTFFTFT
0512	TFTFTFTFTF
0618	TTTFFTTFTF
0619	FFFFFFFFFF
0687	TFTTFTTFTF
0700	FTFFTTFFFT
0712	FTFTFTFTFT
0837	TFTFTTFTFT

Write a program that first reads in the answer string representing the ten correct answers (use `FTFFTFFTFT` as data). Next, for each student, read the student's data, compute and store the number of correct answers for each student in one array, and store the student ID number in the corresponding element of another array. Determine the best score, `Best`. Then print a three-column table displaying the ID number, the score, and the grade for each student. The grade should be determined as follows: If the score is equal to `Best` or `Best-1`, give an A; if it is `Best-2` or `Best- 3`, give a C. Otherwise, give an F.

6. The results of a survey of the households in your town have been made available. Each record contains data for one household, including a four-digit integer identification number, the annual income for the household, and the number of members of the household. Write a program to read the survey results into three arrays and perform the following analyses:
   a. Count the number of households included in the survey and print a three-column table displaying the data read in. (You may assume that no more than twenty-five households were surveyed.)
   b. Calculate the average household income and list the identification number and income of each household that exceeds the average.
   c. Determine the percentage of households having incomes below the poverty level. Compute the poverty-level income using the formula

$$p = \$6500.00 + \$750.00 * (m - 2)$$

where m is the number of members of each household. This formula shows that the poverty level depends on the number of family members, m, and that the poverty level increases as m gets larger.

Test your program on the following data.

Identification number	*Annual income*	*Household members*
1041	$12,180	4
1062	13,240	3
1327	19,800	2
1483	22,458	8
1900	17,000	2
2112	18,125	7
2345	15,623	2
3210	3,200	6
3600	6,500	5
3601	11,970	2
4725	8,900	3
6217	10,000	2
9280	6,200	1

7. Assume a set of sentences is to be processed. Each sentence consists of a sequence of words, separated by one or more blank spaces. Write a program that will read these sentences and count the number of words with one letter, two letters, and so on, up to ten letters.

8. Write an interactive program that plays the game of Hangman. Read the word to be guessed, string `Word`. The player must guess the letters belonging to `Word`. The program should terminate when either all letters have been guessed correctly (player wins) or a specified number of incorrect guesses have been made (computer wins). Hint: Use a string `Solution` to keep track of the solution so far. Initialize `Solution` to a string of symbols `*`. Each time a letter in `Word` is guessed, replace the corresponding `*` in `Solution` with that letter.

9 ▸ Records

THE PREVIOUS CHAPTER introduced the array, a data structure fundamental to programming and included in almost every high-level programming language. This chapter will introduce an additional data structure, the record, which is available in most modern high-level languages. The use of records can make it easier to organize and represent information in Modula-2.

Like an array, a record is a collection of related data items. Unlike an array, however, the individual components of a record can contain data of different types. We can use a record to store a variety of information about a person, such as his or her name, marital status, age, date of birth, and so on. Each data item is stored in a separate record field; we can reference each data item stored in a record through its field name.

This chapter will also introduce an abstract data type for complex arithmetic. This abstract data type will consist of a record type and associated operators.

9.1 The Record Data Type

A *data base* is a collection of information or facts stored in a computer memory or a disk file. A data base is subdivided into records; a *record* normally contains all the information we want to save regarding a particular data object. For example, the description of a person, place, or thing would be stored as a record.

Record Type Declaration

Before a record can be created or saved, the record format must be specified through a record type declaration.

EXAMPLE 9.1 ▶ We want to store the following descriptive information as a record in a data base of employees. ◀

```
ID  : 1234
Name: Caryn Jackson
Sex : FEMALE
Number of Dependents: 3
Hourly Rate: 3.98
Taxable Salary (for 40 hour week): 130.40
```

We can declare a record type `Employee` to store this information. There must be at least six *fields* in the record type. We must specify the name of each field and the type of information stored in each field. The names will be chosen in the same way as all other identifiers in this book: they should describe the nature of the information represented. The contents of each field are used to determine the appropriate data type. For example, the employee's name should be stored in a string field.

The record type `Employee` declared below has six distinct fields. One is a string, two are type `REAL`, one is type `CARDINAL`, one is a subrange type, and one (`Sex`) is an enumeration type. As shown, the data type of a field can be declared within the record type, for example, the enumeration type (`Female, Male`).

```
TYPE
  IDRange = [1111..9999];
  String20 = ARRAY [0..19] OF CHAR;

  Employee = RECORD
               ID : IDRange;
               Name : String20;
               Sex : (Female, Male);
               NumDepend : CARDINAL;
               Rate, TaxSal : REAL
             END; (* Employee *)
```

The record type declaration is a template that describes the format of each record and the name of each individual data element. A record variable declaration is required to allocate storage space for a record. The record variable `Clerk` is declared next.

```
VAR
  Clerk : Employee;
```

The record variable `Clerk` is structured as defined in the declaration for record type `Employee`. Thus, the memory allocated for `Clerk` consists of storage space for six distinct values. The record variable `Clerk` is pictured as follows, assuming the values shown earlier are stored in memory.

Record variable Clerk

ID	1234
Name	Caryn Jackson@??????
Sex	Female
NumDepend	2
Rate	3.98
TaxSal	130.40

As illustrated in the type declaration for `Employee`, each field of a record can be a standard data type or a user-defined simple or structured data type. The record-type declaration is described in the next display.

Record Type Declaration ▶

FORM:

```
TYPE
  rec type = RECORD
               id list1 : type1 ;
               id list2 : type2;
                  .
                  .
                  .
               id listn : typen
             END;
```

EXAMPLE:

```
TYPE
  Complex = RECORD
              RealPart, ImaginaryPart : REAL
            END;
```

INTERPRETATION: The identifier *rec type* is the name of the record structure being described. Each *id list*$_i$ is a list of one or more field names separated by commas; the data type of each field in *id list*$_i$ is specified by *type*$_i$.

Note: *type*$_i$ can be any standard or user-defined data type, including a structured type. If *type*$_i$ is a user-defined data type, it can be defined either before the record or as part of the record description.

Manipulating Individual Fields of a Record

We can reference a record field by using a *field selector* that consists of the record variable name followed by the field name. A period separates the field name and the record name.

EXAMPLE 9.2 ▶ Fig. 9.1 gives an example of the record variable `Clerk`. The data shown earlier could be stored in `Clerk` through the sequence of assignment statements ◀

Figure 9.1 ▶ *Record Variable Clerk*

```
Clerk.ID := 1234;
Clerk.Name := 'Caryn Jackson';
Clerk.Sex := Female;
Clerk.NumDepend := 2;
Clerk.Rate := 3.98
Clerk.TaxSal := Clerk.Rate * 40.0 - FLOAT(Clerk.NumDepend) * 14.40
```

Once data are stored in a record, they can be manipulated in the same way as other data in memory. For example, the preceding assignment statement computes the clerk's taxable salary by deducting $14.40 for each dependent from the gross salary (`Clerk.Rate * 40.0`). The computed result is saved in the record field named `Clerk.TaxSal`.

The statements

```
WriteString ('The clerk is ');
CASE Clerk.Sex OF
  Female : WriteString ('Ms. ')
| Male   : WriteString ('Mr. ')
END; (* CASE *)
WriteString (Clerk.Name)
```

display the clerk's name after an appropriate title (`'Ms. '` or `'Mr. '`). For the preceding data above, the output would be

```
The clerk is Ms. Caryn Jackson
```

Abstract Record

The following specification for an abstract record summarizes our discussion of records.

Specification for Abstract Record ▶

STRUCTURE: A record is a collection of related data values of different types. Each data value is stored in a separate field of the record.

OPERATORS: There are two basic operations that act on fields of a record: store and retrieve. The store operation inserts a value into the record field. If `A` is a record with a field named `B`, and `C` is an expression that is assignment compatible with the type of field `B`, the statement

```
A.B := C
```

stores the contents of `C` in field `B` of record `A`. If `C` is a variable that is assignment compatible with the type of field `B`, the statement

```
C := A.B
```

retrieves the value in field `B` of record `A` and copies it into `C`.

The assignment operator can also be used to copy the contents of one record to another of the same type. If `A` and `D` are *assignment compatible records* (i.e., their types are the same or are renamings of the same type), the statement

```
A := D
```

copies all values associated with record `D` to record `A`.

SELF-CHECK EXERCISES FOR SECTION 9.1

1. Each part in an inventory is represented by its part number, a three-letter code, the quantity on hand, and the price. Declare a record type `Part`.
2. A catalog listing for a book consists of the author's name, title, publisher, and year of publication. Declare a record type `CatalogEntry` and variable `Book` and store the relevant data for this textbook in `Book`.

9.2 The WITH Statement

It becomes tedious to write the complete field selector each time you reference a field of a record. You can use the `WITH` statement to shorten the field selector.

```
WITH Clerk DO
  WriteString ('The clerk is ');
  CASE Sex OF
    Female : WriteString ('Ms. ')
  | Male   : WriteString ('Mr. ')
  END; (* CASE *)
  WriteString (Name);  WriteLn;

  TaxSal := Rate * 40.0 - FLOAT(NumDepend) * 14.40;
  WriteString ("The clerk's taxable salary is $ ");
  WriteReal (TaxSal, 12);  WriteLn
END (* WITH *)
```

As shown, it is not necessary to specify both the record variable and the field names inside a `WITH` statement. The record variable `Clerk` is identified in the `WITH` statement header; consequently, only the field name is needed, not the complete field selector (e.g., `Rate` instead of `Clerk.Rate`). The `WITH` statement is particularly useful when several fields of the same record variable are being manipulated.

WITH Statement ▶

FORM: `WITH` *record var* `DO`
  statement sequence
`END`

EXAMPLE:

```
WITH Clerk DO
  Rate := 1.5 * Rate
END
```

INTERPRETATION: *Record var* is the name of a record variable. Within the *statement sequence,* any field of *record var* can be referenced by specifying only its field name.

EXAMPLE 9.3 ▶ The program in Fig. 9.2 computes the distance from an arbitrary point on the *x-y* plane to the origin (intersection of the *x*-axis and the *y*-axis). The values of the *x* and *y* coordinates are entered as data and stored in the fields `X` and `Y` of the record variable `Point1`. The formula used to compute the distance, `d`, from the origin to an arbitrary point (*X*, *Y*) is

$$d = \sqrt{X^2 + Y^2}$$

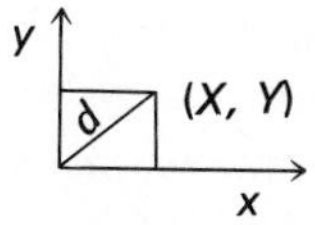

Since the record variable `Point1` is specified in the `WITH` statement header, only the field names `X` and `Y` are needed to reference the coordinates of the data point. Each coordinate is read separately because there are no input procedures available that accept a record variable as a parameter.

Figure 9.2 ▸
Distance from Point to Origin

```
MODULE DistOrigin;

(* Finds the distance from a point to the origin. *)

  FROM InOut IMPORT
    WriteString, WriteLn;

  FROM RealInOut IMPORT
    ReadReal, WriteReal;

  FROM MathLib0 IMPORT
    sqrt;

  TYPE
    Point = RECORD
              X, Y : REAL
            END;  (* Point *)

  VAR
    Point1 : Point;              (* input - the data point *)
    Distance : REAL;             (* output - its distance to the
                                    origin *)

BEGIN (* DistOrigin *)
  WITH Point1 DO
    WriteString ('X> ');  ReadReal (X);  WriteLn;
    WriteString ('Y> ');  ReadReal (Y);  WriteLn;
    Distance := sqrt(X * X + Y * Y);
    WriteString ('Distance to origin is ');
    WriteReal (Distance, 12);
    WriteLn
  END (* WITH *)
END DistOrigin.

X> 3.00
Y> 4.00
Distance to origin is  5.0000E+000
```

Program Style

A Word of Caution about the WITH Statement

Although the `WITH` statement is helpful in shortening the length of program statements that manipulate record components, it can also reduce the clarity of these statements. For example, in Fig. 9.2 it is not obvious that the statement

```
Distance := sqrt(X * X + Y * Y);
```

is multiplying two record fields (`Point1.X` and `Point1.Y`) and not two variables.
The possibility of confusion and error increases when there are two record variables (say, `Point1` and `Point2`) being manipulated. In this case, if the field name `X` is referenced by itself, it is not apparent whether we mean `Point1.X` or `Point2.X`. Modula-2 uses the record variable specified in the closest `WITH` statement header.

SELF-CHECK EXERCISE FOR SECTION 9.2

1. Write the Modula-2 statements required to print the values stored in `Clerk` in the form shown at the beginning of Example 9.1.

9.3 Records as Operands and Parameters

Because arithmetic and logical operations can be performed only on individual memory cells, record variables cannot be used as the operands of arithmetic and relational operators. These operators must be used with individual fields of a record, as shown in the previous section.

Record Assignment

It is possible to copy all the fields of one record variable to another record variable using a record copy (assignment) statement. If `Clerk` and `Janitor` are assignment compatible records, the statement

```
Clerk := Janitor                (* copy Janitor to Clerk *)
```

copies each field of `Janitor` into the corresponding field of `Clerk`. Two records are *assignment compatible* if their types are identical or they are renamings of the same type.

Records as Parameters

A record can be passed as a parameter to a function or a procedure, provided the actual parameter is assignment compatible with its corresponding formal parameter. The use of records as parameters can shorten parameter lists considerably, because one parameter (the record variable) can be passed instead of several related parameters.

EXAMPLE 9.4 ▶ In a grading program, the vital statistics for an exam might consist of the average score, the highest and lowest scores, and the number of students taking the exam. In previous problems, these data would be stored in separate variables; however, it makes sense to group them together as a record.

```
TYPE
  ExamStats = RECORD
                Low, High : [0..100];
                Average, StandardDev : REAL
              END; (* ExamStats *)

VAR
  Exam : ExamStats;
```

A procedure that computes one of these results (e.g., `Average`) could be passed a single record field (e.g., `Exam.Average`). A procedure that manipulates more than one of these fields could be passed the entire record. An example would be procedure `PrintStat` shown in Fig. 9.3. ◂

Figure 9.3 ▸
Procedure PrintStat

```
PROCEDURE PrintStat (Exam (* input *) : ExamStats);
(*
   Prints the exam statistics.
   Pre : The fields of record variable Exam are assigned values.
   Post: Each field of Exam is displayed.
*)

BEGIN (* PrintStat *)
  WITH Exam DO
    WriteString ('High score: ');
    WriteCard (High, 3);          WriteLn;
    WriteString ('Low score: ');
    WriteCard (Low, 3);           WriteLn;
    WriteString ('Average: ');
    WriteReal (Average, 5);       WriteLn;
    WriteString ('Standard deviation: ');
    WriteReal (StandardDev, 5);   WriteLn
  END (* WITH *)
END PrintStat;
```

EXAMPLE 9.5 ▸ In a computer simulation, we want to keep track of the time of day as the simulated event or experiment progresses. Normally, the time of day is updated after a certain amount of time has elapsed. The record type `Time` is declared assuming a 24-hour clock.

```
TYPE
  Time = RECORD
           Hour : [0..23];
           Minute, Second : [0..59]
         END; (* Time *)
```

Procedure `ChangeTime` in Fig. 9.4 updates the time of day, `TimeOfDay` (type `Time`), after a time interval, `ElapsedTime`, which is expressed in seconds.

Each statement that uses the MOD operator updates a particular field of the record represented by TimeOfDay. The MOD operator ensures that each updated value is within the required range; the DIV operator converts multiples of 60 seconds to minutes and multiples of 60 minutes to hours. ◂

Figure 9.4 ▸ *Procedure ChangeTime*

```
PROCEDURE ChangeTime (ElapsedTime (* input *) : CARDINAL;
                      VAR TimeOfDay (* input/output *) : Time);
(*
   Updates the time of day, TimeOfDay, assuming a 24-hour clock and
   an elapsed time of ElapsedTime in seconds.
   Pre : ElapsedTime and record TimeOfDay are assigned values.
   Post: TimeOfDay is "incremented" by ElapsedTime.
*)
   VAR
     NewHour, NewMin, NewSec : CARDINAL;      (* temporary values *)

BEGIN (* ChangeTime *)
  WITH TimeOfDay DO
    NewSec := Second + ElapsedTime;              (* total seconds *)
    Second := NewSec MOD 60;                    (* seconds mod 60 *)
    NewMin := Minute + (NewSec DIV 60);          (* total minutes *)
    Minute := NewMin MOD 60;                    (* minutes mod 60 *)
    NewHour := Hour + (NewMin DIV 60);             (* total hours *)
    Hour := NewHour MOD 24                        (* hours mod 24 *)
  END (* WITH *)
END ChangeTime;
```

Reading a Record

Normally we use a procedure to read data into a record. Procedure ReadEmployee in Fig. 9.5 could be used to read data into the first five fields of a record variable of type Employee. Since we are passing a record variable to ReadEmployee, only one parameter is needed, not five. The procedure call statement

```
ReadEmployee (Clerk)
```

causes the data read to be stored in record variable Clerk.

Figure 9.5 ▸ *Procedure ReadEmployee*

```
PROCEDURE ReadEmployee (VAR OneClerk (* output *) : Employee);
(*
   Reads one employee record into OneClerk.
   Pre : None
   Post: Data are read into record OneClerk.
*)
   VAR
     SexChar : CHAR;                  (* letter indicating sex *)
```

```
BEGIN (* ReadEmployee *)
  WITH OneClerk DO
    WriteString ('ID: ');  ReadCard (ID);  WriteLn;
    WriteString ('Name: ');
    ReadString (Name);   WriteLn;
    WriteString ('Sex (F or M): ');  Read (SexChar);  WriteLn;
    CASE CAP(SexChar) OF
      'F' : Sex := Female
    | 'M' : Sex := Male
    ELSE
      WriteString ('Invalid character ');
      Write (SexChar);  WriteLn
    END; (* CASE *)

    WriteString ('Number of dependents: ');
    ReadCard (NumDepend);  WriteLn;
    WriteString ('Hourly rate: ');  ReadReal (Rate);  WriteLn
  END (* WITH *)
END ReadEmployee;
```

SELF-CHECK EXERCISE FOR SECTION 9.3

1. Write a procedure to read in the data for a record variable of type `CatalogEntry`. (See Exercise 2 at the end of Section 9.1.)

9.4 Abstract Data Types Revisited

Abstraction is a powerful programming tool. The use of abstraction enables us to focus on the operations that we want to perform without having to provide immediately the details of how each operation will be implemented.

Data abstraction is the technique of focusing on the data and the operations to be performed without being concerned about how the data are actually represented in memory. Modula-2 facilitates the practice of data abstraction by enabling us to package a data type and its operators as a separate module called an abstract data type (see Section 6.6). A client module can import the data type and its associated operators. Then the client module can declare and manipulate objects of this type and use these operators without knowing the details of the internal representation of the data type or the implementation of its operator modules. In this way, the use of the data and the operators (by the client module) is separated from the representation and implementation (by the abstract data type). As you will see in Chapter 13, it is possible to change the internal representation of the data type without having to modify or recompile any of its client modules.

CASE STUDY: ABSTRACT DATA TYPE FOR COMPLEX ARITHMETIC

This section explains how to specify and implement an abstract data type for complex arithmetic.

Problem: An engineering professor would like us to write a set of procedures that can be used to perform arithmetic on complex numbers. A complex number is a number with a real and an imaginary part. For example, the complex number $a + ib$ [also written as (a, b)] has a real part of a and an imaginary part of b, where the symbol i represents $\sqrt{-1}$. The professor would like us to provide a module for creating, defining, reading, and displaying a complex number. The module should also contain procedures for performing complex arithmetic (e.g., addition, subtraction, multiplication, and division of complex numbers). There should also be operators for extracting real and imaginary parts and finding the absolute value (magnitude) of the complex number.

Discussion: We will implement module `ComplexType` to represent the abstract data type for complex numbers with operators for each of the previously listed tasks. In Modula-2, the definition module for an abstract data type serves as its specification. The definition module for `ComplexType` is shown in Fig. 9.6. The descriptions of the data structure and its operators follow the export statement.

Figure 9.6 ▶ *Definition Module for ComplexType*

```
DEFINITION MODULE ComplexType;
(*
   Specification of the abstract data type for representing
   and manipulating complex numbers.
   Procedure CreateComplex should be called before a complex number
   is manipulated.
*)
   EXPORT QUALIFIED
     Complex,                                         (* type *)
     CreateComplex, SetComplex,                       (* procedures *)
     ReadComplex, WriteComplex,
     AddComplex, SubtractComplex,
     MultiplyComplex, DivideComplex,
     GetReal, GetImaginary, AbsComplex;               (* functions *)

(* Data type -
   A record of type Complex consists of a pair of REAL values
   such that the first number represents the real part of a complex
   number and the second number represents the imaginary part.
*)
```

```
   TYPE
     Complex = RECORD
                 RealPart, ImaginaryPart : REAL
               END; (* Complex *)

(* Operators *)

   PROCEDURE CreateComplex (VAR C (* output *) : Complex);
   (*
      Creates a complex number C and initializes it to (0.0, 0.0).
      Pre : None
      Post: C is initialized to (0.0, 0.0)
   *)

   PROCEDURE SetComplex (X, Y (* input *) : REAL;
                      VAR C (* output *) : Complex);
   (*
      Sets the real part of a complex number to X
      and the imaginary part to Y.
      Pre : C is initialized.
      Post: C is the complex number (X, Y).
   *)

   PROCEDURE ReadComplex (VAR C (* output *) : Complex);
   (*
      Reads a pair of values into complex number C.
      Pre : C is initialized.
      Post: The first real number read is the real part of C;
            the second real number read is the imaginary part of C.
   *)

   PROCEDURE WriteComplex (C (* input *) : Complex);
   (*
      Displays complex number C.
      Pre : C is assigned a value.
      Post: Prints the real and imaginary parts of C.
   *)

   PROCEDURE AddComplex (A, B  (* input *)  : Complex;
                      VAR C (* output *) : Complex);
   (*
      Complex number C is the sum of complex numbers A and B.
      Pre : A and B are assigned values and C is initialized.
      Post: C is the complex sum of A and B.
   *)

   PROCEDURE SubtractComplex (A, B  (* input *)  : Complex;
                           VAR C (* output *) : Complex);
   (*
      Complex number C is the difference of complex numbers A and B.
      Pre : A and B are assigned values and C is initialized.
      Post: C is the complex difference of A and B.
   *)
```

```
  PROCEDURE MultiplyComplex (A, B  (* input *)  : Complex;
                            VAR C (* output *) : Complex);
  (*
     Complex number C is the product of complex numbers A and B.
     Pre : A and B are assigned values and C is initialized.
     Post: C is the complex product of A and B.
  *)

  PROCEDURE DivideComplex (A, B  (* input *)  : Complex;
                          VAR C (* output *) : Complex);
  (*
     Complex number C is the quotient of complex numbers A and B.
     Pre : A and B are assigned values and C is initialized.
     Post: C is the complex quotient of A and B.
  *)

  PROCEDURE GetReal (A : Complex) : REAL;
  (*
     Returns the real part of complex number A.
     Pre : A is assigned a value.
     Post: The real part of A is returned.
  *)

  PROCEDURE GetImaginary (A : Complex) : REAL;
  (*
     Returns the imaginary part of complex number A.
     Pre : A is assigned a value.
     Post: The imaginary part of A is returned.
  *)

  PROCEDURE AbsComplex (A : Complex) : REAL;
  (*
     Returns the absolute value of complex number A.
     Pre : A is assigned a value.
     Post: The absolute value of A is returned.
  *)

END ComplexType.
```

The definition module for `ComplexType` shown in Fig. 9.6 contains all the information needed by a user of the abstract data type. The data type `Complex` and all its operator procedures are exported. Any of the names listed in the export statement may appear in an import statement found in a client module.

The data type `Complex` is fully declared in the definition module; however, only header statements are provided for the operators (procedures). This is enough information for a user of a procedure to know how to call it and for the Modula-2 compiler to process a call to the procedure in a client module.

The comments under the header statements provide additional documentation for any potential users of the module.

The first operator listed in Fig. 9.7 is `CreateComplex`. `CreateComplex` initializes each variable of type `Complex` to `(0.0, 0.0)`. Every abstract data type should have an operator like `CreateComplex` that is used to initialize each instance of the specified data type before it is manipulated. The remaining operators are self-explanatory and consist of procedures for defining the value of a complex number (`SetComplex` and `ReadComplex`), displaying a complex number (`WriteComplex`), performing complex arithmetic operations (`AddComplex`, etc.), extracting the real and imaginary parts (`GetReal`, `Get-Imaginary`), and finding the absolute value (`AbsComplex`).

The definition module can be compiled as soon as it is completed. Once the definition module is compiled, other programmers can write client modules that use the abstract data type `ComplexType`. These client modules can also be compiled. However, they cannot be linked or executed until the implementation module for `ComplexType`, containing the actual procedure declarations, is compiled. A partially completed implementation module is shown in Fig. 9.7. (See Section 6.2 for a review of definition and implementation modules.)

Figure 9.7 ▸ *Implementation Module for ComplexType*

```
IMPLEMENTATION MODULE ComplexType;
(*
   Implementation module for the abstract data type
   for representing and manipulating complex numbers.
*)

(* Type Complex is declared in the definition module *)

   FROM InOut IMPORT
     Write, WriteString, WriteLn;

   FROM RealInOut IMPORT
     WriteReal, ReadReal;

(* Operators *)

   PROCEDURE CreateComplex (VAR C (* output *) : Complex);
   (*
      Creates a complex number C and initializes it to (0.0, 0.0).
      Pre : None
      Post: C is initialized to (0.0, 0.0)
   *)
   BEGIN (* CreateComplex *)
     C.RealPart := 0.0;  C.ImaginaryPart := 0.0
   END CreateComplex;

   PROCEDURE SetComplex (X, Y (* input *) : REAL;
                         VAR C (* output *) : Complex);
```

```
(*
   Sets the real part of a complex number to X
   and the imaginary part to Y.
   Pre : C is initialized.
   Post: C is the complex number (X, Y).
*)
BEGIN (* SetComplex *)
  C.RealPart := X;  C.ImaginaryPart := Y
END SetComplex;

PROCEDURE ReadComplex (VAR C (* output *) : Complex);
(*
   Reads a pair of values into complex number C.
   Pre : C is initialized.
   Post: The first real number read is the real part of C;
         the second real number read is the imaginary part of C.
*)
BEGIN (* ReadComplex *)
  WriteString ('Real part: ');
  ReadReal (C.RealPart);  WriteLn;
  WriteString ('Imaginary part: ');
  ReadReal (C.ImaginaryPart);  WriteLn
END ReadComplex;

PROCEDURE WriteComplex (C (* input *) : Complex);
(*
   Displays complex number C.
   Pre : C is assigned a value.
   Post: Prints the real and imaginary parts of C.
*)
BEGIN (* WriteComplex *)
  Write ('(');  WriteReal (C.RealPart, 12);
  Write (',');  WriteReal (C.ImaginaryPart, 12);  Write (')')
END WriteComplex;

PROCEDURE AddComplex (A, B  (* input *)  : Complex;
                      VAR C (* output *) : Complex);
(*
   Complex number C is the sum of complex numbers A and B.
   Pre : A and B are assigned values and C is initialized.
   Post: C is the complex sum of A and B.
*)
BEGIN (* AddComplex *)
  C.RealPart := A.RealPart + B.RealPart;
  C.ImaginaryPart := A.ImaginaryPart + B.ImaginaryPart
END AddComplex;

PROCEDURE SubtractComplex (A, B  (* input *)  : Complex;
                           VAR C (* output *) : Complex);
(*
   Complex number C is the difference of complex numbers A and B.
   Pre : A and B are assigned values and C is initialized.
```

```
   Post: C is the complex difference of A and B.
*)
BEGIN (* SubtractComplex *)
  C.RealPart := A.RealPart - B.RealPart;
  C.ImaginaryPart := A.ImaginaryPart - B.ImaginaryPart
END SubtractComplex;

PROCEDURE MultiplyComplex (A, B  (* input *)  : Complex;
                           VAR C (* output *) : Complex);
(*
   Complex number C is the product of complex numbers A and B.
   Pre : A and B are assigned values and C is initialized.
   Post: C is the complex product of A and B.
*)
BEGIN (* MultiplyComplex stub *)
  WriteString ('Procedure MultiplyComplex called.');  WriteLn
END MultiplyComplex;

PROCEDURE DivideComplex (A, B  (* input *)  : Complex;
                         VAR C (* output *) : Complex);
(*
   Complex number C is the quotient of complex numbers A and B.
   Pre : A and B are assigned values and C is initialized.
   Post: C is the complex quotient of A and B.
*)
BEGIN (* DivideComplex stub *)
  WriteString ('Procedure DivideComplex called.');  WriteLn
END DivideComplex;

PROCEDURE GetReal (A : Complex) : REAL;
(*
   Returns the real part of complex number A.
   Pre : A is assigned a value.
   Post: The real part of A is returned.
*)
BEGIN (* GetReal *)
  RETURN A.RealPart
END GetReal;

PROCEDURE GetImaginary (A : Complex) : REAL;
(*
   Returns the imaginary part of complex number A.
   Pre : A is assigned a value.
   Post: The imaginary part of A is returned.
*)
BEGIN (* GetImaginary *)
  RETURN A.ImaginaryPart
END GetImaginary;

PROCEDURE AbsComplex (A : Complex) : REAL;
(*
```

```
      Returns the absolute value of complex number A.
      Pre : A is assigned a value.
      Post: The absolute value of A is returned.
   *)
   BEGIN (* AbsComplex *)
     RETURN A.RealPart * A.RealPart +
            A.ImaginaryPart * A.ImaginaryPart
   END AbsComplex;

END ComplexType.
```

The complex addition and subtraction operators are implemented as procedures `AddComplex` and `SubtractComplex`, respectively. From these procedures, we see that the sum (or difference) of two complex numbers is obtained by adding (or subtracting) the real and imaginary parts separately. Function `AbsComplex` computes the absolute value of a complex number according to the formula below.

$$| a + ib | = (a + ib) \times (a - ib) = a^2 + b^2$$

After the definition and implementation modules are compiled, the engineering professor can compile, link, and execute client modules (programs) that use the abstract data type for complex arithmetic. Each client module must import the data type `Complex` and any required operators from module `ComplexType`.

The implementation module shown in Fig. 9.7 contains stubs for procedures `MultiplyComplex` and `DivideComplex`. When these procedures are completed (see the exercise at the end of this section), they can be substituted for the stubs and used by a client module. It will be necessary only to recompile the implementation module for `ComplexType` and relink the client module. It is not necessary to recompile the definition module or the client module. A client module that uses abstract data type `ComplexType` is shown in Fig. 9.8.

Figure 9.8 ▸ *Using Complex Arithmetic Abstract Data Type*

```
MODULE TestComplex;
(*
   Reads two complex numbers and displays their sum and difference.
   Also displays the absolute value of one of the numbers.
   Uses the abstract data type ComplexType.
*)
   FROM InOut IMPORT
     WriteString, WriteLn;

   FROM RealInOut IMPORT
     WriteReal;
```

```
  FROM ComplexType IMPORT
    Complex,                                      (* data type *)
    CreateComplex, ReadComplex, WriteComplex,     (* procedures *)
    AddComplex, SubtractComplex,
    AbsComplex;                                   (* function *)

  VAR
    A, B, C : Complex;              (* three complex numbers *)

BEGIN (* TestComplex *)
  (* Create three complex numbers. *)
  CreateComplex (A);
  CreateComplex (B);
  CreateComplex (C);

  (* Read in complex numbers A and B. *)
  WriteString ('Enter the first complex number.');   WriteLn;
  ReadComplex (A);  WriteLn;
  WriteString ('Enter the second complex number.');  WriteLn;
  ReadComplex (B);  WriteLn;

  AddComplex (A, B, C);                         (* form the sum *)
  WriteString ('The complex sum is ');
  WriteComplex (C);  WriteLn;                (* display the sum *)

  SubtractComplex (A, B, C);             (* form the difference *)
  WriteString ('The complex difference is ');
  WriteComplex (C);  WriteLn;         (* display the difference *)

  WriteString ('The absolute value of the first complex number is ');
  WriteReal (AbsComplex(A), 12);  WriteLn
END TestComplex.


Enter the first complex number.
Real part: 3.5
Imaginary part: 5.2

Enter the second complex number.
Real part: 2.5
Imaginary part: 1.2

The complex sum is ( 6.0000E+000, 6.4000E+000)  .
The complex difference is ( 1.0000E+000, 4.0000E+000)
The absolute value of the first complex number is  3.9290E+001
```

Module `TestComplex` imports the data type `Complex` and six associated operators. The only procedures imported are those used in the body of `Test-Complex`.

The body of TestComplex begins with three calls to procedure CreateComplex, one for each variable (A, B, C) used for storing a complex number. Next, data are read into complex numbers A and B, and the sum and difference of these complex numbers are saved in C and displayed. Finally, the absolute value of complex number A is displayed.

A program or procedure that uses module ComplexType does not need to know the actual internal representation of data type Complex. All required operations (addition, subtraction, etc.) can be performed without this knowledge. In fact, it is better to hide this information from the user to prevent the calling program from directly manipulating the individual fields of a complex variable. Chapter 13 discusses how to hide the data type declaration.

Program Style

Referencing Individual Fields of an Imported Data Type

Since the program in Fig. 9.8 imports procedure WriteReal, the statements

```
WriteString ('The real part of the sum is ');
WriteReal (C.RealPart, 12);
```

could be used to display the real part only of the sum of A and B. This is a bad programming practice, because the field name C.RealPart is based on a particular internal representation (record with fields RealPart and ImaginaryPart) of the data type Complex. If we later decide to use a different internal representation and to rewrite module ComplexType, the field name C.RealPart may no longer be correct, and the client module would have to be modified.

It would be much better to import procedure GetReal from module ComplexType and use the statements

```
WriteString ('The real part of the sum is ');
WriteReal (GetReal(C), 12);
```

In the second line, GetReal extracts the real part of complex number C before it is displayed. Now the client module would always be correct regardless of the internal representation used for data type Complex.

SELF-CHECK EXERCISE FOR SECTION 9.4

1. Write procedures MultiplyComplex and DivideComplex to implement the operations of multiplication and division of complex numbers as defined below.

$$(a, b) * (c, d) = (a * c - b * d, a * d + b * c)$$

$$(a, b) / (c, d) = \left(\frac{a * c + b * d}{c^2 + d^2}, \frac{b * c - a * d}{c^2 + d^2}\right)$$

9.5 Hierarchical Records

In solving any programming problem, you must select data structures that allow efficient representation in the computer of different kinds of information. The selection of data structures is an important part of the problem-solving process. The data structures you use can have a profound effect on the efficiency and simplicity of the completed program.

The data-structuring facilities in Modula-2 are powerful and general. In the previous examples, all record fields were simple types or strings. It is possible to declare a record type with fields that are other structured types (e.g., a string is an array of characters). A record type with one or more fields that are record types is a *hierarchical record*.

We began our study of records by introducing a record type `Employee`. In this section, we will modify that record by adding new fields for storage of the employee's starting date and date of birth. The record type `NewEmployee` is declared in Fig. 9.9. Data type `Month` must be imported from module `DatesADT` (see Fig. 6.8).

Figure 9.9 ▸ *Declaration of a Hierarchical Record*

```
FROM DatesADT IMPORT
  Month;                  (* data type *)

TYPE
  String20 = ARRAY [0..19] OF CHAR;
  IDRange = [1111..9999];

  Employee = RECORD
               ID : IDRange;
               Name : String20;
               Sex : (Female, Male);
               NumDepend : CARDINAL;
               Rate, TaxSal : REAL
             END;  (* Employee *)

  Date = RECORD
           ThisMonth : Month;
           Day : [1..31];
           Year : [1900..1999]
         END;  (* Date *)

  NewEmployee = RECORD
                  PayData : Employee;
                  StartDate, BirthDate : Date
                END;  (* NewEmployee *)

VAR
  Programmer : NewEmployee;
```

If `Programmer` is a record variable of type `NewEmployee`, the hierarchical structure of `Programmer` is illustrated in Fig. 9.10. The diagram shows that `Programmer` is a record with fields `PayData`, `StartDate`, and `BirthDate`. Each field is itself a record (a *subrecord* of `Programmer`). The fields of each subrecord are indicated under it.

Figure 9.10 ▶ *Record Variable Programmer (Type NewEmployee)*

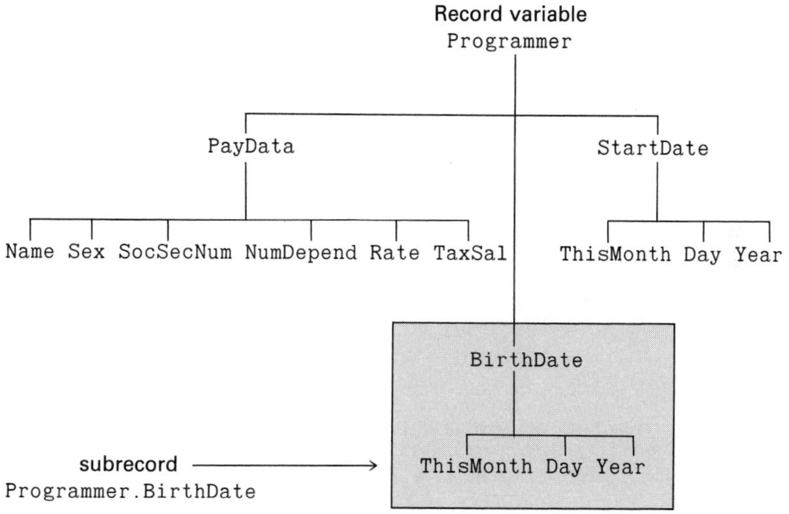

To reference a field in the diagram, we must trace a complete path to it starting at the top of the diagram. For example, the field selector

```
Programmer.StartDate
```

references the subrecord `StartDate` (type `Date`) of the variable `Programmer`. The field selector

```
Programmer.StartDate.Year
```

references the `Year` field (type `[1900..1999]`) of the subrecord `Programmer.StartDate`. The field selector

```
Programmer.Year
```

is incomplete (which `Year` field?) and would cause a syntax error.

The record copy statement

```
Programmer.StartDate := DayOfYear
```

is legal if `DayOfYear` is a record variable of type `Date`. This statement copies each field of `DayOfYear` into the corresponding field of the subrecord `Programmer.StartDate`.

In many situations, the WITH statement can be used to shorten the field selector. The statements

```
WITH Programmer.StartDate DO
  WriteString ('Year started: ');
  WriteCard (Year, 4);  WriteLn;
  WriteString ('Day started: ');
  WriteCard (Day, 2);   WriteLn
END
```

displays two fields of the subrecord Programmer.StartDate. The computation for taxable salary could be written as

```
WITH Programmer.PayData DO
  TaxSal := Rate * 40.0 - FLOAT(NumDepend) * 14.40
END
```

The following WITH statement

```
WITH Programmer DO
  WriteString (PayData.Name);
  WriteString (' started working here in ');
  WriteCard (StartDate.Year, 4);  WriteLn
END
```

displays an output line of the form

```
Caryn Jackson started working here in 1976
```

It is also possible to nest WITH statements. The following nested WITH statement also displays the preceding output line:

```
WITH Programmer DO
  WITH PayData DO
    WITH StartDate DO
      WriteString (Name);
      WriteString (' started working here in ');
      WriteCard (Year, 4);  WriteLn
    END
  END
END
```

The record variable name (Programmer) must precede the subrecord names. The order of the field names PayData and StartDate is not important.

Procedure ReadNewEmp in Fig. 9.11 could be used to read in a record of type NewEmployee. It calls procedures ReadEmployee (see Fig. 9.5) and ReadDate (see the exercise at the end of this section).

Figure 9.11 ▶ *Procedure ReadNewEmp*

```
PROCEDURE ReadNewEmp (VAR NewEmp (* output *) : NewEmployee);
(*
  Reads a record into record variable NewEmp. Uses
  procedures ReadEmployee and ReadDate.
```

```
   Pre : None
   Post: Reads data into all fields of record NewEmp.
*)

BEGIN (* ReadNewEmp *)
  WITH NewEmp DO
    ReadEmployee (PayData);
    ReadDate (StartDate);
    ReadDate (BirthDate)
  END (* WITH *)
END ReadNewEmp;
```

SELF-CHECK EXERCISE FOR SECTION 9.5

1. Write procedure `ReadDate`.

9.6 Variant Records

All record variables of type `NewEmployee` have the same form and structure. It is possible, however, to define record types that have some fields that are the same for all variables of that type (fixed part) and some fields that may be different (variant part).

For example, we might want to include additional information about an employee based on the employee's marital status. For all married employees, we might want to know the spouse's initials and number of children. For all divorced employees, we might want to know the date of the divorce. For all single employees, we might want to know if the employee lives alone.

This new employee type, `Executive`, is declared in Fig. 9.12. It uses several data types declared earlier in Fig. 9.9.

Figure 9.12 ▶ *Record Type Executive and Record Variable Boss*

```
FROM DatesADT IMPORT
  Month;                        (* data type *)

TYPE
  String20 = ARRAY [0..19] OF CHAR;
  IDRange = [1111..9999];

  Employee = RECORD
               ID : IDRange;
               Name : String20;
               Sex : (Female, Male);
               NumDepend : CARDINAL;
               Rate, TaxSal : REAL
             END; (* Employee *)
```

```
Date = RECORD
         ThisMonth : Month;
         Day : [1..31];
         Year : [1900..1999]
       END; (* Date *)

NewEmployee = RECORD
                PayData : Employee;
                StartDate, BirthDate : Date
              END; (* NewEmployee *)

MaritalStatus = (Married, Divorced, Single);
Executive = RECORD
              (* fixed part *)
              PayData : Employee;
              StartDate, BirthDate : Date;

              (* variant part *)
              CASE MS : MaritalStatus OF
                Married  : SpouseName : String20;
                           NumberKids : CARDINAL
              | Divorced : DivorceDate : Date
              | Single   : LivesAlone : BOOLEAN
              END (* CASE *)
            END; (* Executive *)

VAR
  Boss : Executive;
```

The fixed part of record type `Executive` has the form of record type `New–Employee`. The variant part begins with the phrase

```
CASE MS : MaritalStatus OF
```

which defines a special field `MS`, of type `MaritalStatus`, called the *tag field*. The value of the tag field (`Married`, `Divorced`, or `Single`) indicates the form of the remainder of the record. If the value of the tag field is `Married`, there are two additional fields, `SpouseName` (type `String20`) and `NumberKids` (type `CARDINAL`); otherwise, there is only one additional field, `DivorceDate` (type `Date`), or `LivesAlone` (type `BOOLEAN`). The symbol | is used to separate variants.

Fig. 9.13 shows three variants of record variable `Boss`, starting with the tag field. The fixed parts of all these records (not shown) have the same form.

Figure 9.13 ▸ *Three Variants of Record Boss*

Boss.MS	Divorced
Boss.DivorceDate.Month	May
Boss.DivorceDate.Day	20
Boss.DivorceDate.Year	1989

Boss.MS	Single
Boss.LivesAlone	TRUE

For each variable of type `Executive`, the compiler will allocate sufficient storage space to accommodate the largest of the record variants shown in Fig. 9.13. The first variant requires more than twenty bytes of storage and will be the largest. Remember, only one of the variants is defined at any given time; this particular variant is determined by the tag field value.

EXAMPLE 9.6 ▶ If the value of `Boss.MS` is `Married`, then only the variant fields `SpouseName` and `NumberKids` can be correctly referenced; all other variant fields are undefined. Assuming the first variant shown in Fig. 9.13 is stored in record `Boss`, the program fragment

```
WITH Boss DO
  WriteString ("The boss' spouse is ");
  WriteString (SpouseName);
  WriteString ('. They have ');
  WriteCard (NumberKids, 2);
  WriteString (' children.');  WriteLn
END (* WITH *)
```

displays the line

```
The boss' spouse is Elliot Koffman. They have  3 children.
```

The programmer must ensure that the variant fields that are referenced are consistent with the current tag field value. The compiler and run-time system do not normally check this. If the value of `Boss.MS` is `Single` or `Divorced` when the preceding fragment is executed, the information displayed will be meaningless. For this reason, a `CASE` statement is often used to process the variant part of a record. Using the tag field as the `CASE` selector ensures that only the currently defined variant is manipulated. ◂

EXAMPLE 9.7 ▶ The fragment in Fig. 9.14 displays the data stored in the variant part of record `Boss`. The value of `Boss.MS` determines what information is displayed. ◂

Figure 9.14 ▶ *Displaying a Variant Record*

```
(* Display the variant part *)
WITH Boss DO
  CASE MS OF
```

```
  Married  : WriteString ("The boss' spouse is ");
             WriteString (SpouseName);
             WriteString ('. They have ');
             WriteCard (NumberKids, 2);
             WriteString (' children.')
 | Divorced : WITH DivorceDate DO
               WriteString ('Divorced on ');
               WriteCard (ORD(ThisMonth)+1, 2);  Write ('/');
               WriteCard (Day, 2);               Write ('/');
               WriteCard (Year, 4)
             END (* WITH *)
 | Single   : IF LivesAlone THEN
               WriteString ('Lives alone')
             ELSE
               WriteString ('Does not live alone')
             END (* IF *)
 END; (* CASE *)
 WriteLn
END (* WITH *)
```

The syntax for a record with fixed and variant parts is described in the following syntax display.

Record Type with Variant Part ▶

FORM: TYPE
rec type = RECORD

id list$_1$: *type*$_1$;		
id list$_2$: *type*$_2$;		
.		
.	*fixed part*	
.		
id list$_n$: *type*$_n$		
CASE *tag* : *tag-type* OF		
label$_1$: *field-list*$_1$		
| *label*$_2$: *field-list*$_2$		
.		
.	*variant part*	
.		
| *label*$_k$: *field-list*$_k$		
END (* CASE *)		
END;		

EXAMPLE:
```
TYPE
  Face = RECORD
           Eyes, Hair : Color;
           CASE HasScars : BOOLEAN OF
             TRUE  : Number : CARDINAL
           | FALSE : (* empty variant *)
           END (* CASE *)
         END; (*Face*)
```

INTERPRETATION: The variant part starts with the reserved word `CASE`. The identifier *tag* is the name of the tag field of the record; a colon separates the tag field name from its type (*tag type*), which must be `BOOLEAN` or a previously defined enumeration type or subrange.

The `CASE` labels (*label*$_1$, *label*$_2$,..., *label*$_k$) are lists of values of the tag field as defined by *tag type*. *Field list*$_i$ describes the record fields associated with *label*$_i$. Each element of *field list*$_i$ specifies a field name and its type; the elements in *field list*$_i$ are separated by semicolons. The symbol | is used as a separator between variants.

Notes: There may be more than one variant part; each begins with the reserved word `CASE` and ends with an `END (* CASE *)`. It is also possible to nest variants.

All field names must be unique. The same field name may not appear in both the fixed and the variant parts or in two field lists of the variant part.

An empty field list (no variant part for a `CASE` label) is allowed.

The `CASE` statement that declares a variant part may have an `ELSE` clause.

When initially storing data into a record with a variant part, the tag field value should be read first. Once the value of the tag field is defined, data can be read into the fields associated with that variant.

9.7 Case Study: Areas and Perimeters of Different Figures

Problem: We want to write a program that will determine the area and the perimeter for a variety of geometric figures.

Discussion: To solve this problem, we will create an abstract data type that represents a geometric figure and contains operators for entering the figure's characteristics, computing its perimeter, computing its area, and displaying its characteristics. Since the characteristics for a figure are related, we would like to save them in a record. However, because the characteristics for each figure shape are different, we must use a record with a variant part. One possibility is declared as follows.

```
TYPE
  FigKind = (Rectangle, Square, Circle, Other);
  Figure = RECORD
             Area, Perimeter : REAL;
             CASE Shape : FigKind OF
               Rectangle : Width, Height : REAL;
             | Square    : Side : REAL;
             | Circle    : Radius : REAL;
             | Other     : (* empty variant *)
             END (* CASE *)
           END; (* Figure *)
```

The definition module for our abstract data type is shown in Fig. 9.15.

Figure 9.15 ▸ *Definition Module Geometry*

```
DEFINITION MODULE Geometry;
(*
  Defines an abstract data type for a geometric figure. Operators
  are provided for reading and displaying a figure's
  characteristics, computing area, and computing perimeter.
  ReadFigure must be called first.
*)
  EXPORT QUALIFIED
    Figure,                                        (* data type *)
    ReadFigure, ComputePerimeter,                 (* procedures *)
    ComputeArea, DisplayFigure;

(* Data Type *)

  TYPE
    FigKind = (Rectangle, Square, Circle, Other);
    Figure = RECORD
               Area, Perimeter : REAL;
               CASE Shape : FigKind OF
                 Rectangle : Width, Height : REAL;
               | Square    : Side : REAL;
               | Circle    : Radius : REAL;
               | Other     : (* empty variant *)
               END (* CASE *)
             END; (* Figure *)

(* Operators *)

  PROCEDURE ReadFigure (VAR OneFig (* output *) : Figure);
  (*
     Enters data into OneFig.
     Pre : None
     Post: The tag field and characteristics of OneFig are defined.
  *)

  PROCEDURE ComputePerimeter (VAR OneFig (* inout *) : Figure);
```

```
   (*
      Defines Perimeter field of OneFig.
      Pre : The tag field and characteristics of OneFig are defined.
      Post: Assigns value to Perimeter field.
   *)

   PROCEDURE ComputeArea (VAR OneFig (* inout *) : Figure);
   (*
      Defines Area field of OneFig.
      Pre : The tag field and characteristics of OneFig are defined.
      Post: Assigns value to Area field.
   *)

   PROCEDURE DisplayFigure (OneFig (* input *) : Figure);
   (*
      Displays the characteristics of OneFig.
      Pre : All fields of OneFig are defined.
      Post: Displays each field of OneFig.
   *)

END Geometry.
```

Once the definition module is completed, we can focus on the implementation of the operators. To read in a figure's characteristics, we must first determine its shape and then read in the data required for a figure of that shape. Procedure `ReadFigure` in Fig. 9.16 calls `ReadShape` (see Exercise 1 at the end of this section) to enter the character (`'R'`, `'S'`, or `'C'`) representing a figure's shape and to store the corresponding scalar value (`Rectangle`, `Square`, `Circle`) in the tag field `Shape`. If the character entered is not one of the previously mentioned letters, the value `Other` should be stored in the tag field. `ReadFigure` then reads the pertinent characteristics for the figure.

Figure 9.16 ▸ *Implementation Module Geometry*

```
IMPLEMENTATION MODULE Geometry;
(*
   Abstract data type for a geometric figure. Operators are
   provided for reading a figure's characteristics, computing
   area, and computing perimeter.
*)
   FROM InOut IMPORT
     Read, Write, WriteString, WriteLn;

   FROM RealInOut IMPORT
     ReadReal, WriteReal;
```

```
CONST
  Pi = 3.14159;

(* Data type Figure is declared in the definition module. *)

(* Operators *)

  PROCEDURE ReadFigure (VAR OneFig (* output *) : Figure);
  (*
    Enters data into OneFig.
    Pre : None
    Post: The tag field and characteristics of OneFig are defined.
  *)
    PROCEDURE ReadShape (VAR OneFig (* output *) : Figure);
    (*
      Reads the shape character and defines OneFig.Shape
      Pre : None
      Post: OneFig.Shape is Rectangle if the data character
            is R, Square if S, Circle if C; otherwise,
            OneFig.Shape is Other.
    *)
    BEGIN  (* ReadShape stub *)
      OneFig.Shape := Circle
    END ReadShape;

  BEGIN  (* ReadFigure *)
    (* Read the shape character and define the tag field *)
    ReadShape (OneFig);

    WITH OneFig DO
      (* Select the proper variant and read pertinent data *)
      CASE Shape OF
        Rectangle : WriteString ('Enter width: ');
                    ReadReal (Width);   WriteLn;
                    WriteString ('Enter height: ');
                    ReadReal (Height);  WriteLn
      | Square    : WriteString ('Enter length of side: ');
                    ReadReal (Side);    WriteLn
      | Circle    : WriteString ('Enter circle radius: ');
                    ReadReal (Radius);  WriteLn
      | Other     : WriteString ('Shape is not defined.');  WriteLn
      END (* CASE *)
    END (* WITH *)
  END ReadFigure;

  PROCEDURE ComputePerimeter (VAR OneFig (* inout *) : Figure);
  (*
    Defines Perimeter field of OneFig.
    Pre : The tag field and characteristics of OneFig are defined.
    Post: Assigns value to Perimeter field.
  *)
```

```
BEGIN (* ComputePerimeter *)
  WITH OneFig DO
    CASE Shape OF
      Rectangle : Perimeter := 2.0 * (Width + Height)
    | Square    : Perimeter := 4.0 * Side
    | Circle    : Perimeter := 2.0 * Pi * Radius
    | Other     : Perimeter := 0.0
    END (* CASE *)
  END (* WITH *)
END ComputePerimeter;

PROCEDURE ComputeArea (VAR OneFig (* inout *) : Figure);
(*
   Defines Area field of OneFig.
   Pre : The tag field and characteristics of OneFig are defined.
   Post: Assigns value to Area field.
*)
BEGIN (* ComputeArea *)
  WITH OneFig DO
    CASE Shape OF
      Rectangle : Area := Width * Height
    | Square    : Area := Side * Side
    | Circle    : Area := Pi * Radius * Radius
    | Other     : Area := 0.0
    END (* CASE *)
  END (* WITH *)
END ComputeArea;

PROCEDURE DisplayFigure (OneFig (* input *) : Figure);
(*
   Displays the characteristics of OneFig.
   Pre : All fields of OneFig are defined.
   Post: Displays each field of OneFig.
*)
BEGIN (* DisplayFigure *)
  WITH OneFig DO
    (* Display shape and characteristics *)
    WriteString ('Figure shape: ');
    CASE Shape OF
      Rectangle : WriteString ('Rectangle');  WriteLn;
                  WriteString ('Height: ');
                  WriteReal (Height, 12);     WriteLn;
                  WriteString ('Width: ');
                  WriteReal (Width, 12);      WriteLn
    | Square    : WriteString ('Square');     WriteLn;
                  WriteString ('Side :');
                  WriteReal (Side, 12);       WriteLn
    | Circle    : WriteString ('Circle');     WriteLn;
                  WriteString ('Radius :');
                  WriteReal (Radius, 12);     WriteLn
    | Other     : WriteString ('No characteristics for figure');
```

```
                     WriteLn
        END; (* CASE *)

        (* Display area and perimeter *)
        WriteString ('Area: ');
        WriteReal (Area, 12);          WriteLn;
        WriteString ('Perimeter: ');
        WriteReal (Perimeter, 12);     WriteLn
      END (* WITH *)
    END DisplayFigure;

END Geometry.
```

In each procedure, a `CASE` statement controls the processing of the data in the variant part. Procedures `ComputePerimeter` and `ComputeArea` define their respective fields in the data structure. A small client module and a sample execution are shown in Fig. 9.17.

Figure 9.17 ▸
Client Module and Sample Run

```
MODULE TestGeometry;

  FROM Geometry IMPORT
    Figure,                          (* data type *)
    ReadFigure, DisplayFigure,       (* procedures *)
    ComputePerimeter, ComputeArea;

  VAR
    MyFig : Figure;                  (* a figure *)

BEGIN (* TestGeometry *)
  ReadFigure (MyFig);  WriteLn;
  ComputePerimeter (MyFig);
  ComputeArea (MyFig);
  DisplayFigure (MyFig)
END TestGeometry.

Enter the object's shape.
Enter R (rectangle), S (square), or C (circle): R
Enter width: 5.0
Enter height: 6.5

Figure shape: Rectangle
Width:  5.0000E+000
Height:  6.5000E+000
Area:  3.2500E+001
Perimeter:  2.3000E+001
```

SELF-CHECK EXERCISES FOR SECTION 9.7

1. Write procedure `ReadShape`. The first two lines of the sample output of Fig. 9.17 are the prompts generated by `ReadShape`.
2. Add the variant

```
Triangle : Side1, Side2, Angle : REAL;
```

to `Figure` and modify the abstract data type to include triangles.

9.8 Common Programming Errors

When using records, the most common error is incorrectly specifying the record field to be manipulated. The full field selector (record variable and field name) must be used, unless the record reference is nested inside a `WITH` statement or the entire record is to be manipulated. The latter option is available only for record copy statements and for records passed as parameters. When reading or writing records at the terminal, you must process each field separately.

If a record variable name is listed in a `WITH` statement header, only the field name is required to reference fields of that record inside the `WITH` statement. The full field selector still must be used to reference fields of any other record variable.

If an abstract data type is defined as a separate module, a client program must import the data type and all required procedures. A client program must not redeclare the data type or manipulate individual fields of any variable of this type.

For variant records, remember that the value of the tag field determines the form of the variant part that is currently defined. Manipulating any other variant will cause unpredictable results. It is the programmer's responsibility to ensure that the correct variant is being processed—the compiler does not check this. Consequently, a variant record should always be manipulated in a `CASE` statement with the tag field used as the `CASE` selector to ensure that the proper variant part is being manipulated.

9.9 Chapter Review

This chapter examined the record data type. Records were shown to be useful for organizing a collection of related data items of different types. We were able to create some very general data structures to model our "real world" data organization through the use of hierarchical records and variant records.

In processing records, you saw how to reference each individual component through the use of a field selector consisting of the record variable name and field name separated by a period. The `WITH` statement was introduced as a means of shortening the field selector. If a record variable name is specified in a `WITH` statement header, the field name may be used by itself inside the `WITH` statement.

Each individual component of a record must be manipulated separately in an input or output operation or in an arithmetic expression. However, it is permissable to assign one record variable to another record variable of the same type (record copy statement) or to pass a record as a parameter to a procedure or function.

New Modula-2 Statements

The new Modula-2 statements introduced in this chapter are described in Table 9.1.

Table 9.1 ▸ *Summary of New Modula-2 Statements*

STATEMENT	EFFECT

Record Declaration
`TYPE`
`  Part = RECORD`
`           ID : [1111..9999];`
`           Quantity : CARDINAL;`
`           Price : REAL`
`         END; (* Part *)`
`VAR`
`  Nuts, Bolts : Part;`
	A record type `Part` is declared with fields that can store two cardinal numbers and a real number. `Nuts` and `Bolts` are record variables of type `Part`.

Record Variant Declaration
`TYPE`
`  ChildKind = (Girl, Boy);`
`  Child = RECORD`
`            First, Last : CHAR;`
`            Age : CARDINAL;`
`            CASE Sex: ChildKind OF`
`              Girl : Sugar, Spice : REAL;`
`            | Boy : NumSnakes, NumSnails,`
`                     NumTails : CARDINAL`
`            END (* CASE *)`
`          END; (* Child *)`
	A record type with a variant part is declared. Each record variable can store two characters and a cardinal number. The tag field `Sex` determines which variant part is stored. One variant part consists of two real numbers, and the other consists of three cardinals. The record variable `Kid` is type `Child`.

Record Reference
`TotalCost := FLOAT(Nuts.Quantity)`
`              * Nuts.Price`
	Multiplies two fields of `Nuts`.

`WriteCard (Bolts.ID, 4)`	Prints `ID` field of `Bolts`.

Record Copy `Bolts := Nuts`	Copies record `Nuts` to `Bolts`.

WITH Statement
`WITH Bolts DO`
`  WriteCard (ID, 4);`
`  WriteReal (Price, 12)`
`END`
	Prints two fields of `Bolts`.

Referencing a Record Variant
`WITH Kid DO`
`  CASE Sex OF`
`    Girl :`
`      WriteString ('Pounds of sugar: ');`
`      ReadReal (Sugar);`
`  | Boy :`
`      WriteString ('Number of snakes: ');`
`      ReadCard (NumSnakes)`
`  END (* CASE *)`
`END (* WITH *)`
	Uses a `CASE` statement to read data into the variant part of record variable `Kid`. If tag field `Sex` is `Girl`, reads a value into the field `Sugar`. If tag field `Sex` is `Boy`, reads a value into the field `NumSnakes`.

CHAPTER 9 ▸

Review Questions

1. Declare a record called `Subscriber` that contains the fields `Name`, `StreetAddress`, `MonthlyBill` (how much the subscriber owes), and which paper the subscriber receives (`Morning`, `Evening`, or `Both`).
2. Write a Modula-2 program to enter and then print out the data in record `Competition` declared as follows:

```
TYPE
  String15 = ARRAY [0..14] OF CHAR;
  OlympicEvent = RECORD
                   Event : String15;
                   Entrant : String15;
                   Country : String15;
                   Place : INTEGER
                 END; (* OlympicEvent *)

VAR
  Competition: OlympicEvent;
```

3. Explain the use of the `WITH` statement.
4. Identify and correct the errors in the following Modula-2 program.

```
MODULE Report;

  TYPE
    String15 = ARRAY [0..14] OF CHAR;
```

```
    SummerHelp = RECORD
                   Name : String15;
                   StartDate : String15;
                   HoursWorked : REAL
                 END; (* SummerHelp *)

  VAR
    Operator : SummerHelp;

BEGIN (* Report *)
  WITH SummerHelp DO
    Name := 'Stoney Viceroy';
    StartDate := 'June 1, 1984';
    HoursWorked := 29.3
  END; (* WITH *)
  WriteString (Name)
END Report.
```

5. Declare the proper data structure to store the following student data: `GPA`, `Major`, `Address` (consisting of `StreetAddress`, `City`, `State`, `ZipCode`), and `ClassSchedule` (consisting of up to six class records, each of which has `Description`, `Time`, and `Days` fields). Use whatever data types are most appropriate for each field.
6. Write the variant declaration for `Supplies`, which consists of `Paper`, `Ribbon`, or `Labels`. For `Paper`, the information needed is the number of sheets per box and the size of the paper. For `Ribbon`, the size, color, and kind (`Carbon` or `Cloth`) are needed. For `Labels`, the size and number per box are needed. For each supply, the cost, number on hand, and the reorder point must also be stored. Use whatever variable types are appropriate for each field.
7. Write the declaration for `Vehicle`. If the vehicle is a `Truck`, then `BedSize` and `CabSize` are needed. If the vehicle is a `Wagon`, `ThirdSeat` is needed (`BOOLEAN`). If the vehicle is a `Sedan`, the information needed is `2-door` or `4-door`. For all vehicles, we need to know if the transmission is `Manual` or `Automatic`; if it has `AirConditioning`, `PowerSteering`, or `PowerBrakes` (all `BOOLEAN`); and the gas mileage. Use whatever data types are appropriate for each field.

CHAPTER 9 ▸

Programming Projects

1. Implement an abstract data type consisting of the data structure described in review question 5 and procedures for reading and displaying an object of that type.

2. Implement an abstract data type consisting of the data structure described in review question 6 and procedures for reading and displaying an object of that type.

3. Implement an abstract data type consisting of the data structure described in review question 7 and procedures for reading and displaying an object of that type.

4. A number expressed in scientific notation is represented by its mantissa (a fraction) and its exponent. Write an abstract data type for scientific notation. Include a procedure that reads the mantissa and exponent separately and stores each number in a record with two fields (one `REAL` and one `INTEGER`). Include a procedure that prints the contents of each record in scientific notation. Also include procedures that compute the sum, product, difference, and quotient of two numbers in scientific notation. Hint: The string −0.1234E20 represents a number in scientific notation; the real fraction −0.1234 is the mantissa and the integer 20 is the exponent.

5. At a grocery store, certain categories of food have been established, and this information is to be computerized. Write a procedure to read and store information into a variant record with appropriately designed types.

   The first letter read will be M, F, or V (indicating meat, fruit, or vegetable). The second set of information (until a blank is encountered) will be the name of the item (maximum of 20 letters). The third item read will be the cost per unit. The fourth item read will be the unit (O for ounces, P for pounds).

   The last field read will be one character indicating information based on the M, F, or V read earlier. For meat, the valid input values are

   R for red meat, P for poultry, and F for fish

   For fruit, the valid input values are

   T for tropical, N for nontropical

   For vegetables, the valid input values are

   B for beans, P for potatoes, O for other

   The procedure should check that each data item is valid before assigning a value to the record parameter. Also, write procedures to print the data stored for all the meats and another to print the data stored for all the potatoes.

10 Arrays with Structured Elements

YOU HAVE SEEN PROGRAMS that use arrays with many different subscript and element types. All the arrays encountered so far had individual elements that were simple types. This chapter will look at arrays whose elements are structured types.

We will begin by examining arrays with elements that are themselves arrays. These arrays of arrays are called multidimensional arrays and are often used to store tables of data or represent multidimensional objects.

We will also examine arrays with elements that are records. Arrays of records are useful data structures that can represent many real-world objects. For example, it is convenient to use an array of records to represent a class of students or the members of a baseball team.

Finally, we will see how to perform some common operations on arrays of records. These operations include searching for a particular record in an array and ordering the array elements according to the values in a particular field (sorting the array).

10.1 Arrays of Arrays: Multidimensional Arrays

So far, each array element has been used to store a simple data value. Array elements can also be data structures. We will begin by looking at arrays of strings.

Arrays of Strings

We have written programs with enumeration types in earlier examples. One drawback of using enumeration types is that their values cannot be read or written directly. The use of arrays of strings can simplify printing enumeration type values, as shown next.

EXAMPLE 10.1 ▶ We first discussed module `DatesADT` in Chapter 6 (See Fig. 6.8). `DatesADT` exports two enumeration types, `Month` and `Day`, with values that correspond to the months of the year and the days of the week, respectively. It also exports operators (procedures) to read and display a month or day value.

A revised implementation module is shown in Fig. 10.1. This module contains a declaration for an array `MonthName`, which is an array of strings representing the names of the months. Since the longest month name is `'September'`, each array element must be a string of length nine. In the new procedure `WriteMonth`, the statement

```
WriteString (MonthName[ThisMonth])
```

displays the array element (a string) whose subscript is `ThisMonth`. The statement sequence (after `BEGIN`) in module `DatesADT` initializes the array `MonthName`. These statements are executed when the `IMPORT` statement for module `DatesADT` is reached in the client module. Fig. 10.2 shows the array `MonthName` after it is initialized. ◂

Figure 10.1 ▸ *Revised Implementation Module for DatesADT*

```
IMPLEMENTATION MODULE DatesADT;
(*
   Contains procedures for reading and displaying values of
   two enumeration types, Day and Month.
*)
   FROM InOut IMPORT
     Read, Write, WriteString;

   FROM SimpleIO IMPORT
     EnterCard;

(* Data types Day and Month are declared in the definition module. *)

(* Operators *)

   TYPE
     String9 = ARRAY [0..8] OF CHAR;

   VAR
     MonthName : ARRAY Month OF String9;  (* array of month names *)

   PROCEDURE WriteMonth (ThisMonth (* input *) : Month);
   (*
      Displays the month string corresponding to ThisMonth.
      Pre : ThisMonth is assigned a value.
      Post: Displays the month name string selected by ThisMonth.
            Each string is displayed using nine characters.
   *)
   BEGIN (* WriteMonth *)
     WriteString (MonthName[ThisMonth])
   END WriteMonth;

(* Insert other operators here - see Fig. 6.9 *)

BEGIN (* DatesADT *)
  MonthName[January]  := 'January  ';
  MonthName[February] := 'February ';
  MonthName[March]    := 'March    ';
  MonthName[April]    := 'April    ';
  MonthName[May]      := 'May      ';
  MonthName[June]     := 'June     ';
  MonthName[July]     := 'July     ';
  MonthName[August]   := 'August   ';
```

```
  MonthName[September] := 'September';
  MonthName[October]   := 'October  ';
  MonthName[November]  := 'November ';
  MonthName[December]  := 'December '
END DatesADT.
```

Figure 10.2 ▸ *Array MonthName after Initialization*

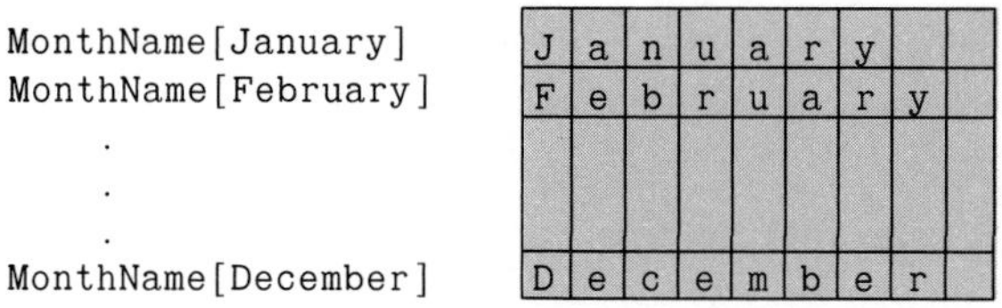

Two-Dimensional Arrays

Since a string is an array of characters, the array `MonthName` is an array of arrays. Such a data structure is called a *two-dimensional array*. To make the two-dimensional nature of `MonthName` more apparent, we could declare it in either of the following ways.

```
VAR
  MonthName : ARRAY Month OF ARRAY [0..8] OF CHAR;
```

or

```
VAR
  MonthName : ARRAY Month, [0..8] OF CHAR;
```

Either declaration could be substituted for the one shown in Fig. 10.1.

EXAMPLE 10.2 ▸ Another two-dimensional object we are all familiar with is a tic-tac-toe board. The declarations

```
TYPE
  BoardRow = ARRAY [1..3] OF CHAR;
  BoardArray = ARRAY [1..3] OF BoardRow;

VAR
  TicTacToe : BoardArray;
```

allocate storage for the array `TicTacToe`. This array has nine storage cells arranged in three rows and three columns. A character value can be stored in each cell.

In the declarations above, `BoardRow` is declared as an array type with three elements of type `CHAR`. `BoardArray` is declared as an array type with three elements of type `BoardRow`. Consequently, the variable `TicTacToe` (type `BoardArray`) is an array of arrays, or a two-dimensional array, as pictured in Fig. 10.3. ◂

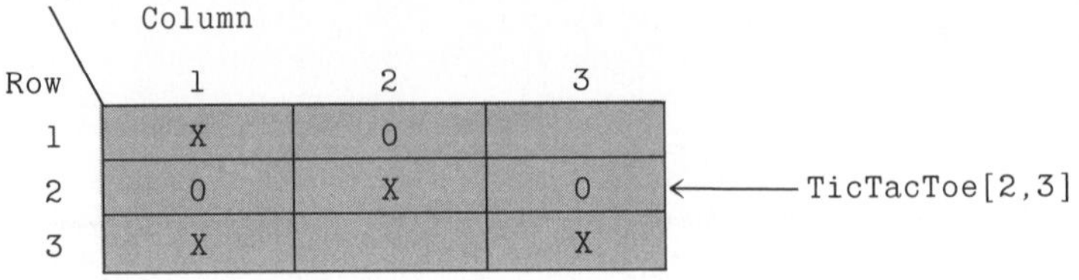

Figure 10.3 ▸ *A Tic-Tac-Toe Board Stored as Array TicTacToe*

The declarations

```
TYPE
  BoardArray = ARRAY [1..3], [1..3] OF CHAR;

VAR
  TicTacToe : BoardArray;
```

are equivalent to the previous ones in that they allocate storage for a two-dimensional array (`TicTacToe`) with three rows and three columns. This array has nine elements, each of which must be referenced by specifying a row subscript (`1`, `2`, or `3`) and a column subscript (`1`, `2`, or `3`). Each array element contains a character value. The array element `TicTacToe[2,3]` pointed to in Fig. 10.3 is in row `2`, column `3` of the array; it contains the character `0`. The diagonal line consisting of array elements `TicTacToe[1,1]`, `TicTacToe[2,2]`, and `TicTacToe[3,3]` represents a win for player X, since each cell contains the character `X`. ◂

Array Type Declaration (Multi-dimensional) ▶

FORM: `ARRAY` *subscript*$_1$ `OF ARRAY` *subscript*$_2$ ... `OF ARRAY` *subscript*$_n$
`OF` *element type*;

or `ARRAY` *subscript*$_1$,*subscript*$_2$, ...*subscript*$_n$ `OF` *element type*;

EXAMPLE: `ARRAY [1900..1999], Month OF CARDINAL;`

INTERPRETATION: *Subscript*$_i$ represents the subscript type of dimension *i* of a multidimensional array. The subscript type can be `BOOLEAN`, `CHAR`, an enumeration type, or a subrange. The *element type* can be any standard data type or a previously defined simple or structured data type.

Although our discussion will focus on arrays with two and three dimensions, there is no limit on the number of dimensions allowed in Modula-2. However, the particular implementation you are using may impose a limit. Be aware that the amount of memory space allocated for storage of a multidimensional array can be quite large. For this reason, avoid passing multidimensional arrays as value parameters.

EXAMPLE 10.3 ▶ The array `Table` declared below

```
VAR
  Table : ARRAY [1..7], [1..5], [1..6] OF REAL;
```

consists of three dimensions: The first subscript may take on values from `1` to `7`; the second, from `1` to `5`; and the third, from `1` to `6`. A total of `7` × `5` × `6`, or 210, real numbers may be stored in the array `Table`. All three subscripts must be specified in each reference to array `Table` (e.g., `Table[2,3,4]`). ◀

Storage of Multidimensional Arrays

Most implementations store multidimensional arrays in adjacent memory cells to simplify accessing the individual elements. The elements of a two-dimensional array are normally stored in order by row (i.e., first row 1, then row 2, and so on). This is called *row-major order*. To access a particular array element, the compiler computes the *offset* of that element from the first element stored. To perform this computation, the compiler must know the size of each element and the number of elements per row. Both values are available from the array-type declaration.

Manipulation of Two-Dimensional Arrays

A row subscript and a column subscript must be specified to reference an element of a two-dimensional array. The type of each subscript must be compatible with the corresponding subscript type specified in the array declaration.

If `I` is type `CARDINAL`, the statement

```
FOR I := 1 TO 3 DO
  Write (TicTacToe[1,I])
END
```

displays the first row of array `TicTacToe` (`TicTacToe[1,1]`, `TicTacToe[1,2]`, and `TicTacToe[1,3]`) on the current output line. The statement

```
FOR I := 1 TO 3 DO
  Write (TicTacToe[I,2]);
  WriteLn
END
```

displays the second column of `TicTacToe` (`TicTacToe[1,2]`, `TicTacToe[2,2]`, and `TicTacToe[3,2]`) in a vertical line.

Nested loops are used to access all elements in a multidimensional array in a predetermined order. In the next examples, the outer loop determines the row being accessed, and the inner loop selects each element in that row.

EXAMPLE 10.4 ▶ Procedure `PrintBoard` in Fig. 10.4 displays the current status of a tic-tac-toe board. A sample output of this procedure is also shown. ◀

Figure 10.4 ▸ *Procedure PrintBoard with Sample Output*

```
PROCEDURE PrintBoard (TicTacToe (* input *) : BoardArray);
(*
   Displays the status of a tic-tac-toe board (array TicTacToe).
   Pre : Array TicTacToe is defined.
   Post: Displays each element of array TicTacToe.
*)
   VAR
     Row, Column : [1..3];

BEGIN (* PrintBoard *)
  WriteString ('-------');  WriteLn;
  FOR Row := 1 TO 3 DO
    (* Print all columns of current row *)
    FOR Column := 1 TO 3 DO
      Write ('|');
      Write (TicTacToe [Row,Column]);
    END; (* FOR Column *)
    Write ('|');
    WriteLn;
    WriteString ('-------');
    WriteLn
  END (* FOR Row *)
END PrintBoard;

-------
|X|O| |
-------
|O|X|O|
-------
|X| |X|
-------
```

EXAMPLE 10.5 ▸ Function `IsFilled` in Fig. 10.5 returns a value of `TRUE` if a tic-tac-toe board is all filled up; it returns a value of `FALSE` if there is at least one cell that contains the constant `Empty` (defined external to the function). `IsFilled` could be called before making a move to determine if there are any possible moves left. The `IF` statement

```
IF IsFilled(TicTacToe) THEN
  WriteString ('Game is a draw!');
  WriteLn
END (* IF *)
```

prints an appropriate message when there are no moves. ◂

Figure 10.5 ▸ *Function IsFilled*

```
PROCEDURE IsFilled (TicTacToe : BoardArray) : BOOLEAN;
(*
  Tests whether the array TicTacToe is filled.
```

```
   Pre : Elements of array TicTacToe are assigned values.
   Post: Returns TRUE if array is filled; otherwise,
         returns FALSE.
*)

   VAR
     Row, Column : [1..3];    (* row and column subscripts *)

BEGIN  (* IsFilled *)
  (* Set BoardFilled to FALSE and return if any cell is empty. *)
  FOR Row := 1 TO 3 DO
    FOR Column := 1 TO 3 DO
      IF TicTacToe[Row,Column] = Empty THEN
        RETURN FALSE       (* board is not filled *)
      END (* IF *)
    END (* FOR Column *)
  END; (* FOR Row *)
  (* assertion: No empty cells were found. *)

  RETURN TRUE                  (* board is filled *)
END IsFilled;
```

EXAMPLE 10.6 ▶ Procedure `EnterMove` in Fig. 10.6 is used to enter a move into the array `TicTacToe`. The character value stored (`'X'` or `'O'`) is determined by the value of `Player`. The move coordinates (`MoveRow`, `MoveColumn`) are read by the procedure.

Figure 10.6 ▶ *Procedure EnterMove*

```
PROCEDURE EnterMove (Player (* input *) : CHAR;
                     VAR TicTacToe (* inout *) : BoardArray);
(*
   Stores an X or O (identity of Player) in the array TicTacToe.
   Pre : Player is 'X' or 'O' and array TicTacToe has at least
         one empty cell.
   Post: The value of Player is stored in the empty cell of
         TicTacToe whose coordinates are read in; the rest
         of array TicTacToe is unchanged.
   Uses: EnterCard from SimpleIO; WriteString, WriteLn from InOut
*)
   VAR
     MoveRow, MoveColumn : CARDINAL;    (* coordinates of
                                           selected cell *)
BEGIN  (* EnterMove *)
  LOOP
    WriteString ('Enter your move row and then the column');
    WriteLn;
    EnterCard (1, 3, MoveRow);     WriteLn;
    EnterCard (1, 3, MoveColumn);  WriteLn;
```

```
    IF TicTacToe[MoveRow, MoveColumn] = Empty THEN
      EXIT
    ELSE
      WriteString ('Cell is occupied - try again');  WriteLn
    END (* IF *)
  END; (* LOOP *)
  (* assertion: A valid move is entered *)

  TicTacToe[MoveRow, MoveColumn] := Player  (* Define cell *)
END EnterMove;
```

EnterMove uses procedure EnterCard from module SimpleIO (see Fig. 6.1) to enter the move coordinates. When a cell is selected that has the value Empty, its value is reset to Player. ◄

Multi-dimensional Arrays with Non-Integer Subscripts

The subscript type for each dimension of the multidimensional array TicTacToe is a subrange of type CARDINAL. It is not necessary for the subscript types to have the same base type. The arrays in the next example have a different subscript type for each dimension.

EXAMPLE 10.7 ► A university offers fifty courses at each of five campuses. We can conveniently store the enrollments of these courses in the array Enroll declared as follows:

```
CONST
  MaxCourse = 50;                        (* maximum number of courses *)

TYPE
  Campus = (Main, Ambler, Center, Delaware, Montco);

VAR
  Enroll : ARRAY [1..MaxCourse] , Campus OF CARDINAL;
```

This array consists of 250 elements, as shown in Fig. 10.7. Enroll[1, Center] represents the number of students in course 1 at Center campus.

If we want to have this enrollment information broken down further according to student rank, we would need a three-dimensional array with 1,000 elements. This array is declared as follows and is shown in Fig. 10.8.

```
CONST
  MaxCourse = 50;          (* maximum number of courses *)

TYPE
  Campus = (Main, Ambler, Center, Delaware, Montco);
  Rank = (Freshman, Sophomore, Junior, Senior);
```

Figure 10.7 ▸ *Two-Dimensional Array Enroll*

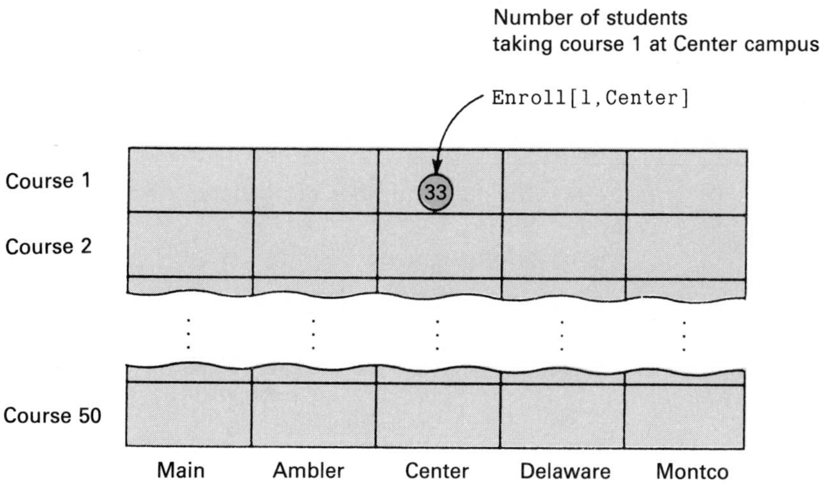

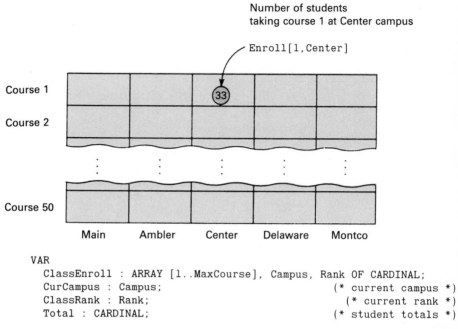

```
VAR
  ClassEnroll : ARRAY [1..MaxCourse], Campus, Rank OF CARDINAL;
  CurCampus : Campus;                              (* current campus *)
  ClassRank : Rank;                                   (* current rank *)
  Total : CARDINAL;                                (* student totals *)
```

The subscripted variable `ClassEnroll[1, Center, Senior]` represents the number of seniors taking course `1` at `Center` campus.

Figure 10.8 ▸ *Three-Dimensional Array ClassEnroll*

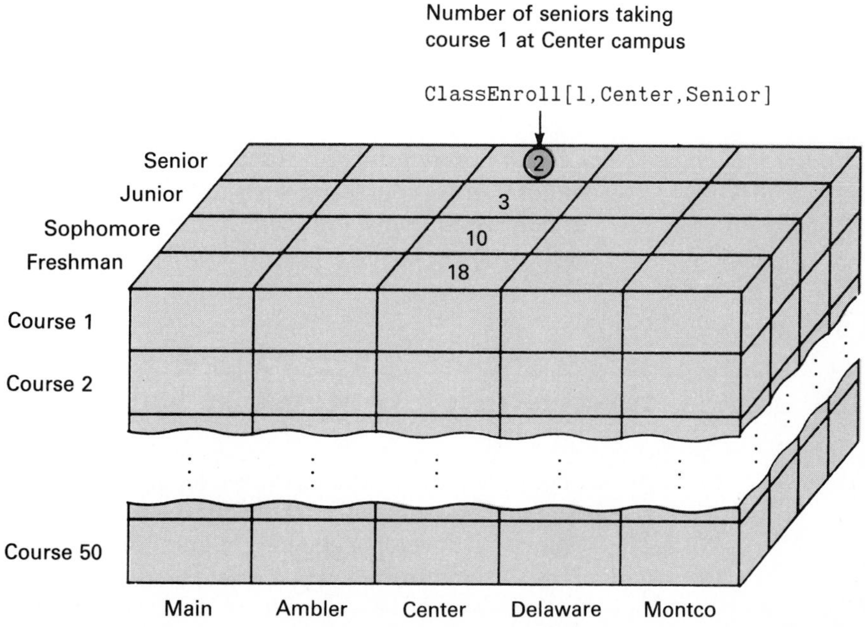

EXAMPLE 10.8 ▶ The program segment

```
Total := 0;
FOR ClassRank := Freshman TO Senior DO
  Total := Total + ClassEnroll[1,Center,ClassRank]
END (* FOR *)
```

computes the total number of students of all ranks in course 1 at Center campus.

The program segment

```
Total := 0;
FOR CurCampus := Main TO Montco DO
  FOR ClassRank := Freshman TO Senior DO
    Total := Total + ClassEnroll[1,CurCampus,ClassRank]
  END (* FOR ClassRank *)
END (* FOR CurCampus *)
```

computes the total number of students in course 1 (regardless of rank or campus). ◀

SELF-CHECK EXERCISE FOR SECTION 10.1

1. Redefine MaxCourse as 5 and write and test program segments that perform the following operations:
   a. Enter the enrollment data.
   b. Find the number of juniors in all classes at all campuses. Students will be counted once for each course in which they are enrolled.
   c. Find the number of sophomores on all campuses who are enrolled in course 2.
   d. Compute and print the number of students at Main campus enrolled in each course and the total number of students at Main campus in all courses. Students will be counted once for each course in which they are enrolled.
   e. Compute and print the number of upperclass students (juniors and seniors) in all courses at each campus, as well as the total number of upperclass students enrolled. Again, students will be counted once for each course in which they are enrolled.

10.2 Case Study: Analysis of Sales Trends

At this point, you have learned quite a lot about Modula-2 and programming. Using arrays of records will enable you to write fairly sophisticated programs. This section will develop a general program that might be used by a company to analyze sales figures.

SALES ANALYSIS PROBLEM

Problem: The High Risk Software Company has employed us to develop a general sales analysis program that they can market to a number of different companies. This program will be menu-driven, which means that each user will be given a choice of options to perform. The menu format is shown in Fig. 10.9. We need to write a program that can perform these operations.

Figure 10.9 ▸ *Menu for Sales Analysis Program*

```
GENERAL SALES ANALYSIS -- choose an option
1. Enter sales data for a specified year range into a table
2. Display sales table
3. Tabulate sales data by year
4. Tabulate sales data by month
5. Display annual totals
6. Display monthly totals
7. Graph sales annual totals
8. Graph monthly totals
9. Exit the program
```

Discussion: We will use data abstraction in solving this problem. An examination of the menu shows that the central data structure will be a table of sales data. The operations to be performed on this table are (1) read data into it, (2) display the table, and (3) decompose it into two smaller tables organized by year and month. Our first task will be to define an abstract data type for the sales table and its operators.

The abstract data type must include a type declaration for the sales table. The sales table must store sales volume data for each month of a given year range. The sales volume data can be stored in a two-dimensional array organized by year and month. This array will be part of a record that also includes the first and last year of the year range, as follows:

```
TYPE
   YearRange = [MinYear..MaxYear];
   SalesArray = ARRAY YearRange, Month OF REAL;
   SalesRecord = RECORD
                   FirstYear, LastYear : YearRange;
                   Volume : SalesArray
                 END; (* SalesRecord *)
```

The data type will accommodate sales data for any specified period. The size of the array field `Volume` depends on the constants `MinYear` and `Max-Year`. They should be chosen so that most companies will be able to use this module without modification. The definition module for `SalesTableADT` is shown in Fig. 10.10. We have included two additional operators, functions `GetFirst` and `GetLast`, in this module.

Figure 10.10 ▸ *Definition Module for SalesTableADT*

```
DEFINITION MODULE SalesTableADT;
(*
   Definition module for abstract data type for a table of sales
   data organized by year and month. The operations performed
   include: reading the sales data, displaying the data, and
   tabulating sums by year or month.
*)
   FROM DatesADT IMPORT
     Month;                                      (* data type *)

   EXPORT QUALIFIED
     MinYear, MaxYear,                           (* constants *)
     SalesRecord, YearRange,                     (* data types *)
     EnterSales, DisplaySales,                   (* procedures *)
     TabYear, TabMonth,
     GetFirst, GetLast;                          (* functions *)

(* Data Types *)

   CONST
     MinYear = 1900;
     MaxYear = 1999;

   TYPE
     YearRange = [MinYear..MaxYear];
     SalesArray = ARRAY YearRange, Month OF REAL;
     SalesRecord = RECORD
                     FirstYear, LastYear : YearRange;
                     Volume : SalesArray
                   END; (* SalesRecord *)

(* operators *)

   PROCEDURE EnterSales (VAR Sales (* output *) : SalesRecord);
   (*
      Reads the sales data into the record Sales.
      Pre : None
      Post: The fields FirstYear and LastYear are defined and
            sales data are read into array Volume for each month of
            years FirstYear..LastYear.
   *)

   PROCEDURE DisplaySales (VAR Sales (* input *) : SalesRecord);
   (*
      Displays the sales data.
      Pre : Record Sales is defined.
```

```
      Post: Displays two-dimensional table of sales volume by
            month for years FirstYear..LastYear.
   *)

   PROCEDURE TabYear (VAR Sales (* input *) : SalesRecord;
                      VAR SumByYear (* output *) : ARRAY OF REAL);
   (*
      Tabulates sales totals by year. Sums are stored in
      array SumByYear.
      Pre : Record Sales is defined.
      Post: Elements SumByYear[FirstYear-MinYear] through
            SumByYear[LastYear-MinYear] are tabulated.
   *)

   PROCEDURE TabMonth (VAR Sales (* input *) : SalesRecord;
                       VAR SumByMonth (* output *) : ARRAY OF REAL);
   (*
      Tabulates sales totals by month. Sums are stored in
      array SumByMonth.
      Pre : Record Sales is defined.
      Post: Elements SumByMonth[January..December] are tabulated for
            the years FirstYear..LastYear.
   *)

   PROCEDURE GetFirst (Sales : SalesRecord) : CARDINAL;
   (*
      Returns the first year of the sales period.
      Pre : Record Sales is defined.
      Post: Returns the FirstYear field.
   *)

   PROCEDURE GetLast (Sales : SalesRecord) : CARDINAL;
   (*
      Returns the last year of the sales period.
      Pre : Record Sales is defined.
      Post: Returns the LastYear field.
   *)

END SalesTableADT.
```

The implementation of each procedure is relatively straightforward. The implementation module is shown in Fig. 10.11.

Figure 10.11 ▸ *Implementation Module for SalesTableADT*

```
IMPLEMENTATION MODULE SalesTableADT;
(*
   Implementation module for abstract data type for a table of sales
   data organized by year and month. The operations performed
```

```
   include: reading the sales data, displaying the data, and
   tabulating sums by year or month.
*)
   FROM InOut IMPORT
     Read, ReadCard, Write, WriteCard, WriteString, WriteLn;

   FROM RealInOut IMPORT
     ReadReal;

   FROM SimpleIO IMPORT
     EnterCard, WriteRealFormat;

   FROM DatesADT IMPORT
     Month,                        (* data type *)
     WriteMonth;                   (* procedure *)

(* Data Type SalesRecord is declared in the definition module. *)

(* Operators *)

   PROCEDURE EnterSales (VAR Sales (* output *) : SalesRecord);
   (*
      Reads the sales data into the record Sales.
      Pre : None
      Post: The fields FirstYear and LastYear are defined and
            sales data are read into array Volume for each month of
            years FirstYear..LastYear.
      Uses: EnterCard from SimpleIO; WriteString, WriteLn from InOut;
            ReadReal from RealInOut.
   *)
      VAR
        CurMonth : Month;                         (* current month *)
        CurYear : YearRange;                      (* current year *)

   BEGIN (* EnterSales *)
     (* Enter first and last years of sales data. *)
     WriteString ('Enter first year of sales data: ');  WriteLn;
     EnterCard (MinYear, MaxYear, Sales.FirstYear);
     WriteLn;
     WriteString ('Enter last year of sales data: ');   WriteLn;
     EnterCard (MinYear, MaxYear, Sales.LastYear);
     WriteLn;  WriteLn;

     (* Enter table data. *)
     FOR CurYear := Sales.FirstYear TO Sales.LastYear DO
       WriteString ('For year ');
       WriteCard (CurYear, 4);
       WriteLn;
       WriteString ('Enter sales amount for each month or 0.0');
       WriteLn;
       FOR CurMonth := January TO December DO
         WriteMonth (CurMonth);
```

```
      WriteString (' $');
      ReadReal (Sales.Volume[CurYear, CurMonth]);
      WriteLn
    END; (* FOR CurMonth *)
    WriteLn
  END (* FOR CurYear *)
END EnterSales;


PROCEDURE DisplaySales (VAR Sales (* input *) : SalesRecord);
(*
   Displays the sales data.
   Pre : Record Sales is defined.
   Post: Displays a two-dimensional table of sales volume
         by month for years FirstYear..LastYear.

   Due to line length limits,
   the first 6 months and last 6 months of each year are shown in
   separate tables. Uses ShowHalf to display each table.
*)

   PROCEDURE ShowHalf (VAR Sales (* input *) : SalesRecord;
                       FirstMonth, LastMonth (* input *) : Month);
   (*
      Displays the sales amounts by year for each of the months
      from FirstMonth to LastMonth.
      Pre : Array Sales and FirstMonth and LastMonth are defined.
      Post: Displays sales volumes in a table whose rows are
            FirstYear..LastYear and whose columns are FirstMonth..
            LastMonth.
      Uses: WriteString, WriteCard, WriteLn from InOut;
            WriteRealFormat from SimpleIO; WriteMonth from
            DatesADT.
   *)
      VAR
        CurMonth : Month;               (* loop-control variable *)
        CurYear : YearRange;            (* loop-control variable *)

   BEGIN (* ShowHalf *)
     (* Print table heading for 6 months of each year. *)
     WriteString ('Year  ');
     FOR CurMonth := FirstMonth TO LastMonth DO
       WriteMonth (CurMonth);           (* Print month names *)
       WriteString ('  ')
     END; (* FOR *)
     WriteLn;                              (* End the heading *)

     (* Print sales figures for 6 months of each year. *)
     FOR CurYear := Sales.FirstYear TO Sales.LastYear DO
       WriteCard (CurYear, 4);
       WriteString ('  ');
       FOR CurMonth := FirstMonth TO LastMonth DO
```

```
        WriteRealFormat (Sales.Volume[CurYear, CurMonth], 9, 2);
        WriteString ('  ')
      END; (* FOR CurMonth *)
      WriteLn
    END (* FOR CurYear *)
  END ShowHalf;

BEGIN (* DisplaySales *)
  (* Display first 6 months of array Sales. *)
  ShowHalf (Sales, January, June);
  WriteLn;

  (* Display last 6 months of array Sales. *)
  ShowHalf (Sales, July, December)
END DisplaySales;

PROCEDURE TabYear (VAR Sales (* input *) : SalesRecord;
                   VAR SumByYear (* output *) : ARRAY OF REAL);
(*
   Tabulates sales totals by year. Sums are stored in
   array SumByYear.
   Pre : Record Sales is defined.
   Post: Elements SumByYear[FirstYear-MinYear] through
         SumByYear[LastYear-MinYear] are tabulated.
*)
   VAR
     CurMonth : Month;                  (* loop-control variable *)
     CurYear : YearRange;               (* loop-control variable *)
     Sum : REAL;                        (* sum for each year *)

BEGIN (* TabYear *)
  (* Find each annual total. *)
  FOR CurYear := Sales.FirstYear TO Sales.LastYear DO
    (* Accumulate sum for 12 months *)
    Sum := 0.0;
    FOR CurMonth := January TO December DO
      Sum := Sum + Sales.Volume[CurYear, CurMonth]
    END; (* FOR CurMonth *)
    SumByYear[CurYear-MinYear] := Sum      (* Store sales total *)
  END (* FOR CurYear *)
END TabYear;


PROCEDURE TabMonth (VAR Sales (* input *) : SalesRecord;
                    VAR SumByMonth (* output *) : ARRAY OF REAL);
(*
   Tabulates sales totals by month. Sums are stored in
   array SumByMonth.
   Pre : Record Sales is defined.
   Post: Elements SumByMonth[January..December] are tabulated for
         the years FirstYear..LastYear.
*)
```

```
  BEGIN (* TabMonth stub *)
    WriteString ('Procedure TabMonth entered.');  WriteLn
  END TabMonth;


  PROCEDURE GetFirst (Sales : SalesRecord) : CARDINAL;
  (*
     Returns the first year of the sales period.
     Pre : Record Sales is defined.
     Post: Returns the FirstYear field.
  *)
  BEGIN (* GetFirst *)
    RETURN Sales.FirstYear
  END GetFirst;


  PROCEDURE GetLast (Sales : SalesRecord) : CARDINAL;
  (*
     Returns the last year of the sales period.
     Pre : Record Sales is defined.
     Post: Returns the LastYear field.
  *)
  BEGIN (* GetLast *)
    RETURN Sales.LastYear
  END GetLast;

END SalesTableADT.
```

Procedures are imported from modules `InOut`, `RealInOut`, `DatesADT`, and `SimpleIO`. Data type `Month` must also be imported from `DatesADT`, because it is used as a type identifier in several procedures.

Procedure `EnterSales` consists of a nested pair of `FOR` loops with loop-control variables `CurYear` and `CurMonth`. It calls `WriteMonth` (see Fig. 10.1) to prompt for the sales data for a particular month, and the statement

```
ReadReal (Sales.Volume[CurYear, CurMonth]);
```

reads each data value into the appropriate element of array `Sales.Volume`.

Procedure `DisplaySales` calls procedure `ShowHalf` twice. The first time, the data in array `Sales.Volume` for the first six months of each year are printed; the second time, the data for the last six months are printed. This is done because many output devices can display only eighty characters per line.

Procedure `TabYear` accumulates the total sales for each year of the period covered in the array `SumByYear`. It does this by accumulating the sum of values across each row (selected by `CurYear`) of the sales table. `TabMonth` (not shown) accumulates the sum of values down each column of the array.

Now that we have an abstract data type for the major data structure of our problem, we can focus on developing the main module. The main module must display the menu and read and perform each option selected by the program user. Procedure EnterCard reads the option, and DoChoice performs it. The main module data requirements and algorithm follow.

PROBLEM INPUTS

the sales data (Sales)
the selected option (Choice : CARDINAL)

PROBLEM OUTPUTS

the sales data displayed by year and month or with sums by year only or by month only and graphical displays

MODULE VARIABLES

the array of month totals (SumByMonth)
the array of year totals (SumByYear)
a program flag indicating whether sales data are read (SalesDataRead : BOOLEAN)
a program flag indicating whether month sums are computed (MonthDone : BOOLEAN)
a program flag indicating whether year sums are computed (YearDone : BOOLEAN)

Algorithm

1. Read in each option selected and perform it.

The BOOLEAN variables SalesDataRead, MonthDone, and YearDone are program flags. They must be initialized to FALSE and may be updated by procedure DoChoice. The structure chart is shown in Fig. 10.12, and the main module in Fig. 10.13.

Figure 10.12 ▸ *Structure Chart for Sales Analysis Problem*

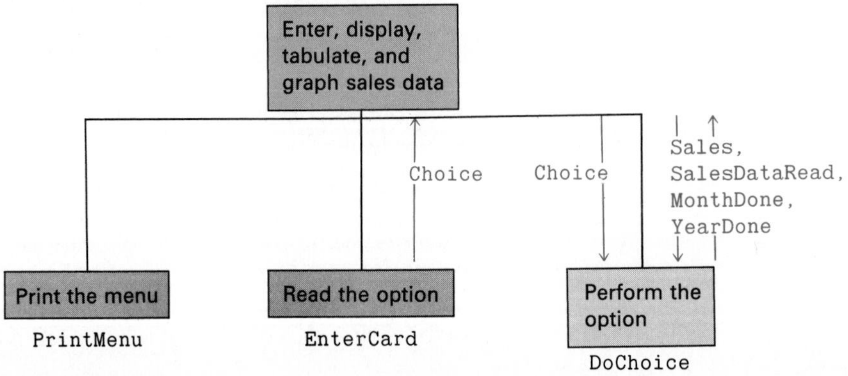

Figure 10.13 ▸ *Main Program for Sales Analysis Problem*

```
MODULE Analyze;
(*
   Analyzes  an  array of sales data. A menu is used to
   determine which operations are performed. The choices
   include: reading the sales data, displaying the data,
   tabulating sums by year or month, and graphing the sums.
*)
   FROM InOut IMPORT
     Read, ReadCard, Write, WriteCard, WriteString, WriteLn;

   FROM RealInOut IMPORT
     ReadReal, WriteReal;

   FROM SimpleIO
     IMPORT EnterCard;

   FROM RealArrayManip IMPORT
     Report, GraphIt;

   FROM DatesADT IMPORT
     Month;                            (* data type *)

   FROM SalesTableADT IMPORT
     MinYear,                          (* constant *)
     SalesRecord, YearRange,           (* data types *)
     TabMonth, TabYear,                (* procedures *)
     EnterSales, DisplaySales,
     GetFirst, GetLast;                (* functions *)

   CONST
     ExitChoice = 9;                   (* quit the program *)

   TYPE
     MonthArray = ARRAY Month OF REAL;
     YearArray = ARRAY YearRange OF REAL;

   VAR
     Sales : SalesRecord;          (* table of sales data *)
     SumByYear : YearArray;        (* sales totals for each year *)
     SumByMonth : MonthArray;      (* sales totals for each month *)
     SalesDataRead,                (* program flag for sales data *)
     YearDone,                     (* program flag for year sums *)
     MonthDone : BOOLEAN;          (* program flag for month sums *)
     Choice : CARDINAL;            (* selection of action taken *)


   PROCEDURE PrintMenu;

   (* Prints the menu. *)
   BEGIN  (* PrintMenu stub *)
     WriteString ('Procedure PrintMenu entered.');  WriteLn
   END PrintMenu;
```

```
  PROCEDURE DoChoice (Choice (* input *) : SmallCard;
                      VAR Sales (* inout *) : SalesRecord;
                      VAR SalesDataRead, MonthDone,
                          YearDone  (* inout *) : BOOLEAN;
                      VAR SumByYear (* inout *) : YearArray;
                      VAR SumByMonth (* inout *) : MonthArray);
  (*
     Performs the option selected by Choice.
     Pre : Choice and Sales are defined.
     Post: Resets SalesDataRead and reads data into Sales if
           Choice is 1. Resets YearDone to TRUE and tabulates
           SumByYear if Choice is 3. Resets MonthDone to TRUE
           and tabulates SumByMonth if Choice is 4.
  *)
  BEGIN  (* DoChoice stub *)
    WriteString ('Procedure DoChoice entered.');  WriteLn
  END DoChoice;


BEGIN  (* Analyze *)
  (* Initialize program flags. *)
  SalesDataRead := FALSE;  MonthDone := FALSE;  YearDone := FALSE;

  (* Read in each option selected and perform it. *)
  REPEAT
    (* Read and validate the user's choice. *)
    PrintMenu;                                (* Display the menu *)
    EnterCard (1, ExitChoice, Choice);        (* Read Choice *)
    WriteLn;
    DoChoice (Choice, Sales, SalesDataRead, MonthDone,
              YearDone, SumByYear, SumByMonth)
  UNTIL Choice = ExitChoice;

  WriteString ('Sales analysis completed.');  WriteLn
END Analyze.
```

Procedure `PrintMenu` consists of a sequence of output operations only and is left as an exercise at the end of this section. Procedure `DoChoice` calls the operator(s) required to carry out the user's selection. `DoChoice` must also check whether the user's selection is valid based on `SalesDataRead`, `Year-Done`, and `MonthDone`. All operators are procedures imported from modules `SalesTableADT` and `RealArrayManip` (see Fig. 8.14). Procedure `DoChoice` is shown in Fig. 10.14.

Figure 10.14 ▸
Procedure DoChoice

```
PROCEDURE DoChoice (VAR Choice (* inout *) : CARDINAL;
                    VAR Sales (* inout *) : SalesRecord;
```

```
                    VAR SalesDataRead, MonthDone,
                            YearDone  (* inout *) : BOOLEAN;
                    VAR SumByYear (* inout *) : YearArray;
                    VAR SumByMonth (* inout *) : MonthArray);
(*
   Performs the option selected by Choice.
   Pre : Choice and Sales are defined.
   Post: Resets SalesData Read to TRUE and reads data into Sales if
         Choice is 1. Resets YearDone to TRUE and tabulates
         SumByYear if Choice is 3. Resets MonthDone to TRUE
         and tabulates SumByMonth if Choice is 4. Resets Choice
         to 0 if ExitChoice was selected by error.
*)
   VAR
     ExitChar : CHAR;      (* used to validate exit request *)

BEGIN (* DoChoice *)
   (* Make sure that option 1 is performed first. *)
   IF NOT SalesDataRead & (1 < Choice) & (Choice < ExitChoice) THEN
     WriteString ('You must enter sales data first.');
     WriteLn;
     RETURN
   END; (* IF *)

   (* Process the option selected. *)
   CASE Choice OF
     1 : EnterSales (Sales);
         SalesDataRead := TRUE
   | 2 : WriteString ('Table of Sales Volume by Year and Month');
         WriteLn;
         DisplaySales (Sales)
   | 3 : TabYear (Sales, SumByYear);
         WriteString ('Year sums tabulated');
         WriteLn;
         YearDone := TRUE
   | 4 : TabMonth (Sales, SumByMonth);
         WriteString ('Month Sums tabulated');
         WriteLn;
         MonthDone := TRUE
   | 5 : IF YearDone THEN
           WriteString ('Table of Sales Totals by Year');
           WriteLn;
           WriteString ('The first table line represents Year ');
           WriteCard (GetFirst(Sales), 4);
           WriteLn;
           WriteString('      Year     Sales'); Write Ln;
           Report (SumByYear, GetFirst(Sales)-MinYear,
                   GetLast(Sales)-MinYear)
         ELSE
           WriteString ('You must tabulate year sums first.');
           WriteLn
         END (* IF *)
```

```
  | 6 : IF MonthDone THEN
          WriteString ('Table of Sales Totals by Month');
          WriteLn;
          WriteString ('The first table line represents January');
          WriteLn;
          WriteString ('     Month      Sales');  WriteLn;
          Report (SumByMonth, 0, 11)
        ELSE
          WriteString ('You must tabulate month sums first.');
          WriteLn
        END (* IF *)
  | 7 : IF YearDone THEN
          WriteString ('The first bar represents Year ');
          WriteCard (GetFirst(Sales), 4);  WriteLn;
          WriteString ('      Year       Sales in Dollars');
          WriteLn;
          GraphIt (SumByYear, GetFirst(Sales)-MinYear,
                   GetLast(Sales)-MinYear)
        ELSE
          WriteString ('You must tabulate year sums first.');
          WriteLn
        END (* IF *)
  | 8 : IF MonthDone THEN
          WriteString ('The first bar represents January');
          WriteLn;
          WriteString ('     Month       Sales in Dollars');
          WriteLn;
          GraphIt (SumByMonth, 0, 11)
        ELSE
          WriteString ('You must tabulate month sums first.');
          WriteLn
        END (* IF *)
  | ExitChoice :  (* verify exit *)
        WriteString ('Are you sure you want to exit?  ');
        WriteString ('Enter Y (yes) or N (no): ');
        Read (ExitChar);  Write (ExitChar);  WriteLn;
        IF CAP(ExitChar) # 'Y' THEN
          Choice := 0              (* cancel exit request *)
        END (* IF *)
  ELSE
    WriteString ('Error in option selected.');  WriteLn
  END; (* CASE *)
  WriteLn
END DoChoice;
```

DoChoice begins with an IF statement that ensures that only options 1 (enter sales data) and ExitChoice (exit the program) can be performed when the sales table is undefined. The CASE statement calls the procedures required to perform a valid option or displays an error message for an invalid option.

Options 1 through 4 use procedures from module SalesTableADT. Options 5 and 6 use procedure Report from module RealArrayManip (see Fig. 8.14) to display the subscripts and element values for a one-dimensional array (SumByYear or SumByMonth). Options 5 and 7 use functions GetFirst and GetLast to define the subscript range for array SumByYear. Options 7 and 8 use GraphIt (Fig. 8.17) from module RealArrayManip to draw a bar graph.

A sample run of the sales analysis program is shown in Fig. 10.15. To save space, only part of the data entry process and the first menu display are shown.

Figure 10.15 ▸ *Sample Run of the Sales Analysis Program*

```
GENERAL SALES ANALYSIS -- choose an option

1. Enter sales data for a specified year range into a table
2. Display sales table
3. Tabulate sales data by year
4. Tabulate sales data by month
5. Display sales data by year
6. Display sales data by month
7. Graph sales data by year
8. Graph sales data by month
9. Exit the program

Enter a cardinal between 1 and 9: 1

Enter first year of sales data:
Enter a cardinal between 1900 and 1999: 1987

Enter last year of sales data:
Enter a cardinal between 1900 and 1999: 1988

For year 1987
Enter sales amount for each month or 0.0
January   $1000.00
February  $600.00
March     $700.00
 ...

For year 1988
Enter sales amount for each month or 0.0
January   $500.00
February  $400.00
March     $400.00
 ...

Enter a cardinal between 1 and 9: 2

Table of Sales Volume by Year and Month
```

```
Year  January    February   March      April      May        June
1987   1000.00     600.00     700.00     800.00    950.00    1000.00
1988    500.00     400.00     400.00     900.00   1000.00      55.00

Year  July       August     September  October    November   December
1987    500.00     500.00     900.00     600.00    950.50    1000.00
1988    300.00     800.00     750.00     900.00    600.00     300.00

Enter a cardinal between 1 and 9: 3

Year sums tabulated

Enter a cardinal between 1 and 9: 5

Table of Sales Totals by Year
The first table line represents Year 1987
      Year     Sales
        87   9500.50
        88   6905.00

Enter a cardinal between 1 and 9: 7

The first bar represents Year 1987
      Year      Sales in Dollars
        87|**************************************************
        88|************************************
      0.00^         ^         ^         ^         ^         ^ 9500.50
Each point represents a value of     190.00

Enter a cardinal between 1 and 9: 9

Are you sure you want to exit?  Enter Y (yes) or N (no): Y

Sales analysis completed.
```

Program Style

Verifying an Exit Request

The `CASE` statement in procedure `DoChoice` requires the program user to verify that he/she wants to exit the sales analysis program when `Choice` is `ExitChoice`. Without this verification step, all data entry and analysis performed so far may have to be repeated if the program user selects option `ExitChoice` by mistake. The verification step prevents this from happening.

SELF-CHECK EXERCISE FOR SECTION 10.2

1. Write procedures `PrintMenu` and `TabMonth`.

10.3 Arrays of Records

Often a data collection contains items of different types. For example, the data representing the performance of a class of students on an exam consists of the student names, exam scores, and grades assigned.

One approach to organizing these data would be to declare separate arrays with identical subscript types for the names, scores, and grades, as shown.

```
CONST
  MaxClassSize = 200;

TYPE
  ClassRange = [1..MaxClassSize];
  String20 = ARRAY [0..19] OF CHAR;

VAR
  Names  : ARRAY ClassRange OF String20;
  Scores : ARRAY ClassRange OF INTEGER;
  Grades : ARRAY ClassRange OF CHAR;
```

These three arrays are called *parallel arrays*, because all the data items with the same subscript (say, *i*) pertain to a particular student (the *i*th student). Related data items are in the same shade of color in the arrays shown in Fig. 10.16. The data for the first student are stored in `Names[1]`, `Scores[1]`, and `Grades[1]`. A better way to organize the student data is shown in the next section.

Figure 10.16 ▸ *Three Parallel Arrays*

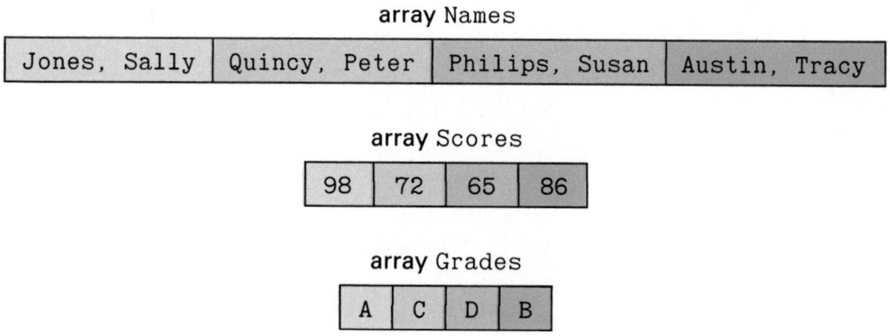

Declaring an Array of Students

A more natural organization of the class performance data is to group all the information pertaining to a particular student in a record. The data structure declared next represents the class data as a single array of records named `Class`. A sample array `Class` is shown in Fig. 10.17.

Figure 10.17 ▸
Array of Records

```
CONST
  MaxClassSize = 200;

TYPE
  ClassRange = [1..MaxClassSize];
  String20 = ARRAY [0..19] OF CHAR;
  Student = RECORD
              Name  : String20;
              Score : INTEGER;
              Grade : CHAR
            END; (* Student *)

VAR
  Class  : ARRAY ClassRange OF Student;
```

array Class

	Name	Score	Grade
Class[1]	Jones, Sally	98	A
Class[2]	Quincy, Peter	72	C
Class[3]	Philips, Susan	65	D
Class[4]	Austin, Tracy	86	B

In Fig. 10.17, the data for the first student are stored in `Class[1]`. The individual data items are `Class[1].NAME`, `Class[1].SCORE`, and `Class[1].GRADE`.

If procedure `ReadOneStudent` is available to read a single student record, the following `FOR` statement can be used to fill the entire array `Class` with data.

```
FOR i := 1 TO MaxClassSize DO
  ReadOneStudent (Class[i])
END (* FOR *)
```

Each time `ReadOneStudent` is called, the record returned will be stored as the *i*th element (1 <= *i* <= `MaxClassSize`) of array `Class`. The following `FOR` statement can be used to display all the names read.

```
FOR i := 1 TO MaxClassSize DO
  WriteString (Class[i].Name)
END (* FOR *)
```

Using the WITH Statement with an Array of Records

Be careful when using a WITH statement to process an array of records. For example, the WITH statement beginning

```
WITH Class[i] DO
```

uses the subscripted variable Class[i] as its record variable. The particular array element referenced depends on the value of i. If i is undefined or out of range, a run-time error will result.

If i is in range but happens to be changed inside the WITH statement, the array element referenced will not be affected. For example, the following statements repeatedly display the first student's name.

```
i := 1;
WITH Class[i] DO
  FOR i := 1 TO MaxClassSize DO
    WriteString (Name);  WriteLn
  END (* FOR *)
END (* WITH *)
```

When the WITH statement is reached, Class[1] is the record selected. Even though the loop-control variable i is changed by the FOR statement, Class[1] is still the record selected.

The correct way to sequence these statements is shown next.

```
FOR i := 1 TO MaxClassSize DO
  WITH Class[i] DO
    WriteString (Name);  WriteLn
  END (* WITH *)
END (* FOR *)
```

Now all student names will be printed, because i is changed by the FOR statement external to the WITH statement. Each time the WITH statement is reached, a new record will be selected. Whenever a FOR statement is used to access an array of records in sequential order, the WITH statement should be nested inside the FOR statement and not vice versa.

SELF-CHECK EXERCISES FOR SECTION 10.3

1. Write a procedure that could be used to read data into the three parallel arrays declared in this section. Assume there are enough students to fill the three arrays.
2. Write procedure ReadOneStudent. Read each student's name and score; leave the grade field undefined.

10.4 Case Study: Grading Program Revisited

The next problem illustrates the use of an array of records. The array of students declared earlier will be manipulated.

GRADING PROBLEM REVISITED

Problem: In Section 4.7, we wrote a program to assign grades to each student taking an exam. Since we could not store strings, only the student's initials were read as data. The grade category (outstanding, satisfactory, unsatisfactory) was determined by comparing the student's exam score to the data values `MinOut` and `MinSat`. We now want to improve this program to read and display the student's last name; to display the low score, high score, average score, and standard deviation; and to assign letter grades more equitably, based on the class average and standard deviation.

Discussion: The input data for the new grading program consists of a name (a string) and exam score (a cardinal) for each student; the output consists of the exam statistics and the grade (a character) assigned to each student. The problem data requirements and algorithm follow.

PROBLEM INPUTS

the name and score of each student taking the exam
the number of students taking the exam

PROBLEM OUTPUTS

the exam statistics including the low score, high score, average score, and standard deviation
the grade assigned to each student

Algorithm

1. Read the student data.
2. Compute the exam statistics.
3. Print the exam statistics.
4. Assign letter grades to each student.
5. Print each student's final record.

We can organize the data for a single student as a record; the data for the entire class can then be stored in an array of records. Each student record should contain storage space for the student's name, score, and the grade to be assigned.

Besides the data on each student, our "gradebook page" must contain a count of the number of students in the class. If we implement our gradebook page and its operators as an abstract data type, the main program module will be easier to write. The definition module for this abstract data type is shown in Fig. 10.18.

Figure 10.18 ▸ *Definition Module for StudentsADT*

```
DEFINITION MODULE StudentsADT;
(*
   Abstract data type for representing a gradebook page. Contains
   procedures for processing all data for a class of students.
*)
   EXPORT QUALIFIED
     Student, GradeBookPage, ScoreArray,         (* data types *)
     ReadStudents, DisplayStudents,              (* procedures *)
     ExtractScores, AssignGrades,
     GetClassSize;                               (* function *)

(* Data Types *)

   CONST
     StringSize = 20;               (* length of each name string *)
     MaxClassSize = 200;            (* maximum number of students *)

   TYPE
     StringIndex = [0..StringSize-1];
     String20 = ARRAY StringIndex OF CHAR;
     Student = RECORD                             (* one student record *)
                 Name : String20;
                 Score : INTEGER;
                 Grade : CHAR
               END; (* Student *)

     ClassRange = [1..MaxClassSize];
     StudentArray = ARRAY ClassRange OF Student; (* array of
                                                     records *)
     ScoreArray = ARRAY ClassRange OF INTEGER;  (* array of
                                                    integers *)

     GradeBookPage = RECORD
                       NumStu : CARDINAL;        (* size of the class *)
                       Class : StudentArray     (* array of students *)
                     END; (* GradeBookPage *)

(* Operators *)

   PROCEDURE ReadStudents (VAR Test (* output *) : GradeBookPage);
   (*
      Reads in the student records for one test and the class size.
      Pre : None
      Post: Record Test is defined.
   *)

   PROCEDURE DisplayStudents (VAR Test (* input *) : GradeBookPage);
   (*
      Displays the student records.
      Pre : Record Test is defined.
```

```
     Post: Displays exam performance data for each student.
  *)

  PROCEDURE AssignGrades (VAR Test (* inout *) : GradeBookPage;
                          Average, StandardDev (* input *) : REAL);
  (*
     Assigns letter grade to each student based on the exam score,
     class average, and standard deviation.
     Pre : All exam scores are stored in Test, and Average and
           StandardDev are defined.
     Post: The letter grade assigned to each student is stored in
           Test.
  *)

  PROCEDURE ExtractScores (VAR Test (* input *) : GradeBookPage;
                           VAR Scores (* output *) : ScoreArray);
  (*
     Extracts the exam scores from Test and stores them in Scores.
     Pre : All exam scores are stored in Test.
     Post: Test.Class[i].Score is copied to Scores[i].
  *)

  PROCEDURE GetClassSize (VAR Test : GradeBookPage) : CARDINAL;
  (*
     Determines the class size for the exam.
     Pre : Record Test is defined.
     Post: Returns Test.NumStu
  *)

END StudentsADT.
```

The data type `GradeBookPage` is a record with a `CARDINAL` field (`NumStu`) for storing the count of students who took the exam and an array field (`Class`) for storing the student records. All procedures manipulate a parameter (`Test`) of type `GradeBook`. `Test` is declared as a variable parameter in `DisplayStudents`, `ExtractScores`, and `GetClassSize`, even though it is used only for input. This is to save the extra time and memory required to make a local copy of this rather large data structure.

Procedure `ExtractScores` copies the exam score field of each record into the corresponding element of an array of integer values. Once this is done, the main module can use another utility module to compute the exam statistics, since they depend only on the scores. The implementation module for `StudentsADT` is shown in Fig. 10.19.

Figure 10.19 ▸ *Implementation Module for StudentsADT*

```
IMPLEMENTATION MODULE StudentsADT;
(*
   Abstract data type for representing a gradebook page. Contains
   procedures for processing all data for a class of students.
```

```
*)
   FROM InOut IMPORT
     ReadInt, ReadString, Write, WriteCard, WriteString, WriteLn;

   FROM RealInOut IMPORT
     WriteReal;

   FROM SimpleIO IMPORT
     EnterCard, MyReadString, WriteStringFormat;

(*
   Data Types GradeBookPage and Student are declared
   in the definition module.

   Operators
*)

   PROCEDURE ReadStudents (VAR Test (* output *) : GradeBookPage);
   (*
      Reads in the student records for one test and the class size.
      Pre : None
      Post: Record Test is defined.
   *)
      VAR
        NextStudent : Student;          (* current student record *)
        i : ClassRange;

      PROCEDURE ReadOneStudent (VAR OneStudent (* output *) :
                                                     Student);

      (* Enters the Name field and Score field of OneStudent. *)
      BEGIN (* ReadOneStudent *)
        WITH OneStudent DO
          WriteString ('Name : ');  MyReadString (Name);  WriteLn;
          WriteString ('Score: ');  ReadInt (Score);      WriteLn
        END (* WITH *)
      END ReadOneStudent;

   BEGIN  (* ReadStudents *)
     WriteString ('How many students took the exam?');  WriteLn;
     EnterCard (1, MaxClassSize, Test.NumStu);
     WriteString ('Enter the data requested for each student.');
     WriteLn;
     FOR i := 1 TO Test.NumStu DO
       WriteString ('Data for student ');
       WriteCard (i, 3);  WriteLn;
       ReadOneStudent (Test.Class[i]);      (* Read next student *)
       WriteLn
     END (* FOR *)
   END ReadStudents;


   PROCEDURE DisplayStudents (VAR Test (* input *) : GradeBookPage);
```

```
(*
   Displays the student records.
   Pre : Record Test is defined.
   Post: Displays exam performance data for each student.
   Uses: WriteStringFormat from SimpleIO.
*)
   VAR
     i : ClassRange;           (* loop-control variable *)

BEGIN (* DisplayStudents *)
  WriteString ('Table of students follows:');
  WriteLn;
  (* Print heading *)
  WriteString ('Name                          Score     Grade');
  WriteLn;

  (* Print each student's data. *)
  FOR i := 1 TO Test.NumStu DO
    WITH Test.Class[i] DO
      WriteStringFormat (Name, StringSize);
      WriteCard (Score, 10);
      WriteString ('        ');
      Write (Grade);
      WriteLn
    END (* WITH *)
  END (* FOR *)
END DisplayStudents;


PROCEDURE AssignGrades (VAR Test (* inout *) : GradeBookPage;
                        Average, StandardDev (* input *) : REAL);
(*
   Assigns letter grade to each student based on the exam score,
   class average, and standard deviation.
   Pre : All exam scores are stored in Test, and Average and
         StandardDev are defined.
   Post: The letter grade assigned to each student is stored in
         Test.
*)
BEGIN (* AssignGrades stub *)
  WriteString ('AssignGrades entered');  WriteLn
END AssignGrades;

PROCEDURE ExtractScores (VAR Test (* input *) : GradeBookPage;
                         VAR Scores (* output *) : ScoreArray);
(*
   Extracts the exam scores and stores them in Scores.
   Pre : All exam scores are stored in Test.
   Post: Test.Class[i].Score is copied to Scores[i].
*)
   VAR
     i : ClassRange;           (* loop-control variable *)
```

```
  BEGIN (* ExtractScores *)
    FOR i := 1 TO Test.NumStu DO
      Scores[i] := Test.Class[i].Score
    END (* FOR *)
  END ExtractScores;


  PROCEDURE GetClassSize (VAR Test : GradeBookPage) : CARDINAL;
  (*
     Determines the class size for the exam.
     Pre : Record Test is defined.
     Post: Returns Test.NumStu
  *)
  BEGIN (* GetClassSize *)
    RETURN Test.NumStu
  END GetClassSize;

END StudentsADT.
```

Procedure `ReadStudents` calls procedure `ReadOneStudent` once for each student who took the exam. `ReadOneStudent` reads the next student's name and score into record `Test.Class[i]`.

Procedure `DisplayStudents` displays a table of student records, one student record per output line. The statement headers

```
FOR i := 1 TO Test.NumStu DO
  WITH Test.Class[i] DO
```

select the record variable, `Test.Class[i]`, to be printed. Since the `WITH` statement is nested inside the `FOR` statement and `i` is the loop-control variable, a different student's record is printed on each output line. It would be an error to attempt to nest the `FOR` statement inside the `WITH` statement.

`DisplayStudents` calls procedure `WriteStringFormat` (see Fig. 8.30) to display the student's name in a field of width `20`. Since the student names are different lengths, the scores and grades would not be aligned in columns if `WriteString` was used to display the names.

In procedure `ExtractScores`, the statement

```
Scores[i] := Test.Class[i].Score
```

simply copies the `Score` field of each student record (`Test.Class[i].Score`) to the corresponding element of the array `Scores` (`Scores[i]`). The array `Scores` is returned to the main module for further processing. Procedure `GetClassSize` returns the count of students as its value.

Finally procedure `AssignGrades` assigns a letter grade to each student. The grade can be determined by comparing the student's score to the class average and standard deviation, which are input parameters. Table 10.1 describes the desired grade assignment.

Table 10.1 ▸ *Decision Table for Assigning Letter Grades*

SCORE RANGE	GRADE
`>= Average + 1.5 * StandardDev`	A
`>= Average + 0.5 * StandardDev`	B
`>= Average - 0.5 * StandardDev`	C
`>= Average - 1.5 * StandardDev`	D
`< Average - 1.5 StandardDev`	F

Procedure `AssignGrades` is shown in Fig. 10.20. The `IF` statement implements the decision table. The `FOR` loop causes this `IF` statement to be repeated once for each student. Because the `IF` statement is also nested inside the `WITH` statement, the fields `Score` and `Grade` reference fields of the record variable `Test.Class[i]` (i.e., the current student record).

Figure 10.20 ▸ *Procedure AssignGrades*

```
PROCEDURE AssignGrades (VAR Test (* inout *) : GradeBookPage;
                        Average, StandardDev (* input *) : REAL);
(*
   Assigns letter grade to each student based on the exam score,
   class average, and standard deviation.
   Pre : All exam scores are stored in Test, and Average and
         StandardDev are defined.
   Post: The letter grade for each student is stored in Test.
*)
   VAR
     i : ClassRange;                (* loop-control variable *)

BEGIN  (* AssignGrades *)
  FOR i := 1 TO Test.NumStu DO
    WITH Test.Class[i] DO
      IF FLOAT(Score) >= Average + 1.5 * StandardDev THEN
        Grade := 'A'
      ELSIF FLOAT(Score) >= Average + 0.5 * StandardDev THEN
        Grade := 'B'
      ELSIF FLOAT(Score) >= Average - 0.5 * StandardDev THEN
        Grade := 'C'
      ELSIF FLOAT(Score) >= Average - 1.5 * StandardDev THEN
        Grade := 'D'
      ELSE
        Grade := 'F'
      END (* IF *)
    END (* WITH *)
  END (* FOR *)
END AssignGrades;
```

Now that we have completed the abstract data type for our gradebook page, we can turn our attention to the main program module. The main program module imports module `StudentsADT` and a second module (`Stat-PackInteger`), which contains procedures that compute the average value and standard deviation for an array of integer values. In the main program module shown in Fig. 10.21, the variable `OneClass` stores the student data, and variable `Exams` stores the exam statistics.

Figure 10.21 ▸ *Main Program for Improved Grading Problem*

```
MODULE NewGrader;
(*
   Reads student names and scores and computes exam statistics such
   as low score, high score, average, standard deviation. Assigns
   letter grades based on the average score. Prints these results.
*)
   FROM InOut IMPORT
     WriteString, WriteLn, WriteInt;

   FROM RealInOut IMPORT
     WriteReal;

   FROM StudentsADT IMPORT
     Student, GradeBookPage, ScoreArray,    (* data types *)
     ReadStudents, DisplayStudents,         (* procedures *)
     AssignGrades, ExtractScores,
     GetClassSize;                          (* function *)

   FROM StatPackInteger IMPORT
     FindAverage, FindLow, FindHigh, FindStandardDev;

   TYPE
     ExamStats = RECORD
                   Low, High : INTEGER;
                   Average, StandardDev : REAL
                 END;  (* ExamStats *)

   VAR
     OneClass : GradeBookPage;              (* a class of students *)
     Exam : ExamStats;                      (* exam statistics *)
     NumScores : CARDINAL;                  (* number of scores *)
     Scores : ScoreArray;                   (* array of scores *)


   PROCEDURE ComputeStat (Scores (* input *) : ScoreArray;
                          NumScores (* input *) : CARDINAL;
                          VAR Exam (* output *) : ExamStats);
   (*
      Computes all exam statistics.
      Pre : Array of exam scores (Scores) is defined.
      Post: Computes low, high, average score and standard deviation.
      Uses: FindHigh, FindLow, FindAverage, FindStandardDev
            from StatPackInteger.
```

```
  *)
  BEGIN (* ComputeStat *)
    WITH Exam DO
      Average := FindAverage(Scores, 0, NumScores-1);
      Low := FindLow(Scores, 0, NumScores-1);
      High := FindHigh(Scores, 0, NumScores-1);
      StandardDev := FindStandardDev(Scores, Average,
                                     0, NumScores-1)
    END (* WITH *)
  END ComputeStat;

  PROCEDURE PrintStat (Exam (* input *) : ExamStats);

  (* Displays all exam statistics. *)
  BEGIN (* PrintStatStub*)
    WriteString ('PrintStat entered.');  WriteLn
  END PrintStat;

BEGIN (* NewGrader *)
  (* Read the student data. *)
  ReadStudents (OneClass);

  (* Compute the exam statistics. *)
  ExtractScores (OneClass, Scores);     (* get the array of scores *)
  NumScores := GetClassSize(OneClass); (* and its size *)
  ComputeStat (Scores, NumScores, Exam);

  (* Print the exam statistics. *)
  PrintStat (Exam);

  (* Assign letter grades to each student. *)
  AssignGrades (OneClass, Exam.Average, Exam.StandardDev);

  (* Print all student records. *)
  DisplayStudents (OneClass)
END NewGrader.
```

Procedure `ComputeStat` calls the procedures imported from `StatPackInteger` to compute the exam statistics and then stores the values returned in record variable `Exam`. Functions `FindLow` and `FindHigh` are similar to function `FindMax` shown in Fig. 8.16. Function `FindAverage` is discussed after the sample run of the program shown in Fig. 10.22.

Figure 10.22 ▸ *Sample Run of Improved Grading Program*

```
How many students took the exam?
Enter a cardinal between 1 and 200: 3
Enter the data requested for each student.
Data for student   1
```

```
Name : Joe Costa
Score: 80

Data for student   2
Name : Lee Hayes
Score: 70

Data for student   3
Name : Bill Titcomb
Score: 60
average     standard deviation      low      high
 70.0              10.0              60       80

Table of students follows:
Name                     Score     Grade
Joe Costa                   80         B
Lee Hayes                   70         C
Bill Titcomb                60         D
```

Function FindAverage

Module `StatPackInteger` consists of a set of functions that compute statistical measures for an array of integer values. One of these, function `Find-Average`, is shown in Fig. 10.23. The `FOR` loop accumulates the sum of the array elements in local variable `Sum`. The statement

```
RETURN FLOAT(Sum) / FLOAT(Max-Min+1)        (* Define result *)
```

divides `Sum` by the number of elements processed and returns the quotient as the function result.

Figure 10.23 ▸ *Function FindAverage*

```
PROCEDURE FindAverage (IntArray : ARRAY OF INTEGER;
                       Min, Max : CARDINAL) : REAL;
(*
   Returns the average of elements IntArray[Min..Max].
   Pre : IntArray is defined and 0 <= Min <= Max <= HIGH(IntArray).
   Post: The average value is returned.
*)
   VAR
     i : CARDINAL;        (* loop control and array subscript *)
     Sum : INTEGER;     (* accumulating sum of array elements *)

BEGIN (* FindAverage *)
  (* Validate parameters *)
  IF (Min < 0) OR (Min > Max) OR
                (Max > HIGH(IntArray)) THEN
    WriteString ('Error in FindAverage parameter');  WriteLn;
    RETURN 0.0
  END; (* IF *)
```

```
  (* Accumulate sum of array element values *)
  Sum := 0;
  FOR i := Min TO Max DO
    Sum := Sum + IntArray[i]
  END; (* FOR *)

  RETURN FLOAT(Sum) / FLOAT(Max-Min+1)        (* Define result *)

END FindAverage;
```

SELF-CHECK EXERCISES FOR SECTION 10.4

1. Write procedure `PrintStat`.
2. Write module `StatPackInteger`. Function `FindStandardDev` should implement the formula

$$\textit{standard deviation} = \sqrt{\frac{\sum_{i=1}^{N} (\textit{score}_i - \textit{average})^2}{N - 1}}$$

where $score_i$ is the ith score and N is the number of scores.

10.5 Searching an Array of Records

A common problem in processing arrays is *searching* an array to determine whether a particular data item is in the array. If the array elements are records, then we must compare a particular field of each record, called the *record key*, to the data item we are seeking. In this section, we will write a `Search` operator for the abstract data type `StudentsADT` (see Fig. 10.18).

EXAMPLE 10.9 ▶ Function `Search` (Fig. 10.24) searches the array `Test.Class` for a record whose `Name` field matches the *target name*, `StuName`. If the target name is located, `Search` returns the index of the student record with that name. Otherwise, it returns one more than the number of records (`Test.NumStu`) currently in the array. `Search` calls function `CompareStr` from module `Strings` (see Section 11.1) to compare names.

Figure 10.24 ▶ *Function Search*

```
PROCEDURE Search (VAR Test : GradeBookPage;
                  StuName : String20) : CARDINAL;
(*
   Searches for StuName in the Name field of array Test.Class.
   Pre : Test and StuName are defined.
   Post: Returns the subscript of StuName if found;
```

```
        otherwise, returns one more than the number of records
        in the array.
   Uses: CompareStr from Strings
*)
   VAR
     CurStu : CARDINAL;                    (* array subscript *)

BEGIN  (* Search *)
  (* Compare each student name to StuName until done. *)
  CurStu := 1;          (* Start with the first record *)
  WITH Test DO
    WHILE
      (* invariant:
           CurStu is <= NumStu+1 and
           StuName is not yet found in the array
      *)
         (CurStu <= NumStu) &
         (CompareStr(Class[CurStu].Name, StuName) # 0) DO
      INC (CurStu)                        (* Get next record *)
    END  (* WHILE *)
  END;   (* WITH *)
  (* assert: StuName is found or CurStu is out of range. *)

  (* Define the function result. *)
  RETURN CurStu                (* Return last subscript value *)
END Search;
```

Each time the `WHILE` loop is repeated, function `CompareStr` compares the student name selected by `CurStu` (`Class[CurStu].Name`) to the target name. If they are equal (function `CompareStr` returns zero), loop exit occurs and the location (`CurStu`) of the target name is returned as the result of `Search`. If the target name does not match the current student name, `CurStu` is incremented by one so the next student name can be checked. When all names have been checked without success (`CurStu > NumStu`), loop exit occurs and `Test.NumStu+1` (value of `CurStu`) is returned as the function result. ◂

Program Style

Taking Advantage of Short-Circuit Evaluation

The `WHILE` loop condition in Fig. 10.24 tests that the array subscript, `CurStu`, is in range before calling `CompareStr` to compare the `Name` fields. Because of the short-circuit evaluation of `BOOLEAN` expressions in Modula-2, the call to `CompareStr` does not occur if `CurStu` is out of range. The order of these tests is intentional. If the order was reversed, the call to `CompareStr` would always occur and would cause a run-time error if `CurStu` is larger than `NumStu`. Think carefully about the order of simple conditions in a `BOOLEAN` expression and use short-circuit evaluation to your advantage.

SELF-CHECK EXERCISE FOR SECTION 10.5

1. Write a procedure to count the number of students with a passing grade on the exam (D or higher).

10.6 Sorting an Array of Records

Section 4.2 discussed a simple sort operation involving three numbers. We performed the sort by examining pairs of numbers and exchanging them if they were out of order. There are many times when we would like to sort the elements in an array, for example, to print a grade report in alphabetical order or in order by score.

This section discusses a fairly intuitive (but not very efficient) algorithm called the *selection sort*. To perform a selection sort of an array with *N* elements (subscripts 1..*N*), we locate the largest element in the array and then switch the largest element with the element at subscript *N*, thereby placing the largest element at position *N*. Then we locate the largest element remaining in the subarray with subscripts 1..*N*–1, and switch it with the element at subscript *N*–1, thereby placing the second largest element at position *N*–1. Then we locate the largest element remaining in subarray 1..*N*–2 and switch it with the element at subscript *N*–2, and so on.

The operation of the selection sort algorithm is traced in Fig. 10.25. The diagram on the left shows the original array. Each subsequent diagram shows the array after the next largest element is moved to its final position in the array. The subarray in the darker color represents the portion of the array that is sorted after each exchange occurs. Note that it will require, at most, `N-1` exchanges to sort an array with `N` elements. The algorithm follows.

Selection Sort Algorithm

1. `FOR i := N TO 2 BY -1 DO`
    2. Find the largest element in subarray `1..i`.
    3. `IF` the largest element is not at subscript `i THEN`
        Switch the largest element with the one at subscript `i`.
       `END (* IF *)`

   `END (* FOR *)`

The refinement of step 2 also contains a `FOR` loop and is shown next.

STEP 2 REFINEMENT

2.1 Save `i` as the position of the largest so far in the subarray
2.2 `FOR j := i-1 TO 1 BY -1 DO`

```
2.3 IF the element at j > largest so far THEN
    2.4 Save j as the position of the largest so far.
  END (* IF *)
END (* FOR *)
```

Figure 10.25 ▸ *Trace of Selection Sort*

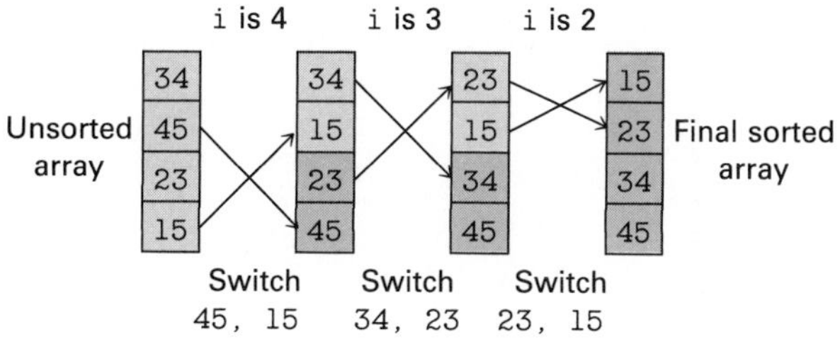

Procedure `SelectSort` in Fig. 10.26 implements the selection sort algorithm for the array field `Class` of parameter `Test`. Local variable `IndexOfMax` holds the location of the largest exam score found so far in the current subarray. After each execution of the inner `FOR` loop, procedure `Switch` is called to exchange the elements with subscripts `IndexOfMax` and `i`, provided that element `i` is not the next largest element. After the execution of procedure `SelectSort`, the student records will be ordered by exam score (record with smallest score first).

Figure 10.26 ▸ *Selection Sort Procedure*

```
PROCEDURE SelectSort (VAR Test (* inout *) : GradeBookPage);
(*
   Orders the data in array Test.Class by exam score.
   Pre : Record Test is defined.
   Post: The records in array Test.Class are ordered by score.
*)
   VAR
     i,                  (* subscript of last element in subarray *)
     j,          (* subscript of element being compared to max *)
     IndexOfMax : CARDINAL;                (* index of max so far *)

   PROCEDURE Switch (VAR Stu1, Stu2 (* inout *) : Student);

   (* Switches records Stu1 and Stu2. *)

      VAR
        TempStu : Student;          (* temporary student record *)

   BEGIN  (* Switch *)
     TempStu := Stu1;  Stu1 := Stu2;  Stu2 := TempStu
   END Switch;
```

```
BEGIN (* SelectSort *)
  WITH Test DO
    (* Order array Test.Class according to Score field. *)
    FOR i := NumStu TO 2 BY -1 DO
      (* Find the element in subarray 1..i with largest Score *)
      IndexOfMax := i;       (* assume element i is largest *)
      FOR j := i-1 TO 1 BY -1 DO
        IF Class[j].Score > Class[IndexOfMax].Score THEN
          IndexOfMax := j    (* element j is largest so far *)
        END (* IF *)
      END; (* FOR j *)
      (* assertion: element at IndexOfMax is largest in subarray *)

      (* Switch element at i with element at IndexOfMax *)
      IF IndexOfMax # i THEN
        Switch (Class[i], Class[IndexOfMax])
      END (* IF *)
    END (* FOR i *)
  END (* WITH *)
END SelectSort;
```

Analysis of Selection Sort

We mentioned earlier that, at most, $N-1$ exchanges are needed to sort an array of N elements. Each exchange occurs after exit from the inner `FOR` loop. An exchange is not performed, however, if the largest element is already at position `i` of subarray `1..i` (i.e., `IndexOfMax` = `i`).

For an array of N elements, there are $N-1$ comparisons of `Score` fields during the first execution of the inner loop, $N-2$ comparisons during the second execution, and so on. The number of `Score` field comparisons, therefore, is represented by the series

$$1 + 2 + 3 + \ldots + N-2 + N-1$$

The value of this series is represented by the closed form below.

$$\frac{N \times (N-1)}{2}$$

Therefore, to sort an array of 10 elements requires $10 \times 9 / 2$, or 45, `Score` field comparisons and at most 9 exchanges.

Finally, there is an additional comparison after each exit from the inner `FOR` loop (`i` is compared to `IndexOfMax`). This comparison takes less time to perform because there is no array reference required. We could eliminate these $N-1$ comparisons and always perform the exchange (even when the largest element was already at position `i`). However, this would be less efficient generally because it would take more time to perform an exchange of records than to do the comparisons.

SELF-CHECK EXERCISES FOR SECTION 10.6

1. Trace the execution of the selection sort on the list below. Show the array after each exchange occurs. How many exchanges are required? How many comparisons? `10 55 34 56 76 5`
2. How could you get the scores in descending order (largest score first)? What changes would be needed to sort the array `Class` by student name instead of score?
3. Since we are ordering the array by `Score` field, we propose changing procedure `Switch` to exchange only the `Score` fields. Describe the effect of this proposal.
4. When looking for the largest element in subarray `1..i`, explain why it is more efficient to start the search with the last element (i.e., `IndexOfMax := i`) rather than the first element.
5. Another method of performing the selection sort is to place the smallest element in position `1`, the next smallest in position `2`, and so on. Write this version.

10.7 Reusable Search and Sort Procedures

Procedures `Search` and `SelectSort` perform their intended tasks and could be incorporated into `StudentsADT`; however, they are not very general because their implementations are based on a particular data type. A major design goal of Modula-2 was to enable programmers to write software that can be reused easily. Obviously neither of these procedures satisfies that goal.

General Search Function

With a little care and forethought, we can write general search and sort procedures. A general search function should be able to search an array with any element type or key type. A general search function also should be able to search only a portion of an array or the entire array. A general search function is shown in Fig. 10.27.

Figure 10.27 ▸ *Function GeneralSearch*

```
PROCEDURE GeneralSearch (VAR Table : ARRAY OF ElementType;
                         TargetKey : KeyType;
                         First, Last : CARDINAL) : CARDINAL;
(*
   Searches for TargetKey in the subarray of array Table
   with subscripts First..Last.
   Pre : Table, TargetKey, First, and Last are defined.
         0 <= First <= Last <= HIGH(Table)
   Post: If TargetKey is found in Table, returns its subscript;
         otherwise, returns Last+1.
```

```
   Uses: KeyType, ElementType, Match declared externally
*)
   VAR
     i : CARDINAL;                  (* array subscript *)

BEGIN (* GeneralSearch *)
  (* Validate subarray bounds. *)
  IF (First < 0) OR (First > Last) OR
                  (Last > HIGH(Table)) THEN
    WriteString ('Invalid GeneralSearch parameter');  WriteLn;
    RETURN HIGH(Table) + 1
  END; (* IF *)

  (* Look for Target in each element until done. *)
  i := First;                    (* Start with first record *)
  WHILE
    (* invariant:
         i is in range First..Last+1 and
         TargetKey not yet found in the array
    *)
       (i <= Last) &
       NOT (Match(TargetKey, Table[i])) DO
    INC (i)                               (* Get next record *)
  END; (* WHILE *)
  (* assert: TargetKey is found or i is out of range. *)

  (* Define the function result. *)
  RETURN i                       (* Return last subscript value *)
END GeneralSearch;
```

Because `Table` is an open array parameter, the calling module must specify the bounds of the subarray to be searched, assuming the first record has a subscript of zero. Since many arrays have an actual lower subscript bound of one, the subscript bounds passed into `GeneralSearch` may be different from the declared subscript range. To indicate a search failure, `GeneralSearch` returns a value that is one more than the value stored in parameter `Last`.

There are two ways to make use of function `GeneralSearch`. We can duplicate the declaration of function `GeneralSearch` in an abstract data type that uses it, or we can place `GeneralSearch` in a separate library module. The first way is easier, but the second way is more general.

Figure 10.28 shows a search operator (function `Search`) that could be included in our abstract data type `StudentsADT`. We can rewrite this operator to call `GeneralSearch` to search the array of student records if we add the type and procedure declarations shown in this figure to the implementation module for `StudentsADT`. The revised function `Search` is shown at the bottom of the figure.

Figure 10.28 ▸ *Using GeneralSearch to Search Student Records*

```
TYPE
  ElementType = Student;
  KeyType = String20;

PROCEDURE Match (TargetKey : KeyType;
                 NextStudent : ElementType) : BOOLEAN;
(*
   Compares TargetKey to NextStudent.Name
   Pre : TargetKey and NextStudent.Name are defined.
   Post: Returns TRUE if the Name field of NextStudent
         is TargetKey; otherwise, returns FALSE.
*)
BEGIN (* Match *)
  RETURN CompareStr(TargetKey, NextStudent.Name) = 0
END Match;

(*  Insert procedure GeneralSearch here *)

PROCEDURE Search (VAR Test : GradeBookPage;
                  StuName : String20) : CARDINAL;
(*
   Searches for StuName in the Name field of array Test.Class.
   Pre : Test and StuName are defined.
   Post: Returns the subscript of StuName if found;
         otherwise, returns one more than the number of values
         in the array.
 *)
BEGIN (* Search *)
  RETURN GeneralSearch(Test.Class, StuName, 0, Test.NumStu-1) + 1
END Search;
```

The type declarations at the top of Fig. 10.28 describe the parameters of function `GeneralSearch` and enable Modula-2 to compile the function. Function `Match` returns `TRUE` only if the two strings being compared are identical. Function `GeneralSearch` should be inserted right after function `Match`.

Function `Search` calls `GeneralSearch` to search for the student whose name is `StuName` in our array `Test.Class`. The actual parameters passed into `First` and `Last` (`0` and `Test.NumStu-1`, respectively) cause the elements of `Test.Class` with subscripts `1..Test.NumStu` to be searched. Because the first record stored in `Test.Class` has a subscript of one (not zero), we must add one to the result returned by `GeneralSearch`.

Program Style

Tradeoffs in Writing General Procedures

Function `GeneralSearch` is a bit more complicated than function `Search`, because it validates its subarray bounds before performing a search. It also appears to be more difficult to use because it calls a user-defined function (`Match`) *to compare* element keys rather than using the utility function `CompareStr`. You might wonder if it is worthwhile to go through all this trouble to implement and use general procedures.

Once `GeneralSearch` has been written, it can search any portion of any array that has type `CARDINAL` subscripts. All that is needed is two type declarations and function `Match`. It is obviously much easier to supply these ingredients than to try to modify function `Search` (see Fig. 10.24) to search an array with a different structure than array `Test.Class`. The potential for error in modifying `Search` is also greater than the potential for error in writing the additional type declarations and function `Match`.

It appears, therefore, that the time spent in writing a general procedure like `GeneralSearch` would be recouped later in shorter program development and debugging time. For this reason, we recommend that you follow this practice whenever possible.

General Selection Sort Procedure

We just implemented a function for searching an array that could be reused relatively easily. To write a general sort procedure, we need to be able to compare field values of two array elements to determine which is the larger. The field being compared (called the *key field*) may contain string data, ordinal data, or real data. A `BOOLEAN` function `Bigger` (declared external to the sort procedure) actually performs the comparison. A general sort procedure is shown in Fig. 10.29.

Figure 10.29 ▸ *General Selection Sort Procedure*

```
PROCEDURE GeneralSort (VAR Table (* inout *) :
                                   ARRAY OF ElementType;
                       Last (* input *) : CARDINAL);
(*
   Orders the data in elements 0..Last of array Table
   by key field.
   Pre : Array Table is defined. Last <= HIGH(Table)
   Post: The records in array Table are ordered by key field.
   Uses: ElementType and Bigger declared externally
 *)
   VAR
     i,                (* subscript of last element in subarray *)
     j,           (* subscript of element being compared to max *)
     IndexOfMax : CARDINAL;              (* index of max so far *)

   PROCEDURE Switch (VAR Rec1, Rec2 (* inout *) : ElementType);
   (*
      Switches records Rec1 and Rec2.
   *)
      VAR
        TempRec : ElementType;   (* temporary student record *)
```

```
  BEGIN (* Switch *)
    TempRec := Rec1;  Rec1 := Rec2;  Rec2 := TempRec
  END Switch;

BEGIN (* GeneralSort *)
  (* Validate Last *)
  IF Last > HIGH(Table) THEN
    WriteString ('Number of elements is out of range.');
    WriteLn;
    Last := HIGH(Table)
  END; (* IF *)

  (* Order the array according to key field *)
  FOR i := Last TO 1 BY -1 DO
    (* Find the largest element in subarray 0..i *)
    IndexOfMax := i;          (* assume element i is largest *)
    FOR j := i-1 TO 0 BY -1 DO
      IF Bigger(Table[j], Table[IndexOfMax]) THEN
        IndexOfMax := j       (* element j is largest so far *)
      END (* IF *)
    END; (* FOR j *)
    (* assertion: element at IndexOfMax is largest in subarray *)

    (* Switch element at i with element at IndexOfMax *)
    IF IndexOfMax # i THEN
      Switch (Table[i], Table[IndexOfMax])
    END (* IF *)
  END (* FOR i *)
END GeneralSort;
```

There is a subtle difference between procedure `GeneralSort` and the earlier selection sort procedure. The loop-control variables `i` and `j` decrease to `1` and `0`, respectively, instead of `2` and `1`. The reason is that the open array parameter has a lower subscript bound of `0`, not `1`.

Figure 10.30 shows the changes needed in the implementation module of `StudentsADT` to enable procedure `SelectSort` to call `GeneralSort` to sort the array `Test.Class`. The actual subscript range, `1..Test.NumStu`, is mapped into the range `0..Test.NumStu-1` for the open array parameter, `Table`, in `GeneralSort`.

Function `Bigger` compares the student name field of adjacent array elements. To order the array by exam score instead, it is necessary only to substitute the `RETURN` statement

```
RETURN Rec1.Score > Rec2.Score
```

for the one currently in `Bigger`. This is another example of the versatility of procedure `GeneralSort`.

Figure 10.30 ▸
Using the General Sort Procedure

```
TYPE
  ElementType = Student;

PROCEDURE Bigger (Recl, Rec2 : ElementType) : BOOLEAN;
(*
   Compares the key fields of Recl and Rec2.
   Pre : Recl and Rec2 are defined.
   Post: Returns TRUE if the key field of Recl >
         key field of Rec2; otherwise, returns FALSE.
*)
BEGIN (* Bigger *)
  RETURN CompareStr(Recl.Name, Rec2.Name) = 1
END Bigger;

(* Insert procedure GeneralSort here. *)

PROCEDURE SelectSort (VAR Test (* inout *) : GradeBookPage);
(*
   Calls GeneralSort to order the array Test.Class
   Pre : Test.Class is defined.
   Post: Test.Class is ordered according to the comparison in
         function Bigger.
*)
BEGIN (* SelectSort *)
  GeneralSort (Test.Class, Test.NumStu-1)
END SelectSort;
```

SELF-CHECK EXERCISE FOR SECTION 10.7

1. Write a module `Elements` containing functions `Bigger` and `Match` and all the type declarations needed by the general search and sort procedures. Place `GeneralSearch` and `GeneralSort` in module `SortSearch`. Write the import and export statements for `StudentsADT` that will enable `Students–ADT` to import and use `GeneralSearch` and `GeneralSort`. Also, write the import and export statements for module `SortSearch`.

10.8 Common Programming Errors

When you use multidimensional arrays, make sure the subscript for each dimension is consistent with its declared type. If any subscript value is out of range, an error will be detected during run-time.

If you use nested `FOR` loops to process the array elements, make sure that the loop-control variables used as array subscripts are in the correct order. The order of the loop-control variables determines the sequence in which the array elements will be processed.

When an array of records is processed, the array name and subscript must be included as part of the field selector (e.g., `X[i].Key` references field `Key` of the *i*th record). If a `FOR` statement is used to process all array elements in sequence, then any `WITH` statement that references the array records must be nested inside the `FOR` statement, as shown next.

```
FOR i := 1 TO N DO
  WITH X[i] DO
    ...
```

As the loop-control variable `i` changes, the next array record is processed by the `WITH` statement. If the nesting order is reversed, as in

```
WITH X[i] DO
  FOR i := 1 to N DO
    ...
```

then the same array record is processed `N` times. The record that is processed is determined by the value of `i` when the `WITH` statement is first reached. Changing the value of `i` inside the `WITH` statement has no effect.

10.9 Chapter Review

Arrays of arrays, or multidimensional arrays, were used to represent tables of information and game boards. Nests of loops are needed to manipulate the elements of a multidimensional array in a systematic way. The correspondence between the loop-control variables and the array subscripts determines the order in which the array elements are processed.

You also saw how to manipulate arrays of records. Arrays of records can be used to represent many real-world data collections. We also introduced methods for searching and sorting arrays of records and discussed writing reusable procedures for these operations.

New Modula-2 Statements

The new Modula-2 statements introduced in this chapter are described in Table 10.2.

Table 10.2 ▸ *Summary of New Modula-2 Statements*

STATEMENT	EFFECT
Declaring Multidimensional Arrays	

`TYPE`
`  Matrix = ARRAY [1..52], Day OF REAL;`
 	
`VAR`
`  Sales : Matrix;`
	`Matrix` describes a two-dimensional array type with 52 rows and 7 columns (days of the week). `Sales` is an array of this type and can store 364 real numbers.

Table 10.2 ▸
(continued)

STATEMENT	EFFECT
Array References	
WriteReal (Sales[3, Monday], 12)	Displays the element of Sales for Monday of week 3.

FOR Week := 1 TO 52 DO
  FOR Today := Sunday TO Saturday DO
    Sales[Week, Today] := 0.0
  END
END
	Initializes each element of Sales to zero.

ReadReal (Sales[1, Sunday])	Reads the value for the rst Sunday into Sales.
Declaring Arrays of Records	

TYPE
  Element = RECORD
      Data : REAL;
      Key : CARDINAL
    END; (* Element *)
  DataArray = ARRAY [1..10] OF Element;
	DataArray is an array type with ten elements of type Element. Each Element has fields named Data and Key.

VAR MyData : DataArray	MyData is a variable of type DataArray.
Referencing an Array of Records	
MyData[1].Data := 3.14159; MyData[10].Key := 9999;	The real value 3.14159 is stored in the first Data field of array MyData; the value 9999 is stored in the last Key field.

CHAPTER 10 ▸

Review Questions

1. Define row-major order.
2. Declare an array that can be used to store each title of the Top 40 hits for each week of the year given that the TitleLength will be twenty characters.
3. Write the declaration of the array YearlyHours to store the hours each of five employees works each day of the week, each week of the year.
4. Write the declarations for the array CPUArray that will hold twenty records of type CPU. The record CPU has the following fields: IDNumber (eleven characters in length), Make (five characters), Location (fifteen characters), and Ports (INTEGER).
5. Use the following declarations to answer questions 5 through 9.

```
CONST
  TotalEmployees = 20;
```

```
TYPE
  Employee = RECORD
               ID : INTEGER;
               Rate,
               Hours : REAL
             END; (* Employee *)
  EmpArray = ARRAY [1..TotalEmployees] OF Employee;

VAR
  Employees : EmpArray;
```

Write the function `TotalGross` that will return the total gross pay, given the data stored in array `Employees`.

6. Explain what is wrong with the following fragment and fix it.

```
(* Display each employee's data *)
i := 1;
WITH Employees[i] DO
  WHILE i <= TotalEmployees DO
    WriteReal (Hours, 12);
    INC (i)
  END (* WHILE *)
END (* WITH *)
```

7. Explain what is wrong with the fragment below and fix it.

```
(* Display each employee until one whose ID = 999 is reached *)
i := 1;
WHILE (Employees[i].ID # 999) & (i <= TotalEmployees) DO
  INC (i);
  WriteString (Employees[i].Name);  WriteLn
END (* WHILE *)
```

8. Write a fragment that displays the ID number of each employee who works between ten and twenty hours per week.
9. Write a fragment that displays the ID number of the employee who works the most hours.
10. How many exchanges are required to sort the list of integers below using selection sort? How many comparisons are performed?

```
20 30 40 25 60 80
```

11. Procedure `SelectSort` in Section 10.6 placed the elements of an array in order by `Score` field. Change the condition in the procedure so that records with the same `Score` value will be ordered by `Name` field (smaller name first). The field `Score` is called the *primary key*, the field `Name` is called the *secondary key*.

CHAPTER 10 ▸

Programming Projects

1. Write a program that generates the Morse code equivalent of a sentence. First, read the Morse code for each letter and punctuation character and save it in an array of strings. Next, read and convert the sentence. Your program should print the Morse code for each word on a separate line.

2. The results of a true-false exam given to a computer science class have been coded for input to a program. The information available for each student consists of a student identification number and the student's answers to ten true-false questions. The available data are as follows:

Student Identification	*Answer String*
0080	FTTFTFTTFT
0340	FTFTFTTTFF
0341	FTTFTTTTTT
0401	TTFFTFFTTT
0462	TTFTTTFFTF
0463	TTTTTTTTTT
0464	FTFFTFFTFT
0512	TFTFTFTFTF
0618	TTTFFTTFTF
0619	FFFFFFFFFF
0687	TFTTFTTFTF
0700	FTFFTTFFFT
0712	FTFTFTFTFT
0837	TFTFTTFTFT

Write a program that first reads in the answer string representing the ten correct answers (use `FTFFTFFTFT` as data). Next, for each student, read the student's data and compute and store the number of correct answers for each student in one array, and store the student ID number in the corresponding element of another array. Determine the best score, `Best`. Then print a three-column table displaying the ID number, score, and grade for each student. The grade should be determined as follows: if the score is equal to `Best` or `Best-1`, give an A; if it is `Best-2` or `Best-3`, give a C. Otherwise, give an F.

3. Write a set of procedures to manipulate a pair of matrices. Provide procedures for addition, subtraction, and multiplication. Each procedure should validate its input parameters (i.e., check all matrix dimensions) before performing the required data manipulation.

4. The results from the mayor's race have been reported by each precinct as follows:

Precinct	*Candidate A*	*Candidate B*	*Candidate C*	*Candidate D*
1	192	48	206	37
2	147	90	312	21
3	186	12	121	38
4	114	21	408	39
5	267	13	382	29

Write a program to do the following:

a. Print out the table with appropriate headings for the rows and columns.
b. Compute and print the total number of votes received by each candidate and the percentage of the total votes cast.

c. If any one candidate received over 50 percent of the votes, the program should print a message declaring that candidate the winner.
d. If no candidate received 50 percent of the votes, the program should print a message declaring a runoff between the two candidates receiving the highest number of votes; the two candidates should be identified by their letter names.
e. Run the program once with the preceding data and once with candidate C receiving only 108 votes in precinct 4.

5. Write a program that reads the five cards representing a poker hand into a two-dimensional array (first dimension is suit, second dimension is rank). Evaluate the poker hand by using procedures to determine if the hand is a flush (all one suit), a straight (five consecutive cards), a straight flush (five consecutive cards of one suit), four of a kind, a full house (three of one kind, two of another), three of a kind, two pairs, or one pair.
6. An array of records can contain descriptions of people, including name, height, weight, sex, color of hair, color of eyes, religion. Write a program that reads and stores data into this array, sorts the array in alphabetical order by name, and prints its contents.
7. Write a program that searches an array of records of type `Employee` (see Section 9.1) to find and print the data stored for all employees who match a target description. The array of employee data should be read in first and then the target data. A blank target name indicates that the `Name` field should be ignored during the matching process. Add a third category (`Unknown`) for the `Sex` field. Enter a pair of numbers denoting a range of values for each numeric target field.
8. The inventory for a warehouse is to be kept on a computer and shipments into and from the warehouse (transactions) are to be processed. Each item will contain an ID number (three digits), name (maximum of ten characters), initial quantity on hand, and cost per item. Write a procedure that will read and store the initial quantities of items into an appropriate array of records until an ID number of zero is read. At this point, write the initial contents of the warehouse.

   Now process the transactions that will consist of the ID number for the item and the quantity of items shipped or received (if negative, the quantity was shipped; otherwise, the items were received). Process these transactions until done.

   After each transaction, display a message indicating the item name, the quantity shipped or received, and the new quantity on hand. The program should check to make sure that there are not more requests for items to be shipped than the number on hand and that the ID number requested for a transaction matches one in the warehouse.

   After all transactions are processed, print a list of all items in the warehouse. Show how many of each item remain and the approximate total value of each item in the inventory.

   Sample input might be:

```
376     BOLTS     350    0.05
142     NUTS      425    0.03
261     HAMMERS   100    10.45
0
142     -27
142     104
261     -75
```

11 ▸ Strings and Sets

So far, we have used procedure `WriteString` to display string data and procedure `ReadString` to read string data into strings (arrays of characters). We used the assignment operator to assign a value to a string variable. We also included two procedures, `MyStringRead` and `WriteStringFormat`, in module `SimpleIO` and used two procedures, `CompareStr` and `Length`, provided in module `Strings`. In this chapter, you will learn more about the procedures in module `Strings`.

We will also examine the set data type. You will learn how to perform the operations of set union, set intersection, and set difference in Modula-2 and how to test for subsets, supersets, and set equality. You will learn how to use sets and the *set membership operator* `IN` to simplify conditions.

11.1 Module Strings

Many computer applications are concerned with the manipulation of character strings or textual data rather than numerical data. For example, a word processor was used to write this text; computerized typesetters are used extensively in the publishing of books and newspapers; "personalized" junk mail is computer generated; computers are used in the analysis of great works of literature; and finally, a Modula-2 program is a sequence of words and symbols that are interpreted by a compiler.

Most Modula-2 systems provide a utility module, called `Strings`, that contains procedures and functions for manipulating strings. This section will describe these procedures and illustrate how they are used. Make sure you import any of these procedures that you want to use in a program.

Length of a String

As you have seen, a string declared to be of length *n* can contain fewer than *n* characters. Consequently, the current length of a string is variable and depends on the data stored in it. There are many applications in which we need to know the current length of a string. Module `Strings` provides the function `Length` for that purpose. The following syntax display shows the header for function procedure `Length` declared in module `Strings`.

Function Length

FORM:
```
PROCEDURE Length (VAR str : ARRAY OF CHAR) : CARDINAL;
```

EXAMPLE:
```
Lenl := Length(Name)   (* Stores the length of string
                          Name in Lenl.            *)
```

INTERPRETATION: Function `Length` returns the number of characters currently stored in string variable *str*. If *str* contains the null character, only characters up to the null character are counted.

EXAMPLE 11.1 ▸ If Name is a string, the statements

```
Name := 'abcde';
WriteString ('Length is ');
WriteCard (Length(Name), 2)
```

assign string value 'abcde' to Name and display the message 'Length is 5'. If the statement

```
Name := 'Leonardo';
```

is executed, the contents and length of string Name become 'Leonardo' and 8, respectively. ◂

EXAMPLE 11.2 ▸ Procedure ReplaceChar (Fig. 11.1) can be used to replace all occurrences of character InChar in the string argument InString with character OutChar. For example, if the symbol '#' is used to represent an embedded blank in a string read by ReadString, RelaceChar could be called to replace all symbols '#' with blank characters. The statements

```
WriteString ('Enter a string, use # for each blank: ');
ReadString (DataString);  WriteLn;
ReplaceChar (DataString, '#', ' ')
```

would accomplish this for string variable DataString. ◂

Figure 11.1 ▸ *Procedure ReplaceChar*

```
PROCEDURE ReplaceChar (VAR InString (* inout *) : ARRAY OF CHAR;
                       InChar, OutChar (* input *) : CHAR);
(*
   Replaces all occurrences of InChar with OutChar.
   Pre : InString, InChar, and OutChar are defined.
   Post: Each character InChar in InString is replaced by OutChar.
   Uses: Length from Strings.
*)
   VAR
     Next : CARDINAL;        (* subscript of next element of string *)

BEGIN (* ReplaceChar *)
  (* Examine each character of InString and replace if needed. *)
  FOR Next := 0 TO Length(InString)-1 DO
    IF InString[Next] = InChar THEN
      InString[Next] := OutChar    (* replace character at Next *)
    END (* IF *)
  END (* FOR *)
END ReplaceChar;
```

In the figure, the last character examined in the `FOR` loop is at position `Length(InString)-1`. This is the last character in the string where the first character is at position `0`.

String Comparison

We can compare individual characters in two strings directly. For example, the condition

```
FirstName[0] < LastName[0]
```

is true if the first character of `FirstName` is less than the first character in `LastName`. It is not possible, however, to use strings as operands of the relational operators. Consequently, we must use function `CompareStr` to compare two strings. We called `CompareStr` in Section 10.7 to compare two strings that were record keys.

The string *str1* is considered equal to *str2* if both strings are identical in contents and length. The string *str1* is considered less than string *str2* if *str1*`[i]` < *str2*`[i]` and the characters in positions `0..i-1` are the same in both strings. For example, when comparing `'abcd'` and `'abfg'`, the order relation is determined by the characters in position 2 (`'c'` and `'f'`). Since `'c'` < `'f'` is true, string `'abcd'` < `'abfg'` is also true. The string `'abc'` is considered less than the string `'abcd'` because the first three characters in both strings are the same and the null character at the end of the shorter string is less than any other character.

Function `CompareStr` returns an integer value (`-1`, `0`, `1`) to indicate the result of a string comparison. `CompareStr` is described in the next display.

Function CompareStr ▶

FORM: `PROCEDURE CompareStr (`*str1*`,` *str2* `: ARRAY OF CHAR) : INTEGER;`

EXAMPLE:
```
CompRes := CompareStr('Ace', 'Zebra')
                            (* stores -1 in CompRes *)
```

INTERPRETATION: Returns an integer value indicating the result of comparing *str1* with *str2*.

Returns −1 if *str1* < *str2*.
Returns 0 if *str1* = *str2*.
Returns 1 if *str1* > *str2*.

EXAMPLE 11.3 ▶ Table 11.1 shows the order relation for several pairs of alphabetic strings (strings of letters) and the result that would be returned by `CompareStr` for each pair of strings. The normal dictionary ordering prevails when two strings of only uppercase letters or only lowercase letters are compared.

Table 11.1 ▸
Order Relation for Alphabetic Strings

STR1	STR2	ORDER RELATION	RESULT OF COMPARESTR(STR1, STR2)	REASON
'ABC'	'BCA'	<	−1	'A' < 'B'
'ACES'	'AS'	<	−1	'C' < 'S'
'Boy '	'Boy '	<	−1	null < ' '
'Boy '	'Boys'	<	−1	' ' < 's'
'Boys'	'Boys'	=	0	identical
'boys'	'Boys'	>	1	'b' > 'B'
'Girls'	'Boys'	>	1	'G' > 'B'

The third and fourth lines are based on the order relation

```
null < ' ' < 's'
```

Two strings cannot be considered identical in Modula-2 unless they are the same length. The sixth line shows that the lowercase letters follow the uppercase letters in the ASCII Code. ◂

Table 11.2 shows the order relation for numeric and mixed strings.

Table 11.2 ▸
Order Relation for Numeric and Mixed Strings

STR1	STR2	ORDER RELATION	RESULT OF COMPARESTR(STR1, STR2)	REASON
'A99'	'B11'	<	−1	'A' < 'B'
'B11'	'B12'	<	−1	'1' < '2'
'123'	'345'	<	−1	'1' < '3'
'1a&'	'1a&'	=	0	identical
'123'	'103'	>	1	'2' > '0'
'34'	'123'	>	1	'3' > '1'
'034'	'123'	<	−1	'0' < '1'

The next to last line shows the curious result that '34' > '123' is true. This is because the condition value depends solely on the characters in position 0 of both strings and not on their numeric value. Remember, we are comparing strings of numeric characters, not numbers. To avoid this kind of result, make sure you include any leading zeros as shown in the last line of the table.

String Assignment

Since a string is an array of characters, the assignment operator := can be used to copy the contents of one string to another of the same type. Procedure Assign can be used when the source and destination strings are not the same type or even the same length.

Procedure Assign

```
FORM:    PROCEDURE Assign (VAR source, dest : ARRAY OF CHAR);

EXAMPLE: Assign (HusbandName, WifeName)   (* Copies the string in
                                             HusbandName to WifeName. *)
```

INTERPRETATION: The contents of string variable *source* are copied into string variable *dest*. If *dest* is too small to hold its new string value, the string value will be truncated.

The previous display indicates that the string value being assigned will be truncated if the string receiving it is too small. This is the case for all procedures in module `Strings`, that is, a string value returned by a procedure will be truncated if it cannot fit in the string receiving it. No error indication will be given when this happens.

Substrings and Procedure Copy

It is often necessary to manipulate *substrings*, or segments, of a larger character string. For example, we might want to examine the three components (month, day, year) of the string `'Jun 25, 1981'`. Procedure `Copy` can be used to do this, as shown next.

EXAMPLE 11.4 ▶ Assume that a date string (stored in `Date`) always has the form `'MMM DD, YYYY'`, where the characters represented by `MMM` are the month name, `DD` the day of the month, and `YYYY` the year. The procedure call statement

```
Copy(Date, 0, 3, MonthStr)
```

returns (in `MonthStr`) the substring of `Date` starting at position `0` and consisting of the first `3` characters. The procedure call statement

```
Copy(Date, 4, 2, Day)
```

returns (in `Day`) the two characters representing the day of the month (positions `4` and `5`). Finally, the procedure call statement

```
Copy(Date, 8, 4, Year)
```

returns the `4` characters representing the year (positions `8` through `11`). `MonthStr`, `Day`, and `Year` must all be declared as string variables.

Procedure Copy

```
FORM:    PROCEDURE Copy (source     : ARRAY OF CHAR;
                         index,
                         len        : CARDINAL;
                         VAR result : ARRAY OF CHAR);
```

EXAMPLE: `Copy ('May 12, 1943', 8, 4, Year)`
`(* Stores '1943' in Year. *)`

INTERPRETATION: The *result* string is the substring of *source* starting at position *index* and consisting of, at most, *len* characters. If *index* is 0, the substring beginning with the first character in *source* is copied to *result*.

Note: The number of characters copied to *result* is limited by the declared length of *result* and the number of characters in the substring of *source* starting at position *index*. If *index* is larger than HIGH(*source*), no characters are copied to *result*.

EXAMPLE 11.5 ▶ The program in Fig. 11.2 reads a data line into string `Sentence` and then displays each individual word on a separate line. It assumes that the symbol `'#'` occurs between words.

The variable `First` always points to the start of the current word and is initialized to zero. During each execution of the `FOR` loop, the `BOOLEAN` expression

```
Sentence[Next] = WordSpace
```

tests whether the next character is the symbol `'#'`. If so, the substring occupying positions `First` through `Next-1` in `Sentence` is copied to `Word` by the statement

```
Copy (Sentence, First, Next-First, Word);
```

The current word is printed, and `First` is reset to `Next + 1`, the position of the first character of the next word.

The calls to `COPY` and `WriteString` at the end of the program display the last word of the sentence. ◀

Figure 11.2 ▶ *Printing the Words in a Sentence*

```
MODULE PrintWords;

(* Displays each word of a sentence on a separate line. *)

  FROM InOut IMPORT
    Write, WriteString, WriteLn, ReadString;

  FROM Strings IMPORT
    Length, Copy;

  CONST
    WordSeparator = '#';
    SentenceSize = 80;
    WordSize = 20;
```

```
  VAR
    Sentence : ARRAY [0..SentenceSize-1] OF CHAR; (* input
                                                    sentence *)
    Word : ARRAY [0..WordSize] OF CHAR;   (* each word *)
    First,                           (* first character in each word *)
    Next   : [0..SentenceSize];      (* position of next character *)

BEGIN (* PrintWords *)
  WriteString ('Enter a sentence. Use the symbol ');
  Write (WordSeparator);  WriteString (' between words.');  WriteLn;
  ReadString (Sentence);  WriteLn;

  (* Display each word of Sentence on a separate line. *)
  First := 0;            (* first word starts at position 0 *)
  FOR Next := 0 TO Length(Sentence)-1 DO
    IF Sentence[Next] = WordSeparator THEN
      Copy (Sentence, First, Next-First, Word);    (* get word *)
      WriteString (Word);  WriteLn;
      First := Next + 1
    END (* IF *)
  END; (* FOR *)

  (* Display last word. *)
  Copy (Sentence, First, Length(Sentence)-First+1, Word);
  WriteString (Word);  WriteLn
END PrintWords.


Enter a sentence. Use the symbol # between words.
This#is#a#sentence.
This
is
a
sentence.
```

Concatenating Strings

The `Copy` procedure is used to reference a substring of a longer string. It is also possible to combine two or more strings to form a new string using the `Concat` procedure.

EXAMPLE 11.6 ▶ The following statements concatenate, or join together, their string arguments. The string result is stored in `Name`. For the string values

Title	First	Last
Ms.	Bo	Peep

the statements

```
Concat (Title, First, Name);
Concat (Name, Last, Name);
```

store the string value `'Ms.BoPeep'` in `Name`. The statements

```
Concat (Last, First, Name);
Concat (Name, Title, Name);
```

store the string value `'PeepBoMs.'` in `Name`. ◂

Procedure Concat ▶

FORM: `PROCEDURE Concat (`*str1*, *str2* `: ARRAY OF CHAR;`
`VAR` *result* `: ARRAY OF CHAR);`

EXAMPLE: `Concat ('two strings ', 'are joined', BigString)`
`(* Stores 'two strings are joined' in BigString. *)`

INTERPRETATION: The string arguments *str1* and *str2* are joined together in the string *result*.

String Search

In processing string data, we often want to locate a particular substring. For example, we might want to know if the string `'and '` appears in a sentence and if so, where? The statement

```
PosAnd := Pos('and ', Sentence)
```

assigns to `PosAnd` the starting position of the first occurrence of `'and '` in string `Sentence`. If the string `'Birds and bees fly all day'` is stored in `Sentence`, the value assigned to `First` is 6 (the a of `'and'` is at position 6.) If the string `'and '` is not in `Sentence`, the `Pos` function returns a value greater than `HIGH(Sentence)`.

Function Pos ▶

FORM: `PROCEDURE Pos (`*pattern*, *source* `: ARRAY OF CHAR) : CARDINAL;`

EXAMPLE: `Posl := Pos('is', "Where's is?") (* Stores 8 in Posl *)`

INTERPRETATION: The string *source* is examined from left to right to determine the location of the first occurrence of the substring *pattern*. If *pattern* is found, the value returned is the position in *source* of the first character of *pattern*; otherwise, a value greater than `HIGH(`*source*`)` is returned.

EXAMPLE 11.7 ▶ A compiler can determine the form of many statements by checking whether the statement begins with a reserved word. If leading blanks and comments are removed from `Statement`, the condition

```
Pos('FOR ', Statement) = 0
```

is true when `Statement` is a `FOR` statement.

Another task of the compiler is to extract the syntactic elements of each statement. A `FOR` statement header has the syntactic form

`FOR` *lcv* := *initial* `TO` *final* `DO`

The first two statements that follow use the `Pos` function to locate the strings `'FOR '` and `':='`. The `IF` statement copies the substring between these symbols into the string `lcv`.

```
PosFOR := Pos('FOR ', Statement);
PosAssign := Pos(':=', Statement);
IF (PosAssign < HIGH(Statement)) & (PosAssign > PosFOR) THEN
   Copy (Statement, PosFOR + 4, PosAssign - PosFOR - 4,lcv)
END (* IF *)
```

Since the string `'FOR '` has four characters, the starting position of the *lcv* is at position `PosFOR` + 4. The number of characters in the *lcv* is determined by the expression `PosAssign` – `PosFOR` – 4. If the string `'FOR ID := 1 TO N DO'` is stored in `Statement`, then the following variable values are assigned by these statements. The symbol □ in `lcv` represents a blank. ◀

PosFOR	PosAssign	lcv
0	7	ID□

Procedures Delete and Insert

Besides the string manipulation functions described so far, there are procedures to insert and delete substrings. They will be illustrated next.

EXAMPLE 11.8 ▶ In this example, assume that `Sentence` contains the string `'This is the example.'` before the first procedure call. The procedure call statement

```
Delete (Sentence, 0, 5)
```

deletes the first five characters from string `Sentence`. The new contents of `Sentence` become `'is the example.'`

The procedure call statement

```
Delete (Sentence, Pos('the ', Sentence), 4)
```

deletes the first occurrence of the four-character string `'the '` from `Sentence`. The new contents of `Sentence` become `'is example'`. Finally, the statements

```
PosTarg := Pos(Target, Source);
IF PosTarg <= HIGH(Source) THEN
  Delete (Sentence, PosTarg, Length(Target))
END
```

delete the first occurrence of string `Target` from `Sentence`, provided `Target` is found. If `Target` is `'ex'`, the new contents of `Sentence` becomes `'is ample.'` ◄

EXAMPLE 11.9 ► Assume that `Sentence` contains the string `'is the stuff'` before the first procedure call. The procedure call statement

```
Insert ('Where ', Sentence, 0)
```

inserts the string `'Where '` at the beginning of string `Sentence`. The new contents of `Sentence` become `'Where is the stuff'`.

The statements

```
PosStuff := Pos('stuff', Sentence);
IF PosStuff <= HIGH(Sentence) THEN
  Insert ('*#@! ', Sentence, PosStuff)
END
```

insert the five symbols `'*#@! '` in front of the string `'stuff'` in `Sentence`. The new contents of `Sentence` become `'Where is the *#@! stuff'`.

Procedure Delete ►

FORM: `PROCEDURE Delete (VAR` *source* `: ARRAY OF CHAR;` *index*, *size* `: CARDINAL)`

EXAMPLE:
```
Delete (Sentence, 0, 5)    (* Removes the first five
                              characters from string Sentence. *)
```

INTERPRETATION: The next *size* characters are removed from string *source* starting with the character at position *index*.

Note: If *index* >= `Length(`*source*`)`, nothing happens. If there are not *size* characters to delete, then all characters to the end of string *source* are deleted.

Procedure Insert ►

FORM: `PROCEDURE Insert (`*pattern* `: ARRAY OF CHAR; VAR` *destination* `: ARRAY OF CHAR;` *index* `: CARDINAL)`

EXAMPLE:
```
Insert('***', Sentence, 0)  (* Inserts three asterisks at the
                               beginning of string Sentence. *)
```

INTERPRETATION: The string *pattern* is inserted before the character currently in position *index* of *destination*.

Note: If `Length(`*destination*`)` <= *index*, then *pattern* is appended to the end of *destination*.

EXAMPLE 11.10 ▶ Procedure `Replace` in Fig. 11.3 replaces a specified target string (`Target`) in a source string (`Source`) with a new string (`Pattern`). It uses function `Pos` to locate `Target`, `Delete` to delete it, and `Insert` to insert `Pattern` in place of `Target`. An error message is displayed if `Target` is not found. ◀

Figure 11.3 ▶
Procedure Replace

```
PROCEDURE Replace (Target, Pattern : ARRAY OF CHAR;
                   VAR Source : ARRAY OF CHAR);
(*
   Replaces first string Target in Source with Pattern if found.
   Pre : Target, Pattern, and Source are defined.
   Post: Source is modified.
   Uses: Pos, Length, Delete, Insert from Strings;
         WriteString, WriteLn from InOut
*)
   VAR
     PosTarg : CARDINAL;               (* position of Target *)

BEGIN  (* Replace *)
  PosTarg := Pos(Target, Source);      (* locate Target *)
  IF PosTarg < Length(Source) THEN
    Delete (Source, PosTarg, Length(Target));
    Insert (Pattern, Source, PosTarg)
  ELSE
    WriteString ('No replacement -- string ');
    WriteString (Target);
    WriteString (' not found.');  WriteLn
  END (* IF *)
END Replace;
```

SELF-CHECK EXERCISES FOR SECTION 11.1

1. Determine the result of the following procedure calls and function designators. Assume `Magic` and `HisMagic` are type `ARRAY [0..9] OF CHAR`.
   a. `Concat ('Abra', 'cadabra', Magic)`
   b. `Length(Magic)`
   c. `Copy ('This string', 1, 9, HisMagic)`
   d. `Delete (HisMagic, 4, 3)`
   e. `Insert ('my', HisMagic, 5)`
   f. `Pos('cey', 'acey deucey')`
   g. `CompareStr('acey', 'deucey')`
   h. `Assign (Magic, HisMagic)`
2. Assume that procedures `Delete` and `Insert` are not available. Implement these procedures using functions `Copy` and `Concat`.

11.2 Case Study: Text Editor

You have been using a text editor to create and edit Modula-2 programs. This is a fairly sophisticated *screen-oriented* editor in which special commands move the cursor around the video screen and specify edit operations. Although we cannot develop such an editor yet, we can write a less sophisticated one.

TEXT EDITOR PROBLEM

Problem: We need an editor to perform some editing operations on a line of text. The editor should be able to locate a specified target string, delete a substring, insert a substring at a specified location, and replace one substring with another.

Discussion: The string manipulation functions and procedures in module `Strings` can be used to make these operations relatively easy to perform. We will write a program that enters a string and then processes a series of edit commands for that string.

PROBLEM INPUTS

the source string (`Source : ARRAY [0..255] OF CHAR`)
each edit command (`Command : CHAR`)

PROBLEM OUTPUTS

the modified source string (`Source : ARRAY [0..255] OF CHAR`)

Algorithm

1. Read the string to be edited into `Source`.
2. Perform each edit operation until done.

The implementation of step 2 will consist of a loop that reads each edit command, calls `DoEdit` to perform it, and then displays the modified text. The structure chart for the text editor is shown in Fig. 11.4; the local variables and algorithm for `DoEdit` follow.

LOCAL VARIABLES

a substring to be found, replaced, or deleted
  (`OldStr : ARRAY [0..255] OF CHAR`)
a substring to be inserted (`NewStr : ARRAY [0..255] OF CHAR`)
an index to the string `Source` (`Index : CARDINAL`)

Algorithm

1. `CASE Command OF`
   - `'D'` : Read the substring to be deleted and delete it.
   - `'I'` : Read the substring to be inserted and its position and insert it.
   - `'F'` : Read the substring to be found and print its position if found.
   - `'R'` : Read the substring to be replaced and replace it.

   `END (* CASE *)`

Figure 11.4 ▸ *Structure Chart for Text Editor Program*

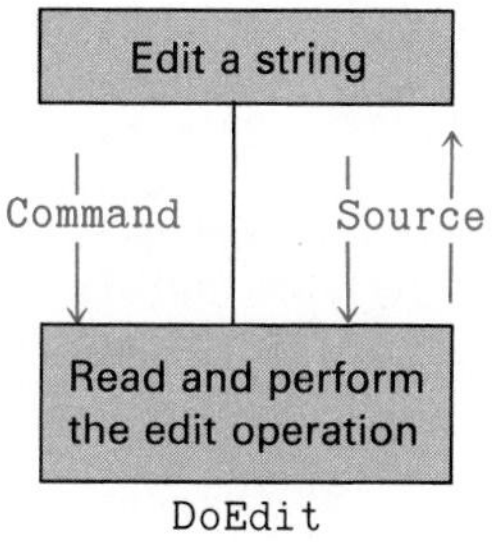

The complete program is shown in Fig. 11.5, along with a sample run.

Figure 11.5 ▸ *Text Editor Program and Sample Run*

```
MODULE TextEdit;

(* Performs text editing operations on a source string. *)

   FROM InOut IMPORT
     Read, ReadCard, Write,
     WriteString, WriteCard, WriteLn;

   FROM SimpleIO IMPORT
     MyReadString;

   FROM Strings IMPORT
     Pos, Length, Insert, Delete;

   CONST
     SourceLen = 255;
     Sentinel = 'Q';                    (* sentinel command *)

   TYPE
     String255 = ARRAY [0..SourceLen-1] OF CHAR;
```

```
VAR
  Source : String255;      (* in/out-the string being edited *)
  Command : CHAR;          (* input-each edit command *)


PROCEDURE DoEdit (Command (* input *) : CHAR;
                  VAR Source : String255);

(* Performs each edit operation. *)

   VAR
     NewStr, OldStr : String255;  (* work strings *)
     Index : [0..SourceLen];      (* index to string Source *)

   (* Insert procedure Replace here. *)

BEGIN (* DoEdit *)
  (* Perform the operation. *)
  CASE Command OF
    'D' : (* Delete *)
          WriteString ('Delete what string? ');
          MyReadString (OldStr);  WriteLn;
          Index := Pos(OldStr, Source);
          IF Index < Length(Source) THEN
            Delete (Source, Index, Length(OldStr))
          ELSE
            WriteString (OldStr);
            WriteString (' not found');
            WriteLn
          END (* IF *)
   | 'I' : (* Insert *)
          WriteString ('Insert what string? ');
          MyReadString (NewStr);  WriteLn;
          WriteString ('At what position? ');
          ReadCard (Index);  WriteLn;
          IF (Index > 0) AND (Index < Length(Source)) THEN
            Insert (NewStr, Source, Index)
          ELSE
            WriteCard (Index, 3);
            WriteString (' out of range');
            WriteLn
          END (* IF *)
   | 'F' : (* Find *)
          WriteString ('Find what string? ');
          MyReadString (OldStr);  WriteLn;
          Index := Pos(OldStr, Source);
          IF Index < Length(Source) THEN
            WriteString (OldStr);
            WriteString (' found at position ');
            WriteCard (Index, 3);
            WriteLn
```

```
            ELSE
              WriteString (OldStr);
              WriteString (' not found');
              WriteLn
            END (* IF *)
        | 'R' : (* Replace *)
            WriteString ('Replace old string? ');
            MyReadString (OldStr);  WriteLn;
            WriteString ('With new string? ');
            MyReadString (NewStr);  WriteLn;
            Replace (OldStr, NewStr, Source)
      ELSE
        WriteString ('Invalid edit character');  WriteLn
      END (* CASE *)
    END DoEdit;

BEGIN  (* TextEdit *)
  (* Read in the string to be edited. *)
  WriteString ('Enter the source string:');  WriteLn;
  MyReadString (Source);  WriteLn;

  (* Perform each edit operation until done. *)
  LOOP
    (* Get the operation symbol. *)
    WriteLn;
    WriteString ('Enter D (Delete), I (Insert), ');
    WriteString ('F (Find), R (Replace), Q (Quit): ');
    Read (Command);  Write (Command);  WriteLn;
    Command := CAP(Command);        (* convert to uppercase *)
    IF Command = Sentinel THEN
      EXIT
    END; (* IF *)
    DoEdit (Command, Source);

    (* Display latest string *)
    WriteString ('New source: ');
    WriteString (Source);
    WriteLn
  END (* LOOP *)
END TextEdit.
```

```
Enter the source string:
Mary had a cute little lamb.

Enter D (Delete), I (Insert), F (Find), R (Replace), Q (Quit): f
Find what string? cute
cute  found at position  11
New source: Mary had a cute little lamb.

Enter D (Delete), I (Insert), F (Find), R (Replace), Q (Quit): i
```

```
Insert what string? very
At what position? 11
New source: Mary had a very cute little lamb.

Enter D (Delete), I (Insert), F (Find), R (Replace), Q (Quit): R
Replace old string? lamb
With new string? lamb chop
New source: Mary had a very cute little lamb chop.

Enter D (Delete), I (Insert), F (Find), R (Replace), Q (Quit): D
Delete what string? very cute
New source: Mary had a lamb chop.

Enter D (Delete), I (Insert), F (Find), R (Replace), Q (Quit): q
New source: Mary had a lamb chop.
```

11.3 Set Data Type

A set is used for storing a collection of simple values when the order of occurrence of these values is not important. Very often we are interested in determining whether a particular item is present in a set of values. Modula-2 provides the set membership operator `IN` for answering this question, along with operators for forming the union, intersection, and difference of two set operands. There are also operators for determining set relationships such as equivalence, subset, and superset.

Declaring and Defining Sets

Many of you have studied sets in mathematics. In mathematics and in Modula-2, a set is represented by a list of *set elements* enclosed in curly braces. For example, the set of odd integers from 1 to 9 is written as {1, 3, 5, 7, 9}. The order in which elements are listed is immaterial; for example, the set {9, 5, 7, 1, 3} is equivalent to the first set.

EXAMPLE 11.11 ▸ The following statements define a set type `DigitSet` and two set variables named `Odd` and `Even`. Each set variable of type `DigitSet` can contain between zero and eleven elements chosen from the integers in the subrange `[-5..5]`. Each combination of these eleven integers is a possible value for the sets `Odd` and `Even`.

```
TYPE
  DigitSet = SET OF [-5..5];

VAR
  Odd, Even : DigitSet;
```

Set variables, like any other variables, are initially undefined. The assignment statements

```
Odd := DigitSet {-5, -3, -1, 1, 3, 5};
Even := DigitSet {-4, -2, 0, 2, 4};
```

define these variables in the expected way; that is, `Odd` contains all the odd integers and `Even` contains all the even integers in the subrange type `[-5..5]`.

The expression

```
DigitSet {-5, -3, -1, 1, 3, 5};
```

is called a *set constructor* because it constructs a value of a set type from its elements. A set constructor can have a range specification instead of individual set elements. For example, the set constructor

```
DigitSet {-5..0, 2, 4};
```

forms the set consisting of all negative integers greater than −6 and all even integers less than 6. Because of the presence of the integer 6, the set constructor

```
DigitSet {0, 2, 4, 6}
```

is invalid and causes the syntax error `element value out of bounds.` ◄

EXAMPLE 11.12 ► A set type `ColorSet` is declared next, along with two sets, `Primary` and `Secondary`.

```
TYPE
  Color = (Red, Blue, Black, Green, Purple, Yellow, Orange, Brown);
  ColorSet = SET OF Color;

VAR
  Primary, Secondary : ColorSet;
```

The assignment statements

```
Primary := ColorSet {Red..Green};
Secondary := ColorSet {Purple..Brown};
```

define two sets of four colors each in the expected way. ◄

Empty Set and Universal Set

An existing set can be modified using the set operators described later in Section 11.5. Before a set can be manipulated, its initial value must be defined using a set assignment statement.

EXAMPLE 11.13 ► Two set variables, `Winter` and `Summer`, with base type `Month` are declared below. `Month` is an enumeration type imported from `DatesADT`.

```
TYPE
  MonthSet =  SET OF Month;

VAR
  Winter, Summer : MonthSet;
```

The assignment statements

```
Winter := MonthSet {January..December};
Summer := MonthSet {};
```

define a particularly hostile climate. The set `Winter` is called the *universal set* and consists of all values in the base type. The set `Summer` is called the *empty set* because it contains no values from the base type. ◂

The set type declaration and set constructor are described in the following syntax display.

Set Type Declaration ▶

FORM: *set type* = `SET OF` *base type*;

EXAMPLE: `TYPE LetterSet = SET OF Letters;`

INTERPRETATION: The identifier *set type* is defined over the values specified in *base type*. A variable declared to be of type *set type* is a set whose elements are chosen from the values in *base type*. The *base type* must be `BOOLEAN`, `CHAR`, an enumeration type, or a subrange.

Note: All implementations impose a limit on the number of values in the *base type* of a set. This limit is usually the same as the number of binary bits in a computer word, for example, 16 or 32. Consequently, the scalar type `CHAR` cannot normally be used as a base type, although a subrange of `CHAR` of limited size may be. A subrange of the scalar types `INTEGER` and `CARDINAL` may also be used as a *base type*.

Set Constructor ▶

FORM: *set type* {*set elements*}

EXAMPLE: `DigitSet {-5, 0, 5}`

INTERPRETATION: A set of type *set type* is constructed that contains the elements in the list *set elements*, where *set elements* is a list of expressions. Each expression in *set elements* is evaluated, and its value is inserted in the set being formed. The type of each expression must be compatible with the base type of a set of type *set type*.

Note: Early versions of Modula-2 allow only constants in the list of *set elements*.

11.4 Type BITSET

The data type `BITSET` is predefined in Modula-2 as

```
BITSET = SET OF [0..w-1];
```

where `w` is the number of bits in a word of memory (the *word size*). The set type may be omitted from a set constructor for a set of type `BITSET`.

EXAMPLE 11.14 ▶ The sets `Odd` and `Even` are declared below as type `BITSET`.

```
VAR
  Odd, Even : BITSET;
```

The assignment statements

```
Odd  := {1, 3, 5, 7, 9, 11, 13, 15};
Even := {0, 2, 4, 6, 8, 10, 12, 14};
```

define these two sets. Compare them with the assignment statements shown in Example 11.11. The data type `BITSET` is particularly useful for performing low-level operations that are beyond the scope of this text. ◀

11.5 Set Operators

This section will discuss the set operators provided in Modula-2. These include operators for forming the union, intersection, and difference of two sets, and operators for testing set relationships such as membership, set equality and inequality, and subset and superset.

Set Membership Test

The set membership operator `IN` can be used to determine whether or not a specified element is in a set. Set membership tests are the most common operations involving sets in Modula-2.

EXAMPLE 11.15 ▶ Assuming `Primary` is the set defined in Example 11.12 and `ColorVal` is type `Color`, the statement

```
IF ColorVal IN Primary THEN
  WriteString ('Primary')
ELSE
  WriteString ('Secondary')
END (* IF *)
```

displays an appropriate message string depending on the value of `ColorVal`. The condition

```
(ColorVal = Black) OR (ColorVal = Red) OR
(ColorVal = Green) OR (ColorVal = Blue)
```

could be used instead of the set membership test, but the set membership test is preferable because it is easier to read and is more efficient. Another option would be to use a `CASE` statement to determine which message string to display.

Be careful when writing the negation of the set membership test. The expression

```
NOT (ColorVal IN Primary)
```

is valid, whereas the expression

```
ColorVal NOT IN Primary
```

is invalid. The operator `IN`, like the relational operators, has the lowest precedence of all Modula-2 operators (see Table 5.9). ◂

Set Union, Intersection, Difference, and Symmetric Difference

The set operators union, intersection, difference, and symmetric difference require two sets of the same type as operands.

- The *union* of two sets (set operator +) is the set of elements contained in either set or both sets.

  `{1,3,4} + {1,2,4}` is `{1,2,3,4}`
  `{1,3} + {2,4}` is `{1,2,3,4}`
  `{'A','C','F'} + {'B','C','D','F'}` is `{'A','B','C','D','F'}`
  `{'A','C','F'} + {'A','C','D','F'}` is `{'A','C','D','F'}`

- The *intersection* of two sets (set operator *) is the set of all elements common to both sets:

  `{1,3,4} * {1,2,4}` is `{1,4}`
  `{1,3} * {2,4}` is `{ }`
  `{'A','C','F'} * {'B','C','D','F'}` is `{'C','F'}`
  `{'A','C','F'} * {'A','C','D','F'}` is `{'A','C','F'}`

- The *difference* of set A and set B (set operator –) is the set of elements in set A but not in set B:

  `{1,3,4} - {1,2,4}` is `{3}`
  `{1,3} - {2,4}` is `{1,3}`
  `{'A','C','F'} - {'B','C','D','F'}` is `{'A'}`
  `{'A','C','F'} - {'A','C','D','F'}` is `{ }`

- The *symmetric difference* of set A and set B (set operator /) is the set of elements in set A or set B but not both:
  `{1,3,4} / {1,2,4}` is `{2,3}`
  `{1,3} / {2,4}` is `{1,2,3,4}`
  `{'A','C','F'} / {'B','C','D','F'}` is `{'A','B','D'}`
  `{'A','C','F'} / {'A','C','F'}` is `{ }`

The operators +, −, *, and / are treated as set operators when their operands are sets. These operators can be used to combine two sets to form a third set. If more than one set operator is used in an expression, the normal precedence rules for the operators +, − , *, and / will be followed (see Table 5.9 in Section 5.4). When in doubt, use parentheses to specify the intended order of evaluation. Don't forget to use the set type in front of each set operand of type other than `BITSET`.

Procedures INCL and EXCL

Often we want to insert a new element in an existing set. This can be accomplished by forming the union of the existing set and the *unit set* containing only the new element. The set `{2}` is a unit set. If `NumSet` is type `BITSET`, the assignment statement

```
NumSet := NumSet + {2}
```

inserts the cardinal 2 in the set `NumSet`.

A common error is omitting the braces around a unit set. The expression

```
NumSet + 2        {invalid unit set}
```

is invalid because one operand is a set and the other is a constant. For this reason, it is better to use the predefined procedure `INCL` to insert a single element into a set. The statement

```
INCL (NumSet, 2)
```

is the preferred way to insert the cardinal 2 into the set `NumSet`.

The statement

```
INCL (Primary, ColorVal)
```

inserts the set element `ColorVal` (type `Color`) into the set `Primary` (see Example 11.12). The statement

```
EXCL (Primary, ColorVal)
```

removes the set element `ColorVal` from the set `Primary`. Its use is preferred over the equivalent assignment statement

```
Primary := Primary - ColorSet {ColorVal}
```

which may be invalid in early versions of Modula-2.

EXAMPLE 11.16 ▶ Procedure `BuildSets` in Fig. 11.6 returns a set of odd numbers (`Odd`) and a set of even numbers (`Even`) in the range `1` to `MaxNum` (a constant). ◀

Figure 11.6 ▶
Procedure BuildSets

```
PROCEDURE BuildSets (VAR Odd, Even (* output *) : BITSET);
(*
   Builds a set of odd integers (Odd) and a set of even
   integers (Even) in the range 1 to MaxNum (a constant).
*)
   VAR
     i : CARDINAL;          (* loop-control variable *)

BEGIN (* BuildSets *)
  ODD := {};                (* initialize ODD to the empty set *)

  (* Build a set of odd integers. *)
  FOR i := 1 TO MaxNum BY 2 DO
    INCL (ODD, i)           (* insert next odd integer in Odd *)
  END; (* WHILE *)

  Even := {1..MaxNum} - Odd (* assign rest of integers to Even *)
END BuildSets;
```

Set Relational Operators

Sets can also be compared through the use of the relational operators. Both operands of a set relational operator must be the same set type. The relational operators = and # (or <>) are used to test whether or not two sets contain the same elements.

```
{1,3} = {1,3} is TRUE      {1,3} # {1,3} is FALSE
{1,3} = {2,4} is FALSE     {1,3} # {2,4} is TRUE
{1,3} = {3,1} is TRUE      {1,3} # {3,1} is FALSE
   {} = {1}   is FALSE        {} # {1}   is TRUE
```

As indicated by the next to last example, the order in which the elements of a set are listed is not important (`{1,3}` and `{3,1}` denote the same set). However, we will normally list the elements of a set in ordinal sequence.

Other relational operators are used to determine subset and superset relationships.

- Set `A` is a *subset* of set `B` (`A <= B`) if every element of set `A` is also an element of set `B`.

```
{1,3}      <= {1,2,3,4} is TRUE
{1,3}      <= {1,3}     is TRUE
{1,2,3,4}  <= {1,3}     is FALSE
{1,3}      <= {}        is FALSE
{}         <= {1,3}     is TRUE
```

As indicated in the last example, the empty set, {}, is a subset of every set.

▸ Set A is a *superset* of set B (A >= B) if every element of B is also an element of A.

```
{1,3}      >= {1,2,3,4} is FALSE
{1,3}      >= {1,3}     is TRUE
{1,2,3,4} >= {1,3}     is TRUE
{1,3}      >= {}        is TRUE
{}         >= {1,3}     is FALSE
```

The set operators are summarized in Table 11.3.

Table 11.3 ▸ *Table of Set Operators*

OPERATOR	EXAMPLE	DESCRIPTION
+ (union)	A + B	Set of all elements in A or B or both
* (intersection)	A * B	Set of all elements in both A and B
– (difference)	A – B	Set of all elements in A but not B
/ (symmetric difference)	A / B	Set of all elements in A or B but not both
INCL (inclusion)	INCL (A, a)	Element a is inserted into set A
EXCL (exclusion)	EXCL (A, a)	Element a is deleted from set A
IN (membership)	a IN A	TRUE if element a is in A
= (equality)	A = B	TRUE if sets A and B are identical
# or <> (inequality)	A # B or A <> B	TRUE if sets A and B are not identical
<= (subset)	A <= B	TRUE if A is a subset of B
>= (superset)	A >= B	TRUE if set A contains set B

Reading and Displaying Sets

There are no utility procedures in Modula-2 for reading or displaying a set. Data items to be stored in a set must be read individually and inserted in an initially empty set using the INCL operator.

EXAMPLE 11.17 ▸ Procedure ReadSet in Fig. 11.7 reads a data line and inserts all data characters in the range 'A'..'P' into the set represented by parameter Letters (maximum of sixteen elements). LetterSet is the set type declared below.

```
TYPE
  LetterSet = SET OF ['A'..'P'];
```

The IF statement condition

```
NextChar IN LetterSet {'A'..'P'}
```

is true only for letters that belong in the set Letters. For the data line

```
abcDEF123XYZ
```

the set {D, E, F} would be returned through Letters. ◂

Figure 11.7 ▶
Procedure ReadSet

```
PROCEDURE ReadSet (VAR Letters (* output *) : LetterSet);
(*
   Reads a data line and inserts the uppercase letters
   in the range 'A'..'P' into the set Letters.
*)
   CONST
     LineSize = 80;

   VAR
     DataString : ARRAY [0..LineSize-1] OF CHAR;  (* data line *)
     NextChar : CHAR;                      (* next input character *)
     i : [0..LineSize-1];        (* loop control and subscript *)

BEGIN  (* ReadSet *)
  Letters := LetterSet {};                 (* initialize Letters *)
  WriteString ('Enter a data string: ');
  ReadString (DataString);  WriteLn;
  FOR I := 0 TO Length(DataString)-1 DO
    NextChar := DataString[i];              (* get next character *)
    IF NextChar IN LetterSet {'A'..'P'} THEN
      INCL (Letters, NextChar)              (* insert NextChar *)
    END (* IF *)
  END (* FOR *)
END ReadSet;
```

To print a set, you must test every possible value in the base type to see whether or not it is a set element. Only values that are set elements should be printed.

EXAMPLE 11.18 ▶ Procedure `PrintSet` in Fig. 11.8 prints the uppercase letters in the range `'A'..'P'` that are in the set represented by its parameter `Letters`. ◀

Figure 11.8 ▶
Procedure PrintSet

```
PROCEDURE PrintSet (Letters (* input *) : LetterSet);

(* Prints the uppercase letters in set Letters. *)

   VAR
     NextLetter : ['A'..'P'];   (* loop control and subscript *)

BEGIN  (* PrintSet *)
  FOR NextLetter := 'A' TO 'P' DO
    IF NextLetter IN Letters THEN
      Write (NextLetter)                  (* print a set member *)
    END (* IF *)
  END (* FOR *)
END PrintSet;
```

SELF-CHECK EXERCISES FOR SECTION 11.5

1. A is the set {1,3,5,7}, B is the set {2,4,6}, and C is the set {1,2,3}. Evaluate the following:
   a. A + (B – C)
   b. A + (B * C)
   c. A + B + C
   d. (C – A) < B
   e. C + (A – C)
   f. C – (A – B)
   g. (C – A) – B
   h. (B + C) = (A + C)
2. Modify PrintSet to print a set of type BITSET.

11.6 Arrays of Sets

The small size of sets in Modula-2 limits their usefulness. It is possible, however, to use an array of sets to represent a larger set.

EXAMPLE 11.19 ▶ In a computer graphics program, an artist can draw pictures on a computer screen by illuminating certain cells of the screen (called *pixels*, for "picture elements") and darkening others. We can represent a line of the screen as a set of pixels; each pixel that is illuminated will be included in the set.

There are eighty columns across the screen, but on many computers only sixteen elements can be included in Modula-2 sets. We can use an array with five set elements to represent a line of a screen, as shown next.

```
TYPE
  PixelSet = ARRAY [0..4] OF BITSET;

VAR
  Line : PixelSet;
```

Assuming the largest value in a set of type BITSET is 15, Line[0] represents pixels 0 through 15 of our screen, Line[1] represents pixels 16 through 31, and Line[4] represents pixels 64 through 79. The assignment statement

```
Line[0] := {0, 1, 2, 14, 15};
```

illuminates pixels 0, 1, 2, 14, and 15. The assignment statement

```
Line[1] := {1, 2, 6, 7, 14, 15};
```

illuminates pixels 17, 18, 22, 23, 30, and 31. The statement

```
INCL (Line[1], 3)
```

illuminates pixel 19; whereas, the statement

```
EXCL (Line[1], 2)
```

darkens pixel 18.

EXAMPLE 11.20 ▶ Procedure `FillLine` in Fig. 11.9 stores the picture represented by its input parameter, `InString`, in its output parameter, `OutLine`. Each character of `InString` is either an asterisk or a blank, where an asterisk denotes a pixel that should be illuminated.

Figure 11.9 ▶
Procedure FillLine

```
PROCEDURE FillLine (InString (* input *) : ARRAY OF CHAR;
                    VAR OutLine (* output *) : PixelSet);
(*
   Defines the picture line OutLine based on the input
   string InString.
   Pre : InString is defined.
   Post: Each member of set OutLine represents an illuminated
         pixel. A pixel is illuminated if an '*' is stored in the
         corresponding position of InString. A pixel is not
         illuminated if a blank is stored in InString.
*)
   CONST
     Illuminated = '*';
     Darkened = ' ';
     ScreenWidth = 80;
     SetSize = 16;     (* maximum number of elements in a set *)

   VAR
     PixelGroup : [0..4];             (* subscript for OutLine *)
     Bit : [0..SetSize-1];     (* current bit of a pixel group *)
     CharPos : [0..ScreenWidth-1];  (* subscript for InString *)

BEGIN (* FillLine *)
  IF Length(InString) > ScreenWidth THEN
    WriteString ('Input string too long.');  WriteLn;
    RETURN
  END; (* IF *)

  (* Black out array OutLine. *)
  FOR PixelGroup := 0 TO 4 DO
    OutLine[PixelGroup] := {}
  END; (* FOR *)

  (* Insert each illuminated pixel in a set of array OutLine. *)
  FOR CharPos := 0 TO Length(InString)-1 DO
    IF InString[CharPos] = Illuminated THEN
      PixelGroup := CharPos DIV SetSize;
      Bit := CharPos MOD SetSize;
      INCL (OutLine[PixelGroup], Bit)
    ELSIF InString[CharPos] # Darkened THEN
      WriteString ('Illegal character ');
      Write (InString[CharPos]);  WriteLn
    END (* IF *)
  END (* FOR *)
END FillLine;
```

In procedure `FillLine`, the statements

```
PixelGroup := CharPos DIV SetSize;
Bit := CharPos MOD SetSize;
INCL (OutLine[PixelGroup], Bit)
```

illuminate a pixel. The value of `PixelGroup` (`0..4`) represents the subscript of the set containing the pixel to be illuminated; the value of `Bit` (`0..15`) represents the set element itself. For example, if the character `'*'` is stored at position `18` of `InString`, element `2` (`18 MOD 16` is `2`) will be inserted in set `OutLine[1]` (`18 DIV 16` is `1`). ◂

SELF-CHECK EXERCISES FOR SECTION 11.6

1. Declare a data structure `Screen` that can be used to represent a screen of 25 rows and 80 columns.
2. Display the picture represented by array `Line`. Display the character `'*'` if a pixel is illuminated; otherwise, display a blank character.
3. Write a procedure to copy the picture represented by array `Line` into a string of length eighty. Represent each pixel by placing the character value `'*'` (for illuminated) or `' '` (for not illuminated) in the corresponding position in the string. Hint: For the array `Line` shown previously, character positions `0, 1, 2, 14, 15, 17, 18, 22, 23, 30,` and `31` should contain the character `'*'`.

11.7 Common Programming Errors

If your program processes strings, make sure to import procedure `ReadString` from module `InOut` and any required utility procedures from module `Strings`. Remember that truncation is automatically performed by the utility procedures in module `Strings` if the string result being returned is longer than the declared length of the variable receiving it. No error indication is given when this happens.

Remember that a set variable, like any variable, must be initialized before it can be manipulated. It is tempting to assume that a set is empty and to begin processing it without initializing it to the empty set {}.

Most of the Modula-2 operators may be used with sets. The meaning of an operator is, of course, different when its operands are sets and not numbers. Don't forget to precede a set value in an expression with the set type identifier unless the set type is `BITSET` (e.g., `ColorSet {Blue Red}`).

11.8 Chapter Review

You saw how to read strings of length n+1 or less into character arrays with index type `[0..n]` using the `ReadString` procedure (part of `InOut`). You saw how to copy a string from one character array to another of the same type and how to assign string values to character arrays. You also learned how to manipulate strings using the utility procedures and functions in module `Strings`.

The set data structure is used to store values of a specified base type. The size of a set is implementation dependent and is likely to be relatively small (e.g., sixteen elements or less). Unlike an array, a value can be saved only once in a set and there is no way to determine the time sequence in which values are stored in a set (e.g., {1, 2, 3} is the same set as {3, 2, 1}).

New Modula-2 Statements

The new Modula-2 statements introduced in this chapter are described in Table 11.4.

Table 11.4 ▸ *Summary of New Modula-2 Statements*

STATEMENT	EFFECT

String Declaration
`TYPE String11 = ARRAY [0..10] OF CHAR;`
`VAR FirstName, LastName, SurName : String11;`
	`FirstName`, `LastName`, and `SurName` are strings of maximum length 11.

String Assignment
`FirstName := 'Daffy';`
`LastName := 'Duck';`
`Assign (LastName, SurName);`
	Saves `'Daffy'` in `FirstName` and `'Duck'` in `LastName` and `SurName`.

String Length `Length(FirstName);`	Returns the current length (5) of `FirstName`.
String Comparison `CompareStr(FirstName, LastName);`	Compares `FirstName` to `LastName` and returns `-1` (<).
String Copy `Copy (FirstName, 0, 3, SurName);`	Copies `'Daf'` to `SurName`.
String Concatenation `Concat (FirstName, LastName, SurName);`	Stores `'DaffyDuck'` in `SurName`.

String Search
`Pos('Du', FirstName);`
`Pos('Du', LastName);`
`Pos('Du', Surname);`
	Returns `11` (`'Du'` not found)
	Returns `0` (`'Du'` found at 0)
	Returns `5` (`'Du'` found at 5)

String Deletion `Delete (SurName, 6, 2);`	Changes `SurName` to `'DaffyDk'`.

String Insertion	
`Insert ('uc', SurName, 6);`	Changes `SurName` to `'DaffyDuck'`.
Set Type Declaration	

`TYPE Color = (Red, Black, Blue, Green);`
`  ColorSet = SET OF Color;`
`VAR MyColors : ColorSet;`
	Declares `MyColors` as a set whose elements are values of type `Color`.

Set Assignment	
`MyColors := ColorSet {Blue, Green};`	`MyColors` is the two-element set `{Blue, Green}`
`MyColors := MyColors + ColorSet {Red};`	`MyColors` is `{Blue,Green,Red}`
`MyColors := MyColors - ColorSet {Blue}`	`MyColors` is `{Green, Red}`
`MyColors := MyColors * ColorSet {Red}`	`MyColors` is `{Red}`
Set Inclusion and Exclusion	
`INCL (MyColors, Black);`	`MyColors` is `{Red, Black}`
`EXCL (MyColors, Red);`	`MyColors` is `{Black}`
Set Relations	
`Black IN MyColors`	Value is `TRUE`
`ColorSet {Black} = MyColors`	Value is `TRUE`
`ColorSet {Black} # MyColors`	Value is `FALSE`
`ColorSet {Black} <= MyColors`	Value is `TRUE`
`MyColors >= ColorSet {Blue, Red}`	Value is `FALSE`

CHAPTER 11 ▸

Review Questions

1. Explain the difference between the current length of a string and the declared length of a string? Which does function `Length` return?
2. How can function `HIGH` be used to determine string length? If the null character is stored in a string, is it counted by `High` or by `Length`?
3. Explain when procedure `Assign` should be used instead of the assignment operator.
4. Write a call to procedure `Copy` that can be substituted for the statement
   `Assign (AString, BString)`
5. Many search functions return a value of zero when the target is not found in the data structure being searched. Explain why function `Pos` cannot do this.
6. Indicate whether each of the following identifiers is a procedure or a function and describe the type of result returned by each.
   `Length, CompareStr, Concat, Pos,`
   `Assign, Copy, Insert, Delete, EXCL, INCL`
7. Explain the difference between a set and a `BITSET`.
8. Why can't we declare a set whose base type is `CHAR`?
9. The following `FOR` loop prints each member of a set whose elements are values of enumeration type `Day`. Write the declaration for set `TestSet`. Rewrite the loop as a `WHILE` loop whose repetition condition is `TestSet # {}`. Use procedure `INC` to

advance to the next value in the enumeration type and procedure EXCL to remove each element from TestSet after it is printed.

```
FOR Today := Sunday to Saturday DO
  IF Today IN TestSet THEN
    WriteDay (Today)
  END (* IF *)
END (* FOR *)
```

CHAPTER 11 ▸

Programming Projects

1. Write a program that removes all the blanks from a character string.

2. Write a program that reads in a sequence of lines and displays a count of the total number of words in those lines and counts of the number of words with one letter, two letters, and so on.

3. Write a program that reads in a sequence of lines and displays each line read with all four-letter words replaced with asterisks.

4. Write a program that reads in a sequence of lines and rewrites each line in a simplified form of pig latin. If the word begins with a consonant, then strip off the first letter and place it at the end of the word followed by the string 'ay'.

5. Write a procedure that reads in a hand of cards and stores it in an array of sets, one set for each suit. Use an enumeration type for the suits and one for the card face values. The data for each card will be presented in the form of a character representing the suit and a character representing the card face value ('2'..'9', 'T', 'J', 'Q', 'K', 'A').

6. Consider a hand of cards read in Problem 5 as a bridge hand and evaluate it. Award points for each card according to the following method:

Card face value	*Points*
two..ten	0
jack	1
queen	2
king	3
ace	4

   Also add one for each suit that has only two cards, two for each suit that has only one card, and three for each suit that is missing.

7. Revise the text editor discussed in Section 11.2 so it will edit a "page" of text. Store each line of the page in a separate element of an array of strings. Maintain a pointer (index) to the line currently being edited. In addition to the edit commands, include commands that move the index to the top of the page, the bottom of the page, and

up and down a specified number of lines. Your program should also be able to delete an entire line, insert a new line preceding the current line, or replace the current line with another. The first two of these new operations will require moving a portion of the array of strings up or down by one element.

8. Write a program that will read 400 characters into a 20-by-20 array. Afterward read in a character string of a maximum of 10 characters that will be used to search the "table" of characters. Indicate how many times the second string occurs in the 20-by-20 array. This should include horizontal, vertical, and right-diagonal occurrences. ("Right diagonal" means going down and to the right.)

12 ▸ Recursion

A RECURSIVE PROCEDURE or function is one that calls itself. This ability enables a recursive procedure to be repeated with different parameter values. Recursion can be used as an alternative to iteration (looping). Generally a recursive solution is less efficient in terms of computer time than an iterative one because of the overhead for the extra procedure calls; however, in many instances the use of recursion enables us to specify a very natural, simple solution to a problem that would otherwise be difficult to solve. For this reason, recursion is an important and powerful tool in problem solving and programming.

12.1 The Nature of Recursion

Problems that lend themselves to a recursive solution have the following characteristics.

- One or more simple cases of the problem (called *stopping cases*) have a simple, nonrecursive solution.
- For the other cases, there is a process (using recursion) for substituting one or more reduced cases of the problem closer to a stopping case.
- Eventually the problem can be reduced to stopping cases only, all of which are relatively easy to solve.

The Towers of Hanoi Problem has these characteristics. The version of the problem shown in Fig. 12.1 has five disks (numbered 1 through 5) and three "towers" or pegs (lettered A, B, and C). The goal is to move the five disks from peg A to peg C, subject to the following rules:

1. Only one disk may be moved at a time, and this disk must be the top disk on a peg.
2. A larger disk can never be placed on top of a smaller disk.

Figure 12.1 ▸ *Towers of Hanoi*

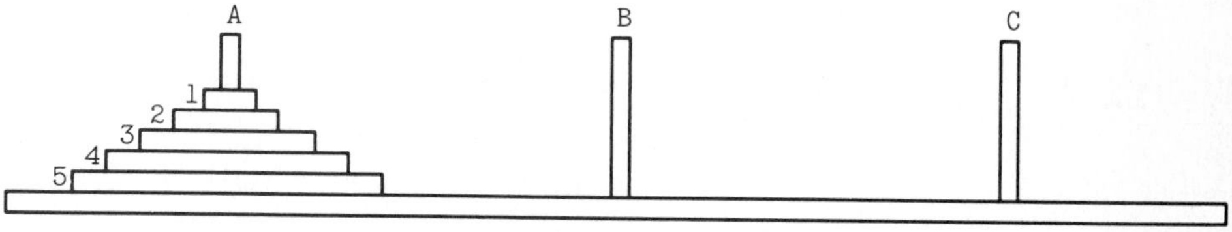

The stopping cases of the problem involve only moving one disk (e.g., "move disk 2 from peg A to peg C"). A simpler case than moving five disks would be to move four disks. Therefore, we want to redefine the original problem (which was to move five disks) in terms of moving four disks, even if this means we have additional steps. By applying recursion, we get the following solution steps:

1. Move four disks from peg A to peg B.
2. Move disk 5 from peg A to peg C.
3. Move four disks from peg B to peg C.

The status of the three towers after steps 1 and 2 are completed verifies that it is indeed valid to substitute these three steps for the original problem (see Fig. 12.2). It should be clear that performing step 3 next will lead to the desired result.

Figure 12.2 ▸ *Towers of Hanoi after Steps 1 and 2*

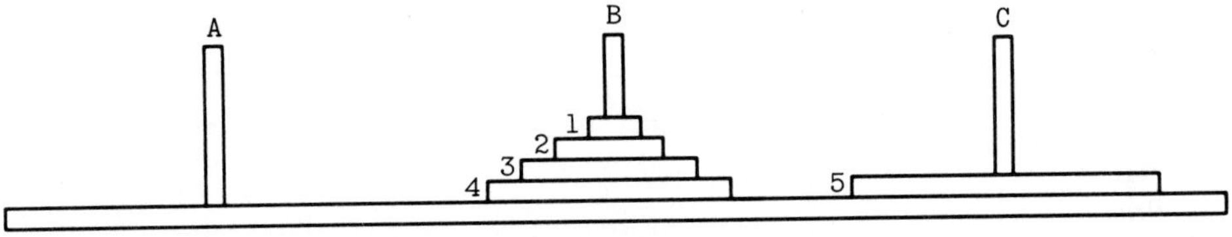

Unfortunately, we still don't know how to perform step 1 or step 3 (step 2 is easy because it's a stopping case). However, both steps involve four disks instead of five, so they are an improvement on the original problem. Applying recursion to step 1 generates the following solution steps:

1.1 Move three disks from peg A to peg C.
1.2 Move disk 4 from peg A to peg B.
1.3 Move three disks from peg C to peg B.

By repeating the process for three disks and then for two disks, we will finally reach all cases of one disk, which we know how to solve. We will write a Modula-2 program that does this later.

12.2 Tracing a Recursive Procedure

Conventional techniques cannot be used to trace the execution of a recursive procedure. We will illustrate how to do this trace by studying a recursive procedure next.

EXAMPLE 12.1 ▸ Procedure `Palindrome` in Fig. 12.3 is a recursive procedure that reads in a string of length `N` and prints it out backward. If the procedure call statement

```
Palindrome (5)
```

is executed, the five characters entered at the screen will be printed in reverse order. If the characters abcde are entered when this procedure is called, the output line

```
edcba
```

will appear on the screen.

If the procedure call statement

```
Palindrome (3)
```

is executed instead, only three characters will be read and the output line

```
cba
```

will appear on the screen. ◂

Figure 12.3 ▸ *Procedure Palindrome*

```
PROCEDURE Palindrome (N (* input *) : CARDINAL);
(*
   Displays a string of length N in
   reverse of the order in which it is entered.
   Pre : N is greater than or equal to one.
   Post: Displays N characters.
*)
   VAR
     Next : CHAR;           (* next data character *)

BEGIN  (* Palindrome *)
  IF N <= 1 THEN
    (* stopping case *)
    Read (Next);
    WriteLn;                (* terminate data entry line *)
    Write (Next)
  ELSE
    (* recursion *)
    Read (Next);
    Palindrome (N-1);
    Write (Next)
  END (* IF *)
END Palindrome;
```

Like most recursive procedures, the body of procedure Palindrome consists of an IF statement that evaluates a *terminating condition*, N <= 1. When the terminating condition is true, the problem has reached a stopping case. The stopping case is a data string of length 1. If N <= 1 is true, the statements

```
Read (Next);
WriteLn;                (* terminate data entry line *)
Write (Next)
```

are executed, causing a single character to be read and displayed. (The WriteLn statement starts the display of the output characters on the next line of the screen.) The procedure END statement is then reached and control is returned back from the procedure.

If the terminating condition is false (N greater than 1), the recursive step (following ELSE) is executed. The Read statement enters the next data character. The procedure call statement

```
Palindrome (N-1);
```

calls the procedure recursively with the parameter value decreased by one. The character just read is not displayed until later. This is because the Write statement comes after the recursive procedure call; consequently, the Write statement cannot be performed until after the procedure execution is completed and control is returned back to the Write statement. For example, the character that is read when N is 3 is not displayed until after the procedure execution for N equal to 2 is done. Hence, this character is displayed after the characters that are read when N is 2 and N is 1.

To fully understand this, it is necessary to trace the execution of the procedure call statement

```
Palindrome (3)
```

This trace is shown in Fig. 12.4, assuming the letters abc are entered as data.

Figure 12.4 ▸ *Trace of Palindrome (3)*

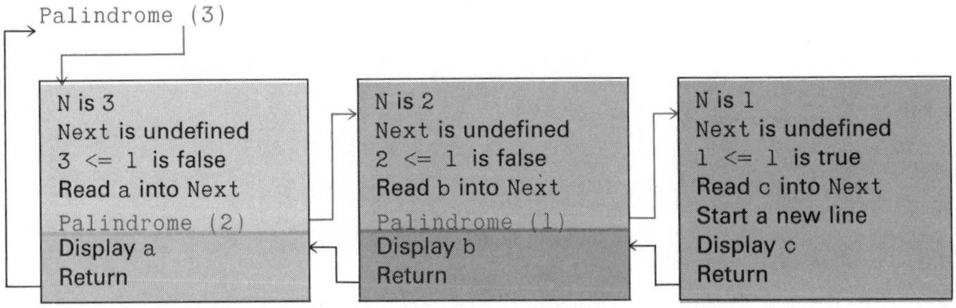

The trace shows three separate *activation frames* for procedure Palindrome. Each activation frame begins with a list of the initial values of N and Next for that frame. The value of N is passed into the procedure when it is called, because N is a value parameter; the value of Next is initially undefined, because Next is a local variable.

Each frame shows the statements that it executes. The statements in color are recursive procedure calls and result in a new activation frame, as indicated by the colored arrows. The darker the color of the activation frame, the greater the depth of recursion. A procedure return occurs when the procedure `END` statement is reached. This is indicated by the word Return in Fig. 12.4 and a black arrow that points to the statement in the calling frame to which the procedure returns.

Tracing the colored arrows and then the black arrows gives us the sequence of events listed below. All the statements for a particular activation frame are indented to the same column.

```
Call Palindrome with N equal to 3.
    Read the first character (a) into Next.
    Call Palindrome with N equal to 2.
        Read the second character (b) into Next.
        Call Palindrome with N equal to 1.
            Read the third character (c) into Next.
            Start a new line.
            Display the third character (c).
            Return from third call.
        Display the second character (b).
        Return from second call.
    Display the first character (a).
    Return from original call.
```

As shown, there are three calls to procedure `Palindrome`, each with a different parameter value. The procedure returns always occur in the reverse order of the procedure calls; that is, we return from the last call first, then we return from the next to last call, and so on. After we return from a particular execution of the procedure, we display the character that was read into `Next` just prior to that procedure call.

Parameter and Local Variable Stacks

You may be wondering how Modula-2 keeps track of the values of `N` and `Next` at any given point. Modula-2 uses a special data structure called a *stack*, which is analogous to a stack of dishes in a cafeteria. When clean dishes are brought into the cafeteria, they are always placed on the top of the stack of dishes. When we need a dish, we always remove the one most recently placed on the stack. This causes the next to last dish placed on the stack to move up to the top of the stack. (The stack data structure is discussed further in Section 13.4.) Whenever a new procedure call occurs, the parameter value associated with that call is placed on the top of the parameter stack. Also, a new cell whose value is initially undefined is placed on top of the stack maintained for the local variable `Next`. Whenever `N` or `Next` is referenced, the value at the top of the corresponding stack is always used. When a procedure return occurs, the value currently at the top of each stack is removed and the next lower value moves to the top.

As an example, look at the stacks for `N` and `Next` right after the first call to `Palindrome`. There is one cell on each stack.

After the first call to Palindrome

The letter `a` is read into `Next` just before the second call to `Palindrome`.

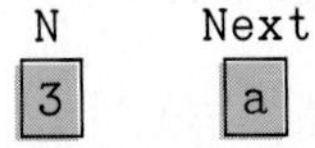

After the second call to `Palindrome`, the number `2` is placed on top of the stack for `N`, and the top of the stack for `Next` becomes undefined again. The darker color cells represent the top of each stack.

After the second call to Palindrome

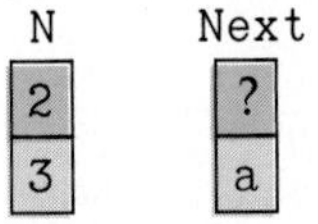

The letter `b` is read into `Next` just before the third call to `Palindrome`.

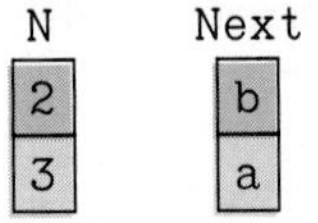

However, `Next` becomes undefined again right after the third call.

After the third call to Palindrome

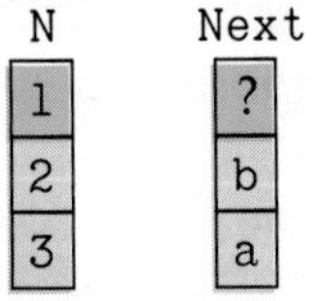

During this execution of the procedure, the letter `c` is read into `Next`; `c` is echo-printed immediately because `N` is `1` (the stopping case).

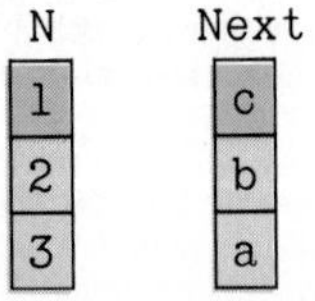

The procedure return causes the values at the top of the stack to be removed.

After the return from the third call

N	Next
2	b
3	a

Because control is returned to a `Write` statement, the value of `Next` (`b`) at the top of the stack is then displayed. Another return occurs, causing the values currently at the top of the stack to be removed.

After the return from the second call

N	Next
3	a

Again control is returned to a `Write` statement, and the value of `Next` (`a`) at the top of the stack is displayed. The return from the first (original) call removes the last pair of values from the stack, and `N` and `Next` both become undefined.

After the return from the first call

N	Next
?	?

SELF-CHECK EXERCISES FOR SECTION 12.2

1. Why is `N` a value parameter in Fig. 12.3?
2. Assume the characters `*+–/` are entered for the procedure call statement

   ```
   Palindrome (4)
   ```

   What output line would appear on the screen? Show the contents of the stacks immediately after each procedure call and return.

12.3 Case Studies of Recursive Procedures

This section will examine two familiar problems and implement recursive procedures to solve them. Both problems involve printing the contents of an array and could easily be solved using iteration. We will also redo the selection sort as a recursive procedure. Finally, we will solve the Towers of Hanoi problem, which is not easily done using iteration.

PRINTING AN ARRAY BACKWARD

Problem: Provide a recursive solution to the problem of printing the elements of an array in reverse order.

Discussion: If the array X has elements with subscripts 0..N, then the element values should be printed in the sequence X[N], X[N-1], X[N-2], ..., X[1], X[0]. The stopping case is printing an array with one element (N is 0); the solution is to print that element. For larger arrays, the recursive step is to print the last array element (X[N]) and then print the subarray with subscripts 0..N-1 backwards. The data description and algorithm are shown next.

PROBLEM INPUTS

an array of integer values (X : ARRAY OF INTEGER)
the subscript of the last element in the array (N : CARDINAL)

PROBLEM OUTPUTS

the array values in reverse order (X[N], X[N-1], ..., X[1], X[0])

Algorithm

1. IF N is 0 THEN
    2. Print X[0]
   ELSE
    3. Print X[N]
    4. Print the subarray with subscripts 0..N-1
   END (* IF *)

Procedure PrintBack in Fig. 12.5 implements this algorithm.

Figure 12.5 ▶ *Procedure PrintBack*

```
PROCEDURE PrintBack  (VAR X (* input *) : ARRAY OF INTEGER;
                      N (* input *) : CARDINAL);
(*
   Prints an array of integers (X) with subscripts 0..N.
   Pre : Array X is defined and 0 <= N <= HIGH(X).
   Post: Displays X[N], X[N-1], ... , X[1], X[0]
*)
BEGIN (* PrintBack *)
  IF N = 0 THEN
    WriteInt (X[0], 3)                    (* stopping case *)
  ELSIF N > HIGH(X) THEN
    WriteString ('Error in parameter for PrintBack');
    WriteLn
  ELSE
```

```
    (* recursive step *)
    WriteInt (X[N], 3);
    PrintBack  (X, N-1)
  END (* IF *)
END PrintBack;
```

Given the declarations

```
TYPE
  IntArray = ARRAY [0..20] OF INTEGER;

VAR
  Test : IntArray;
```

and the procedure call statement

```
PrintBack  (Test, 2)
```

three `WriteInt` statements will be executed in the order indicated, and the elements of `Test` will be printed backward, as desired.

```
WriteInt (Test[2]);
WriteInt (Test[1]);
WriteInt (Test[0])
```

To verify this, we trace the execution of the preceding procedure call statement in Fig. 12.6. Tracing the color arrows and then the black arrows leads to the sequence of events listed below.

Call `PrintBack` with parameters `Test` and `2`.
  Print `Test[2]`.
  Call `PrintBack` with parameters `Test` and `1`.
    Print `Test[1]`.
    Call `PrintBack` with parameters `Test` and `0`.
      Print `Test[0]`.
      Return from third call.
    Return from second call.
  Return from original call.

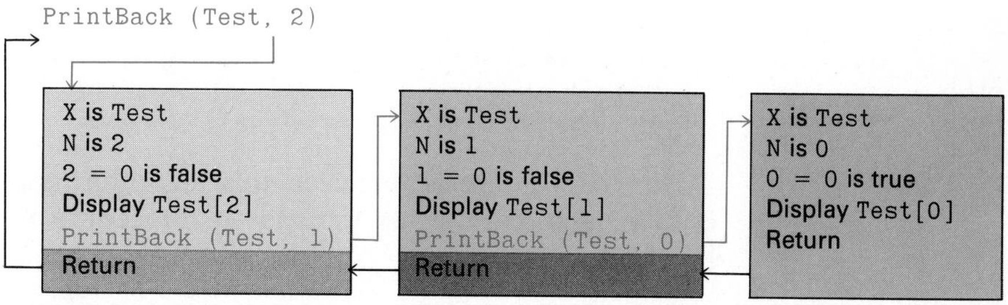

Figure 12.6 ▸ *Trace of PrintBack (Test, 2)*

As shown, there are three calls to procedure `PrintBack`, each with different parameters. The procedure returns always occur in the reverse order of the procedure calls; that is, we return from the last call first, then from the next to last call, and so on. This time there are no statements left to execute after the returns, because the recursive call

```
PrintBack (X, N-1)
```

occurs at the end of the recursive step.

Although it is not part of the algorithm, we have added an `ELSIF` clause to test for a value of `N` that exceeds the declared size of the array. In this case, the procedure will be called just once and will display an error message. As always, this is a good programming practice.

PRINTING AN ARRAY IN NORMAL ORDER

Problem: Provide a recursive procedure that prints the elements of an array in normal order.

Discussion: We can use the approach just followed to print the elements of an array in normal order. Again the stopping case is an array with just one element. The data description and algorithm follow.

PROBLEM INPUTS

an array of integer values (`X : ARRAY OF INTEGER`)
the subscript of the last element in the array (`N : CARDINAL`)

PROBLEM OUTPUTS

the array values in normal order (`X[0]`, `X[1]`, ..., `X[N-1]`, `X[N]`)

Algorithm

```
1. IF N is 0 THEN
      2. Print X[0]
   ELSE
      3. Print the subarray with subscripts 0..N-1
      4. Print X[N]
   END (* IF *)
```

The only difference between this algorithm and the one shown earlier is that steps 3 and 4 are transposed. Procedure `PrintNormal` is shown in Fig. 12.7.

Figure 12.7 ▸ *Procedure PrintNormal*

```
PROCEDURE PrintNormal (VAR X (* input *) : ARRAY OF INTEGER;
                       N (* input *) : CARDINAL);
(*
   Prints an array of integers (X) with subscripts 0..N.
   Pre : Array X is defined and 0 <= N <= HIGH(X).
   Post: Displays X[0], X[1], ... , X[N-1], X[N]
*)
BEGIN (* PrintNormal *)
  IF N = 0 THEN
    WriteInt (X[0], 3)              (* stopping case *)
  ELSIF N > HIGH(X) THEN
    WriteString ('Invalid parameter for PrintNormal');
    WriteLn
  ELSE
    (* recursive step *)
    PrintNormal (X, N-1);
    WriteInt (X[N], 3)
  END (* IF *)
END PrintNormal;
```

The trace of `PrintNormal (Test, 2)` is shown in Fig. 12.8. The black return arrows to each activation frame point to the display operation (`WriteInt`); therefore, the display operation is performed after the return. Following the color arrows and then the black arrows shows the following sequence of events. This time there are no statements that precede the recursive calls.

Call `PrintNormal` with parameters `Test` and `2`.
    Call `PrintNormal` with parameters `Test` and `1`.
        Call `PrintNormal` with parameters `Test` and `0`.
            Print `Test[0]`.
            Return from third call.
        Print `Test[1]`.
        Return from second call.
    Print `Test[2]`.
    Return from original call.

Figure 12.8 ▸ *Trace of PrintNormal (Test, 2)*

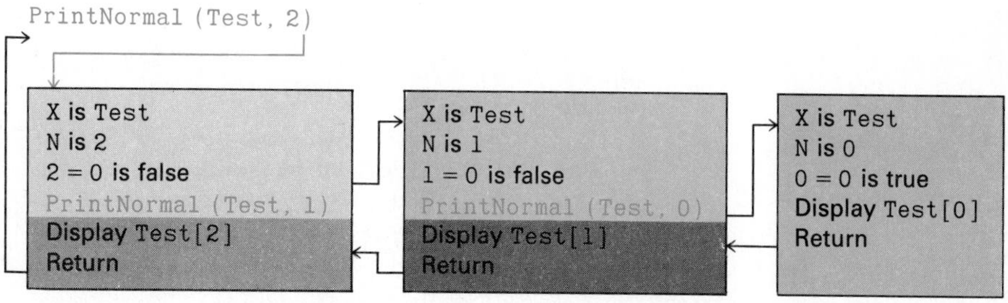

EXAMPLE 12.2 ▶ We have discussed and implemented an iterative version of the selection sort algorithm. A recursive algorithm for selection sort follows.

Recursive Algorithm for Selection Sort

1. IF N is 0 THEN
    2. The array is sorted.

   ELSE
    3. Place the largest array element in X[N].
    4. Sort the subarray with subscripts 0..N-1.

   END (* IF *)

This algorithm is implemented as a recursive procedure at the bottom of Fig. 12.9. Procedure PlaceLargest performs step 3 of the algorithm. The recursive procedure is simpler to understand than the one shown in Fig. 10.26 because it contains an IF statement instead of nested FOR loops. However, the recursive version will execute more slowly because of the extra overhead due to the recursive procedure calls. ◀

Figure 12.9 ▶ *PlaceLargest and Recursive SelectSort*

```
PROCEDURE PlaceLargest (VAR X (* inout *) : ARRAY OF INTEGER;
                        N (* input *) : CARDINAL);
(*
   Finds the largest element in array X[0]..X[N] and exchanges
   it with the element at X[N].
   Pre : Array X and N are defined and 0 <= N <= HIGH(X).
   Post: X[N] contains the largest value.
*)
   VAR
     Temp : INTEGER;      (* temporary copy for exchange *)
     j,                   (* array subscript and loop control *)
     MaxIndex : CARDINAL; (* index of largest so far *)

BEGIN (* PlaceLargest *)
  MaxIndex := N;                    (* assume X[N] is largest *)
  FOR j := N-1 TO 0 BY -1 DO
    IF X[j] > X[MaxIndex] THEN
      MaxIndex := j                 (* X[j] is largest so far *)
    END (* IF *)
  END; (* FOR *)

  (* assertion: MaxIndex is subscript of largest element *)
  IF MaxIndex # N THEN
    (* exchange X[N] and X[MaxIndex] *)
    Temp := X[N];  X[N] := X[MaxIndex];  X[MaxIndex] := Temp
  END (* IF *)
END PlaceLargest;
```

```
PROCEDURE SelectSort (VAR X (* input *) : ARRAY OF INTEGER;
                      N (* input *) : CARDINAL);
(*
   Sorts an array of integers (X) with subscripts 0..N.
   Pre : Array X is defined and 0 <= N <= HIGH(X).
   Post: The array elements are in numerical order.
*)
BEGIN (* SelectSort *)
  IF N = 0 THEN
    RETURN                    (* stopping case *)
  ELSIF N > HIGH(X) THEN
    WriteString ('Invalid parameter for SelectSort');
    WriteLn
  ELSE
    (*
       recursive step:
         Place largest value in X[N] and sort subarray 0..N-1.
    *)
    PlaceLargest (X, N);
    SelectSort (X, N-1)
  END (* IF *)
END SelectSort;
```

Program Style

Avoiding Value Array Parameters in Recursive Procedures

X is declared as a variable parameter in procedures PrintBack and PrintNormal even though it is used for input only. If X was a value parameter, each recursive call would generate a local copy of the actual array corresponding to X in each activation frame. This can result in a tremendous waste of time and memory space. For example, if X corresponds to an array with 10 elements and we want to print the entire array, there will be 10 activation frames, so storage space will be needed for 100 integer values. If X corresponds to an array with 100 elements, then storage space is needed for 100 × 100, or 10,000, integer values.

The next case study is considerably more complicated than the preceding ones. It leads to a recursive procedure that solves the Towers of Hanoi problem.

TOWERS OF HANOI PROBLEM

Problem: Solve the Towers of Hanoi problem for N disks where N is a parameter.

Discussion: The solution to the Towers of Hanoi problem consists of a printed list of individual disk moves. A general recursive procedure is needed that can be used to move any number of disks from one peg to another using a third peg as an auxiliary. The data description and algorithm for this procedure follow.

PROBLEM INPUTS

the number of disks to be moved (N : INTEGER)
the *from* peg (FromPeg : 'A'..'C')
the *to* peg (ToPeg : 'A'..'C')
the *auxiliary* peg (AuxPeg : 'A'..'C')

PROBLEM OUTPUTS

a list of individual disk moves

Algorithm

1. IF N is 1 THEN
    2. Move disk 1 from the *from* peg to the *to* peg
   ELSE
    3. Move N-1 disks from the *from* peg to the *auxiliary* peg using the *to* peg.
    4. Move disk N from the *from* peg to the *to* peg.
    5. Move N-1 disks from the *auxiliary* peg to the *to* peg using the *from* peg.
   END (* IF *)

The recursive step (following ELSE) will generate the three subproblems listed earlier when N is 5, the *from* peg is 'A', the *to* peg is 'C', and the *auxiliary* peg is 'B'. The implementation of this algorithm is shown as procedure Tower in Fig. 12.10. Procedure Tower has four parameters. The stopping case (move disk 1) is handled by the true statement sequence. Each recursive step consists of a sequence of output statements sandwiched between two recursive calls to procedure Tower. The first recursive call moves N-1 disks to the *auxiliary* peg. The output statements "move" disk N to the *to* peg. The second recursive call to Tower moves the N-1 disks from the *auxiliary* peg to the *to* peg.

Figure 12.10 ▸ *Recursive Procedure Tower*

```
PROCEDURE Tower (FromPeg,
                 ToPeg,
                 AuxPeg  (* input *) : CHAR;
                 N       (* input *) : CARDINAL);
(* Moves N disks from FromPeg to ToPeg
   using AuxPeg as an auxiliary. *)
BEGIN  (* Tower *)
   IF N = 1 THEN
      WriteString ('Move disk 1 from peg ');
      Write (FromPeg);
      WriteString (' to peg ');
      Write (ToPeg);
      WriteLn
   ELSE
      (* recursive step *)
```

```
      Tower (FromPeg, AuxPeg, ToPeg, N-1);
      WriteString ('Move disk ');
      WriteCard (N, 1);
      WriteString (' from peg ');
      Write (FromPeg);
      WriteString (' to peg ');
      Write (ToPeg);
      WriteLn;
      Tower (AuxPeg, ToPeg, FromPeg, N-1)
   END (* IF *)
END Tower;
```

The procedure call statement

```
Tower ('A', 'C', 'B', 5)
```

generates the solution to the original problem. The procedure call statement

```
Tower ('A', 'C', 'B', 3)
```

solves the simpler three-disk problem. Its execution is traced in Fig. 12.11, and the output generated is shown in Table 12.1. Verify for yourself that this solves the three-disk problem.

Figure 12.11 ▶ *Trace of Tower ('A','C','B',3)*

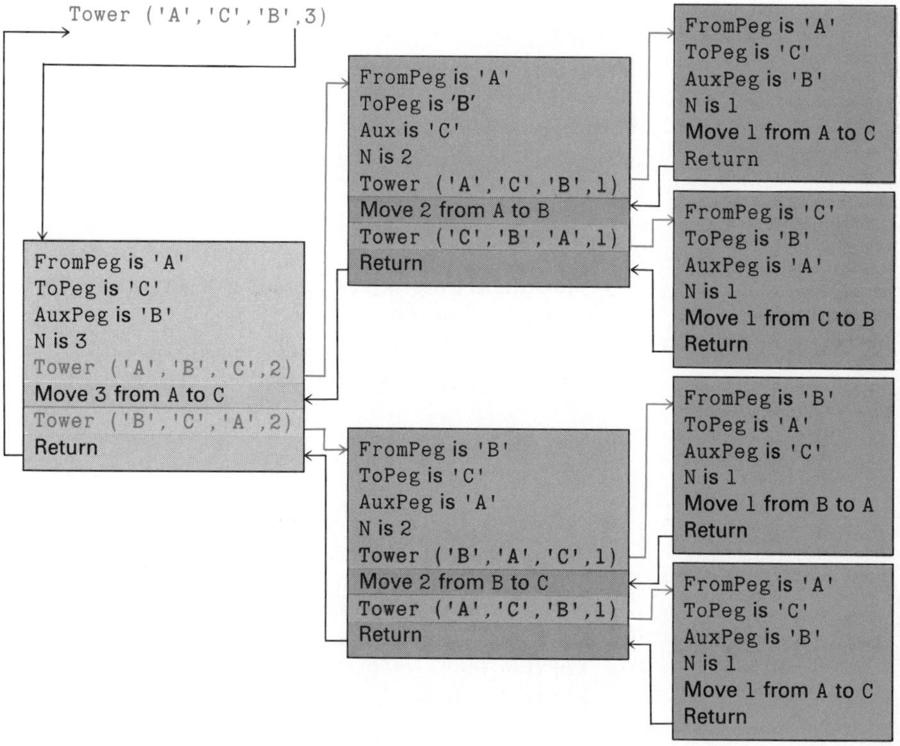

Table 12.1 ▸ *Output Generated by Tower ('A','C','B',3)*

```
Move disk 1 from A to C
Move disk 2 from A to B
Move disk 1 from C to B
Move disk 3 from A to C
Move disk 1 from B to A
Move disk 2 from B to C
Move disk 1 from A to C
```

Comparison of Iteration and Recursive Procedures

It is interesting to consider that procedure `Tower` in Fig. 12.10 will solve the Tower of Hanoi problem for any number of disks. The three-disk problem results in a total of seven calls to procedure `Tower` and is solved by seven disk moves. The five-disk problem would result in a total of thirty-one calls to procedure `Tower` and is solved in thirty-one disk moves. Since each procedure call requires the allocation and initialization of a local data area in memory, the computer time increases exponentially with the problem size (2^3 is 8, 2^5 is 32). For this reason, be careful about running this program with a value of `N` that is larger than 10.

The dramatic increase in processing time for larger towers is a function of this problem, not recursion. In general, however, if there are recursive and iterative solutions to the same problem, the recursive solution will require more time and space because of the extra procedure calls. Section 12.9 will discuss algorithm efficiency more completely.

Although recursion was not really needed to solve the simpler problems in this section, it was extremely useful in formulating an algorithm for the Towers of Hanoi problem. For certain problems, recursion leads naturally to solutions that are much easier to read and understand than their iterative counterparts. In those cases, the benefits gained from increased clarity far outweigh the extra cost (in time and memory) of running a recursive program.

SELF-CHECK EXERCISES FOR SECTION 12.3

1. Write a main program that reads in a data value for `N` (the number of disks) and calls procedure `Tower`.
2. Show the solution that would be generated for the four-disk problem.
3. Provide an iterative procedure that is equivalent to `PrintBack` in Fig. 12.6.

12.4 Case Studies of Recursive Functions

The process described in the previous section can be followed to write recursive functions. This process involves identifying the stopping cases of a problem. For the other cases, there must be a means of reducing the problem to one that is closer to a stopping case.

SUMMING THE VALUES IN AN ARRAY

Problem: We want to write a recursive function that finds the sum of the values in an array X with subscripts 0..N.

Discussion: The stopping case occurs when N is 0—the sum is X[0]. If N is not 0, then we must add the sum of the values in the subarray with subscripts 0..N-1 to X[N].

PROBLEM INPUTS

an array of integer values (X : ARRAY OF INTEGER)
the subscript of the last element in the array (N : CARDINAL)

PROBLEM OUTPUTS

the sum of the array values

Algorithm

```
1. IF N is 0 THEN
     2. The sum is X[0]
   ELSE
     3. Add X[N] to the sum of values in the subarray with
        subscripts 0..N-1
   END (* IF *)
```

Function FindSum in Fig. 12.12 implements this algorithm. The result of calling FindSum for a small array (N is 2) with element values 5, 10, -7 is also shown.

Figure 12.12 ▸ *Using Recursive Function FindSum*

```
MODULE TestFindSum;

(* Tests function FindSum. *)

   FROM InOut IMPORT
     WriteInt, WriteString, WriteLn;

   VAR
     X : ARRAY [0..10] OF INTEGER;

   PROCEDURE FindSum (VAR X : ARRAY OF INTEGER;
                      N : CARDINAL) : INTEGER;
   (*
      Finds the sum of the values in elements 0..N of array X.
      Pre : Array X is defined and consists of at least X[0].
      Post: Returns sum of first N elements of X.
   *)
   BEGIN (* FindSum *)
```

```
    IF N = 0 THEN
      RETURN X[0]
    ELSE
      RETURN X[N] + FindSum(X, N-1)
    END (* IF *)
  END FindSum;

BEGIN  (* TestFindSum *)
  X[0] := 5;  X[1] := 10;  X[2] := -7;
  WriteString ('The array sum is ');
  WriteInt (FindSum(X, 2), 0);
  WriteLn
END TestFindSum.
```

```
The array sum is 8
```

A recursive function will generally have two RETURN statements. In Fig. 12.12, the statement

```
RETURN X[0]
```

returns the function value, X[0], when the stopping step is reached. The expression in the second return

```
RETURN X[N] + FindSum(X, N-1)
```

contains a recursive call to FindSum. Therefore, the function result for N equals 2 cannot be determined until after the function result for N equals 1 is returned.

A trace of the function call FindSum(X, 2) is shown in Fig. 12.13. As before, each recursive function call is in color, and a colored arrow points to the activation frame for a recursive call. The black arrows indicate the return point (the operator +) after each function execution. The value returned is indicated alongside the arrow. The value returned for the original call, FindSum(X, 2), is 8, and this value is printed.

Functions that return BOOLEAN values (TRUE or FALSE) can also be written recursively. These functions do not perform a numeric computation; however, the function result is still determined by evaluating a BOOLEAN expression containing a recursive call. We will write recursive functions that search an array and compare two arrays.

EXAMPLE 12.3 ▶ The BOOLEAN function Member in Fig. 12.14 returns the value TRUE if the argument Target is in the array X with subscripts 0..N; otherwise, it returns the value FALSE. If N is 0 (the stopping case), the result is determined by comparing X[0] and Target. If N is not 0 (the recursive step),

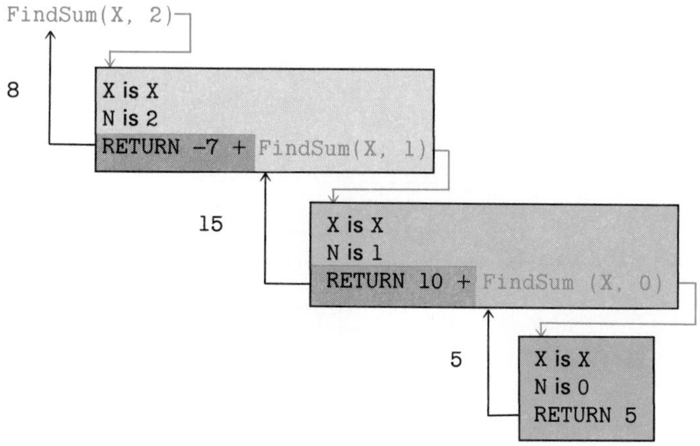

Figure 12.13 ▸ *Trace of FindSum(X, 2)*

then the result is true if either `X[N]` is `Target` or `Target` occurs in the subarray with subscripts `0..N-1`. The recursion is activated by the `RETURN` statement

```
RETURN (X[N] = Target) OR Member(X, Target, N-1)
```

in Fig. 12.14.

Figure 12.14 ▸ *Recursive Function Member*

```
PROCEDURE Member (VAR X : ARRAY OF INTEGER;
                  Target : INTEGER;
                  N      : CARDINAL) : BOOLEAN;
(*
   Searches for Target in array X with subscripts 0..N.
   Pre : Target, N and array X are defined and X has at least one
         element.
   Post: Returns TRUE if Target is located in array X; otherwise,
         returns FALSE.
*)
BEGIN (* Member *)
  IF N = 0 THEN
    RETURN X[0] = Target
  ELSE
    RETURN (X[N] = Target) OR Member(X, Target, N-1)
  END (* IF *)
END Member;
```

The function designator `Member(X, 10, 2)` is traced in Fig. 12.15 for the array `X` defined in Fig. 12.12. The value returned is `TRUE`, because the expression `X[N] = Target` is `TRUE` when `N` is `1`. ◂

Figure 12.15 ▸ *Trace of Function Member*

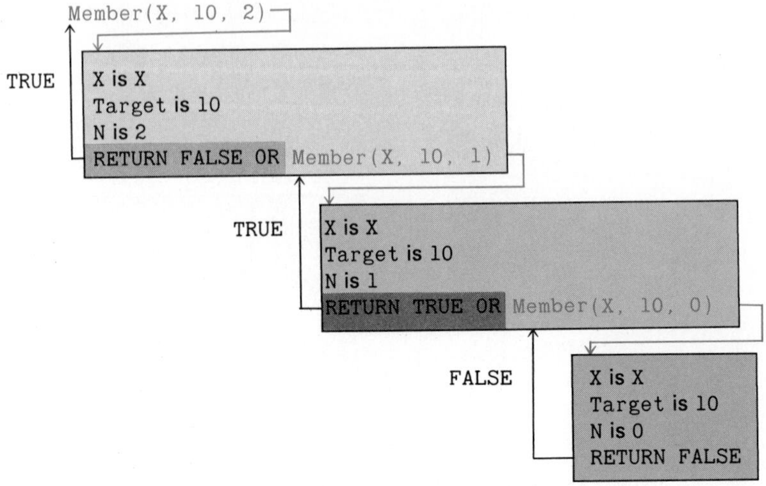

EXAMPLE 12.4 ▸ The BOOLEAN function EQUAL returns the value TRUE if two arrays, say, X and Y, of N elements are the same (i.e., X[0] = Y[0], X[1] = Y[1], ..., X[N] = Y[N]). This function (see Fig. 12.16) looks similar to function Member. For the stopping case, single-element arrays, the function result depends on whether X[0] = Y[0]. For larger arrays, the result is TRUE if X[N] = Y[N] and the subarrays with subscripts 0..N– 1 are equal. ◂

Figure 12.16 ▸ *Recursive Function Equal*

```
PROCEDURE Equal (VAR X, Y : ARRAY OF INTEGER;
                 N : CARDINAL) : BOOLEAN;
(*
   Compares arrays X and Y with elements 0..N.
   Pre : N and arrays X and Y are defined and both arrays have at
         least one element.
   Post: Returns TRUE if arrays X and Y are equal; otherwise,
         returns FALSE.
*)
BEGIN (* Equal *)
  IF N = 0 THEN
    RETURN X[0] = Y[0]
  ELSE
    RETURN (X[N] = Y[N]) & Equal(X, Y, N-1)
  END (* IF *)
END Equal;
```

Comparison of Iterative and Recursive Functions

It is interesting to consider the iterative version of function Member shown in Fig. 12.17. A FOR loop is needed to examine each array element. If Target is stored in the array, the statement

```
RETURN TRUE
```

inside the FOR loop is executed; otherwise, the statement

```
RETURN FALSE
```

is executed after loop exit.

Figure 12.17 ▸ *Iterative Function Member*

```
PROCEDURE Member (VAR X : ARRAY OF INTEGER;
                  Target : INTEGER;
                  N      : CARDINAL) : BOOLEAN;
(*
   Searches for Target in array X with subscripts 0..N.
   Pre : Target, N and array X are defined and X has at least one
         element.
   Post: Returns TRUE if Target is located in array X; otherwise,
         returns FALSE.
*)

   VAR
     I : CARDINAL;          (* subscript and loop-control variable *)

BEGIN (* Member *)
  (* Search array X for Target. *)
  FOR I := 0 TO N DO
    IF X[I] = Target THEN
      RETURN TRUE                  (* stop search - Target found *)
    END (* IF *)
  END; (* FOR *)

  (* assertion:  Target not found *)
  RETURN FALSE
END Member;
```

Many would argue that the recursive version of Member (see Fig. 12.14) is esthetically more pleasing. It is certainly more compact (a single IF statement) and requires no local variables. Once you are used to thinking recursively, the recursive form is somewhat easier to read and understand than the iterative form.

Some programmers like to use recursion as a conceptual tool. Once the recursive form of a function or procedure is written, it can always be translated into an iterative version if runtime efficiency is a major concern.

12.5 Recursive Mathematical Functions

Many mathematical functions are defined recursively. An example is the factorial of a number n ($n!$).

- 0! is 1
- $n!$ is $n \times (n-1)!$, for $n > 0$

Thus, 4! is $4 \times 3 \times 2 \times 1$, or 24. It is easy to implement this definition as a recursive function in Modula-2.

EXAMPLE 12.5 ▶ Function `Factorial` in Fig. 12.18 computes the factorial of its argument `N`. The statement

```
RETURN N * Factorial(N-1)
```

implements the second line of the preceding factorial definition. This means that the result of the current call (argument `N`) is determined by multiplying the result of the next call (argument `N-1`) by `N`.

Figure 12.18 ▶
Function Factorial

```
Procedure Factorial (N : CARDINAL) : CARDINAL;
(*
   Pre : N is defined.
   Post: Returns N!
*)
BEGIN (* Factorial *)
  IF N = 0 THEN
    RETURN 1
  ELSE
    RETURN N * Factorial(N-1)
  END (* IF *)
END Factorial;
```

A trace of

```
Fact := Factorial(3)
```

is shown in Fig. 12.19. The value returned from the original call, `Factorial(3)`, is 6, and this value is assigned to `Fact`.

Although the recursive implementation of function `Factorial` follows naturally from its definition, this function can be implemented easily using iteration. The iterative version is left as an exercise at the end of this section. ◀

EXAMPLE 12.6 ▶ The Fibonacci numbers are a sequence of numbers that have many varied uses. They were originally intended to model the growth of a rabbit colony. Although we will not go into details of the model here, the Fibonacci sequence 1,1,2,3,5,8,13,21,34,... certainly seems to increase rapidly enough. The fifteenth number in the sequence is 610 (that's a lot of rabbits!).

Figure 12.19 ▸ *Trace of Fact := Factorial(3)*

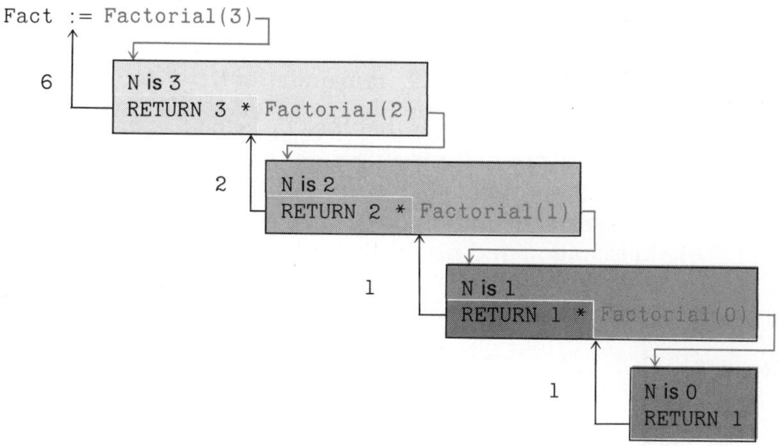

The Fibonacci sequence is defined as follows:

- Fib_1 is 1
- Fib_2 is 1
- Fib_n is $\text{Fib}_{n-2} + \text{Fib}_{n-1}$, for $n > 2$.

Verify for yourself that the sequence of numbers shown is correct. A recursive function that computes the `N`th Fibonacci number is shown in Fig. 12.20. ◂

Figure 12.20 ▸ *Recursive Function Fibonacci*

```
PROCEDURE Fibonacci (N : CARDINAL) : CARDINAL;
(*
   Pre : N is defined.
   Post: Returns the Nth Fibonacci number.
*)
BEGIN (* Fibonacci *)
  IF (N = 1) OR (N = 2) THEN
    RETURN 1
  ELSE
    RETURN Fibonacci(N-2) + Fibonacci(N-1)
  END (* IF *)
END Fibonacci;
```

Although easy to write, the Fibonacci function is not very efficient, because each recursive step generates two calls to function `Fibonacci`. This is similar to procedure `Tower`, so the execution time grows exponentially as `N` increases.

EXAMPLE 12.7 ▸ Euclid's algorithm for finding the greatest common divisor of two cardinal values, `GCD(M,N)`, is defined recursively below. The *greatest common divisor* of two cardinals is the largest cardinal that divides them both.

- `GCD(M,N)` is `N` if `N` <= `M` and `N` divides `M`
- `GCD(M,N)` is `GCD(N,M)` if `M` < `N`
- `GCD(M,N)` is `GCD(N,` remainder of `M` divided by `N)` otherwise

This algorithm states that the `GCD` is `N` if `N` is the smaller number and `N` divides `M`. If `M` is the smaller number, then the `GCD` determination should be performed with the arguments transposed. If `N` does not divide `M`, then the answer is obtained by finding the `GCD` of `N` and the remainder of `M` divided by `N`. The declaration and use of the function `GCD` is shown in Fig. 12.21.

Figure 12.21 ▸ *Euclid's Algorithm for the Greatest Common Divisor*

```
MODULE FindGCD;

(* Prints the greatest common divisor of two cardinals. *)

   FROM InOut IMPORT
      ReadCard, WriteCard, WriteString, WriteLn;

   VAR
      M, N : CARDINAL;                    (* two data items *)

   PROCEDURE GCD (M, N : CARDINAL) : CARDINAL;
   (*
      Pre : M and N are defined.
      Post: Returns the greatest common divisor of M and N.
   *)
   BEGIN (* GCD *)
     IF (N <= M)  (M MOD N = 0) THEN
       RETURN N
     ELSIF M < N THEN
       RETURN GCD(N, M)
     ELSE
       RETURN GCD(N, M MOD N)
     END (* IF *)
   END GCD;

BEGIN (* FindGCD *)
  WriteString ('Enter a cardinal number: ');
  ReadCard (M);  WriteLn;
  WriteString ('Enter another cardinal number: ');
  ReadCard (N);  WriteLn;  WriteLn;
  WriteString ('Their greatest common divisor is ');
  WriteCard (GCD(M, N), 0);
  WriteLn
END FindGCD.

Enter a cardinal number: 24
Enter another cardinal number: 84

Their greatest common divisor is 12
```

SELF-CHECK EXERCISES FOR SECTION 12.5

1. Write an iterative version of function `Factorial`.
2. Write an iterative version of function `GCD`.

12.6 Case Study: Counting Cells in a Blob

The next problem is a good illustration of the power of recursion. Its solution is relatively easy to write recursively; however, the problem would be much more difficult without using recursion.

Problem: We have a two-dimensional grid of cells, each of which may be empty (contents are `' '`) or filled (contents are `'#'`). The filled cells that are connected form a blob. There may be several blobs on the grid. We would like a function that accepts as input the coordinates of a particular cell and returns the size of the blob containing the cell.

There are three blobs in the sample grid. If the function parameters represent the x and y coordinates of a cell, the result of `BlobCount(3, 4)` is `5`; the result of `BlobCount(1, 2)` is `2`; the result of `BlobCount(5, 5)` is `0`; the result of `BlobCount(5, 1)` is `4`.

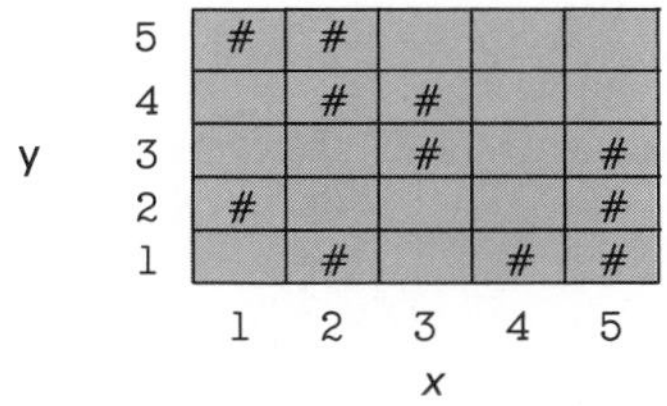

Discussion: Function `BlobCount` must test the cell specified by its arguments to see if it is filled. There are two stopping cases: the cell (`X, Y`) is not on the grid or the cell (`X, Y`) is empty; in either case, the value returned by `BlobCount` is `0`. If the cell is on the grid and filled, the value returned is `1` plus the size of the blobs containing each of its eight neighbors. To avoid counting a cell more than once, we will mark it as empty once we have counted it. The data description and algorithm follow.

PROBLEM INPUTS

the grid (a global array)
the x and y coordinates of the point being tested (`X, Y : INTEGER`)

PROBLEM OUTPUTS

the number of the cells in the blob containing point (`X, Y`)

Algorithm

1. IF cell (X, Y) is not in the array THEN
    2. BlobCount is 0

   ELSIF cell (X, Y) is empty THEN
    3. BlobCount := 0

   ELSE
    4. Mark cell (X, Y) as empty
    5. Add 1 to the size of the blobs containing the eight neighbors of cell (X, Y)

   END (* IF *)

The recursive function BlobCount is shown in Fig. 12.22 assuming the following declarations:

```
CONST
  MaxX = 100;
  MaxY = 100;

TYPE
  BlobArray = ARRAY [1..MaxX], [1..MaxY] OF (Filled, Empty);

VAR
  Grid : BlobArray;
```

The global array Grid is type BlobArray with element values Empty or Filled. The constants MaxX and MaxY represent the largest X and Y coordinate in Grid, respectively.

Figure 12.22 ▸ *The Function BlobCount*

```
PROCEDURE BlobCount (X, Y : CARDINAL) : CARDINAL;
(*
   Counts the number of filled cells in the blob containing
   point (X, Y).
   Pre : Global array Grid is defined.
   Post: Returns the size of the blob containing point (X,Y).
         Resets the status of each cell in the blob to Empty.
*)
BEGIN (* BlobCount *)
  IF (X < 1) OR (X > MaxX) OR (Y < 1) OR (Y > MaxY) THEN
    RETURN 0                              (* cell not in grid *)
  ELSIF Grid[X, Y] = Empty THEN
    RETURN 0                                 (* cell is empty *)
  ELSE (* cell is filled *)
    (* recursive step *)
    Grid[X, Y] := Empty;
    RETURN 1 + BlobCount(X-1, Y+1) + BlobCount(X, Y+1) +
               BlobCount(X+1, Y+1) + BlobCount(X+1, Y) +
```

```
                BlobCount(X+1, Y-1) + BlobCount(X, Y-1) +
                BlobCount(X-1, Y-1) + BlobCount(X-1, Y)
  END (* IF *)
END BlobCount;
```

In the recursive step, function BlobCount is called eight times with the neighbors of the current cell passed as arguments. The cells are passed in a clockwise manner, with the neighbor above and to the left being passed first. If a cell is off the grid or empty, a value of zero will be returned immediately. The function result is defined as the sum of all values returned plus one (for the current cell).

The sequence of operations performed in function BlobCount is important. The IF statement tests whether the cell (X, Y) is on the grid before testing whether (X, Y) is empty. If the order is reversed, the run-time error range error occurs whenever (X, Y) is off the grid.

Also, the recursive step resets Grid [X, Y] to Empty before checking the neighbors of point (X, Y). If this is not done first, cell (X, Y) is counted more than once since it is a neighbor of all its neighbors. A worse problem is that the recursion does not terminate. When each neighbor of the current cell is tested, BlobCount is called again with the coordinates of the current cell as arguments. If the current cell is Empty, an immediate return occurs. If the current cell is still Filled, the recursive step is executed erroneously. Eventually the program runs out of time or memory space; the latter is often indicated by a stack overflow message.

A side effect of the function execution is that all cells that are part of the blob being processed are reset to Empty. It would be necessary to save a copy of array Grid before the first call to BlobCount if its original status was important. This could also be achieved by making Grid a value parameter in procedure BlobCount; however, this would waste a lot of memory because a new copy of array Grid would be made each time BlobCount was called.

SELF-CHECK EXERCISES FOR SECTION 12.6

1. Write a recursive function FindMin that finds the smallest value in an integer array X with subscripts 0..N.
2. Trace the execution of function BlobCount for the coordinate pairs (1,1) and (1,2) in the sample grid.

12.7 A Recursive Array Search—Binary Search

We discussed searching an array in Section 10.5 and wrote a function that returned the index of a target value in an array if the target was present. To do this, it was necessary to compare array element values to the target value, starting with the first array element value. The comparison process was terminated when the target value was found or the end of the array was reached.

Often we want to search an array that is already sorted in ascending (increasing) order. We can take advantage of the fact that the array is sorted and terminate our search when an array element value greater than or equal to the target value is reached. Since the array is sorted, there is no need to look any further in the array because all other values must be too large.

Computer scientists are concerned about the efficiency of an algorithm as it relates to the number of elements being processed. If there are `N` elements in the array, then we would need to examine on the average `N/2`, or half, of the elements to either locate the target or determine that it is not in the array using our improved search algorithm. In the original algorithm, all `N` elements need to be examined when the target is not in the array.

BINARY SEARCH

The array search just described is called a *linear search* because its execution time increases linearly with the number of array elements. For very large arrays (say, `N` > 1000), the time required to perform a linear search becomes excessive. Consequently, we often use the *binary search algorithm* for large sorted arrays.

Problem: The binary search algorithm can be used to search an ordered array. It takes advantage of the fact that the array is ordered to eliminate half of the array elements with each probe into the array. Consequently if the array has 1,000 elements, it will either locate the target value or eliminate 500 elements with its first probe, 250 elements with its second probe, 125 elements with its third probe, and so on. It turns out that only 10 probes will be needed to completely search an array with 1,000 elements. (Why?) The binary search algorithm can be used to find a name in a large metropolitan phonebook using 30 probes or less.

Discussion: Because the array is ordered, all we have to do is compare the target value with the middle element of the subarray we are searching. If their values are the same, we are done. If the middle value is larger than the target, then we should search the lower half of the array next; otherwise, we should search the upper half of the array next.

The subarray to be searched has subscripts `First..Last`. The variable `Middle` is the subscript to the middle element in this range. The upper half of the array (subscripts `Middle..Last`) is eliminated by the first probe shown in the diagram below.

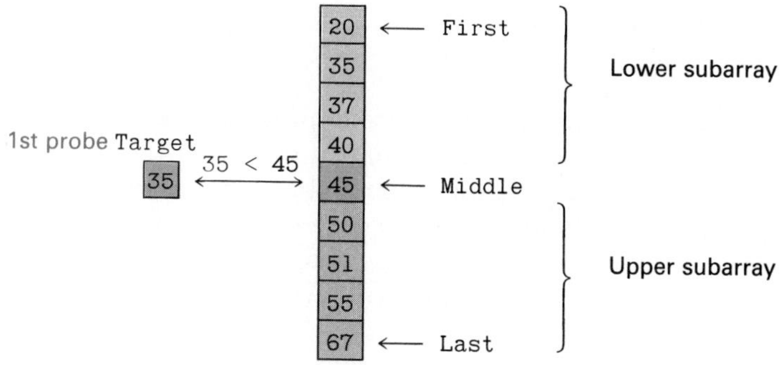

Last should be reset to Middle-1 to define the new subarray to be searched, and Middle should be redefined, as shown next. The target value, 35, would be found on this probe.

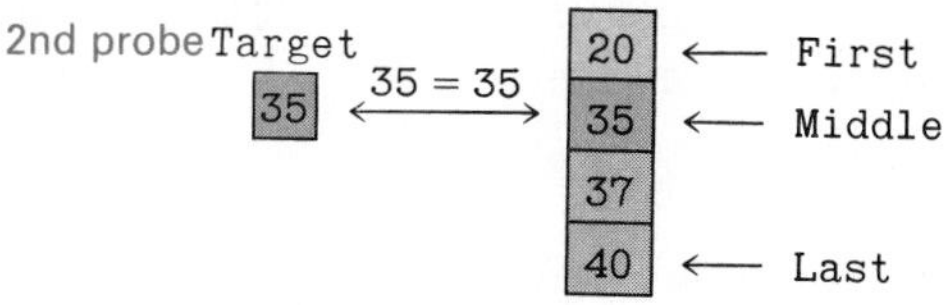

The binary search algorithm can be stated clearly using recursion. The stopping cases are:

- The array bounds are improper (First > Last).
- The middle value is the target value.

In the first case, the function should return a number that is one more than the size of the array; in the second case, the function result is Middle. The recursive step is to search the appropriate subarray. The data requirements and the algorithm for a recursive binary search function follow.

PROBLEM INPUTS

array to be searched (Table : ARRAY OF INTEGER)
target being searched for (Target : INTEGER)
the first subscript in the subarray (First : INTEGER)
the last subscript in the subarray (Last : INTEGER)

PROBLEM OUTPUTS

the location of the Target value or HIGH(Table) + 1 if the
 Target value is not found

Algorithm

1. Compute the subscript of the middle element
2. IF the array bounds are improper THEN
    3. Return a result of HIGH(Table) + 1
   ELSIF the middle value is the target THEN
    4. Return the subscript of the middle element
   ELSIF the middle value is larger than the target THEN
    5. Search the subarray with subscripts First..Middle-1
   ELSE
    6. Search the subarray with subscripts Middle+1..Last
   END (* IF *)

For each of the recursive steps (steps 5 and 6), the bounds of the new subarray must be listed as actual parameters in the recursive call. The actual parameters define the search limits for the next probe into the array.

In the initial call to the recursive procedure, `First` and `Last` should be defined as the first and last elements of the entire array, respectively. For example, the procedure call statement

```
BinarySearch(X, 35, 0, HIGH(X))
```

could be used to search an array `X` for the target value 35 (assuming `X` is an array of integers). Function `BinarySearch` is shown in Fig. 12.23.

Figure 12.23 ▸ *Recursive Binary Search Function*

```
PROCEDURE BinarySearch (VAR Table : ARRAY OF INTEGER;
                        Target : INTEGER;
                        First, Last : INTEGER) : INTEGER;
(*
   Performs a recursive binary search of an ordered array of integer
   values with suscripts First..Last.
   Pre : Target, First, Last and array Table are defined.
         0 <= First <= HIGH(Table), -1 <= Last <= HIGH(Table)
   Post: Returns the subscript of Target if found in array Table;
         otherwise, returns HIGH(Table) + 1.
*)
   VAR
    Middle : INTEGER;       (* the subscript of the middle element *)

BEGIN (* BinarySearch *)
  Middle := (First + Last) DIV 2;                  (* define Middle *)

  (* Determine if Target is found or missing or redefine subarray. *)
  IF First > Last THEN
    RETURN HIGH(Table) + 1         (* stopping case: Target missing *)
  ELSIF Table[Middle] = Target THEN
    RETURN Middle                    (* stopping case: Target found *)
```

```
  ELSIF Table[Middle] > Target THEN       (* search lower subarray *)
    RETURN BinarySearch(Table, Target, First, Middle-1)
  ELSE                                    (* search upper subarray *)
    RETURN BinarySearch(Table, Target, Middle+1, Last)
  END (* IF *)
END BinarySearch;
```

The assignment statement

```
Middle := (First + Last) DIV 2;                (* define Middle *)
```

computes the subscript of the middle element by finding the average of `First` and `Last`. This value has no meaning when `First` is greater than `Last`, but it does no harm to compute it.

If the target value is smaller than the element at position `Middle`, the statement

```
RETURN BinarySearch(Table, Target, First, Middle-1)
```

redefines `Last` as `Middle-1` in the next recursive call to `BinarySearch`, causing the lower subarray to be searched. If the target value is smaller than all array element values, this statement will be executed each time `BinarySearch` is called. Eventually, the value of `Middle-1` will become less than `First`, and a stopping state will be reached. If `First` is zero, the final value of `Middle-1` will be minus one. Since `CARDINAL` expressions cannot be negative, `First`, `Last`, and `Middle` are declared as type `INTEGER`.

An iterative version of the binary search function is shown in Fig. 12.24. Before performing the search, it is necessary to test that the array bounds passed to the function are proper (i.e., `First <= Last` is `TRUE`).

Figure 12.24 ▸ *Iterative Binary Search Function*

```
PROCEDURE BinarySearch (VAR Table : ARRAY OF INTEGER;
                        Target : INTEGER;
                        First, Last : INTEGER) : INTEGER;
(*
   Performs an iterative binary search of an ordered array of integer
   values with suscripts First..Last.
   Pre : Target, First, Last and array Table are defined.
         First and Last are >= 0 and <= HIGH(Table).
   Post  Returns the subscript of Target if found in array Table;
         otherwise, returns HIGH(Table) + 1.
*)
   VAR
     Middle : INTEGER;          (* the subscript of the middle
                                   element *)

BEGIN (* BinarySearch *)
```

```
  (* Compare Target to middle element and reduce search subarray *)
  IF First <= Last THEN
    REPEAT
      (* invariant: First <= Last and Target not yet found *)
      Middle := (First + Last) DIV 2;              (* define Middle *)
      IF Table[Middle] > Target THEN
        Last := Middle - 1                  (* search lower subarray *)
      ELSIF Table[Middle] < Target THEN
        First := Middle + 1                 (* search upper subarray *)
      END (* IF *)
    UNTIL (First > Last) OR (Table[Middle] = Target)
  END; (* IF *)

  (* Assertion:  Target is found or improper array bounds. *)
  IF First <= Last THEN
    RETURN Middle                                 (* Target is found *)
  ELSE
    RETURN HIGH(Table) + 1                     (* Target not found *)
  END (* IF *)
END BinarySearch;
```

SELF-CHECK EXERCISES FOR SECTION 12.7

1. Trace the search of the array `Table` shown in this section for a `Target` of 40. Specify the values of `First`, `Middle`, and `Last` during each recursive call.
2. Write a recursive function that finds the length of its string argument. Do not use the function `Length`. Assume that the null character is always stored at the end of a string.

12.8 A Recursive Array Sort—QuickSort

A binary search can be performed only on a sorted array. Section 10.6 discussed a simple but inefficient sorting algorithm, the selection sort. This section will describe a recursive algorithm for sorting an array.

The time required to sort an array using a simple sorting algorithm increases with the square of the number of array elements. This means that the time required to sort an array with N elements is proportional to N^2.

SORTING AN ARRAY

Problem: A faster algorithm is needed for sorting an array. We would like to see an improvement similar to that provided by binary search over simple search.

Discussion: The *quicksort* algorithm works in the following way. Given an array with subscripts `First..Last` to sort, the algorithm rearranges the array so that all element values smaller than a selected *pivot value* are first, followed by the pivot value, followed by all element values larger than the pivot value. After this rearrangement (called a *partition*), the pivot value is in its proper place. All element values smaller than the pivot value are closer to where they belong as they precede the pivot value. All element values larger than the pivot value are closer to where they belong as they follow the pivot value.

An example of this process follows. Assume that the first array element is arbitrarily selected as the pivot. A possible result of the partitioning process is shown beneath the original array.

Pivot

44

Original array

44	75	23	43	55	12	64	77	33

Array after 1st partition

12	33	23	43	44	55	64	77	75

After the partitioning process, the fifth array element contains the pivot value, 44. All values less than 44 are in the left subarray (color background); all values greater than 44 are in the right subarray (grey background), as desired. The next step would be to apply quicksort recursively to both subarrays. The data requirements and algorithm for quicksort follow. We will describe how to do the partitioning later.

PROBLEM INPUTS

the array being sorted (`Table : ARRAY OF INTEGER`)
the first subscript (`First : CARDINAL`)
the last subscript (`Last : CARDINAL`)

PROBLEM OUTPUTS

the sorted array (`Table`)

LOCAL VARIABLES

the subscript of the pivot value after partitioning
(`PivIndex : CARDINAL`)

Algorithm

1. `IF First < Last THEN`
    2. Partition the elements in the subarray `First..Last` so that the pivot value is in place (subscript is `PivIndex`)
    3. Apply quicksort to the subarray `First..PivIndex-1`

4. Apply quicksort to the subarray PivIndex+1..Last
END (* IF *)

The recursive algorithm above shows that nothing is done for the trivial case First >= Last. If First > Last is true, then the array bounds are improper; if First = Last is true, then a one-element array exists, which is sorted by definition. The implementation of procedure QuickSort is shown in Fig. 12.25. The procedure call statement

Figure 12.25 ▸ *Procedure QuickSort*

```
PROCEDURE QuickSort (VAR Table (* input/output *) : ARRAY OF INTEGER;
                     First, Last (* input *) : INTEGER);
(*
   Recursive procedure to sort the subarray of Table with
   subscripts First..Last.
   Pre : First, Last, and array Table are defined. First and Last
         are >= 0 and <= HIGH(Table).
   Post: Table is sorted.
*)
   VAR

     PivIndex : INTEGER;          (* subscript of pivot value -
                                     returned by Partition    *)

   PROCEDURE Partition (VAR Table (* in/out *) : ARRAY OF INTEGER;
                        First, Last (* input *) : INTEGER;
                        VAR PivIndex (* output *) : INTEGER);
   (*
      Partitions the subarray of Table with subscripts First..Last
      into two subarrays.
      Pre : First, Last, and array Table are defined. First and Last
            are >= 0 and <= HIGH(Table).
      Post: PivIndex is defined such that all values less than or
            equal to Table[PivIndex] have subscripts < PivIndex; all
            values greater than Table[PivIndex] have subscripts >
            PivIndex.
   *)
   BEGIN  (* Partition *)
      WriteString ('Procedure Partition entered.');  WriteLn
   END Partition;

BEGIN (* QuickSort *)
  IF First < Last THEN
    (* Split into two subarrays separated by value at PivIndex *)
    Partition (Table, First, Last, PivIndex);
    QuickSort (Table, First, PivIndex-1);
    QuickSort (Table, PivIndex+1, Last)
  END (* IF *)
END QuickSort;
```

```
QuickSort (Table, 0, HIGH(Table))
```

could be used to sort array `Table`.

The two recursive calls to `QuickSort` in Fig. 12.25 will cause the quicksort procedure to be applied to the subarrays that are separated by the value at `PivIndex`. If any subarray contains just one element (or zero elements), an immediate return will occur.

Procedure `Partition` selects the pivot and performs the partitioning operation. When we are selecting the pivot, if the arrays are randomly ordered to begin with, it does not really matter which element is used as the pivot value. For simplicity, we will choose the element with subscript `First`. We will then search for the first value at the left end of the subarray that is greater than the pivot value. When we find it, we search for the first value at the right end of the subarray that is less than or equal to the pivot value. These two values are exchanged, and we repeat the search and exchange operations. This is illustrated as follows with `Up` pointing to the first value greater than the pivot and `Down` pointing to the first value less than or equal to the pivot value.

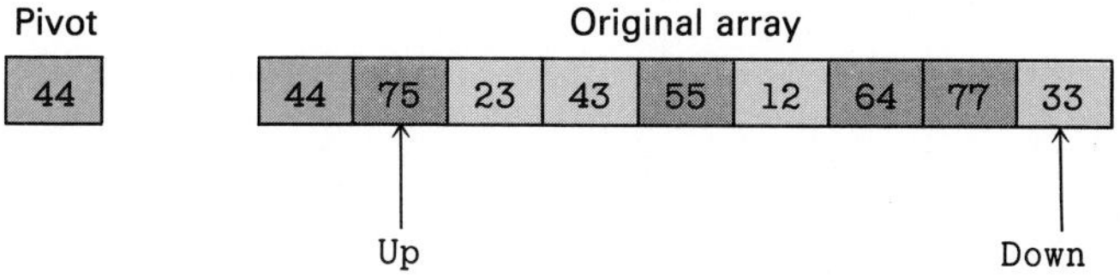

75 is the first value at the left end of the array that is larger than 44; 33 is the first value at the right end that is less than or equal to 44, so these two values are exchanged. The *pointers* `Up` and `Down` are then advanced from their current positions to the positions below.

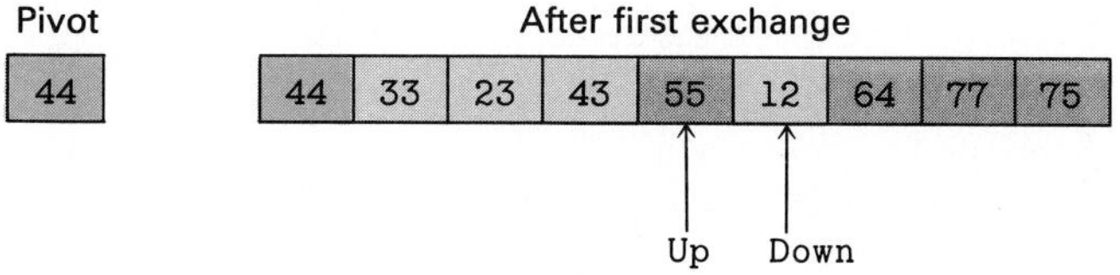

55 is the next value at the left end that is larger than 44; 12 is the next value at the right end that is less than or equal to 44, so these two values are exchanged, and `Up` and `Down` are advanced again.

After the second exchange, the first five array elements contain the pivot value and all values less than or equal to the pivot; the last four elements contain all values larger than the pivot. 55 is selected by `Up` once again as the

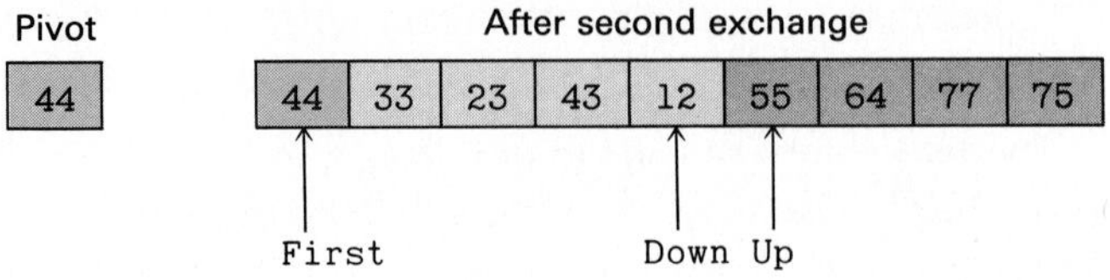

next element larger than the pivot; 12 is selected by Down as the next element less than or equal to the pivot. Since Up has now "passed" Down, these values are not exchanged. Instead, the pivot value (subscript is First) and the value at position Down are exchanged. This puts the pivot value in its proper position (new subscript is Down), as shown next.

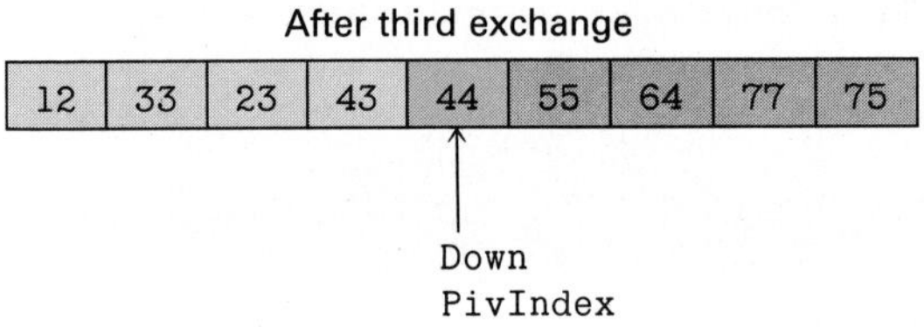

The partitioning process is now complete, and the value of Down is returned as the pivot index (PivIndex). QuickSort will be called recursively to sort the left subarray and the right subarray. The algorithm for Partition follows. This algorithm is implemented in Fig. 12.26.

Algorithm for Partition

1. Define the pivot value as the contents of Table[First].
2. Initialize Up to First and Down to Last.
3. REPEAT
    4. Assign the subscript of the next element greater than the pivot value to Up.
    5. Assign the subscript of the next element less than or equal to the pivot value to Down.
    6. IF Up < Down THEN
        7. Exchange their values.

        END (* IF *)

    UNTIL Up meets or passes Down
8. Exchange Table[First] and Table[Down].
9. Define PivIndex as Down.

Figure 12.26 ▶
Procedure Partition

```
PROCEDURE Partition (VAR Table (* input/output *) : ARRAY OF INTEGER;
                     First, Last (* input *) : INTEGER;
                     VAR PivIndex (* output *) : INTEGER);
(*
   Partitions the subarray of Table with subscripts First..Last into
   two subarrays.
   Pre : First, Last, and array Table are defined. First and Last
         are >= 0 and <= HIGH(Table).
   Post: PivIndex is defined such that all values less than or equal
         to Table[PivIndex] have subscripts < PivIndex; all values
         greater than Table[PivIndex] have subscripts > PivIndex.
*)
   VAR
     Pivot,                          (* the pivot value *)
     Up,                             (* pointer to values > Pivot *)
     Down : INTEGER;                 (* pointer to values <= Pivot *)

   PROCEDURE Exchange (VAR X, Y (* input/output *) : INTEGER);

   (* Switches the values in X and Y. *)

      VAR
        Temp : INTEGER;                (* temporary cell for exchange *)

   BEGIN (* Exchange *)
      Temp := X;        X := Y;         Y := Temp
   END Exchange;

BEGIN  (* Partition *)
   Pivot := Table[First];     (* define leftmost element as the
                                 pivot *)

   (* Find and exchange values that are out of place. *)
   Up := First;                (* set Up to point to leftmost
                                  element *)
   Down := Last;             (* set Down to point to rightmost
                                element *)
   REPEAT
     (* Move Up to the next value larger than Pivot. *)
     WHILE (Table[Up] <= Pivot) & (Up < Last) DO
       INC (Up)
     END; (* WHILE *)
     (* assertion:  Table[Up] > Pivot or Up is equal to Last *)

     (* Move Down to the next value less than or equal to Pivot. *)
     WHILE Table[Down] > Pivot DO
       DEC (Down)
     END; (* WHILE *)
     (* assertion:  Table[Down] <= Pivot *)

     (  * Exchange out of order values. *)
```

```
    IF Up < Down THEN
      Exchange (Table[Up], Table[Down])
    END (* IF *)
  UNTIL Up >= Down;                (* until Up meets or passes
                                      Down *)
  (*
     assertion:
       values <= Pivot have subscripts <= Down and
       values > Pivot have subscripts > Down
  *)

  (* Put pivot value where it belongs and define PivIndex. *)

  PivIndex := Down
END Partition;
```

The two `WHILE` loops in Fig. 12.26 are used to advance pointers `Up` and `Down` to the right and left, respectively. Since `Table[First]` is equal to `Pivot`, the second loop will stop if `Down` happens to reach the left end of the array (`Down` is `First`). The extra condition (`Up < Last`) is added to the first `WHILE` loop to ensure that it also stops if `Up` happens to reach the right end of the array.

SELF-CHECK EXERCISES FOR SECTION 12.8

1. Complete the trace of `QuickSort` for the subarrays remaining after the first partition.
2. In the event an array contains some duplicate values, in which subarray (left or right) will all values that are equal to the pivot value be placed?

12.9 Analysis of Algorithms—Big O Notation

The quicksort procedure works better for some arrays than it does for others. It works best when the partitioning process splits each subarray into two subarrays of almost the same size. The worst behavior results when one of the subarrays has `0` elements and the other has all the rest except for the pivot value. Ironically, this worst-case behavior results when quicksort is applied to an array that is already sorted. The pivot value remains in position `First`, and the rest of the elements are in the subarray with subscripts `2..Last`.

The relationship between the number of array elements, N, and the time required to perform quicksort is on the order of $N \times \log_2 N$ as compared to $N \times N$ for selection sort. We denote this by stating that quicksort is an $O(N \times \log N)$ algorithm and selection sort is an $O(N^2)$ algorithm using an abbreviation called *big O notation*. We can also say that selection sort is a quadratic algorithm and quicksort is a logarithmic algorithm.

To give you some idea of the difference in performance between $O(N^2)$ algorithms and $O(N \times \log N)$ algorithms, Table 12.2 provides a comparison of these formulas for different values of N. By moving down a column of the table, we see the relative effect of increasing N; obviously, $N \times \log_2 N$ increases much more slowly than does N^2.

Table 12.2 ▸ *Comparison of Effect of N on Sort Algorithms*

N	N^2 (SELECTION SORT)	$N \times LOG_2N$ (QUICKSORT)
32	1024	160
64	4096	384
128	16384	896
256	65536	2048
512	262144	4608

A similar table can be drawn to compare the expected performance difference between a linear search, $O(N)$, and a binary search, $O(\log N)$, for different values of N (see Table 12.3).

Table 12.3 ▸ *Comparison of Effect of N on Search Algorithms*

N (LINEAR SEARCH)	LOG_2N (BINARY SEARCH)
32	5
64	6
128	7
256	8
512	9

These tables provide some of the story, but they don't give all of it. For example, it may require considerably more time to perform each step of a logarithmic algorithm than a linear algorithm. So even though there are fewer steps, the actual time saved may be less than expected. Also, the performance of quicksort can deteriorate significantly if the array to be sorted is nearly in order to begin with, while the performance of selection sort is improved in this case.

12.10 Common Programming Errors

The most common problem with a recursive procedure is that it does not terminate properly. For example, if the terminating condition is not correct or is incomplete, the procedure may call itself indefinitely or until all available memory is used up. Normally a stack overflow run-time error indicates that a recursive procedure is not terminating. Make sure you identify all stopping cases and provide a terminating condition for each one. Also be sure that each recursive step leads to a situation that is closer to a stopping case and that repeated recursive calls will eventually lead to stopping cases only.

The use of large arrays or other data structures as value parameters can quickly consume all available memory. Unless absolutely essential for data protection, arrays should be passed as variable parameters. Expressions such as `N-1` must be passed as value parameters.

Sometimes it is difficult to observe the result of a recursive procedure execution. If each recursive call generates a large number of output lines and there are many recursive calls, the output will scroll down the screen more quickly than it can be read. On most systems it is possible to stop the screen temporarily by pressing a control character sequence (e.g., CONTROL-S). If this cannot be done, you can still stop your output temporarily by displaying a prompting message followed by a `Read (NextChar)` operation before each recursive call. Your program will resume execution when you enter a data character.

One problem with search and sort procedures is the possibility of going beyond the bounds of a subarray and generating a `subscript-range error`. Some subscript-range errors can be avoided by taking advantage of short-circuit evaluation to test the subscript expression before accessing the array. If a subscript type is `CARDINAL`, a cardinal overflow error occurs when the value of the expression to be assigned to the subscript is negative.

When you are debugging a search or sort procedure, it is best to use relatively small arrays (e.g., ten elements). Make sure you print the new contents of the array after each pass through a sort procedure. Verify that a search procedure works correctly when the target is the first or last array element.

12.11 Chapter Review

This chapter provided many examples of recursive procedures and functions. Studying them should have given you some appreciation of the power of recursion as a problem-solving and programming tool. It may take some time to feel comfortable thinking about programming in this new way, but it is certainly worth the effort.

We studied the binary search technique, which is a significant improvement for searching larger arrays. Binary search is an $O(\log_2 N)$ algorithm, which means that the time required to perform a binary search increases very slowly. For example, it should take only about twice as long to perform a binary search on an array with 256 elements ($\log_2 256$ is 8) as it would take to perform a binary search on an array with 16 elements ($\log_2 16$ is 4).

This chapter also discussed a new sorting algorithm (quicksort) and provided a recursive implementation of an old one (selection sort). Selection sort is an $O(N \times N)$ algorithm, which means that the time required to sort an array using selection sort is proportional to the square of the number of elements. For larger arrays, it is best to use quicksort, which is an $O(N \times \log_2 N)$ algorithm.

CHAPTER 12 ▸

Review Questions

1. Explain the nature of a recursive problem.
2. Discuss the efficiency of recursive procedures.
3. Differentiate between stopping cases and a terminating condition.
4. Write a Modula-2 recursive procedure that has a character-string parameter (maximum length of six). The procedure should print the accumulating sum of ordinal values corresponding to each character in the string until a null character is encountered or all six characters have been summed.
5. Write a Modula-2 recursive function that will return the sum of ordinal values corresponding to the characters in a character-string parameter (maximum length of six). The function should add up the ordinal values until a null character is encountered or all six characters have been summed.
6. Convert the following program from an iterative process to a recursive function that calculates an approximate value for *e*, the base of the natural logarithms, by summing the series

   $$1 + 1/1! + 1/2! + \ldots 1/N!$$

   until additional terms do not affect the approximation.

```
MODULE eLog;
  FROM InOut IMPORT
    WriteString, WriteLn;
  FROM RealInOut IMPORT
    WriteReal;

VAR
  e, Delta, Fact : REAL;
  N : CARDINAL;
```

```
BEGIN (* Elog *)
  e := 1.0;
  N := 1;
  Fact := 1.0;
  Delta := 1.0;
  REPEAT
    e := e + Delta;
    INC (N);
    Fact := Fact * FLOAT(N);
    Delta := 1.0 / Fact
  UNTIL e = (e + Delta);
  WriteString ('The value of e is ');
  WriteReal (e, 18);  WriteLn
END eLog.
```

7. Write a function that will recursively search a string of maximum length of thirty characters and return the position of the first comma in the string. If the string does not contain a comma, then return 30.

CHAPTER 12 ▸

Programming Projects

1. Write a procedure that reads each row of an array as a string and converts it to a row of `Grid` (see Fig. 12.22). The first character of row 1 corresponds to `Grid[1,1]`, the second character to `Grid[1,2]`, and so on. Set the element value to `Empty` if the character is blank; otherwise, set it to `Filled`. The number of rows in the array should be read first. Use this procedure in a program that reads in cell coordinates and prints the number of cells in the blob containing each coordinate pair.

2. The expression for computing $c(n,r)$, the number of combinations of n items taken r at a time is

$$c(n,r) = \frac{n!}{r!(n-r)!}$$

   Write and test a function for computing $c(n,r)$ given that $n!$ is the factorial of n.

3. A palindrome consists of a word that is spelled exactly the same when the letters are reversed, for example, level, deed, and mom. Write a recursive function that returns the `BOOLEAN` value `TRUE` if a word, passed as a parameter, is a palindrome.

4. Write a recursive function that returns the value of the following recursive definition:

$$F(X,Y) = X - Y \quad \text{if X or Y} < 0$$
$$F(X,Y) = F(X-1,Y) + F(X,Y-1) \quad \text{otherwise}$$

5. Write a recursive procedure that lists all two-letter subsets for a given set of letters. For example:

```
['A', 'C', 'E', 'G'] => ['A', 'C'], ['A', 'E'], ['A', 'G'],
                        ['C', 'E'], ['C', 'G'], ['E', 'G']
```

6. Write a procedure that accepts an 8 by 8 array of characters that represents a maze. Each position can contain either an `'X'` or a blank. Starting at position `[1,1]`, list any path through the maze to get to location `[8,8]`. Only horizontal and vertical moves are allowed (no diagonal moves). If no path exists, write a message indicating this.

   Moves can be made only to locations that contain blanks. If an `'X'` is encountered, that path is blocked and another must be chosen. Use recursion.

7. One method of solving a continuous numerical function for a root implements a technique similar to the binary search. Given a numerical function, defined as *f(X)*, and two values of X that are known to bracket one of the roots, an approximation to this root can be determined through a method of repeated division of this bracket.

   For a set of values of X to bracket a root, the value of the function for one X must be negative and the other must be positive, as illustrated in the following diagram, which plots *f(X)* for values of X between *X1* and *X2*.

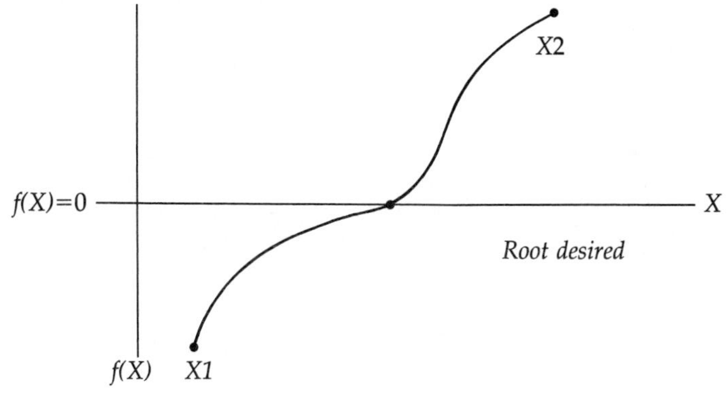

   The algorithm requires that the midpoint between the left X and the right X be evaluated in the function—if it equals zero, the root is found; otherwise, the left X (X1) or right X (X2) is set to this midpoint. To determine whether to replace either X1 or X2, the sign of the midpoint is compared against the signs of the values of *f*(X1) and *f*(X2). The midpoint replaces the X (X1 or X2) whose function value has the same sign as its function value.

   This routine can be written recursively. The terminating conditions are true when either the midpoint evaluated in the function is zero or the absolute value of the left X minus the right X is less than some small predetermined value (e.g., 0.0005). If the second condition occurs, the root is said to be approximately equal to the midpoint of the last set of left and right Xs.

8. We can use a merge technique to sort two arrays. The *mergesort* begins by taking adjacent pairs of array values and ordering the values in each pair (first pair has subscripts `1, 2`, second pair has subscripts `3, 4`, etc). It then forms groups of four elements by merging adjacent pairs (first pair with second pair, third pair with fourth pair, etc.) into another array. It then takes adjacent groups of four elements from this new array and merges them back into the original array as groups of eight, and so on. The process terminates when a single group is formed that has the same number of elements as the array. The mergesort is illustrated in Fig. 12.27 for an array with eight elements. Write a `MergeSort` procedure.

Figure 12.27 ▸ *Illustration of mergesort*

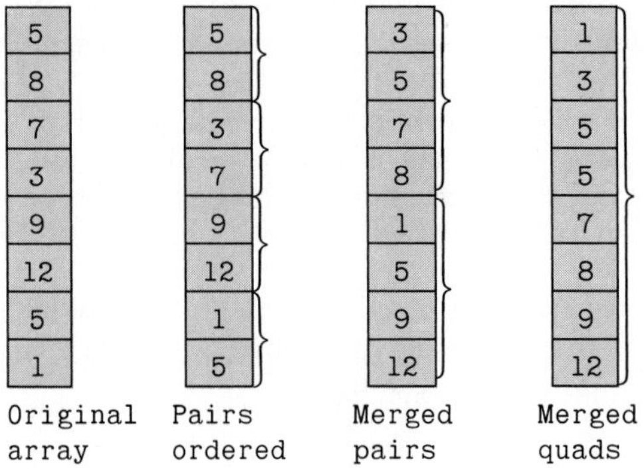

13 ▸ Pointer Types, Opaque Types, Stacks, and Queues

OUR STUDY OF abstract data types has stressed the importance of manipulating a data object using only the operators imported from the abstract data type. Although we cannot prevent a client module from manipulating a data object directly, this is poor programming practice and we advise against it (see Section 9.4).

In this chapter, you will learn how to hide information about the internal representation of a data type by removing it from the definition module and placing it in the implementation module. Hiding the internal representation in this way prevents a client module from directly manipulating a data object.

This chapter will introduce a new data type, the pointer type. The use of pointer types is necessary to accomplish information hiding. We will also use pointer types in the next chapter to build new data structures.

Finally, we will introduce two data structures that are important in computer science: the stack and the queue. We will implement and use abstract data types for both of these structures.

13.1 Information Hiding and Opaque Types

By reexamining an earlier example, we will show how to hide the internal representation of a data structure. In Section 9.4, we defined and implemented an abstract data type for complex arithmetic. Part of the definition module for this abstract data type is repeated in Fig. 13.1.

Figure 13.1 ► *Start of Definition Module for ComplexType*

```
DEFINITION MODULE ComplexType;
(*
   Specification of the abstract data type for representing
   and manipulating complex numbers.
*)
   EXPORT QUALIFIED
     Complex,                                    (* type *)
     CreateComplex, SetComplex,                  (* procedures *)
     ReadComplex, WriteComplex,
     AddComplex, SubtractComplex,
     MultiplyComplex, DivideComplex,
     GetReal, GetImaginary;                      (* functions *)

(*
   Data type - A record of type Complex consists of a pair of Real
   values such that the first number represents the real part of a
   complex number and the second number represents the imaginary
   part.
*)
```

```
  TYPE
    Complex = RECORD
      RealPart, ImaginaryPart : REAL
    END;  (* Complex *)
(* Operators *)
```

Since the declaration of data type `Complex` appears in the definition module shown in Fig. 13.1, `Complex` is considered a *transparent type*. Its structure is known to any client module, and so its individual fields can be manipulated by a client module. To prevent this manipulation, Modula-2 allows us to hide the structure of a data type, as discussed next.

Opaque Types

If the declaration

```
TYPE
  Complex;           (* opaque type *)
```

appears in the definition module instead, the only information given about `Complex` to a client module is that `Complex` is a data type. Because its exact structure (internal representation) is not known, the data type `Complex` is considered an *opaque type*, and its individual fields cannot be referenced or manipulated by a client module. This is the only change required for the definition module shown in Fig. 13.1.

If the structure of data type `Complex` is hidden in the definition module, then it must be specified in the implementation module. Therefore, `Complex` must be declared in the implementation module, as follows:

```
TYPE
  Complex = POINTER TO ComplexObject;
  ComplexObject = RECORD
                    RealPart, ImaginaryPart : Real
                  END; (* Complex *)
```

The first line in the type declaration specifies that `Complex` is a pointer type where a *pointer* is the address (location in memory) of a data structure. Furthermore, the data structure whose address is stored in a variable of type `Complex` must be type `ComplexObject`, a record with fields `RealPart` and `ImaginaryPart` (both type `REAL`). In Modula-2, all opaque types that are data structures must be declared using pointer types; simple data types can be declared as opaque without using pointer types.

13.2 Pointer Types and the NEW Statement

We can declare variables (called *pointer variables*) whose types are pointer types. For example, the declaration

```
VAR
  P : Complex;
```

specifies that `P` is a pointer variable of type `Complex`. This means that `P` can be used to store the address of a record of type `ComplexObject`.

The statement

```
NEW (P);
```

allocates storage for a record of type `ComplexObject` and places the address of this new record in pointer variable `P`. Once storage is allocated for the record that is pointed to by `P`, we can store data in that record and manipulate it.

We can represent the value of a pointer variable by an arrow drawn to a record. The following diagram

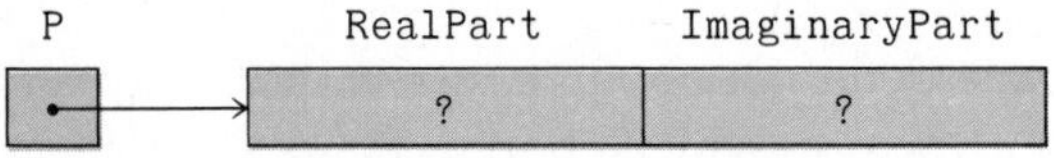

shows that pointer variable `P` points to a record of type `ComplexObject` with fields `RealPart` and `ImaginaryPart` that are currently undefined. This is the situation that exists just after `NEW(P)` is executed. The exact location in memory of this particular record is immaterial.

The symbols `P^` (or `P` ↑) denote the record pointed to by pointer variable `P`. The symbol ^ (caret) or ↑ (uparrow) is called the *dereferencing operator*. (Don't confuse the symbol ↑ with a cursor movement key that may be on your keyboard.) The assignment statements

```
P^.RealPart := 15.0;  P^.ImaginaryPart := 0.0
```

store data in record `P^`, as shown below.

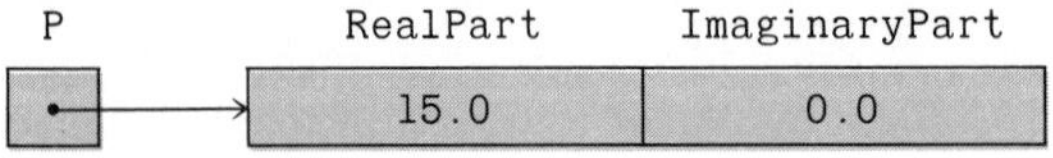

The statement

```
WriteReal (P^.RealPart, 12)
```

displays the value (`15.0`) of field `RealPart` of record `P^`.

Pointer Type Declaration

FORM: `TYPE` *ptype* `= POINTER TO` *dtype*

INTERPRETATION: Pointer type *ptype* is a data type whose values are memory cell addresses. A data structure whose address is stored in a variable of type *ptype* must be type *dtype*.

NEW Procedure

FORM: `NEW (`*pvar*`)`

INTERPRETATION: Storage for a new data structure is allocated, and the address of this data structure is stored in pointer variable *pvar*. The internal representation of this data structure is determined by its data type. If *pvar* is type *ptype*, the type of the new data structure is specified by the last identifier appearing in the declaration for *ptype*. The symbols *pvar*^ (or *pvar* ↑) are used to reference this data structure.

A module that calls procedure `NEW` must contain the statement

```
FROM Storage IMPORT
  ALLOCATE;
```

where `Storage` is a module containing the procedures that are used by the Modula-2 system to allocate and deallocate memory cells during execution of a program (called *dynamic allocation*). Procedure `ALLOCATE` is a low-level procedure used by the Modula-2 system to allocate additional memory cells whenever procedure `NEW` is called in a program. The details of how this is done do not concern us; however, we must remember to list `ALLOCATE`, not `NEW`, in the import statement.

13.3 Using Opaque Types in an Implementation Module

In the implementation module for `ComplexType` shown in Fig. 13.2, the declaration for the opaque type `Complex` follows the `IMPORT` statements. Since `Complex` is now a pointer type, the statements that manipulate a parameter of type `Complex` must all be modified to include the dereferencing operator ^. For example, the body of procedure `SetComplex` becomes

```
BEGIN (* SetComplex *)
  C^.RealPart := X;  C^.ImaginaryPart := Y
END SetComplex;
```

Similar changes occur in all other procedures shown in Fig. 13.2.

Figure 13.2 ▸ *Implementation Module for ComplexType Using an Opaque Type*

```
IMPLEMENTATION MODULE ComplexType;
(*
   Implementation module for the abstract data type
   for representing and manipulating complex numbers.
*)
   FROM InOut IMPORT
     Write, WriteString, WriteLn;

   FROM RealInOut IMPORT
     WriteReal, ReadReal;

   FROM Storage IMPORT
     ALLOCATE;

(* Data Type *)

   TYPE
     Complex = POINTER TO ComplexObject;
     ComplexObject = RECORD
                         RealPart, ImaginaryPart : REAL
                       END; (* Complex *)

(* Operators *)

   PROCEDURE CreateComplex (VAR C (* output *) : Complex);
   (*
      Creates a complex number C and initializes it to (0.0, 0.0).
      Pre : None
      Post: C is initialized to (0.0, 0.0)
   *)
   BEGIN (* CreateComplex *)
     NEW (C);
     C^.RealPart := 0.0;  C^.ImaginaryPart := 0.0
   END CreateComplex;

   PROCEDURE SetComplex (X, Y (* input *) : REAL;
                         VAR C (* output *) : Complex);
   (*
      Sets the real part of a complex number to X
      and the imaginary part to Y.
      Pre : C is initialized.
      Post: C is the complex number (X, Y).
   *)

   BEGIN (* SetComplex *)
     C^.RealPart := X;  C^.ImaginaryPart := Y
   END SetComplex;

   PROCEDURE ReadComplex (VAR C (* output *) : Complex);
   (*
      Reads a pair of values into complex number C.
```

```
   Pre : C is initialized.
   Post: The first real number read is the real part of C;
         the second real number read is the imaginary part of C.
*)
BEGIN (* ReadComplex *)
  WriteString ('Real part: ');
  ReadReal (C^.RealPart);  WriteLn;
  WriteString ('Imaginary part: ');
  ReadReal (C^.ImaginaryPart);  WriteLn
END ReadComplex;

PROCEDURE WriteComplex (C (* input *) : Complex);
(*
   Displays complex number C.
   Pre : C is assigned a value.
   Post: Prints the real and imaginary parts of C.
*)
BEGIN (* WriteComplex *)
  Write ('(');  WriteReal (C^.RealPart, 12);
  Write (',');  WriteReal (C^.ImaginaryPart, 12);  Write (')')
END WriteComplex;

PROCEDURE AddComplex (A, B  (* input *)  : Complex;
                      VAR C (* output *) : Complex);
(*
   Complex number C is the sum of complex numbers A and B.
   Pre : A and B are assigned values and C is initialized.
   Post: C is the complex sum of A and B.
*)
BEGIN (* AddComplex *)
  C^.RealPart := A^.RealPart + B^.RealPart;
  C^.ImaginaryPart := A^.ImaginaryPart + B^.ImaginaryPart
END AddComplex;

PROCEDURE SubtractComplex (A, B  (* input *)  : Complex;
                           VAR C (* output *) : Complex);
(*
   Complex number C is the difference of complex numbers A and B.
   Pre : A and B are assigned values and C is initialized.
   Post: C is the complex difference of A and B.
*)
BEGIN (* SubtractComplex *)
  C^.RealPart := A^.RealPart - B^.RealPart;
  C^.ImaginaryPart := A^.ImaginaryPart - B^.ImaginaryPart
END SubtractComplex;

PROCEDURE MultiplyComplex (A, B  (* input *)  : Complex;
                           VAR C (* output *) : Complex);
(*
   Complex number C is the product of complex numbers A and B.
   Pre : A and B are assigned values and C is initialized.
   Post: C is the complex product of A and B.
```

```
  *)
  BEGIN (* MultiplyComplex Stub *)
    WriteString ('Procedure MultiplyComplex called.');  WriteLn
  END MultiplyComplex;

  PROCEDURE DivideComplex (A, B  (* input *)  : Complex;
                           VAR C (* output *) : Complex);
  (*
     Complex number C is the quotient of complex numbers A and B.
     Pre : A and B are assigned values and C is initialized.
     Post: C is the complex quotient of A and B.
  *)
  BEGIN (* DivideComplex Stub *)
    WriteString ('Procedure DivideComplex called.');  WriteLn
  END DivideComplex;

  PROCEDURE GetReal (A : Complex) : REAL;
  (*
     Returns the real part of complex number A.
     Pre : A is assigned a value.
     Post: The real part of A is returned.
  *)
  BEGIN (* GetReal *)
    RETURN A^.RealPart
  END GetReal;

  PROCEDURE GetImaginary (A : Complex) : REAL;
  (*
     Returns the imaginary part of complex number A.
     Pre : A is assigned a value.
     Post: The imaginary part of A is returned.
  *)
  BEGIN (* GetImaginary *)
    RETURN A^.ImaginaryPart
  END GetImaginary;

  PROCEDURE AbsComplex (A : Complex) : REAL;
  (*
     Returns the absolute value of complex number A.
     Pre : A is assigned a value.
     Post: The absolute value of A is returned.
  *)
  BEGIN (* AbsComplex *)
    RETURN A^.RealPart * A^.RealPart +
           A^.ImaginaryPart * A^.ImaginaryPart
  END AbsComplex;

END ComplexType.
```

Procedure `CreateComplex` must be called to initialize any variable of type `Complex` before it can be manipulated. Since `Complex` is a pointer type, any variable of type `Complex` is a pointer variable. The statement

```
NEW (C);
```

allocates storage for the pointer variable represented by `C`. The statements

```
C^.RealPart := 0.0;  C^.ImaginaryPart := 0.0
```

initialize the complex number referenced by `C^` to (`0.0`, `0.0`).

The client module shown in Fig. 9.8 can be used with the modified definition and implementation modules discussed above. However, since the definition module was changed to make `Complex` an opaque type, it will be necessary to recompile and relink the client module.

When to Recompile Client Modules

Besides the fact that the details of data type `Complex` are hidden from any client module, there is another advantage to using opaque types. The definition module serves as the interface between the abstract data type and any client module that uses it. If we decide later to change the internal representation of the data structure (e.g., from rectangular to polar coordinates), the implementation module must be modified (and recompiled) but not the definition module. Consequently, it will not be necessary to recompile the definition module for `ComplexType` or any of its client modules.

On the other hand, if data type `Complex` is transparent, any change in its internal representation is reflected in its definition module. Consequently, the definition module and all client modules must be recompiled. In a large program library, this is liable to be a laborious task.

Returning Pointer Values

Another more subtle advantage to using opaque types is that it permits us to implement operators that compute new values for a data structure as functions instead of procedures. For example, the operation of complex addition returns a complex number as its value. We originally implemented this operator as a procedure that returns the complex sum of two input parameters through an output parameter (see Fig. 13.2). This was necessary because a function can return only a single value, not a data structure.

If `Complex` is a pointer type, the procedure header

```
PROCEDURE AddComplex (A, B : Complex) : Complex;
```

redefines `AddComplex` as a function procedure with two input arguments. Function `AddComplex` returns a pointer value of type `Complex`. This is valid because a Modula-2 function can return a pointer value as its result, but not a record. The complete function declaration is shown in Fig. 13.3.

Figure 13.3 ▸ *Function AddComplex*

```
PROCEDURE AddComplex (A, B : Complex) : Complex);
(*
   Pre : A and B are assigned values.
   Post: Returns the complex sum (a record) of A and B.
*)
   VAR
     Temp : Complex;       (* local result *)

BEGIN (* AddComplex *)
  NEW (Temp);
  Temp^.RealPart := A^.RealPart + B^.RealPart;
  Temp^.ImaginaryPart := A^.ImaginaryPart + B^.ImaginaryPart;
  RETURN Temp
END AddComplex;
```

Each time `AddComplex` is executed, storage is allocated for a new complex number that is pointed to by `Temp`. The sum of the complex numbers represented by A and B is saved in record `Temp^`, and the address of this record is returned to the calling program. The *pointer assignment* statement

```
C := AddComplex(A, B)
```

could be used in a client module to store the address returned in pointer variable `C`, replacing the address currently in `C`.

This situation is depicted in Fig. 13.4, assuming `C` points to the complex number (`0.0`, `0.0`) before the function call. The old value of pointer variable `C` is represented by the grey arrow; the new value is represented by the colored arrow. After the function return, `C` points to the same record as did pointer `Temp`, and `C` no longer points to the complex number (`0.0`, `0.0`).

Figure 13.4 ▸ *Effect of a Pointer Assignment*

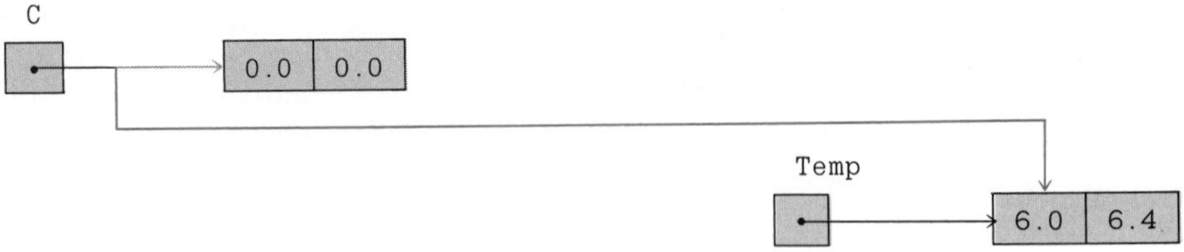

13.4 Stacks

In this section we will discuss a data abstraction, the stack, that is very useful in computer science applications such as writing compilers. We already introduced the stack in Section 12.2 and discussed how stacks might be used to implement recursion.

A stack is characterized by the property that at any one time only the top element of the stack is accessible. Some of the operations that we might wish to perform on a stack are summarized in the specification below.

Specification of an Abstract Data Type Stack ▶

ELEMENTS: A stack consists of a collection of elements that are all the same data type.

STRUCTURE: The elements of a stack are ordered according to when they were placed on the stack. Only the element that was last inserted into the stack may be removed or examined. New elements are inserted at the top of the stack.

OPERATORS: In the following descriptions, assume these parameters:
- `S` represents the stack
- `X` has the same data type as the stack elements
- `Success` is type `BOOLEAN` and indicates whether or not the operation succeeds.

`CreateStack (VAR S)`: Creates an empty stack.

`Push (VAR S, X, VAR Success)`: If stack `S` is not full, the value in `X` is placed on the top of the stack and `Success` is set to `TRUE`. Otherwise, the top of the stack is not changed and `Success` is set to `FALSE`.

`Pop (VAR S, VAR X, VAR Success)`: If stack `S` is not empty, the value at the top of the stack is removed and placed in `X`, and `Success` is set to `TRUE`. If the stack is empty, `X` is not defined and `Success` is set to `FALSE`.

`Retrieve (S, VAR X, VAR Success)`: If stack `S` is not empty, the value at the top of the stack is copied into `X`, and `Success` is set to `TRUE`. If the stack is empty, `X` is not defined and `Success` is set to `FALSE`. In either case, the stack is not changed.

`IsEmpty(S)`: Returns `TRUE` if stack `S` is empty; otherwise, returns `FALSE`.

`IsFull(S)`: Returns `TRUE` if stack `S` is full; otherwise, returns `FALSE`.

EXAMPLE 13.1 ▶ A stack `S` of character elements is shown in Fig. 13.5. This stack has four elements; the first element placed on the stack was `'2'`; the last element placed on the stack was `'*'`.

Figure 13.5 ▶
Stack S

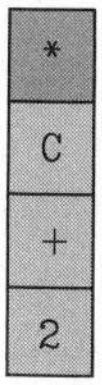

For stack `S` in Fig. 13.5, the value of `IsEmpty(S)` is `FALSE`. The value of `IsFull(S)` is `FALSE` if stack `S` can store more than four elements; otherwise, the value of `IsFull(S)` is `TRUE`. The procedure call statement

```
Retrieve (S, X, Success)
```

stores `'*'` in `X` (type `CHAR`) without changing `S`. The procedure call statement

```
Pop (S, X, Success)
```

removes `'*'` from `S` and stores it in `X`. The new stack `S` contains three elements and is shown in Fig. 13.6.

Figure 13.6 ▸ *Stack S after Pop Operation*

The procedure call statement

```
Push (S, '/', Success)
```

pushes `'/'` onto the stack; the new stack `S` contains four elements and is shown in Fig. 13.7. The value of `Success` (type `BOOLEAN`) after each operation should be `TRUE`. ◂

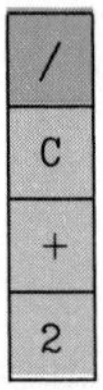

Figure 13.7 ▸ *Stack S after Push Operation*

13.5 Implementing a Stack of Characters

This section will discuss how to implement the stack data type in Modula-2. We will use an opaque type so there is no need to specify any of the details of the stack in the definition module shown in Fig. 13.8. The definition module follows naturally from the specification shown earlier.

Figure 13.8 ▸ *Definition Module for StackADT*

```
DEFINITION MODULE StackADT;

(* Specification for the abstract data type stack. *)
```

```
  EXPORT QUALIFIED
    Stack,                                (* data type *)
    CreateStack, Push, Pop, Retrieve,     (* procedures *)
    IsEmpty, IsFull;                      (* functions *)

(* Data type *)

  TYPE
    Stack;                              (* opaque type *)


(* Operators *)

  PROCEDURE CreateStack (VAR S (* out *) : Stack);
  (*
     Creates an empty stack.
     Pre : None
     Post: S is an empty stack.
  *)

  PROCEDURE Push (VAR S (* in/out *) : Stack;
                  X (* in *) : CHAR;
                  VAR Success (* out *) : BOOLEAN);
  (*
     Pushes X onto stack S.
     Pre : X is defined and S is a stack.
     Post: Sets Success to indicate success (TRUE) or failure
           (FALSE) of push operation.
  *)

  PROCEDURE Pop (VAR S (* in/out *) : Stack;
                 VAR X (* out *) : CHAR;
                 VAR Success (* out *) : BOOLEAN);
  (*
     Pops the top of stack S into X.
     Pre : S is a stack.
     Post: Contents of X is character at top of stack S, which is
           then removed from S. Sets Success to indicate success
           (TRUE) or failure (FALSE) of pop operation.
  *)

  PROCEDURE Retrieve (S (* input *) : Stack;
                      VAR X (* out *) : CHAR;
                      VAR Success (* out *) : BOOLEAN);
  (* Copies the value at the top of the stack into X.
     Pre : S is a stack.
     Post: Contents of X is character at top of stack S; S is
           unchanged. Sets Success to indicate success (TRUE) or
           failure (FALSE).
  *)

  PROCEDURE IsEmpty (S : Stack) : BOOLEAN;
  (*
```

```
      Pre : S is a stack.
      Post: Returns TRUE if stack S is empty;
            otherwise, returns FALSE.
   *)
   PROCEDURE IsFull (S : Stack) : BOOLEAN;
   (*
      Pre : S is a stack.
      Post: Returns TRUE if stack S is full;
            otherwise, returns FALSE.
   *)

END StackADT.
```

For simplicity, assume that the elements of a stack are characters. We will use the following data type in the implementation module.

```
TYPE
  Stack = POINTER TO StackObject;
  StackObject = RECORD
                  Top : [0..MaxStack];
                  Items : ARRAY [1..MaxStack] OF CHAR
                END; (* StackObject *)
```

A variable of type `Stack` is a pointer to a record of type `StackObject`, which represents a stack. `StackObject` is a record with a `CARDINAL` field, `Top`, and an array field (`Items`) used for storing a collection of character elements. The `CARDINAL` field `Top` is an array index whose value will be used to select the element of array field `Items` that is currently at the top of the stack. The constant `MaxStack` determines how many elements can be stored in the stack.

EXAMPLE 13.2 ▶ In the stack shown to the left of Fig. 13.9, `Top` has a value of 3, so `Items[3]` (value is `'C'`) is the element at the top of the stack. Before a new item is pushed onto the stack, `Top` will be incremented to 4 and the new item (`'*'`) will be stored in `Items[4]`, as shown to the right of the figure.

Figure 13.9 ▶ *Stack before and after Push Operation*

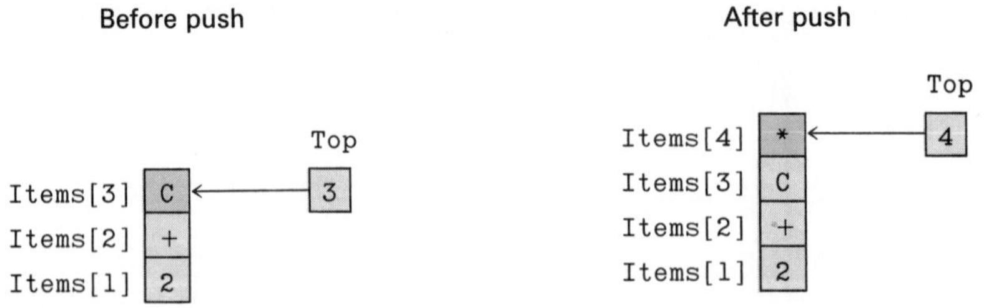

The array index `Top` is often called the *top-of-stack pointer*, since its value points to the element currently at the top of the stack. The implementation module for `StackADT` is shown in Fig. 13.10. ◀

Figure 13.10 ▸ *Implementation Module for StackADT*

```
IMPLEMENTATION MODULE StackADT;

(* Implementation for the abstract data type stack. *)

   FROM Storage IMPORT
     ALLOCATE;

   CONST
     MaxStack = 100;                  (* maximum size of the stack *)

(* Data type -
   A variable of type Stack is a pointer to a record of type
   StackObject. A record of type StackObject consists of a
   CARDINAL value (Top) representing the top of a stack and
   an array (Items) of stack elements.
*)
   TYPE
     Stack = POINTER TO StackObject;
     StackObject = RECORD
                     Top : [0..MaxStack];
                     Items : ARRAY [1..MaxStack] OF CHAR
                   END; (* StackObject *)

(* Operators *)

   PROCEDURE CreateStack (VAR S (* out *) : Stack);
   (*
      Creates an empty stack.
      Pre : None
      Post: S is an empty stack.
   *)
   BEGIN (* CreateStack *)
     NEW (S);                      (* allocate a stack *)
     S^.Top := 0                   (* stack is empty *)
   END CreateStack;

   PROCEDURE Push (VAR S (* in/out *) : Stack;
                   X (* in *) : CHAR;
                   VAR Success (* out *) : BOOLEAN);
   (*
      Pushes X onto stack S.
      Pre : X is defined and S is a stack.
      Post: Sets Success to indicate success (TRUE) or failure
            (FALSE) of push operation.
   *)
   BEGIN (* Push *)
     IF IsFull(S) THEN
       Success := FALSE             (* no room on stack *)
     ELSE
       INC (S^.Top);                (* increment top of stack pointer *)
       S^.Items[S^.Top] := X;       (* push X onto stack *)
```

```
    Success := TRUE
  END (* IF *)
END Push;

PROCEDURE Pop (VAR S (* in/out *) : Stack;
               VAR X (* out *) : CHAR;
               VAR Success (* out *) : BOOLEAN);
(*
   Pops the top of stack S into X.
   Pre : S is a stack.
   Post: Contents of X is character at top of stack S which is
         then removed from S. Sets Success to indicate success
         (TRUE) or failure (FALSE) of pop operation.
*)
BEGIN (* Pop *)
  IF IsEmpty(S) THEN
    Success := FALSE
  ELSE
    X := S^.Items[S^.Top];        (* pop top of stack into X *)
    DEC (S^.Top);                 (* decrement top of stack
                                     pointer *)
    Success := TRUE
  END (* IF *)
END Pop;

PROCEDURE Retrieve (S (* in *) : Stack;
                    VAR X (* out *) : CHAR;
                    VAR Success (* out *) : BOOLEAN);
(* Copies the value at the top of the stack into X.
   Pre : S is a stack.
   Post: Contents of X is character at top of stack S; S is
         unchanged. Sets Success to indicate success (TRUE) or
         failure (FALSE).
*)
BEGIN (* Retrieve *)
  IF IsEmpty(S) THEN
    Success := FALSE
  ELSE
    X := S^.Items[S^.Top];      (* copy top of stack into X *)
    Success := TRUE
  END (*IF *)
END Retrieve;

PROCEDURE IsEmpty (S : Stack) : BOOLEAN;
(*
   Pre : S is a stack.
   Post: Returns TRUE if stack S is empty;
         otherwise, returns FALSE.
*)
BEGIN (* IsEmpty *)
  RETURN S^.Top = 0
END IsEmpty;
```

```
    PROCEDURE IsFull (S : Stack) : BOOLEAN;
    (*
       Pre : S is a stack.
       Post: Returns TRUE if stack S is full;
             otherwise, returns FALSE.
    *)
    BEGIN (* IsFull *)
      RETURN S^.Top = MaxStack
    END IsFull;

END StackADT.
```

Since `Stack` is a pointer type and parameter `S` is type `Stack`, the symbols `S^` must be used to denote individual fields of the record pointed to by `S`. The qualified identifier `S^.Top` references the top-of-stack pointer.

Procedure `CreateStack` must be called before the stack can be manipulated. In `CreateStack`, the statements

```
NEW (S);                    (* allocate a stack *)
S^.Top := 0                 (* stack is empty *)
```

initialize a stack by allocating a record of type `StackObject` and setting its top-of-stack pointer to zero. The address of this new record is saved in the pointer variable that corresponds to formal parameter `S`. If you attempt to perform any other operation before calling `CreateStack`, Modula-2 interprets whatever value happens to be stored in the actual parameter corresponding to `S` as a record address; this could lead to a run-time error.

Procedure `Push` increments the top-of-stack pointer before pushing a new value onto the stack. Procedure `Pop` copies the value at the top of the stack (denoted by `S^.Items[S^.Top]`) into `X` before decrementing the top-of-stack pointer. Procedure `Retrieve` copies the value at the top of the stack into `X` without changing the top-of-stack pointer. Function procedures `IsFull` and `IsEmpty` test the top-of-stack pointer to determine the stack status.

Program Style

Efficiency versus Readability

Procedure `Push` in Fig. 13.10 uses the function designator `IsFull(S)` to determine if the stack represented by `S` is full. It would be more efficient to substitute the condition `S^.Top = MaxStack` for this function designator in procedure `Push`. A similar case could be made for substituting the condition `S^.Top = 0` for the function designator `IsEmpty(S)` in procedure `Pop`. Some would argue, however, that the resulting procedures would be less readable with this change. This substitution is not allowed in a client module, because the field `Top` cannot be manipulated external to the implementation module.

Using the Stack of Characters

A client module that uses a stack of characters is shown in Fig. 13.11. This program simply reads a sequence of characters and pushes them onto a stack. It then pops each character from the stack and displays it, thereby printing the sequence in reverse order.

Figure 13.11 ▸ *Program PrintReverse*

```
MODULE PrintReverse;
(*
   Reads a sequence of characters and displays it in reverse order.
   Uses the abstract data type stack.
*)

   FROM InOut IMPORT
     Write, Read, WriteString, WriteLn, EOL;

   FROM StackADT IMPORT
     Stack,                       (* data type *)
     CreateStack, Push, Pop,      (* procedures *)
     IsFull, IsEmpty;             (* functions *)

   VAR
     S : Stack;                   (* the stack of characters *)

   PROCEDURE FillStack (VAR S (* in/out *) : Stack);

   (* Reads data characters and pushes them onto the stack. *)

     VAR
       NextCh : CHAR;                  (* the next character *)
       Success : BOOLEAN;              (* flag *)

   BEGIN (* FillStack *)
     WriteString ('Enter a string of one or more characters.');
     WriteLn;  WriteString ('Press return when done.');  WriteLn;
     REPEAT
       Read (NextCh);  Write (NextCh);  (* read and echo character *)
       Push (S, NextCh, Success)        (* push it onto stack *)
     UNTIL (NextCh = EOL) OR NOT Success;
     WriteLn;

     (* Print an error if stack overflows. *)
     IF NOT Success THEN
       WriteString ('Stack overflow error - string too long');
       WriteLn
     END (* IF *)
   END FillStack;

   PROCEDURE DisplayStack (VAR S (* in/out *) : Stack);

   (* Pops each stack character and displays it. *)
```

```
      VAR
        NextCh : CHAR;                    (* the next character *)
        Success : BOOLEAN;                (* flag *)

    BEGIN (* DisplayStack *)
      Pop (S, NextCh, Success);
      WHILE Success DO
        Write (NextCh);
        Pop (S, NextCh, Success)
      END; (* WHILE *)
      WriteLn
    END DisplayStack;

BEGIN (* PrintReverse *)
  CreateStack (S);                       (* start with an empty stack *)

  (* Fill the stack. *)
  FillStack (S);

  (* Display the characters in reverse order. *)
  DisplayStack (S);

  (* Display status of stack S. *)
  IF IsEmpty(S) THEN
    WriteString ('Stack is empty')
  ELSIF IsFull(S) THEN
    WriteString ('Stack is full')
  END;
  WriteLn
END PrintReverse.

Enter a string of one or more characters.
Press return when done.
This is a short string.

.gnirts trohs a si sihT
Stack is empty
```

The `REPEAT-UNTIL` loop in procedure `FillStack` reads the data characters (at least one) and pushes them onto the stack. The `IF` statement displays an error message if the input string is too long. This would happen if the program user entered more than `MaxStack` characters before pressing Return.

The `WHILE` loop in procedure `DisplayStack` pops each character from the stack and displays it. The loop is repeated as long as there are characters remaining on the stack (`Success` is `TRUE`). After `DisplayStack` is finished, the stack is empty.

SELF-CHECK EXERCISES FOR SECTION 13.5

1. Draw the stack S shown in Fig. 13.9 after all the following operations have been performed. Assume that Y (type CHAR) contains the character '#'. What will be the final values of X and Success?

```
Pop (S, X, Success);
Pop (S, X, Success);
Push (S, '&', Success);
Pop (S, X, Success);
Push (S, X, Success);
Push (S, Y, Success);
Pop (S, X, Success);
```

2. Write an operator SizeOfStack that returns the number of elements currently on the stack. What changes would be needed to include this operator in the definition and implementation modules for StackADT?

13.6 Queues

A queue is a data abstraction that can be used to model things such as a line of customers waiting at a checkout counter or a stream of jobs waiting to be printed by a printer in a computer center. A queue differs from a stack in that new elements are inserted at one end (the rear of the queue) and existing elements are removed from the other end (the front of the queue). In contrast, stack elements are pushed onto (inserted) and popped off (removed) the same end (the top of the stack).

A queue of three passengers on a waiting list for an airline flight is shown in Fig. 13.12. The passenger who has been waiting the longest is 'Brown' (pointed to by Front); the most recent arrival is 'Carson' (pointed to by Rear). The passenger pointed to by Front will be the first one removed. Since this is also the passenger who has been waiting the longest, a queue is sometimes called a *FIFO list* (first-in first-out). [A stack is called a *LIFO list* (last-in first-out)]. The last passenger who will be removed is the one most recently inserted (pointed to by Rear).

Note that the passengers are listed in order of arrival into the queue rather than in alphabetical order. If an opening occurs on the flight, passenger 'Brown' will be removed from the queue and placed on the flight, and Front will be reset to point to passenger 'Watson'. If another passenger is added to the waiting list, the new passenger will be added after 'Carson', and Rear will be reset to point to the new passenger.

The specification for the abstract data type Queue follows; compare it with the earlier specification for an abstract stack.

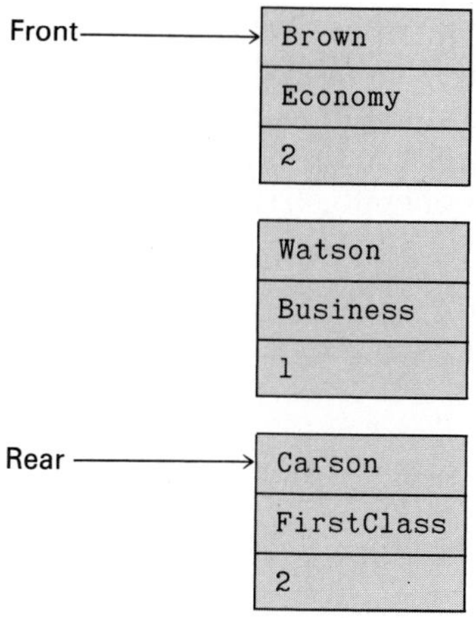

Figure 13.12 ▸
A Passenger Queue

Specification of Abstract Data Type Queue ▸

ELEMENTS: A queue consists of a collection of elements that are all the same data type.

STRUCTURE: The elements of a queue are ordered according to time of arrival. The element first inserted into the queue is the only one that can be removed or examined. Elements are removed from the *front* of the queue and inserted at the *rear* of the queue.

OPERATORS: In the following descriptions, assume these parameters:

`Q` represents the queue.
`El` has the same data type as the queue elements.
`Success` is type `BOOLEAN` and indicates whether the operation succeeds.

`CreateQueue (VAR Q)`: Creates an empty queue `Q`.

`Insert (VAR Q, El, VAR Success)`: If queue `Q` is not full, the value in `El` is inserted at the rear of the queue and `Success` is set to `TRUE`. Otherwise, the queue is not changed and `Success` is set to `FALSE`.

`Remove (VAR Q, VAR El, VAR Success)`: If queue `Q` is not empty, the element at the front of the queue is removed and copied to `El`, and Success is set to `TRUE`. If the queue is empty, `El` is not changed and `Success` is set to `FALSE`.

`Retrieve (Q, VAR El, VAR Success)`: If queue `Q` is not empty, the element at the top of the queue is copied into `El`, and `Success` is set to `TRUE`. If the queue is empty, `El` is not defined and `Success` is set to `FALSE`. In either case, the queue is not changed.

`IsEmpty(Q)`: Returns `TRUE` if queue `Q` is empty; otherwise, returns `FALSE`.
`IsFull(Q)`: Returns `TRUE` if queue `Q` is full; otherwise, returns `FALSE`.

The DEFINITION Module for QueueADT

To make our queue data type as flexible as possible, assume that its element type, `Element`, is imported from module `ElementType`. The definition module provided in Fig. 13.13 declares `Queue` as an opaque type. Because the operator procedures are similar to the ones provided earlier for `StackADT`, the comments describing each operator have been abbreviated.

Figure 13.13 ▸ *Definition Module for QueueADT*

```
DEFINITION MODULE QueueADT;

(* Specification of abstract data type queue. *)

  FROM ElementType IMPORT
    Element;                    (* type of each queue element *)

  EXPORT QUALIFIED
    Queue,                                          (* opaque type *)
    CreateQueue, Insert, Remove, Retrieve,          (* procedures *)
    IsFull, IsEmpty;                                (* functions *)

(* Data type Queue is an opaque type. *)

  TYPE
    Queue;

(* Operators *)

  PROCEDURE CreateQueue (VAR Q (* out *) : Queue);
  (* Creates an empty queue. *)

  PROCEDURE Insert (VAR Q (* in/out *) : Queue;
                    El (* in *) : Element;
                    VAR Success (* out *) : BOOLEAN);
  (*
     Inserts El in queue Q. Sets Success to indicate success or
     failure of insert operation.
  *)

  PROCEDURE Remove (VAR Q (* in/out *) : Queue;
                    VAR El (* out *) : Element;
                    VAR Success (* out *) : BOOLEAN);
  (*
     Removes the element at the front of queue Q and copies it into
     El. Sets Success to indicate success or failure.
  *)

  PROCEDURE Retrieve (Q (* in *) : Queue;
                      VAR El (* out *) : Element;
                      VAR Success (* out *) : BOOLEAN);
```

```
   (*
      Copies the value at the front of the queue into El without
      removing it. Sets Success to indicate success or failure.
   *)

   PROCEDURE IsEmpty (Q : Queue) : BOOLEAN;
   (* Returns TRUE if queue Q is empty; otherwise, returns FALSE. *)

   PROCEDURE IsFull (Q : Queue) : BOOLEAN;
   (* Returns TRUE if queue Q is full; otherwise, returns FALSE. *)

END QueueADT.
```

Another advantage to using an opaque type is that we can compile the above definition module and then write and compile client modules before we even decide on the data structure used to represent the queue. However, an implementation module for `QueueADT` must be written before we can link and run any of these client modules.

13.7 Implementing and Using the Queue Data Type

Each pointer variable of type `Queue` will contain the address of a data structure representing a queue. We will use a record structure that consists of three `CARDINAL` fields (`Front`, `Rear`, `NumItems`), and an array, `Items`, of queue elements. This record structure is declared as follows:

```
TYPE
  Queue = POINTER TO QueueObject;
  QueueObject = RECORD
                  Front, Rear : [1..MaxSize];
                  NumItems : [0..MaxSize];
                  Items : ARRAY [1..MaxSize] OF Element
                END; (* QueueObject *)
```

Fields `Front` and `Rear` are pointers to the queue elements at the front and the rear of the queue, respectively. Field `NumItems` is used to keep track of the actual number of items in the queue and facilitates determining whether the queue is empty (`NumItems` is `0`) or full (`NumItems` is `MaxSize`).

It is a good idea to represent the array `Items` as a *circular array*. In a circular array, the elements wrap around so that the first element actually follows the last.

EXAMPLE 13.3 ▶ Fig. 13.14 shows the effect of inserting a new element in a queue that is represented as a circular array of characters with `MaxSize` equal to seven. As shown on the left of the figure, there are four characters in this queue (stored in `Items[4]` through `Items[7]`). The symbol `?` in `Items[1]` through `Items[3]` indicates that the values stored in these elements have been removed from the queue. The cells that are currently unused are shown in grey.

Since `Rear` is equal to `MaxSize` (7), it might appear that the queue is full; there are, however, three available slots. The right side of Fig. 13.14 shows the queue after insertion of a new element (`'*'`). The value of `Rear` is "incremented" to `1`, and the next element is inserted into `Items[1]`. This queue element "follows" the element (`'&'`) in `Items[7]`. The next queue element would be inserted in `Items[2]`.

Figure 13.14 ▶ *A Queue as a Circular Array*

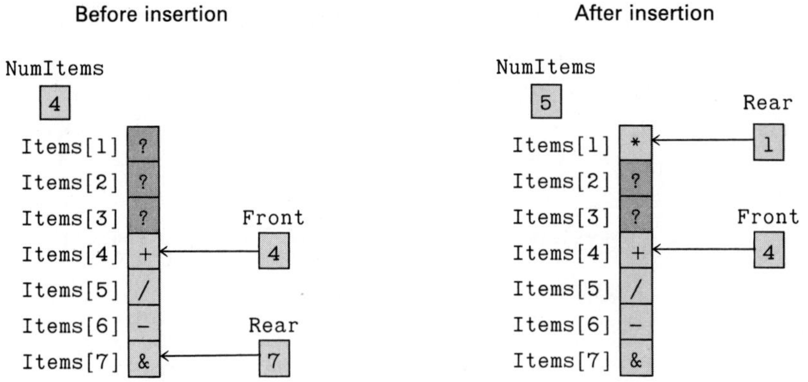

The implementation module for the abstract data type queue is shown in Fig. 13.15. ◂

Figure 13.15 ▶ *Implementation Module for Abstract Data Type Queue*

```
IMPLEMENTATION MODULE QueueADT;

(* Implementation of abstract data type queue. *)

   FROM ElementType IMPORT
     Element;

   FROM Storage IMPORT
     ALLOCATE;

(*
   Data type -
   A pointer variable of type Queue contains the address of a record
   of type QueueObject that represents a queue. Each record contains
   two pointer fields (Front, Rear), a CARDINAL field NumItems, and
```

```
   an array field, Items, to hold the queue elements. The element
   type, Element, is imported from module ElementType.
*)
   CONST
     MaxSize = 100;             (* maximum size of queue *)

   TYPE
     Queue = POINTER TO QueueObject;
     QueueObject = RECORD
                     Front, Rear : [1..MaxSize];
                     NumItems : [0..MaxSize];
                     Items : ARRAY [1..MaxSize] OF Element
                   END; (* QueueObject *)

(* Operators *)

   PROCEDURE CreateQueue (VAR Q (* out *) : Queue);
   (*
      Creates an empty queue.
   *)
   BEGIN (* CreateQueue *)
     NEW (Q);                    (* allocate a queue *)
     Q^.NumItems := 0;           (* queue is empty *)
     Q^.Front := 1;
     Q^.Rear := MaxSize          (* queue is circular *)
   END CreateQueue;

   PROCEDURE Insert (VAR Q (* in/out *) : Queue;
                     El (* in *) : Element;
                     VAR Success (* out *) : BOOLEAN);
   (*
      Inserts El in queue Q. Sets Success to indicate success or
      failure of insert operation.
   *)
   BEGIN (* Insert *)
     IF IsFull(Q) THEN
       Success := FALSE
     ELSE
       (* Insert El at the rear of the queue. *)
       Q^.Rear := (Q^.Rear MOD MaxSize) + 1;     (* increment Rear *)
       Q^.Items[Q^.Rear] := El;
       INC (Q^.NumItems);
       Success := TRUE
     END (* IF *)
   END Insert;

   PROCEDURE Remove (VAR Q (* in/out *) : Queue;
                     VAR El (* out *) : Element;
                     VAR Success (* out *) : BOOLEAN);
   (*
      Removes the element at the front of queue Q and copies it into
      El. Sets Success to indicate success or failure.
   *)
```

```
  BEGIN (* Remove *)
    IF IsEmpty(Q) THEN
      Success := FALSE
    ELSE
      (* Remove the element at the front of the queue. *)
      El := Q^.Items[Q^.Front];
      Q^.Front := (Q^.Front MOD MaxSize) + 1;  (* increment Front *)
      DEC (Q^.NumItems);
      Success := TRUE
    END (* IF *)
  END Remove;

  PROCEDURE Retrieve (Q (* in *) : Queue;
                      VAR El (* out *) : Element;
                      VAR Success (* out *) : BOOLEAN);
  (*
     Copies the value at the front of queue Q into El without
     removing it. Sets Success to indicate success or failure.
  *)
  BEGIN (* Retrieve *)
    IF IsEmpty(Q) THEN
      Success := FALSE
    ELSE
      (* Retrieve the item at the front of the queue. *)
      El := Q^.Items[Q^.Front];
      Success := TRUE
    END (* IF *)
  END Retrieve;

  PROCEDURE IsEmpty (Q : Queue) : BOOLEAN;
  (*
     Returns TRUE is queue Q is empty; otherwise, returns FALSE.
  *)
  BEGIN (* IsEmpty *)
    RETURN Q^.NumItems = 0
  END IsEmpty;

  PROCEDURE IsFull (Q : Queue) : BOOLEAN;
  (*
     Returns TRUE if queue Q is full; otherwise, returns FALSE.
  *)
  BEGIN (* IsFull *)
    RETURN Q^.NumItems = MaxSize
  END IsFull;

END QueueADT.
```

In procedure `CreateQueue` of Fig. 13.15, the statements

```
NEW (Q);                     (* allocate a queue *)
Q^.NumItems := 0;            (* queue is empty *)
```

are used to create an empty queue, and procedure CreateQueue must be called first. Array element Q^.Items[1] is considered the front of the empty queue (Q^.Front is 1). Q^.Rear is initialized to MaxSize because the queue is circular.

In procedure Insert, the statement

```
Q^.Rear := (Q^.Rear MOD MaxSize) + 1;        (* increment Rear *)
```

is used to increment the value of Q^.Rear. When Q^.Rear is less than MaxSize, this statement simply increments its value by one. But when Q^.Rear is equal to MaxSize, this statement sets Q^.Rear to 1 (MaxSize MOD MaxSize is 0), thereby wrapping the last element of the queue around to the first element. Since Q^.Rear is initialized to MaxSize, the first queue element will be placed in Items[1], as desired.

In procedure Remove, the element currently stored in Items[Front] is copied into El before Q^.Front is incremented. In procedure Retrieve, the element at Items[Front] is copied into El, but Q^.Front is not changed.

The number of elements in the queue is changed by procedures Insert and Remove, so Q^.NumItems must be incremented by one in Insert and decremented by one in Remove. The value of Q^.NumItems is tested in both IsFull and IsEmpty to determine the status of the queue.

The Module ElementType

So far we have not said anything about module ElementType other than that the structure of each queue element is declared in this module. Also, any procedures that depend on this structure (e.g., procedures for data entry and display) should be implemented in this module. Although these procedures are not needed by QueueADT, they will most likely be imported (along with data type Element) by any client module that uses QueueADT. Think of ElementType as an abstract data type for a queue element and its operators.

Fig. 13.16 contains the definition module for an abstract data type that consists of a record for storing the airline passenger data shown in Fig. 13.12. The data type Element is declared as a transparent type in the definition module. The operator ReadPass is declared in the implementation module (see Fig. 13.17). Procedure WritePass and function ClassConvert are left as exercises.

Figure 13.16 ▸ *Definition Module for ElementType*

```
DEFINITION MODULE ElementType;

(* Specification for an airline passenger abstract data type. *)

   EXPORT QUALIFIED
     Element,                    (* data type *)
     ReadPass, WritePass;        (* procedures *)
```

```
(* Data type *)

   CONST
     MaxLetters = 20;
     MaxSeats = 30;

   TYPE
     ClassType = (FirstClass, Business, Economy, Standby,
                  Undesignated);
     NameType = ARRAY [0..MaxLetters] OF CHAR;
     Element = RECORD
                 Name : NameType;
                 Class : ClassType;
                 NumSeats : [1..MaxSeats]
               END;  (* Element *)

(* Operators *)

   PROCEDURE ReadPass (VAR OnePass : Element);
   (* Reads one record of type Element. *)

   PROCEDURE WritePass (OnePass : Element);
   (* Displays one record of type Element. *)

END ElementType.
```

Figure 13.17 ▸ *Implementation Module for ElementType*

```
IMPLEMENTATION MODULE ElementType;

(* Implementation module for airline passenger abstract data type.

   FROM InOut IMPORT
     Read, ReadCard, ReadString,
     Write, WriteCard, WriteLn, WriteString;

(* Data type Element is declared in the definition module. *)

(* Operators *)

   PROCEDURE ReadPass (VAR OnePass : Element);
   (*
      Reads one record of type Element.
   *)
      VAR
        ClassCh : CHAR;          (* character for class type *)

      PROCEDURE ClassConvert (ClassCh : CHAR) : ClassType;
      (*
         Converts a character to a class type.
```

```
    *)
    BEGIN (* ClassConvertStub *)
      RETURN Economy
    END ClassConvert;

  BEGIN (* ReadPass *)
    WITH OnePass DO
      WriteString ('Passenger name: ');
      ReadString (Name);  WriteLn;
      WriteString ('Class (F, B, E, S): ');
      Read (ClassCh);  Write (ClassCh);  WriteLn;
      Class := ClassConvert(ClassCh);
      WriteString ('Number of Seats (1 to 30): ');
      ReadCard (NumSeats);  WriteLn;
      IF NumSeats > 30 THEN
        NumSeats := 30;
        WriteString ('Only 30 seats can be assigned now.')
      END (* IF *)
    END (* WITH *)
  END ReadPass;

  PROCEDURE WritePass (OnePass : Element);
  (*
     Displays one record of type Element.
  *)
  BEGIN (* WritePass stub *)
    WriteString ('Procedure WritePass Entered.');  WriteLn;
    WriteString ('Name: ');
    WriteString (OnePass.Name);  WriteLn
  END WritePass;

END ElementType.
```

Declaring Element as an Opaque Type

Although it was not necessary to do so, we could have declared `Element` as an opaque type in the definition module for `ElementType`. To do so would require moving the `CONST` and `TYPE` declarations from the definition module to the implementation module with the `TYPE` declarations modified as shown next:

```
TYPE
  Element = POINTER TO ElementObject;
  ElementObject = RECORD
                    Name : NameType;
                    Class : ClassType;
                    NumSeats : [1..MaxSeats]
                  END;  (* ElementObject *)
```

Since `Element` is now a pointer type, procedure `ReadPass` would begin with the statements

```
NEW (OnePass);          (* allocate a new record *)
WITH OnePass^ DO
```

Similarly, the second `WriteString` statement in the stub for `WritePass` must be changed to

```
WriteString (OnePass^.Name);
```

It would not be necessary to modify any of `ElementType`'s client modules. A benefit of making this change would be the extra protection afforded opaque types.

A Client Module for QueueADT

All that remains is to write a client module that uses the abstract data type `QueueADT`. A menu-driven program is shown in Fig. 13.18. This program begins by creating an empty queue and then processes a set of requests to insert or remove queue elements or to display the element at the head of the queue. Within the `REPEAT-UNTIL` loop, the statement

```
WriteString ('Enter I(nsert), R(emove), D(isplay), or Q(uit): ');
```

displays the menu on the current output line. After the selection is read into `Choice`, procedure `ModifyQueue` calls the appropriate procedures from `QueueADT` and `ElementType` to perform that operation.

Figure 13.18 ▸ *Program UseQueue*

```
MODULE UseQueue;
(*
   Manipulates a queue of airline passengers.
   Uses the abstract data types queue and element.
*)
   FROM InOut IMPORT
     WriteString, Read, Write, WriteLn;

   FROM ElementType IMPORT
     Element, ReadPass, WritePass;

   FROM QueueADT IMPORT
     Queue, CreateQueue, Insert, Remove, Retrieve;

   VAR
     Q : Queue;                   (* a passenger queue *)
     Choice : CHAR;               (* operation request *)
     Success : BOOLEAN;           (* program flag *)

   PROCEDURE ModifyQueue (VAR Q (* in/out *) : Queue;
                          Choice (* input *) : CHAR);
   (*
     Performs the operation indicated by Choice on the queue Q.
   *)
     VAR
       NextPass : Element;        (* a passenger *)
```

```
      Success : BOOLEAN;        (* program flag *)

    BEGIN (* ModifyQueue *)
      CASE CAP(Choice) OF
        'I' : (* insert *)
              WriteString ('Enter passenger data.');  WriteLn;
              ReadPass (NextPass);
              Insert (Q, NextPass, Success);
              IF NOT Success THEN
                WriteString ('Queue is full - no insertion');
                WriteLn
              END (* IF *)
      | 'R' : (* remove *)
              Remove (Q, NextPass, Success);
              IF Success THEN
                WriteString ('Passenger removed from queue follows.');
                WriteLn;
                WritePass (NextPass)
              ELSE
                WriteString ('Queue is empty - no deletion');
                WriteLn
              END (* IF *)
      | 'D' : (* display *)
              Retrieve (Q, NextPass, Success);
              IF Success THEN
                WriteString ('Passenger at head of queue follows.');
                WriteLn;
                WritePass (NextPass)
              ELSE
                WriteString ('Queue is empty - no passenger');
                WriteLn
              END (* IF *)
      | 'Q' : (* quit *)
              WriteString ('Leaving passenger queue.');  WriteLn
      ELSE
        WriteString ('Incorrect choice - try again.');  WriteLn
      END; (* CASE *)
      WriteLn
  END ModifyQueue;

BEGIN (* UseQue *)
  CreateQueue(Q);                   (* start with an empty queue *)

  (* Process all requests until done. *)
  REPEAT
    WriteString ('Enter I(nsert), R(emove), D(isplay), or Q(uit): ');
    Read (Choice);  Write (Choice);  WriteLn;

    (* Process current request. *)
    ModifyQueue (Q, Choice)
  UNTIL CAP(Choice) = 'Q'
END UseQueue.
```

In the sample run of program `UseQueue` shown in Fig. 13.19, passenger `Brown` is inserted first, followed by passenger `Watson`. After passenger `Brown` is removed from the queue, the new passenger at the front of the queue (`Watson`) is displayed.

Figure 13.19 ▸ *Sample Run of Program UseQueue*

```
Enter I(nsert), R(emove), D(isplay), or Q(uit): I
Enter passenger data.
Passenger Name: Brown
Class (F, B, E, S): E
Number of Seats: 2

Enter I(nsert), R(emove), D(isplay), or Q(uit): I
Enter passenger data.
Passenger Name: Watson
Class (F, B, E, S): B
Number of Seats: 1

Enter I(nsert), R(emove), D(isplay), or Q(uit): R
Passenger removed from queue follows.
Brown
Economy Class
 2 Seats

Enter I(nsert), R(emove), D(isplay), or Q(uit): D
Passenger at head of queue follows.
Watson
Business Class
 1 Seat

Enter I(nsert), R(emove), D(isplay), or Q(uit): Q
Leaving passenger queue.
```

Compilation Order for an Abstract Data Type and Its Client

The following compilation sequence could be used to develop a client module that imports the abstract data type `QueueADT`.

1. Compile the definition module for `ElementType`.
2. Compile the implementation module for `ElementType`.
3. Compile the definition module for `QueueADT`.
4. Compile the implementation module for `QueueADT`.
5. Compile the client module.

The only requirements are that step 1 be performed before step 3 and step 3 before step 5. Each implementation module can be compiled at any time after its corresponding definition module is compiled.

If a definition module is changed, it must be recompiled and all the compilations that depend on it must be redone. However, if an implementation module is changed, only that implementation module has to be recompiled.

SELF-CHECK EXERCISES FOR SECTION 13.7

1. Provide procedure `WritePass` and function `ClassConvert` for Fig. 13.15.
2. The program in Fig. 13.18 displays the element at the front of the queue. It is useful to be able to display the entire queue contents (from `Front` to `Rear`, inclusive). Write a procedure that accomplishes this. In which module `QueueADT` or `ElementType` should this procedure be placed?
3. Redo the definition and implementation modules for `ElementType` with `Element` declared as an opaque type.

13.8 Common Programming Errors

Be consistent in your use of definition and implementation modules for an abstract data type. Make sure that a data type is declared as either a transparent type or an opaque type in the definition module. Only data types that are opaque should be declared in the implementation module.

Don't forget to use the dereferencing operator (^ or ↑) when accessing a record field referenced by a pointer. If `Object` is a pointer variable, use the name `Object^` to denote the record pointed to by `Object`. This is the case for any procedure that operates on a data structure whose type is opaque. The parameter representing the data structure must be a pointer type, and all references to fields of that data structure are through the pointer.

Make sure you always use the `NEW` statement to allocate storage for a new record referenced by a pointer. If you forget to use the `NEW` statement, the system will use whatever value happens to be stored in the pointer. If your program is reading in a collection of records referenced by the same pointer, each record entered will overwrite the last one entered unless you use the `NEW` statement to allocate a separate block of storage for each new record.

It is difficult to debug a program involving pointers, because the value of a pointer is a memory cell address and normally cannot be displayed. Hence, if a pointer value is invalid or incorrect, there may be no way of finding out exactly what that erroneous value happens to be.

13.9 Chapter Review

This chapter discussed the concept of information hiding, and you learned how to declare and use opaque types. If an abstract data type uses a data type declared as an opaque type, the declaration of the data type is placed in the implementation module for the abstract data type, not the definition module.

Therefore, only the operators declared in the implementation module for the abstract data type can manipulate individual fields of any object of that type. The actual structure of the data object is not known to any client modules because it is not described in the module interface (the definition module). Thus, declaring a data structure as an opaque type prohibits access to its individual fields by a client module.

Two data structures, stacks and queues, were introduced. Stacks are used to implement recursion and expression translation. A stack is a last-in-first-out data structure. This means that the last item inserted will be the first one removed. In contrast, a queue is a first-in-first-out data structure. Queues are used to implement waiting lists. We provided definition and implementation modules for both abstract data types and sample client modules.

New Modula-2 Statements

The new Modula-2 statements introduced in this chapter are described in Table 13.1.

Table 13.1 ▸ *Summary of New Modula-2 Statements*

STATEMENT	EFFECT

Pointer Type Declaration
`TYPE`
`  Point = POINTER TO Object;`
`  Object = RECORD`
`             ID : CARDINAL;`
`             Quantity : INTEGER`
`           END; (* Object *)`
`VAR`
`  Head : Point;`
	The identifier `Point` is declared as a pointer to a record of type `Object`, where `Object` is a record type containing fields `ID` and `Quantity`. `Head` is a pointer variable of type `Point`.

NEW Statement `NEW (Head)`	A new record is allocated of type `Object`. This record is pointed to by `Head`.

Using a Pointer Variable
`Head^.ID := 1111;`
`Head^.Quantity := -5;`
`WITH Head^ DO`
`  WriteCard (ID, 4);`
`  WriteInt (Quantity, 0);`
`  WriteLn`
`END (* WITH *)`
	The fields `ID` and `Quantity` of the record pointed to by `Head` are assigned values. These values are then displayed.

CHAPTER 13 ▸

Review Questions

1. What kind of value is contained in a pointer variable?
2. Give the necessary statements to create a pointer variable `Q` that points to a record type `Numbers` consisting of three integer fields called `A`, `B`, and `C`. Also indicate at what point actual space is allocated for `Q` and one occurrence of `Numbers`.
3. Use the declarations below to answer questions 3 through 6.

```
TYPE
  Point = POINTER TO Person;
  Person = RECORD
             Name : ARRAY [0..19] OF CHAR;
             Age : INTEGER
           END; (* Person *)
VAR
  Me, You : Person;
```

   Write statements that allocate storage for a record pointed to by `Me` and store `'George Washington', 300` in that record.

4. Correct the following statements. What does your corrected version do?

```
WITH You^ DO
  NEW (You);
  You.Name := Me.Name;
  You.Age := Me.Age - 100
END (* WITH *)
```

5. What is the effect of executing the following fragment?

```
NEW (Me);
Me^.Name := 'Jones';
Me^.Age := 97;
NEW (You);
You^ := Me^;
```

6. Why is the `NEW` statement needed in the program fragment in question 5? What would happen if it was omitted?
7. The declaration

```
TYPE
  Point;
```

   appears in the definition module for `ADT`, and the declaration for `Point` shown in question 3 appears in the implementation module for `ADT`. What can you say about data type `Point`? If module `MeToo` imports data type `Point`, and variables `OnePer-son` and `Individual` are declared as type `Point` in `MeToo`, which of the following statements are valid in `MeToo`?

```
NEW (Individual);
Individual := OnePerson;
```

```
Individual^ := OnePerson^;
Individual^.Name := OnePerson^.Name;
Individual.Age := Oneperson.Age;
```

8. To execute `MeToo` as a main program module, specify the sequence of module compilations that must be performed.

CHAPTER 13 ▸

Programming Projects

1. Extend the abstract data type `QueueADT` to include operators that display a queue and determine the size of a queue. Change `Element` to represent a customer at a bank. Store the customer's name, transaction type, and amount in the customer record. Write a client module that simulates a typical session for a bank teller. After every five customers are processed, display the size of the queue and the names of the customers who are waiting.

2. Modify the abstract data type for a stack to enable a record of a prespecified type to be placed on the stack. The record type will be imported into the stack module. Carry out project 1 using a stack instead of a queue.

3. Use the stack abstract data type to determine if an expression is balanced with respect to parentheses. Assume that the symbols `(`, {, and `[` denote opening parentheses and that `)`, }, and `]` are the respective closing parentheses. Place each opening parenthesis on the stack. When a closing parenthesis is encountered, pop the top of the stack. If it is the matching opening parenthesis, continue processing; otherwise, indicate that parentheses are not balanced. If parentheses are balanced, the stack should be empty when the end of the string is reached. A balanced input string is `'(X[y,z{a,b}+c]{d,e})'`. Ignore all characters except the parentheses.

4. Write a program to moniter the flow of an item into and out of a warehouse. The warehouse will have numerous deliveries and shipments for this item (a widget) during the time period covered. A shipment out is billed at a profit of 50 percent over cost. Unfortunately, each shipment received may have a different cost. The accountants for the firm have instituted a last-in, first-out system for filling orders. This means that the newest widgets are the first ones sent out to fill an order. This method of inventory can be represented using a stack. The `Push` procedure will insert a shipment received. The `Pop` procedure will delete a shipment out. Each data record will consist of:

   `S or O` — for shipment received or an order to be sent
   `#` — a quantity received or shipped out
   `Cost` — the cost per widget (for a shipment received only)
   `Vendor` — character string naming company sent to or received from

   Write the necessary procedures to store the shipments received and to process orders. The output for an order will consist of the total cost for all the widgets in the order as well as the quantity. Hint: Each widget price is 50 percent higher than its cost. The widgets used to fill an order may come from multiple shipments with different costs.

5. Redo project 4 assuming the widgets are shipped using a first-in, first-out strategy. Use a queue to store the widget orders.

6. Write a client module for the stack abstract data type that can be used to compile a simple arithmetic expression without parentheses. For example, the expression

```
A + B * C - D
```

should be compiled as the table

operation	*operandl*	*operand2*	*result*
*	B	C	Z
+	A	Z	Y
–	Y	D	X

The above table shows the order in which the operations are performed (*, +, –) and the operands for each operator. The result column gives the name of an identifier (working backward from Z) chosen to hold each result. Assume the operands are the letters A through F and the operators are (+, –, *, /).

Your program should read each character and process it as follows: if it is a blank, ignore it; if it is an operand, push it onto the operand stack; if it is not an operator, display an error message and terminate the program; if it is an operator, compare its precedence with that of the operator on top of the stack (* and / have higher precedence than + and –). If the new operator has higher precedence than the one currently on top (or if the stack is empty), it should be pushed onto the stack.

If the new operator has the same or lower precedence, the operator on the top of the stack must be evaluated next. This is done by popping it off the operator stack along with a pair of operands from the operand stack and writing a new line of the output table. The character selected to hold the result should then be pushed onto the operand stack. Next, the new operator should be compared to the new top of the operator stack. Continue to generate output table lines until the top of the operator stack has lower precedence than the new operator or until the stack is empty. At this point, push the new operator onto the top of the stack and examine the next character in the data string. When the end of the string is reached, pop any remaining operators along with its operand pair, as just described. Remember to push the result character onto the operand stack after each table line is generated.

14 ▸ Dynamic Data Structures

THIS CHAPTER WILL DISCUSS how Modula-2 can be used to create *dynamic data structures*. Dynamic data structures are data structures that expand and contract as a program executes. A dynamic data structure is a collection of elements (called *nodes*) that are records. Unlike an array that always contains storage for a fixed number of elements, the number of records stored in a dynamic data structure changes as the program executes.

Dynamic data structures are extremely flexible. It is relatively easy to add new information by creating a new node and inserting it between two existing nodes. It is also relatively easy to delete a node.

Several examples of dynamic data structures are examined in this chapter, including lists, stacks, queues, circular lists, multiple-linked lists, trees, and binary search trees. You will learn how to use these data structures for storing information and how to process information saved in these structures.

14.1 Review of Pointers and the NEW Procedure

Section 13.2 introduced the concept of a pointer variable. The declarations

```
TYPE
  Complex = POINTER TO ComplexObject;
  ComplexObject = RECORD
                    RealPart, ImaginaryPart : REAL
                  END; (* ComplexObject *)

VAR
  P : Complex;
```

were used to declare P as a pointer variable. Since the value of a pointer variable is a memory address, we used the following diagram

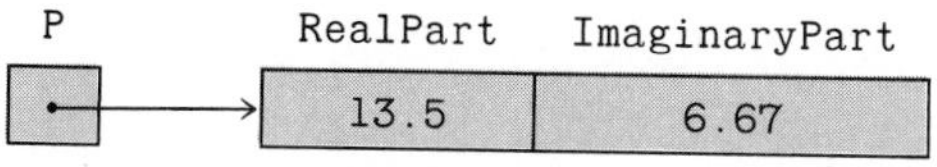

to show that pointer variable P references a record of type ComplexObject. In the diagram, the value of P^.RealPart is 13.5; the value of P^.ImaginaryPart is 6.67.

The statement

```
NEW (P)
```

allocates memory for a new record of type ComplexObject; the address of this new record is stored in pointer variable P. Next, you will see how the NEW procedure can be used to allocate nodes of a dynamic data structure.

Manipulating Pointers

Since we don't know beforehand how many nodes will be in a dynamic data structure, we cannot allocate storage for a dynamic data structure in the conventional way, that is, through a variable declaration. Instead, we must allocate storage for each individual node as needed and, somehow, join this node to the rest of the structure.

We can connect two nodes if we include a pointer field in each node. The declarations

```
TYPE
  NodePointer = POINTER TO Node;
  Node = RECORD
           Current : ARRAY [0..1] OF CHAR;
           Volts : CARDINAL;
           Link : NodePointer
         END; (* Node *)

VAR
  P, Q, R : NodePointer;
```

identify `NodePointer` as a pointer type. A pointer variable of type `Node–Pointer` points to a record of type `Node` with three fields: `Current`, `Volts`, and `Link`. The `Link` field is also type `NodePointer`. We can use this field to point to the "next" node in a dynamic data structure. The next section will illustrate how to connect two nodes.

Variables `P`, `Q`, and `R` are pointer variables and can be used to reference records of type `Node` (denoted by `P^`, `Q^`, and `R^`). An address can be stored in a pointer variable in one of two ways. The statements

```
NEW (P);  NEW (Q);
```

allocate storage for two records of type `Node`. The memory address of the first of these records is stored in `P`, and the memory address of the second of these records is stored in `Q`. All three fields of these two nodes are initially undefined.

The assignment statements

```
P^.Current := 'AC';    P^.Volts := 115;
Q^.Current := 'DC';    Q^.Volts := 12;
```

define two fields of these nodes, as shown in Fig. 14.1. The `Link` fields are still undefined. Note that it makes no difference where the arrow representing the value of a pointer variable touches its node.

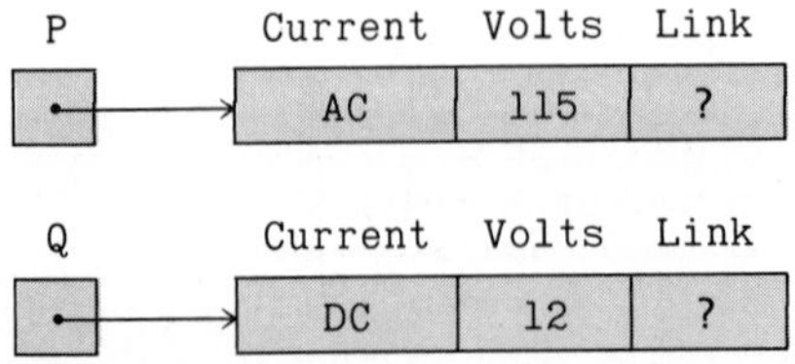

Figure 14.1 ▸ *Nodes P^ and Q^*

Besides using a NEW statement, we can also use an assignment statement to store an address in a pointer variable. The assignment statement

```
R := P;
```

copies the value of pointer variable P into pointer variable R. This means that pointers P and R contain the same memory address and, therefore, point to the same node, as shown in Fig. 14.2.

Figure 14.2 ▸ *Nodes R^/P^ and Q^*

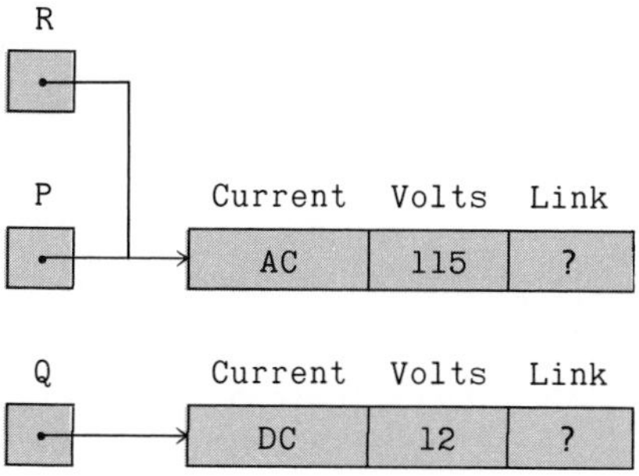

The pointer assignment statements

```
P := Q;  Q := R;
```

would have the effect of exchanging the nodes pointed to by P and Q as shown in Fig. 14.3.

Figure 14.3 ▸ *Nodes R^/Q^ and P^*

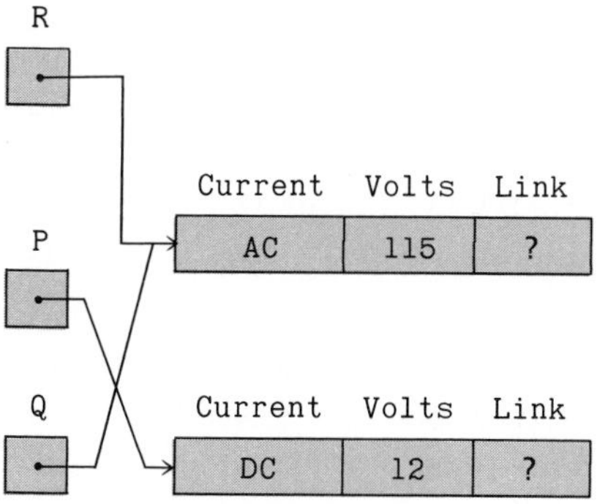

The statements

```
WriteString (Q^.Current);  WriteString (P^.Current);
```

display the Current fields of the records pointed to by Q and P. For the situation depicted in Fig. 14.3, the line

```
ACDC
```

would be displayed.
The statement

```
NEW (Q)
```

changes the value of Q to the address of a new node, thereby disconnecting Q from its previous node. The new values of pointer variables P, Q, and R are shown in Fig. 14.4. The data fields of the new node pointed to by Q are initially undefined.

Figure 14.4 ▸
*Nodes R^, P^, and Q^*

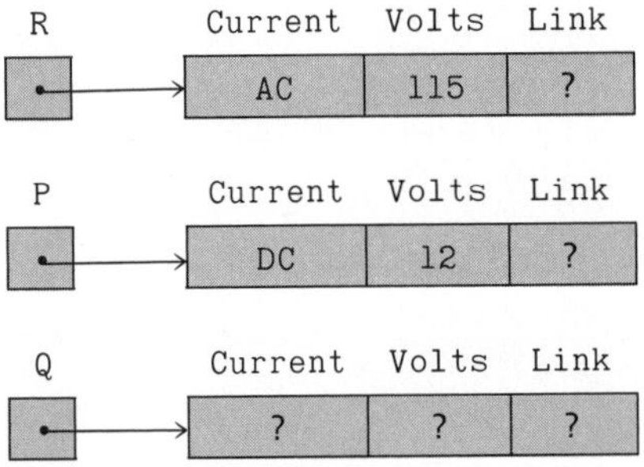

Pointers P, Q, and R are analogous to subscripts in that they select a particular node or element of a data structure. Unlike subscripts, however, their range of values is not declared and their values (memory cell addresses) cannot be printed.

It is important that you understand the difference between using P and P^ in a program. P is a pointer variable (type NodePointer) and is used to store the address of a data structure of type Node. P can be assigned a new value through a pointer assignment or execution of a NEW statement. P^ is the name of the record pointed to by P and can be manipulated like any other record in Modula-2. The field selectors P^.Current and P^.Volts can be used to reference data (a string and an integer) stored in this record.

Connecting Nodes

One purpose of dynamically allocated nodes is to be able to grow data structures of varying size. We can accomplish this by connecting individual nodes. If you look at the nodes allocated in the last subsection, you will see that their Link fields are undefined. Since the Link fields are type NodePointer, they can be used to store a memory cell address. The assignment statement

```
R^.Link := P;
```

copies the address stored in P into the Link field of Node R^. In this way, nodes R and P become connected. Similarly, the assignment statement

```
P^.Link := Q
```

copies the address stored in pointer variable Q into the Link field of node P^, thereby connecting nodes P and Q. The situation after execution of these two assignment statements is shown in Fig. 14.5. The arrows that represent the new values of R^.Link and P^.Link are shown in color.

Figure 14.5 ▸ *Connecting Nodes R^, P^, and Q^*

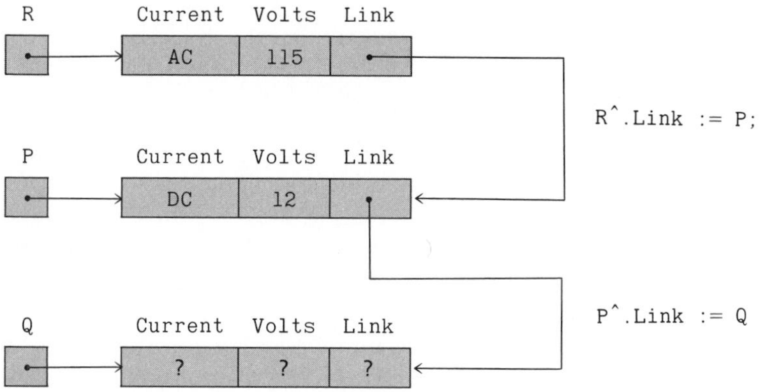

The data structure pointed to by R has now grown to include all three nodes. The first node is referenced by R^. The second node can be referenced by P^ or R^.Link^. Finally, the third node can be referenced by Q^ or P^.Link^ or even R^.Link^.Link^.

SELF-CHECK EXERCISES FOR SECTION 14.1

1. For Fig. 14.5, explain the effect of each legal assignment statement below.

a. R^.Current := 'CA'	e. R^.Link^.Volts := 0
b. P^ := R^	f. P := R
c. P.Current := 'HT'	g. R^.Link^.Link^.Current := 'XY'
d. P := 54	h. Q^.Volts := R^.Volts

2. The assignment statements

```
R := P;   P := Q;   Q := R
```

exchange the values of pointer variables R and Q (type NodePointer). What do the following assignment statements do?

```
R^.Current := P^.Current;
P^.Current := Q^.Current;
Q^.Current := R^.Current
```

14.2 Manipulating the Heap

In the last section, you saw that a new record is created whenever the NEW procedure is executed. You may be wondering where in memory the new record is stored. Modula-2 maintains a storage pool of available memory cells called a *heap;* memory cells from the heap are allocated whenever procedure NEW is executed.

Effect of NEW Statement on the Heap

The statement

```
NEW (P)
```

causes the allocation of memory space for the storage of two characters, an integer variable, and an address. These cells are originally undefined (they retain whatever data were last stored in them) and the memory address of the first cell allocated is stored in P. The cells allocated are no longer considered part of the heap. The only way to reference these cells is through pointer variable P (e.g., P^.Current, P^.Volts, or P^.Link).

Fig. 14.6 shows the pointer variable P and the heap before and after the execution of NEW(P). The before diagram shows pointer variable P as undefined before the execution of NEW(P). The after diagram shows P pointing to the first of three memory cells allocated for the new record (assuming that three memory cells can accommodate a record of type Node). In Fig. 14.6, the cells still considered part of the heap have the darker color.

Figure 14.6 ▸ *Heap before and after NEW (P)*

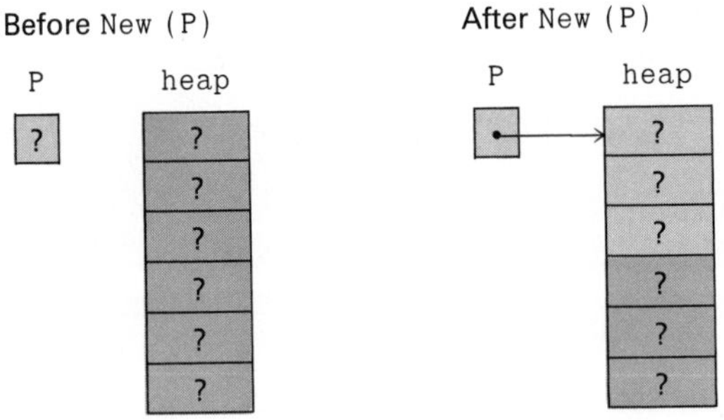

As an example, if the memory cells with addresses 1000 through 1005 were originally in the heap, then after the execution of NEW (P) only the memory cells with addresses 1003 through 1005 would be considered part of the heap. The address 1000 would be stored in pointer variable P, and that cell would be named P^.Current; memory cells 1001 and 1002 would be named P^.Volts and P^.Link, respectively.

Returning Cells to the Storage Pool

The procedure call statement

```
DISPOSE (P)
```

returns the memory cells pointed to by P to the storage pool. The value of pointer variable P becomes undefined, and the data formerly associated with P^ are no longer accessible. The three cells returned to the storage pool can be reused later when another NEW statement is executed.

To use the standard procedures NEW and DISPOSE, a Modula-2 program must include the statement

```
FROM Storage IMPORT ALLOCATE, DEALLOCATE;
```

Modula-2 uses these lower-level procedures to perform the allocation and deallocation of dynamic storage when procedures NEW and DISPOSE are called in a program. We will have no need to call them directly, but we must import them for use by NEW and DISPOSE.

Often more than one pointer will point to the same record. For this reason, you must be careful when returning the storage occupied by a record to the heap. Errors will result if the cells returned are later referenced by another pointer that still points to them. Make sure you have no need for a particular record before returning the storage occupied by it.

The DISPOSE Procedure ▶

FORM: DISPOSE (*pvar*)

EXAMPLE: DISPOSE (P)

INTERPRETATION: The memory cells that make up the record whose address is stored in pointer *pvar* are returned to the heap. These cells may be reallocated when procedure NEW is called.

Note: to call DISPOSE, the calling program must import procedure DEALLOCATE from Storage.

Testing for Available Cells

Because it is possible to exhaust the supply of cells on the heap, it is sometimes advisable to test that there are enough cells available before you attempt to allocate a new node.

EXAMPLE 14.1. ▶ The following IF statement either allocates a new node P^ or displays an error message if there are not enough cells on the heap.

```
IF Available(TSIZE(Node)) THEN
  NEW (P)
ELSE
  WriteString ('No cells available on storage heap');
  WriteLn
END (* IF *)
```

The condition in the `IF` statement header is `TRUE` if there are enough memory cells available on the heap to allocate a new node of type `Node`. Function `TSIZE` (imported from `SYSTEM`) returns the number of bytes required by a record of type `Node`. Function `Available` (imported from `Storage`) returns `TRUE` if the heap contains at least the number of bytes specified by its argument. ◂

You can normally assume that there are enough memory cells available on the heap without explicitly testing that this is so. However, when you write large programs that create sizable data structures, it is a good idea to call function `Available` before calling procedure `NEW`, as was demonstrated in Example 14.1.

Function TSIZE ▶

FORM: `TSIZE(`*rectype*`)`

INTERPRETATION: Returns a cardinal value representing the number of bytes in a variable of type *rectype*. `TSIZE` must be imported from module `SYSTEM`.

Function Available ▶

FORM: `Available(`*NumBytes*`)`

INTERPRETATION: Returns `TRUE` if there are at least *NumBytes* bytes (a `CARDINAL`) available on the storage heap; otherwise, returns `FALSE`. `Available` must be imported from module `Storage`.

14.3 Linked Lists

This section will introduce an important data structure called a *linked list* or simply *list*. We will see how to build and manipulate lists in Modula-2.

Abstract Lists

An abstract list is a sequence of nodes in which each node is linked or connected to the node following it. An abstract list with three nodes follows.

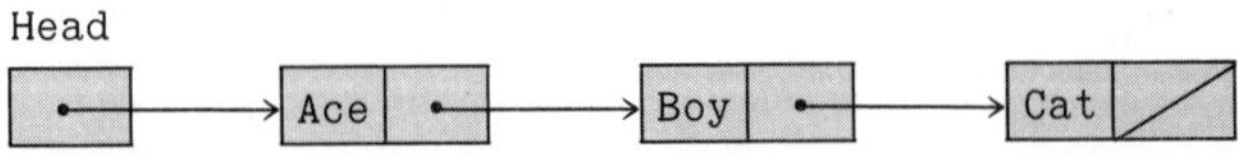

Each node in the list has two fields: the first field contains data, the second field is a pointer (represented by an arrow) to the next list element. There is a pointer (Head) to the first list element, or *list head*. The last list element always has a diagonal line in its pointer field.

Lists are an important data structure because they can be modified easily. For example, a new node containing the string 'Bye' can be inserted between the strings 'Boy' and 'Cat' by changing only one pointer value (the one from 'Boy') and setting the pointer from the new node to point to 'Cat'. This is true regardless of how many elements may be in the list. The list shown next is after the insertion; the new pointer values are shown in color.

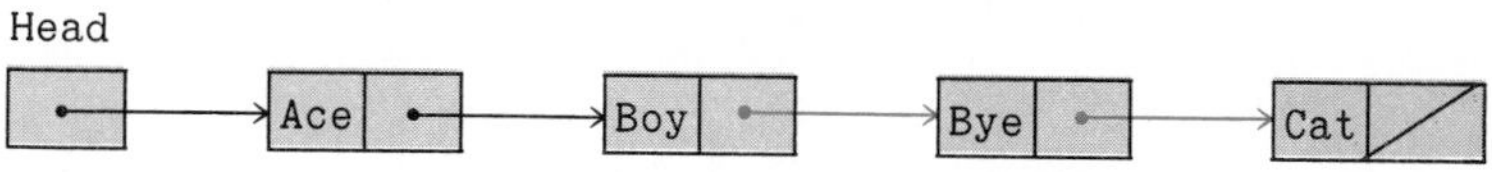

Similarly, it is quite easy to delete a list element. Only one pointer value has to be changed—the pointer that currently points to the element being deleted. The linked list is redrawn as follows after deleting the string 'Boy' by changing the pointer from the node 'Ace'. The node containing the string 'Boy' is effectively disconnected from the list since there is no longer a pointer to it. The new list consists of the strings 'Ace', 'Bye', 'Cat'.

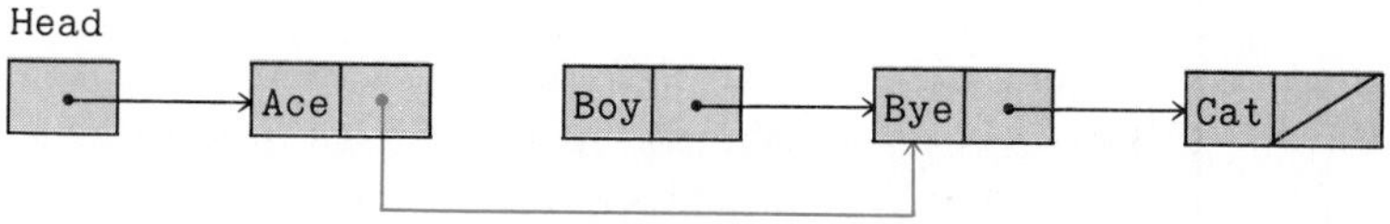

Implementing Lists Using Pointers

The preceding abstract list is relatively easy to create in Modula-2 using pointers and dynamic allocation. In Section 14.1, you saw how to connect three nodes with pointer fields. Although you didn't know it at the time, the data structure shown in Fig. 14.5 could be considered a list of three nodes with pointer variable R as the pointer to its head.

The pointer value NIL is reserved in Modula-2 to indicate the end of a list. After the assignment statement

```
Q^.Link := NIL
```

is executed, the data structure in Fig. 14.5 implements the following linked list. Each node has two data fields (Current and Volts) and one pointer field (Link). The pointer value NIL is drawn as a diagonal line.

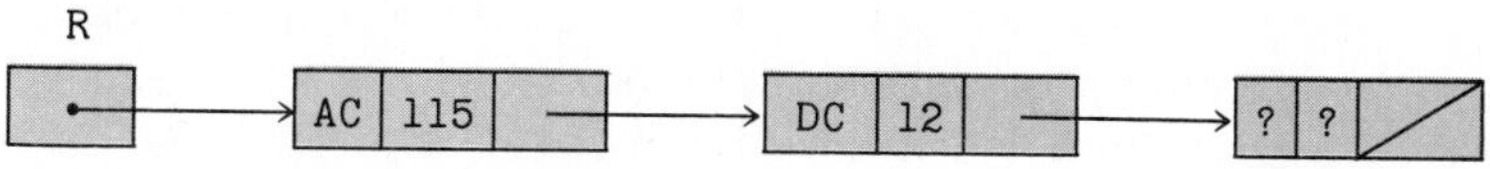

Array Implementation of Linked Lists

You can also implement lists by using arrays of records in which a `CARDINAL` field stores the pointer to the next list element. Fig. 14.7 shows the previous abstract list implemented as an array of records. The last field of each record contains the subscript of the next element. The variable `R` contains the subscript of the first list element. The three list nodes are stored in array elements `2`, `4`, and `1`, in that order. Element `1` has a link field of `0`, which indicates the end of the list.

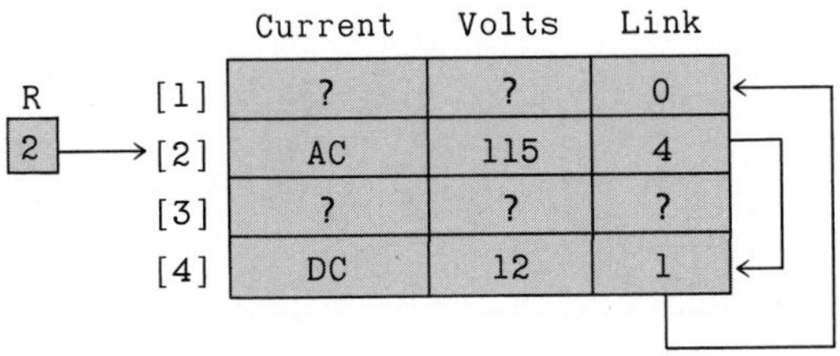

Figure 14.7 ▸ *Array Implementation of a Linked List*

Program Style

Storage Considerations for Array Implementations of Lists

Lists stored in arrays are just as easy to modify as lists that are implemented with pointer variables. To insert or delete a list element, it is only necessary to change one or more subscript values. The disadvantage, however, is that memory space for the entire array must be allocated at one time. If a list is built using pointer variables and dynamic allocation, the size of the list in memory will grow and shrink as needed and the storage allocated to it will change accordingly. For this reason, we recommend implementing lists using pointers.

Creating a List

This section and the ones that follow will consider some common list-processing operations and show how they are implemented using pointer variables. We will assume that the structure of each list node corresponds to type `ListNode` declared as follows:

```
TYPE
  String3 = ARRAY [0..2] OF CHAR;
  ListPointer = POINTER TO ListNode;
  ListNode = RECORD
               Word : String3;
               Link : ListPointer
             END; (* ListNode *)
```

Procedure `CreateList` in Fig. 14.9 creates a linked list by reading in a sequence of data strings ending with a sentinel (`'***'`) and storing each string in a list. If the data lines

```
Hat
Boy
Cat
***
```

are entered, the following list will be created. Note that the sentinel string is not stored.

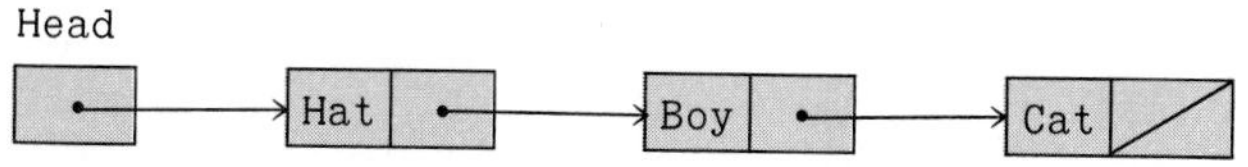

Procedure `CreateList` first displays the user's instructions and then reads the first data word into `FirstWord`. If `FirstWord` is the sentinel, `Head` is set to `NIL` to indicate an *empty list*. If the first word is not the sentinel, the statements

```
NEW (Head);                        (* create the list head *)
Head^.Word := FirstWord;          (* store it in list head *)
FillRest (Head)                      (* fill rest of list *)
```

allocate a new node `Head^` into which `FirstWord` is copied. Next, procedure `FillRest` is called to append the rest of the list to node `Head^`.

The `WHILE` loop in `FillRest` is repeated until the sentinel is read. Each time the loop is repeated, the statements

```
(*1*) NEW (Last^.Link);           (* attach a new node to Last^ *)
(*2*) Last := Last^.Link;         (* reset Last to new list end *)
      Last^.Word := NextWord;        (* store last word read *)
```

append a new node to the current end of the list, reset `Last` to point to the new end of the list, and then store the data word in node `Last^`. The list after the first execution of these statements is shown in Fig. 14.8. Each new pointer value is shown in color, along with the label of the statement that defines it; the initial value of `Last` is shown in grey.

Figure 14.8 ▸ *Partial List*

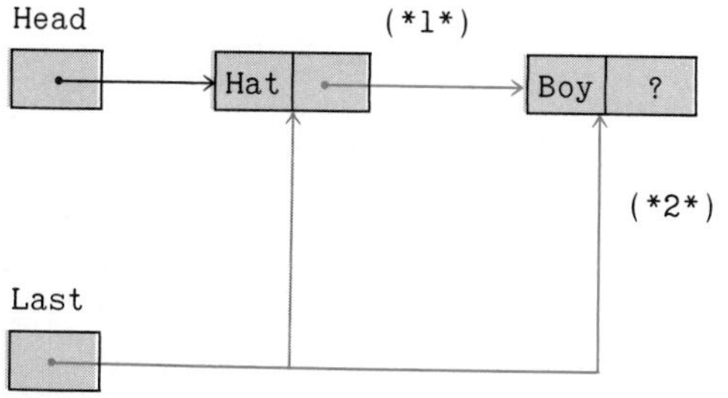

After loop exit, the statement

```
Last^.Link := NIL                           (* mark end of list *)
```

is used to mark the end of the list.

Figure 14.9 ▶ *Procedure CreateList*

```
PROCEDURE CreateList (VAR Head (* output *) : ListPointer);
(*
   Creates a linked list of strings pointed to by Head.
   Each new string is appended to the end of the list so
   the strings will be stored in the order in which they were read.
   Pre : None
   Post: Head points to the first string entered. Head is
   set to NIL if the sentinel string is the first string.
   Uses: CompareStr from Strings, NEW (ALLOCATE) from Storage,
         ReadString, WriteString, and WriteLn from InOut.
*)
   CONST
     Sentinel = '***';

   VAR
     FirstWord : String3;             (* first data word *)

   PROCEDURE FillRest (Last (* input *) : ListPointer);
   (*
      Appends new nodes to the end of a list.
      Pre : Last points to the last node in a list of length n.
      Post: Last points to the last node in a list of length >= n.
            Each data string is stored in a new node in the order
            in which it was read. The last node contains the data
            string just before the sentinel.
   *)
      VAR
        NextWord : String3;          (* next data word *)

   BEGIN (* FillRest *)
     ReadString (NextWord);  WriteLn;
     WHILE
       (* invariant:
            Last points to the last node in a list and
            the last string read is stored in node Last^ and
            no prior data string was the Sentinel
       *)
         CompareStr(NextWord, Sentinel) # 0 DO
       NEW (Last^.Link);           (* attach a new node to Last^ *)
       Last := Last^.Link;         (* reset Last to new list end *)
       Last^.Word := NextWord;         (* store last word read *)
       ReadString (NextWord);  WriteLn      (* read next word *)
     END; (* WHILE *)
     (* assert: The last string read was the Sentinel *)
```

```
      Last^.Link := NIL                          (* mark end of list *)
    END FillRest;

BEGIN (* CreateList *)
  (* Display instructions to user. *)
  WriteString ('Enter each data string on a line.');  WriteLn;
  WriteString ('Enter "');          WriteString (Sentinel);
  WriteString ('" when done.');    WriteLn;

  (* Create and fill the list head. *)
  ReadString (FirstWord);  WriteLn;             (* read first word *)
  IF CompareStr(FirstWord, Sentinel) = 0 THEN
    Head := NIL                                       (* empty list *)
  ELSE
    NEW (Head);                                (* create the list head *)
    Head^.Word := FirstWord;                   (* store it in list head *)
    FillRest (Head)                             (* fill rest of list *)
  END (* IF *)
END CreateList;
```

Traversing a List

In many list-processing operations, we must process each node in the list in sequence; this is called *traversing* a list. To traverse a list, we must start at the list head and follow the list pointers.

Procedure `PrintList` in Fig. 14.10 displays the `Word` fields of each node in a list starting with the node pointed to by `Head`. Consequently, `PrintList` can be used to print the words stored in a list created by procedure `CreateList`. For the list

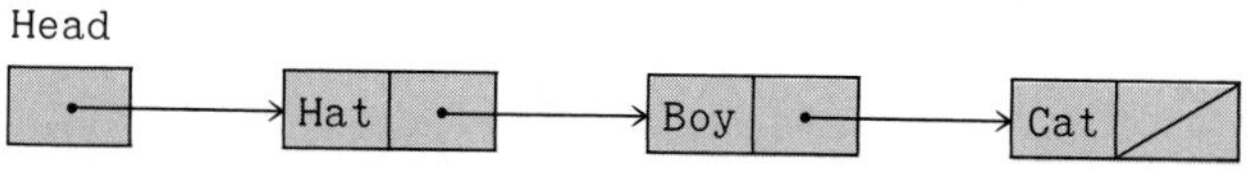

the output of `PrintList` would be

```
Hat
Boy
Cat
```

Figure 14.10 ▸
Procedure PrintList

```
PROCEDURE PrintList (Head (* input *) : ListPointer);
(*
   Displays the list pointed to by Head.
*)
BEGIN (* PrintList *)
  (* Traverse the list until the end is reached. *)
  WHILE
    (* invariant:
```

```
         No prior value of Head was NIL.
    *)
       Head # NIL DO
    WriteString(Head^.Word);  WriteLn;
    Head := Head^.Link                    (* advance to next node *)
  END (* WHILE *)
END PrintList;
```

The statement

```
Head := Head^.Link          (* advance to next node *)
```

advances the pointer `Head` to the next list element, which is pointed to by the `Link` field of the current list element. The `WHILE` loop is exited when `Head` becomes `NIL`. Since `Head` is a value parameter, a local copy of the pointer to the first list element is established when the procedure is entered. This local pointer is advanced; however, the corresponding pointer in the calling program remains unchanged.

Searching a List for a Target

List-processing operations can be formulated naturally using recursion. As an example, consider the problem of searching a list to find a string `Target`. The result will be a pointer to the list element containing `Target`; if `Target` is not found, the result will be `NIL`. One stopping state would be an empty list; in this case, the `Target` cannot be present. The other stopping state would be finding `Target` at the head of the list. The recursion step is to search the rest of the list (excluding the current list head) for `Target`. This algorithm is summarized as follows: function Search is shown in Fig. 14.11.

Algorithm for List Search

1. `IF` the list is empty `THEN`
    2. `Target` is not present—the result is `NIL`.

   `ELSIF` `Target` is in the list head `THEN`
    3. `Target` is found—the result is a pointer to the list head.

   `ELSE`
    4. Search for `Target` in the rest of the list.

   `END`

Figure 14.11 ▸ *Function Search*

```
PROCEDURE Search (Head : ListPointer;
                  Target : String3)   : ListPointer;
(*
   Searches a list for a specified Target string.
   Pre : Head points to a list and Target is defined.
```

```
  Post: Returns a pointer to Target if found;
        otherwise, returns NIL if Target is not found.
*)
BEGIN (* Search *)
  IF Head = NIL THEN
    RETURN NIL             (* empty list -- Target not found *)
  ELSIF CompareStr(Head^.Word, Target) = 0 THEN
    RETURN Head                          (* Target is in Head *)
  ELSE
    RETURN Search(Head^.Link, Target) (* search rest of list *)
  END (* IF *)
END Search;
```

As indicated by the function header, a pointer value can be returned as a function result. In the recursive step

```
RETURN Search(Head^.Link, Target) (* search rest of list *)
```

the function `Search` is called recursively to search the rest of the list (pointed to by `Head^.Link`). Eventually a stopping state will be reached, and a value will be returned. The value returned from a lower-level call is not modified; it is simply passed up as the function result.

A trace of

```
P := Search(Head, 'Boy')
```

is shown in Fig. 14.12 for our sample list `'Hat'`, `'Boy'`, `'Cat'`. Since the `Target` string `'Boy'` is in the second list element, there is one recursive call to `Search` after the original function call. The result is a pointer to the node containing the string `'Boy'`, as desired. The address of this node is saved in pointer variable `P`.

Figure 14.12 ▸ *Trace of P := Search(Head, 'Boy')*

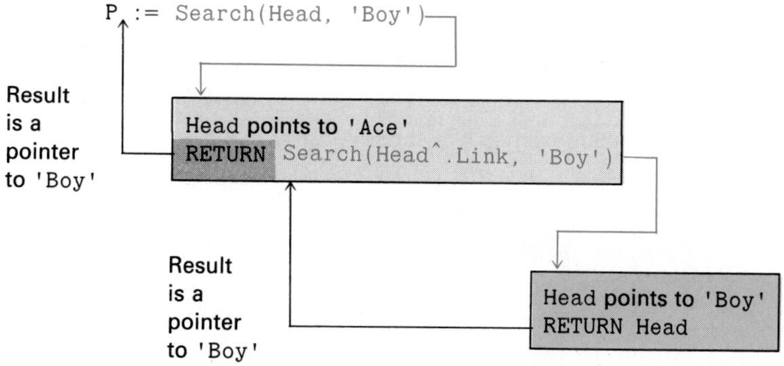

Program Style

Testing for an Empty List

The order of evaluation of the terminating conditions in Fig. 14.11 is very important. The value of `Head^.Word` is not defined if the list is empty (`Head` is `NIL`); consequently, the terminating condition `Head=NIL` must be evaluated before `Head^.Word=Target`. In all list-processing operations, make sure your program does not attempt to reference a field pointed to by `NIL`. This illegal reference to undefined data is a common error.

SELF-CHECK EXERCISES FOR SECTION 14.3

1. Write procedure `PrintList` as a recursive procedure.
2. Write an iterative version of function `Search`.
3. Write a recursive function that finds the length of a list.

14.4 Stacks, Queues, and Circular Lists

Chapter 13 introduced the stack and queue abstract data types and showed how to implement them using arrays for storage of the individual elements of a stack or a queue. Since the number of elements in a stack or a queue is dynamic, it makes sense to implement these data structures as linked lists.

A stack can be thought of as a linked list in which all insertions and deletions are performed at the list head. A list representation of a stack is shown in Fig. 14.13. The pointer `Top` points to the top of the stack. If a new node is pushed onto the stack, it should be inserted in front of the node currently pointed to by `Top`. The stack after the insertion of the letter `A` is shown at the bottom of Fig. 14.13.

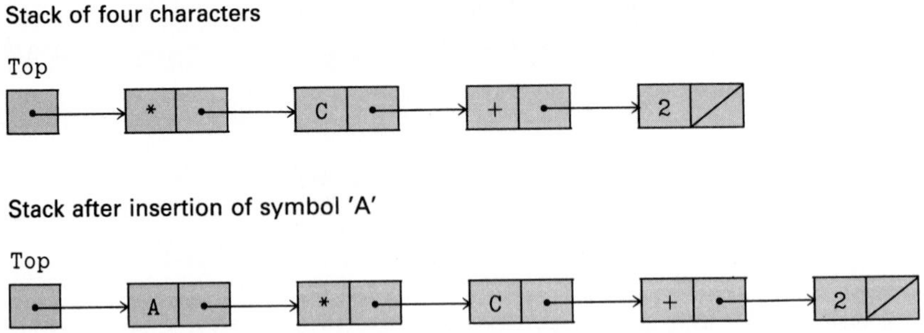

Figure 14.13 ▸ *List Representation of a Stack*

Each element of the stack can be stored in a node with a type `CHAR` field and a pointer field declared as follows:

```
TYPE
  StackNext = POINTER TO StackNode;
  StackNode = RECORD
                Item : CHAR;
                Next : StackNext
              END; (* StackNode *)
```

The stack itself is represented by a pointer to a record of type `StackObject`, which consists of a single field, `Top`. `Top` is the top of stack pointer declared as follows:

```
Stack = POINTER TO StackObject;
StackObject = RECORD
                Top : StackNext
              END; (* StackObject *)
```

You will recall that one of the important advantages of using opaque types is that we can change the implementation module for an abstract data type without having to change its definition module or recompile any other modules. The linked list implementation module for `StackADT` is shown in Fig. 14.14. In this module, parameter `S` (type `Stack`) represents a stack, and procedures `CreateStack`, `Push`, and `Pop` manipulate this stack.

Figure 14.14 ▸ *Implementing StackADT as a Linked List*

```
IMPLEMENTATION MODULE StackADT;

(* Linked list implementation of StackADT *)

  FROM Storage IMPORT
    ALLOCATE, DEALLOCATE, Available;

  FROM SYSTEM IMPORT
    TSIZE;

(* Data Structure *)
  TYPE
    StackNext = POINTER TO StackNode;
    StackNode = RECORD
                  Item : CHAR;
                  Next : StackNext
                END; (* StackNode *)

    Stack = POINTER TO StackObject;
    StackObject = RECORD
                    Top : StackNext
                  END; (* StackObject *)

(* Operators *)
```

```
PROCEDURE CreateStack (VAR S (* out *) : Stack);
(*
   Creates an empty stack.
   Pre : None
   Post: S is an empty stack.
*)
BEGIN (* CreateStack *)
  NEW (S);
  S^.Top := NIL             (* set top of stack pointer to NIL *)
END CreateStack;

PROCEDURE Push(VAR S (* in/out *) : Stack;
               X (* in *) : CHAR;
               VAR Success (* out *) : BOOLEAN);
(*
   Pushes X onto stack S.
   Pre : X is defined and S is a stack.
   Post: Sets Success to indicate success (TRUE) or failure (FALSE)
         of push operation.
*)
   VAR OldTop : StackNext;         (* pointer to old top of stack *)

BEGIN (* Push *)
  IF IsFull(S) THEN
    Success := FALSE
  ELSE
    OldTop := S^.Top;          (* save old top of stack *)
    NEW (S^.Top);              (* allocate new node at top of stack *)
    S^.Top^.Next := OldTop;    (* link new node to stack *)
    S^.Top^.Item := X;         (* define new stack item *)
    Success := TRUE
  END (* IF *)
END Push;


PROCEDURE Pop (VAR S (* in/out *) : Stack;
               VAR X (* out *) : CHAR;
               VAR Success (* out *) : BOOLEAN);
(*
   Pops the top of stack S into X.
   Pre : S is a stack.
   Post: Contents of X is character at top of stack S which is then
         removed from S. Sets Success to indicate success (TRUE)
         or failure (FALSE) of pop operation.
*)
   VAR
     OldTop : StackNext;          (* pointer to old top of stack *)

BEGIN (* Pop *)
  IF IsEmpty(S) THEN
    Success := FALSE
```

```
    ELSE
      X := S^.Top^.Item;              (* copy top of stack into X *)
      OldTop := S^.Top;               (* save old top of stack *)
      S^.Top := S^.Top^.Next;         (* pop top node *)
      DISPOSE (OldTop);               (* return top node to the heap *)
      Success := TRUE
    END (* IF *)
  END Pop;


  PROCEDURE Retrieve (S (* in *) : Stack;
                      VAR X (* out *) : CHAR;
                      VAR Success (* out *) : BOOLEAN);
  (*
     Copies the value at the top of the stack into X.
     Pre : S is a stack.
     Post: Contents of X is character at top of stack S; S is
           unchanged. Sets Success to indicate success (TRUE) or
           failure (FALSE).
  *)
  BEGIN (* Retrieve *)
    IF IsEmpty(S) THEN
      Success := FALSE
    ELSE
      X := S^.Top^.Item;                 (* copy top of stack into X *)
      Success := TRUE
    END (* IF *)
  END Retrieve;


  PROCEDURE IsEmpty (S : Stack) : BOOLEAN;
  (*
     Pre : S is a stack.
     Post: Returns TRUE if stack S is empty; otherwise, returns FALSE
  *)
  BEGIN (* IsEmpty *)
    RETURN S^.Top = NIL
  END IsEmpty;


  PROCEDURE IsFull (S : Stack) : BOOLEAN;
  (*
     Pre : S is a stack.
     Post: Returns TRUE if stack S is full; otherwise, returns FALSE.
  *)
  BEGIN (* IsFull *)
    RETURN NOT Available(TSIZE(StackNode))
  END IsFull;

END StackADT.
```

In Fig. 14.14, procedure `CreateStack` creates an empty stack, `S`, by setting the top of stack pointer, `S^.Top`, to `NIL`. `CreateStack` must be called first.

Each call to procedure `Push` places a new node on the stack. The statements

```
(*1*) OldTop := S^.Top;           (* save old top of stack *)
(*2*) NEW (S^.Top);               (* allocate new node at top of
                                     stack *)
(*3*) S^.Top^.Next := OldTop;     (* link new node to stack *)
```

allocate a new node (pointed to by `S^.Top`) and connect this node to the former top of the stack (pointed to by `OldTop`). Fig. 14.15 shows a stack before and after the letter `A` is pushed onto it. The original value of `S^.Top` is shown in grey, and the new value is shown in color. The comment preceding each statement appears as a label for the pointer value it defines.

Figure 14.15 ▸ *Pushing the Letter 'A' onto a Stack*

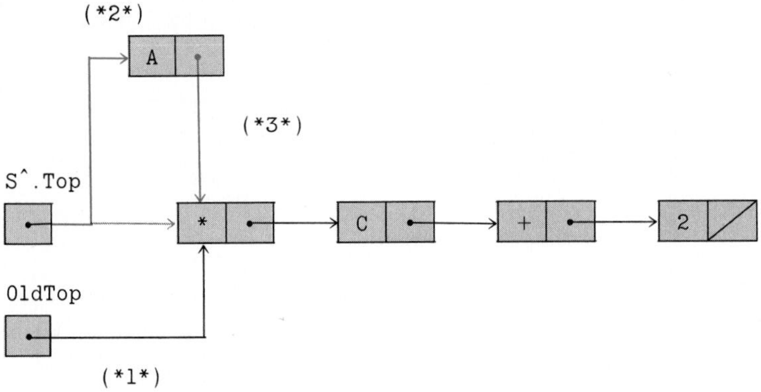

Procedure `Pop` first copies the value at the top of the stack into `X`. Next, the statement with label `(*2*)`

```
(*1*) OldTop := S^.Top;           (* save old top of stack *)
(*2*) S^.Top := S^.Top^.Next;     (* pop top node *)
(*3*) DISPOSE (OldTop);           (* return top node to the heap *)
```

pops the stack by resetting `S^.Top` to point to the node following the current top node. The statement with label `(*3*)` returns the former top node to the heap so that its memory cells can be reallocated. The effect of popping the letter `A` is shown in Fig. 14.16.

Procedure `IsEmpty` returns a value of `TRUE` if the top-of-stack pointer value is `NIL`. Procedure `IsFull` uses the statement

```
RETURN NOT Available(TSIZE(StackNode))
```

to report back whether the stack is full. This statement returns a value of `TRUE` if there are not enough storage cells available on the heap to allocate a new node of type `StackNode`. Function `TSIZE` (imported from `SYSTEM`) returns the

Figure 14.16 ▸
Popping the Stack

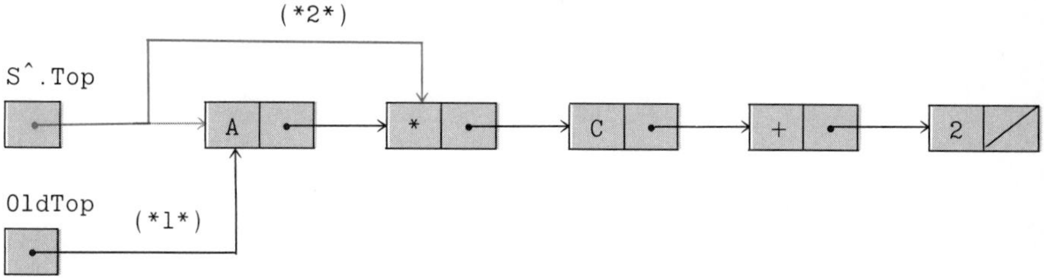

number of bytes in a record of type `StackNode`. Function `Available` (imported from `Storage`) returns `TRUE` if the heap contains at least the number of cells specified by its argument.

We can replace the implementation module shown in Fig. 13.10 with the implementation module shown in Fig. 14.14. The new implementation module can be compiled without any change to the definition module, because `Stack` was declared as an opaque type in the definition module. Since the definition module is unchanged, any client modules can be run using this new stack implementation without recompilation. Before running a client module, however, it is necessary to relink it.

Program Style

Time and Space Tradeoffs for Stack Implementations

The advantage of using pointer variables to implement a stack is that we can increase the size of the stack when we push on a new element and decrease its size when we pop off an element. In this way, the storage space allocated to the stack expands and contracts as the number of stack elements changes. In the array implementation shown earlier, the entire array is allocated at once whether or not it is all needed.

You should realize that this apparent saving of memory is not without cost. Each stack element requires an additional field that is used for storage of the address of the next stack element. In an array implementation, this extra field is not required because the elements of an array are implicitly linked together.

With respect to time, it is usually more costly for a compiler to access elements of a stack stored in an array. This is because the compiler must compute the actual memory address corresponding to a subscript value stored in the top-of-stack pointer. In a linked-list implementation, the top-of-stack pointer contains the memory address, so no computation is required.

Implementing a Queue as a Linked List

We can also implement a queue (see Sections 13.6 and 13.7) as a linked list that grows and shrinks as elements are inserted and deleted. We can use two pointers, `Front` and `Rear`, to point to elements of the queue, as shown in Fig. 14.17.

Figure 14.17 ▸ *Representing a Queue as a Linked List*

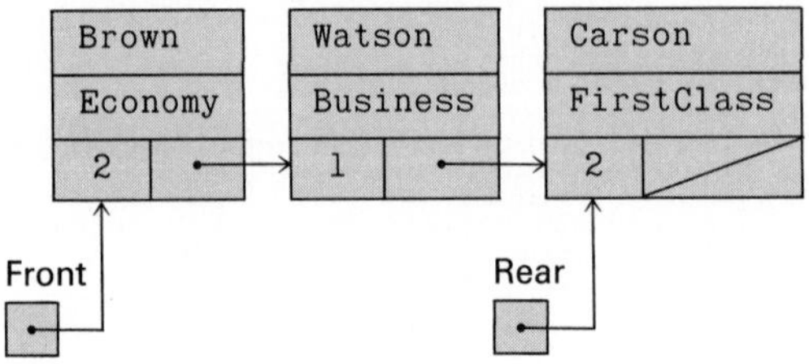

The following declarations could be used in an implementation module based on this representation.

```
TYPE
  QueueNext = POINTER TO QueueNode;
  QueueNode = RECORD
                Item : Element;
                Next : QueueNext
              END QueueNode;

  Queue = POINTER TO QueueObject;
  QueueObject = RECORD
                  Front, Rear : QueueNext;
                  NumItems : [0..MaxSize]
                END; (* QueueObject *)
```

Compare these declarations with the declaration for `QueueObject` in Section 13.6. In the preceding declarations, a variable of type `QueueObject` contains two pointers, `Front` and `Rear`, and the queue expands and contracts as records of type `Element` are inserted and removed. In Section 13.6, it was necessary to allocate an entire array of `MaxSize` records (type `Element`) for storage of a queue's elements. The implementation module for `QueueADT` using these declarations is left as an exercise.

Implementing a Queue as a Circular List

Section 13.7 demonstrated that a circular array was a convenient data structure for storing the elements of a queue. This section will show you how to represent and manipulate a queue using a *circular list*.

Fig. 14.18 shows a queue of three elements represented as a circular list. This is called a *circular list* because the pointer field of the last list element

Figure 14.18 ▸ *A Queue as a Circular List*

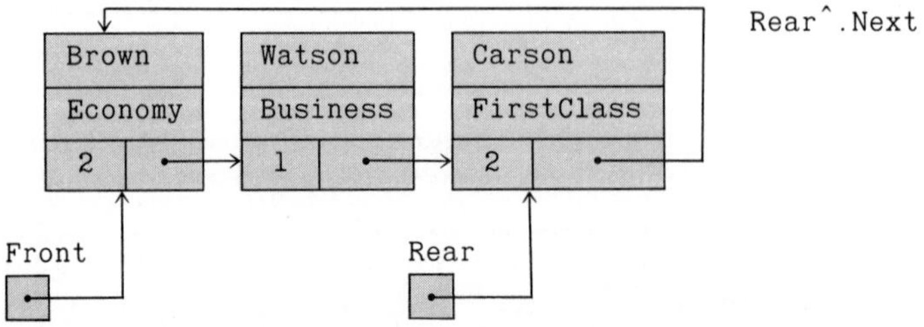

(passenger 'Carson') points back to the first list element (passenger 'Brown'). Only the pointer variable Rear is required to access the queue because the pointer variable Rear^.Next points to the same record as pointer variable Front.

If a new node is inserted in the preceding queue, it should be attached to the node currently pointed to by Rear, and Rear should be reset to point to the new node. Passenger McMann is inserted in Fig. 14.19. The original values of pointers that are changed are shown in grey; the new pointer values are in color.

Figure 14.19 ▶ *Queue after Insertion*

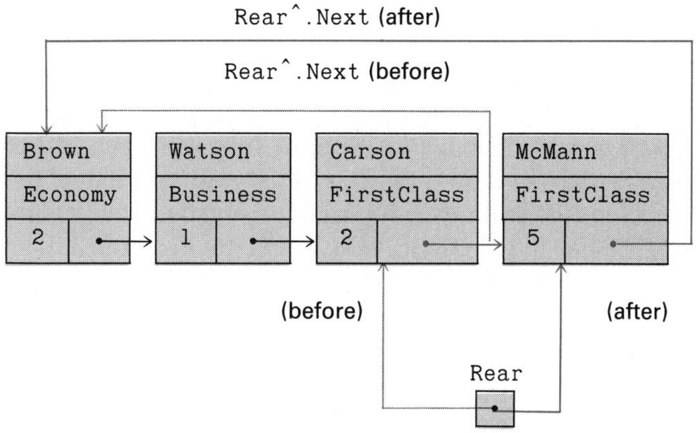

To remove a node, the pointer Rear should be reset to point to the node following the one that is currently at the front of the queue (Rear^.Next becomes Rear^.Next^.Next). Fig. 14.20 shows the queue above after a passenger ('Brown') is removed from the queue. The new value of Rear^.Next is shown in color; the old value is in grey.

Figure 14.20 ▶ *Queue after Deletion*

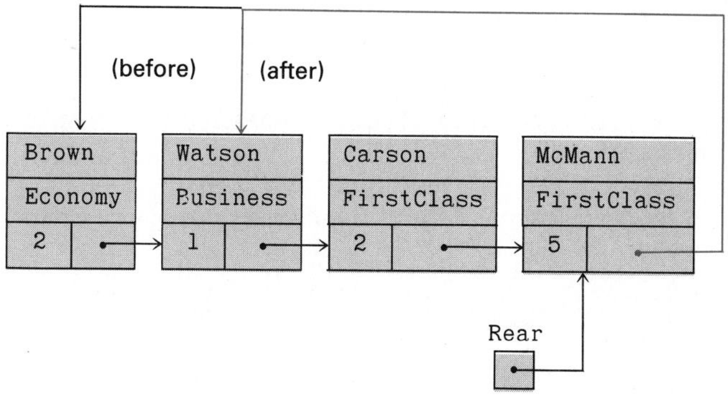

The implementation module for QueueADT as a circular list is left as a programming project at the end of this chapter.

SELF-CHECK EXERCISE FOR SECTION 14.4

1. Rewrite the implementation module shown in Section 13.7 using the linked list representation of a queue shown in Fig. 14.17 (not the circular list).

14.5 Specification of an Ordered List Abstract Data Type

This section will consider the problem of maintaining an ordered list of records. We would like to be able to automatically insert a new record into the list and know that the list will still be in order after the insertion. Similarly, after a record is deleted, the remaining elements should still be in order. As long as we maintain the order of list elements as we perform each deletion or insertion, we will never have to sort the list. It will also be easier to search for a particular list element if the elements are in order.

The specification of an abstract data type consisting of an ordered list and its operators follows.

Specification of Ordered List Abstract Data Type ▶

DATA STRUCTURE: An ordered list consists of a collection of elements that are records (type `Element`). Each record has a key field (type `KeyType`) and a data field. For simplicity, assume that there are no duplicate keys. The elements of an ordered list are always in sequential order by key field.

OPERATORS: For the following descriptions, assume the parameters:

- `List` represents the ordered list
- `El` is a list record
- `Target` is a key value
- `Success` is a `BOOLEAN` flag indicating success (`TRUE`) or failure (`FALSE`) of an operation

`CreateList (VAR List)`: Creates an ordered list. Must be called before any other operators.

`SizeOfList(List)`: Returns the number of nodes currently in the ordered list.

`Search (List, Target, VAR Success)`: Searches a list to find the key `Target`. If the `Target` is found, sets `Success` to `TRUE`; otherwise, sets `Success` to `FALSE`.

`Insert (VAR List, El, VAR Success)`: Inserts item `El` into the list maintaining the list order and sets `Success` to `TRUE`. If there is already an element with the same key value as `El`, `Success` will be set to `FALSE` and no insertion is performed.

`Delete (VAR List, Target, VAR Success)`: Deletes the element whose key value is `Target`, maintaining the list order, and sets `Success` to `TRUE`. If `Target` is not located, sets `Success` to `FALSE`.

`Retrieve (VAR List, Target, VAR El, VAR Success)`: Copies the record whose key is `Target` into `El`, and sets `Success` to `TRUE`. If there is no element with key `Target`, `El` is not defined and `Success` is `FALSE`.

`Replace (List, El, VAR Success)`: Replaces the element whose key value is the same as the key value of `El` and sets `Success` to `TRUE`. If there is no element whose key value matches the key value of `El`, sets `Success` to `FALSE`.

`Traverse (List, Visit)`: Traverses the elements in sequential order. Calls procedure `Visit` to process each item.

The last operator requires some discussion. Traversing a list means processing all list elements in sequence. As each element is reached, procedure `Traverse` will call a procedure to perform a desired operation (e.g., display selected fields of that record). Later, you will see how to specify the desired operation as a parameter of `Traverse`.

The Definition Module

We can write the definition module for the ordered list abstract data type without knowing the details of the implementation. It is based on the specification and is shown in Fig. 14.21.

Figure 14.21 ▸ *Definition Module for Ordered List Abstract Data Type*

```
DEFINITION MODULE OrderList;
(*
   Specification of the abstract data type for an ordered list of
   records. Procedure CreateList must be called first to initialize
   the ordered list.
*)
   FROM ElementType IMPORT
     Element, KeyType;                          (* data types *)

   EXPORT QUALIFIED
     ListPointer,                               (* data type *)
     CreateList, Insert, Delete, SizeOfList,    (* procedures *)
     Search, Replace, Retrieve, Traverse;


(* Data Structure *)

   TYPE
     ListPointer;                               (* opaque type *)
```

```
(* Operators *)

   PROCEDURE CreateList (VAR List (* output *) : ListPointer);
   (*
      Creates an ordered list. Must be executed first.
      Pre : None
      Post: List points to the header node for an ordered list.
   *)

   PROCEDURE SizeOfList (List : ListPointer) : CARDINAL;
   (* Returns the number of elements in an ordered list. *)

   PROCEDURE Search (List (* input *) : ListPointer;
                     Target (* input *) : KeyType;
                     VAR Success (* output *) : BOOLEAN);
   (*
      Searches an ordered List for Target.
      Pre : List points to the header node for an ordered list.
      Post: Success is TRUE if Target is found; otherwise,
            Success is FALSE.
   *)

   PROCEDURE Insert (VAR List (* in/out *) : ListPointer;
                     El (* input *) : Element;
                     VAR Success (* in/out *) : BOOLEAN);
   (*
      Inserts item El into an ordered list.
      Pre : List points to the header node for an ordered list.
      Post: Success is TRUE if insertion is performed; Success is
            FALSE if insertion is not performed because there is
            already an element with the same key as El.
   *)

   PROCEDURE Delete (VAR List (* in/out *) : ListPointer;
                     Target (* input *) : KeyType;
                     VAR Success (* in/out *) : BOOLEAN);
   (*
      Deletes the element with key Target from an ordered list.
      Pre : List points to the header node for an ordered list.
      Post: Success is TRUE if deletion is performed; Success is
            FALSE if deletion is not performed because there is no
            element whose key is Target.
   *)

   PROCEDURE Replace (VAR List (* in/out *) : ListPointer;
                      El (* input *) : Element;
                      VAR Success (* output *) : BOOLEAN);
   (*
      Replaces the element of an ordered List with the same key as
      El by the contents of El.
      Pre : List points to the header node for an ordered list.
```

```
      Post: Success is TRUE if the replacement is performed; Success
            is FALSE if there is no element with the same key as El.
   *)

   PROCEDURE Retrieve (List (* input *) : ListPointer;
                       Target (* input *) : KeyType;
                       VAR El (* output *) : Element;
                       VAR Success (* output *) : BOOLEAN);
   (*
      Copies the element whose key is Target into El.
      Pre : List points to the header node for an ordered list.
      Post: Success is TRUE if the copy is performed; Success is
            FALSE if there is no element whose key is Target.
   *)

   TYPE
     VisitType = PROCEDURE (VAR Element);

   PROCEDURE Traverse (List (* input *) : ListPointer;
                       Visit (* procedure *) : VisitType);
   (*
      Repeatedly calls procedure Visit (a parameter) to
      process each element of an ordered list.
      Pre : List points to the header node of an ordered list.
      Post: Each element is operated on in turn by procedure Visit.
   *)

END OrderList.
```

The data type ListPointer (an opaque type) is exported from module OrderList along with the list operators. For generality, data types Element and KeyType are imported from module ElementType.

14.6 Procedure Types

So far, we have used procedures and procedural abstraction in most of our programming, where each procedure encapsulates part of an algorithm. Modula-2 also enables us to regard procedures as objects of a particular data type and to manipulate them like other objects. In Fig. 14.21, the lines

```
TYPE
  VisitType = PROCEDURE (VAR Element);
```

declare VisitType to be a *procedure type*. This declaration means that any procedure of type VisitType must have a single parameter that is a variable parameter of type Element.

The variable declaration

```
VAR
  Operation : VisitType;
```

declares Operation to be a "variable" that can be assigned a procedure name as its value. Assuming procedures Proc1 and Proc2 have a single variable parameter of type Element, the IF statement

```
IF Choice = 1 THEN
  Operation := Proc1
ELSE
  Operation := Proc2
END; (* IF *)
```

assigns either Proc1 or Proc2 as the value of procedure variable Operation. The procedure call statement

```
Operation (OneElement)
```

calls the procedure assigned to Operation with OneElement (type Element) as its parameter.

Passing Procedures as Parameters

The use of procedure types also enables us to pass procedures as parameters to other Modula-2 procedures. In the heading for procedure Traverse, parameter Visit is declared to be a procedure of type VisitType. Therefore, whenever procedure Traverse is called, it must be passed a procedure of type VisitType. This facility enables a different operation to be performed each time Traverse is called; the operation is determined by the procedure that is passed to Traverse.

The comment in procedure Traverse implies that the specified operation will be performed uniformly on all list records. For example, the procedure call statement

```
Traverse (List, WritePass)
```

will cause procedure WritePass to be performed on all records of the ordered list pointed to by List. This call statement is valid only if List is type ListPointer and WritePass has the required formal parameter list (a variable parameter of type Element).

Procedure Type Declaration ▶

FORM: TYPE *ProcName* = PROCEDURE (*FormalTypeList*);
TYPE *ProcName* = PROCEDURE (*FormalTypeList*) : *FuncType*;

EXAMPLE:
```
TYPE DoArray = PROCEDURE (VAR ARRAY OF REAL, CARDINAL);
                        (* two parameters: a variable array of reals
                                                and a CARDINAL value *)

TYPE DoFunc = PROCEDURE (REAL, REAL) : REAL;
                                    (* two REAL value parameters
                                                and a REAL result *)
```

INTERPRETATION: The identifier *ProcName* is declared to be a procedure type. The formal parameters of any procedure of type *ProcName* must match the parameter types provided in *FormalTypeList*. If *ProcName* is a function procedure type, the type of the result returned is specified by *FuncType*.

Note: The procedure type `PROC` is predefined and denotes a procedure type without parameters.

14.7 Implementation of an Ordered List Abstract Data Type

So far in this chapter, you have seen many advantages to using pointer variables and dynamic allocation to implement linked lists. We have repeatedly emphasized the ease with which insertions and deletions can be performed on such a list. For these reasons, we will use a list node with a pointer field (type `NodePointer`) to represent each element of our ordered list, declared as follows.

```
TYPE
  NodePointer = POINTER TO ListNode;
  ListNode = RECORD
               Item : Element;      (* includes the key field *)
               Link : NodePointer
             END; (* ListNode *)
```

The key field of each list node is part of field `Item` and is type `KeyType`. Besides the data types `KeyType` and `Element`, we must also import any procedures from `ElementType` that are needed to manipulate the record keys. Procedures `InsertKey` and `ExtractKey` define and retrieve a record key, respectively. Function `Bigger` compares two key values, where `Bigger(Key1, Key2)` is true if `Key1` is larger than `Key2`.

Each instance of an ordered list will be represented by a pointer to a record of type `ListObject` containing a pointer field, `Head`, and a `CARDINAL` field, `NumItems`. `Head` points to the first node in the linked list; `NumItems` is a count of the number of list nodes.

```
TYPE
  ListPointer = POINTER TO ListObject;
  ListObject = RECORD
                 Head : NodePointer;
                 NumItems : CARDINAL
               END; (* ListObject *)
```

The import statements and type declarations required in the implementation module are shown in Fig. 14.22. We will discuss some of the operator procedures after the figure.

Figure 14.22 ▸ *Import Statement and Type Declarations for OrderList*

```
IMPLEMENTATION MODULE OrderList;
(*
   Implementation of ordered list abstract data type.
   Procedure CreateList must be called first to initialize
   the ordered list to a list of 2 dummy nodes
   containing keys of MinKey and MaxKey. All actual element
   keys will be greater than MinKey and less than MaxKey.
*)
   FROM ElementType IMPORT
     Element, KeyType,                (* data types *)
     Bigger,                          (* function *)
     ExtractKey, InsertKey,           (* procedures *)
     MinKey, MaxKey;                  (* constants *)
     (*
        Function procedure Bigger is used to compare two keys.
        Bigger(Key1, Key2) returns TRUE if Key1 is larger than Key2;
        otherwise, Bigger(Key1, Key2) returns FALSE.

        Procedures InsertKey and ExtractKey are used to define
        and retrieve the key field of a record of type Element.
     *)

   FROM Storage IMPORT
     ALLOCATE, DEALLOCATE;


(* Data Structure *)

   TYPE
     NodePointer = POINTER TO ListNode;
     ListNode = RECORD
                  Item : Element;
                  Link : NodePointer
                END; (* ListNode *)

     ListPointer = POINTER TO ListObject;
```

```
    ListObject = RECORD
                   Head : NodePointer;
                   NumItems : CARDINAL
                 END; (* ListObject *)

(* Operators -- to be inserted *)

END OrderList.
```

The type declarations in Fig. 14.22 indicate that each instance of an ordered list will be represented by a record of type `ListObject`. This record contains a pointer, `Head`, to the first node of a linked list and a `CARDINAL` field, `NumItems`, which represents a count of list nodes.

It will simplify the list-processing operations if we assume that an ordered list always begins and ends with two dummy nodes. The dummy node at the head of the list should have a key value (`MinKey`) that is smaller than all the list keys; the dummy node at the end of the list should have a key value (`MaxKey`) that is larger than all the list keys. The constants `MinKey` and `MaxKey` are imported from module `ElementType`, where they are defined.

The dummy nodes are analogous to sentinels. The presence of the first dummy node means that we never have to change the value of `Head` when a new node is inserted. The presence of the second dummy node keeps us from "falling off" the end of the list when searching for a target key. An "empty" list always contains two dummy nodes, as shown in Fig. 14.23. The symbol ? indicates that only the key fields of each node are defined. The procedure call statement

```
CreateList (MyList)
```

builds the list shown in Fig. 14.23.

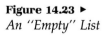

Figure 14.23 ▸ *An "Empty" List*

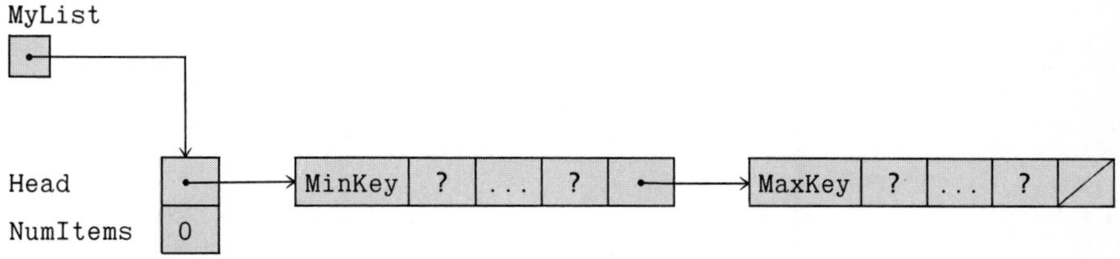

Figure 14.24 ▸ *Procedure CreateList*

```
PROCEDURE CreateList (VAR List (* output *) : ListPointer);
(*
   Creates an ordered list containing two dummy nodes whose keys
   are the constants MinKey and MaxKey.
   Pre : None
   Post: List points to the header node for an ordered list.
*)
BEGIN (* CreateList *)
  NEW (List);                                 (* Create a new list *)
  NEW (List^.Head);                    (* allocate first dummy node *)
  NEW (List^.Head^.Link);             (* allocate second dummy node *)
  InsertKey (List^.Head^.Item, MinKey);
  InsertKey (List^.Head^.Link^.Item, MaxKey);
  List^.Head^.Link^.Link := NIL;     (* second node is last node *)
  List^.NumItems := 0                 (* dummy nodes don't count *)
END CreateList;
```

The first NEW statement in Fig. 14.24 allocates storage for one record of type ListObject that is pointed to by List. The next two NEW statements allocate storage for two dummy list nodes that are connected. The pointer List^.Head points to the first dummy node in the empty list; List^.Head^.Link points to the second dummy node. Procedure InsertKey stores MinKey and MaxKey as key values in the dummy nodes. The field NumItems in the node of type ListObject is set to zero because the dummy nodes aren't counted as actual list nodes.

Procedure Search is used to determine if a particular target key is present in the list; it returns a BOOLEAN value to indicate the search result. Search calls procedure Locate to perform the actual search. Procedure Search is shown in Fig. 14.25.

Figure 14.25 ▸ *Procedure Search*

```
PROCEDURE Search (List (* input *) : ListPointer;
                  Target (* input *) : KeyType;
                  VAR Success (* output *) : BOOLEAN);
(*
   Searches an ordered List for Target.
   Pre : List points to the header node for an ordered list.
   Post: Success is TRUE if Target is found; otherwise,
         Success is FALSE.
*)
   VAR
     Previous,                  (* pointer to previous node *)
     Next      : NodePointer;   (* pointer to current node *)
```

```
BEGIN (* Search *)
  (* Start search at first dummy node. *)
  Previous := List^.Head;
  (* Perform search and define Success *)
  Locate (Target, Previous, Next, Success)
END Search;
```

In writing procedure `Locate`, we can take advantage of the fact that the key values are in ascending sequence. Consequently, while searching for the target key, if we reach a list element whose key value is larger than the target key, we know the target key cannot be present in the list.

Procedure `Locate` advances pointer `Next` down the list until it reaches a node whose key value is greater than or equal to the target key. If the stopping key value is equal to the target key, `SearchSuccess` is set to `TRUE`; otherwise, `SearchSuccess` is set to `FALSE`.

Pointer `Previous` always points to the node just before the one pointed to by `Next`. Before `Locate` is called, `Previous` is initialized to the dummy node with key value `MinKey`. When `Locate` is entered, `Next` is initialized to the node following `Previous`. When `Locate` is finished, `Next` points to the last node tested and `Previous` points to its predecessor.

Figure 14.26 shows the effect of calling `Locate` to search for the `Target` key `'ALPH'` in a list of four-letter words. `MinKey` and `MaxKey` are `'AAAA'` and `'ZZZZ'`, respectively. Pointer `Next` has advanced down the list to the node containing the key `'BOYS'`, which is the first key greater than or equal to the target `'ALPH'`. Since the target was not found, the value `FALSE` should be returned as the search result. Procedure `Locate` is shown in Fig. 14.27.

Figure 14.26 ▶ *Final Pointer Values in Search for 'ALPH'*

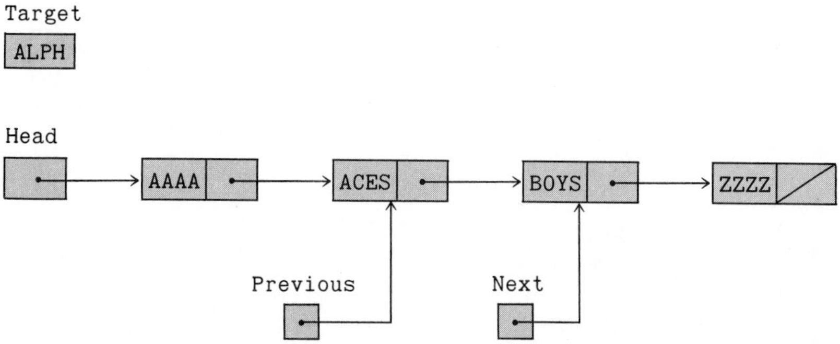

Figure 14.27 ▸
Procedure Locate

```
PROCEDURE Locate (Target (* input *) : KeyType;
                  VAR Previous, (* in/out *)
                      Next      (* output *) : NodePointer;
                  VAR SearchSuccess (* output *) : BOOLEAN);
(*
   Attempts to locate a node with key value Target in the
   list whose first node is pointed to by Previous.
   Pre : Target is defined; Previous points to the first dummy node.
   Post: If Target is located, SearchSuccess is set to TRUE;
         otherwise, SearchSuccess is set to FALSE.
         Previous points to the last list node with key < Target;
         Next points to the first list node with key >= Target.
   Uses: Bigger, ExtractKey from ElementType.
*)
   VAR
     NextKey : KeyType;           (* key of node Next^ *)

BEGIN (* Locate *)
  (* Search for first node with key >= Target. *)
  (* Start with first actual node. *)
  Next := Previous^.Link;
  ExtractKey (Next^.Item, NextKey);      (* get first key *)
  WHILE
    (* invariant:
         Target > key of each node pointed to by Next so far.
    *)
       Bigger(Target, NextKey) DO
    Previous := Next;                    (* advance Previous *)
    Next := Next^.Link;                  (* advance Next *)
    ExtractKey (Next^.Item, NextKey)     (* get next key *)
  END; (* WHILE *)
  (* assert: Target is located or NextKey is larger than Target. *)

  (* Set flag to indicate search results. *)
  SearchSuccess := NOT Bigger(NextKey, Target)
END Locate;
```

The procedure call statement

```
ExtractKey (Next^.Item, NextKey)
```

is used in `Locate` to get each key. In the `WHILE` loop header, the function designator

```
Bigger(Target, NextKey)
```

compares each key to `Target` and causes the `WHILE` loop to be exited when `Next` reaches a node whose key value, `NextKey`, is greater than or equal to `Target`. After loop exit, function `Bigger` compares `NextKey` to `Target`. If `NextKey` is greater than `Target`, `SearchSuccess` is set to `FALSE`; otherwise, `NextKey` must be equal to `Target`, so `SearchSuccess` is set to `TRUE`.

Procedure `Insert` is used to insert a node in the ordered list. It first calls `Locate` to search for the key value of the new record and, in this way, determines where the new record should be inserted. For example, a new record with key value `'ALPH'` should be inserted between nodes `Previous^` and `Next^` in the list shown in Fig. 14.26. If there is already a node with the same key value as the new record, `Locate` sets `SearchSuccess` to `TRUE` and the insertion is not performed. Procedure `Insert` is shown in Fig. 14.28.

Figure 14.28 ▸
Procedure Insert

```
PROCEDURE Insert (VAR List (* in/out *) : ListPointer;
                  El (* input *) : Element;
                  VAR Success (* in/out *) : BOOLEAN);
(*
   Inserts item El into an ordered list.
   Pre : List points to the header node for an ordered list.
   Post: Success is TRUE if insertion is performed; Success is FALSE
         if insertion is not performed because there is already
         an element with the same key as El.
   Uses: NEW (ALLOCATE) from Storage; Bigger, ExtractKey from
         ElementType.
*)
   VAR
     Previous,              (* pointer to node preceding El *)
     Next : NodePointer;    (* pointer to node following El *)
     SearchSuccess : BOOLEAN;              (* search result *)
     ElKey : KeyType;                   (* key of record El *)

BEGIN (* Insert *)
  (* Validate ElKey and search for a valid key. *)
  ExtractKey (El, ElKey);
  IF Bigger(MinKey, ElKey) OR Bigger(ElKey, MaxKey) THEN
    Success := FALSE        (* ElKey is out of range *)
  ELSE
    (* Search the list for ElKey. *)
    Previous := List^.Head;           (* start at first dummy node *)
    Locate (ElKey, Previous, Next, SearchSuccess);
    Success := NOT SearchSuccess   (* ElKey is new if search fails *)
  END; (* IF *)

  (* Insert if ElKey is in range and is a new key *)
  IF Success THEN
    NEW (Previous^.Link);          (* join new node to Previous^ *)
    Previous^.Link^.Link := Next;      (* join new node to Next^ *)
    Previous^.Link^.Item := El;          (* store El in new node *)
    INC (List^.NumItems)
  END (* IF *)
END Insert;
```

Procedure `Insert` begins by extracting `ElKey` from `El` and validating it. If `ElKey` is within the range `MinKey` to `MaxKey`, procedure `Locate` is called. If `ElKey` is in range and is a new key, record `El` is inserted. The statements

```
(*1*) NEW (Previous^.Link);          (* join new node to Previous^ *)
(*2*) Previous^.Link^.Link := Next;  (* join new node to Next^ *)
      Previous^.Link^.Item := El;    (* store El in new node *)
```

perform the actual insertion. Fig. 14.29 illustrates their effect in inserting a new node with key `'ALPH'`. The new pointer values are in color; the original pointer values are in grey.

Figure 14.29 ▶ *Inserting 'ALPH' between Nodes Previous^ and Next^*

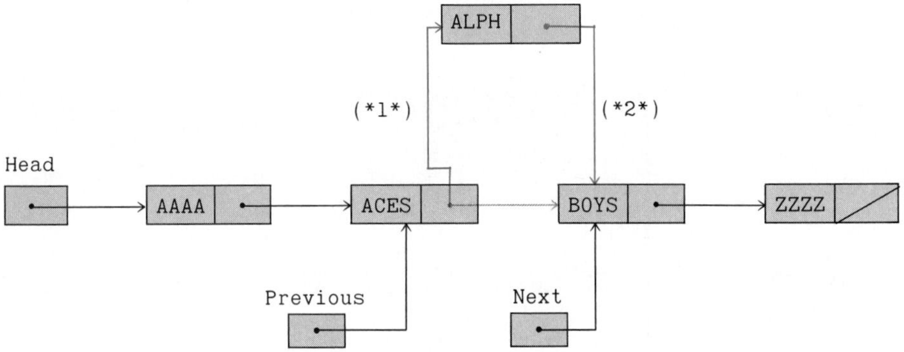

Before we can delete a node containing a specified key (`Target`), procedure `Locate` must advance `Next` to point to the node with that key. If the search succeeds, the statement

```
Previous^.Link := Next^.Link;          (* disconnect node Next^ *)
```

redirects `Previous^.Link` to point to the first node whose key is greater than `Target`, thereby disconnecting the node with key `Target`. Procedure `Delete` is shown in Fig. 14.30. Procedures `Retrieve` and `Replace` are quite similar and are left as an exercise, along with function procedure `SizeOfList`.

Figure 14.30 ▶ *Procedure Delete*

```
PROCEDURE Delete (VAR List (* in/out *) : ListPointer;
                  Target (* input *) : KeyType;
                  VAR Success (* in/out *) : BOOLEAN);
```

```
(*
   Deletes the element with key Target from an ordered list.
   Pre : List points to the header node for an ordered list.
   Post: Success is TRUE if deletion is performed; Success is FALSE
         if deletion is not performed because there is no element
         whose key is Target.
   Uses: Dispose (DEALLOCATE) from Storage.
*)
   VAR
     Previous,             (* pointer to last list key < ElKey *)
     Next : NodePointer;   (* pointer to first list key >= ElKey *)
     Temp : NodePointer;   (* temporary variable *)

BEGIN (* Delete *)
  (* Search the list for the key Target. *)
  Previous := List^.Head;  (* Previous points to first dummy node *)
  Locate (Target, Previous, Next, Success);

  (* If Target is found, delete it. *)
  IF Success THEN
    Temp := Next;          (* point Temp to the node being deleted *)
    Previous^.Link := Next^.Link;         (* disconnect node Next^ *)
    DISPOSE (Temp);                         (* deallocate storage *)
    DEC (List^.NumItems)
  END (* IF *)
END Delete;
```

Finally, procedure `Traverse` traverses the ordered list, visiting each actual node, but not the dummy nodes. Procedure `Traverse` is shown in Fig. 14.31. `List` is a variable parameter because it may be necessary for procedure `Visit` to update each node of the list (e.g., increase each salary by 10 percent).

Figure 14.31 ▸
Procedure Traverse

```
PROCEDURE Traverse (VAR List (* in/out *) : ListPointer;
                    Visit (* procedure *) : VisitType);
(*
   Repeatedly calls procedure Visit (a parameter) to
   process each element of an ordered list.
   Pre : List points to the header node of an ordered list.
   Post: Each element is operated on in turn by procedure Visit.
   Uses: ExtractKey from ElementType
*)
   VAR
     Next : NodePointer;      (* pointer to each list node *)
     NextKey : KeyType;       (* key of node Next^ *)

BEGIN (* Traverse *)
```

```
  Next := List^.Head^.Link;     (* start with first node after dummy *)
  ExtractKey (Next^.Item, NextKey);                  (* get node key *)
  WHILE
    (* invariant:
         MaxKey > key of each prior node pointed to by Next
    *)
      Bigger(MaxKey, NextKey) DO
    Visit (Next^.Item);                             (* visit node *)
    Next := Next^.Link;                           (* advance Next *)
    ExtractKey (Next^.Item, NextKey)
  END (* WHILE *)
END Traverse;
```

Analysis of Operations on an Ordered List

We have gone through considerable effort to maintain our linked list in ascending order by key value; however, the improvement in search efficiency that results is relatively modest. If we assume that a target key is equally likely to be at the front of a list as at the end of a list, then we will have to examine, on the average, half of the list elements. This is the same whether or not the target key is in the list. If a list is not ordered, we will have to examine all of its elements to determine that a key is not in the list, but only half of its elements, on the average, to find a key that is in the list. Therefore, list search is an O(n) process for both an ordered list and an unordered list.

It takes considerably longer to insert an item in an ordered list than in an unordered list. In an unordered list, we can arbitrarily insert a new element at the list head. In an ordered list, we must first search for the appropriate position of the new element before inserting it.

The main advantage to using ordered lists occurs when displaying the list contents. If the list is unordered, we must find some way to sort it before we can display it. An ordered list is always ready to be printed or displayed.

Using the Ordered List Table Abstract Data Type

All of the procedures in the previous section are, of course, part of the implementation module for the ordered list abstract data type. Once module `ElementType` is defined, client modules can be written that use this abstract data type to build and maintain an ordered list. Building an ordered list is accomplished by performing a sequence of `Insert` operations.

The abstract data type can be reused to manipulate different list structures simply by redefining and recompiling module `ElementType`. The abstract data type `OrderList` and its client modules will also have to be recompiled.

We can use this abstract data type to maintain an ordered list of airline passengers where each passenger has the record format described in Section 13.7. The definition module for `ElementType` shown in Fig. 14.32 is an expansion of the module in Fig. 13.16. The passenger name is used as the record key (`TYPE KeyType = NameType`). We have changed the parameter of the procedure `WritePass` from value to variable, so that `WritePass` can be used as a procedure parameter for `Traverse`.

Figure 14.32 ▸ *Definition Module for ElementType*

```
DEFINITION MODULE ElementType;

(* Interface for module that uses data type Element. *)

  EXPORT QUALIFIED
    Element, KeyType, NameType, (* data types *)
    MinKey, MaxKey,             (* constants *)
    Bigger,                     (* function *)
    ExtractKey, InsertKey,      (* procedures *)
    ReadPass, WritePass;

  CONST
    MaxLetters = 20;
    MaxSeats = 30;
    MinKey = 'AAAAAAA';
    MaxKey = 'zzzzzzz';

(* Data Structure *)

  TYPE
    ClassType = (FirstClass, Business, Economy, Standby,
                 Undesignated);
    NameType = ARRAY [0..MaxLetters] OF CHAR;
    KeyType = NameType;
    Element = RECORD
                Name : NameType;
                Class : ClassType;
                NumSeats : [1..MaxSeats]
              END;  (* Element *)

(* Operators *)

  PROCEDURE ReadPass (VAR OnePass (* output *) : Element);
  (* Reads one record of type Element. *)

  PROCEDURE WritePass (VAR OnePass (* input *) : Element);
  (* Displays one record of type Element. *)

  PROCEDURE InsertKey (VAR OnePass (* output *) : Element;
                       Key (* input *) : KeyType);
  (* Inserts the key value in record OnePass. *)

  PROCEDURE ExtractKey (OnePass (* input *) : Element;
                        VAR Key (* output *) : KeyType);
```

```
  (* Extracts the key of record OnePass. *)

  PROCEDURE Bigger (Key1, Key2 (* input *) : KeyType) : BOOLEAN;
  (* Compares Key1 and Key2 and returns TRUE if Key1 > Key2. *)

END ElementType.
```

In addition to the procedures shown earlier in Fig. 13.17, the implementation module must contain procedures `ExtractKey`, and `InsertKey` and function `Bigger`. These three procedures are shown in Fig. 14.33. Procedure `CompareStr` (called by `Bigger`) must be imported from module `Strings`.

Figure 14.33 ▸ *ExtractKey, InsertKey, and Bigger*

```
PROCEDURE ExtractKey (OnePass (* input *) : Element;
                      VAR Key (* output *) : KeyType);

(* Extracts the key of record OnePass. *)

BEGIN (* ExtractKey *)
  Key := OnePass.Name
END ExtractKey;


PROCEDURE InsertKey (VAR OnePass (* output *) : Element;
                     Key (* input *) : KeyType);

(* Inserts the key value in record OnePass. *)

BEGIN (* InsertKey *)
  OnePass.Name := Key
END InsertKey;


PROCEDURE Bigger (Key1, Key2 : KeyType) : BOOLEAN;

(* Compares Key1 and Key2 and returns TRUE if Key1 > Key2. *)

BEGIN (* Bigger *)
  RETURN CompareStr(Key1, Key2) = 1
END Bigger;
```

A simple client module that uses the abstract data type `OrderList` to build an ordered list of three passengers and display it is shown in Fig. 14.34; a sample run of this program is shown in Fig. 14.35. More robust client modules are described in the programming projects at the end of this chapter.

Figure 14.34 ▸
Client Module for OrderListADT

```
MODULE BuildOrdList;

(* Builds an ordered list using the abstract data type OrderList *)

   FROM InOut IMPORT
     WriteString, WriteLn, WriteCard;

   FROM OrderList IMPORT
     ListPointer,                               (* type *)
     CreateList, Insert, Traverse, Delete,      (* procedures *)
     SizeOfList;                                (* function *)


   FROM ElementType IMPORT
     Element,                                   (* type *)
     ReadPass, WritePass;                       (* procedures *)

   CONST
     MaxPass = 4;                           (* maximum list size *)

   VAR
     PassList : ListPointer;                (* ordered list *)
     OnePass : Element;                     (* a passenger *)
     i : [1..MaxPass];                      (* counter *)
     Success : BOOLEAN;                     (* program flag *)

BEGIN (* BuildOrdList *)
  (* Initialize the list *)
   CreateList (PassList);

  (* Read and insert up to four passengers in PassList *)
  FOR i := 1 TO MaxPass DO
    WriteString ('Enter data for next passenger.');  WriteLn;
    ReadPass (OnePass);
    Insert (PassList, OnePass, Success);
    IF Success THEN
      WriteString ('Passenger inserted.')
    ELSE
      WriteString ('Already booked - no insertion.')
    END; (* IF *)
    WriteLn;  WriteLn
  END; (* FOR *)

  (* Delete Smith *)
  Delete (PassList, 'Smith', Success);
  IF Success THEN
    WriteString ('Smith deleted.');  WriteLn;  WriteLn
  END; (* IF *)

  (* Display the passenger list. *)
```

```
  WriteString ('The ordered passenger list follows.');  WriteLn;
  Traverse (PassList, WritePass);
  WriteString ('The number of nodes in the list is ');
  WriteCard (SizeOfList(PassList), 2);  WriteLn
END BuildOrdList.
```

Figure 14.35 ▸ *Sample Run of Program in Fig. 14.34.*

```
Enter data for next passenger.
Passenger name: Jones
Class (F, B, E, S): E
Number of Seats (1 to 30): 3
Passenger inserted.

Enter data for next passenger.
Passenger name: Smith
Class (F, B, E, S): B
Number of Seats (1 to 30): 2
Passenger inserted.

Enter data for next passenger.
Passenger name: Jones
Class (F, B, E, S): F
Number of Seats (1 to 30): 1
Already booked - no insertion.

Enter data for next passenger.
Passenger name: Brown
Class (F, B, E, S): B
Number of Seats (1 to 30): 2
Passenger Inserted.

Smith deleted.

The ordered passenger list follows.
Brown
Business Class
  2 seats
Jones
Economy Class
  3 seats

The number of nodes in the list is 2
```

SELF-CHECK EXERCISES FOR SECTION 14.7

1. Write function procedure `SizeOfList` and procedures `Retrieve` and `Replace`.
2. In specifying the ordered list abstract data type, the assumption was made that there would be no insertion if the key of a new record was already present in the list. Modify procedure `Insert` in Fig. 14.28 to insert a record

with a duplicate key before the first record with that key currently in the list. Discuss what changes would be required to insert the new record after the last record with that key currently in the list.

3. The two dummy records (see Fig. 14.23) were placed in the list to ensure that there would be no need to insert a record into an empty list or in front of the first list node (i.e., all valid keys follow the key `MinKey` in the first dummy node). Discuss what changes would be necessary for `Locate`, `Insert`, and `Delete` if these nodes were not present.

14.8 Multiple-Linked Lists and Trees

All the examples seen so far have involved elements or nodes with a single pointer field. It is possible to have a list of elements with more than one link. For example, each element in the list below has a forward pointer that points to the next list element and a backward pointer that points to the previous list element. This allows us to traverse the list in either the left or right direction.

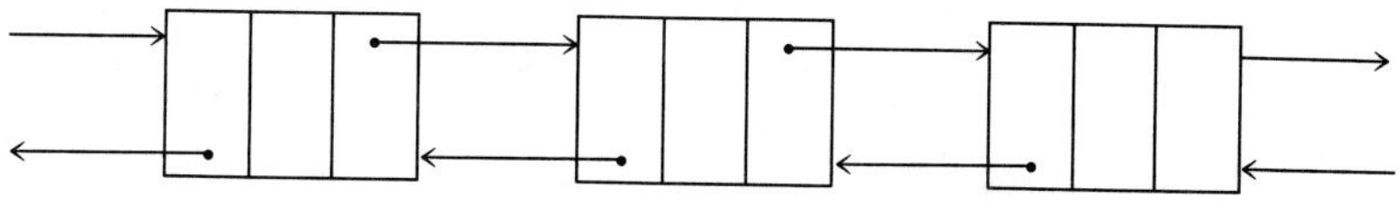

This structure is called a *doubly linked list*. The declarations below describe a general node of such a list.

```
TYPE
  MultiLink = POINTER TO MultiNode;
  MultiNode = RECORD
                .....
                .....  } Data Fields
                .....

                Left, Right : MultiLink
              END; (* MultiNode *)
```

Introduction to Trees

A special kind of multiple-linked list that has wide applicability in computer science is a data structure called a *tree*. A sample tree is in Fig. 14.36.

Trees in computer science actually grow from the top down rather than the ground up. The topmost element is called the *root of the tree*. The pointer, `Root`, points to the root of the tree in Fig. 14.36. Each tree node shown has a single data field and two pointer fields called the *left branch* and the *right branch*, respectively.

Figure 14.36 ▸
Tree

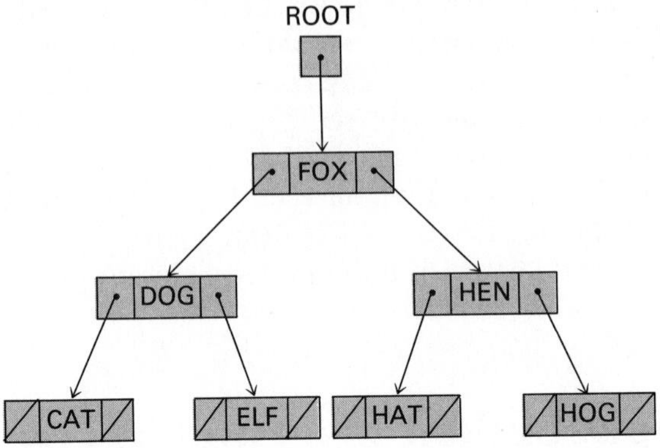

Family tree terminology is used to describe computer science trees. The node containing the string `'HEN'` is the *parent* of the nodes containing the strings `'HAT'` and `'HOG'`. Similarly, the nodes `'HAT'` and `'HOG'` are *siblings,* since they are both *children* of the same parent node. The root of the tree is an *ancestor* of all other nodes in the tree, and they in turn are all *descendants* of the root node.

Each node in a tree may be thought of as the root node of its own *subtree*. Since each node has two branches, it spawns two subtrees, a *left subtree* and a *right subtree*. Either one or both of these subtrees may be empty (denoted by a branch value of `NIL`). A node with two empty subtrees is called a *leaf node*. The *left (right) child* of a node is the root node of its left (right) subtree.

The following statements describe the form of a tree node in Fig. 14.36. Since each node can have at most two children, such a tree is called a *binary tree*.

```
TYPE
  Branch = POINTER TO TreeNode;
  TreeNode = RECORD
               Info : ARRAY [0..2] OF CHAR;
               Left, Right : Branch
             END; (* TreeNode *)
```

Field `Info` contains the data associated with the tree node, a string of three characters.

Trees may be used for representing expressions in memory. For example, the expression

```
(X + Y) * (A - B)
```

could be represented as the tree drawn in Fig. 14.37. This tree has the same shape as the one drawn in Fig. 14.36.

Figure 14.37 ▸ *Expression Stored in a Tree*

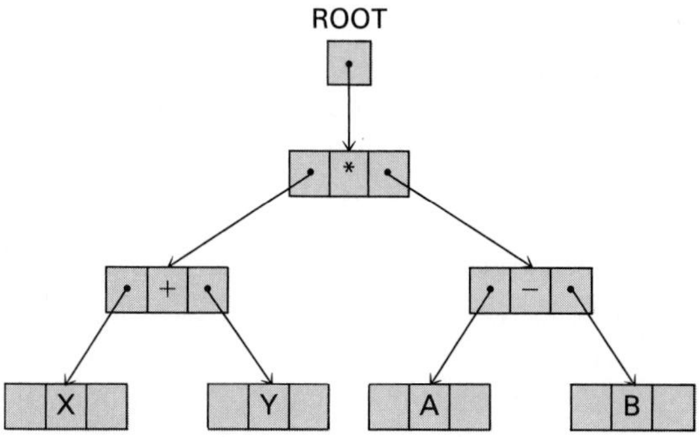

The root node contains the operator (*) that is evaluated last in the expression. Each subtree is also an expression and contains either the subexpression operator (+ or –) in its root or a variable (X, Y, A, or B). There are subtrees for the subexpressions (X + Y) and (A – B).

Trees are also used to organize related data items to facilitate efficient search and retrieval for a desired item. For example, the *binary search tree* shown in Fig. 14.36 is arranged so that the left child of each node alphabetically precedes its parent and the right child alphabetically follows its parent. Thus, in searching for a particular key at any level of this tree, the left subtree should be examined if the key value is "less than" the current node value, and the right subtree should be examined if the key value is "greater than" the current node value. (What if the key value equals the current node value?) This can reduce the search space by a factor of two each time, since all the descendants in the other subtree are ignored. Binary search trees will be discussed in detail later.

Traversing a Tree

To process the data stored in a tree, we need to be able to traverse the tree, or visit each node, in a systematic way. The first approach that will be illustrated is called an *inorder traversal*. The algorithm for an inorder traversal is described as follows:

Algorithm for Inorder Traversal

1. Traverse the left subtree.
2. Visit the root node.
3. Traverse the right subtree

You will recall that the left subtree of any node is the part of the tree whose root is the left child of that node. The inorder traversal for the tree shown in Fig. 14.36 would visit the nodes in the sequence

```
'CAT'  'DOG'  'ELF'  'FOX'  'HAT'  'HEN'  'HOG'
```

If we assume that each node's data are printed when it is visited, the strings will be printed in alphabetical order, as shown.

In Fig. 14.38, a numbered circle is drawn around each subtree. The subtrees are numbered in the order that they are traversed. Subtree 1 is the left subtree of the root node. Its left subtree (numbered 2) has no left subtree (or right subtree); thus, the string `'CAT'` would be printed first. The root node for subtree 1 would then be visited and `'DOG'` would be printed. Its right subtree consists of the leaf node containing the string `'ELF'` (number 3). After `'ELF'` is printed, the root node for the complete tree is visited (`'FOX'` is printed), and the right subtree of the root node (number 4) is traversed in a like manner.

Figure 14.38 ▸
Subtrees of a Tree

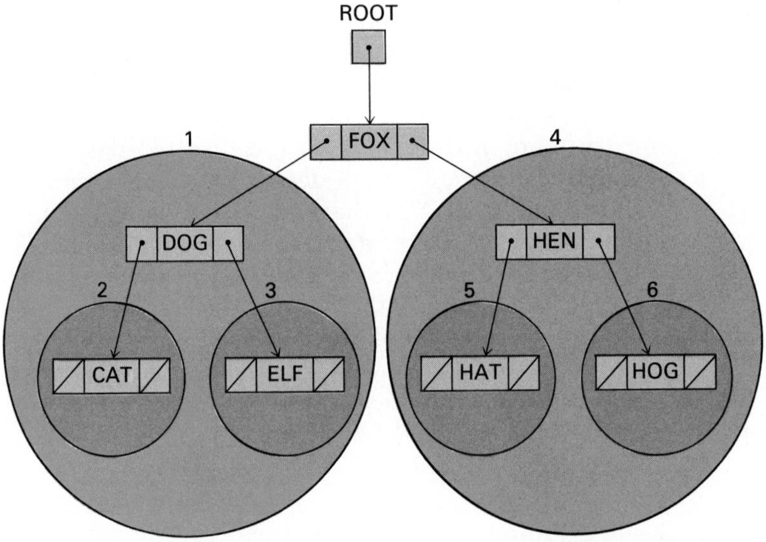

Procedure `Traverse` in Fig. 14.39 is a recursive procedure that performs an inorder traversal of a tree and displays each node's data. The parameter `Root` represents the pointer to the root node of the tree being traversed. If the tree is empty (root = `NIL`), an immediate return occurs. Procedure `Traverse`, like most procedures that process trees, can be written much more simply with recursion than without it.

Figure 14.39 ▸
Procedure Traverse

```
PROCEDURE Traverse (Root (* input *) : Branch);
(*
   Performs an inorder traversal of a binary tree.
   Pre : Root points to a binary tree or is NIL.
   Post: Displays each node visited.
*)
```

```
BEGIN (* Traverse *)
  IF Root # NIL THEN
    (* recursive step *)
    Traverse (Root^.Left);          (* traverse left subtree *)
    WriteString (Root^.Info);           (* print root value *)
    WriteLn;
    Traverse (Root^.Right)         (* traverse right subtree *)
  END (* recursive step *)
END Traverse;
```

As we saw earlier, an inorder traversal of the tree shown in Fig. 14.36 would visit the nodes in alphabetical sequence. If we performed an inorder traversal of the expression tree in Fig. 14.37, the nodes would be visited in the sequence

```
X + Y * A - B
```

Except for the absence of parentheses, this is the form in which we would normally write the expression. The expression above is called an *infix* expression, because each operator is in between its operands.

An easy way to determine the order in which the nodes of a tree are visited is to outline the contour of the tree, following all indentations as shown in Fig. 14.40. Move your finger along the tree contour, starting to the left of the root node. As your finger passes under a node (indicated by a colored arrow head), that node is visited in an inorder traversal.

Figure 14.40 ▸ *Outlining the Contour of a Tree*

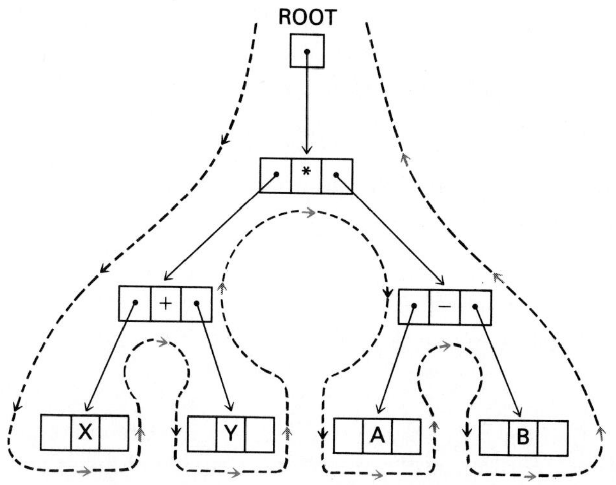

Switching the sequence of the three statements in the IF statement shown in Fig. 14.39 will produce rather different results. The sequence

```
WriteString (Root^.Info);      (* print root value *)
WriteLn;
Traverse (Root^.Left);      (* traverse left subtree *)
Traverse (Root^.Right)      (* traverse right subtree *)
```

displays the root node before traversing its subtrees; consequently, the data field of the root node will be displayed before the data fields of its subtrees. This is called a *preorder* traversal. The nodes in Fig. 14.36 would be visited in the sequence

```
FOX    DOG    CAT    ELF    HEN    HAT    HOG
```

The nodes in the expression tree in Fig. 14.37 are visited in the sequence shown below.

```
* + X Y - A B
```

The previous expression is called a *prefix* expression, because each operator precedes its operands. The operands of + are X and Y; the operands of – are A and B; the operands of * are the two triples + X Y and – A B.

To find the sequence in which the nodes are visited in a preorder traversal, trace the contour of the tree shown in Fig. 14.40. As your finger passes to the left of a node (indicated by black arrow head), that node is visited. Your finger should be moving in a downward direction when a node is visited.

Finally, the sequence

```
Traverse (Root^.Left);    (* traverse left subtree *)
Traverse (Root^.Right); (* traverse right subtree *)
WriteString (Root^.Info)      (* print root value *)
WriteLn;
```

displays the root node after traversing each of its subtrees; consequently, each root value will be printed after all values in its subtrees. This is called a *postorder* traversal. The nodes in Fig. 14.36 would be visited in the sequence

```
CAT    ELF    DOG    HAT    HOG    HEN    FOX
```

The nodes in the expression tree in Fig. 14.36 would be visited in the sequence

```
X Y + A B - *
```

The previous expression is called a *postfix* expression, because each operator follows its operands. The operands of + are X and Y; the operands of – are A and B; the operands of * are the two triples X Y + and A B –.

To find the sequence in which the nodes are visited in a postorder traversal, trace the contour of the tree shown in Fig. 14.40. As your finger passes to the right of a node (indicated by grey arrow head), that node is visited. Your finger should be moving in an upward direction when a node is visited.

Note that for all three methods the left subtree is always traversed before the right subtree.

SELF-CHECK EXERCISES FOR SECTION 14.8

1. Draw the binary tree representation of the following expressions.

```
X * Y / (A + B) * C
X * Y / A + B * C
```

2. What would be printed by the inorder, preorder, and postorder traversals of the following tree?

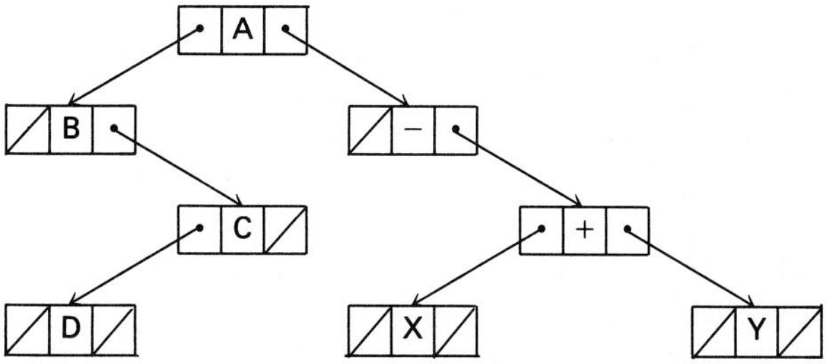

14.9 Binary Search Tree Abstract Data Type

We mentioned earlier that the tree in Fig. 14.36 is a binary search tree. A binary search tree has the property that for any node, all key values less than that node's key value are in its left subtree and all key values greater than that node's key value are in its right subtree.

Trying to locate an item in a binary search tree is analogous to performing a binary search on an array that has already been sorted. To find a particular item, we compare its key (the target key) to the key of the root node. If the target key is less than the root key, we can eliminate the right subtree and search only the left subtree, thereby cutting the number of nodes to be searched in half. For this reason, the binary tree search is an $O(\log_2 n)$ algorithm. The algorithm for searching a binary tree follows.

Algorithm for Binary Tree Search

1. `IF` the tree is empty `THEN`
    2. The target key is not in the tree.

   `ELSIF` the target key matches the root key `THEN`

3. The target key is found in the root node.
ELSIF the target key is larger than the root key THEN
4. Search the right subtree.
ELSE
5. Search the left subtree.
END (* IF *)

Steps 2 and 3 are stopping steps. We will implement this algorithm in the next section.

Implementing the Binary Search Tree Abstract Data Type

The binary search tree abstract data type must include the same operators as for the ordered list abstract data type discussed earlier. The following operations must be performed: create an empty tree, search for a target key, insert a node, delete a node, retrieve a node, replace a node, traverse the tree, and return its size.

Space precludes us from covering the binary search tree abstract data type with the same thoroughness as the ordered list. We will simply state that its definition module is similar to the one shown in Fig. 14.21. Rather than provide the complete implementation module, we will implement three of its operators, `CreateTree`, `Search`, and `Insert`.

We will assume the following data structure for the search tree.

```
TYPE
  Branch = POINTER TO TreeNode;
  TreeNode = RECORD
               Item : Element;
               Left, Right : Branch
             END; (* TreeNode *)

  SearchTree = POINTER TO TreeObject;
  TreeObject = RECORD
                 Root : Branch;
                 NumItems : CARDINAL
               END; (* TreeObject *)
```

Each node of the tree consists of a field `Item` (type `Element`) containing a key (type `KeyType`) and two pointers, `Left` and `Right` (type `Branch`). Data types `Element` and `KeyType` are imported from module `ElementType`. The field `Root` (type `Branch`) points to the root of the tree.

Procedure `CreateTree` is shown in Fig. 14.41. It simply creates a record of type `TreeObject` with a `Root` field of `NIL` and a count field (`NumItems`) of zero. The result of `CreateTree (MyTree)` follows.

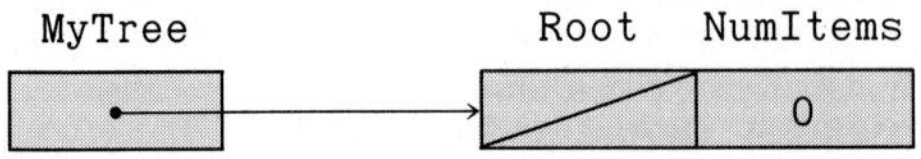

Figure 14.41 ▸ *Procedure CreateTree*

```
PROCEDURE CreateTree (VAR Tree (* output *) : SearchTree);
(*
   Creates an empty tree. Must be called first.
   Pre : None
   Post: Tree points to the header node for a binary tree.
*)
BEGIN (* CreateTree *)
  NEW (Tree);
  Tree^.Root := NIL;
  Tree^.NumItems := 0
END CreateTree;
```

Procedure `Search` is shown in Fig. 14.42. It starts the search at the tree root by calling `DoSearch` with a parameter of `Tree^.Root`. `DoSearch` implements the recursive algorithm shown earlier. In `DoSearch`, we are assuming that the key field is type `KeyType` and that procedures `ExtractKey` and `Bigger` are used to extract and compare keys (see Fig. 14.33).

Figure 14.42 ▸ *Procedure Search*

```
PROCEDURE Search (Tree (* input *) : SearchTree;
                  Target (* input *) : KeyType;
                  VAR Success (* output *) : BOOLEAN);
(*
   Searches for Target in a binary search tree.
   Pre : Tree points to the header node of a binary search tree.
   Post: If Target is located, Success is TRUE;
         otherwise, Success is FALSE.
*)
   PROCEDURE DoSearch (Parent (* input *) : Branch;
                       Target (* input *) : KeyType;
                       VAR Success (* output *) : BOOLEAN);
   (*
      Searches the subtree pointed to by Parent.
      Pre : Target and Parent are defined.
      Post: If Target is not found, Success is FALSE; otherwise,
            Success is TRUE.
      Uses: ExtractKey, Bigger from ElementType
   *)
      VAR
        NextKey : KeyType;        (* key of node Parent^ *)

   BEGIN (* DoSearch *)
     IF Parent = NIL THEN
       Success := FALSE              (* tree is empty *)
     ELSE
       ExtractKey (Parent^.Item, NextKey);
```

```
        IF Bigger(Target, NextKey) THEN
          DoSearch (Parent^.Right, Target, Success)
        ELSIF Bigger(NextKey, Target) THEN
          DoSearch (Parent^.Left, Target, Success)
        ELSE (* Target = NextKey *)
          Success := TRUE
        END (* IF *)
      END (* IF *)
    END DoSearch;

BEGIN (* Search *)
    DoSearch (Tree^.Root, Target, Success)
END Search;
```

Finally, procedure `Insert` is shown in Fig. 14.43. It stores the key of `El` in `ElKey`. Then it calls `DoInsert` to perform a recursive search for `ElKey`, starting at the tree root. There are two stopping states for the recursion. If `DoInsert` passes a leaf node (both pointers `NIL`) without finding `ElKey`, it attaches a new node to the leaf node, stores `El` in the new node, and sets `Success` to `TRUE` before returning. If `DoInsert` finds `ElKey` in the tree, it sets `Success` to `FALSE` and returns. Otherwise, `DoInsert` calls itself recursively to process the left subtree or right subtree of its current tree. After the return from the original call to `DoInsert`, procedure `Insert` increments the count of tree nodes if the insertion was performed.

Figure 14.43 ▸
Procedure Insert

```
PROCEDURE Insert (VAR Tree (* in/out *) : SearchTree;
                  El (* input *) : Element;
                  VAR Success (* in/out *) : BOOLEAN);
(*
   Inserts item El into a binary tree.
   Pre : El is defined and Tree points to the header node of a tree.
   Post: Success is TRUE if the insertion is performed. If there is
         a node with the same key value as El, Success is FALSE.
*)
   VAR
     ElKey : KeyType;            (* key of record El *)

   PROCEDURE DoInsert (VAR Parent (* in/out *) : Branch;
                       El (* input *) : Element;
                       ElKey (* input *) : KeyType;
                       VAR Success (* in/out *) : BOOLEAN);
```

```
    (* Inserts item El in the subtree with root Parent. *)

      VAR
        NextKey : KeyType;        (* key of Parent^ *)

    BEGIN (* DoInsert *)
      (* Check for empty tree. *)
      IF Parent = NIL THEN
        (* Attach new node containing El to Parent *)
        NEW (Parent);
        Parent^.Left := NIL;
        Parent^.Right := NIL;
        Parent^.Item := El;
        Success := TRUE
      ELSE (* search for correct insertion point *)
        ExtractKey (Parent^.Item, NextKey);
        IF Bigger(ElKey, NextKey) THEN
          DoInsert (Parent^.Right, El, ElKey, Success)
        ELSIF Bigger(NextKey, ElKey) THEN
          DoInsert (Parent^.Left, El, ElKey, Success)
        ELSE (* ElKey is in tree *)
          Success := FALSE
        END (* IF *)
      END (* IF *)
    END DoInsert;

BEGIN (* Insert *)
  ExtractKey (El, ElKey);                  (* get key *)
  DoInsert (Tree^.Root, El, ElKey, Success);
  IF Success THEN
    INC (Tree^.NumItems)                   (* new node in tree *)
  END (* IF *)
END Insert;
```

Analysis of Binary Tree Search and Insert

The order in which data items are stored in a binary tree has a profound effect on the efficiency of the search and insert algorithms discussed in the last section. For example, if the data words arrive in the sequence `'FOX'`, `'DOG'`, `'CAT'`, `'HEN'`, `'HOG'`, `'HAT'`, `'ELF'`, the result is the nicely balanced binary tree shown earlier in Fig. 14.36. Verify this by tracing the incomplete trees that are formed as each word is inserted. This trace is shown in Fig. 14.44. The pointers passed as parameters to procedure `DoInsert` are shown in color in each tree diagram. The lowest level pointer points to the word being inserted.

Figure 14.44 ▸ *Building a Binary Search Tree*

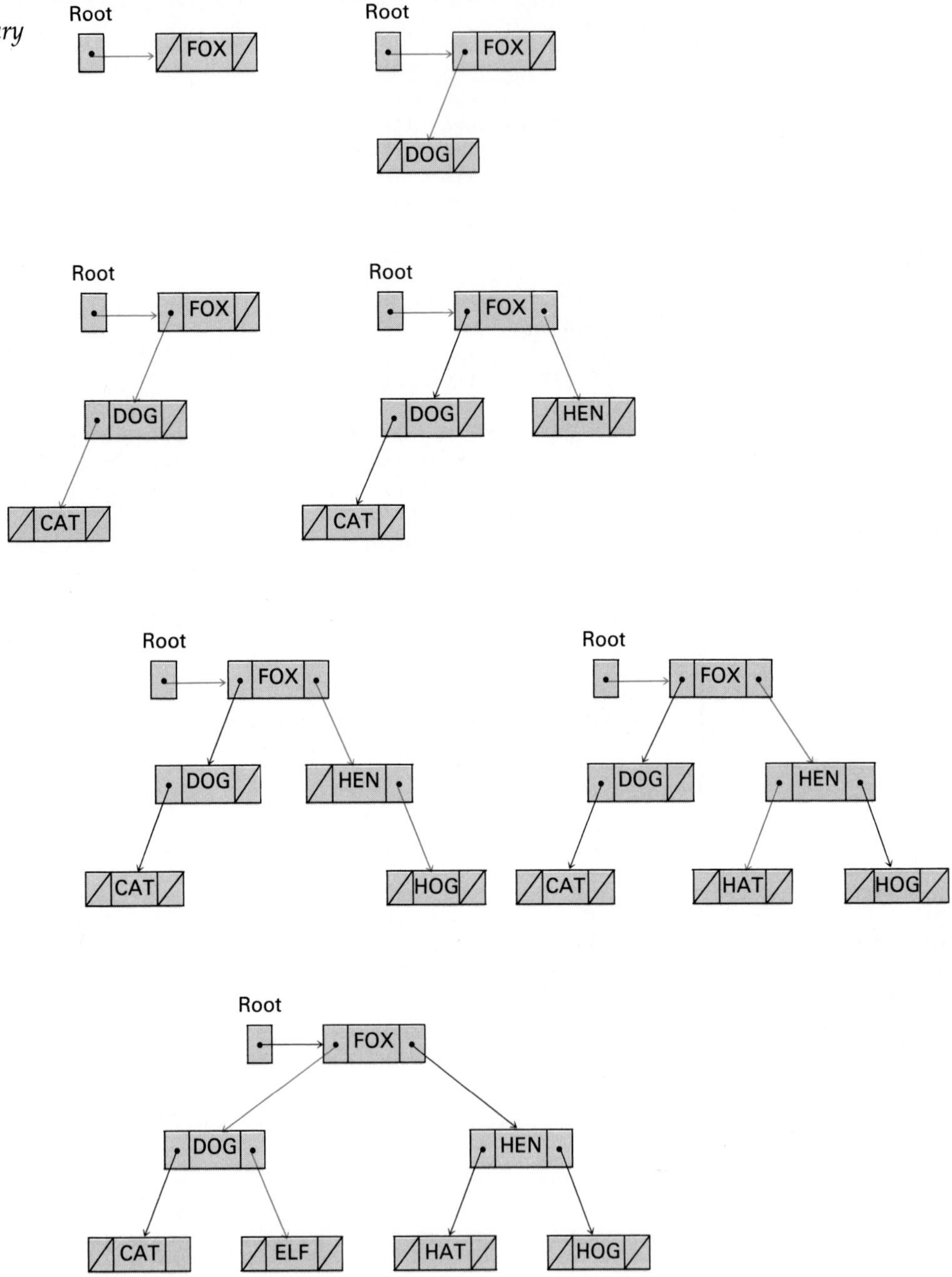

Since the tree is nicely balanced, search and insert operations are performed in time proportional to $O(\log_2 n)$. However, if the data words arrive in the sequence `'CAT'`, `'DOG'`, `'ELF'`, `'FOX'`, `'HAT'`, `'HEN'`, `'HOG'`, the result is the very unbalanced tree shown in Fig. 14.45, which resembles an ordered linked list. In this case, search and insert operations are performed in time proportional to $O(n)$.

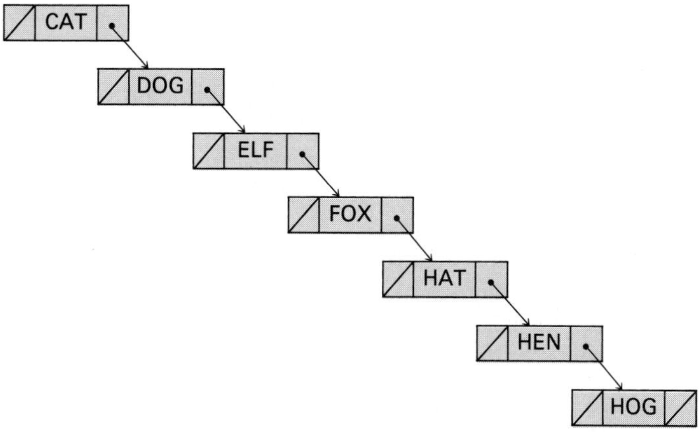

Figure 14.45 ▸ *An Unbalanced Tree*

Given the random nature of data to be inserted in a tree, the actual situation will be somewhere between the best and worst cases illustrated above. Although beyond the scope of this text, there are algorithms that maintain tree balance by switching the positions of data items in tree nodes as the tree is formed.

SELF-CHECK EXERCISE FOR SECTION 14.9

1. Write procedures `Traverse` for the search tree abstract data type. `Traverse` should have parameters for type `SearchTree` and `VisitType` (see Fig. 14.21) and perform an in-order traversal.

14.10 Common Programming Errors

When processing linked data structures, make sure that the pointer to the next node is not `NIL`. If pointer `Next` has the value `NIL`, the record `Next^` is undefined. Therefore, the condition

```
(Next^.ID # 9999) & (Next # NIL)
```

will lead to an execution error when `Next` is `NIL`, whereas the logically equivalent condition

```
(Next # NIL) & (Next^.ID # 9999)
```

will not lead to an error because of short-circuit evaluation.

If your program gets stuck in an infinite loop while creating a dynamic data structure, it is possible to consume all memory cells on the storage heap. This situation will lead to a "heap overflow" run-time error.

Debugging Tips

Because the value of a pointer variable cannot be printed, it is difficult to debug programs that manipulate pointers. You will have to trace the execution of such a program by printing an information field that uniquely identifies the list element being processed instead of the pointer value itself.

When you are writing driver programs, it is often helpful to create a sample linked structure using the technique discussed in Section 14.1. The data and pointer fields of the structure can be defined using assignment statements.

14.11 Chapter Review

This chapter introduced several dynamic data structures. We discussed the use of pointers to reference and connect elements of a dynamic data structure. The procedure `NEW` was used to allocate additional elements or nodes of a dynamic data structure.

Many different aspects of manipulating linked lists were covered. We showed how to build or create a linked list, how to traverse a linked list, and how to insert and delete elements of a linked list.

We revisited stacks and queues and showed how to implement them as linked data structures. We provided new implementation modules using linked lists for the abstract data types stack and queue.

We discussed techniques for maintaining an ordered collection of records and studied two data structures for this purpose. We provided definition and implementation modules for the first data structure, the ordered list. We showed how to write similar operators for the second, the binary search tree.

Finally, we discussed binary trees in general and showed how they could be used to represent expressions in memory. We discussed the differences between inorder, preorder, and postorder traversal and related these three methods to infix, prefix, and postfix expressions.

New Modula-2 Statements

The new Modula-2 statements introduced in this chapter are described in Table 14.1.

Table 14.1 ▸ *Summary of New Modula-2 Statements*

STATEMENT	EFFECT
DISPOSE Procedure	
`DISPOSE (Head)`	The memory space occupied by the record `Head^` is returned to the storage pool.
Pointer Assignment	
`Head := Head^.Link`	If `Head` is a pointer and `Link` is a pointer field, `Head` is advanced to the next node in the dynamic data structure pointed to by `Head`.
Functions Available and TSIZE	
`Available(TSIZE(Node))`	Returns `TRUE` if the number of cells in the storage heap is sufficient to allocate a record of type `Node`.

CHAPTER 14 ▸

Review Questions

1. Differentiate between dynamic and nondynamic data structures.
2. Define a simple linked list. Indicate how the pointers are utilized to establish a link between nodes. Also indicate any other variables that would be needed to reference the linked list.
3. Write a procedure that will link a node to an existing list. Parameters will be a pointer to the head of the linked list and a pointer to the node to be inserted. Assume dummy sentinel records exist at the beginning and end of the linked list and that there are no duplicate records.

   Given the following record definition, insert the new element preserving `ID` order:

```
TYPE
  String10 = ARRAY [0..9] of CHAR;
  PTR = POINTER TO Node;
  Node = RECORD
           ID : INTEGER;
           Name : String10;
           GPA : REAL;
           Link : PTR
         END;
```

4. Write an algorithm to remove a node (identified by `TargetID`) from an ordered list that does not contain a dummy mode at the beginning.
5. Write the necessary procedures to duplicate all elements with a grade point average (GPA) of 3.5 or above in one linked list in another linked list. The original

list is ordered by ID number; the new list should be ordered by GPA. Do not remove nodes from the existing list. Assume the list nodes are type Node as described in question 3.

Parameters will be a pointer to the head of the existing list and to the head of the new linked list (GPAHead).

6. Declare a node for a two-way or doubly linked list and indicate how a traversal would be made in reverse order (from the last list element to the list head). Include any necessary variables or fields.
7. Discuss the differences between a simple linked list and a binary tree. Consider such things as numbers of pointer fields per node, search technique, and insertion algorithm.
8. Write a procedure to delete all males over 25 from an existing linear linked list, given the following declarations (assume no dummy records).

```
TYPE
  PTR = POINTER TO Node;
  Node = RECORD
    Name : String10;
    Age : INTEGER;
    Sex : (Male, Female);
    Link : PTR
END;
```

The procedure parameter is a pointer to the head of the list.

9. How can you determine whether a node is a leaf?
10. Traverse the tree below in inorder, preorder, and postorder.

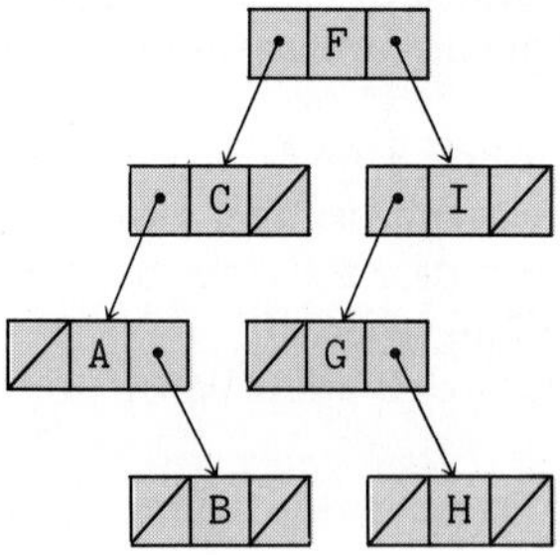

Provide one sequence that would create this ordered binary tree. Are there any letters that must occur before other letters?

11. Discuss how you might delete a node from a binary tree. Consider nodes with zero or one child first.

CHAPTER 14 ▸ Programming Projects

1. Complete the implementation module for an ordered list shown in Section 14.7. Use this abstract data type to maintain an airline passenger list. The main program

should be menu driven and should allow its user to display the data for a particular passenger, display the entire list, create a list, insert a node, delete a node, and replace the data for a particular passenger.

2. Redo project 1 using a binary search tree for storage of the airline passenger list. When deleting a node, simply change the number of seats assigned to zero and leave the passenger's node in the tree.

3. The set capability is limited in the number of elements that can be stored in a set (often only sixteen). A more universal system can be implemented using list representation to store sets.
   Write the necessary routines needed to insert and delete integer values from a set. Also, write the routines necessary to implement the set difference, intersection, and union operations. To verify the results, display the contents of the sets before and after each operation.

4. When you are preparing mailing lists, it is often useful to be able to reference the information by using either the person's name or zip code. This can be done if each list node has a pointer to the next node by name and a pointer to the next node by zip code. The nodes representing each person's data should be linked together in both name and zip code order; there should be only one copy of the data for each person. Provide a header node that has pointers to the first element in each of the two lists.
   Write a program that reads a record containing first name (`String15`), last name (`String15`), street address (`String50`), city (`String20`), state (`String2`), and zip code (`String6`) and connects each new record to the appropriate nodes of both lists. After all the information has been entered, display a list of the information in name order and a second list in zip code order.

5. In this chapter, we wrote recursive procedures to perform preorder, inorder, and postorder tree traversals. A tree traversal can be written without using recursion. In this case, it is necessary to push the address of a tree node that is reached during the traversal onto a stack. The node will be popped off later when it is time to traverse the tree rooted at this node. For example, the algorithm for a nonrecursive preorder traversal follows.

```
1. Push NIL onto the stack.
2. Assign the root node as the current node.
3. WHILE the current node is not NIL DO
     4. Print the current node.
     5. IF the current node has a right subtree THEN
          Push the right subtree root onto the stack.
        END (* IF *)
     6. IF the current node has a left subtree THEN
          Make it the current node
        ELSE
          Pop the stack and make the node removed the current node.
        END (* IF *)
   END (* WHILE *)
```

In this algorthim, each right subtree pointer that is not NIL is pushed onto the stack; the stack is popped when the current left subtree pointer is NIL.

Implement and test a nonrecursive procedure for preorder traversal. Write a nonrecursive algorithm for inorder traversal and implement and test it as well.

6. If an arithmetic expression is written in prefix or postfix notation, there is no need to use parentheses to specify the order of operator evaluation. For this reason, some compilers translate infix expressions to postfix notation first and then evaluate the postfix string.

   Write a procedure that simulates the operation of a calculator. The input will consist of an expression in postfix notation. The operands will all be single-digit numbers. Your program should print the expression value. For example, if the input string is '54+3/', the result printed should be three (the value of (5 + 4) / 3).

   To accomplish this, examine each character in the string in left-to-right order. If the character is a digit, push its numeric value onto a stack. If the character is an operator, pop the top two operands, apply the operator to them, and push the result onto the stack. When the string is completely scanned, there should be only one number on the stack and that should be the expression value. Besides the operators +,–,*, and /, use the operator ^ to indicate exponentiation.

7. A polynomial can be represented as a linked list where each node contains the coefficient and exponent of a term of the polynomial. The polynomial $4x^3 + 3x^2 - 5$ would be represented as the following linked list.

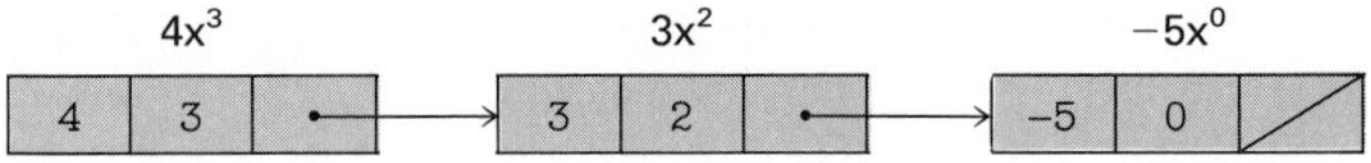

   Write an abstract data type for polynomials that has operators for creating a polynomial, reading a polynomial, and adding and subtracting a pair of polynomials. Hint: To add or subtract two polynomials, traverse both lists. If a particular exponent value is present in either one, then it should be present in the result polynomial unless its coefficient is zero.

8. Since the students in a university take a varying number of courses, the registrar has decided to use a linked list to store each student's class schedule and an array of records to represent the whole student body. A portion of this data structure follows.

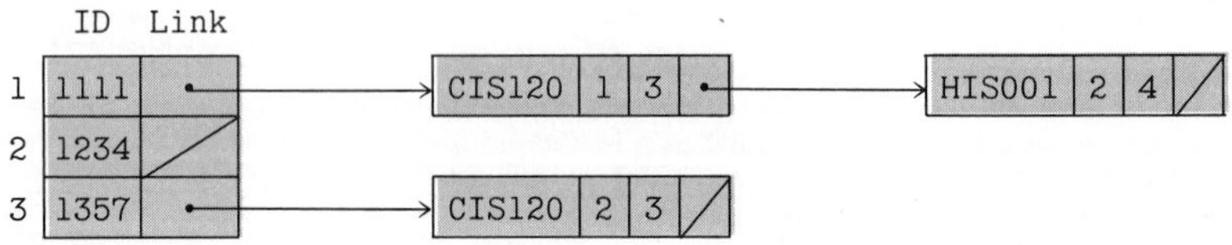

The records show that the first student (ID is 1111) is taking section 1 of CIS120 for 3 credits and section 2 of HIS001 for 4 credits; the second student (ID is 1234) is not currently enrolled, and so on. Write an abstract data type for this data structure. Provide operators for creating the original array of student ID numbers, inserting a student's initial class schedule, adding a course, and dropping a course. Write a menu-driven program that uses this abstract data type.

Appendix A
Reserved Words, Standard Identifiers, Operators and Delimiters, Predefined Procedures and Functions

Reserved Words

AND	LOOP
ARRAY	MOD
BEGIN	MODULE
BY	NOT
CASE	OF
CONST	OR
DEFINITION	POINTER
DIV	PROCEDURE
DO	QUALIFIED
ELSE	RECORD
ELSIF	REPEAT
END	RETURN
EXIT	SET
EXPORT	THEN
FOR	TO
FROM	TYPE
IF	UNTIL
IMPLEMENTATION	VAR
IMPORT	WHILE
IN	WITH

Standard Identifiers

ABS	CARDINAL
BITSET	CHAR
BOOLEAN	CHR
CAP	DEC

DISPOSE	NEW
EXCL	NIL
FALSE	ODD
FLOAT	ORD
HALT	PROC
HIGH	REAL
INC	TRUE
INCL	TRUNC
INTEGER	VAL

Operators and Delimiters

+	unary plus, addition, set union
−	unary minus, subtraction, set difference
*	multiplication, set intersection
/	real division, symmetric set difference
:=	assignment
&	logical and
=	equal
<>	not equal
#	not equal
<	less than
<=	less than or equal
>	greater than
>=	greater than or equal
(,)	parentheses for expressions and parameter lists
[,]	array subscript brackets
{ , }	set braces
(* , *)	comment delimiters
..	subrange delimiter
.	qualified identifier delimiter
,	list delimiter
;	statement separator, parameter list delimiter
:	type delimiter
|	CASE alternative delimiter
^	dereference delimiter

Predefined Procedures and Functions

Function	*Description*
ABS(*x*)	absolute value function; *x* is numeric
CAP(*c*)	capitalization function; *c* is a character
CHR(*n*)	character transfer function; *n* is a cardinal number

`DEC` (*x*)	decrement procedure; *x* is an ordinal value,
`DEC` (*x*, *n*)	*n* is a cardinal number
`DISPOSE` (*p*)	storage deallocation procedure; *p* is a pointer
`EXCL` (*s*, *x*)	exclude procedure; *s* is a set, *x* is an element of the base type of the set
`FLOAT`(*n*)	real conversion function; *n* is a cardinal number
`HALT`	halt procedure
`INC` (*x*)	increment procedure; *x* is an ordinal value,
`INC` (*x*, *n*)	*n* is a cardinal number
`INCL` (*s*, *x*)	include procedure; *s* is a set, *x* is an element of the base type of the set
`NEW` (*p*)	storage allocation procedure; *p* is a pointer
`ODD`(*n*)	odd function; *n* is an integer or cardinal number
`ORD`(*x*)	ordinal number function; *x* is an ordinal value
`TRUNC`(*r*)	truncate function; *r* is a nonnegative real
`VAL`(*t*, *n*)	value transfer function; *t* is an ordinal type identifier, *n* is a cardinal number

Appendix B
Standard Module Definitions

This appendix provides abbreviated definition modules for some of the standard modules of Modula-2. Included are modules `InOut`, `RealInOut`, `Mathlib0`, `Strings`, `Storage`, and SYSTEM.

```
DEFINITION MODULE InOut;
(*
   Performs high-level formatted input/output,
   allowing for redirection to/from files
*)

   EXPORT QUALIFIED
     EOL, Done, termCH, Read, ReadString, ReadInt, ReadCard,
     Write, WriteLn, WriteString, WriteInt, WriteCard, WriteOct,
     OpenInput, OpenOutput, CloseInput, CloseOutput;

   CONST
     EOL = 36C;  (* end-of-line character *)

   VAR
     Done : BOOLEAN;  (* flag indicating result of an operation *)
     termCH : CHAR;   (* character terminating a read operation *)

   PROCEDURE Read (VAR ch  : CHAR);
   (*
      Reads the next data character into ch.  Done is set to TRUE
      unless the input file is positioned beyond its last character.
   *)

   PROCEDURE ReadString (VAR s : ARRAY OF CHAR);
   (*
      Reads a string into s.
      Leading blanks are accepted and thrown away, then
      characters are read into s until a blank or control
      character is entered. ReadString truncates the input
      string if it is too long for s.  The terminating
      character is left in termCH.  If input is from the
      terminal, BS (backspace) and DEL (delete) are allowed for editing.
   *)

   PROCEDURE ReadInt (VAR x : INTEGER);
   (*
      Reads an INTEGER representation into x.
```

```
   ReadInt is like ReadString, but the string is converted to
   an INTEGER value if possible.  The first non-blank may be "+",
   "-", or a digit.  The remaining characters must be digits.
   Done is set to TRUE if some conversion was performed.
*)

PROCEDURE ReadCard (VAR x : CARDINAL);
(*
   Reads an unsigned decimal number into x.
   ReadCard is like ReadInt, but the first non-blank
   character must be a digit.
*)

PROCEDURE Write (ch : CHAR);
(* Writes the character in ch. *)

PROCEDURE WriteLn;
(* Writes an end-of-line sequence. *)

PROCEDURE WriteString (s : ARRAY OF CHAR);
(* Writes the string in s. *)

PROCEDURE WriteInt (x : INTEGER; n : CARDINAL);
(*
   Writes the integer in x in right-justified decimal format.
   The decimal representation of x (including '-' if x is
   negative) is written using n characters and
   more if needed.  Leading blanks are written if necessary.
*)

PROCEDURE WriteCard (x, n : CARDINAL);
(*
   Writes the cardinal number in x in decimal format.
   The decimal representation of the value x is written,
   using n characters and more if needed.
   Leading blanks are written if necessary.
*)

PROCEDURE WriteOct (x, n : CARDINAL);
(*
   Writes the cardinal number in x in octal format.
   [see WriteCard above]
*)

PROCEDURE OpenInput (defext : ARRAY OF CHAR);
(*
   Accepts a file name from the terminal and opens it for
   input.  If the file name that is read doesn't have an extension,
   then defext is appended to the file name.
   If OpenInput succeeds, Done is set to TRUE and subsequent
   input is taken from the file until CloseInput is called.
```

```
   *)

   PROCEDURE OpenOutput (defext : ARRAY OF CHAR);
   (*
      Accepts a file name from the terminal and opens it for
      output.  If the file name that is read doesn't have an
      extension, then defext is appended to the file name.
      If OpenOutput succeeds, Done is set to TRUE and subsequent
      output is written to the file until CloseOutput is called.
   *)

   PROCEDURE CloseInput;
   (* Closes current input file and reverts to terminal for input. *)

   PROCEDURE CloseOutput;
   (* Closes current output file and reverts to terminal for output. *)

END InOut.
```

```
DEFINITION MODULE RealInOut;
(* Performs input/output of type REAL values. *)

   EXPORT QUALIFIED
     ReadReal, WriteReal, WriteRealOct, Done;

   VAR Done: BOOLEAN;  (* flag indicating success or failure of read *)

   PROCEDURE ReadReal (VAR x : REAL);
   (*
      Reads a real number into x, skipping over leading
      blanks.  Data entry terminates when a control character
      or space is read.  DEL (delete) or BS (backspace) is used for
      backspacing.  The variable Done indicates whether a valid number
      was read.
   *)

   PROCEDURE WriteReal (x : REAL; n : CARDINAL);
   (*
      Writes the type REAL value of x right-justified in n columns.
      If fewer than n characters are needed, leading blanks are
      displayed.  More characters will be displayed if needed.
   *)

   PROCEDURE WriteRealOct (x : REAL);
   (* Writes the type REAL value of x in octal form. *)

END RealInOut.
```

```
DEFINITION MODULE MathLib0;

(* Real Math Functions *)

   EXPORT QUALIFIED
     sqrt, exp, ln, sin, cos, arctan, real, entier;

   PROCEDURE sqrt (x : REAL): REAL;
   (* Returns the square root of x.  The argument x must be positive. *)

   PROCEDURE exp (x : REAL): REAL;
   (* Returns e^x where e = 2.71828. *)

   PROCEDURE ln (x : REAL): REAL;
   (*
      Returns the natural logarithm with base e = 2.71828... of x.
      The argument x must be positive and not zero
   *)

   PROCEDURE sin (x : REAL): REAL;
   (* Returns sin(x) where x is given in radians. *)

   PROCEDURE cos (x : REAL): REAL;
   (* Returns cos(x) where x is given in radians. *)

   PROCEDURE arctan (x : REAL): REAL;
   (* Returns arctan(x) in radians. *)

   PROCEDURE real (x : INTEGER): REAL;
   (* Returns the real number equivalent in value to the integer x. *)

   PROCEDURE entier (x : REAL): INTEGER;
   (* Returns the largest integer less than or equal to x. *)

END MathLib0.
```

```
DEFINITION MODULE Strings;
(*
   Processes variable-length character strings.  If the user does not
   provide a variable large enough to contain the result of a string
   operation, truncation may result without any error notification.
   String variables have the following characteristics:
   - They are of type ARRAY OF CHAR.
   - The array lower bound must be zero.
   - The length of the string is the size of the string
     variable, unless a null character (0C) occurs in
     the string to indicate end of string.
*)
```

```
EXPORT QUALIFIED
  Assign, Insert, Delete,
  Pos, Copy, Concat, Length, CompareStr;

PROCEDURE Assign (VAR source, dest : ARRAY OF CHAR);
(*
   Assigns the contents of string variable source to
   string variable dest.
*)

PROCEDURE Insert (substr : ARRAY OF CHAR;
                  VAR str : ARRAY OF CHAR;
                  inx : CARDINAL);
(*
   Inserts the string substr into str, starting at str[inx].
   If inx is greater than or equal to Length(str), substr
   is appended to the end of str.
*)

PROCEDURE Delete (VAR str : ARRAY OF CHAR;
                  inx,
                  len : CARDINAL);
(*
   Deletes len characters from str, starting at str[inx].
   If inx >= Length(str) then nothing happens.  If there are
   not len characters to delete, all characters to the end of the
   string are deleted.
*)

PROCEDURE Pos (substr, str : ARRAY OF CHAR) : CARDINAL;
(*
   Returns the index in str of the first occurrence of substr.
   Pos returns a value greater than HIGH(str) if no
   occurrence of the substring substr is found.
*)

PROCEDURE  Copy (str : ARRAY OF CHAR;
                 inx,
                 len : CARDINAL;
                 VAR result : ARRAY OF CHAR);
(*
   Copies at most len characters from str into result, starting at
   index inx in str.
*)

PROCEDURE Concat (s1, s2 : ARRAY OF CHAR;
                  VAR result : ARRAY OF CHAR);
(* Stores s1 concatenated with s2 in result. *)

PROCEDURE Length (VAR str : ARRAY OF CHAR) : CARDINAL;
(* Returns the number of characters in string str. *)
```

```
   PROCEDURE CompareStr (s1, s2 : ARRAY OF CHAR) : INTEGER;
   (*
      Compares strings s1 and s2.
      Returns an integer value indicating the comparison result:
       -1 if s1 is less than s2;
        0 if s1 equals s2;
        1 if s1 is greater than s2
   *)

END Strings.
```

```
DEFINITION MODULE Storage;
(*
    Provides storage management for dynamic variables. Calls
    to the Modula-2 standard procedures NEW and DISPOSE are
    translated into calls to ALLOCATE and DEALLOCATE.
*)

    FROM SYSTEM IMPORT ADDRESS;

    EXPORT QUALIFIED
      ALLOCATE, DEALLOCATE, Available;

    PROCEDURE ALLOCATE (VAR a : ADDRESS; size : CARDINAL);
    (*
       Allocates size bytes of dynamic storage.  Returns the address
       of this storage in a.
    *)

    PROCEDURE DEALLOCATE (VAR a : ADDRESS; size : CARDINAL);
    (* Releases size bytes of dynamic storage located at address a. *)

    PROCEDURE Available (size : CARDINAL)  : BOOLEAN;
    (*
       Tests whether size bytes could be allocated.  Returns TRUE if
       space is available; otherwise, returns FALSE.
    *)

END Storage.
```

```
DEFINITION MODULE SYSTEM;

(* Performs system level operations. *)

   TYPE
     WORD;                          (* a memory storage cell *)
     ADDRESS = POINTER TO WORD;     (* memory address *)
```

```
    PROCEDURE ADR (VAR x : anytype) : ADDRESS;
    (* Returns the memory address of variable x of type anytype. *)

    PROCEDURE SIZE (VAR x : anytype) : CARDINAL;
    (*
       Returns the number of bytes of storage allocated to
       variable x of type anytype.
    *)

    PROCEDURE TSIZE (anytype) : CARDINAL;
    (*
       Returns the number of bytes of storage allocated to
       variables of type anytype.
    *)

END SYSTEM.
```

Appendix C
Modula-2 Syntax Diagrams

compilation unit

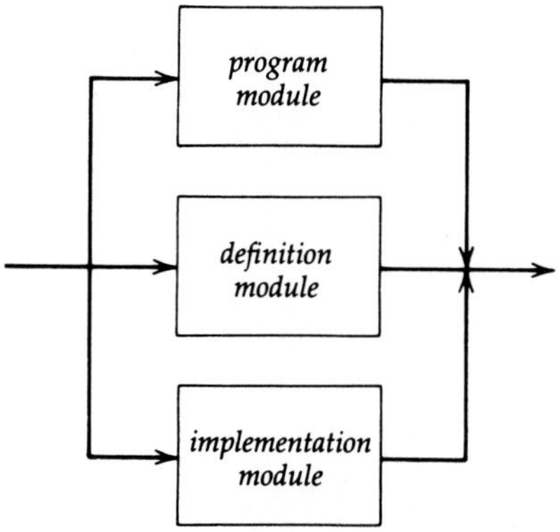

program module

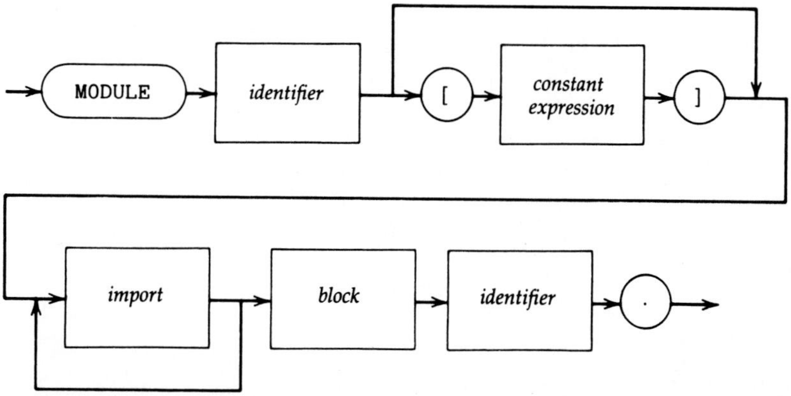

"The syntax diagrams in this appendix are from: Ford, G. A. and Wiener, R. S.: Modula-2: A Software Development Approach. Copyright © 1985 by John Wiley and Sons, Inc. Reprinted by permission of John Wiley and Sons, Inc."

definition module

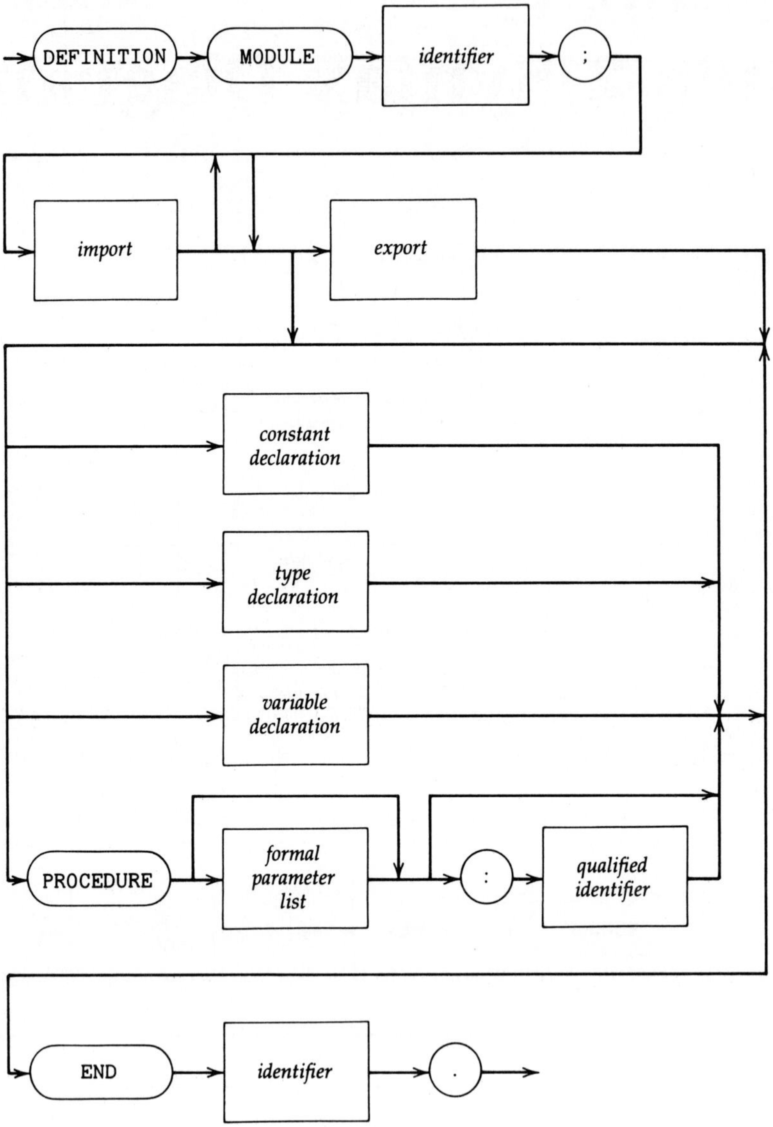

implementation module

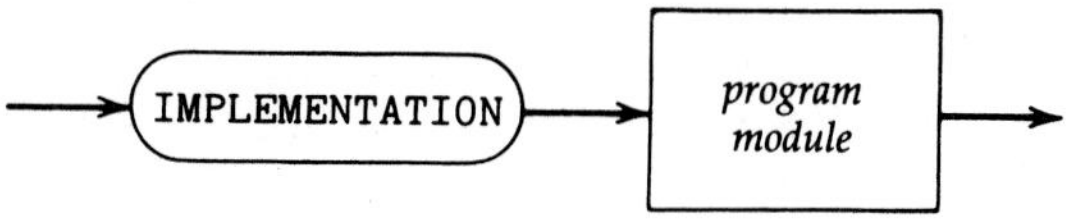

import

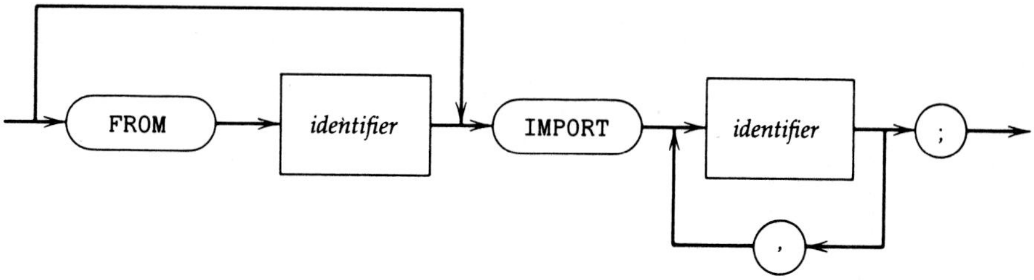

export

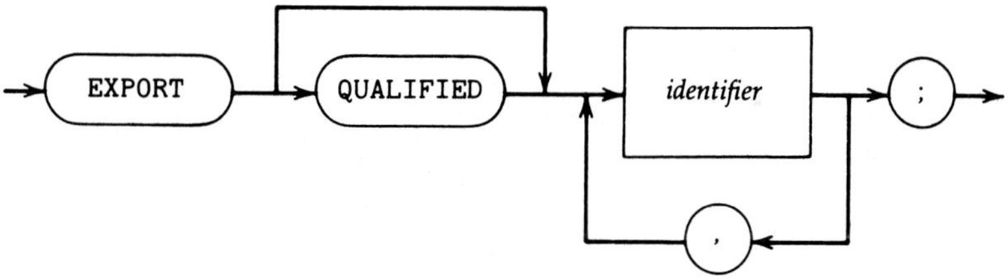

block

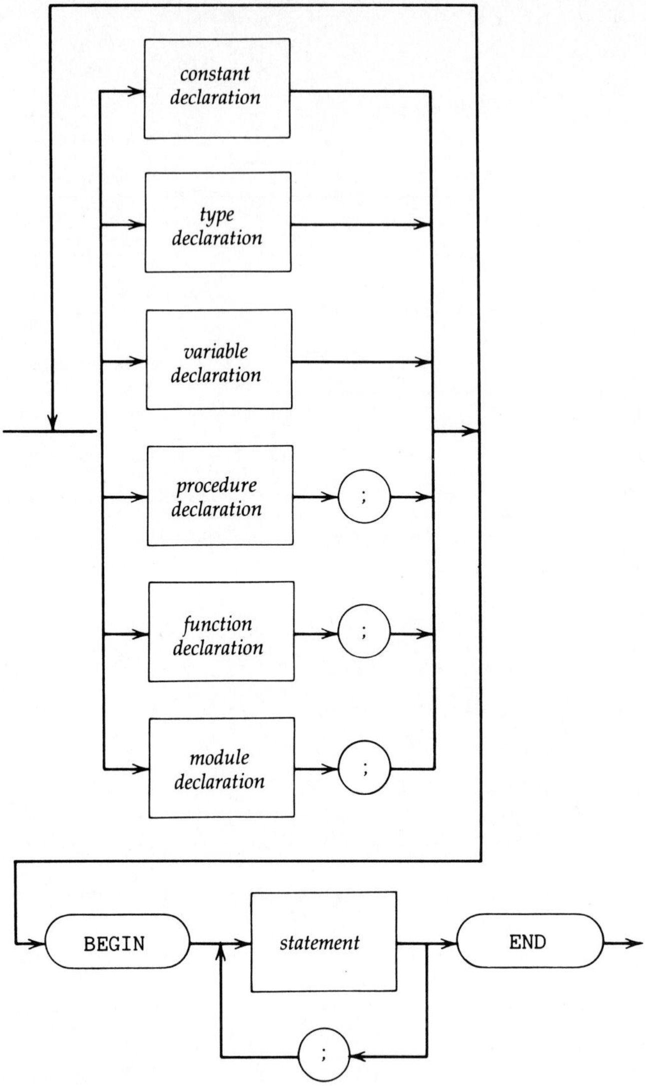

procedure declaration

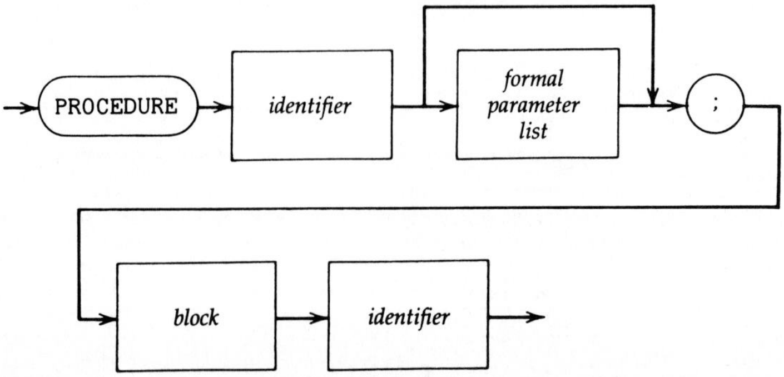

function declaration

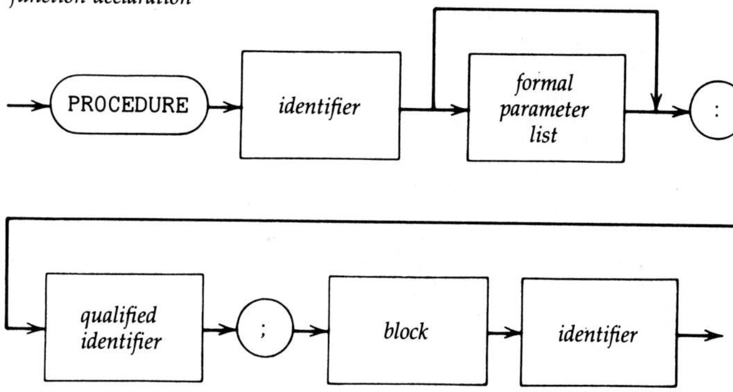

formal parameter list

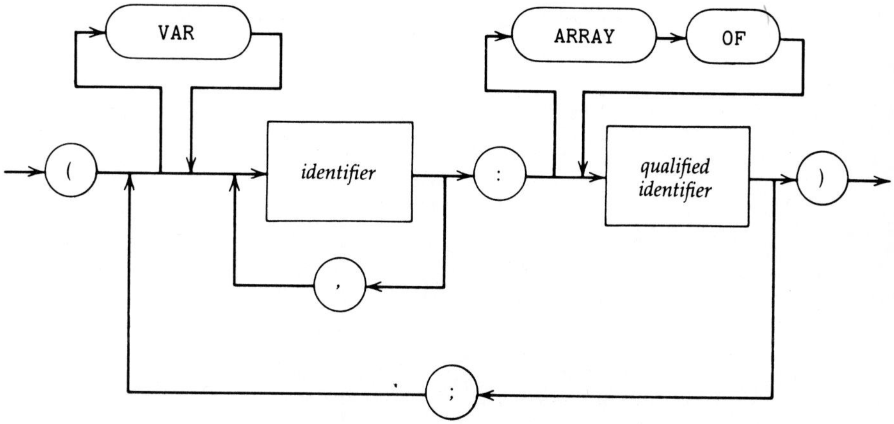

module declaration

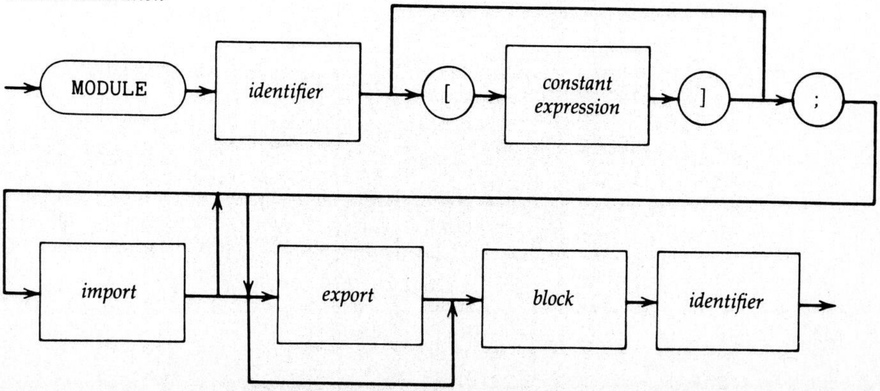

statement

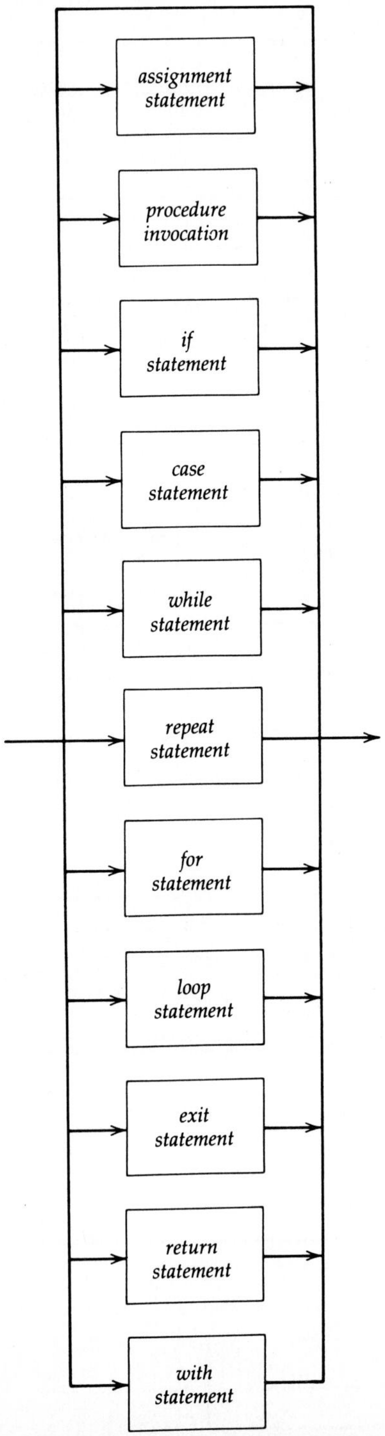
assignment statement
procedure invocation
if statement
case statement
while statement
repeat statement
for statement
loop statement
exit statement
return statement
with statement

assignment statement

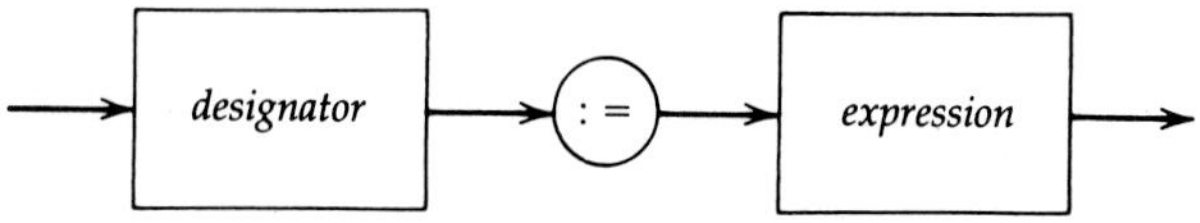

if statement

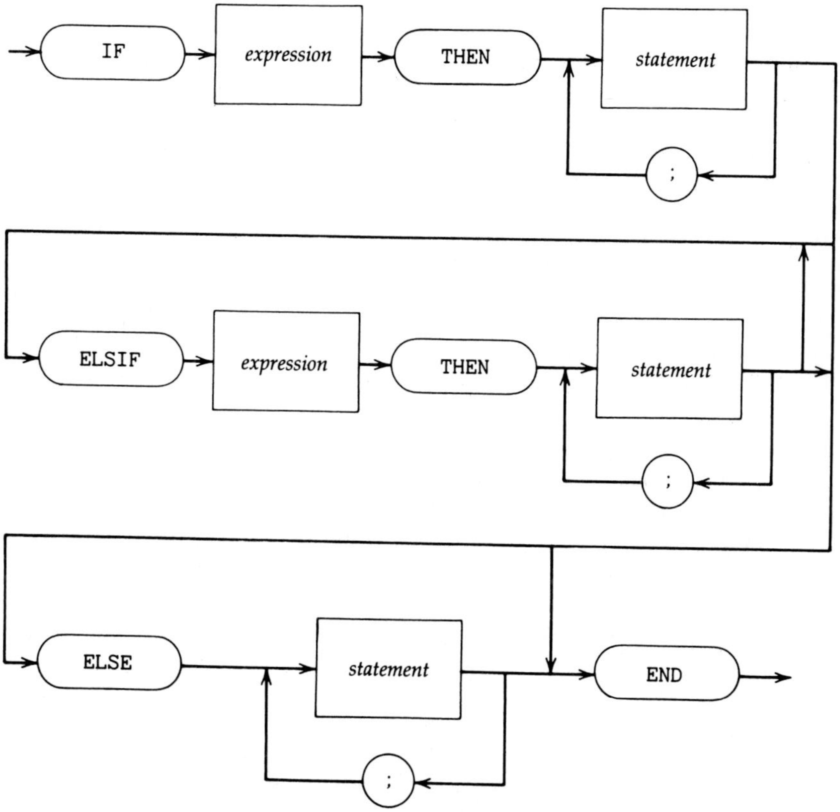

case statement

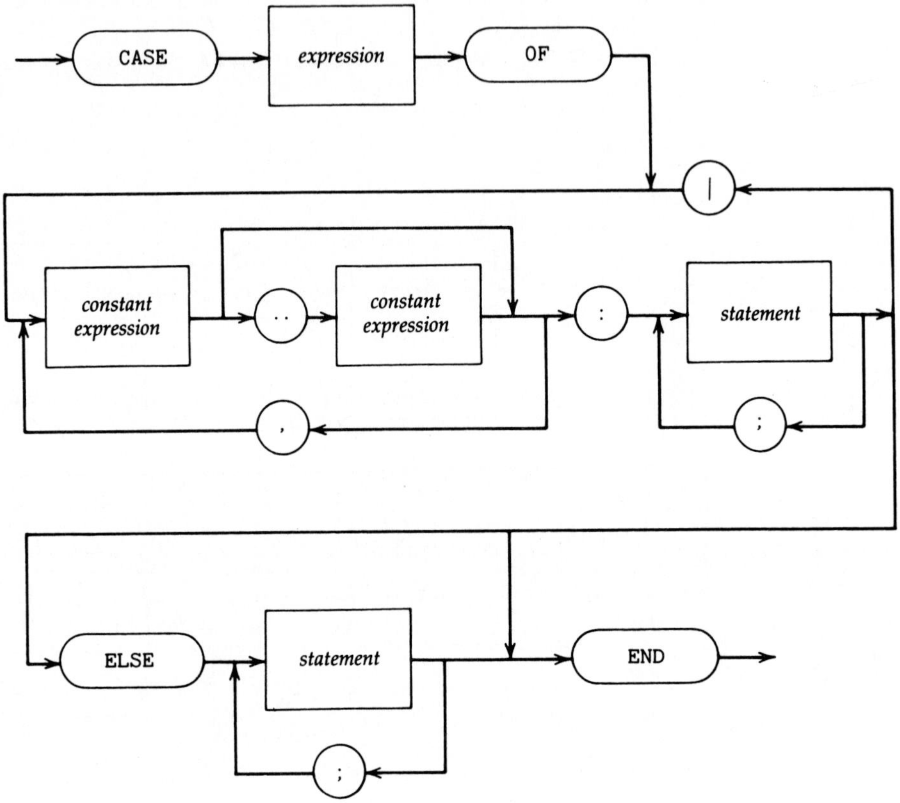

variable declaration

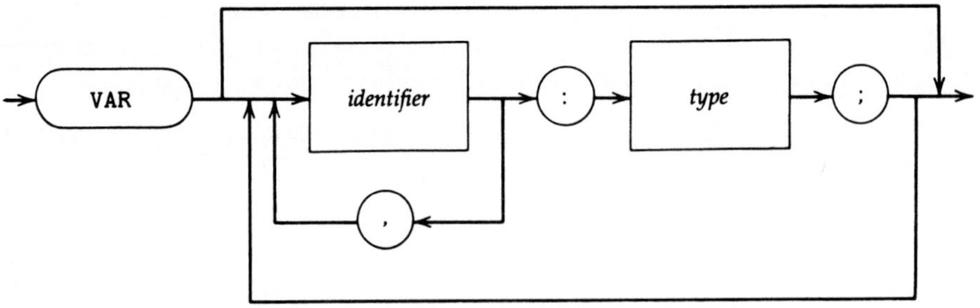

expression

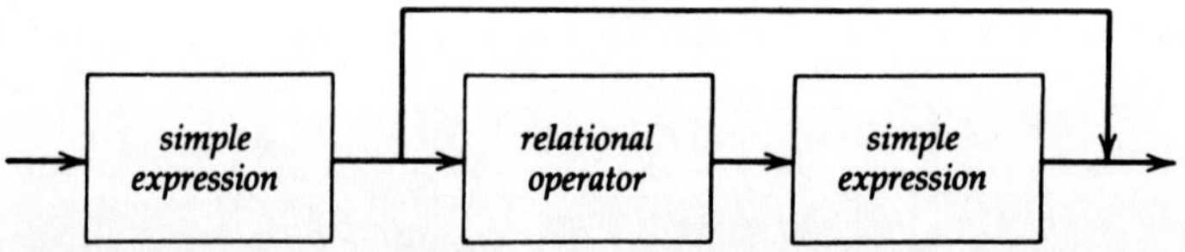

simple expression

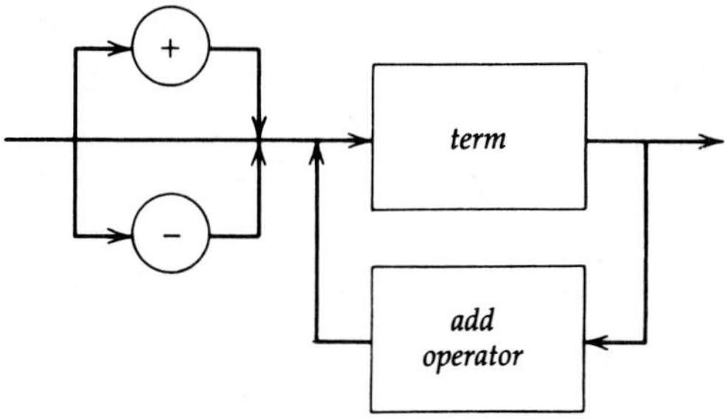

term

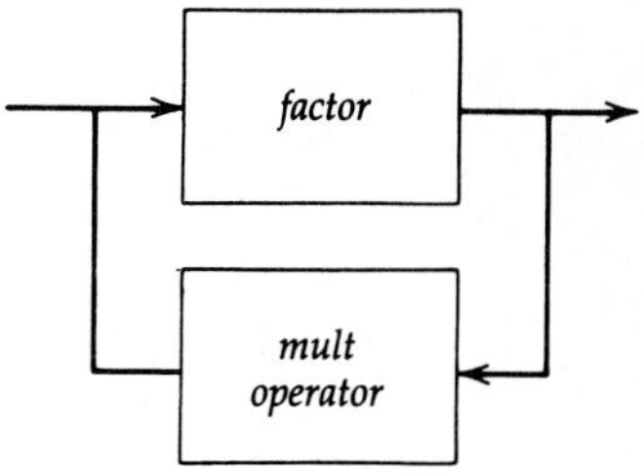

factor

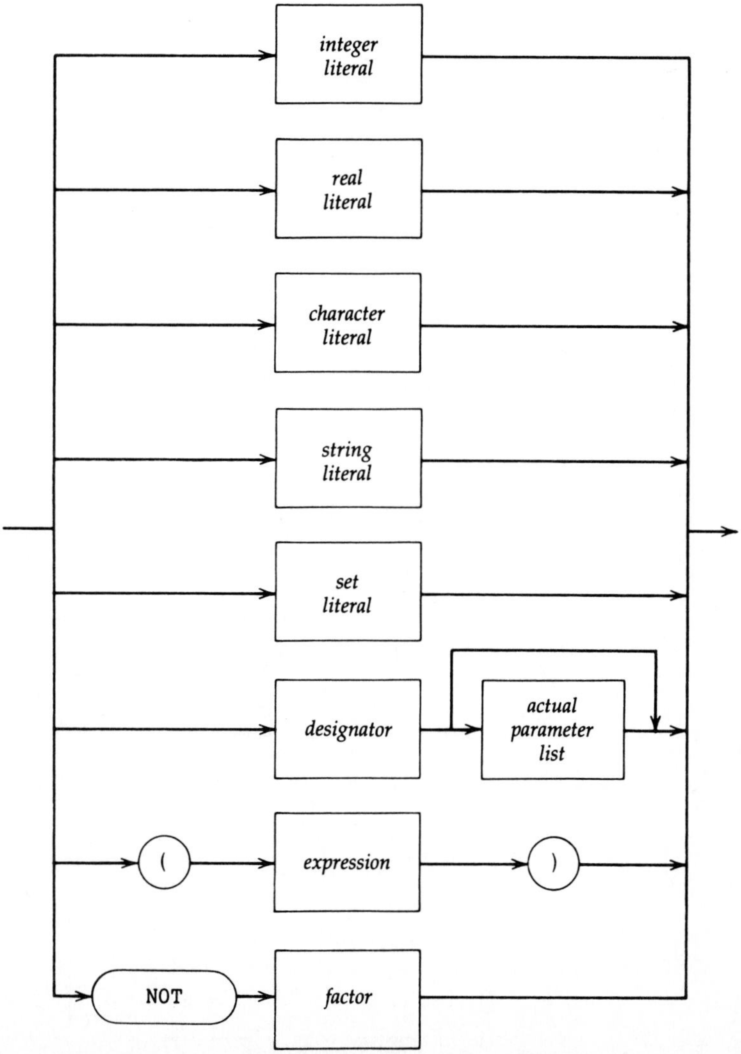

designator

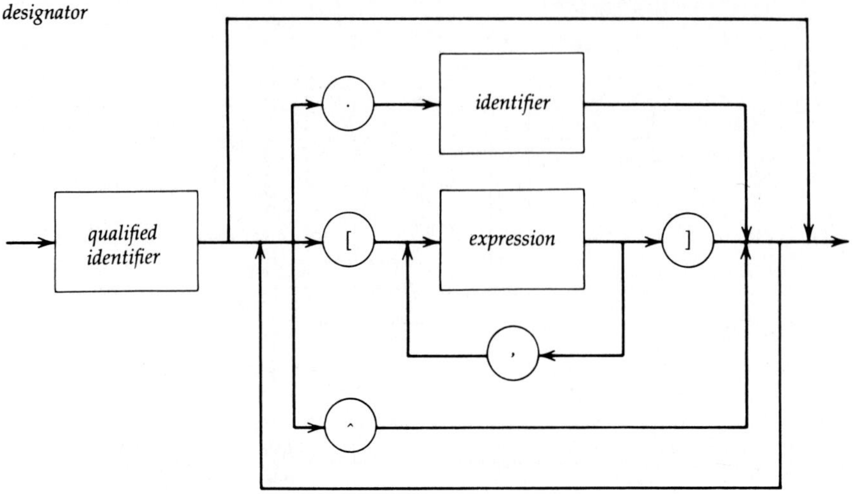

constant expression

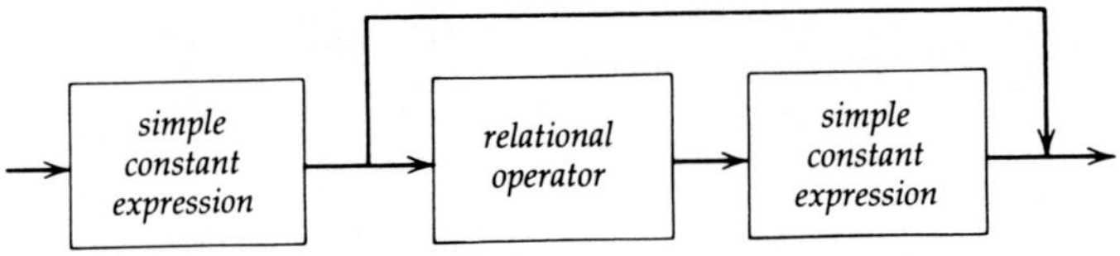

simple constant expression

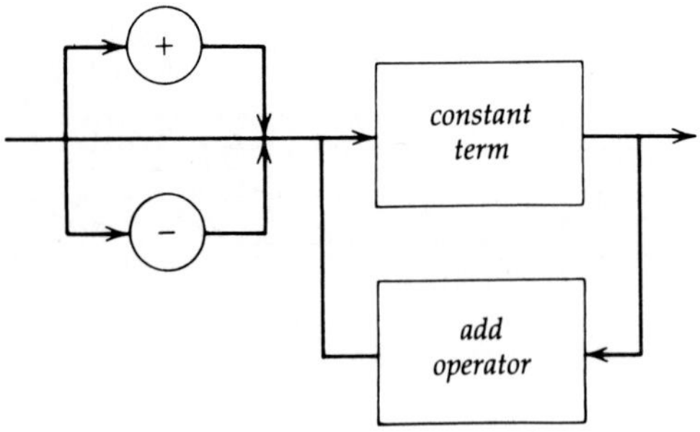

constant term

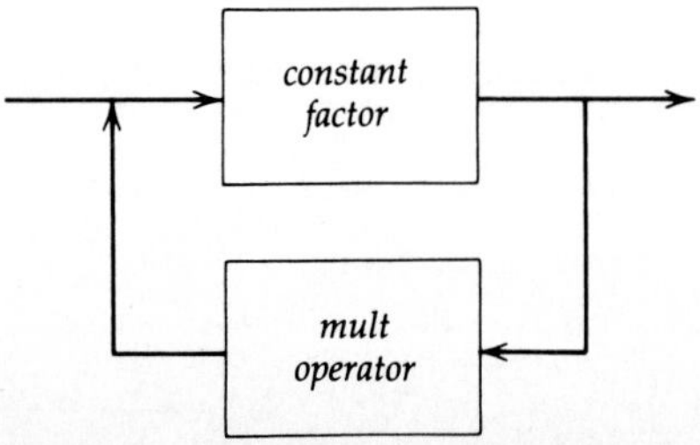

constant factor

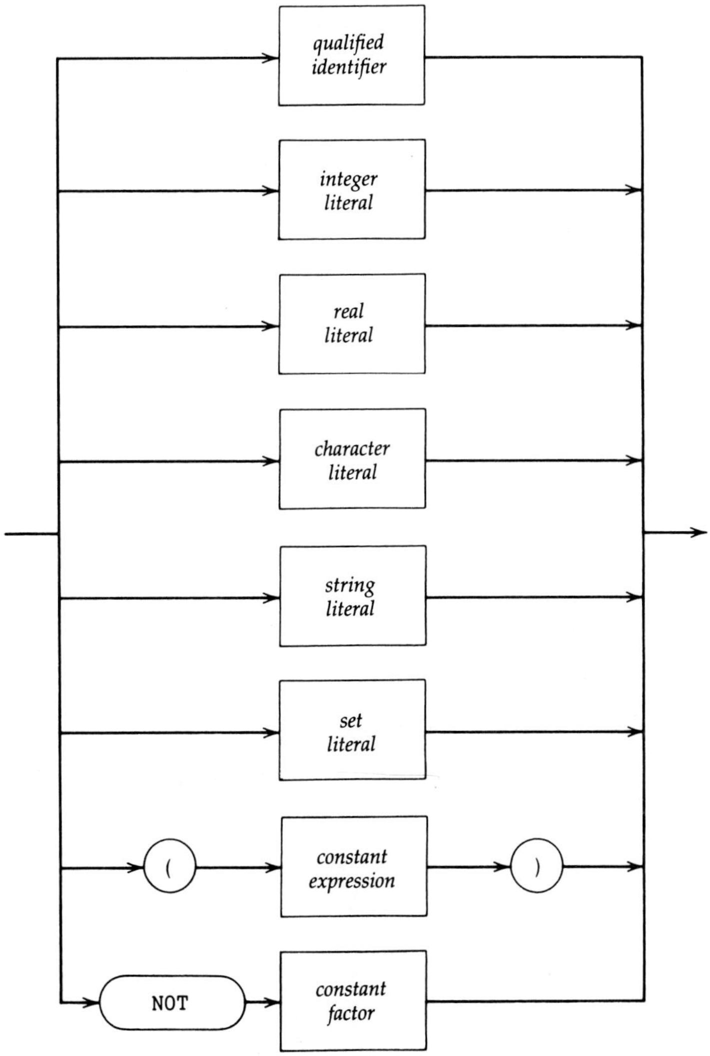

relational operator

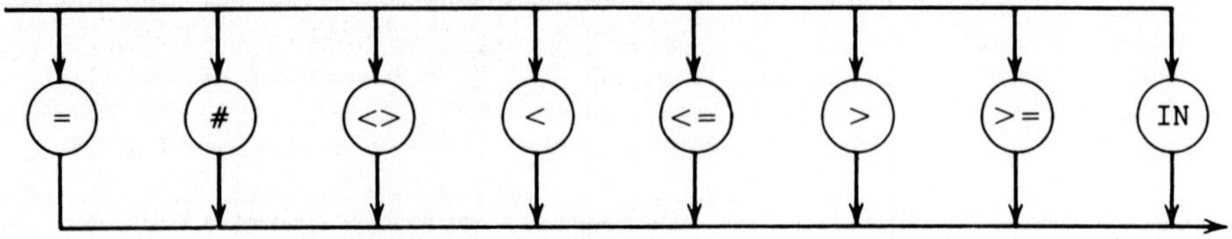

add operator

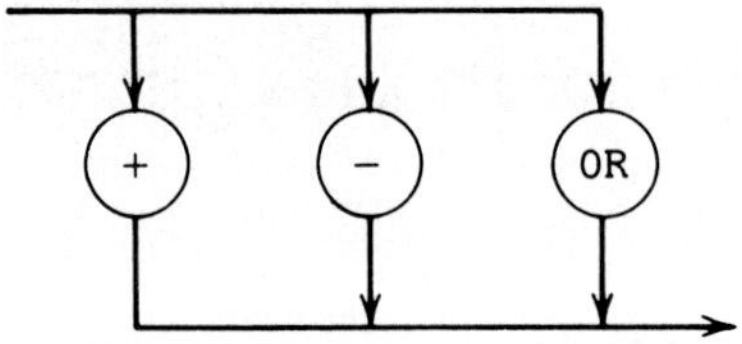

mult operator

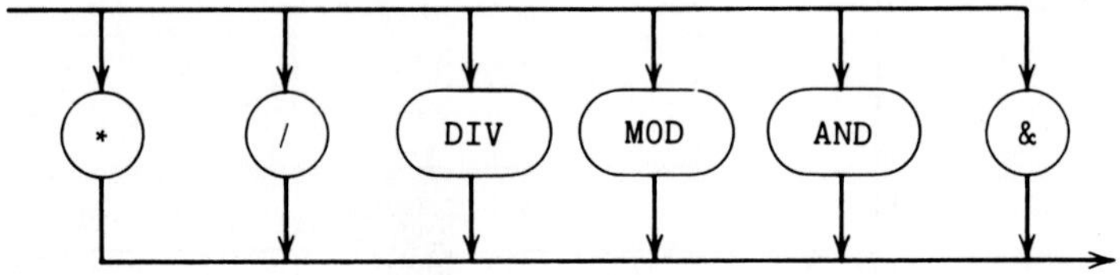

integer literal

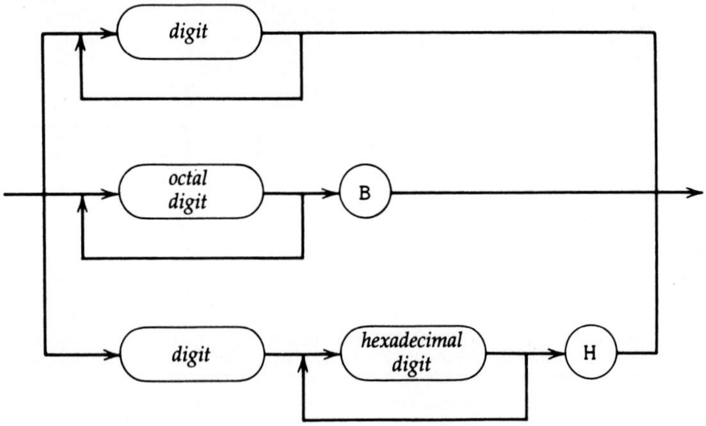

real literal

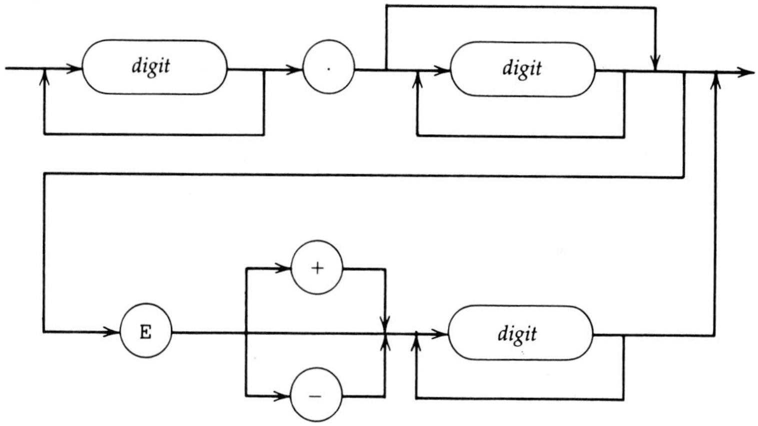

character literal

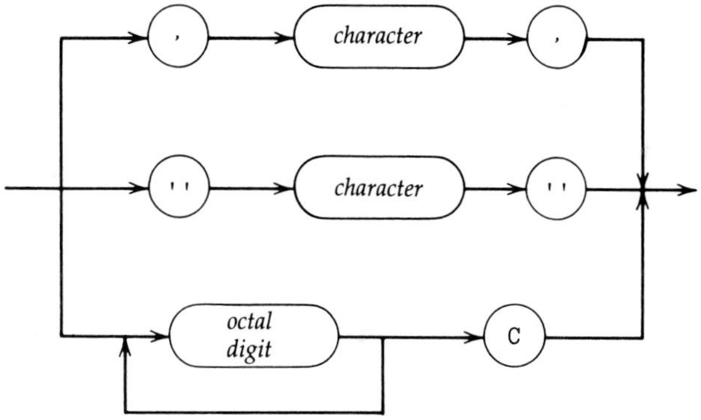

string literal

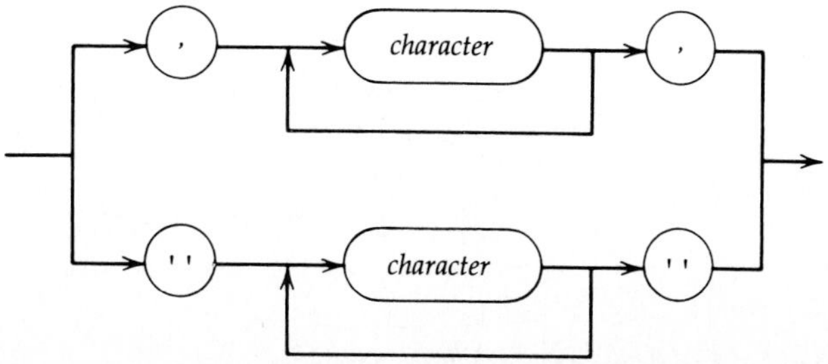

set literal

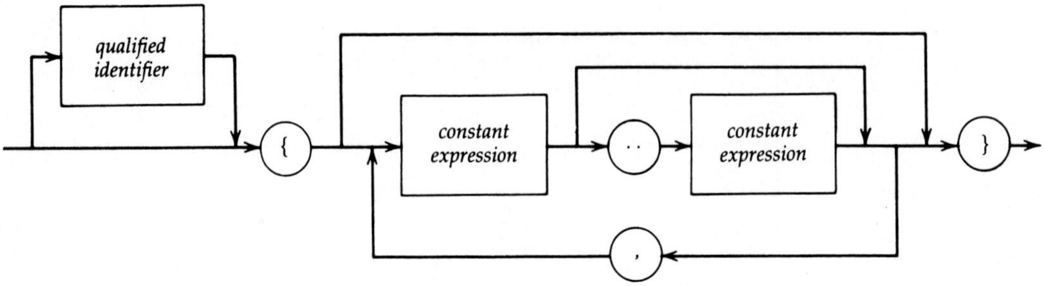

identifier

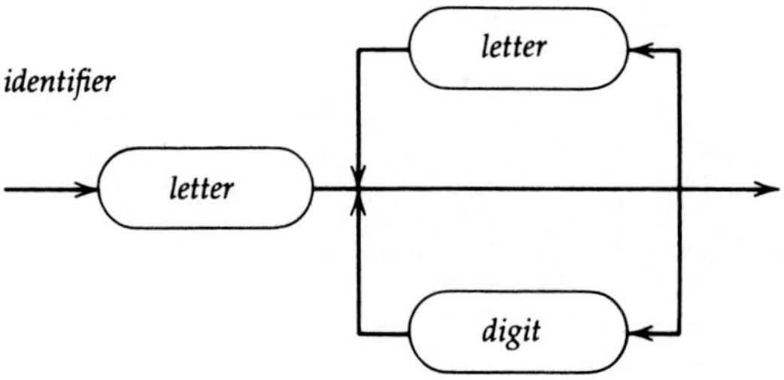

qualified identifier

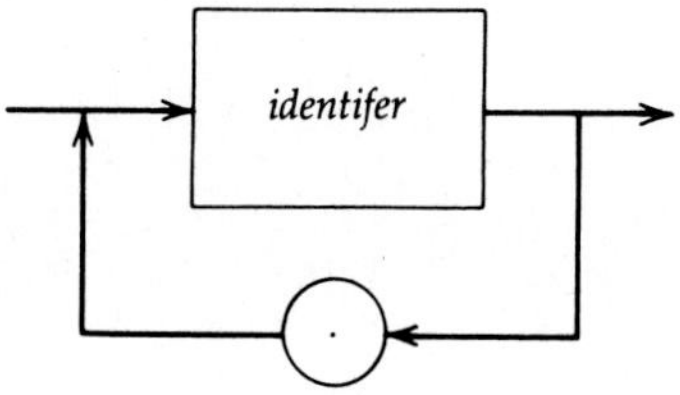

while statement

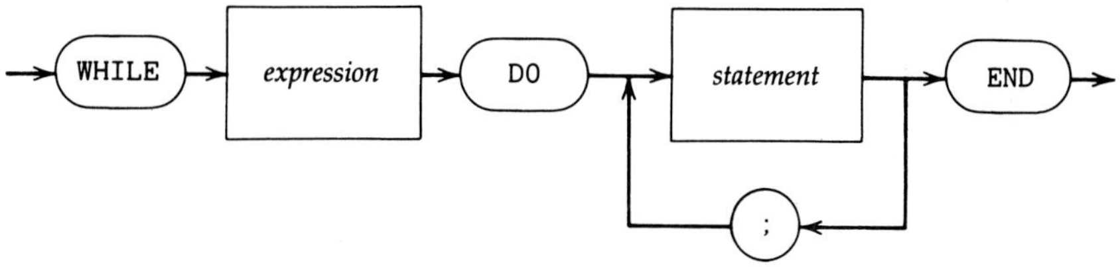

repeat statement

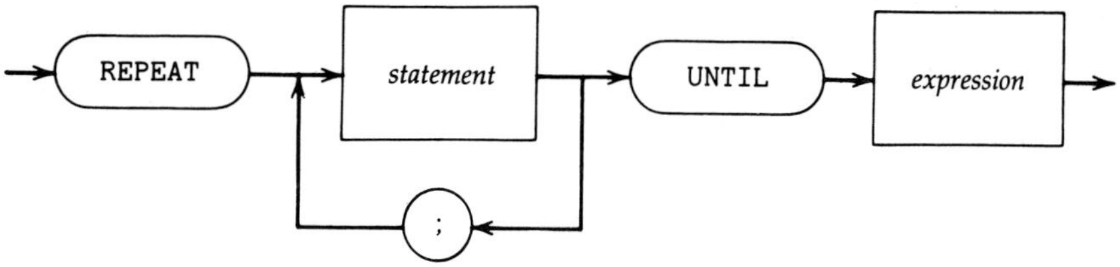

for statement

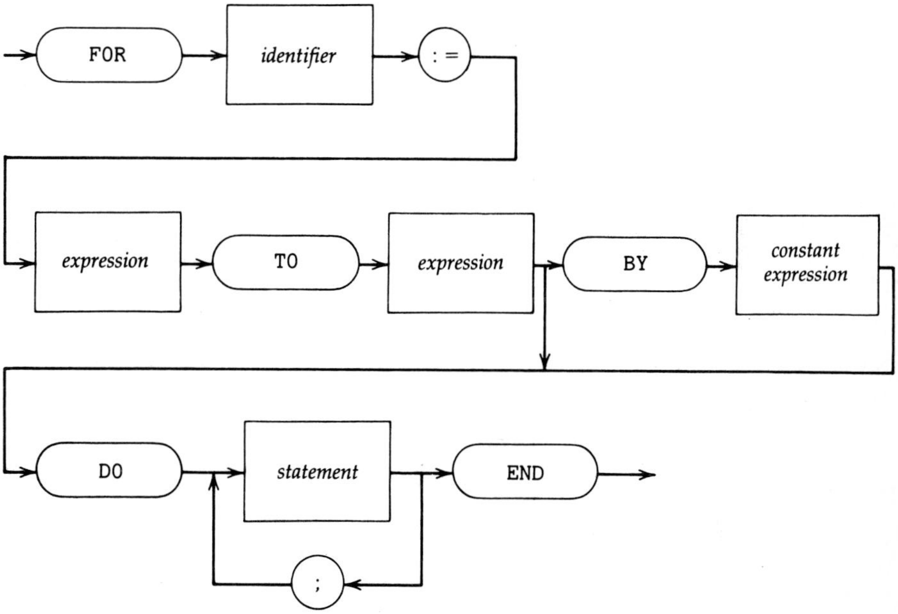

loop statement

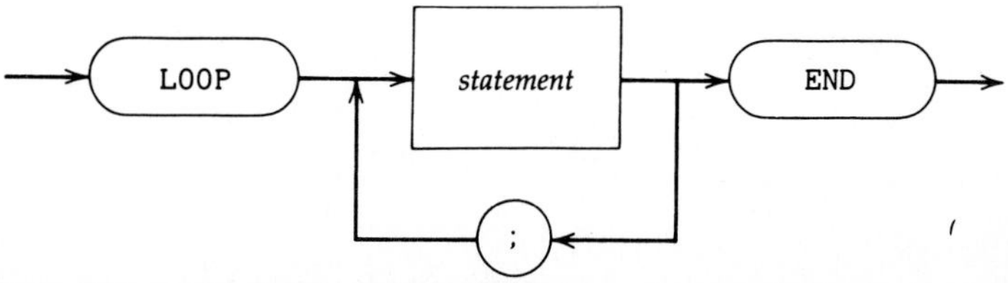

exit statement

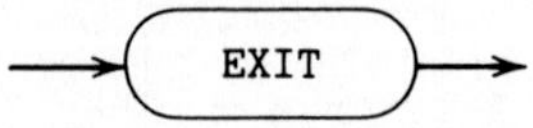

with statement

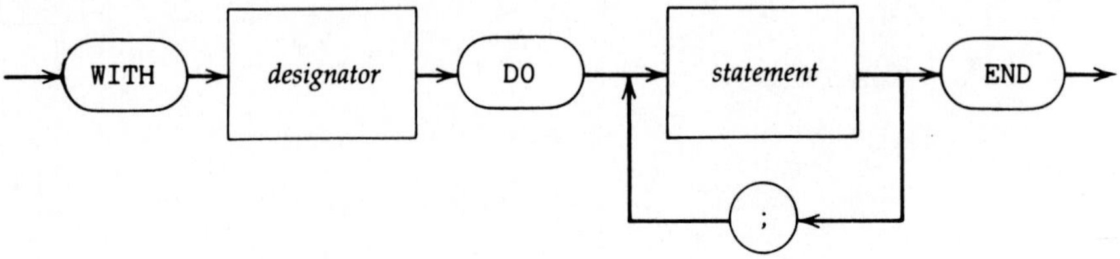

procedure invocation

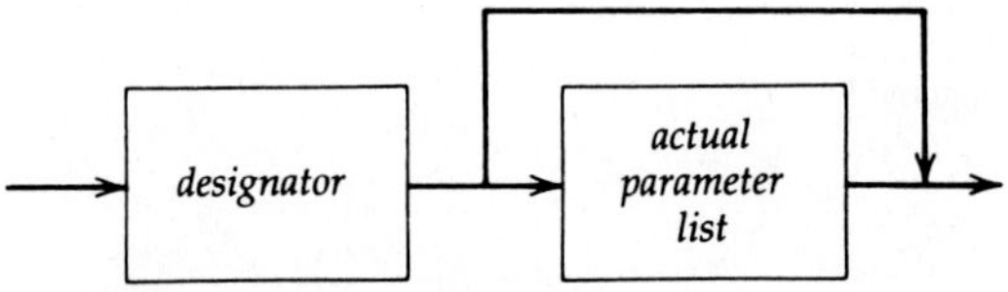

actual parameter list

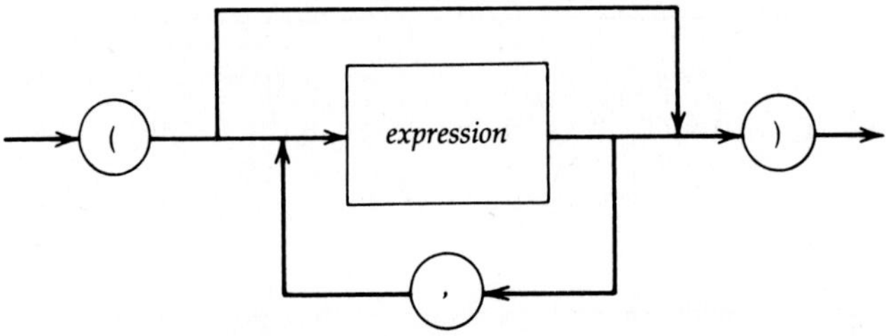

return statement

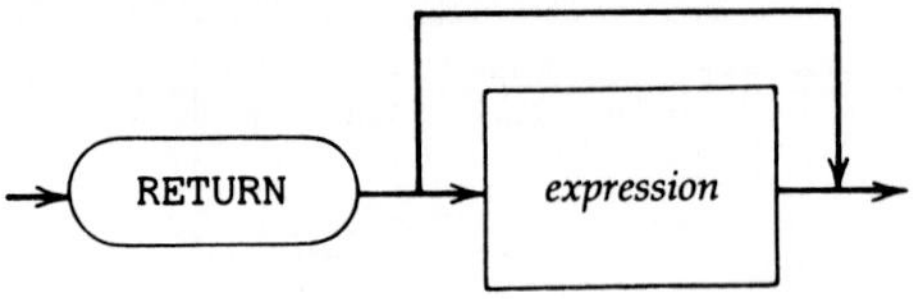

constant declaration

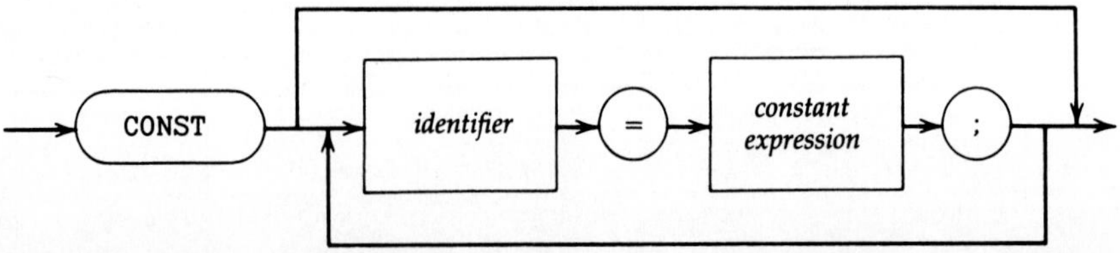

type declaration

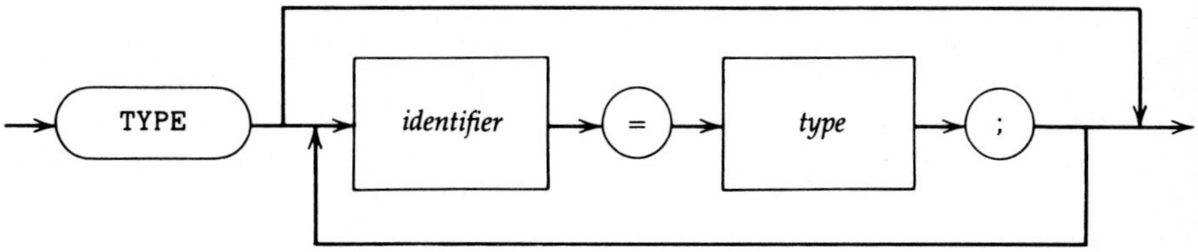

type

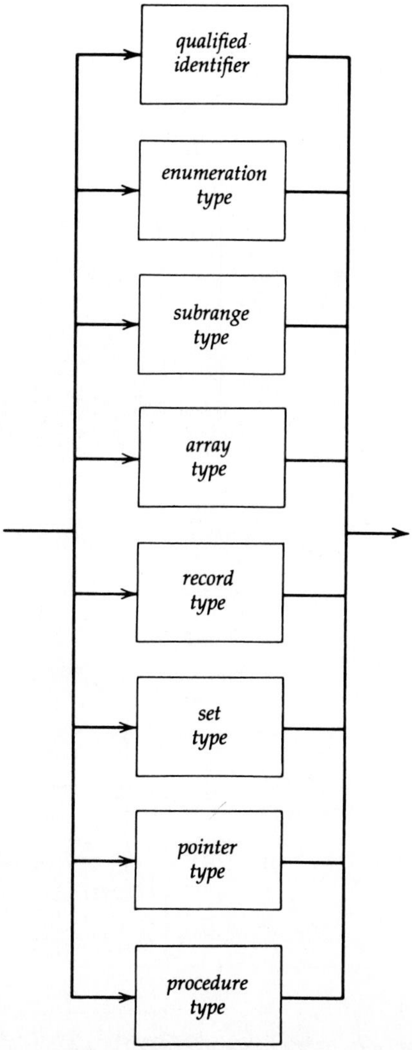

enumeration type

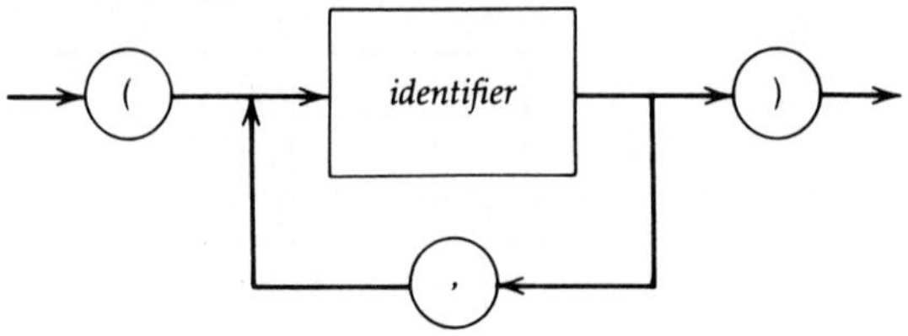

subrange type

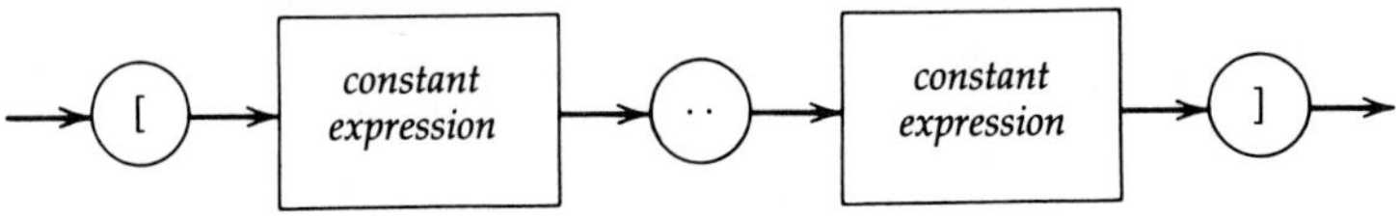

array type

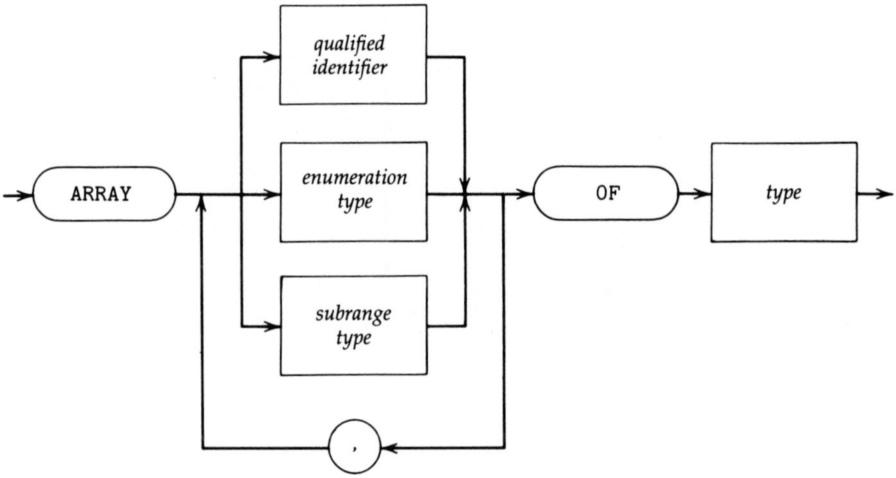

record type

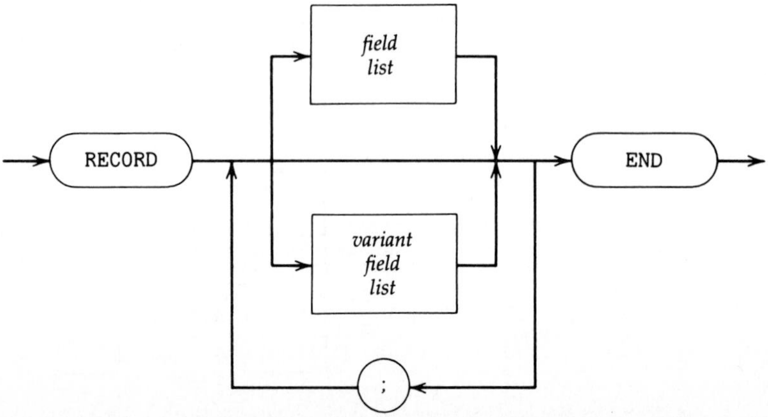

field list

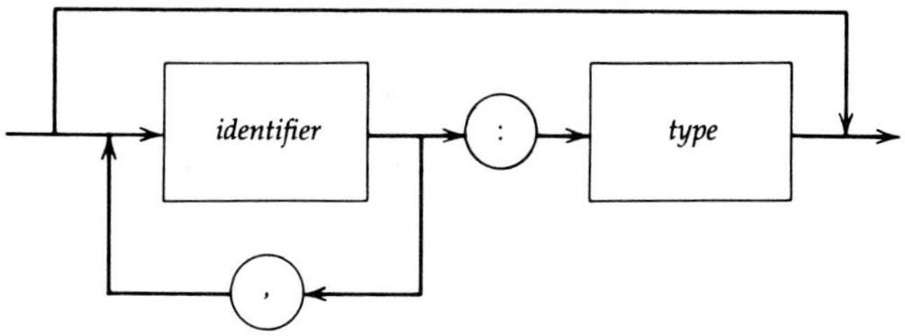

variant field list

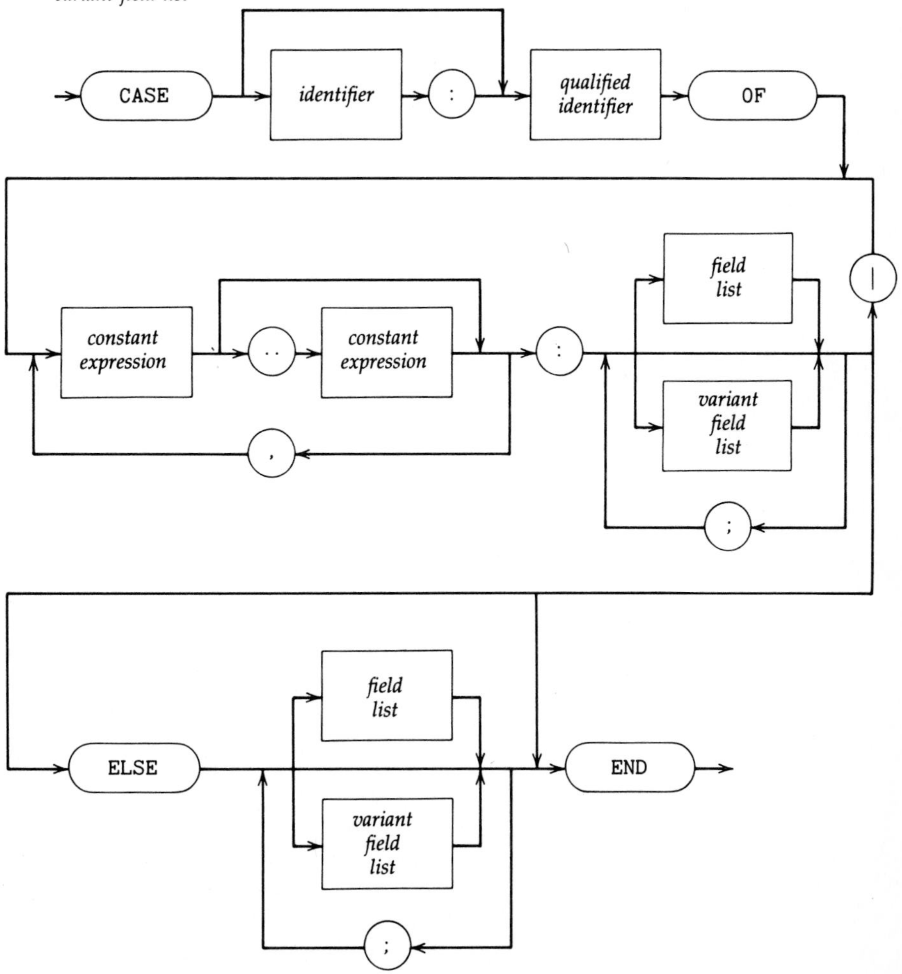

set type

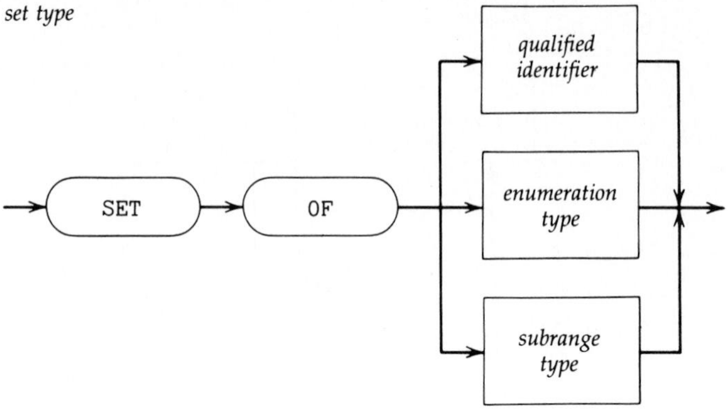

pointer type

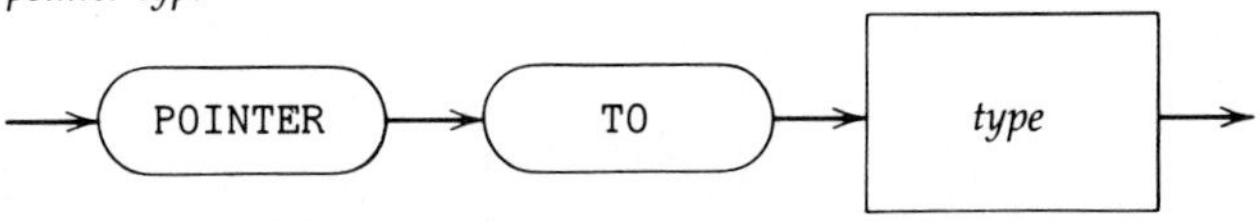

procedure type

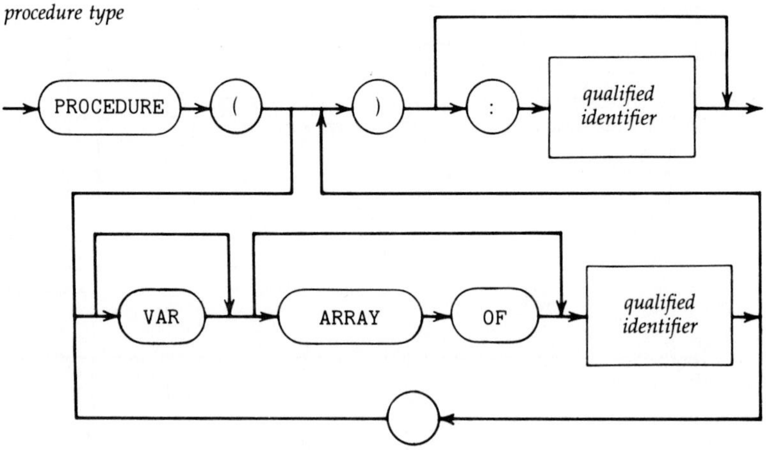

Appendix D
ASCII Character Set

Table D.1 provides the ASCII character set. The printable characters have codes from 32 (blank or space) to 126 (symbol ~). The other codes represent nonprintable control characters.

Table D.1 ▸ *Table of ASCII Characters*

CODE	CHAR	CODE	CHAR	CODE	CHAR	CODE	CHAR
0	NUL	32		64	@	96	'
1	SOH	33	!	65	A	97	a
2	STX	34	"	66	B	98	b
3	ETX	35	#	67	C	99	c
4	EOT	36	$	68	D	100	d
5	ENQ	37	%	69	E	101	e
6	ACK	38	&	70	F	102	f
7	BEL	39	'	71	G	103	g
8	BS	40	(	72	H	104	h
9	HT	41	)	73	I	105	i
10	LF	42	*	74	J	106	j
11	VT	43	+	75	K	107	k
12	FF	44	,	76	L	108	l
13	CR	45	-	77	M	109	m
14	SO	46	.	78	N	110	n
15	SI	47	/	79	O	111	o
16	DLE	48	0	80	P	112	p
17	DC1	49	1	81	Q	113	q
18	DC2	50	2	82	R	114	r
19	DC3	51	3	83	S	115	s
20	DC4	52	4	84	T	116	t
21	NAK	53	5	85	U	117	u
22	SYN	54	6	86	V	118	v
23	ETB	55	7	87	W	119	w
24	CAN	56	8	88	X	120	x
25	EM	57	9	89	Y	121	y
26	SUB	58	:	90	Z	122	z
27	ESC	59	;	91	[	123	{
28	FS	60	<	92	\	124	|
29	GS	61	=	93	]	125	}
30	RS	62	>	94	^	126	~
31	US	63	?	95	_	127	DEL

The following meanings are attached to the control characters frequently used in keyboard, terminal, or printer programming. Many of the others are used in remote communications.

`NUL`	Means "nothing"; terminates Modula-2 strings
`EOT`	End of transmission or file
`BEL`	Make audible sound on terminal ('Ring bell')
`BS`	Backspace
`HT`	Horizontal tab (across the page/screen)
`LF`	Line feed (move a line down but don't move back to margin)
`VT`	Vertical tab (down the page)
`FF`	Form feed (clear the screen or start new page)
`CR`	Carriage return (new line, starting at margin); called `EOL` in Modula-2
`ESC`	Escape (next character(s) do not have conventional meaning)
`DEL`	Delete

Appendix E
File Processing Procedures in Modula-2

The file is an external data structure and is an aggregate of characters or bytes stored on disk. Input/output operators that process files are provided in each Modula-2 system through modules named `Files` and/or `FileSystem`. Since each computer system performs input/output operations in its own way, these modules may have minor differences. This appendix examines one such module, `FileSystem`, as provided in the LOGITECH MODULA-2/86 system.

So far, we have learned how to use the `OpenInput`/`OpenOutput` operators in module `InOut` to redirect input/output from the terminal to a file whose name was entered at the keyboard. Once these operators were executed, the keyboard and screen were disconnected and all input and output operations were performed on the designated files using operators such as `Read`, `Read–Int`, `Write`, `WriteInt`, `ReadReal`, `WriteReal`, etc. from modules `InOut` and `RealInOut`. If we use the operators in module `FileSystem` instead, we can use files for input and output without having to disconnect the terminal.

Text Files

First we will learn how to process files of characters or *text files*. The program in Fig. E.1 copies the contents of one file to another. It uses procedure `Lookup` to *open* (prepare for processing) the input and the output files, procedures `ReadChar` and `WriteChar` to read and write each individual character from the input to the output file, and procedure `Close` to terminate the processing of the files.

Figure E.1 ▸ *Copying a File*

```
MODULE CopyFile;

  FROM InOut IMPORT
    WriteCard, WriteLn, WriteString;

  FROM FileSystem IMPORT
    File, Response,                      (* types *)
    Lookup, Close, WriteChar, ReadChar;  (* procedures *)
```

```
  VAR
    InFile,                          (* the input file *)
    OutFile : File;                  (* the output file *)
    NextChar : CHAR;                 (* each data character *)
    NumChars : CARDINAL;             (* count of characters *)

BEGIN (* CopyFile *)
  (* Open the input and output files *)
  Lookup (InFile, 'InData.TXT', FALSE);
  IF InFile.res = notdone THEN
    WriteString ('Error - input file not opened');  WriteLn;
    HALT
  END; (* IF *)
  Lookup (OutFile, 'OutData.TXT', TRUE);

  (* Copy the data from InFile to OutFile, counting each character *)
  NumChars := 0;
  ReadChar (InFile, NextChar);
  WHILE NOT InFile.eof DO
    WriteChar (OutFile, NextChar);
    INC ( NumChars);
    ReadChar (InFile, NextChar)
  END; (* WHILE *)

  (* Display the result *)
  WriteString ('File copy completed.');  WriteLn;
  WriteCard (NumChars, 0);  WriteString (' characters copied.');
  WriteLn;

  (* Close files *)
  Close (InFile);  Close (OutFile)
END CopyFile.


File copy completed.
307 characters copied.
```

InFile and OutFile are declared as type File which is a record consisting of several fields. Two of which, res (type Response) and eof (type BOOLEAN), are manipulated in Fig. E.1. The statement

```
Lookup (InFile, 'InData.TXT', FALSE);
```

searches the disk for a file named InData.TXT. If the file is found, it is associated with the internal name InFile and the value done is stored in InFile.res. If the file is not found, no action is taken and the value of InFile.res is set to notdone. The IF statement following the first call to Lookup aborts the program if the data file is not found.

The statement

```
Lookup (OutFile, 'OutData.TXT', TRUE);
```

searches the disk for a file named `OutData.TXT`. If the file is found, it is associated with the internal name `OutFile`. If the file is not found, a new permanent file named `OutData.TXT` is created. In either case, the value of `OutFile.res` is set to `done`.

The two calls to `Lookup` have different results when the file being searched for is not found. The reason for the difference is that the third parameter is `FALSE` in one call and `TRUE` in the other. When the third parameter is `TRUE`, a new file is opened if there is no existing file with the file name passed to `Lookup`.

The external file names, `'InData.TXT'` and `'OutData.TXT'`, were provided as string values in the calls to `Lookup`. It is also possible to read each value into a string variable and pass the string variable as a parameter to `Lookup`.

The `WHILE` loop copies each individual character from file `InFile` to `OutFile`. Each call to procedure `ReadChar` reads the next character of file `InFile` into `NextChar` and sets the `eof` field of `InFile` to `TRUE` or `FALSE` as a side effect. The `eof` field signals whether or not all characters in the file have been processed. The `eof` field is set to `TRUE` if a read operation fails because the last character in the file was already processed; otherwise, the `eof` field is set to `FALSE`. Therefore, the `WHILE` condition (`NOT InFile.eof`) is `TRUE` after each character in file `InFile` is read, and the statements

```
WriteChar (OutFile, NextChar);
INC ( NumChars);
```

copy the character in `NextChar` to file `OutFile` and increment `NumChars`. If a read operation is attempted after the last character in `InFile` has been read, `InFile.eof` becomes `TRUE` so `NOT InFile.eof` is `FALSE` and the `WHILE` loop is exited.

Finally, the `Close` procedure is called to terminate the processing of each file. A special character is written to the output file, `OutData.TXT`, to denote the end of the file. The new operators are summarized in the following displays. Note that the file parameter, *f*, is always a `VAR` (variable) parameter.

File Variable Declaration ▶

FORM: `VAR` *f* `: File;`

EXAMPLE: `VAR InFile : File;`

INTERPRETATION: The variable *f* is declared as type `File` where `File` is a predefined record including fields `eof` (type `BOOLEAN`) and `res` (type `Response`) among others. The field selector *f*`.eof` indicates whether the last file access was past the end of the file (value is `TRUE`) or within the file (value is `FALSE`). The field selector *f*`.res` contains an enumeration type value which indicates the result of the last operation. Two of these values, `done` and `notdone`, indicate the success or failure, respectively, of the last operation.

Lookup Procedure (in module FileSystem) ▶

FORM: `PROCEDURE Lookup (VAR` *f* `: File;`
filename `: ARRAY OF CHAR;`
newfile `: BOOLEAN);`

EXAMPLE:
```
Lookup (InFile, 'MyData.TXT', FALSE);
Lookup (OutFile, 'MyOut.TXT', TRUE)
```

INTERPRETATION: The disk directory is searched for string *filename*. If *filename* is found, file variable *f* is associated with that file, *f*`.res` is set to `done`, and the file is positioned at its first character. If *filename* is not found and *newfile* is `TRUE`, a new file named *filename* is created on the disk and *f*`.res` is set to `done`. If *filename* is not found and *newfile* is `FALSE`, no action takes place and *f*`.res` is set to `notdone`.

ReadChar Procedure (in module FileSystem) ▶

FORM: `PROCEDURE ReadChar (VAR` *f* `: File; VAR` *char* `: CHAR);`

EXAMPLE: `ReadChar (InFile, NextCh)`

INTERPRETATION: The next character in file *f* is read into *char*, and the file will be positioned at the character following the one just read. If there are no characters remaining to be read, the null character is stored in *char*.

WriteChar Procedure (in module FileSystem) ▶

FORM: `PROCEDURE WriteChar (VAR` *f* `: File;` *char* `: CHAR);`

EXAMPLE: `WriteChar (OutFile, NextCh)`

INTERPRETATION: Writes the character *char* to the current position in file *f*. The file will be repositioned just beyond this character.

Close Procedure (in module FileSystem) ▶

FORM: `PROCEDURE Close (VAR` *f* `: File);`

EXAMPLE: `Close (MyFile)`

INTERPRETATION: Terminates processing of file *f*. If file *f* is a text file being closed after writing, the end-of-file character code (`32C`) is written at the current file position.

Binary Files

Next we will consider processing *binary files* where a binary file is a file consisting of binary values, not necessarily characters. Module `FileSystem` contains procedures for transferring binary values stored in core memory directly to a file and vice versa. Procedure `ReadNBytes` reads a specified number of bytes from a file into a given address in memory; procedure `WriteNBytes` writes a specified number of bytes from a given address in memory to a file.

The program in Fig. E.2 creates a binary file. It does this by calling procedure `ReadPart` to read data into record variable `Part`. Next, the statement

```
WriteNBytes (OutFile, ADR(Part), SIZE(Part), Actual);
```

calls `WriteNBytes` to write the contents of `Part` to file `OutFile`. The second parameter specifies the address in memory of variable `Part`; the third parameter specifies how many bytes to write. The actual number of bytes written is returned in the fourth parameter and should be the same as the value of the third parameter. If they are not the same, the `IF` statement at the end of the loop displays a warning message.

Figure E.2 ▸
Module CreateFile

```
MODULE CreateFile;

(* Creates a binary file of records of type FileRec. *)

   FROM InOut IMPORT
     WriteCard, WriteLn, ReadInt, ReadString, WriteString;

   FROM RealInOut IMPORT
     ReadReal;

   FROM Strings IMPORT
     CompareStr;

   FROM FileSystem IMPORT
     File,                                        (* type *)
     Lookup, Close, WriteNBytes, ReadNBytes;      (* procedures *)

   FROM SYSTEM IMPORT
     ADR, SIZE;                                   (* procedures *)

   CONST
     Sentinel = '***';                            (* sentinel name *)

   TYPE
     String12 = ARRAY [0..11] OF CHAR;
     FileRec = RECORD
       Name : String12;
       Quantity : INTEGER;
       Price : REAL
     END; (* FileRec *)
```

```
  VAR
    OutFile : File;                     (* the output file *)
    NumRecords : CARDINAL;              (* count of file records *)
    OutName : String12;                 (* file directory name *)
    Part : FileRec;                     (* file record *)
    Actual : CARDINAL;                  (* number of bytes written *)

  PROCEDURE ReadPart (VAR OnePart (* output *) : FileRec);
  (*
     Reads a record of type FileRec into OnePart.
     Pre : None
     Post: OnePart is defined.
     Uses: CompareStr from Strings
  *)
  BEGIN (* ReadPart *)
    WITH OnePart DO
      WriteString ('Enter part name or *** to stop: ');
      ReadString (Name);  WriteLn;
      IF CompareStr(Name, Sentinel) # 0 THEN
        WriteString ('Enter quantity: ');
        ReadInt (Quantity);  WriteLn;
        WriteString ('Enter price: ');
        ReadReal (Price);  WriteLn
      END (* IF *)
    END (* WITH *)
  END ReadPart;

BEGIN (* CreateFile *)
  (* Open output file. *)
  WriteString ('Output file: ');  ReadString (OutName);  WriteLn;
  Lookup (OutFile, OutName, TRUE);

  (* Read each record into Part and write it to OutFile. *)
  NumRecords := 0;
  ReadPart (Part);
  WHILE CompareStr(Part.Name, Sentinel) # 0 DO
    WriteLn;
    WriteNBytes (OutFile, ADR(Part), SIZE(Part), Actual);
    INC (NumRecords);
    IF Actual # SIZE(Part) THEN
      WriteString ('Error in file write.');  WriteLn
    END; (* IF *)
    ReadPart (Part)
  END; (* WHILE *)

  (* Display results and close files *)
  WriteString ('File creation completed.');  WriteLn;
  WriteCard (NumRecords, 0);
  WriteString (' records written to output file.');  WriteLn;
  Close (OutFile)
END CreateFile.
```

```
Output file: Inventry.Bin
Enter part name or *** to stop: nuts
Enter quantity: 300
Enter price: 0.25

Enter part name or *** to stop: bolts
Enter quantity: 250
Enter price: 0.36

Enter part name or *** to stop: ***
File creation completed.
2 records written to output file.
```

After a binary file is created, each of its records can be read into memory and processed. The program in Fig. E.3 updates the `Price` field of a file of records of type `FileRec`. It does this by creating a new file whose records have the same values as those in the old file except for the `Price` field.

The statement

```
ReadNBytes (InFile, ADR(Part), SIZE(Part), InActual);
```

reads the next record of file `InFile` into record variable `Part`. Next, the statements

```
Part.Price := Part.Price * (1.0 + PerCentChange);
WriteNBytes (OutFile, ADR(Part), SIZE(Part), OutActual);
```

add a specified percentage (`PerCentChange`) to field `Price` and then write the modified record to file `OutFile`. After completion of the program, there will be the same number of records in both files; the only difference will be in the `Price` field of corresponding records.

Figure E.3 ▸ *Updating a Binary File*

```
MODULE ChangePrice;

(* Creates a new file with updated price field values. *)

   FROM InOut IMPORT
     WriteCard, WriteLn, ReadString, WriteString;

   FROM RealInOut IMPORT
     ReadReal;

   FROM Strings IMPORT
     CompareStr;

   FROM FileSystem IMPORT
```

```
    File, Response,                              (* types *)
    Lookup, Close, WriteNBytes, ReadNBytes;      (* procedures *)

  FROM SYSTEM IMPORT
    ADR, SIZE;                                   (* procedures *)

  TYPE
    String12 = ARRAY [0..11] OF CHAR;
    FileRec = RECORD
      Name : String12;
      Quantity : INTEGER;
      Price : REAL
    END; (* FileRec *)

  VAR
    InFile,                          (* the input file *)
    OutFile : File;                  (* the output file *)
    NumRecords : CARDINAL;           (* count of file records *)
    InName,                          (* input file directory name *)
    OutName : String12;              (* output file directory name *)
    Part : FileRec;                  (* file record *)
    InActual,                        (* number of bytes read *)
    OutActual : CARDINAL;            (* number of bytes written *)
    PerCentChange : REAL;            (* percentage change in price *)

BEGIN (* ChangePrice *)
  (* Open the input file and the output file. *)
  WriteString ('Input file : ');  ReadString (InName);  WriteLn;
  Lookup (InFile, InName, FALSE);
  IF InFile.res = notdone THEN
    WriteString ('Error - input file not opened');  WriteLn;
    HALT
  END; (* IF *)
  WriteString ('Output file: ');  ReadString (OutName);  WriteLn;
  Lookup (OutFile, OutName, TRUE);

  (* Update price of each record. *)
  WriteString ('Enter price change percent as a decimal fraction: ');
  ReadReal (PerCentChange);  WriteLn;
  NumRecords := 0;
  ReadNBytes (InFile, ADR(Part), SIZE(Part), InActual);
  WHILE NOT InFile.eof DO
    Part.Price := Part.Price * (1.0 + PerCentChange);
    WriteNBytes (OutFile, ADR(Part), SIZE(Part), OutActual);
    INC (NumRecords);
    IF (InActual # OutActual) OR (InActual # SIZE(Part)) THEN
      WriteString ('Error in number of bytes read or written');
      WriteLn
    END; (* IF *)
    ReadNBytes (InFile, ADR(Part), SIZE(Part), InActual)
  END; (* WHILE *)
```

```
  (* Display results and close files. *)
  WriteString ('Price change completed.');  WriteLn;
  WriteCard (NumRecords, 0);
  WriteString (' records modified.');  WriteLn;
  Close (InFile);  Close (OutFile)
END ChangePrice.


Input file : Inventry.Bin
Output file: NewInven.Bin
Price change completed.
2 records modified.
```

The displays that follow summarize the new operators.

ADDR Function (in module SYSTEM) ▶

FORM: `PROCEDURE ADDR (`*variable*`) : ADDRESS;`

EXAMPLE: `ADDR(Part)`

INTERPRETATION: Returns the memory address of *variable*.

SIZE Function (in module SYSTEM) ▶

FORM: `PROCEDURE SIZE (`*variable*`) : CARDINAL;`

EXAMPLE: `SIZE(Part)`

INTERPRETATION: Returns the size (number of bytes) of *variable*.

ReadNBytes Procedure (in module FileSystem) ▶

FORM: `PROCEDURE ReadNBytes (VAR` *f* `: File;`
bufptr `: ADDRESS;`
numberbytes `: CARDINAL;`
`VAR` *bytesread* `: CARDINAL);`

EXAMPLE: `ReadNBytes (InFile, ADR(Part), SIZE(Part), InActual)`

INTERPRETATION: The number of bytes specified by *numberbytes* is read from the current position of file *f* and stored in memory at the address specified by *bufptr*. The actual number of bytes read is stored in *bytesread*. The file will be repositioned just past the last byte read.

WriteNBytes Procedure (in module FileSystem) ▶

FORM: `PROCEDURE WriteNBytes (VAR f : File;`
`bufptr : ADDRESS;`
`numberbytes : CARDINAL;`
`VAR byteswritten : CARDINAL);`

EXAMPLE: `WriteNBytes (OutFile, ADR(Part), SIZE(Part), OutActual)`

INTERPRETATION: The number of bytes specified by *numberbytes* is written from the memory address specified by *bufptr* to the current position of file *f*. The actual number of bytes written is stored in *byteswritten*. The file will be repositioned just past the last byte written.

Random Access Binary Files

In the examples shown so far, all the records of a file were processed in sequence, starting with the first record, and a file was used either for input or for output, but not for both in the same program. This method of file access is called *sequential access*. We can also treat a file on disk in a manner analogous to an array in memory and process its records in any order we wish (*random access*), and perform both read and write operations on the same file.

The *file position pointer* denotes the disk address where the next file access will occur. Procedure `Lookup` initializes the file position pointer to the disk address of the first byte in the file. After a read or write operation, the file position pointer is automatically advanced just beyond the last byte that was processed. Procedure `SetPos` enables us to move the file position pointer to any disk address in the file.

Program `UpdateFile` updates the `Quantity` field of selected file records where the first record is designated as record number `0`. The statement

```
SetPos (InOutFile, 0, ORD(RecNum) * SIZE(Part));
```

moves the file position pointer to the start of the record denoted by `RecNum`. The third parameter determines where to move the file position pointer and represents an *offset* from the first byte in the file. Since each record has `SIZE(Part)` bytes, the file position pointer is advanced past the first `RecNum` records to the first byte of record `RecNum`. The second parameter is zero unless the offset is too large to be represented as a cardinal number.

After the file is positioned to record number `RecNum`, the statement

```
ReadNBytes (InOutFile, ADR(Part), SIZE(Part), InActual);
```

attempts to read a record at the current disk address. If the read operation succeeds, the new value of the `Quantity` field is entered and the statements

```
SetPos (InOutFile, 0, ORD(RecNum) * SIZE(Part));
WriteNBytes (InOutFile, ADR(Part), SIZE(Part), OutActual);
```

write the updated record back out to file `InOutFile`. Note that we must reset the file position pointer before performing the write operation.

Figure E.4 ▸
Random Access File Update

```
MODULE UpdateFile;
(*
   Updates the quantity field of selected records. Demonstrates
   random access.
*)

   FROM InOut IMPORT
     WriteCard, WriteLn, ReadString, WriteString, ReadInt;

   FROM FileSystem IMPORT
     File, Response,                                  (* type *)
     Lookup, Close, WriteNBytes, ReadNBytes, SetPos; (* procedures *)

   FROM SYSTEM IMPORT
     ADR, SIZE, TSIZE;                                (* procedures *)

   CONST
     Sentinel = -1;

   TYPE
     String12 = ARRAY [0..11] OF CHAR;
     FileRec = RECORD
       Name : String12;
       Quantity : INTEGER;
       Price : REAL
     END; (* FileRec *)

   VAR
     InOutFile : File;             (* the file being updated *)
     InOutName : String12;         (* the file directory name *)
     Part : FileRec;               (* file record *)
     InActual,                     (* number of bytes read *)
     OutActual : CARDINAL;         (* number of bytes written *)
     RecNum : INTEGER;             (* number of record to update *)

BEGIN (* UpdateFile *)
  (* Open the input/output file. *)
  WriteString ('Input/output file: ');
  ReadString (InOutName);  WriteLn;
  Lookup (InOutFile, InOutName, FALSE);
  IF InOutFile.res = notdone THEN
    WriteString ('Error - input/output file not opened');  WriteLn;
    HALT
  END; (* IF *)
```

```
 (* Update selected records until done. *)
 WriteString ('Enter the number of each record to update.');
 WriteLn;
 WriteString ('The first file record has record number 0.');
 WriteLn;
 WriteString ('Enter -1 to stop.');  WriteLn;
 LOOP
   WriteString ('Record number: ');  ReadInt (RecNum);  WriteLn;
   IF RecNum = Sentinel THEN
     EXIT
   END; (* IF *)

   (* Get existing record. *)
   SetPos (InOutFile, 0, ORD(RecNum) * SIZE(Part));
   ReadNBytes (InOutFile, ADR(Part), SIZE(Part), InActual);
   IF NOT InOutFile.eof THEN
     (* Modify record and write new record. *)
     WriteString ('Enter new quantity for item ');
     WriteString (Part.Name);  WriteString (': ');
     ReadInt (Part.Quantity);  WriteLn;
     SetPos (InOutFile, 0, ORD(RecNum) * SIZE(Part));
     WriteNBytes (InOutFile, ADR(Part), SIZE(Part), OutActual)
   ELSE
     WriteString ('Error - attempt to read past end of file.');
     WriteLn
   END; (* IF *)
   WriteLn
 END; (* WHILE *)

 WriteString ('File update completed.');  WriteLn;
 Close (InOutFile)
END UpdateFile.
```

```
Input/output file: Inventry.Bin
Enter the number of each record to update.
The first file record has record number 0.
Enter -1 to stop.
Record number: 1
Enter new quantity for item bolts: 50

Record number: 0
Enter new quantity for item nuts: 100

Record number: 2
Error - attempt to read past end of file.

Record number: -1
File update completed.
```

Random access methods should be used whenever a file's records are processed in arbitrary (non-sequential) order or when only a small percentage of the file's records are updated. If most of the file's records are processed in a uniform manner, it is more efficient to use sequential access as demonstrated in Figs. E.2 and E.3. Procedure `SetPos` is described next.

SetPos Procedure

FORM:
```
PROCEDURE SetPos (VAR f : File;
                      highpos,
                      lowpos : CARDINAL);
```

EXAMPLE: `SetPos (InOutFile, 0, ORD(RecNum) * SIZE(Part))`

INTERPRETATION: Moves the file position pointer for file *f* to the byte whose offset is specified by *highpos* and *lowpos*. If sixteen bits are used for storage of a cardinal number, the offset would be $highpos * 2^{16} + lowpos$.

Answers to Odd-Numbered Self-Check Exercises

Chapter 1

Section 1.2

1. Cell 0: −27.2
   Cell 999: 75.62

   Letter X is in Cell 998
   Fraction 0.005 is in Cell 2

Section 1.4

1. The statement "`X := A + B + C`" means "add the values represented by the names `A`, `B` and `C` together and place the sum in the memory cell represented by the name `X`."
   The statement "`X := Y / Z`" means "divide the value represented by `Y` by the value represented by `Z`, and place the result in the memory cell represented by `X`."
   The statement "`D := C - B + A`" means "subtract the value represented by `B` from the value represented by `C` and then add the value represented by `A`, placing the result in the memory cell represented by `D`."

Section 1.5

1. A compiler attempts to translate a high-level language program into machine language.
   A syntax error is an error found in a statement in a high-level language program which does not follow the syntax rules of the language. A syntax error would be found in the source file.

Section 1.7

1. `END`, `MODULE`, `BEGIN`, and `CONST` are Modula-2 reserved words. There are no standard identifiers.
   `Readln`, `BILL`, `Rate`, `OPERATE`, `START`, `XYZ123`, and `ThisIsALongOne` are identifiers.
   `SUE'S`, `123XYZ`, and `Y=Z` are invalid identifiers.

3. The necessary statements are:

```
WriteString ('The value of X is ');
WriteCard (X, 10);
WriteString (' pounds.');
WriteLn;
```

Section 1.9

Value	*Type*	
15	CARDINAL	
'XYZ'		invalid (a string)
'*'	CHAR	
$		invalid
25.123	REAL	
15.	REAL	
-999	INTEGER	
.123		invalid
'x'	CHAR	
"x"	CHAR	
'9'	CHAR	
'-5'		invalid (a string)

Chapter 2

Section 2.1

1. problem inputs
    the three numbers (`Num1,Num2,Num3 : REAL`)

   problem outputs
    the sum of the three numbers (`Sum : REAL`)
    the average of the three numbers (`Average : REAL`)

   algorithm
    1. read the values of the three numbers
    2. find the sum
    3. find the average
    4. print the sum and the average

   step 2 refinement
    2.1 add the three numbers together

   step 3 refinement
    3.1 divide the sum of the three numbers by `3.0`

Section 2.2

1.
```
PROCEDURE PrintH;

(* Prints the block letter "H". *)
BEGIN (* PrintH *)
  WriteString ("*      *");  WriteLn;
  WriteString ("*      *");  WriteLn;
  WriteString ("*      *");  WriteLn;
  WriteString ("********");  WriteLn;
  WriteString ("*      *");  WriteLn;
  WriteString ("*      *");  WriteLn;
  WriteString ("*      *");  WriteLn;
  WriteLn
END PrintH;

PROCEDURE PrintI;

(* Prints the block letter "I". *)
BEGIN (* PrintI *)
  WriteString ("   **");  WriteLn;
  WriteString ("   **");  WriteLn;
  WriteString ("   **");  WriteLn;
  WriteString ("   **");  WriteLn;
  WriteString ("   **");  WriteLn;
  WriteString ("   **");  WriteLn;
  WriteString ("   **");  WriteLn;
  WriteLn
END PrintI;

PROCEDURE PrintO;

(* Prints the block letter "O". *)
BEGIN (* PrintO *)
  WriteString ("  ****");  WriteLn;
  WriteString (" **  **");  WriteLn;
  WriteString ("**    **");  WriteLn;
  WriteString ("*      *");  WriteLn;
  WriteString ("**    **");  WriteLn;
  WriteString (" **  **");  WriteLn;
  WriteString ("  ****");  WriteLn;
  WriteLn
END PrintO;
```

Section 2.3

1.

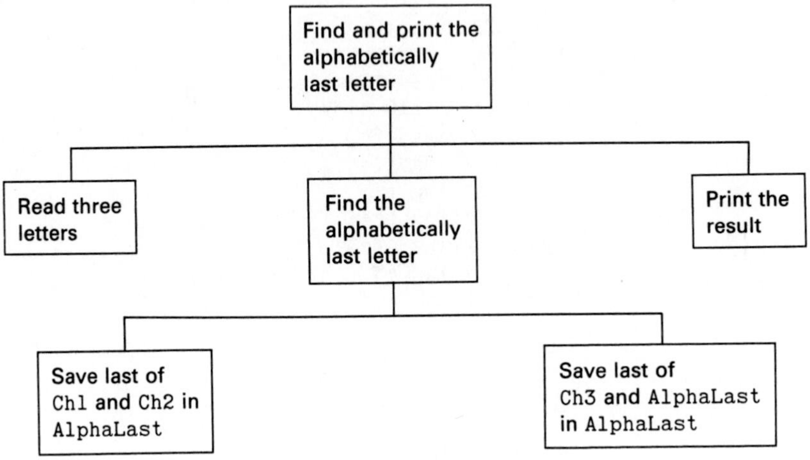
Find and print the alphabetically last letter
Read three letters
Find the alphabetically last letter
Print the result
Save last of Ch1 and Ch2 in AlphaLast
Save last of Ch3 and AlphaLast in AlphaLast

```
MODULE LastLetter;

(* Finds and prints the alphabetically last letter. *)

  FROM InOut IMPORT
    Read, Write, WriteString, WriteLn;

  VAR
    Ch1, Ch2, Ch3,               (* input  - three letters *)
    AlphaLast       : CHAR;      (* output - alphabetically
                                              last letter *)

BEGIN  (* LastLetter *)
  (* Read three letters *)
  WriteString ('Enter any three letters: ');
  Read (Ch1);  Write (Ch1);
  Read (Ch2);  Write (Ch2);
  Read (Ch3);  Write (Ch3);
  WriteLn;

  (* Save the larger of Ch1 and Ch2 in AlphaLast *)
  IF Ch1 > Ch2 THEN
    AlphaLast := Ch1       (* Ch1 comes after Ch2 *)
  ELSE
    AlphaLast := Ch2       (* Ch2 comes after Ch1 *)
  END;

  (* Save the larger of Ch3 and AlphaLast in AlphaLast *)
  IF Ch3 > AlphaLast THEN
    AlphaLast := Ch3       (* Ch3 comes after AlphaLast *)
  END;
```

```
    (* Print result *)
    Write (AlphaLast);
    WriteString (' is the last letter alphabetically');
    WriteLn
  END LastLetter.
```

3. a.
```
IF Item # 0 THEN
  Product := Product * Item
END;
WriteReal (Product, 12)
```
b.
```
IF X > Y THEN
  Z := X - Y
ELSE
  Z := Y - X
END
```
c.
```
IF X = 0 THEN
  ZeroCount := ZeroCount + 1
ELSIF X < 0 THEN
  MinusSum := MinusSum + X
ELSE
  PlusSum := PlusSum + X
END
```

Section 2.4

1.
Case 2:

PROGRAM STATEMENT	Ch1	Ch2	Ch3	AlphaFirst	EFFECT
	?	?	?	?	
`WriteString ('Enter ...')`					Prints a prompt
`Read (Ch1);`	H				Reads `Ch1`
`Read (CH2);`		T			Reads `Ch2`
`Read (Ch3);`			E		Reads `Ch3`
`IF Ch1 < Ch2 THEN`	H	T			Is `'H' < 'T'` ? value is true
`  AlphaFirst := Ch1`				H	`'H'` is first
`IF Ch3 < AlphaFirst THEN`			E	H	Is `'E' < 'H'` ? value is true
`  AlphaFirst := Ch3`				E	`'E'` is first

`Write (AlphaFirst);` `WriteString (' is first...')`	Prints E is the first letter...

Case 3:

PROGRAM STATEMENT	Ch1	Ch2	Ch3	AlphaFirst	EFFECT
	?	?	?	?	
`WriteString ('Enter ...')`					Prints a prompt
`Read (Ch1);`	E				Reads Ch1
`Read (CH2);`		T			Reads Ch2
`Read (Ch3);`			H		Reads Ch3
`IF Ch1 < Ch2 THEN`	E	T			Is 'E' < 'T' ? value is true
`AlphaFirst := Ch1`				E	'E' is first
`IF Ch3 < AlphaFirst THEN`			H	E	Is 'H' < 'E' ? value is false
`Write (AlphaFirst);` `WriteString ('is first...')`					Prints E is the first letter...

Case 4:

PROGRAM STATEMENT	Ch1	Ch2	Ch3	AlphaFirst	EFFECT
	?	?	?	?	
`WriteString ('Enter ...')`					Prints a prompt
`Read (Ch1);`	H				Reads Ch1
`Read (CH2);`		E			Reads Ch2
`Read (Ch3);`			T		Reads Ch3
`IF Ch1 < Ch2 THEN`	H	E			Is 'H' < 'E' ? value is false
`AlphaFirst := Ch2`				E	'E' is first
`IF Ch3 < AlphaFirst THEN`			T	E	Is 'T' < 'E' ? value is false
`Write (AlphaFirst);` `WriteString ('is first...')`					Prints E is the first letter...

Section 2.5

1.
```
MODULE ModPay;
(*
   Computes and prints gross pay, net pay and overtime pay
   given an hourly rate and the number of hours worked.
   Deducts a tax of $25 if gross salary exceeds $100;
   otherwise, deducts no tax.
*)
   FROM InOut IMPORT
     WriteString, WriteLn;

   FROM RealInOut IMPORT
     ReadReal, WriteReal;

   CONST
     TaxBracket = 100.00;  (* maximum salary for no deduction *)
     Tax = 25.00;                              (* tax amount *)
     MaxHours = 40.0;    (* maximum hours without overtime pay *)

   VAR
     Hours, Rate,   (* inputs - hours worked, hourly rate *)
     Gross, Net   : REAL; (* outputs - gross pay, net pay *)

BEGIN (* ModPay *)
  (* Enter Hours and Rate *)
  WriteString ('Hours worked? ');
  ReadReal (Hours);  WriteLn;
  WriteString ('Hourly rate? ');
  ReadReal (Rate);  WriteLn;

  Gross := Hours * Rate;        (* Compute gross salary *)

  (* Add overtime pay to Gross *)
  IF Hours > MaxHours THEN
    Gross := Gross + ((Hours - MaxHours) * Rate)
  END;

  (* Compute net salary *)
  IF Gross > TaxBracket THEN
    Net := Gross - Tax      (* Deduct a tax amount *)
  ELSE
    Net := Gross            (* Deduct no tax *)
  END;

  (* Print Gross and Net *)
  WriteString ('Gross salary is $');
  WriteReal (Gross, 12);
  WriteLn;
  WriteString ('Net salary is $');
  WriteReal (Net, 12);
  WriteLn
END ModPay.
```

3.
```
IF Claims = 0.0 THEN
  Dividend := Premium * (FixedRate + BonusRate)
ELSE
  Dividend := Premium * FixedRate
END
```

Section 2.6

1.
```
MODULE SumIntegers;
  (*
     Finds and prints the sum of all integers from 1 to N
     using two methods and compares the results.
  *)
     FROM InOut IMPORT
       ReadCard, WriteCard, WriteString, WriteLn;

     VAR
       N,                 (* input   - the last integer added *)
       Sum1, Sum2,        (* outputs - the sums being calculated *)
       i    : CARDINAL;   (* loop control - next integer added *)

  BEGIN (* SumIntegers *)
    (* Read the last integer N *)
    WriteString ('Enter the last integer in the sum: ');
    ReadCard (N);  WriteLn;

    (* Find the sum (Sum1) of all integers from 1 to N *)
    Sum1 := 0;                (* Initialize Sum1 to zero *)
    FOR i := 1 TO N DO
      Sum1 := Sum1 + i        (* Add the next integer to Sum1 *)
    END;

    (* Find the sum (Sum2) using the algebraic method *)
    Sum2 := (N * (N + 1)) DIV 2;

    (* compare the results *)
    IF Sum1 = Sum2 THEN
      WriteString ('The results match.');  WriteLn;
      WriteString ('The sum is ');
      WriteCard (Sum1, 5);  WriteLn
    ELSE
      WriteString ('The results do not match.');  WriteLn
    END
  END SumIntegers.
```

Section 2.7

1.
```
MODULE MultiplyItems;

  (* Finds and prints the product of a list of data items. *)

     FROM InOut IMPORT
```

```
      ReadCard, WriteString, WriteLn;

    FROM RealInOut IMPORT
      ReadReal, WriteReal;

    VAR
      NumItems : CARDINAL; (* input  -  the number of data items *)

      Item,                (* input  - the next data item *)
      Product : REAL;      (* output - accumulated product *)
      Count : CARDINAL;    (* loop control - count of items
                                         multiplied so far *)

BEGIN (* MultiplyItems *)
  (* Read the number of data items to be multiplied *)
  WriteString ('Number of items to be muliplied? ');
  ReadCard (NumItems);  WriteLn;

  (* Find the product (Product) of NumItems data items *)
  Product := 1.0;                (* Initialize Product to one *)
  FOR Count := 1 TO NumItems DO
    WriteString ('Next item to be multiplied? ');
    ReadReal (Item);                     (* Read next data item *)
    WriteLn;
    IF Item # 0.0 THEN
      Product := Product * Item      (* Multiply it by Product *)
    END (* IF *)
  END;  (* FOR *)

  (* Print the final value of Product *)
  WriteString ('The product is ');
  WriteReal (Product, 12);  WriteLn
END MultiplyItems.
```

Chapter 3

Section 3.1

1. Diagrams used: FOR statement, identifier, expression, statement.
   To check identifier (I), examine letter.
   To check expression (1), examine simple expression, term, factor, integer literal.
   To check expression (N), examine simple expression, term, factor, designator, qualified identifier, identifier.
   To check statement, examine assignment statement.

   To check assignment statement (Sum := Sum + I), examine designator, expression.
   To check designator (Sum), examine qualified identifier, identifier, letter.
   To check expression (Sum + I), examine simple expression, add operator, term, factor, designator.

The identifier N is used as an expression in the FOR statement.
The identifier Sum is used as a designator in the assignment statement and as a term in the expression part of the assignment statement. The identifier I is used as an identifier in the FOR statement and as a term in the expression part of the assignment statement.

Section 3.2

1.
```
IF X > Y THEN
  Larger := X;
  Smaller := Y;
  WriteString ('X Larger');  WriteLn
ELSE (* Y > X *)
  Larger := Y;
  Smaller := X;
  WriteString ('Y Larger');  WriteLn
END
```
3. Negative values for Tax would be accepted and erroneous results would be computed.
5.
```
IF GPA < 1.0 THEN
  WriteString ('Failed semester -- registration suspended')
ELSIF GPA < 2.0 THEN
  WriteString ('On probation for next semester')
ELSIF GPA < 3.0 THEN
  Write (' ')
ELSIF GPA < 3.5 THEN
  WriteString ('Deans list for the semester')
ELSE
  WriteString ('Highest honors for semester')
END
```

Section 3.3

1. 2 4 8 16 32 64 128 256 512 1024

Section 3.4

1. ▸ Height is equal to Tower before the loop begins.
   ▸ t is equal to 0.0 before the loop begins.
   ▸ t during pass i is equal to t during pass i−1 + DeltaT (for i > 1).
   ▸ Height during pass i is equal to Tower − 0.5gt^2 (for i > 1).
   ▸ Just after loop exit, Height = 0.0

Section 3.5

1.
```
(* invariant:
     t during pass i is equal to DeltaT * (i-1) (for i > 1) and
     Height is equal to Tower - 0.5gt^2
*)
```

Section 3.6

1. If one data value besides the sentinel value is supplied, the product will equal that value. If the assignment statement is performed after the read statement, `LastNum` would be the same as `NextNum` so the product would equal the first value entered.

Section 3.7

1.
```
MODULE PowersOfN;

(*
   Prints a table of powers and n raised to those powers
   while the results are less than MaxPower
*)

  FROM InOut IMPORT
    ReadCard, WriteString, WriteCard, WriteLn;

  VAR
    N,                       (* base value *)
    Power,                   (* power to which N is raised *)
    PowerOfN,                (* N raised to the power  *)
    MaxPower : CARDINAL;     (* Maximum power for N *)

BEGIN  (* PowersOfN *)
  (* Read in values for N and MaxPower *)
  WriteString ('Please enter a value for n: ');
  ReadCard (N);
  WriteString ('Please enter the maximum value to raise n to:');
  ReadCard (MaxPower);

  (* Print table headings *)
  WriteString ('  Power n^Power  ');  WriteLn;
  WriteString ('  ----- ---------');  WriteLn;

  (* Initialize Power and N to the Power values *)
  Power := 0;
  PowerOfN := 1;

  (* Print table *)
  WHILE PowerOfN < MaxPower DO
    WriteCard (Power, 5);
    WriteCard (PowerOfN, 7);  WriteLn;
    INC (Power);
    PowerOfN := PowerOfN * N
  END (* WHILE *)
END PowersOfN.
```

Chapter 4

Section 4.2

1.

Actual Parameter	*Formal Parameter*	*Description*
Num1	X	REAL variable
Num3	Y	REAL variable

Actual Parameter	*Formal Parameter*	*Description*
Num2	X	REAL variable
Num3	Y	REAL variable

Section 4.4

1.

Actual Parameter	*Formal Parameters*	*Description*
M	A	INTEGER, value
MaxInt	B	INTEGER, value
Y	C	REAL, variable
X	D	REAL, variable
Next	E	CHAR, variable

For the second list, 35 corresponds to A and M * 10 corresponds to B. The rest of the table is the same.

3. a. Data type of third actual parameter is incorrect.
   b. correct
   c. correct
   d. Data type of first actual parameter is incorrect.
   e. First and second parameters are not variables.
   f. correct
   g. A and B are not declared in the main program.
   h. correct
   i. First two parameters are expressions, not variables.
   j. Data type of first actual parameter, X (type REAL), is incorrect.
   k. There are too many parameters.
   l. correct

Section 4.5

1.

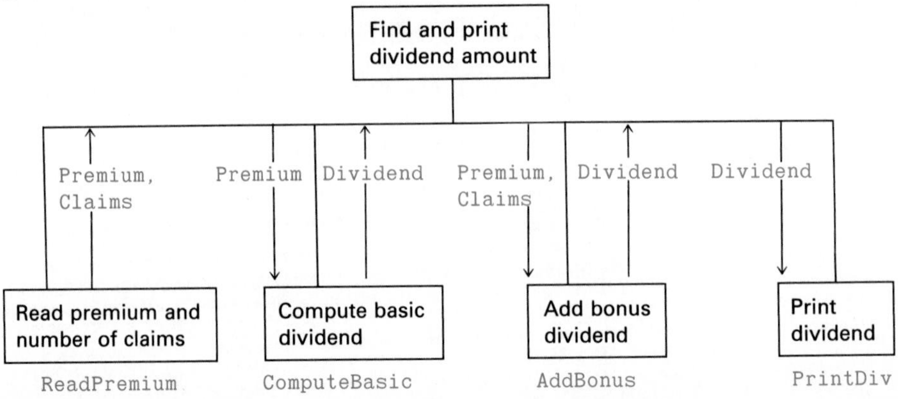

```
PROCEDURE ReadPremium (VAR Premium, Claims (* output *) : REAL);

(* Reads number of premiums and Claims. *)

BEGIN (* ReadPremium *)
  WriteString ('Premium amount: $');
  ReadReal (Premium);  WriteLn;
  WriteString ('Number of claims: ');
  ReadReal (Claims);  WriteLn
END ReadPremium;

PROCEDURE ComputeBasic (Premium (* input *) : REAL;
                        VAR Dividend (* output *) : REAL);

(* Computes basic dividend. *)
CONST
  FixedRate = 0.045;

BEGIN (* ComputeBasic *)
  Dividend := Premium * FixedRate;
END ComputeBasic;

PROCEDURE AddBonus (Premium, Claims (* input *) : REAL;
                    VAR Dividend (* input/output *) : REAL);

(* Adds bonus dividend for zero claims. *)
CONST
  BonusRate = 0.005;

BEGIN (* AddBonus *)
  IF Claims = 0.0 THEN
    Dividend := Dividend + (Premium * BonusRate)
  END (* IF *)
END AddBonus;

PROCEDURE PrintDiv (Dividend (* input *) : REAL);

(* Displays dividend value. *)
BEGIN (* PrintDiv *)
  WriteString ('Total dividend is $');
  WriteReal (Dividend, 12);  WriteLn
END PrintDiv;
```

Section 4.6

1. The scope of variable `N` declared in `Outer` is procedure `Outer`. The main program body and procedure `Too` are not included in the scope of `N`. `Inner` is excluded; because `N` is declared as a local variable in `Inner`.
3. For `Outer`: parameter `X` is set to `5.5`; global variable `Y` is set to `6.6`; local variables `M` and `N` are set to `2` and `3`, respectively; identifier `O` is undeclared.

   For `Too` and `Nested`: Global variables `X` and `Y` are set to `5.5` and `6.6`, respectively; identifiers `M`, `N`, and `O` are undeclared.

Section 4.7

1. Declare a local variable `NumOverDraft` (initial value `0`) in `Process` and pass it as a variable parameter to `Update`. Declare a local constant `Penalty` (value is `15.0`) in `Update` and change the `IF` statement in `Update` as follows:

```
IF TranType = Deposit THEN
  CurBal := CurBal + Amount;
  INC (Deposit);
  IF CurBal >= 0.0 THEN
    NumOverDraft := 0
  END (* IF *)
ELSIF TranType = Check THEN
  CurBal := CurBal - Amount;
  INC (NumCheck);
  IF CurBal < 0.0 THEN
    CurBal := CurBal - Penalty;
    INC (NumOverDraft)
  END (* IF *)
END (* IF *)
```

Pass `NumOverDraft` to `DisplayTran` and modify the `IF` statement nested inside the alternative that is executed when `TranType = Check` as follows:

```
ELSIF TranType = Check THEN
  IF CurBal < 0.0 THEN
    WriteString ('Overdraft #');
    WriteCard (NumOverDraft, 4);  WriteLn
  END (* inner IF *)
```

3. This should cause the value of `MinSat` to be larger than the value of `MinOut`. Consequently, all scores would be considered unsatisfactory or outstanding; there would be no satisfactory scores. Add the `IF` statement below at the end of `ReadScale`.

```
IF MinSat > MinOut THEN
  WriteString ('Switching MinSat and MinOut values');  WriteLn;
  TempScore := MinSat;  MinSat := MinOut;  MinOut := TempScore
END (* IF *)
```

Chapter 5

Section 5.2

1. If `Base` is `2` instead of `10`, `PrintDigits` displays the binary number corresponding to its parameter. When `Base` is `2`, `PrintDigits (23)` displays the binary digits `1,1,1,0,1` (the binary number `10111` has the decimal value `23`); `PrintDigits (64)` displays the binary digits `0,0,0,0,0,0,1` (the binary number `1000000` has the decimal value `64`). When `Base` is `8`, `PrintDigits` displays octal (base `8`) numbers. When

Base is 8, PrintDigits (23) displays 7,2 (the octal number 27 has the decimal value 23); PrintDigits (64) displays 0,0,1 (the octal number 100 has the decimal value 64).

3. a. 3 b. −3 c. invalid, REAL operand for MOD d. −3.14159 e. invalid use of integer division operator with REAL operands f. invalid use of real division operator with INTEGER operands g. invalid assignment of INTEGER expression to REAL variable h. invalid, division by 0 i. invalid, negative divisor for MOD j. 3 k. −3.0 l. invalid assignment of REAL expression to INTEGER variable m. invalid REAL operand for DIV n. 0 o. 1 p. invalid, division by 0 q. 3
5. a. White is 1.6666... b. Green is 0.6666... c. Orange is 0 d. Blue is −3.0 e. Lime is 2 f. Purple is 0.6666...

Section 5.3

1.
```
PROCEDURE RaiseBtoA (a, b (* input *) : REAL;
                     VAR BtoA (* output *) : REAL);

(* Computes b ^ a (b raised to the power a). *)
BEGIN (* RaiseBtoA *)
  BtoA := exp(a * ln(b))
END RaiseBtoA;
```
3.
```
PROCEDURE EtoX (X (* input *) : REAL;
                N (* input *) : CARDINAL;
                VAR ExpX (* output *) : REAL);

VAR
  Term : REAL;          (* next series term *)
  i : CARDINAL;         (* loop control variable *)

BEGIN (* EtoX *)
  Term := 1.0;
  ExpX := 1.0;
  FOR i := 1 TO N DO
    Term := (Term * X) / FLOAT(i);
    ExpX := ExpX + Term
  END (* FOR *)
END EtoX;
```

The main program follows.

```
MODULE TestEtoX;

  FROM InOut IMPORT ReadCard, WriteString, WriteLn;
  FROM RealInOut IMPORT ReadReal;
  FROM MathLib0 IMPORT exp;

  VAR
    X, Result : REAL;
    N : CARDINAL;

  (* insert procedure EtoX here. *)
```

```
BEGIN (* TestEtoX *)
  ReadReal (X);
  ReadCard (N);
  EToX (X, N, Result);
  IF ABS(Result - exp(X)) <= 0.001 THEN
    WriteString ('O.K.')
  ELSE
    WriteString ('Not O.K.')
  END; (* IF *)
  WriteLn
END TestEtoX.
```

Section 5.4

1.
```
        TRUE    4.0   2.0  3.0  2.0
  NOT (Flag OR ((Y + Z) >= (X - Z)))

                   +          -

                  6.0          1.0

                        >=

       TRUE          TRUE

            OR

       TRUE

            NOT

       FALSE
```

3. `Divisor := (N MOD M) = 0`

Section 5.5

1. a. `1` b. `' '` c. `'F'` d. `1` e. `0` f. `'Z'` g. `2`

Section 5.6

1. a. `TRUE` b. `TRUE` c. `FALSE` d. `FALSE` e. `32` f. `'C'` g. `'C'` h. `'A'`

Section 5.7

1. invalid subranges: a, d, e, f

Section 5.8

1.
```
PROCEDURE PrintPrimes (N (* input *) : CARDINAL);

  (* Displays all divisors of N. *)
```

```
    VAR
      i : CARDINAL;      (* loop control variable *)

  BEGIN (* PrintPrimes *)
    WriteString ('List of divisors of ');
    WriteCard (N, 0);  WriteLn;
    FOR i := 1 TO N DO
      IF N MOD i = 0 THEN
        WriteCard (N, 4);
        WriteLn
      END (* IF *)
    END (* FOR *)
  END PrintPrimes;
```

Chapter 6

Section 6.3

1. Insert the statement

```
FROM SimpleIO IMPORT EnterCard;
```

and remove the declaration of procedure `EnterCard` from the main program.

Section 6.5

1. a. `1` b. `4` c. `Saturday` d. `FALSE` e. `Saturday` f. `Tuesday` g. `Sunday` h. `TRUE`

Section 6.7

1.
```
PROCEDURE ReadDay (VAR InDay (* output *) : Day;
                    VAR ValidDay (* output *) : BOOLEAN);
(*
   Reads a value into InDay and sets ValidDay to indicate success
   or failure.
*)
   VAR
     Chl, Ch2 : CHAR;

BEGIN (* ReadDay *)
  WriteString ('Enter the first 2 letters of the day name: ');
  Read (Chl);  Write (Chl);  Read (Ch2);  Write (Ch2);  WriteLn;
  Chl := CAP(Chl);  Ch2 := CAP(Ch2);

  IF (Chl = 'S') & (Ch2 = 'U') THEN
    InDay := Sunday;     ValidDay := TRUE
  ELSIF (Chl = 'M') & (Ch2 = 'O') THEN
    InDay := Monday;     ValidDay := TRUE
  ...
  ELSIF (Chl = 'S') & (Ch2 = 'A') THEN
```

```
      InDay := Saturday;  ValidDay := TRUE
    ELSE
      ValidDay := FALSE
    END (* IF *)
  END ReadDay;
```

Section 6.8

1. The program body follows.

```
BEGIN (* Main *)
  WriteString ('Enter a data line after the prompt ">" ');
  WriteLn;
  FOR i := 1 TO 3 DO
    Write ('>');
    EchoLine
  END (* FOR *)
END Main.
```

Chapter 7

Section 7.1

1.
```
IF OneDay = Sunday THEN
    WriteString ('Sunday')
  ELSIF OneDay = Monday THEN
    WriteString ('Monday')
  ELSIF OneDay = Tuesday THEN
    WriteString ('Tuesday')
  ELSIF OneDay = Wednesday THEN
    WriteString ('Wednesday')
  ELSIF OneDay = Thursday THEN
    WriteString ('Thursday')
  ELSIF OneDay = Friday THEN
    WriteString ('Friday')
  ELSIF OneDay = Saturday THEN
    WriteString ('Saturday')
  END (* IF *)
```
3.
```
CASE NextCh OF
    '+','-','*','=','#','<','>','&'
            : WriteString ('NextCh is an operator symbol')
  | ',',';','(',')','[',']','|'
            : WriteString ('NextCh is a punctuation symbol')
  | 0..9    : WriteString ('NextCh is a digit')
  | 'A'..'Z': WriteString ('NextCh is a letter')
  | 'a'..'z': WriteString ('NextCh is a letter')
  ELSE
    WriteString ('NextCh is something else')
  END (* CASE *);
```

Equivalent IF Statement

```
IF (NextCh = '+') OR (NextCh = '-') OR (NextCh = '*') OR
   (NextCh = '=') OR (NextCh = '#') OR (NextCh = '<') OR
   (NextCh = '>') OR (NextCh = '&') THEN
  WriteString ('NextCh is an operator symbol')
ELSIF (NextCh = ',') OR (NextCh = ';') OR (NextCh = '(') OR
      (NextCh = ')') OR (NextCh = '[') OR (NextCh = ']') OR
      (NextCh = '|') THEN
  WriteString ('NextCh is a punctuation symbol')
ELSIF (NextCh >=0) & (NextCh <= 9) THEN
  WriteString ('NextCh is a digit')
ELSIF ((NextCh >= 'A') & (NextCh <= 'Z')) OR
      ((NextCh >= 'a') & (NextCh <= 'z')) THEN
  WriteString ('NextCh is a letter')
ELSE
  WriteString ('NextCh is something else')
END (* IF *)
```

Section 7.2

1.
```
FOR Digit := 0 TO 9 DO
   Write (Digit);  WriteString ('    ');
   WriteCard (ORD(Digit));  WriteLn
 END (* FOR *)
```

Section 7.3

1.
```
PROCEDURE  PrintStatMenu;

(* Prints a menu for choosing an option *)

BEGIN
   WriteString ('1. Compute an average'); WriteLn;
   WriteString ('2. Compute a standard deviation');WriteLn;
   WriteString ('3. Find the median'); WriteLn;
   WriteString ('4. Find the smallest and largest value');WriteLn;
   WriteString ('5. Plot the data'); WriteLn;
   WriteString ('6. Exit the program'); WriteLn
END PrintStatMenu;
```

3.
```
FOR Num := 10 TO 90 BY 10 DO
   WriteCard (Num, 2);
   WriteLn
END (* FOR *)


Num := 10;
REPEAT
  WriteCard (Num,2);
  WriteLn;
  INC (Num,10)
UNTIL Num = 100;
```

5.
```
PROCEDURE Exponent ( X, Delta (* input *) : REAL;
                     VAR Total (* output *) : REAL);

  (* This gives an approximation of the exp function. *)

    VAR
      ApproxError, Term : REAL;
      N : CARDINAL;

  BEGIN
    Total := 1.0;
    N := 1;
    Term := 1.0;
    REPEAT
      Term := Term * X / FLOAT(N);
      Total := Total + Term;
      INC (N);
      ApproxError := ABS(Total - exp(X))
    UNTIL ApproxError < Delta
  END Exponent;
```

Section 7.4

1.
```
Power := 1;
LOOP
  IF Power >= 1000 THEN
    EXIT
  END; (* IF *)
  WriteCard (Power, 5);
  Power := Power * 2
END (* LOOP *)
```

Section 7.5

1.
```
MODULE MultTable;

  (* prints a multiplication table *)

    FROM InOut IMPORT WriteString, WriteCard, WriteLn;

    CONST  MaxDigit = 9;                (* largest digit *)

    TYPE  SmallInt = [0..MaxDigit];     (* digit range *)

    PROCEDURE Heading;

    (* Print table headings*)

      VAR
        Operand2 : SmallInt;

    BEGIN (* Heading *)
```

```
      WriteString ('*');
      FOR Operand2 := 0 TO MaxDigit DO
        WriteCard (Operand2, 4)      (* print digits in heading*)
      END; (* FOR *)
      WriteLn
    END Heading;

    PROCEDURE Table;

    (* Print table body *)

      VAR
        Product: CARDINAL;
        Operand1, Operand2 : SmallInt;

    BEGIN (* Table *)
      FOR Operand1 := 0 TO MaxDigit DO
        (* print each row of the table *)
        WriteCard (Operand1, 1);
        FOR Operand2 := 0 TO MaxDigit DO
          Product := Operand1 * Operand2;
          WriteCard (Product, 4)
        END; (* FOR Operand2 *)
        WriteLn
      END (* FOR Operand1 *)
    END Table;

  BEGIN (* MultTable *)
    Heading;
    Table
  END MultTable.
```

3.
```
FOR  I := 1 TO 4 DO
  FOR J := 1 TO I DO
    WriteCard (J, 3)
  END; (* FOR J *)
  WriteLn
END (* FOR I*);

FOR I := 3 TO 1 BY -1 DO
  FOR J := 1 TO I DO
    WriteCard (J, 3)
  END; (* FOR J *)
  WriteLn
END (* FOR I *);
```

Section 7.6

1.
```
PROCEDURE Cube (X : REAL) : REAL;

BEGIN (* Cube *)
  RETURN X * X * X
END Cube;
```

3.
```
PROCEDURE Exponent (Number, Power : REAL) : REAL;

(* Raises Number to a given Power *)

BEGIN (* Exponent *)
  RETURN exp(Power * ln(Number))
END Exponent;
```

5.
```
PROCEDURE IsLowercase (Ch:CHAR) : BOOLEAN;

(* Determines if Ch is lowercase *)

BEGIN
  RETURN Ch = CAP(Ch)
END IsLowercase;


PROCEDURE IsLowercase(Ch:CHAR) : BOOLEAN;

(* determines if Ch is lower case *);

BEGIN
  RETURN ((Ch >= 'a') & (Ch <= 'z'))
END IsLowercase;
```

Chapter 8

Section 8.2

1. Displays 8.0; displays 2.5; displays 3.5; displays 12.0; illegal attempt to display `X[10]`; illegal attempt to display `X[10]`; displays 12.0; assigns 12.0 to `X[5]`; assigns 12.0 to `X[5]`; illegal assignment; assigns 17.5 to `X[8]`

Section 8.3

1.
```
PROCEDURE Copy (InArray : AnArray; Size : CARDINAL;
                VAR OutArray : AnArray);

(* copies each value in array InArray to array OutArray *)

   VAR I:INTEGER;

BEGIN
  FOR I := 1 TO Size DO
    OutArray[I] := InArray[I]
  END (* FOR *)
END Copy;
```

Section 8.5

1.
```
DEFINITION MODULE RealArrayManip;

   EXPORT QUALIFIED Initialize, Report;
```

```
  PROCEDURE Initialize (VAR X (* output *) : ARRAY OF REAL);

  PROCEDURE Report (X (* input *) : ARRAY OF REAL;
                    Min, Max (* input *) : CARDINAL);

END RealArrayManip.
```

3.
```
TYPE
  Index = [1..MaxSize];
  AnArray = ARRAY Index OF CHAR;
  BoolArray = ARRAY Index OF BOOLEAN;

PROCEDURE Compare (X, Y (* input *) : AnArray;
                   N (* input *) : Index;
                   VAR Z (* output *) : BoolArray);

(*  Assigns TRUE to Z[I] if X[I] = Y[I]; assigns  FALSE
    otherwise   *)

    VAR I : Index;

BEGIN (* Compare *)
  FOR I := 1 TO N DO
    Z[I] := X[I] = Y[I]
  END (* FOR *)
END Compare;
```

Section 8.6

1. a. An array of characters with 20 elements and subscripts of 1 to 20.
   b. An array of BOOLEAN type values with 10 elements and the subscripts are digit characters from '0' to '9'.
   c. An array of real numbers with 11 elements and subscripts of the integers −5 to 5.
   d. An array of characters with 2 elements and subscripts of FALSE and TRUE.

Section 8.7

1.
```
CONST
  nul = 00C;

TYPE
  STRING = ARRAY [0..StringSize-1] OF CHAR;

PROCEDURE Length (InString : STRING) : INTEGER;

(* finds the actual length of InString excluding blanks *)

   VAR
     I : CARDINAL;

BEGIN
```

```
    FOR I := 0 TO StringSize-1 DO
      IF InString[I] = nul THEN
        RETURN I
      END (* IF *)
    END; (* FOR *)
    (* assertion: end of string reached without finding nul. *)

    (* Define result. *)
    RETURN StringSize
  END Length;
```

3.
```
MODULE Palindrome;
    FROM Strings IMPORT Length;
    FROM InOut IMPORT ReadString, WriteString, WriteLn;
    CONST StringSize = 80;
    TYPE
      STRING = ARRAY [0..StringSize-1] OF CHAR;

    VAR
      InString, OutString : STRING;
      I : CARDINAL;

    (* Insert procedure Reverse. *)

  BEGIN
    ReadString (InString);
    Reverse (InString, OutString);

    (* Compare two strings. *)
    I := 0;
    WHILE (I < Length(InString)) & (InString[I] = OutString[I]) DO
      INC (I)
    END; (* WHILE *)
    (* assertion: end of strings reached or non-match found. *)

    IF I = Length(InString) THEN
      WriteString ('String is a palindrome')
    ELSE
      WriteString ('String is not a palindrome')
    END; (* IF *)
    WriteLn
  END Palindrome
```

Section 8.9

1. Add the following export statement to the definition module.

```
EXPORT QUALIFIED WriteStringFormat, MyReadString;
```

Add the procedure headers to the definition module and the complete procedure declarations to the implementation module. Also add the following import statement to the implementation module.

```
FROM InOut IMPORT EOL, Read, Write, WriteString;
FROM Strings IMPORT Length;
```

Chapter 9

Section 9.1

1.
```
TYPE
  String3 : ARRAY [0..2] OF CHAR;

  Part = RECORD
           PartNum : String3;
           Quantity : INTEGER;
           Price : REAL
         END; (* Part *)
```

Section 9.2

1.
```
WITH Clerk DO
  WriteString ('ID number : ');  WriteCard (ID, 4);  WriteLn;
  WriteString ('Name: ');  WriteString (Name);  WriteLn;
  WriteString ('Sex: ');
  CASE Sex OF
    Female : WriteString ('Female ')
  | Male   : WriteString ('Male ')
  END; (* CASE *);
  WriteLn;
  WriteString ('Number of dependents : ');
  WriteCard (NumDepend, 2);  WriteLn;
  WriteString ('Hourly Rate : ');  WriteReal (Rate, 12);  WriteLn;
  WriteString ('Taxable Salary: ');
  WriteReal (TaxSal, 12);  WriteLn
END (*WITH*);
```

Section 9.3

1.
```
PROCEDURE BookEntry (VAR OneBook (* output *) : CatalogueEntry);

BEGIN (* BookEntry *)
  WITH OneBook DO
    WriteString ("Author's name : ");
    ReadString (Author);     WriteLn;
    WriteString ('Title : ');
    ReadString (Title);      WriteLn;
    WriteString ('Publisher : ');
    ReadString (Publisher);  WriteLn;
    WriteString ('Date published : ');
    ReadCard (PubDate);      WriteLn
  END (* WITH *)
END BookEntry;
```

Section 9.4

1.
```
PROCEDURE MultiplyComplex (A, B   (*input*) : Complex;
                           VAR C (*output*) : Complex);
(*
   Complex number C is the product of complex numbers A and B.
   Pre  : A and B are assigned values and C is initialized.
   Post : C is the complex product of A and B.
*)
BEGIN (* MultiplyComplex *)
     C.RealPart := A.RealPart * B.RealPart -
                   A.ImaginaryPart * B.ImaginaryPart;
     C.ImaginaryPart := A.RealPart * B.ImaginaryPart +
                        A.ImaginaryPart * B.RealPart;
END MultiplyComplex;


PROCEDURE DivideComplex (A, B  (* input *)  : Complex;
                         VAR C (* output *) : Complex);
(*
   Complex number C is the quotient of complex numbers A and B.
   Pre  : A and B are assigned values and C is initialized.
   Post : C is the complex quotient of A and B.
*)
  VAR
    Divisor : REAL;

BEGIN (* DivideComplex *)
  Divisor := B.RealPart * B.RealPart +
             B.ImaginaryPart * B.ImaginaryPart;
  C.RealPart := (A.RealPart * B.RealPart +
                 A.ImaginaryPart * B.ImaginaryPart) / Divisor;
  C.ImaginaryPart := (A.ImaginaryPart * B.RealPart -
                      A.RealPart * B.ImaginaryPart) / Divisor
END DivideComplex;
```

Section 9.5

1.
```
PROCEDURE ReadDate (VAR NewDate (*output*) : Date);
(*
   Pre : None
   Post: Returns a record of type Date in NewDate.
   Uses: ReadMonth from DatesADT; EnterCard from SimpleIO;
         WriteString, WriteLn from InOut.
*)
BEGIN (* ReadDate *)
  WITH NewDate DO
    WriteString ('Enter month ');
    ReadMonth (ThisMonth);
    WriteLn;
    WriteString ('Enter day: ');  WriteLn;
    EnterCard (Day, 1, 31);
```

```
    WriteString ('Enter year: ');  WriteLn;
    EnterCard (Year, 1900, 1999)
  END (* WITH*);
END ReadDate;
```

Section 9.7

1.
```
PROCEDURE ReadShape (VAR OneFig (* output *) : Figure;

(*
   Reads the shape character and defines OneFig.Shape.
   Pre : None
   Post: The tag field of OneFig is defined based
         on the data character read.
*)

   VAR Letter : CHAR;

BEGIN
  WriteString('Enter the object's shape.'); WriteLn;
  WriteString('Enter R (rectangle), S (square), or C (circle) : ');
  Read(Letter);
  CASE Letter OF
    'R': OneFig.Shape := Rectangle;
   | 'S': OneFig.Shape := Square;
   | 'C': OneFig.Shape := Circle
  ELSE
    OneFig.Shape := Other
  END (* CASE *)
END ReadShape;
```

Chapter 10

Section 10.1

1. Declare `CampusName` and `ClassName` as arrays of strings and initialize them so that `CampusName[Delaware]` is `'Delaware'` and `ClassName[Junior]` is `'Junior'`.

```
CONST
  MaxCourse = 5;
```

a.
```
(* enter enrollment data *)
FOR OurCampus :=  Main TO Montco DO
  FOR I := 1 TO MaxCourse DO
    FOR ClassRank := Freshman TO Senior DO
      WriteString ('Enter No. of ');
      WriteString (ClassName[ClassRank]);
      WriteString (' students in class # ');  WriteCard (I, 1);
      WriteString (' at ');  WriteString (CampusName[OurCampus]);
      WriteString (' campus: ');
      ReadCard (ClassEnroll[I,OurCampus,ClassRank]);  WriteLn
```

```
    END (* FOR ClassRank *)
  END (* FOR I *)
END (* FOR OurCampus *)
```

b.
```
ClassSum := 0;
FOR OurCampus := Main TO Montco DO
  FOR I := 1 TO MaxCourse DO
    ClassSum := ClassSum + ClassEnroll[I,OurCampus,Junior];
  END (* FOR I *)
END (* FOR OurCampus *)
```

c.
```
ClassSum := 0;
FOR OurCampus := Main TO Montco DO
  ClassSum := ClassSum + ClassEnroll[2,OurCampus,Sophomore]
END (* FOR *);
```

d.
```
StudentTotal := 0;
WriteString ('ENROLLMENT AT MAIN CAMPUS ');  WriteLn;
WriteString ('--------------------------');  WriteLn;
WriteString ('  Course #     Students  ');  WriteLn;
FOR I := 1 TO MaxCourse DO
  ClassSum := 0;
  FOR ClassRank := Freshman TO Senior DO
    ClassSum := ClassSum + ClassEnroll[I,Main,ClassRank]
  END; (* FOR ClassRank *)
  WriteCard (I,6);
  WriteCard (ClassSum,14); WriteLn;
  StudentTotal := StudentTotal + ClassSum
END; (* FOR I *)

WriteString ('Total students enrolled at Main campus : ');
WriteCard (StudentTotal, 4);  WriteLn
```

e.
```
UpperClassTotal := 0;
WriteString ('ENROLLMENT OF UPPERCLASS STUDENTS BY CAMPUS');
  WriteLn;
WriteString ('-------------------------------------------');
  WriteLn;
WriteString ('        Campus              Enrollment ');  WriteLn;
FOR OurCampus := Main TO Montco DO
  ClassSum := 0;
  FOR ClassRank := Junior TO Senior DO
    FOR I := 1 TO MaxCourse DO
      ClassSum := ClassSum + ClassEnroll[I,OurCampus,ClassRank]
    END (* FOR I *)
  END; (* FOR ClassRank *)
  WriteString (CampusName[OurCampus]);
  WriteCard (ClassSum, 15);  WriteLn;
  UpperClassTotal := UpperClassTotal + ClassSum
END; (* FOR OurCampus *)

WriteString ('Total enrolled upperclass students is : ');
WriteCard (UpperClassTotal, 5)
```

Section 10.2

1. `PrintMenu` is implemented as a sequence of `WriteString` statements. `TabMonth` must compute and save the sales amounts for `January` of all years covered in

SumByMonth[January], etc. It will be similar to TabYear except that the order of the loop control variables should be reversed. The assignment statement

```
SumByMonth[CurMonth] := Sum
```

should appear at the end of the inner loop.

Section 10.3

1.
```
PROCEDURE ReadData (VAR Names : NameArray;
                    VAR Scores : ScoreArray;
                    VAR Grades : GradeArray);
(* Read data into 3 parallel arrays *)

   VAR I : CARDINAL;

BEGIN (* ReadData *)
  FOR I := 1 TO MaxClassSize DO
    WriteString ('Enter student name : ');
    ReadString (Names[I]);  WriteLn;
    WriteString ('Enter score (0-100) : ');
    ReadInt (Scores[I]);  WriteLn;
    WriteString ('Enter grade ('A-F') : ');
    Read (Grades[I]);  WriteLn;  WriteLn
  END (* FOR *)
END ReadData;
```

Section 10.4

1.
```
PROCEDURE PrintStat (Exam (*input*) : ExamStats);

(* Displays all exam statistics *)

BEGIN (* PrintStat *)
  WITH Exam DO
    WriteString ('Low score on exam : ');
    WriteInt (Low, 3);          WriteLn;
    WriteString ('High score on exam : ');
    WriteInt (High, 3);         WriteLn;
    WriteString ('Average score : ');
    WriteReal (Average, 6);     WriteLn;
    WriteString ('Standard deviation : ');
    WriteReal (StandardDev, 6); WriteLn;
  END (* WITH *)
END PrintStat;
```

Section 10.5

1.
```
PROCEDURE PassCheck (Test (* input *) : GradeBookPage;
                     VAR PassCount (* output *) : CARDINAL);
(*
   Returns in PassCount the number of students with a grade of
   D or better
   Pre  : Class and NumStu are defined
```

```
    Post : Returns the number of passing students in PassCount.
*)
    VAR
     CurStu : CARDINAL;                    (* array subscript *)

BEGIN (* PassCheck *)
  PassCount := 0;
  WITH Test DO
    FOR CurStu := 1 TO NumStu DO
      IF Class[CurStu].Grade >= 'D' THEN
        PassCount := PassCount + 1
      END (* IF *)
    END (* FOR *)
  END (* WITH *)
END PassCheck;
```

Section 10.6

1. Unsorted ... Sorted

Unsorted					Sorted
10	10	10	10	10	5
55	55	55	5	5	10
34	34	34	34	34	34
56	56	5	55	55	55
76	5	56	56	56	56
5	76	76	76	76	76
switch 5 and 76	switch 5 and 56	switch 55 and 5		switch 10 and 5	
5 comp. 1 exch.	4 comp. 1 exch.	3 comp. 1 exch.	2 comp. 0 exch.	1 comp. 1 exch.	

   Total exchanges = 4
   Total comparisons = 15

3. The records would stay in the same order but the scores would be sorted so everyone would end up with a different score.

5.
```
WITH Test DO
  (* order array Test.Class according to Score field *)
  FOR I := 1 TO NumStu - 1 DO
    (* Find the element in subarray 1..I with largest Score *)
    IndexOfMin := I;
    FOR J := I+1 TO NumStu DO
      IF Class[J].Score < Class[IndexOfMin].Score THEN
        IndexOfMin := J
      END (* IF *)
    END; (* FOR J *)

    (* assertion: element at IndexOfMin is smallest in subarray *)
    (* switch element at I with element at IndexOfMin *)
    IF IndexOfMin # I THEN
      Switch (Class[I], Class[IndexOfMin])
```

```
    END (* IF *)
  END (* FOR I *)
END (* WITH *)
```

Chapter 11

Section 11.1

1. a. Magic array elements are `Abracadabr`
   b. 10
   c. HisMagic array elements are `his strin`
   d. HisMagic array elements are `his in`
   e. HisMagic array elements are `his imyn`
   f. 1
   g. −1
   h. HisMagic array elements are `Abracadabr`

Section 11.5

1. a. {1,3,4,5,6,7} b. {1,2,3,5,7} c. {1,2,3,4,5,6,7} d. TRUE
   e. {1,2,3,5,7} f. {2} g. {} h. FALSE

Section 11.6

1.
```
CONST
  ScreenRows = 25;

TYPE
  Row = [0..ScreenRows];
  PixelSet = ARRAY [0..4] OF BITSET;
  FullScreen = ARRAY Row OF PixelSet;

VAR
  Screen : FullScreen;
```

3.
```
PROCEDURE CopyPic (Line : PixelSet; VAR String : ARRAY OF CHAR);

(* copy picture represented by Line array into String. *)

CONST
  ScreenWidth = 80;
  SetSize = 16;

VAR
  PixelGroup : [0..4];         (* subscript for Line *)
  Bit : [0..15];               (* current bit of pixel group*)
  I : CARDINAL;                (* loop control *)

BEGIN (* CopyPic *)
  FOR I := 0 TO ScreenWidth-1 DO
    PixelGroup := I DIV SetSize;
    Bit := I MOD SetSize;
```

```
      IF Bit IN Line[PixelGroup] THEN
        String[I] := '*'
      ELSE
        String[I] := ' '
      END (* IF *)
    END (* FOR I *)
  END CopyPic;
```

Chapter 12

Section 12.1

1. The actual parameter in the procedure call `Palindrome (N-1)` is an expression and must correspond to a value parameter.

Section 12.3

1.
```
MODULE  TestHanoi;

(* Tests the Towers of Hanoi procedure *)

VAR
  NumDiscs   : CARDINAL;          (* number of discs to be moved*)

(* Insert procedure Tower here *)

BEGIN (*TestHanoi*)
   WriteString ('How many discs do you wish moved?');
   ReadCard (NumDiscs);
   Tower ('A', 'C', 'B', NumDiscs)
END TestHanoi;
```

3.
```
BEGIN (* PrintBack *)
  FOR I := N TO 0 BY -1 DO
    WriteCard (X[I], 3);
  END (* FOR *)
END PrintBack;
```

Section 12.5

1.
```
PROCEDURE Factorial (N : CARDINAL) : CARDINAL;
(*
   Pre  : N is defined
   Post : Returns N!
*)
   VAR
     J, Product : CARDINAL;

BEGIN (* Factorial *)
```

```
  Product := 1;
  FOR J := N TO 2 BY -1 DO
    Product := Product * J
  END; (* FOR *)
  RETURN Product
END Factorial;
```

Section 12.6

1.
```
PROCEDURE FindMin (VAR X : ARRAY OF INTEGER;
                       N : INTEGER) : INTEGER;
(*
   Finds the smallest value in array X[0]..X[N]
   Pre  : X and N are defined
   Post : Returns the smallest element in X
*)
   VAR
     MinOfRest : INTEGER;

BEGIN (* FindMin *)
  IF N = 0 THEN
    RETURN X[0]
  ELSE
    MinOfRest := FindMin(X, N-1);
    IF MinOfRest < X[N]  THEN
      RETURN MinOfRest
    ELSE
      RETURN X[N]
    END (* IF *)
  END (* IF *)
END FindMin;
```

Section 12.7

1.

First Call			Second Call			Third Call			Fourth Call		
First	Last	Middle	First	Last	Middle	First	Last	Middle	First	Last	Middle
0	8	4	0	3	1	2	3	2	3	3	3

The result is 3

Section 12.8

1. For Subarray 12, 33, 23, 43 the pivot value is the smallest value. New Subarray to sort is 33, 23, 43. When pivot value is placed in the middle, two single element arrays are left.
   For Subarray 55, 64, 77, 75, the pivot value is the smallest value. New Subarray to sort is 64, 77, 75. Pivot value is smallest. New Subarray to sort is 77, 75 - it becomes 75, 77

Chapter 13

Section 13.5

1.

	Pop	Pop	Push	Pop	Push	Push	Pop
*	C	+	&	+	&	#	&
C	+	2	+	2	+	&	+
+	2		2		2	+	2
2						2	

Final value of X = '#'; final value of Success = TRUE

Section 13.7

1.
```
PROCEDURE WritePass (OnePass (* input *) : Element);
(* Displays one record of type OnePass. *)

BEGIN (* WritePass *)
  WriteString ('Name : ');
  WriteString (OnePass.Name);  WriteLn;
  WriteString ('Class : ');
  CASE OnePass.Class OF
    FirstClass    : WriteString ('FirstClass');
   | Business     : WriteString ('Business');
   | Economy      : WriteString ('Economy');
   | Standby      : WriteString ('Standby');
   | Undesignated : WriteString ('Undesignated')
  END; (* CASE *)
  WriteLn;
  WriteString ('Number of seats : ');
  WriteCard (OnePass.NumSeats, 3);  WriteLn;  WriteLn
END WritePass;


PROCEDURE ClassConvert (ClassCh : CHAR) : ClassType;
(* Converts a character to a ClassType. *)

BEGIN (* ClassConvert *)
  CASE ClassCh OF
    'F' : RETURN FirstClass;
   | 'B' : RETURN Business;
   | 'E' : RETURN Economy;
   | 'S' : RETURN Standby
  END (* CASE *)
END ClassConvert;
```

Chapter 14

Section 14.1

1. a. The string `'CA'` is stored in the `Current` field of the record pointed to by `R`.
   b. The record pointed to by `R` is copied into the record pointed to by `P`.
   c. Illegal, `P.Current` should be written as `P^.Current`.
   d. Illegal, `P` cannot be assigned an integer value.
   e. The integer `0` is stored in the `Volts` field of the record pointed to by the `Link` field of the record pointed to by `R`.
   f. Pointer `P` is reset to point to the same record as pointer `R`.
   g. The string `'XY'` is stored in the `Current` field of the 3rd record where the first record is pointed to by `R`. This is the node pointed to by `Q` in the figure preceding the exercises.
   h. The `Volts` field of the record pointed to by `R` is copied into the `Volts` field of the record pointed to by `Q`.

Section 14.3

1.
```
PROCEDURE PrintList (Head (* input *) : ListPointer);

(* Displays the list pointed to by Head *)

BEGIN (* PrintList *)
  IF Head # NIL THEN
    WriteString (Head^.Word);  WriteLn;
    PrintList (Head^.Link)
  END (* IF *)
END PrintList;
```
3.
```
PROCEDURE Length (Head : ListPointer) : INTEGER;

(* Finds the length of the list pointed to by Head. *)

BEGIN (* Length *)
  IF Head = NIL THEN
    Length := 0
  ELSE
    Length := 1 + Length(Head^.Link)    (* 1 + length of rest
                                                 of list *)
  END (* IF *)
END Length;
```

Section 14.4

1. In `CreateQueue`, replace the assignments to `Q^.Rear` and `Q^.Front` with

```
Q^.Rear  := NIL;
Q^.Front := NIL;
```

In `Insert`, add local pointer variable `Temp` (type `QueueNext`) and replace the `ELSE` clause with

```
ELSE
  Success := TRUE;  INC (Q^.NumItems);
  NEW (Temp);
  Temp^.Item := El;  Temp^.Link := NIL;     (* store El *)
  IF IsEmpty(Q) THEN
    Q^.Front := Temp;
    Q^.Rear := Temp
  ELSE (* connect El to current end of queue *)
    Q^.Rear^.Link := Temp;  Q^.Rear := Temp
  END (* inner IF *)
END (* outer IF *)
```

Change the `ELSE` clause of `Remove`:

```
ELSE
  El := Q^.Front^.Item;
  Temp := Q^.Front;
  Q^.Front := Q^.Front^.Link;
  DISPOSE (Temp);
  DEC (Q^.NumItems);
  Success := TRUE
END (* IF *)
```

Change the `ELSE` clause of `Retrieve`:

```
ELSE
  El := Q^.Front^.Item;
  Success := TRUE
END (* IF *)
```

Change `IsFull`:

```
RETURN NOT Available(TSIZE(QueueNode))
```

Section 14.7

1.
```
PROCEDURE SizeOfList (List (* input *) : ListPointer) : CARDINAL;
(* Returns the number of elements in an ordered list. *)

BEGIN (* SizeOfList *)
  RETURN List^.Numitems
END SizeOfList;
```

Procedure `Retrieve` begins like `Delete`. The `IF` statement below should be used instead of the one in `Delete`.

```
IF Success THEN
  El := Next^.Item
END (* IF *)
```

Procedure `Replace` begins like `Insert`. In the first `IF` statement, change the assignment to `Success`:

```
Success := SearchSuccess
```

Replace the second `IF` statement with:

```
IF Success THEN
  Next^.Item := El
END (* IF *)
```

3. In `Locate`, it would be necessary to test whether or not `Next` was `NIL` before removing its key; the `WHILE` loop should be exited when `Next` is `NIL`. `Insert` will have to differentiate between insertion at the head of a list and within the list.

Section 14.8

1. Inserting parentheses according to the algebraic rules for expression evaluation gives us the two expressions and trees below.

((X * Y) / (A + B)) * C

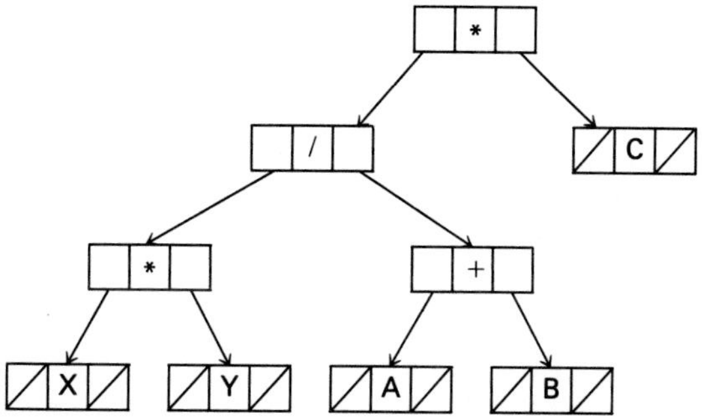

((X * Y) / A) + (B * C)

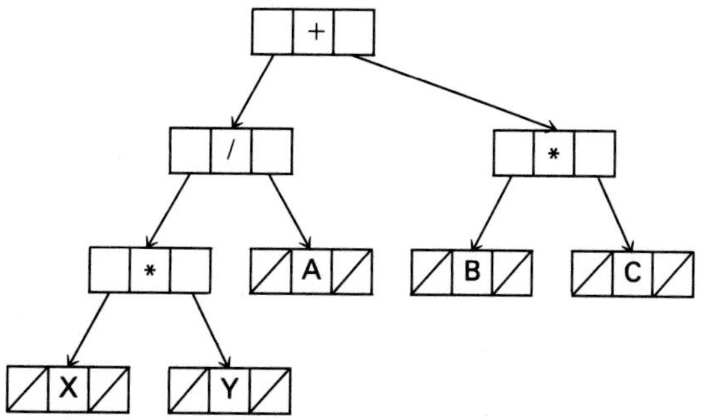

Section 14.9

1.
```
PROCEDURE Traverse (Tree (* input *) : SearchTree;
                    Visit (* procedure *) : VisitType);
(*
   Repeatedly calls procedure Visit (a parameter) to
   process each element of a tree.
   Pre : Tree points to header node of a tree
   Post: The nodes are visited in order.
*)

   PROCEDURE DoTraverse (Root (* in/out *) : Branch);
   (*
      Traverses the subtree pointed to by Root. *)
      Pre : none
      Post: Displays the information fields at Root.
      Uses: Visit from ElementType to visit each node.
   *)
   BEGIN (* DoTraverse *)
     IF Root # NIL THEN
       DoTraverse (Root^.Left);
       Visit (Root^.Item);
       DoTraverse (Root^.Right)
     END (* IF *)
   END; (* DoTraverse *)

BEGIN (* Traverse *)
  DoTraverse (Tree^.Root)
END; (* Traverse *)
```

Index